Peter & Olson
Consumer Behavior and Marketing
Strategy
Fifth Edition

Rangan
Business Marketing Strategy: Cases,
Concepts & Applications
First Edition

Rangan, Shapiro & Moriarty
Business Marketing Strategy:
Concepts and Applications
First Edition

Rossiter & Percy
Advertising Communications and
Promotion Management
Second Edition

Stanton, Spiro & Buskirk
Management of a Sales Force
Tenth Edition

Sudman & Blair
Marketing Research: A Problem Solving
Approach
First Edition

Ulrich & Eppinger
Product Design and Development
Second Edition

Walker, Boyd & Larreche
Marketing Strategy: Planning and
Implementation
Third Edition

Weitz, Castleberry & Tanner
Selling: Building Partnerships
Fourth Edition

Zeithaml & Bitner
Services Marketing
Second Edition

INTERNET MARKETING

Readings and Online Resources

Paul Richardson
Loyola University Chicago

Boston   Burr Ridge, IL   Dubuque, IA   Madison, WI   New York   San Francisco   St. Louis
Bangkok   Bogotá   Caracas   Kuala Lumpur   Lisbon   London   Madrid   Mexico City
Milan   Montreal   New Delhi   Santiago   Seoul   Singapore   Sydney   Taipei   Toronto

McGraw-Hill Higher Education

A Division of The McGraw-Hill Companies

INTERNET MARKETING: READINGS AND ONLINE RESOURCES
International Edition 2001

10 09 08 07 06 05 04 03 02 01
20 09 08 07 06 05 04 03 02 01 00
CTP KKP

Library of Congress Cataloging-in-Publication Data
Internet Marketing : reading and online resources / [edited by] Paul Richardson.
      p.   cm. (McGraw-Hill/Irwin series in marketing)
    ISBN 0-07-242793-0
    Includes bibliographical references.
    1.   Internet marketing.   I. Richardson, Paul, 1962- II. Series.
HF5415.1265I568 2001
658'.8'4dc—21   00-056868

www.mhhe.com

When ordering this title, use ISBN 0-07-118809-6

Printed in Singapore

PREFACE

The Internet continues to grow at exponential rates in the United States and around the world. In 1998 there were some 2.8 million websites on the Internet. By the beginning of 2000 this number had increased to over 9 million. E-commerce revenues are forecasted to increase tenfold between 1998 and 2003. This astonishing pace of change has given rise to the expression that "one Internet year is equal to three months."

For the student of Internet marketing, the key challenge is to not only master Internet marketing principles and concepts but to stay abreast of technological advances and industry trends. Professors likewise require teaching resources that maintain relevancy in the classroom over time. Toward this end, we offer the first "nonperishable," integrated approach to Internet marketing education. Our approach to the subject consists of **three reinforcing components.**

Component One stresses understanding of Internet marketing theory and concepts. To achieve this, we turn to current, important, and interesting research conducted by acknowledged masters of the field, including Dr. Hanson of Stanford University, Professors Hoffman and Novak of Vanderbilt University, Dr. Kaplan of the University of Chicago, Dr. Maes of the Massachusetts Institute of Technology, Dr. Sawhney of Northwestern University, and Dr. Varian of the University of California, Berkeley—to name just a few. In addition, the book's website and a free electronic newsletter keep the student and professor informed of breakthrough academic research as it is published between editions.

Component Two shows how concepts are applied in the real world. A website companion to the book (http://www.mhhe.com/richardson01) provides students with hundreds of links to industry news, articles, forecasts, software demonstrations, e-commerce tutorials, and directories relevant to each chapter module. By visiting these resources, students see firsthand how Internet marketing theory is applied using the latest techniques and best practices. These online resources are updated and revised on a continual basis to ensure high relevancy and interest.

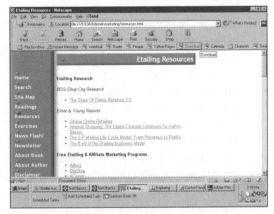

Component Three stresses the development of advanced Internet marketing abilities and skills. At the end of each module, students are asked to perform a series of exercises. By completing these exercises, students master the latest cutting-edge Internet marketing techniques. Students learn, for example, how to evaluate web business models and measure website quality, how to create web advertising programs and calculate advertising ROI, how to "e-commerce enable" websites for payment processing and implement closed loop promotional programs, how to conduct competitor analyses and improve search engine positioning—to name just a few! These online exercises are updated on a continual basis to ensure relevancy for students.

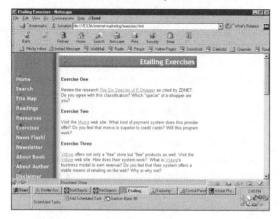

The course is arranged into twelve chapters in a modular fashion.

Module One introduces students to the Internet and shows how leading firms are successfully integrating the Internet into their business processes.

Module Two provides foundations of Internet marketing and discusses how commercial websites can be classified.

Module Three presents research concerning the business-to-consumer Internet marketing environment and discusses characteristics of the Internet shopper.

Module Four describes how electronic shopping agents and robots are influencing consumer behavior online.

Module Five presents research concerning Internet advertising and web marketing communications.

Module Six discusses key issues related to interactivity and community and how these factors drive website quality.

Module Seven describes the rise of business-to-business marketing on the web and shows the various B2B models that are emerging.

Module Eight describes how the Internet is impacting the marketing research process.

Module Nine discusses the Internet and international marketing.

Module Ten presents research concerning the Internet and public policy.

Module Eleven discusses how the Internet presents special challenges for the pricing and delivery of information and informational components of products and services.

Module Twelve is a bonus online module that presents examples of winning strategic Internet marketing plans and links to decision tools and resources for Internet entrepreneurs and startups.

Professors will be pleased with the extensive teaching support available through the website at http://www.mhhe.com/richardson01. The website resources, content, and exercises have been developed and exhaustively tested by the author in his own undergraduate and MBA Internet marketing classes. In addition, the pedagogical approach–which mixes offline articles with online resources–has been evaluated in real classroom environments with great success over a period of four years. Instructor resources on the website include PowerPoint slides for each module and an Instructor's Manual with answers to online exercises, suggested syllabi, and teaching tips. Finally, a free course electronic newsletter and continual website updates keep course content fresh and interesting for all.

Paul Richardson

LIST OF AUTHOR AFFILIATIONS

Alba, Joseph.   *University of Florida*

Boza, María-Eugenia.   *University of Massachusetts—Amherst*

Briggs, Rex.   *Millward Brown Interactive*

Chen, Qimei.   *University of Minnesota*

Clark, Bruce H.   *Northwestern University*

Cornwell, T. Bettina.   *University of Memphis*

Donthu, Naveen.   *Georgia State University*

Dou, Wenyu.   *University of Wisconsin—Milwaukee*

Drèze, Xavier.   *University of Southern California*

Garcia, Adriana.   *United Parcel Service*

Ghose, Sanjoy.   *University of Wisconsin—Milwaukee*

Haeckel, Stephan H.   *IBM's Advanced Business Institute*

Hagel, John.   *McKinsey & Company*

Hanson, Ward.   *Stanford University*

Harvey, Bill.   *Next Century Media*

Hoffman, Donna L.   *Vanderbilt University*

Hollis, Nigel.   *Millward Brown International*

Janiszewski, Chris.   *University of Florida*

Kaplan, Steven.   *University of Chicago*

Korgaonkar, Pradeep K.   *Florida Atlantic University*

Lutz, Richard.   *University of Florida*

Lynch, John.   *Duke University*

Maes, Pattie.   *Massachusetts Institute of Technology*

Milne, George R.   *University of Massachusetts—Amherst*

Nicovich, Stef.   *University of Memphis* (Ph.D. student)

Novak, Thomas P.   *Vanderbilt University*

Petty, Ross D.   *Babson College*

Quinn, Chad.   *Manugistics*

Samiee, Saeed.   *University of Tulsa*

Sawhney, Mohanbir.   *Northwestern University*

Sawyer, Alan.   *University of Florida*

Shapiro, Carl.   *University of California—Berkeley*

Sheehan, Kim Bartel.   *University of Oregon*

Varian, Hal R.   *University of California—Berkeley*

Wallace, John.   *Marshall University*

Weible, Rick.   *Marshall University*

Weitz, Barton.   *University of Florida*

Wells, William D.   *University of Minnesota*

Wolin, Lori D.   *Florida Atlantic University* (Ph.D. student)

Wood, Stacy.   *University of Florida* (Ph.D. student)

Zufryden, Fred.   *University of Southern California*

BRIEF CONTENTS

CONTENTS

INTERNET MARKETING

Readings and Online Resources

INTRODUCTION TO INTERNET MARKETING

From humble beginnings as a modest U.S. government project, the Internet has exploded on the world stage. The world's first multimedia web browser, Mosaic, was developed in 1994. Since this time, the Internet has grown faster than any medium or technology in history. However, even in this short period of time, we are witnessing three distinct revolutions.

The first Internet revolution is characterized by rapid growth in the business-to-consumer market. Amazon.com pioneered retailing on the Internet. Yahoo! defined the emerging role of cybermediaries. eBay created the world's largest consumer-to-consumer auction market. Priceline showed how consumer power could force airlines and other service providers to bid for business. Business-to-consumer revenue growth continues unabated.

The second Internet revolution is characterized by even faster growth than the first. This second revolution focuses on the business-to-business market. Ariba and CommerceOne are creating global web-based electronic procurement portals for industrial operating supplies and parts. Freemarkets.com and Vertical.Net have established the viability of business-to-business auctions for a variety of industrial commodities and products. HoustonStreet.com and Arbinet are among the world's first pioneers of successful Internet exchanges.

The third revolution is occurring within the firm itself. Private web sites called intranets and extranets are transforming corporate relationships. Intranets are designed for internal marketing purposes. Intranets have grown from simple web sites hosting corporate communication information to sophisticated internal portals for sales force training, expense and timesheet reporting, collaboration, and knowledge management among employees. Extranets are used to manage vendor, partner, and customer relationships. Through the use of extranets, firms may automatically procure needed supplies or manufacturing parts, collaborate with vendors and partners on project designs, and offer preferential pricing or terms to preferred channel members.

In this way, the web is transforming customer, supplier, and employee relationships.

What will we witness in the fourth revolution? Are the signs already here? Probably. In the first article in this chapter, Dr. Ward Hanson suggests that the growth of the web is remarkably similar to the growth of the radio. In both markets, there was initial ambiguity regarding the appropriate application of the technology followed by unexpected and rapid consumer adoption. Only after a shake-out and some chaos did successful business models emerge.

In the second article, Dr. Haeckel states that the Internet and related technologies are creating a new form of interactive marketing. Professor Haeckel suggests that new technologies are often adopted first to increase efficiency and then to increase effectiveness. Later, the technologies are applied in ways that were inconceivable at the time of original adoption. Dr. Haeckel suggests ways to imagine where technologies such as the Internet may lead us in the future.

Finally, in the third article, Mr. Quinn compares business environments to ecosystems. Just as creatures need air, water, and food, businesses need effective marketing, sales, and fulfillment. Mr. Quinn suggests that the Internet must be integrated into the marketing, sales, and fulfillment business ecosystem in a way that enhances the unique strengths of the firm. Quinn provides several case studies of leading firms that have been successful with their integration efforts.

Please visit the textbook's web site, where you will find supporting resources and exercises.

The Original WWW: Web Lessons from the Early Days of Radio

Ward Hanson

How do you evaluate a technology that has completely captured the public's imagination? A technology perceived as so rich in promise that thousands of articles in newspapers and magazines explain its workings to their readers. A technology that has come to indicate innovativeness, where failure to appreciate it is taken as a sure sign of belonging to the wrong side of a generational divide. Which has led, almost overnight, to the creation of new companies, brands, industries, and fortunes. One that commentators claim will revolutionize not only public culture, but also education and commerce. And, in moments of excess, a technology hailed as the best new chance for creating a peaceful world.

Such a dilemma confronted the radio analyst in 1922. The technology was the original WWW, World Wide Wireless. When the RCA Corporation took this logo in 1920, it felt that its new technology promised profits and a reasonable business opportunity in the wireless provision of telegraphy. In 1922 radio suddenly transitioned from a low-cost niche alternative to transcontinental cable to a consumer phenomenon. It was "top of the charts," and seemed to point the very way to the future.

Radio created much more than just a product or an industry. Although it now seems hardly more than a useful appliance, the impact of radio in the 1920s was huge. It changed the way the average person thought about distance and time. Listeners now heard global events as they happened. Performances in distant cities appeared instantly in the neighbor's living room. Fast breaking stories, or simply news about impending weather, was available with a flip of the switch.

Radio caused a wide range of spillovers and changes in the conduct of business. Radio dramatically accelerated the economy's push to a mass market. New national brands sprung up. A firm could launch marketing campaigns across the country simultaneously, backed with a nationally created image.

As part of this transformation, we suddenly had the concept of scheduled mass culture. As early as 1923 the Happiness Boys had become famous as "your Friday night date, from seven thirty to eight" (Smulyan, 1994, p. 93). Time slots, lead-ins, and prime time became familiar concepts. This change in the everyday life of millions of listeners affected every aspect of their lives, from church attendance to newspaper reading (Lazarsfeld, 1940).

In making the transition from hobby to industry, radio struggled with the most fundamental requirement of any technology: generating a self-sustaining revenue base. This was neither a smooth transition nor one with which participants felt comfortable. There were major differences and competing visions of the future. There was explosive growth and there were captivating possibilities. Even in the heady early days there was a gnawing awareness that the sources of fascination and growth fueling the early days could not last, and that a more permanent basis of support was needed. There were times participants felt the industry might be lagging, with the luster gone and the difficulties still present. There was both satisfaction and deep disappointment in the way the commercial foundations developed.

Modern-day participants in a similar evolution, the commercial growth of the World Wide Web, can learn much from the early days of radio. There have been striking parallels in the timing of investment, the concerns surrounding the financial basis of content, and the importance that popular fascination can play in stimulating the takeoff of a new medium. Jobs (1996) noted:

The Web is going to be very important. Is it going to be a life-changing event for millions of people? No. I mean, maybe. But it's not an assured Yes at this point. And it'll probably creep up on people. It's certainly not going to be like the first time somebody saw a television. It's certainly not going to be as profound as when someone in Nebraska first heard a radio broadcast. It not going to be that profound.

There are likely to be further parallels as well. Radio's experience of shakeouts and eventual maturity seems to be especially relevant.

RADIO'S COMMERCIAL BEGINNINGS IN AMERICA

Radio was originally known as wireless telegraphy or wireless telephony, a reflection of its main early market. Between the original innovations in 1897 and the outbreak of World War I, the British Marconi interests created a global capability for wireless messaging, which effectively competed against telephones and telegraphy. Key markets were those where it was either expensive or impossible to lay a cable; between ships, from ship to shore, across a long expanse of difficult terrain, and through undeveloped areas.

Radio telephony's commercialization showed many of the characteristics expected of a network technology. A single company, Marconi, emerged as the de facto standard. Central to their success were first-mover advantages, investment ahead of demand, and a growing stable of protective patents.

World War I disrupted this commercial dominance. During the war many combatants nationalized and controlled the use of radio. This military application froze the commercial side of things, but also created many of the preconditions for the explosive growth of radio that happened in the 1920s. Numerous technical improvements in broadcast and reception sensitivity owed their existence to military needs for distance or miniaturization. Perhaps most importantly, it created a cadre of technically trained people who did not forget their skills when they returned to civilian life. This created a considerable pool of skilled amateurs, willing to continue using radio as an interesting hobby and potential career.

As the world emerged from global conflict it appeared that Marconi would be able to reestablish its almost complete control over this wireless global communications medium. However, as part of negotiations following the end of the war, elements of the U.S. government came to demand an end of British control over this strategic asset. This led, in 1919, to the forced sale of American Marconi assets and patents to the Westinghouse Company. (Archer, 1926; Archer, 1939; Jome, 1925)

It quickly became apparent that successful radio development required alliances. Several companies owned key technological advances. General Electric controlled vital patents in areas of both radio transmission and reception. The Bell System controlled key patents on vacuum tube technology, which made amplification of signals and quality reception feasible for the first time. United Fruit had been active early in using radio to communicate with its Central American plantations, and had vital technology for powerful broadcasting.

These companies created the Radio Corporation of America, as the sole legitimate seller of radio reception equipment. Stock ownership

TABLE 1.1	RCA Ownership 1921		
Partner	Common	Preferred	Percent of Total
GE	2,364,826	620,800	30.1%
Westinghouse	1,000,000	1,000,000	20.6
AT&T	500,000	500,000	10.3
United Fruit	200,000	200,000	4.1
Others/Public	1,667,174	1,635,174	34.9

cemented the alliance. Table 1.1 shows the RCA ownership structure.

Wireless telephony and telegraphy resumed their growth following the lifting of World War I restrictions. Table 1.2 shows the breakdown for the world messaging radio industry in this early post-war period. By June of 1921, there were over 23,000 wireless stations in the world committed to wireless telegraphy and telephony (Jome, 1925, p. 69). Radio was again a viable industry.

RCA executives of the time viewed their market as based on one-to-one or one-to-few communication, in competition with submarine cables. These wireless markets did develop, and formed a profitable and increasing market for RCA. Transoceanic communication revenues were $2.1 million in 1921, with half a million from marine service. (David Sarnoff, a leading executive of RCA, owed part of his fame to this marine connection. While still a teenager, he was the sole radio operator on call when the messages about the sinking of the Titanic started to arrive. It was Sarnoff who relayed the messages to the newspapers.)

RCA's early venture used a well-understood revenue model, fee for service. Each message had a price; either the sender or the recipient could pay. As messages always had a pair of interested parties, there was no problem in assigning benefits and charges or excluding nonpaying customers.

RCA's value proposition was clear. High-power radio broadcast facilities had the capability for low-cost communication to Europe, Asia, and South America. For example, the 1920 standard wire-based telegraph rates to England were 25 cents per word. The cost to Norway was 35 cents. RCA undercut this price by approximately 30%, to secure a valuable but relatively modest niche market.

This focus on wireless messaging provides us with our first lesson from the radio story. Highly involved company and industry participants are often surprised by fundamentally new sources of growth in their markets. While visionary exceptions can usually be found, the mainstream participants are commonly caught short by what is later realized to be a basic sea change in use. (David Sarnoff received large amounts of praise for his prescient forecast of the capabilities of the consumer market in radio generating huge amounts of sales in the 1922–1924 time period. In late 1920 he had forecast RCA unit sales to follow a growth path of 100,000 units in 1922, 300,000 in 1923, and 600,000 in 1924. His revenue projections were $7.5 million, $22.5 million and $45 million, respectively. RCA's actual sales for those years corresponded to $11 million, $22.5 million, and $50 million. This is quite amazing in its insight—although Sarnoff was also known for making numerous forecasts that were not nearly so accurate.

TABLE 1.2	Classification of Wireless Stations				
	1920	1921	1922	1923	1924
Amateurs	5,922	10,809	15,504	16,570	15,545
Special land	164	383	525	566	665
U.S. commercial—land	94	139	185	236	289
U.S. commercial—ship	2,808	2,978	2,773	2,723	2,741
Government stations	1,574	1,385	1,478	1,299	1,249
Foreign stations	6,842	8,154	11,462	11,349	11,979
Broadcast (U.S. only)	—	—	382	573	535
Total	17,404	23,848	32,309	33,316	33,003

TABLE 1.3	Purposes of Broadcasters 1924		
Incentive for Launching Radio Station	**Total**	**Only Purpose**	**1 of 2 or More Purposes**
1. To help maintain sale of receiving sets	31	2	29
2. To profit from goodwill developed	44	8	36
3. To profit by direct sale of advertising time	2	0	2
4. To serve public generally	146	46	100
5. To serve some special group or clientele	26	6	20
6. Research purposes	13	4	9
7. Police information	8	2	6
8. University extension work	1	1	0

However, as the Annual Report quote makes clear, the established wisdom at RCA was not anywhere as rosy as was Sarnoff's.)

BROADCASTING AND THE EUPHORIA OF 1912

A fundamental change in the radio industry occurred in 1922. During that year the commercial role of radio made a transition from point-to-point communication to broadcast. Just as fundamentally, it made a transition from a clear-cut business model to a situation where industry participants knew there was incredible demand but couldn't see how to collect revenue.

At first it didn't matter. Merely the presence of a radio station in a town created a rush to buy radio sets. Radio receiver sales in 1922 quickly dwarfed revenues from all other of RCA's lines of business combined. This was a surprise to many of the participants. Even the most interested parties, such as RCA, expressed amazement and shock at how fast the market exploded. The 1922 Annual Report of RCA commented:

"At the time your Corporation was formed in 1919, for the purpose of building up a world-wide international wireless communication system, wireless telephony had not passed out of the experimental stage, and it was not at that time foreseen that the broadcasting art would ever reach the high point of popularity that it has in the last year. The engineers and scientists had anticipated the development of wireless telephony for communication purposes, but no one had visualized the phenomenal expansion of wireless telephony as used today for broadcasting.

In the last year the number of broadcasting stations has grown from less than twenty to almost six hundred. The art itself is advancing very fast, and the ultimate effect of broadcasting upon the economic, social, religious, political, educational life of the country and the world, is comparable only with that of the discovery of printing 500 years ago."

Figure 1-1 shows how lucrative the sale of receiver equipment was. By 1922, RCA radio sales exceeded $10 million. It doubled to more than $20 million in 1923; it doubled again to over $50 million in 1924. Industry sales for radio receivers followed a similar pattern of doubling. They mushroomed to $60 million in 1922, $136 million by 1923, and an amazing $358 million in sales in 1924.

What makes this level of sales so remarkable is the rudimentary state of radio receivers during this time of extraordinary growth. It was not until 1924 that radios were sold with wall plugs. Radio users had to struggle with heavy batteries, typically 12-volt lead acid. Next, there were no speakers. All listening had to take place with earphones. Acceptable reception required an extensive antenna system. This made radio listening a complicated—and in a summer thunderstorm, potentially dangerous—pastime.

Less obvious is the difficulty most of these sets had in locking on to signals. Indeed, there was a constant need to "comb the ether" to keep a weak signal connected. All too often this signal was also varying, as improperly configured broadcast stations would wander around their basic frequency.

Frequency sharing by stations was common. This necessitated extensive time sharing arrangements between regional broadcasters to avoid mutual jamming of each other's signal. Local newspapers published extensive listening and time guides. High-power stations would follow low power stations, causing listener discomfort and a rush to control the volume.

Why spend so much money on a flimsy, hard-to-use gadget? The first part of that answer is the very rapid growth of stations throughout the country [Table 1.3]. During this era essentially anyone wishing to launch a radio station could do so. The regulatory agency with any jurisdiction over the granting of licenses in the U.S. was the Commerce Department. In 1926 the Secretary of Commerce's power was strengthened, and Hoover could take a more restrictive or directive role in assigning or denying station license petitions; but until then the department's regulatory power was very weak. Commerce was essentially compelled to grant a unique set of call letters and an operating license to anyone who requested and maintained a station. For the critical window of 1922–1926 anyone believing that they could benefit and profit from a radio station could enter the market.

Many chose to do so. In 1922 it seemed that broadcast stations were appearing every day, with wonderfully creative and adventurous uses of the time they had available. By the end of 1922, the first real year of broadcasting, there were 576 broadcasting stations in the U.S. These early stations were a mixture of amateurs, speculators, nonprofit centers such as universities, companies looking for goodwill from sponsorship, and radio manufacturers and retailers looking to further seed and promote the sales of radios.

But the real driver of both set sales and broadcasting stations was the combination of hype, media coverage, and public fascination that came to be called the "Euphoria of 1922." Popular discussion of radio was everywhere. This ran from newspaper accounts of any new radio station opening up to the achievement of some new record for distance listening, from technical pieces in journals describing new radio developments to get-rich-quick schemes popping up in investment circles.

The intellectual as well as the popular media were full of analysis and insights around the long-term impacts of this amazing new technology. Hot debates emerged on the impact of radio on education, the music industry, politics, church attendance, and global understanding. The fundamental value of social interaction was questioned. Why leave the privacy of one's own living room when many cultural events could be experienced for free?

The impact of three forces propelled the explosion of radio: rapid radio set sales, mushrooming growth in signal sources, and intense public attention. This is a powerful, autocatalytic process. Fascination leads to sales, sales lead to stations, new stations lead to more fascination.

The intensity of attention showered on the World Wide Web in 1995–1997, the explosion of servers (i.e., "broadcasters"), and the rapid expansion of Web connections and browser use (i.e., "receivers") is highly reminiscent of radio in 1922–1923. It is also highly likely that observers 10 or 20 years from now will look back at the features, bandwidth, connection difficulties, and general "kludginess" of Internet technology with bemusement and incredulity. But at the same time, it is unlikely that the level of societal focus will ever be as high. We may already have seen the peak of the Web positive feedback loop—but nowhere near the peak of its economic or true social impact.

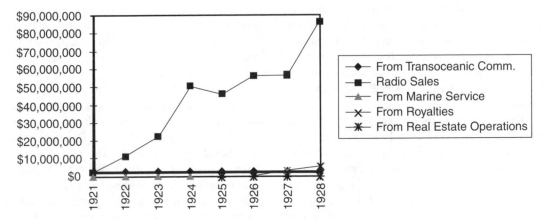

Figure 1-1   Sources of RCA Revenue: 1921–1928

SHAKEOUTS AND BUSINESS MODELS

The 23,848 radio stations in existence in 1921 were for two-way communication. The broadcast revolution dramatically changed this. Suddenly there were millions of receivers. While the number of broadcasting stations during this period never exceeded 1,000, the number of receiving sets expanded to dwarf the number used in all previous applications. This one-to-many structure meant that the message sent needed to be sufficiently general that a widespread group of listeners would benefit. But the public good nature of the radio signal meant that the old model of pricing by individual message no longer worked.

Broadcast radio was a fundamental change in the business use of radio. The revenue model for direct communication was clear-cut. Broadcast was a puzzle of indirect communication. High quality content requires revenue. Pay-as-you-go was infeasible. Somehow third parties must support the effort.

At first the goals of broadcasters were a combination of hard-headed good business, wild-eyed speculation, and public-spirited altruism. Fortunately, a researcher captured this spread with a study conducted in 1924.

Several striking features are present in this survey. First is the role of the major radio "hardware" companies. They were among the key sponsors of many stations. The logic and benefit is simple—people will buy radios only if they have something to listen to. With a sufficiently large share of the market, key manufacturers and retailers will find it profitable to engage in category development.

Generalized goodwill was a common motive. Many early radio sponsors were well-known department stores, car dealers, or newspapers. Their names would occasionally be mentioned, merged into the name of the show, or even made part of the call letters. Among the leading shows were the Eveready Hour, the Happiness Boys, and the Michelin Troubadours. (This was eventually spoofed on the floor of Congress by Representative Emmanuel Celler of New York, introducing a bill to the House: "This is BLAA, broadcasting station of the Jumbo Peanut Company at Newark, New Jersey. You will now have the pleasure of listening to the *Walk Up One Flight Clothing Company's* orchestra. Their first number will be *You Don't Wear Them Out if You Don't Sit Down*.") In Chicago, the Chicago Tribune sponsored the radio station WGN—the World's Greatest Newspaper.

Sponsors hoped that public relations and name recognition would somehow translate into loyal retail customers.

Participants at the time realized that both of these rationales were insufficient. Eventually the market would mature, and motivating replacement radio sales would be much less lucrative. Also, entry into retailing and manufacturing threatened to destroy the incentives for hardware manufacturers to support broadcasts. Below some critical market share, free riding becomes the dominant strategy and individual companies will not find it worthwhile to actively provide free content. Anticipating these realities, as early as 1922 many of the key companies providing broadcasting were actively raising the question of "Who Will Pay for Radio?"

Of course, we know what the answer turned out to be—advertising. But in 1922 there were several very serious problems with advertising. One was public hostility. Commerce Secretary Herbert Hoover, RCA Chairman David Sarnoff, most industry magazines, and many members of the public opposed advertising.

It was also hard to tell if advertising worked. There was no infrastructure to provide meaningful measurement of audience size and demographics. Shows relied on postcards and letters sent in by listeners to provide some measure of the reach and frequency of their listening audience. There was

little knowledge about the effectiveness of radio advertising. Existing advertising agencies had no knowledge of how to make ads meaningful and effective in this new, non-text–based medium.

But the most important factor was legal. The Bell system owned and operated station WEAF in New York City. Bell interpreted the initial patent sharing arrangements strictly. It claimed that all use of wireless telephony for hire (that is, with advertising) was a direct violation of its monopoly of telephony retained under the patent arrangement. Any station attempting to sell advertising was potentially incurring the wrath of the legal department of the mighty Bell system, and the termination of its access to long distance service.

While this threatening posture by AT&T didn't prevent all use of radio spots, it dramatically limited them. An arbitration in 1926 between AT&T and RCA removed this restriction. The arbiter in the case ruled quite decisively for RCA, after which AT&T provided very low-cost licensing arrangements to all takers. Thus, almost five years after the initial explosion of sales and interest, the stage was set for the modern American method of broadcasting.

Meanwhile, there was a very active debate surrounding the business model for radio. A wide range of possible support mechanisms was proposed. The most popular among many of the observers, especially the trade publications, was public support through some method of tax support. Proposals included general tax revenues, a receiver set tax, or a tube tax.

Those arguing for general revenue support stressed the public good nature of the broadcast signal. All potentially benefit, so why shouldn't all pay? Appeals to listeners could augment the tax support. Modern-day public broadcasting follows this plan. Set manufacturers were especially strong backers of the public model.

Others claimed that radio was only partially a public good, in that it was necessary to buy a radio receiver to benefit from the signals. This led to a proposed set tax, where radio buyers would pay an

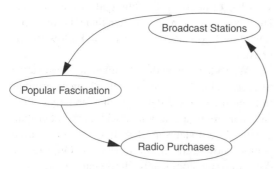

Figure 1-2   The Euphoria of 1922 Cycle

increment in the purchase price that would go to the general fund to support radio. This is the basic form of support for the British Broadcasting Company, and tended to be very popular among the trade commentators.

Supporters of a tube tax argued that it better matched usage to payment. Radios used vacuum tubes. Like a light bulb, vacuum tubes wear out with use. A tube tax would indirectly meter usage. One difficulty was separating out tubes meant for radio and those used for other purposes. Of course, manufacturers of vacuum tubes opposed the tube tax.

Influential members of industry and government opposed all of these mechanisms. Their opposition was less economic than political. They did not wish to confer onto government the power to disperse funding. It was already clear that radio had large scale potential for shaping public opinion and debate. Few of the business people or members of the Coolidge administration had any taste for granting the power of radio's purse strings to Federal government control.

In other countries, different arguments proved persuasive. The "American System" of broadcasting, based solely on radio as a commercial medium, was popular in North and South America. By 1936, 22 countries had embraced this approach. It stressed private ownership, and tended to result in a large variety of stations. The more popular method, as measured by adoption, was actually the set tax. Over 40 countries, mostly in Europe and Asia adopted the "BBC system." This led to fewer channels, owned and sponsored by the government.

As early as mid-1922 the lack of a solid financial foundation for broadcasting started to show up as stations folded. One of the few regulatory powers the Commerce Department had was the rubber-stamping of radio license approvals and deletions. This created a data set of additions and deletions of stations. Figure 1-3 shows the exponential growth in stations during the first half of 1922 followed by a steady stream of station failures. Indeed, by late 1922 a roughly constant total

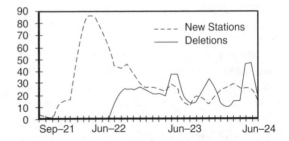

Figure 1-3   Monthly Rate of Station Creation and Death: 1921–1924.

number of radio stations broadcast in the United States. However, this steady number hid a large amount of churn. Stations opened and closed at roughly the same rates, with deletions gaining the upper hand in 1924.

Another measure of this churn is what happened to the pioneering radio stations. All of the 48 states then in the U.S. had radio stations operating by the third quarter of 1922. Of the 48 stations that were first in their state, 17 of them are still active. Fully 27 of the other 31 went out of business before the end of 1924. The toll was 7 in 1922, 15 in 1923, and 5 in 1924.

A key reason for this turnover was the high cost of quality broadcasting. Entry costs for most stations were relatively modest. Operating costs were close to the initial costs for small stations. This led to churn at the low end of station size. High-power stations had better financial backing, relatively lower operating costs, and a lower failure rate.

Web sites exaggerate the low entry cost status of early radio. However, it is much more difficult to track the exit and deletions of Web pages. Web sites tend to disappear with a whimper, rather than a bang. Site updates are less frequent, innovative content slows, and traffic tapers off. Only rarely does the site completely disappear. Even so, a growing number of obvious "ghost sites" or sites with stale content are emerging.

SUCCESSFUL RADIO

Early on it was realized that affordable quality content was driven by audience size. The largest stations, such as those in New York and Chicago, could be more professional and have better talent. Artists were often willing to donate time for the image and sales boost if the audience was big enough. This led to the innovation of "silent nights" where local radio stations would go off the air so residents could suddenly hear distant stations and the stars of Broadway or the Chicago Opera. Silent nights lowered the direct profits of local broadcasters, but were felt to stimulate the entire growth of the radio market.

There were proposals for radio to rely on super stations, perhaps 10 or 15 in number, with a signal so strong that they could blanket the United States. This would mean a limited number of stations to staff and create content for. This was a strong favorite of Sarnoff and RCA, who viewed it as a reliable way to provide a reason to use their receivers. RCA also had high power transmission capabilities.

Events quickly eliminated the clear channel possibility. By the end of 1922 there were close to 600 broadcasting stations on the air. They were not about to relinquish their investment. Still, the logic of national stations was sound. A solution combining national content, local presence, and a strong business model was required. This was provided by the final piece of the financial puzzle, the radio network.

RCA launched a national radio network in 1926, the National Broadcasting Company. In 1928 this split into two networks, the NBC Blue and NBC Red Networks. Entry occurred in 1929 with the formation of CBS.

The growth of networks solved many of the financial problems of radio. The audience was now large enough to generate ample audience size and advertising dollars. This in turn allowed radio to pay top dollar to the most popular stars. The growth of the networks was hand in hand with the growth of the star system. This "first copy cost" of talent could be spread over a large number of broadcast outlets.

The network system was also superior to the super station model in its ability to mix local and national advertising. Local affiliates could tap into the large number of local advertisers. National advertising could support national shows by national brands. Spot advertising permits a much more effective use of this national/local audience mix than a completely national or completely local model.

Advertising was critical to the success of radio in the United States. Other sources of support were running out of energy. And just as importantly, the hyperactivity caused by the positive feedback cycle was losing one of its main drivers—public fascination. By 1925 articles were already appearing claiming that radio was "old hat."

It was becoming clear that radio wouldn't end war and bring universal culture. Many of the wild predictions and exaggerated hopes for radio result from a trick of the technological imagination. Users confronting a radically new technology pay much more attention to the direction the technology is taking them than to the limitations of the current realizations. They experience snippets of music broadcast from the Broadway stage; they extrapolate and imagine the global availability of only the best music. They hear an interesting 10-minute discussion of a scientific topic; they make the jump to a "university of the air" which provides universal higher education. They learn about a distant event, they make the nonsequitar connection that surely familiarity must lower barriers to people and support peace.

As the World Wide Web enters the delicate transition between explosive imagination and normal industry, the search for an "NBC" continues. If it is again advertising, the potential of the Web is highly constrained. Incumbent technologies, such as radio, television, and direct mail have extensive infrastructures and momentum to overcome. Each will fight back to protect its turf.

The executives of radio solved their business problem when they followed the logic of the medium. It took time for them to move from the well-understood metered service of wireless telegraphy to the new world of broadcasting. Radio created fundamental new capabilities of achieving national reach with local presence. At the same time, it worked best when all could hear and there wasn't an artificial barrier put on access to the signal.

The executives of the World Wide Web must also follow the logic of this new medium. Digital networks have new capabilities and there is always the possibility of surprise. (For an extensive discussion of these capabilities, see Hanson [1998].) Paradoxically, it is now executives familiar with broadcast, publishing, and brand management that must discover the benefits of direct communication, personalization, and dialogue. These are the new tools shaping successful and profitable uses of the Web, and are likely to be the basis of the core

successful business models. Web sites must also handle the merger of local, national, and global. Governments must decide their proper role as well.

There is one more fundamental lesson from the early days of radio. Modern society has a truly incredible ability to assimilate technology. What was revolutionary becomes humdrum. What was a grand adventure of science and hobbyists becomes an appliance. Business practices that seemed odd, even disturbing, become part of the background noise of our life. Capabilities which changed the very way we viewed time and space become as habitual to the next generation as reaching for the radio dial as we get in the car each morning.

Ward Hanson is with the Graduate School of Business, Stanford University, and Director of the Stanford Internet Marketing Project.

REFERENCES AND KEY SOURCES

Archer, G. *Big Business and Radio.* New York: Arno Press, 1939; reprinted in 1971.

Archer, G. *History of Radio to 1926.* New York: American Historical Society, 1938.

Barnouw, E. *A History of Broadcasting in the United States,* vol. I, *A Tower in Babel.* New York: Oxford University Press, 1966.

Barnouw, E. *A History of Broadcasting in the United States,* vol. II, *The Golden Web.* New York: Oxford University Press, 1966.

Broadcasting (various years).

Hanson, W. *Principles of Internet Marketing.* ITP South-Western, 1998.

Jobs, Steve. *Wired Magazine* (February 1966).

Jome, H. *Economics of the Radio Industry.* Chicago: A. W. Shaw, 1925.

Lazarsfeld, P. *Radio and the Printed Page.* New York: Duell, Sloan, and Pearce, 1940.

Lumley, F. *Measurement in Radio.* Columbus: Ohio State Press, 1934.

Radio Broadcast (various years).

Radio Corporation of America (years from 1921–1930). *Annual Report.*

Smulyan, S. *Selling Radio: The Commercialization of American Broadcasting 1920–1934.* Washington: Smithsonian Institution Press, 1994.

About the Nature and Future of Interactive Marketing

Stephan H. Haeckel

ABSTRACT

The essence of interactivity is exchange. Degree of contingency and frequency are among the more important dimensions of a marketing exchange. Technology enables and enhances these dimensions on a scale and scope unprecedented in human history. The author argues that information technology and the collaborative potential of the Internet may eventually change human cognitive processes as much or more than writing technology did. He offers anecdotal evidence that technology-assisted human collaboration can systematically lead to synergetic, "previously unthinkable," (and therefore unpredictable) breakthroughs. While it is therefore not reasonable to expect accurate predictions of what the breakthroughs in interactive marketing and "e-business" will be, it is possible to think about ways to discover them earlier. Two areas of research are suggested as being of special interest: whether or not the collaborative potential of technology is likely to transform business-as-games-against-competitors into business-as-games-with-customers; and what are the necessary and sufficient conditions for interactive technology to lead to breakthrough creativity.

Many conferences with important but vague themes such as *Leadership, Trust,* or *Organizational Learning* suffer from a common malady: the term meant to be the organizing concept event is never defined and variously interpreted. In such cases it usually becomes clear early on that the group literally doesn't know what it's talking about. To minimize the probability of this outcome, organizers of a May 1996 Harvard Business School Conference on the Future of Interactive Marketing sent a pre-conference questionnaire to all participants, asking for their definition of the term *interactivity* and for the dimensions of interaction they thought most important in establishing its quality. What follows is an attempt at a synthesized definition based on this input, and some ideas this exercise provoked concerning how we might think strategically about the unpredictable future of interactive marketing.

Table 1.4 contains a representative set of participant definitions, and the factors each individual thought were most important in determining the impact of a given interaction.

SOME OBSERVATIONS

The submissions tended to cluster in three groups: interactivity as specifically a communication exchange; as any action with effects; or as a particular type of interentity relationship.

Communication was the group's favorite synonym. *Dialogue,* with its connotation of mutual learning, suggests two-way communication. The notion of mutuality was reinforced by several mentions of *degree of contingency* as an important dimension. The extent that one agent's response is shaped by the previous response of another would presumably affect the intensity and impact of an interaction—as would the frequency with which the exchanges take place. Contingency as a quality of interactivity might therefore logically be associated with marketing concepts such as customer intimacy.

A systems-theoretic definition of interactivity is given in row 4 of Table 1.4. Any number of entities may be involved in an interactive system, but the interactions are always paired, and only one of the entities need be affected. Furthermore, it allows for a change in the *mental,* as well as physical, state of an entity, which the Oxford English

Dictionary definition in row 6 appears to exclude. From a marketing perspective, changing mental states is an important issue. The mention of *consciousness* as a dimension (row 9) draws attention to the fact that this can take place on either a conscious or subconscious level.

Sensory involvement was given as a dimension of importance by several participants. And the attribute *synchronous* evokes concepts such as cadence, interference, and flow—all of which would presumably enhance the quality and impact of an interaction.

SYNTHESIZED DEFINITION

Here is an attempt to capture the sense of what *interactivity* meant to the people attending this conference.

> Marketing interactivity is a person-to-person or person-to-technology exchange designed to effect a change in the knowledge or behavior of at least one person.

Because it seems clear that technology is doing something to interactivity—and because, after all, it's *marketing* interactivity that is of interest— it seemed appropriate to add the qualifiers *technology* and *designed,* and to exclude physical exchanges.

DIMENSIONS OF INTERACTIVITY

Somewhere down the road, we will surely want to subdivide and categorize interactivity and its effects; and it would undoubtedly be very useful if we were able to predict the intensity, or impact, of a given interaction. So perhaps more interesting than the definition itself are the ideas and potentials implicit in the dimensions of interactivity that participants collectively nominated.

Here are some of the dimensions submitted that, intuitively at least, appear to relate to impact.

$$I = f(N, C, F, SI, CI, T, CT, SY, M),$$

where

I	=	impact of interaction,
N	=	number of entities involved,
C	=	degree of contingency,
F	=	frequency of exchange,
SI	=	degree of sensory involvement,
CI	=	degree of cognitive involvement,
T	=	types of entities involved,
CT	=	content t being exchanged,
SY	=	degree of synchronicity, and
M	=	type of media involved

Two business examples of important outcomes that could not have occurred without a high degree of technology-augmented interactivity illustrate the potential significance of some of these dimensions.

REXX is a systems control language that became such a successful IBM product its creator was awarded the highest technical honor the company can bestow—designation as an IBM Fellow. The product was born in IBM's first worldwide network, a 1960s implementation of a network of networks connecting all the development and research laboratories around the world. REXX's British inventor sent his original idea to a colleague in San Jose, who made some comments and forwarded it to several others in different labs in Germany and France, who appended their own comments and criticisms, and sent the composite on to colleagues. Out of this highly contingent, worldwide multiplexing of ideas emerged REXX, a product that was never in any IBM plan, and for which there was no budget. It was literally a manifestation of interactivity on a network.

In an early 1970s project to measure the effect of technology on human productivity, IBM researchers discovered that, regardless whether it was an accountant or a particle physicist at work on a terminal, when system response time was reduced to less than 1 second, a quantum improvement in productivity routinely occurred. The apparent explanation is that with exchange delays of less than 1 second, the human mind, rather than the technology, establishes the pace at which ideas develop.

These two instances afford anecdotal evidence that interactive technologies will do more than help us communicate faster; that in fact we are likely to see a wide range of unexpected, emergent effects. But if these effects are truly unpredictable, how could we think about interactivity in a way that raises our chances of anticipating some

---

TABLE 1.4   Representative Definitions and Dimensions of *Interactivity* from Attendees at the Harvard Conference on Marketing Interactivity, May, 1996.

Definition	Dimensions
Interactivity is . . .	
• . . . a two-way dynamic dialogue.	• Number of people/things involved
• . . . person-to-person *communications,* permitting feedback.	
• . . . two-way *communication* in which the response made by each party is contingent on, or a function of, the response made by the other party	• Degree of contingency • Frequency of exchange
• . . . an *exchange* between two entities that changes the state of at least one of them.	• Frequency, reaction time of exchange • Degree of sensory involvement
• . . . a synchronous *exchange* of information.	• Types of entities interacting • Content of exchange
• . . . reciprocal *action,* the action or influence of persons or things on each other (Oxford English Dictionary, 1832).	
• . . . behavior over time by two or more parties, if each party's behavior at a particular time is at least partly in response to earlier and/or concurrent behavior by the others.	• Locus of control • Degree of synchronicity
• . . . the *way* two or more organisms relate to each other.	• Senses involved • Cost • Intimacy • Consciousness
• . . . an *expression* of the extent that in a given series of communication exchanges, any third (or later) transmission (or message) is related to the degree to which previous exchanges referred to even earlier transmission.	• Mediated or person-to-person • Degree of user ability to modify form and content of exchange in real time

of the surprises that are in store? A logical place to start is by considering the role of technology in fostering surprise.

HOW MIGHT INTERACTIVE TECHNOLOGY CHANGE MARKETING?

The important applications of any significant new technology are usually unthinkable in advance. Faraday confessed he had no idea what his discovery of electrical induction might be useful for, and Edison thought the primary application of the phonograph would be dictation. New developments in information technology—including interactive technologies—are particularly fraught with mystery about how they might impact the way we work, live, and think.

A version of Figure 1-4 was shown to a 1984 Harvard Business School Conference on Electronic Marketing. It depicts the conclusion of a study made in the early 1980s on the evolution of leading-edge computer applications over the previous 25 years. (Haeckel, 1985)

The way mainframe applications—and later on PC applications—changed over time appeared

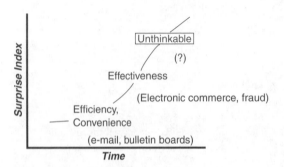

Figure 1-4   Assimilation of New Technologies

to reveal a consistent three-stage pattern to human assimilation of significantly new technologies. Collectively, at least, it seems people do not solve new problems with an unfamiliar technology. We start by solving familiar problems more efficiently; then we solve these same problems differently; and only when we have truly internalized the capabilities of the technology do we apply our ingenuity to new problem areas.

After an initial stage of experimentation—largely by *heat seekers*—a class of efficiency/convenience applications emerges. In the late 1950s and early 1960s, for example, inventory recordkeeping systems were converted from punched-card tabulating equipment to stored-program computers—with virtually no change in function. Later in the decade, exponential smoothing algorithms, economic lot size calculations, and other theory that had been on the shelves for many years were incorporated, transforming inventory recordkeeping applications into inventory management systems. This was a more effective way of solving an existing business problem: inventory management. It was made possible by the increased speed of computers, enabling the application of computationally intense theory for the first time.

The third stage, *previously unthinkable* applications, is exemplified by the "just-in-time" systems that have emerged in the last decade or so. Now the *problem* is recast as managing logistics, not inventory. This is called *previously unthinkable,* because no forecaster in 1958 could have thought of including inventory-less production systems in a long-term forecast for computer capacity demand.

That phenomenon explains the famous forecast of a dozen or so computers given to Thomas Watson, Jr. in the early 1950s as the maximum computational capacity that would ever be required on earth. Together with a rather modest gradient in the learning curve of IBM forecasters over the next quarter century, it also helps explain a 1980 forecast of 280,000 personal computers by 1990.

Global positioning systems, magnetic resonance imaging, virtual Boeing 777 prototypes, and a $30 trillion financial derivatives market are other examples of previously unthinkable computer applications. It is this category that will provide us with surprises in the future of interactive marketing.

GETTING TO STAGE 3

Given that we can't think in advance *of* such applications, how might we think *about* them? What can we do to reduce the time required to understand the potential of the Internet for doing things better and differently, a prerequisite to the truly surprising ideas of stage 3?

For starters, we might ask why the Internet itself is such a surprise. It has been around for almost 30 years, but wasn't taken seriously by the business community until quite recently. Then, a few years ago, without anyone planning or decreeing it, a very simple set of browser and server protocols emerged as universal Internet standards. Suddenly, and basically without warning, the internet became a plausible and economic solution to a seemingly intractable problem that had plagued business since the 1960s: integrating increasingly heterogeneous information technology systems between and within organizations. The World Wide Web now offers providers and seekers of information around the globe an ease of access to one another that proprietary systems will never provide, but which they can easily benefit from. The lesson here is that it pays to use important, well-understood problems as an initial filter for thinking about the aggregate impact of technological change, especially when the changes seem unrelated and incremental.

It is also important to learn from early adapters. Electronic commerce is currently a hot topic. As presently conceived it will let some companies do business more efficiently, and others differently. But e-commerce is not new. It is happening on the internet more than 10 years after McGraw-Hill and CitiCorp launched a large-scale electronic global petroleum trading company called GEMCO.

GEMCO was a virtual enterprise operating on a private network connecting 70 information providers, hundreds of traders, and a bank. Every aspect of the business, from gathering information to negotiating and striking deals, to making and clearing payment was conducted on the network. The technology worked, the business model was robust, and the investors had deep pockets. It should have succeeded. One wonders how many of those planning electronic commerce ventures today understand why it didn't: GEMCO failed primarily because the traders—an "old boy" network of a few hundred people—*didn't want to work with each other (i.e., interact) the way GEMCO's designers thought they should.*

That result suggests that the impact of technology on the future of interactive marketing may depend on the way technology affects how people work together. If so, it is important to think about the latter. And, because there are no data on the future, we must resort to scenarios, or thought experiments, to do that.

A Thought Experiment on the Future of Work

Walter Ong (1982), in *Orality and Literacy,* argues convincingly that writing and printing technologies changed forever human cognitive processes. The ability to systematically codify and build on prior knowledge eventually effected a neural rewiring that makes analytic thought second nature to modern humans. Writing it down and looking it up are prerequisites to the elaborated deductive and inductive reasoning underlying the "proof" that two triangles are congruent, the "history" of the Civil War, contract law, the 49ers' game plan, fly-by-wire airplanes, much of theology, and the whole of the "scientific method." It is what enabled Isaac Newton to stand on the shoulders of giants.

Writing technology endowed humans with external memory. It allowed us to begin decomposing complex problems into successively more manageable chunks without losing the larger picture. This intellectual process led eventually (and logically) to the physical decomposition of work into successively smaller units, and to the *division of labor* managerial concept. Writing technology first changed the way we think, and then the way we work.

Since at least the late 1950s managers and academics have been exploring how information and communication technologies change the way we work. Information technology has become personal, ubiquitous and, with the sudden advent of the worldwide web, globally networked. The question of how we will work is an urgent operational issue for many organizations. One way of addressing this question is to do good field research and observe how work is changing as it changes. Another way of gaining insight is to ask, "How will networked—and therefore potentially interactive—information technologies change the way we think, once we have internalized them to the extent we have writing and printing technologies?"

Writing gave us external memory, and printing the means for authors to reach large audiences. Information technology externalizes and automates logical inferencing, while low-cost global digital networks give us the potential to collaborate with one another in a new medium, on a scale unprecedented in human history. It is not unreasonable to assume that learning to exploit these potentials might require the development of substantially different cognitive processes.

Walter Ong (1982) cites Plato, in his *Phaedrus,* warning about the damage writing will wreak on humankind: it will weaken the mind, destroy memory, and subvert the give-and-take of ideas between people. In spite of Plato's dire prediction, humans did not lose the capacity to remember things. We did, however, stop trying to memorize the classics by heart. And we did learn new techniques for processing information, among them the idea that remembering where to look something up is often more useful than remembering the content. Indexing supplements, rather than replaces, mnemonic association. We can write down the indices, and make indices of indices. In effect, we've taken memory processes up a notch, by remembering what to remember, and forgetting a lot of what Plato thought we shouldn't forget. Only since the advent of the printing press have a large number of humans been able to accumulate knowledge by putting the bulk of cognitive processing into building on what's already there, rather than memorizing it.

By analogy, we should not expect information technology to destroy our capacity for logical inferencing, but lead to the development of a complementary mental faculty.

It is important to stress the difference between technology that stores the result of logical inferencing, and technology that does the inferencing. One no longer has to learn an algorithm for taking square roots, nor even how to look them up. The only requirement is pushing a button on a calculator and then deciding whether or not to believe the result. The first few times we use a calculator, we might well make a back-calculation to check the result; if the technology passes this test, we might reduce our testing to a duplication of the exercise, in order to check for the possibility of input error, as well as logical error. A next stage might be one of simply checking the result for reasonableness, and a final (not to be recommended) state might be accepting whatever result is shown on the display. Each of these steps represents it greater degree of internalization of the technology, and frees up brain time for other things. What other things? A prime candidate is: intuitive thinking.

Imhotep, architect of the first pyramid, Hammurabi, the first law-giver, and Homer earned their places in history with brains wired to recall and apply proven formulas, and to hear the voices of the gods as inspiration for what to do in unprecedented situations. But it is very difficult to believe that they were totally bereft of analytic thought processes, relatively primitive as these might have been. Similarly, we are not devoid of intuitive thought, although since at least the Age of Reason it has been considered less reliable and useful than analytic thought.

But things are changing again, and we are finding that the rate and unpredictability of that change render inadequate the linear approximations deeply baked into many of our models of the world and what happens in it. Scientists who specialize in the category of nonlinear systems called complex adaptive (of which humans are perhaps the primary exemplars), tell us that *such systems can only be controlled intuitively.* It is therefore reasonable to assume that, as what goes on in our lives and businesses becomes more obviously nonlinear, we will place a greater premium on the development of our intuitive mental processes. The increased interest in "drawing/thinking on the right side of the brain" and thinking "outside the box" may be anecdotal evidence that such a shift is already well underway.

One of the most nonlinear, intuitive things we do is interact with other nonlinear systems—the people that we live and deal with every day. Technology is in the process of changing by several orders of magnitude the number of people with whom we can interact.

A special type of interaction, one in which people interact to achieve a common purpose, is called *collaboration.* It is highly contingent, requiring reconciliation of intents, beliefs, and activities among the collaborators. Although humans have been collaborating since the dawn of history, it has never been contemplated at the scale or in the medium now possible. Furthermore, I am not aware of any theory of collaboration—that is, a systematic way of predicting such things as who will collaborate well with whom in what kinds of enterprises, what principles and processes are most likely to increase the efficiency and effectiveness of what kinds of collaborations, and what kind of social, psychological, and cognitive skills will be needed to maximize the likelihood of a successful result in a given collaboration. Yet it seems

quite possible, even likely, that this will emerge as the predominant mode of work for many of us.

Plato's diatribe against literacy triggered the notion that useful insights on the future of work might spring from thinking about the future of thought. One such exercise suggests that our future work will indeed be highly interactive. It will entail collaborating in cyberspace, and we will get better and better at it as we develop our ability to think intuitively.

Professor Gerald Zaltman's second-year Harvard Business School MBA class was asked for their ideas about how to complete the analogy: "Writing is to analytic thinking as computers are to . . ." Their responses included "holistic thinking," "conceptual thinking," and "synthesis"—not a bad way of describing the kind of nonlinear thinking at which one would want our future leaders to excel.

SOME PREREQUISITES FOR REALIZING STAGE 3 IDEAS

Asking about the impact of technology on marketing led us to consider its impact on working, and ultimately to its impact on thinking. Out of that came the notion that collaboration is likely to become an especially important form of interactivity. And that, in turn, invites the concept of collaborative marketing, i.e., a *recasting of business as a game with customers, rather than as a game against competitors.* Now we have a truly important potential transformation to consider.

Using this possibility as a filter to scan the current environment for indications that such a scenario may be coming about makes it more likely that we will, for instance, notice the article by W. Chan Kim and Renee Mauborgne reporting on five years of research into what differentiates successful high growth companies from the rest of the pack. They found that it was not size, access to the latest technology nor deep pockets. Rather:

The less successful companies were stuck in the trap of competing. Their strategic logic centered around building competitive advantages. They benchmarked the competition and focused on outperforming rivals. The result was a perpetual cycle of offering a little more for a little less than competitors. The competition, not the customer, set the parameters of their strategic thinking. . . .

By contrast, high-growth companies [in the study] paid little heed to matching or beating the competition. Instead, they sought to make the competition irrelevant by offering buyers a quantum leap in value. (Kim and Mauborgne, 1997)

A related technique for thinking about the previously unthinkable is the development of propositions about necessary conditions for creative breakthroughs to emerge.

Consider, for example, the hypothesis that each of the following must be present:

1. A common representational schema, robust enough to abstract and codify the essential characteristics of an idea, so that it can be faithfully reproduced.
2. A structural format that comprehends the potential of existing technology, and that disciplines, but does not overly constrain, creative expression.

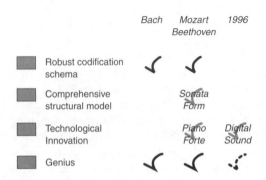

Figure 1-5   What Makes Classical Music So Classical?

3. A substantial technological advance, not previously internalized by human beings.
4. Genius.

Let's test this model on music. I know many musicians who think that Bach was the greatest musician that ever lived. Many of these same people believe that Mozart and Beethoven composed the best music ever written. How could that be?

With our hypothesis, we could explain the continued pre-eminence of classical period music by showing that Bach—certainly the best composer of the baroque period—lacked both the *structure* provided by the sonata form and the *technology* of the *forte piano* and clarinet. Bach never heard a clarinet, and therefore obviously could not think of a clarinet concerto. So Benny Goodman's favorite composer was Mozart, much as he admired Bach's genius.

In fact, Bach did not even think of a concerto in the same way Mozart did. Bach never wrote in the sonata form, the structure that enabled . . . the sonata—and that transformed the concerto and symphony. Its simple but powerful *statement, development, recapitulation* format provided a framework of structural integrity to harness the improvisational genius of Mozart and Beethoven.

Bach never owned a *forte piano,* although it had appeared on the scene toward the latter part of his life. His keyboard instruments were the organ, clavichord, and harpsichord. Harpsichord technology features one plectrum plucking one string. The hammers in a *forte piano,* however, struck two strings, with a volume and duration determined by the touch of the pianist. This permitted overtones, dynamics, sonorities, and an expressiveness that Beethoven applied to glorious effect, but that were simply not in Bach's tool kit. The *forte piano* also had more keys, which gave classical period composers more notes to work with, an advantage Beethoven exploited in his remarkable late sonatas.

All three of these men used the same notational scheme—two centuries old in their time, and still the standard today. But only Mozart and Beethoven—especially Beethoven—were able to exploit the potential of the new technology within the new sonata form paradigm. The result is what for many of us is better music than anyone has written before or since.

Today we have technology that can produce an almost infinite number of notes, of virtually any timbre, and in the style of virtually any orchestra or performer. But after decades of trying, no one has produced a notational scheme *or* a structural paradigm rich enough to encompass and discipline the capability of the technology. Which means, according to our hypothesis, that even if we assume a Mozart is walking the earth today, he lacks the necessary ingredients to produce a masterpiece for digital synthesizers.

At the risk of overtaxing the sophistication of our model, let's briefly apply its logic to the so-called interactive book. Can we expect more than audience exploration of a preplanned set of modular plot options, created in advance by authors? This is at best a marginal change in the presently passive creative role played by readers. Or will some new form emerge that substantially enhances contingency—modeled, for example, after the team stories that many of us have built with others sitting around a campfire or dinner table?

It may be that the representational schema of interactive books will be primarily visual, rather than textual, and that books and films will merge

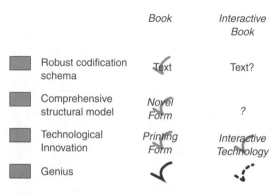

Figure 1-6   Toward an Interactive "War and Peace"

into a new category of cyberstory. Whatever our conjectures may be, until the emergence of robust new notational and structural paradigms, it is at least doubtful that we will see major creative breakthroughs in the artistic application of interactive technology.

IMPLICATIONS

This discussion of what we mean about interactivity, and how previously unthinkable things get thought, suggests that we might want to keep an eye peeled for research about, and indications of:

- technological developments permitting greater contingency, frequency, simultaneity, and sensory involvement
- a notational scheme for collaboration that encompasses these dimensions
- a robust paradigm that provides structural discipline for creative, *collaborative* genius.

Collaboration is an especially important type of interaction. How people work together (and how people and technology work together) to establish common purpose and coordinate behaviors is a very important thing to understand when thinking about the application of interactive technologies. In fact, understanding how the quality of collaboration can be improved may even be prerequisite to thinking about certain kinds of presently unthinkable applications. Since Descartes, our model of thinking has been linear and sequential sense-making. But the best collaborations will probably feature nonlinear and parallel thinking.

What, to summarize, might help us better anticipate and manage the surprises in our collaborative, interactive future? Knowing that surprises are fundamental to progress in exploiting interactive technology, and that developments in collaboration are a likely source of many of them. Understanding that there are no shortcuts up the learning curve of efficiency and effectiveness to the previously unthinkable, but that there are ways of climbing it faster. Recognizing that implicit in the Web is a potential for collaboration of a scale and kind we are only beginning to appreciate. Keeping an eye on research that can help us understand how people will change the way they think and work with each other and with machines.

William Gibson, Jules Verne of the information age, wrote in the July 14, 1996, *New York Times Magazine*:

> The Web is new, and our response to it has not yet hardened. That is a large part of its appeal.

It is something half-formed, growing. Larval. It is not what it was six months ago; in another six months it will be something else again. It was not planned; it simply happened, is happening. It is happening the way cities happened. It is a city. (Gibson, 1996)

Stephan H. Haeckel is Director of Strategic Studies at IBM's Advanced Business Institute, and Chairman of the Marketing Science Institute.

I am grateful to Jim Harrison, former professor and chairman of the Department of Music at Hunter College, for sharing his musicological knowledge about changes that occurred between the times of Bach and Mozart.

REFERENCES

Gibson, W. *New York Times Magazine,* July 14, 1996.

Haeckel, S. H. In *Marketing in an Electronic Age,* R. Buzzell (ed.), Cambridge, MA: Harvard Business School Press, 1985, p. 320.

Kim, W. C., and R. Mauborgne. "Value Innovation: The Strategic Logic of High Growth." *Harvard Business Review 75,* 1 January–February 1997.

Lloyd, S. "Learning How to Control Complex Systems." *Bulletin & the Santa Fe Institute* (Spring 1995).

Ong, W. J. *Orality and Literacy,* Routledge, 1982.

Oxford English Dictionary.

Chad Quinn

ABSTRACT

Chad Quinn discussed these issues in his speech at the Direct Marketing Association's 1998 net. marketing Conference, held April 1998.

INTRODUCTION

Before I address new business strategies, I would like to start with all of us taking a second to look back. The visual for us today is 15 to 20 years in the past. Imagine we are not at an Internet conference; we are at a banking brainstorming session, discussing ways in which the banking community can add value to our customers, decrease costs, and increase customer service. While exploring ways to become more effective, get closer to customers, and increase value, somebody says, "I've got a great idea. Why don't we take a whole bunch of cash and put it in a box? Keep it unsecured, put that box in a mall and let the general public have at it. They can make withdrawals, deposits, no guard, no anything. That's what we think would do it." How would you have judged that idea 20 years ago? At face value, that is a pretty crazy idea, but that is today's ATM machine—to the tune of over 600,000 ATM machines out there. Fast-forward 20 years: it is stranger today to go to a teller than an ATM machine.

Tomorrow's Business Standard

I think it's important to emphasize this point: what appears crazy, what appears to be fiction today will become tomorrow's business standard. You may look at the ideas at the conferences and the exhibits we are at today and wonder if this is really happening in your own business. Is this really going to be a viable way for you to conduct business? The real-life ATM example points to *yes.* So we need to change the way that we are thinking about our Internet channel, and about how we market, sell and fulfill over the Internet.

Exchange of Ideas

There is simply no greater asset that we have in today's economy than exchanging knowledge and ideas. Take a look at a company like Exxon. Exxon has $87.4 billion worth of capital, yet has less value and less shareholder wealth than Microsoft, which has $5.7 billion worth of capital. That to me is an eye-opening message: it may not be the physical assets that a company has, because Microsoft's assets are in tee shirts and ponytails with ideas. It is the knowledge you bring that is important. It is the way you think differently that has value in the marketplace today. We need to share ideas and transfer knowledge because that's the best intellectual capital.

In that spirit, I want to advance some new, perhaps strange, thoughts and terms to have a dialogue on how we can market, sell, and fulfill over the Internet. There are a lot of stories and examples that are commonly used. I'm going to try to use uncommon examples, and maybe some uncommon terms, to spur on some thoughts. My objective is to generate an idea that you can bring back to your business. One new term that I'm coining is the *business ecosystem.* It needs to be the first discussion point because what I'm asking us to do is look at marketing, selling, and fulfilling in a whole different light, not just Internet-centric, but more from a big-picture perspective. I want to share with you what has and has not worked at FedEx as it relates to the Internet. I can give you some time-tested methods using FedEx as a case study. We will look at how an "airline" has harnessed the power of the Internet and made it effective. Finally, we will take a look at two leading companies and two smaller companies you may not have heard of, but that you will hear of soon because of their unique strategies and the tactics that they have in place.

THE BUSINESS ECOSYSTEM

I just came back from Jackson Hole, Wyoming, where I had a chance to go to Yellowstone Park. So that is one reason why I'm interested in nature and this whole ecosystem idea right now. If you look at an ecosystem, it is the most perfect example of pure integration. There is no better analogy for business than an ecosystem with different organisms living in balance within a community. In nature, widely different organisms—everything from sea plankton to a whale—live in unison and in synergy. From the business perspective, you have many different channel strategies that you are launching. You have to keep them synchronized, not just have the Internet as the total goal or just a minor part, but in balance. This is critical to the way that you need to think. In our consulting experience with companies, the people that look at it from that holistic perspective are the successful ones.

The Basics of Survival

What are the essential elements for sustaining life, whether you are in an ecosystem or a business? From nature's standpoint there are three: oxygen, food, and water. All organisms need these to sustain life. From a business standpoint, the three disciplines are marketing, sales, and fulfillment.

Whatever your tactic—whether you are going to interact with your customers though a direct sales force, direct marketing campaigns, or the Internet—you will be able to grow and live and sustain. All three business operations are necessary to effectively compete in today's marketplace. Each channel strategy that you provide needs a marketing element tied to a selling application and then back-end integration into the fulfillment process.

A New Beast: The Internet

We have in our business ecosystem a new organism that we are all trying to get our arms around and understand better. That is why we have come to this conference, to answer the question, "How do I fit this Internet, which has a lot of elements and power to it, within my business ecosystem today?" What we are really saying is "How do I integrate it into existing channels so that it *is* in balance?" First, you have to understand how the Internet has changed the experience of the customer. I can unequivocally say we have seen some pretty big changes from our own customer research. It has definitely moved from a broad, mass-market approach to a very personalized one-on-one experience. If I want to buy a computer, I can go to a store such as CompUSA. I am limited to the selection they have on the shelf, the vendors they choose to show and the pricing that they offer. It is very much an "appeal to the masses" type of environment. On the Internet, I can go to a web page and configure per *my* requirements, per *my* demand, what kind of CPU I want, what kind of hard drive, mousepad, or monitor. I can truly configure and personalize my experience. The tectonic shift from a physical way of buying things to the Internet is definitely in place and has changed the customer's experience.

The Internet has also heightened customer intimacy. You can learn much more about your customers' behaviors, trends, and understanding, and in essence become much more involved in their needs. I'll give you an example. I typically go to the Internet to buy CDs, and I like jazz and blues. CDNow has captured my information and knows my preferences, so now they are able to become much closer to me. When there are specials on blues music, they appear right on my browser, right at my desktop. That is a way of becoming more intimate with a customer, as opposed to a call center agent who might not remember a particular customer's preferences. There is no mass-market capture mechanism that happens, whereas on the Internet that capture technology is built-in.

The Internet has dissolved barriers of time, distance and space. In the physical world, you could not have a million books in inventory and be able to shelve them as quickly as Amazon.com has done. The Internet has also made location irrelevant. It does not matter where you are or who you're next to. The promotional aspects are powerful, but the most powerful aspect is that traditional barriers companies have faced have dissolved, which in turn has shaped the customer's experience.

Finally, the Internet really is the great equalizer. It allows you to compete on your knowledge, on your content, and on what you bring to the customer. General Motors, with $100 billion in assets, is just as relevant as a small entrepreneurial company in terms of the Internet. There is a great cartoon with two dogs on the Internet looking at the screen. One turns to his canine buddy and says, "You see, on the Internet no one cares that you're a dog." That is true—it is democracy in its greatest form. It does not matter who you are or what your resources are, you have an equal voice in this medium. That enables the smaller, growing companies to make a strong impact on their customers.

Integrate

If we agree conceptually that the Internet has changed the experience of a customer, let's go back and see how we can take this "organism," if you will, and move it into our current business strategies. The Internet has to be tied to existing channels. We have consulted with companies that

have tried to have it be everything that they move towards, and we have consulted with companies that just want to put up a web page so that they have a URL on their business card. Those are the two ends of the spectrum. In our estimation, the ones that have been able to capture the market quickly are those that say, "What do I do best? What are my existing channels? How do I integrate this new entity into my existing way of doing business?" These are the time-tested methods that actually drive a successful strategy. Like anything, you have to feed it. An animal would not choose to say, "I'm only going to feed myself once every three days." To sustain life it has to feed daily, and you have to think of your Internet channel as a daily resource that you feed, nurture and develop. It has to be something that you take a long-term approach to. I have often gone on pages that say, "Last time updated September 1996." How likely are you to order from that page? You do not know the relevancy or the frequency. Are you nurturing and developing it? Are you in real-time with that medium? Are you signaling to your customer that this is something that you consider to be important? Then again, can it coexist with other channels? Is it perceived by your company as a competitor or a complementor? Answering that will tell you a lot. If it's complementing channels and driving traffic to traditional sites, then you are on the right track. If you are looking at this in competition with other channels, then it is a divided effort that will not realize its full potential.

FEDERAL EXPRESS: A CASE STUDY

Let's look at Federal Express as a case study and understand how it has shaped the customer's experience. Why is a company that you think instinctively of as an airline delivering packages? If anything, the Internet would be looked at as a major competitor. You might think, "I don't need to deliver packages, I can get my information on the Internet." So what was Federal Express's Hopefully, some of the pain we wen well as some of the success, will help you in your business.

We looked at the Internet from a standpoint of harmony, not hype. There is an incredible amount of hype about the Internet, about what it can do, and about people or a company having a Web presence. Our thought was not to get too hyped on the research, the information, and the market opportunity. We were not going to reinvent our business or try to do something that wasn't our core competency. People get wowed by the potential and think, "I can put a couple of products on the web, do something totally new that I haven't done before in my business, and capture all this incremental revenue." We took the holistic approach of incorporating it harmoniously into what we do now. Being mindful of the inherent channel differences, we hoped to harness the power of the Internet.

PowerShip

Federal Express has had an initiative for the last decade that hopefully some of you are involved in already. About 15 to 20 years ago, we decided to take this little computer box, which has a retail value of about $4000, and give it to customers. This was one of those ideas that, like an ATM machine, sounds crazy. I can just imagine the reaction to the person at FedEx that presented that idea, the initial frowns of "Why would you give a computer to a customer?" The thought was, if we provided the technology for you to see information about us, to go on and fill out an airway bill, or to track your package, you as a customer would be more efficient and be more satisfied. We started that about a decade ago. Meanwhile, the Internet started to evolve and expand. Our strategy was not to scrap all that we had just done with these boxes, and all jump blindly onto the Internet. We migrated what we had already done with these computer systems and incorporated the Internet into them. Right now, system-wide, there are over a quarter of a million people transacting with us online. We have linked these computer devices to the Internet so

that you can ship and track online. That is pretty powerful, because we extended from our current base. We made it harmonious with our prior initiative and did not try to make the Internet a competitive channel.

You need to figure out what your company does well, what is its strategic advantage, and how the Internet can complement that. Federal Express's advantage is our network, which serves 211 countries directly. We realized very quickly that we have a physical network with which we can move packages. This Internet provides an even more powerful information network. How could we tie the two together to complement each other and not act as competitors? We took our existing efforts, layered them into the aspects that the Internet possessed, and developed PowerShip. That refers to the computer devices that I was talking about. The ability for you as a customer to ship online has come in many different forms: big computers for high volume, small for light software, and also now InternetShip. We took our existing backbone through the PowerShip network, the online customers through our software, our client server network that supports this, our Electronic Data Interchange (EDI) billing network, and the infrastructure of Information Technology professionals we had, and built upon this with our Internet strategy.

A large portion (80%) of our customers are using automation in one sense or another, either through the Internet or being accessed through the Internet through these devices that we distributed. That has incurred a lot of cost savings for us. The idea of giving out a computer wasn't altruism; it wasn't because we wanted to be charitable. Guess what happened when we gave customers a computer? They shipped a lot more—to the tune of 40% more system-wide—because they found that it was easier to use and that there was more information to gain than from a FedEx competitor. Think of that same business principle in terms of your customer base and your competitors. How can you take information and make it easier for customers to deal with you? Open up what you do best through the Internet, and use it as a strategic advantage.

Do Work on the Web

We became a pioneer on the Web very quickly because we did not look to start anything new. Our first Web initiative was basically to give the customer base more information, and show everything that we were doing internally in order to make better-informed decisions. So what would normally be perceived as a modest ambition (not trying to reinvent anything, just show what we already do within our company) became something that got a lot of press, because our Web site allowed customers to do the things I have listed here. In essence, without the fancy terms, people were able to *do* work on the Web. Allow your customers to take care of some of their daily tasks with you. Allow them to do that on the Web on their terms, 24 hours a day, 7 days a week, at their convenience. If you can achieve that objective within your business, that alone puts you in a group of only 2% of sites out there today. Ninety-eight percent of the Web sites are what I call "dead Webs." Basically when you go there, you can see a lot of brochures or read a mission statement, but there is no work to be done. Until you can get somebody to see some benefit and utility in it, whose page is it really? Is it your page or is it your customers'? That perspective shift needs to happen. Ask yourself, "How can I help my customers, like FedEx tried to do with these PowerShips, do work?" For us, work is defined as tracking packages, shipping, downloading software to schedule pick-ups, e-mail notification forms, getting transportation rates or drop-offs. The more content we put up, the more the site grew. This site has never received one commercial. It has never received much of an advertising budget because what we realized is the best advertisement is if you can actually do something. If you have content that is rich, people say, "I'm going to bookmark this site because I can plug in a couple of numbers and I get information

back on what is being shipped to me." That is the greatest way for a site to grow.

The site has grown at a clip of about 10 to 15% per month in traffic since 1995, representing over 3 million hits per month. These are customers that are looking to do a business transaction. They are not here to read about FedEx's mission statement. In fact, most customers will not even go to the first splash page. They are there to do something and move and get out. 800,000 packages are tracked per month off the Net. Look at it in terms of cost reduction and adding value. Over 170,000 copies of software that we would probably have had to FedEx to customers are now downloaded. So digital distribution is another powerful tool. How can you provide content or downloads to your customers? We have been able to build upon the relationship, adding value by the convenience of the Internet on a customer's terms. You and I go to an ATM machine because we do not want to be confined to a teller's hours. The same concept is here on the Internet. There are business principles behind all of this. We did this for a reason. What is most potent for us is that half of the Web customers tell us they would have called our 1-800 number. We get about 600,000 calls a day. Factoring in this half having to go through our phones at a call handling cost to have a human being answer their question, or type in information from a work-screen and give them a tracking number, was expensive and time-consuming. Now that we have been able to migrate transactions over to the Internet, it has led to a substantial cost savings.

We have basically reinvented the customer relationship, because we have improved our retention rate, increased the amount of information that we are providing, and raised our customer market share. More people are doing business with us because of the functionality that we have off the Net. This has also provided an incremental revenue stream. Once more, back to this ecosystem, the Net is nothing more than a fourth sales channel. It is not the be-all and end-all, and then again it is not something that you should passively look should be part of a channel, but inte other channel strategies: direct marketing, a sales force and call centers, along with an Internet presence. The convergence of the four, complementing and referring back to each other, is so powerful. We have taken care to make sure that each channel supports the others. The Internet has really provided a lower cost way of serving our customers. Where else could you interact with more customers at a reduced cost? That is the net of the Net. The bottom line is that this provides opportunity, and helps our customers build their businesses. If we were to look at this as just a FedEx-win, not a customer-win scenario, it would be ephemeral. Our biggest challenge right now is how to make sure that we stay ahead of the great jobs UPS and other transportation companies do. I love that competition because that just gets us better. We have to keep raising the bar.

The Next Step

By now we have made an impact on the Internet. We have demonstrated a way that helps you by giving you information. This in turn helps our relationships with customers. We have gained some cost savings and market share from it. Our next big mountain to climb is, "How do we affect your customer?" That is on our strategy drawing board right now, to be very candid with you. This raises the bar on the level of service and information that we need to provide. We've developed a virtual customer service relationship. Many people tell us that they prefer to go to the Net for information than to call us up, as evidenced by that survey I shared with you. So we have now created a whole population of customers out there and allowed them to be serviced over the Web. The measurement in ROI on this is absolutely tangible. You can look at click streams and other report mechanisms that show you the incremental purchase activity and retention off the Net. Because you can understand somebody's online behavior on the Net, you can understand the measurements and have the

ability to see the return on your investment. The fact that we have brought customers from a call center to the Net has funded this initiative on its own. Again, this is the point of adding value, with half of the tracking requests going to the Net. It was factored into one of our business plan models that we would have had to hire about 20,000 more employees to deal with our demand if we didn't have a Net presence. That is a substantial investment. Since this channel complements our existing channels, we can provide high levels of service to our customers.

Measures of Success

So why was it successful? Because we looked at integrating it with our own systems. One of the huge differentiators that we see in customer feedback is operational excellence. When FedEx picks up a package, we use scanners and track it throughout the system; we have all these control mechanisms. We saw that was valuable, along with our name and reputation, so we took the Internet and enhanced our positive value. We couldn't find enough ways to show you our tracking and proof of delivery, to show you what we do well. That is what we think is so powerful. What is inside your company that makes you different? Make sure the Net positively enforces that in as many different mediums as possible, and positions you in comparison to your competition, because that's where the difference is going to be highlighted. That is where we saw the difference.

Back to the elements of survival, we focused on our oxygen, food, and water. We didn't try to launch something new. We tried to keep it consistent, based on marketing being our oxygen, creating a Web site that was very personalized and one-to-one. Customers could look at tracking numbers, schedule their own pick-ups, with a very customized look and feel. Our food in this case would be the sales, the ability for us to garner increased traffic and orders through our Web page.

The fulfillment was the water, making sure that whatever our customers saw and clicked on came out with a FedEx shipping label. They had total visibility into their order. So focusing in on the sales, marketing, and fulfillment, and making sure that those three disciplines were in our Internet strategy and complement our existing channels, is the reason for our success. We wanted the Internet to be a complement, not a competitor. Instinctively our sales force thought, "If people can ship off the Internet, how do I fit into that equation?" We harnessed them as the advocates of it. They became the people that educated our customer about our Web initiative. You want your salespeople to gravitate toward it, not see it as a threat to job security.

Finally, it may seem very simple, but you have to be able to do something on your web site. I don't know how else to explain it other than in 20 years of consulting with over 750 companies, mid-sized, small, and large, one take-away is when your customers go to your site, they have to be able to perform some function. They should not only see a bunch of brochureware or eye-candy or nice-to-haves, but also be able to do something there that helps people, saves time, or gives them more information. We've talked with so many folks that get wrapped up into the cosmetics of it: "I want an animated image here" or "I want my logo to come out." Those are nice-to-haves, but remember this is a commerce site. What do you need to grow your business? You need the same functions you need in other channels, but highlight them on this channel.

I started out by saying, "Why is an airline on the Internet?" and it lot of people asked that question when we first did it. You look at this quote, and you can tell what we have been able to do in a short period of time. The CEO of a top computer company is referencing us as a networking company. That is a pretty big mind shift for our company. We have been able to shift people towards this paradigm because we are more about sharing the information on your package with you than on us just having that information, and we let the In-

ternet prove that to you. Now we have positive marketplace feedback on what our customers are doing in using us as referrals. I wanted to make another note of this because I want you to think about it within your own business plan.

Once you get to a function that adds value, your next step is raising the bar on your competitors. The key here is how to help your customer with their customers. I do not know the answer within each of your industries and businesses, but think through that. That is where we are moving towards right now. We believe that tracking and shipping is now standard; others will have that. If they do not already have it, they will be roadkill on the information highway. What we need to do next is help our customers' customers.

Supply Chain Initiatives

We are looking at three ways to network in the supply chain. One is virtual order, a solution that allows companies to put their product catalog on the Internet, and have an interactive experience with full integration to fulfillment, order status capability and tracking. That happens on the order demand creation side. We can come in with a SWAT–team style initiative and work with an account to get it up and running very quickly with our resources. Again, our 15 years of experience with electronic commerce and also struggling on the Internet helps. I should make this qualifier though: we are still doing things wrong. We have server outages, we have issues with going from one look and feel on our home page to another. So we are not doing everything right, but we are making our mistakes faster than hopefully our competitors are, so we are learning from them and adjusting. We are taking a solution outside of our relationship with our customers and giving it to them to give to their customers.

The second supply chain initiative deals with, once you receive orders, how to get them to inventory management sites and distribution centers, or to vendors for a direct ship scenario. We have a whole EDI-based solution in place that allows companies like L.L. Bean to manage inventory. They do not want to hold all of your products in one warehouse up in Maine. So they came to FedEx and asked, "How can I tie the orders right to my vendors and have them ship it, but have all the information on the package, right down to what's inside the box?" We provided their vendors with full-view capability, with all of the information clearly displayed on their packages now

The final initiative is what we call "reverse logistics." When somebody has a return, or wants a warranty upgrade, how do you manage the Return Material Authorization (RMA) process? It is a golden opportunity to create customer loyalty. NetReturns is an Internet-based solution for small companies to authorize and schedule pick-ups.

LEADING-EDGE COMPANIES

Let's talk about other leading-edge companies. Two you probably know very well, and two you may not know. I chose these companies because I want you to think about what they are doing and why they are successful.

Hewlett Packard

First, let's take it look at Hewlett Packard (HP). Again, we are going to use our oxygen, food, and water analogy. The first, oxygen, is marketing. What they are doing from that standpoint is leveraging their strong brand. Market research shows that consumers and companies at most remember two to three brands: Nike, Reebok, Adidas maybe; FedEx, UPS, maybe Airborne. So the ability to create brand awareness is very powerful. HP realizes that. They are not going to go out and try to create a new brand on the Internet. Again, they're going to be harmonious, thinking of their own ecosystem. They are going to try to bring all the

value inherent in their name and tie it into their Internet site. They are going to make it one-on-one. When you and I go there and we want an HP printer, we can really configure on demand, and have the product that we want on our terms, at our price points, and at our convenience. From a sales standpoint, this whole process involves configurator type of technology, which is just componentry. As you and I go through their site, we look at and pick a certain printer. There may be accessory items for that printer, but we do not have to know that. This technology provides all of the accessory items plus substitutable items if they are out of stock, so there is a lot of cross-selling and tip-selling potential there. As HP is moving towards this customized experience, they are going to get higher order values and more frequent orders. So think about that within your own business. The more you can make decisions for your customer or provide relevant information on a product that they're looking at, the more they're going to see that site as successful. Finally, on fulfillment, they have outsourced their entire logistics operations: warehousing, time-definite delivery and inventory management. Personally, I think they are smart, because they want to be HP, not a fulfillment house. By outsourcing that part of the business, they can have key integration with a vendor who they feel is a long-term player. Then HP can push the envelope again and again on the logistics side and stick to what they do best.

Staples

The next company is Staples. Think in terms of Staples in a corporation perspective, not how Staples interacts with the general public. Their corporate offices are lining up all the key companies that they do business with and provide office supplies to, and they're creating individualized catalogs for each one of those key customers. They are pursuing Extranets. This is a term you have probably heard of and will continue to hear about. Market research by both Forrester's and Gartner shows that by the year 2002, 40% of the business to business transactions on the Internet will go through an Extranet. That is what you and I and other people will be talking about when we come back to these conferences over the next two to three years as this migration occurs. Extranets are here to stay, and they are powerful. As a review, an Extranet is a secured community between a buyer, a product, and the suppliers that the buyer sources from. So Staples thought, "Our companies, big Fortune 500 companies, are setting up Extranets. We need to get a piece of that, because that is where the traffic, transactions and commerce are moving towards. What if we offer them a specific Chase Manhattan product catalog with all the office supplies they want to look at, on their pricing terms, and on their delivery schedules? We could put that catalog on Chase's Intranet, so whole departments could be at a desktop location and order their office supplies." That is a powerful concept because what happens normally to Staples (and they will be the first to tell you) is they have a lot of leakage. They set up a big contract with a customer, then are not as effective in getting the message out to the whole company, so people go out and do renegade purchasing. Employees run over to Kinko's and buy something at list rates, not at the contract that the company negotiated, and they wind up paying more as a company. Bringing ordering to a browser allows it to happen faster, easier and more conveniently, which keeps them locked into these customer relationships. So the Extranet strategy that Staples is providing is very powerful and makes them a leading edge company in what they are trying to do.

Again, the final element is fulfillment, full integration into the back-end. This is what we feel is the next frontier. A lot of people are looking at this. I have sales input. I have an email form where you can order from me. Providing back-end visibility to your customers is where you are going to keep the loyalty. Loyalty today is so ephemeral. Customers are fickle, they will move and not worry.

They will stay if they can go to the same site where they ordered something to find out where it is in your process: whether it's being credit-verified or approved, whether it is in a pick-pack area, whether it has been shipped, what's the proof of delivery, where is it going? That whole back-end is the next frontier where people will be able to differentiate their sites. To Staples' credit, they are looking at full integration into those systems.

RISING COMPANIES

PC Parts

The last two companies you may not have heard about. This one excites me because the company is very small. It is headquartered in Harrisburg, Pennsylvania. It probably has less than $100 million in total revenue, but it will have a name because it has the right equation to it. PC Parts is a small computer peripheral and accessory distributor. They sell a lot of secondhand IBM parts and other accessory items in the computer industry, but they are limited to the amount that they can warehouse. Again there is this whole issue of limitation by space, location and distance. What PC Parts is doing now is integrating with their trading partners to offer products that they will never even touch. Right now they have a catalog that has 6000 SKUs on it. Over the course of the next year, they will be offering 30,000 different items that you can buy. They are going to become a virtual distributor, because they are integrating these trading partners into routing orders and tracking visibility when it comes from the vendor direct to the customer. They are using the Web as their front-end order entry and order management channel, and linking with EDI to be able to back-end to the suppliers to route the orders. That combination is very robust because a lot of the back-end systems are EDI-based. They have the infrastructure in place right now to take advantage of the supplier network. Finally, they are taking the fulfillment process and leveraging it as a customer service tool. They are saying, "I'm not going to allow what's perceived as a mundane activity like fulfillment just lie there. I'm going to make it a differentiator." They are going to do so by passing back visibility via their Web page to their customers for the whole life of that product right up until the point it is delivered. Again, this negates call-ins, "where's my order?" queries, and a lot of the servicing issues that are happening now on a manual mode and on the phone by their call center agents.

Sun Data

The last company, Sun Data, is a $200 million company, a little bigger than PC Parts. Based in Atlanta, Georgia, they are a workstation configurator of Sun Microsystems. They offer a very compelling business plan because they are taking the Web from the marketing standpoint, with an interactive Web site, and they're using it as a vehicle to achieve global reach. They are expanding into markets that they have not been able to penetrate before. Their Vice President of Sales was telling me that they have received orders from South America and from Europe. They had never dealt with an international order before, so they did not know how to process it and send it out—but those are the kind of problems I guess you *want* to have. They are taking this global reach and trying to expand their business without the costs of getting a sales force hired and up and running in foreign areas. They are using the Net to gain a global reach to a whole new customer base. They have a very well-balanced approach. In fact, Sun Data was referenced in *Electronic Commerce World* magazine as having $1.5 million worth of incremental business come in off their interactive Web page. The interesting thing is that business is not all from orders off the Web page. The fact that they are now marketing through their Web presence has allowed their traditional channels to grow to the point of $1.5 million. People are going on, placing orders, and Sun Data's revenues are increasing on the In-

ternet site, but people are also going on, learning for the first time, seeing it being interactive, and then maybe calling up or going through other traditional channels. They have taken a balanced approach of coordinating, so when a call center agent receives that phone call, he or she is aware of what happened on the Net and what the customers' experiences on the Net were, and it is almost seamless to the point when the agent gets back on the phone with the customer. Or a salesperson receives an incentive when Net orders occur from Sun Data. So this whole crossover balance approach of all the channels is showing in hard dollars, through the amount of incremental revenue that they have been able to produce. Finally, they are going to offer something called "Total Order Status," which they see as their real competitive weapon. Regardless of whether you order from them on the Internet, on the phone, or through one of their sales reps, you can go to one area on the web site, click on Order Status, and have total visibility on everything and where it is. Over time this negates the callbacks, the "where's my order?" calls, and the manual processes that they entail. They are going to use fulfillment as the last leg to provide that visibility, and not just on the Web track. On all the mediums that they use with the customer you'll have the ability to see the order status capability.

CONCLUSION

So, to review our discussion points:
- A business ecosystem: keep it well-balanced. Do not launch something separate; launch something that highlights your core competencies and that interrelates to your existing channels. Learn from the case study. Take a core competency and make it available in as many different ways as you can from the Internet—for us it was tracking and shipping and visibility.
- From these leading companies, think through how they are raising the bar on how they are servicing their customers through things like

configurators, helping them make decisions on ordering, order status capability, total visibility into their internal processes, integration into their fulfillment and Extranets. How you can apply these strategies as a small company to be able to do business with a bigger company by working to get a product catalog on one of the company's Intranets, for example. Extranet traffic is growing substantially. This is a huge theme, with a good deal of support.

QUESTIONS AND ANSWERS

Q: UPS now offers similar online services such as tracking. What do you feel is the difference between FedEx and its competitors on the Web?

A: UPS and FedEx are in a leapfrog situation right now. UPS has matched us in terms of our early success on tracking and shipping. One distinction we see is that the level of detail we provide about our network is, according to our customer focus groups, far greater. When I say level of detail, I mean the ability to tell you that your package was not just picked up and delivered, but everything in between. People value that. However, you bring up a good point. That is why we feel we need to affect not just you, the customer, and your business, but also your *customers'* business. We do not see UPS having those supply chain tools right now. Probably next year, they will have these tools and we will have to think about some other competitive advantage.

Q: Is there any human interaction available on the site?

A: What we are doing now is very relevant to that. We are coming out with a new technology called *Interactive Answers.* When you go on to an Internet site through Federal Express to track something, you may need an agent's help. You will be able to call up and have an agent on the line at the same time as you are on the site. We believe that this fits with the ecosystem. You have to merge everything together, keep it in balance. We want to bring the human contact together with the digital contact.

Q: Who uses the FedEx.com site and how do you reach your target audience?

A: Looking at the demographics and the target audience, our Web users are business sales, marketing, and operations contacts that are in any need of tracking and shipping information. Predominantly it is most heavily used by the operations side, then second would be sales and third would be marketing, in terms of input. We do not do commercials on it, as noted, and that is because the content has spoken for itself. People have just bookmarked the page and it has grown. Companies like Cisco actively promote that you can have free FedEx tracking off their site. What we are finding is a kind of reactive approach. Companies call us to ask for our logo and a link to our site, because that helps them on their sites. We have set up a network now. At first we were doing it kind of ad hoc, and now we have a formalized process to go through. The short answer is growth has been based more on word of mouth about the content and the fact that it works and less on a big splash of PR with nothing behind it.

Q: How do you determine where your future growth will be, and how do you prepare for it?

A: We struggle with that all the time, frankly. A lot of the research and growth has focused on the business to business side. Obviously, given the traffic and the installed base of computers in business, we're definitely committed to harnessing that. You have to have a network that supports the consumer as well. We're looking at the costs from a FedEx perspective, so the metrics for us are tough. We would much rather go to a business where we can pick up *and* deliver, whereas a far remote residential delivery is less cost effective for us. That does not mean we want to back away from it. We want to find ways to engineer our network so that business to customer transactions remain competitive and make sense for both the customer and for us, the provider.

Q: During the UPS strike last year, did FedEx take any specific actions or use different online strategies?

A: We did a lot of manual labor. I actually had to volunteer in the hub to deliver. A lot of employees had to come together to handle the extra work. The other thing was, we thought people would come to us for a short period of time and go back to their existing courier. That has not happened. People came and they stayed, so we have had to develop a lot more infrastructure to support the volume. To the question of what we did on the site, that is probably one of the few times that we did take a promotional aspect to our site, because we realized that was a lower cost way to serve customers. So we did some PR to drive traffic to the site, as opposed to customers going and manually filling out airbills or calling us up on our 1-800 number.

Q: Are you looking to penetrate online communities?

A: Absolutely. There are communities that we feel are going to evolve on the Web. These business communities are going to support the type of time-definite transportation that we provide. This will be mainly in the pharmaceutical, automotive, medical device, computer hardware and peripherals industries, based on the companies we looked at. We are definitely looking to link directly into and become a valued extension of these pods or communities.

Q: Can you provide a specific example of how to integrate the sales force with Internet initiatives for smaller companies?

A: I can even give you one example on Sun Data as a small company. Sun Data took the orders that came off the Internet and matched the zip code of the customer against the territory of a salesperson. They would give that person an incentive or some type of bonus payoff on the customer. So what happened was the salespeople, instead of just allowing it to happen, became proactive. On sales calls that would penetrate internally, they could say, "If I'm not here and you have a routine order, here's the site to go towards." That has worked much better for them than some of their PR releases or direct mail pieces.

Q: How do you manage the costs of maintaining and upgrading your site?

A: That's a good question. In terms of our cost structure, we have to practice what we preach. Some of it on the creative side is in a core competency. You will notice that the Web page has changed dramatically in the last six months. We outsourced the creative look and feel to a very close third party vendor. Stuff like the tracking or the core we keep in-house. We have structured that based on our IT group that does those loads and changes. We also have a very thin marketing team that will either manage a project themselves or outsource it to some best-degree third party of front-end companies that we work with. So those are some of the ways that we've been able to offset some internal costs from the site.

At the time of writing, Chad Quinn was manager of electronic commerce at Federal Express Corporation. He is now vice president leading Internet strategy for Manugistics, a provider of solutions for supply chain optimization.

CONCEPTUAL FOUNDATIONS OF INTERNET MARKETING

Outline

Early attempts at Internet marketing were largely ineffective for most firms. Many firms rushed online with web sites that mimicked corporate brochures. There was little, if any, consideration given to the strategic value of the Internet to the firm.

As marketers gained knowledge, web sites were created with a greater focus on strategic objectives. Customer support databases and interactive features were implemented. A greater number of web sites could perform valuable functions for visitors.

The seamless integration of the web with traditional support and distribution channels is now a priority for many firms. The power of the Internet as a value proposition is no longer questioned. Instead, firms are seeking to discover and implement strategies to more effectively leverage the web for corporate success.

The starting point in formulating an effective Internet marketing strategy is to identify the needs of customers or stakeholders who will visit the web site. The content of the site should be structured such that the needs of various visitors are given first priority. In short, site content and structure should match visitor needs and abilities.

In the first article of this chapter, Donna Hoffman and Thomas Novak present a network navigation model that provides the foundation for understanding principles of Internet marketing. The central construct of their model is *flow*. When flow is positive, it is more likely that the visitor will respond to the site in the desired manner. Flow is indirectly determined by individual, site, and situational characteristics. Individual characteristics include the relationship between skills and challenges. Site characteristics include interactivity and vividness. Situational characteristics include motivation and benefits sought.

In the second reading, Bruce Clark presents a framework for classifying web sites. Clark distinguishes between supplemental and virtual approaches to Internet marketing and defines different revenue models used on the Internet. Clark also provides a number of useful recommendations to management.

In the third reading, Pradeep Korgaonkar and Lori Wolin show that web usage can be explained by a relatively small number of motivations and concerns. These include social escapism, transaction-based security and privacy concerns, information motivation, interactive control motivation, socialization motivation, nontransactional privacy concerns, and economic motivation. These findings show the importance of understanding visitors' motivations and concerns when building a web presence.

The online resources and content are designed to complement the chapter readings. Please visit the textbook's web site to enhance your understanding.

Marketing in Hypermedia Computer-Mediated Environments: Conceptual Foundations

Donna L. Hoffman
Thomas P. Novak

The authors address the role of marketing in hypermedia computer-mediated environments (CMEs). Their approach considers hypermedia CMEs to be large-scale (i.e., national or global) networked environments, of which the World Wide Web on the Internet is the first and current global implementation. They introduce marketers to this revolutionary new medium, propose a structural model of consumer navigation behavior in a CME that incorporates the notion of flow, and examine a series of research issues and marketing implications that follow from the model.

Firms communicate with their customers through various media. Traditionally, these media follow a passive one-to-many communication model, whereby a firm reaches many current and potential customers, segmented or not through marketing efforts that allow only limited forms of feedback from the customer. For several years, a revolution has been developing that is dramatically altering this traditional view of advertising and communication media. This revolution is the Internet, the massive global network of interconnected packet-switched computer networks, which as a new marketing medium has the potential to radically change the way firms do business with their customers.

The Internet operationalizes a model of distributed computing that facilitates interactive multimedia many-to-many communication (for a complete history, see Hafner and Lyon 1996). As such, the Internet supports discussion groups (e.g., USENET news, moderated and unmoderated mailing lists),

multiplayer games and communication systems (e.g., MUDs [Multiuser Dungeons], IRC [Internet Relay Chat], chat, MUSEs [Multiuser Shared Environment]), file transfer, electronic mail, and global information access and retrieval systems (e.g., archie, gopher, World Wide Web).[1] The business implications of this model, in which "the engine of democratization sitting on so many desktops is already out of control, is already creating new players in a new game" (Carroll 1994, p. 73), will be played out in as yet unknown ways for many years to come.

We focus on the marketing implications of commercializing hypermedia computer-mediated environments (CMEs), of which the World Wide Web (Berners-Lee et al. 1993) on the Internet is the first and current networked global implementation. Although we provide a formal definition of a hypermedia CME subsequently, at this point we informally define it as a distributed computer network used to access and provide hypermedia content (i.e., multimedia content connected across the network with hypertext links). Although other CMEs are relevant to marketers, including private bulletin board systems; conferencing systems such as The WELL (Rheingold 1992); and commercial on-line services such as America Online, CompuServe, Prodigy, and the Microsoft Network, we restrict our focus to marketing activities in hypermedia CMEs accessible via the Web on the Internet.

From a commercial perspective, the Web consists of locations, or sites, that firms erect on servers and consumers visit. On the Web, consumer-oriented network navigation consists

---

[1]For a discussion of the technical terms used in this paper, consult one of the many reference books on the Internet (e.g., December and Randall 1995). A comprehensive listing of books about the Internet can be found at http://www.switch.ch/switch/InternetBooks.txt. The http address is a Uniform Resource Locator (URL) that specifies the exact location of a document on the Internet. Note that URLs are used in the Reference list to indicate where on-line versions of documents can be identified. Although these URLs were accurate at the time this article was written, it is possible that over time, some of these URLs may have changed or no longer exist.

Reprinted with Permission from the *Journal of Marketing,* published by the American Marketing Association, Donna L. Hoffman & Thomas P. Novak, July 1996, Vol. 60, pp. 50–68.

of visiting a series of *Web sites* to search for information and/or advertising about products and services or consumer content (possibly advertiser-supported) or place an order for a product.

Consumers visit a site by directly entering its Web address in the browser or clicking on a hypertext link leading to it from some other site. Once there, consumers navigate through the site using a series of point-and-click motions with a mouse or entering textual information into pop-up windows and "fill-out forms" with keyboard strokes. From there, the consumer chooses where to go next in the site. Often, the offerings are presented as a nonlinear graphical menu or map of choices to the consumer. The navigation process continues, terminated only when the consumer jumps to another off-site hypertext link within the Web or exits the Web navigation experience entirely.

The Internet is an important focus for marketers for several reasons. First, consumers and firms are conducting a substantial and rapidly increasing amount of business on the Internet.[2] Although there is some controversy surrounding the estimates of the size of the Internet, surveys performed to date by O'Reilly, FIND/SVP, Times Mirror, and Hoffman, Kalsbeek, and Novak (1996) suggest that there are at least 10 million Internet users in the United States alone. The number of

computers (hosts) connected to the Internet topped 9.47 million (Network Wizards 1996) as of January 1996 and has been doubling every year since 1982. Note that a single host supports anywhere from a single user to, in some cases, thousands of users. As of March 21, 1996, Open Market's (1996) directory of "Commercial Services on the Net" listed 24,347 firms, and there were 54,800 entries in the "Companies" directory of Yahoo's (1996) guide to the Web, with the total number of Web sites doubling approximately every two months.

Second, as Malone (1995) has argued, the market prefers the decentralized, many-to-many Web for electronic commerce to the centralized, closed-access environments provided by the on-line services. Significantly, all the major on-line services now offer Web access to their subscribers and have or are expected to announce plans to allow members to self-publish their own *home pages* on the Web, as well. Additionally, virtually all the major communications conglomerates have Web sites, as they shift their strategic orientations away from so-called interactive television applications to Web-based publishing, communication, and multimedia marketing efforts.

Third, and this follows from the first and second points, the World Wide Web represents the broader context within which other hypermedia CMEs exist. Indeed, much of the foundation we develop here is relevant to on-line services, particularly as they begin to function more as full-service Internet access providers and less as closed, proprietary networks. Thus, restricted on-line services are special cases of the open-access World Wide Web. Open access results in lower entry barriers so that virtually anyone can both access and provide content to the Internet. In essence, the Web "levels the playing field."

Both the Web and proprietary on-line services are examples of developments in *electronic commerce,* which, as Rangaswamy and Wind (1994) have noted, include such developments as EDI (electronic data interchange), kiosks, electronic classified advertisements, and on-line services such as CompuServe and Minitel, the French

---

[2]The most recent figures decision makers are using for business planning and research purposes are that the total core economy for electronic commerce on the Internet will approach $45.8 billion by the year 2000 (Modahl 1995), including $14.2 billion for infrastructure, $2.8 billion for consumer content, $6.9 billion for business content, and $21.9 billion in on-line trade (made up of $6.9 billion in retail and $15 billion in EDI). Additionally, Modahl (1995) forecasts that $46.2 billion in consumer assets will be managed over the Internet by the year 2000, broken down as $29.9 billion in mutual funds and $16.3 billion in deposits. However, analysts at Hambrecht and Quist (1995, www.hambrecht.com) estimate a much larger Internet economy of $73 billion by the year 2000, comprised of $13 billion in infrastructure, $10 billion in content, and $50 billion in transactions. On the other hand, Alex, Brown and Sons (Clark 1995) forecast a much smaller Internet economy, between $13.5 billion and $16 billion by 1998, composed of a $6 billion infrastructure, $5 billion to $7 billion in communication access, and $2.5 billion in content. Currently, the total Internet economy is estimated at $2 billion (Modahl 1995). Additionally, the market for the largely digital electronic convergence of content systems, publishing, and so on is already estimated at over $1 trillion (Oliver 1995). None of these forecasts include efficiency savings from moving processes and transactions on-line.

videotex system (Cats-Baril and Jelassi 1994). With the possible exception of EDI, which is moving to the Internet because its "open architecture" system is more inclusive and offers numerous advantages over private networks, none of these mechanisms for facilitating commerce electronically has the same far-reaching scope and potential for transformation of the business function as does the World Wide Web.

Fourth, the Web provides an efficient channel for advertising, marketing, and even direct distribution of certain goods and information services. For example, Verity and Hof (1994) suggest that it may be nearly one-fourth less costly to perform direct marketing through the Internet than through conventional channels. Neece (1995) reports that SunSolve Online™ has saved Sun Microsystems over $4 million in "FAQs"[3] alone since Sun "reengineered information processes around the WWW [Web]." A recent study by IBM Corporation (1995) suggests that on-line catalogs on the Internet can save firms up to 25% in processing costs and reduce cycle time by up to 62%. Along with the suspected increases in efficiency, the anecdotal evidence mounts that marketing on the net also may be more effective than marketing through traditional media. For example, one vendor estimated that his marketing efforts on the Web resulted in "10 times as many units [sold] with 1/10 the advertising budget" (Potter 1994).

GOALS AND ORGANIZATION OF THE PAPER

Although there have been recent scholarly efforts detailing the impact of new information technologies on marketing (e.g., Blattberg, Glazer, and Little 1994; Glazer 1991), the existing research does not discuss the impact that hypermedia CMEs such as the World Wide Web have on marketing theory and business practice. Despite the massive

amount of attention given to the Internet in the popular press (see, e.g., the more than 6000 references to the Internet in *ABI Inform* through November 1995) and the belief in many business circles that the Web represents a phenomenal marketing opportunity, virtually no scholarly effort has been undertaken by marketing academics to understand hypermedia CMEs, both as media for marketing communications and as markets in and of themselves. We draw from the relevant literatures in psychology, communications, media studies, organizational behavior, and human-computer interaction, and concentrate our efforts on developing a conceptual foundation for understanding consumer behavior in hypermedia CMEs.

Therefore, our goals are to introduce marketers to this revolutionary new medium, propose a preliminary process model of consumer navigation behavior in a hypermedia CME, examine the research issues that correspond to the process model, and derive marketing implications for electronic commerce all to stimulate critical inquiry in this emerging area. To that end, the article is organized as follows: We discuss three models of communication that underlie traditional and new media and develop a media typology that reveals new insight into the distinctions among traditional media and CMEs. Then, using an expanded concept of flow (Csikszentmihalyi 1977, 1990), we introduce a preliminary process model of network navigation in CMEs. We next present a series of 15 research issues involving the flow construct and process model, while paying attention to the marketing implications that follow from the research issues. Finally, we offer conclusions about the importance of this emerging area of inquiry to both marketing scholars and practitioners interested in electronic commerce.

HYPERMEDIA COMPUTER-MEDIATED ENVIRONMENTS

We begin by outlining a series of three communication models that serve to identify several unique characteristics of hypermedia CMEs such as the

---

[3]A FAQ is a frequently asked question to which standardized replies are both readily available and desirable.

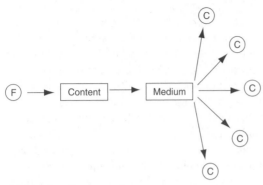

Note: F = firm; C = consumer.

Figure 2-1 Traditional One-to-Many Marketing Communications Model for Mass Media

Web. We then describe a new media typology that positions the Web in the broader context of new and traditional media and discuss the marketing implications of the communication models and typology.

Communication Models

Model 1: Mass Media

In Figure 2-1, we present a simplified model that underlies many models of mass communication (e.g., Katz and Lazarsfeld 1955; Lasswell 1948). The primary feature of Figure 2-1 is a one-to-many communications process, whereby the firm (F) transmits content through a medium to consumers (C). Depending on the medium (i.e., broadcast, print, and billboards), either static (i.e., text, image, and graphics) and/or dynamic (i.e., audio, full-motion video, and animation) content can be incorporated. No interaction between consumers and firms is present in this model. Virtually all contemporary models of mass media effects are based on this traditional model of the communication process (e.g., see Kotler 1994, Chapter 22).

Model 2: Interpersonal and Computer-Mediated Communications

In Figure 2-2, we present a simplified model of interpersonal communication that is based on traditional models of communication from sender to receiver. The solid and dashed lines indicate communication flows through a medium for two distinct persons. This model incorporates a feedback view of interactivity, which is consistent with Rafaeli's (1988, p. 111) definition of interaction as "an expression of the extent that in a given series of communication exchanges, any third (or later) transmission (or message) is related to the degree to which previous exchanges referred to even earlier transmissions." Although Figure 2-2 is shown here for one-to-one communication between two consumers, the model can be easily extended to represent many-to-many interpersonal communication (i.e., teleconference, face-to-face group meetings, or on-line chat rooms). Note that unmediated face-to-face interpersonal communication is a special case of Figure 2-2. From a marketing perspective, the model in Figure 2-2 is implicit in developments of word-of-mouth communication models.

Person-interactivity, the key feature distinguishing Figure 2-2 from Figure 2-1, is defined as interactivity between people that occurs through a medium or is unmediated, as in the case of face-to-face communication. In this view of interactivity,

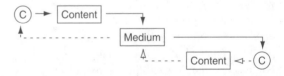

Note: C = consumer.

Figure 2-2 Model of Interpersonal and Computer-Mediated Communication

media are "important only as a conduit, as a means of connecting sender and receiver, and are only interesting to the extent that they contribute to or otherwise interfere with the transmission of messages from sender to receiver" (Steuer 1992, p. 77–78).

Hypermedia CMEs

Nearly 50 years ago, Busch (1945, p. 106) proposed a hypertext-like system called *Memex,* which would consist of "a device in which an individual stores all his books, records, and communications, and which is mechanized so that it may be consulted with exceeding speed and flexibility." Nelson (1967) discussed hypertext in terms of a network of paths and associations, with an emphasis on approximating the way the human brain connects information. Bornman and von Solms (1993, p. 260) provide a current definition: "*Hypertext* suggests the concept of non-sequential writing of information that allows the user to connect information together by means of different paths or links." *Multimedia* uses a computer to integrate and provide interactive access to both static (i.e., text, image, and graphics) and dynamic (i.e., audio, full-motion video, and animation) content, whereas hypermedia combines the node-and-link access of hypertext with multimedia content. Gygi (1990) and Smith and Wilson (1993) provide more extensive discussion of hypertext and hypermedia.

We define a *hypermedia CME* as a dynamic distributed network, potentially global in scope, together with associated hardware and software for accessing the network, which enables consumers and firms to (1) provide and interactively access hypermedia content (i.e., "machine interactivity") and (2) communicate through the medium (i.e., "person interactivity"). We further define *network navigation* as the process of self-directed movement through a hypermedia CME. This nonlinear search and retrieval process provides essentially unlimited freedom of choice and greater control for the consumer and may be contrasted with the restrictive navigation options available in traditional media such as televi-

sion or print. Furthermore, network navigation permits much greater freedom of choice than the centrally controlled interactive multimedia systems, such as video-on-demand and home-shopping applications of so-called Interactive Television; the text-based French Minitel system (Cats-Baril and Jelassi 1994); the menu-based information-acceleration approach of Hauser, Urban, and Weinberg (1993); or the experimental systems for monitoring information processing, such as Mouselab (e.g., Payne, Bettman, and Johnson 1993).

Model 3: A New Model for Hypermedia CMEs

In Figure 2-3, we present a many-to-many communication model for hypermedia CMEs. The content in Figure 2-3 is hypermedia, and the medium is a distributed computer network. Figure 2-3 differs

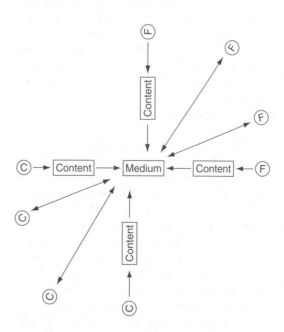

Note: F = firm; C = consumer.

Figure 2-3   A Model of Marketing Communications in a Hypermedia CME

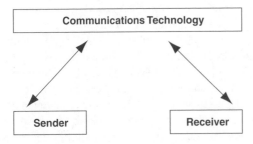

Figure 2-4   Mediated Communication
Note: Adapted from Steuer (1992).

from Figure 2-2 in that interactivity can also be *with* the medium (i.e., machine interactivity) in addition to *through* the medium (i.e., person interactivity).

Figure 2-3 is based on a communication model outlined by Steuer (1992) and shown in Figure 2-4. The mediated model represented in Figure 2-4 suggests that the primary relationship is not between the sender and the receiver, but rather with the mediated environment with which they interact. According to this view, information or content is not merely transmitted from a sender to a receiver; instead, "mediated environments are created and then experienced" (Steuer 1992, p. 78). In Steuer's model of mediated communication, *machine interactivity* is "the extent to which users can participate in modifying the form and content of a mediated environment in real time" (p. 84). Steuer calls his model a *telepresence view* of mediated communication, where *presence* is defined as "the natural perception of an environment" and *telepresence* is defined as "the mediated perception of an environment" (p. 76). Following Steuer, when interacting with a computer-mediated environment, the consumer perceives two environments: (1) the physical environment in which he or she is present and (2) the environment defined by the hypermedia CME. The strength of the experience of telepresence is a function of the extent to which a person feels present in the hypermedia CME, rather than in his or her immediate physical environment.

In Figure 2-3, we show the range of communication relationships possible in a hypermedia

CME. Consumers can interact with the medium (e.g., "surf the Web" using browsing software) as can firms (e.g., business-to-business marketing in CommerceNet). In addition, firms can provide content to the medium (e.g., a firm establishes a corporate Web server). Finally—in perhaps the most radical departure from traditional marketing environments—consumers can put product-related content in the medium. For example, individual consumers have established Web pages for automobiles (e.g., the Ford Probe, Porsche, car audio equipment, and solar cars), toys (e.g., Legos and Barbie Dolls), and television shows (e.g., Friends, The X-Files, Married With Children, and Rugrats). Furthermore, note that Figures 2-1 and 2-2 are contained within Figure 2-3. Thus, a hypermedia CME also can be used for computer-mediated communication among consumers and/or firms (*through* the medium, or person interactivity), as well as potentially for one-to-many mass communication, though applications of the latter have met with considerable consumer resistance (e.g., Godwin 1994).

Media Characteristics

Studying media characteristics provides a structured context for comparing different media types, including traditional media and new media (Valacich et al. 1993; Williams, Strover, and Grant 1994). Traditional media include both mass media (e.g., television, radio, newspaper, magazines, direct mail), and personal communications (e.g., word of mouth). New media encompass interactive media, such as videotex, interactive CD-ROM, on-line services, and hypermedia CMEs, as well as emerging so-called interactive multimedia, such as pay-per-view, video-on-demand, and interactive television.

The media typologies referenced in Table 2.1 reveal that media differ along many different dimensions, for example, channel characteristics (Reardon and Rogers 1988; Rogers 1986), social presence (Rice 1992, 1993), and uses and gratifications (Perse and Courtright 1993). However,

TABLE 2.1	Review of Media Comparisons	
Source	Communication Media Compared	Characteristics of Communication Media
Dennis and Valacich (1994)	Face-to-face, phone, memo, voice mail, video conference, email, electronic phone, and group support systems	Feedback, symbol variety, concurrency, persistence, ability to rehearse
Perse and Courtright (1993)	Television, video cassette recorder, movies, conversation, phone, computer, newspapers, magazines, books, and radio	11 communication needs (relaxation, entertainment, forget work, friendship, learning, pass time, excitement, feel less lonely, satisfy habits, acknowledge feelings, get someone to do something for me) and social presence
Reardon and Rogers (1988)	Interpersonal communication, interactive media, and mass media	Message flow, source knowledge of the audience, segmentation, interactivity, feedback, asynchronicity, emotional versus task-related content, control, privacy
Steuer (1992)	44 new and old media including newspapers, fax, interactive television, three-dimensional films, sensorama, and the Star Trek Holodec	Subjective classification according to vividness and interactivity
Stewart and Ward (1994)	Television, radio, magazines, and newspapers	27 characteristics for "gross media comparisons"
Rice (1992)	Email, voice mail, videoconferencing, and on-line databases	Social presence, information
Rice (1993)	Face-to-face, email, meetings, phone, desktop video, text, and voice mail	Social presence, appropriateness for ten communication activities (exchange information, negotiate, get to know someone, ask questions, stay in touch, exchange time-sensitive information, generate ideas, resolve disagreements, make decisions, confidentiality)
Valacich and colleagues (1993)	Distributed verbal, face-to-face verbal, distributed electronic, and face-to-face electronic	Communication concurrency
van Dijik (1993)	Two-way cable, videotex, data networks, email, videophone, and interactive video	Kinds of information, mode of communication

TABLE 2.2 Objective Characteristics of Media

	Person-Interactivity	Machine-Interactivity	Number of Linked Sources	Communication Model	Content[a]	Media Feedback Symmetry	Temporal Synchronicity
Mass Media							
Billboards	no	no	one	one-to-many	T, I	yes	n/a
Newspapers	no	no	one	one-to-many	T, I	yes	n/a
Magazines	no	no	one	one-to-many	T, I	yes	n/a
Direct mail	no	no	one	one-to-many	T, I	yes	n/a
Radio	no	no	few	one-to-many	A	no	n/a
Broadcast television	no	no	few	one-to-many	A, V, (T)	no	n/a
Cable television	no	no	few	one-to-many	A, V, (T)	no	n/a
Satellite television	no	no	many	one-to-many	A, V, (T)	no	n/a
500 channel cable television	no	no	many	one-to-many	A, V, (T)	no	n/a
Interactive Media							
Local hypertext	no	yes	one	one-to-many	T	yes	yes
Local hypermedia	no	yes	one	one-to-many	T, I, A, V	no	yes
Dial-up bulletin board service (information only)	no	yes	one	one-to-many	T	yes	yes
CD-Interactive	no	yes	one	one-to-many	T, I, A, V	no	yes
Videotex	no	yes	few	one-to-many	T	yes	yes
Pre-Web On-line Services	no	yes	few	one-to-many	T, I	no	yes
Interactive television	no	yes	few	one-to-many	T, I, A, V	no	yes
World Wide Web	no	yes	many	many-to-many	T, I, A, V	no	yes
Interpersonal Communication							
Mail	yes	no	one	one-to-one	T	yes	no
Fax	yes	no	one	one-to-one	T	yes	no
Telephone	yes	no	one	one-to-one	A	yes	yes
Videophone	yes	no	one	one-to-one	A, V	yes	yes
Face-to-face	yes	no	one	one-to-one	A, V, E	yes	yes
Face-to-face (group)	yes	no	few	few-to-few	A, V, E	yes	yes
Town meeting	yes	no	many	many-to-many	A, V, E	yes	yes

TABLE 2.2 Objective Characteristics of Media (*continued*)

	Person-Interactivity	Machine-Interactivity	Number of Linked Sources	Communication Model	Content[a]	Media Feedback Symmetry	Temporal Synchronicity
Computer-Mediated Communication							
Email	yes	yes	one	one-to-one	T	yes	no
Voice mail	yes	yes	one	one-to-one	A	yes	no
Talk program	yes	yes	one	one-to-one	T	yes	yes
Email (carbon copy: list)	yes	yes	one	one-to-few	T	yes	no
Multiparty chat	yes	yes	few	few-to-few	T	yes	yes
MUDs	yes	yes	few	few-to-few	T	yes	yes
See you see me	yes	yes	few	few-to-few	A, V	yes	yes
Mailing lists	yes	yes	many	many-to-many	T	yes	no
Usenet newsgroups	yes	yes	many	many-to-many	T	yes	no
Web (forms/annotation)	yes	yes	many	many-to-many	T, I	yes	no
Internet Relay Chat	yes	yes	many	many-to-many	T	yes	yes

[a]T = text; I = image; A = audio; V = video; E = experiential. (T) = there is a minor amount of text content.

hypermedia CMEs were not in existence at the time these typologies were proposed. Although the typologies cited include the computer as a communications medium, it is defined narrowly in terms of email, bulletin boards, and computer conferencing.

Furthermore, many of the characteristics listed in Table 2.1 are either subjective in nature or require the application of valid measurement procedures. Therefore, we propose a new media typology based on seven objective characteristics. Although objective characteristics do not allow the media to be compared with respect to such psychological dimensions as communication needs, social presence, or control, they do permit a relatively error-free classification. Thus, in Table 2.2, we characterize 35 traditional and new media with respect to seven objective characteristics. We have already discussed person-interactivity and machine-interactivity and the distinction between one-to-many and one-to-few (Figure 2-1), one-to-one and few-to-few (Figure 2-2), and many-to-many (Figure 2-3) communication models. Content simply identifies whether static or dynamic information can be delivered by the medium. For unmediated interpersonal communication, experiential content includes stimuli affecting additional sensory modalities, such as tactile, proprioceptive, or olfactory senses.

The remaining three characteristics may be defined briefly as follows: The *number of linked sources available* specifies how many sources of content are readily accessible or available to the user at any given usage opportunity. *Media feedback symmetry* refers to whether different parties in the communication process employ differing media bandwidths for sending information. For example, in an Interactive CD, feedback is asymmetric, because the Interactive CD sends high bandwidth information, but the consumer sends low bandwidth information. From the consumer's perspective, this facilitates interactivity because a few simple cursor, mouse, or joystick movements produce dramatic modifications in the environment. When there is symmetric media feedback,

all sources in the communication process employ the same media bandwidth for sending information—for example, telephone, mail, and face-to-face communication. *Temporal synchronicity* is a property of interactive media only, does not apply to mass media, and means interaction occurs in real time.

In Figure 2-5, we present a perceptual map, produced by plotting object scores for 35 media types resulting from a nonlinear principal components analysis (Gifi 1990) of the data from Table 2.2. The nonlinear principal components analysis is equivalent to a multiple correspondence analysis (Hoffman and de Leeuw 1992), with ordinal restrictions imposed on category quantification of variables assumed to have a known underlying ordering of categories.[4] To simplify presentation, only the object scores for the rows of Table 2.2, and not the category quantifications for the columns of Table 2.2, are plotted.

Following orthogonal rotation of axes, Figure 2-5 has a clear interpretation. The horizontal axis differentiates from personal from personal communication media, and the vertical axis differentiates dynamic from static media. Reardon and Rogers (1988, p. 297) argue that "new communication technologies are interactive in nature, and thus cannot be easily categorized as either interpersonal or mass media channels." Indeed, Figure 2-5 shows that traditional mass media channels occupy positions at the upper left (broadcast media) and lower left (print media), whereas interpersonal media occupy the upper-right position and mail and fax occupy the lower-right position. New media occupy largely intermediate positions, in agreement with Reardon and Rogers (1988), who view new interactive media as

---

[4]In this case, ordinal restrictions were imposed on the number of linked sources (one, few, many) and the three-category variable specifying presence of text content. The communication model also was treated as two separate ordinal variables—the number of senders (one, few, many) and the number of receivers (one, few, many). Because all other variables were either binary (person-interactivity, machine-interactivity, audio, video, image, experiential, and media feedback symmetry) or nominal (temporal synchronicity), no other ordinal restrictions were imposed.

combining properties of mass (impersonal) and face-to-face (personal) communication channels.

Figure 2-5 identifies two points for the Web, one assuming text, image, and audio content (Web alone) and one assuming text, image, audio, and video content (Web plus video). Web plus video content occupies a central position in Figure 2-5; that is, it is the most "typical" of all communications, sharing characteristics with a wide variety of other media types. The many-to-many communication model underlying the Web positions the Web closer to the personal side of the horizontal axis than it does traditional mass media.

The central position of the Web in Figure 2-5 corresponds to an important strategic interpretation of the Web as a marketing medium; namely the Web combines elements from a variety of traditional media, yet is more than the sum of the

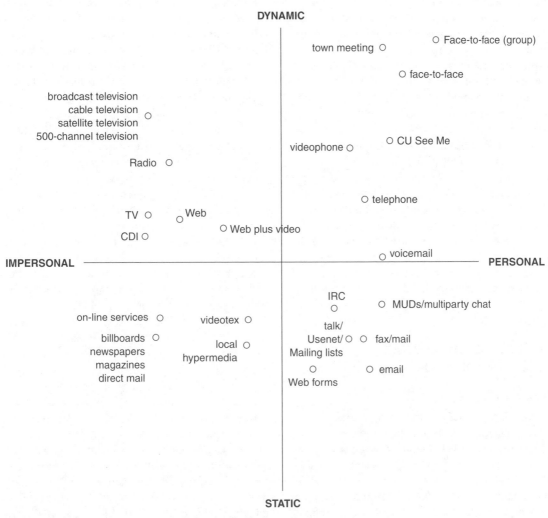

Figure 2–5   Media Typology Based on Objective Characteristics

parts. For example, broadcast media in the top left quadrant of Figure 2-5 provide relatively short-term exposure with low information content, whereas the print media in the bottom left quadrant provide relatively long-term exposure with high information content. Advertising strategy on the Web must account for both short-term (decision of which link to select next) and long-term (reading detailed information provided at a commercial site) exposure.

We next discuss a process model of network navigation in hypermedia CMEs such as the Web. There are several unique features of CMEs as media and marketing environments that motivate the process model. As virtual hypermedia environments incorporating interactivity with both people and computers, CMEs are not simulations of real-world environments, but alternatives to them. Within the virtual environment, both experiential (e.g., net-surfing) and goal directed (e.g., on-line shopping) activities compete for consumers' attention. Consumer skill in functioning in the virtual environment, as well as challenges posed by the environment, introduce a competency issue that does not exist in such a fundamental manner in the physical world. This issue of whether consumers' skills are competent to meet the challenges of the virtual environment plus the telepresence created by immersion in an interactive hypermedia environment bear directly on the construct of flow, which underlies the process model.

A PROCESS MODEL OF NETWORK NAVIGATION IN HYPERMEDIA CMEs

The Flow Construct

Although consumer researchers have explored the role of play in the consumption experience (e.g., Holbrook et al. 1984), we believe the concept of flow in a hypermedia CME holds wider applicability and underlies many crucial components of the consumer's interaction with the firm and its offerings. Simply stated, *flow* is the process of optimal *experience* (Csikszentmihalyi 1977; Csikszentmi-

halyi and LeFevre 1989; p. 816, emphasis added) preceded by a set of antecedent conditions necessary for the experience to be achieved and followed by a set of consequences that occurs as a result of the process.

We define the *flow experience* in a CME as the state occurring during network navigation, which is (1) characterized by a seamless sequence of responses facilitated by machine interactivity, (2) intrinsically enjoyable, (3) accompanied by a loss of self-consciousness, and (4) self-reinforcing. In the flow experience, which formalizes and extends a sense of playfulness (Csikszentmihalyi 1977; Csikszentmihalyi and LeFevre 1989), consumers are so acutely involved in the act of network navigation in the hypermedia CME that "nothing else seems to matter" (Csikszentmihalyi 1990, p. 4).

Two primary antecedents must be present in sufficiently motivated users of a hypermedia CME for the flow experience to occur. Consumers must focus their attention on the interaction, narrowing their focus of awareness so that irrelevant perceptions and thoughts are filtered out, and they must perceive a balance between their skills and the challenges of the interaction.

The key consequences of the flow experience for consumers are increased learning, exploratory and participatory behaviors, positive subjective experiences, and a perceived sense of control over their interactions in the hypermedia CME.

When in the flow state, irrelevant thoughts and perceptions are screened out and the consumer focuses entirely on the interaction. The flow experience involves a merging of actions and awareness, with concentration so intense that there is little attention left to consider anything else. A consumer's action in the flow state is experienced as a "unified flowing from one moment to the next, in which he is in control of his actions, and in which there is little distinction between self and environment, between stimulus and response, or between past, present and future" (Csikszentmihalyi 1977, p. 36). Self-consciousness disappears, the consumer's sense of time becomes distorted, and the resulting state of mind is extremely gratifying.

Flow has been previously noted as a useful construct for describing human-computer interactions (Csikszentmihalyi 1990; Ghani, Supnick, and Rooney 1991; Trevino and Webster 1992; Webster, Trevino, and Ryan 1993). Our conceptualization extends these ideas by explicitly developing the flow construct in the context of network navigation in a hypermedia CME and arguing that flow consists of a process state that requires a set of antecedents to occur and results in a set of consequences.

On first inspection, the flow experience may appear to be similar to attention and involvement, as well as other construct events (Privette and Bundrick 1987) of peak experience and peak performance. Privette's (1983) and Privette and Bundrick's (1987) distinction between flow, peak experience, and peak performance is helpful for understanding how flow differs from these related construct events, as well as from attention and involvement. Privette considers attention and involvement to be common qualities of flow, peak experience, and peak performance, but attention and involvement do not differentiate between the three. Flow is characterized by fun and occurs in structured activities in which action follows action. Peak performance is characterized by a clear focus, a strong sense of self (rather than loss of self, as in flow), and a sense of fulfillment, whereas peak experience is characterized by a transpersonal and spiritual quality that has much higher levels of experienced joy than flow has.

Flow is a central construct because of the nature of commercial activity in a CME such as the World Wide Web. It is important to understand that commercial activity on the Web consists of much more than purchasing products in on-line storefronts. Hoffman, Novak, and Chatterjee (1995) identify six functional categories of commercial activity on the Web: on-line storefronts, Internet presence sites, content sites, malls, incentive sites, and search agents. To date, Internet presence sites, rather than on-line storefronts,

dominate commercial activity. Using the typology proposed by Hoffman, Novak, and Chatterjee, Kaul (1995) found that only 18% of a random sample of 290 Web sites served as on-line storefronts. The remaining 82% were informational or image-based Internet presence sites or directories of other commercial sites.

Internet presence sites either provide detailed information on a firm's offerings (e.g., the Web sites of Federal Express, Sun Microsystems, Volvo) or create an image and attempt to build an ongoing relationship with the consumer (e.g., the Web sites of Zima, Reebok, David Letterman). Internet presence sites are a new form of nonintrusive advertising, in which the customer actively chooses to visit and interact with the firm's marketing communication efforts. Recent efforts involve the merging of information and image in innovative ways (see, e.g., L. L. Bean's sophisticated "trail metaphor" Web site at www.llbean.com). Measures of duration time spent at an Internet presence site, depth of search through the site, navigation patterns through the site, and repeat visits to the site are crucial outcome measures for evaluating the effectiveness of such sites. Flow affects all of these outcome measures and is an important consideration for understanding consumer behavior in commercial Web sites.

The process model described subsequently has direct implications for understanding experiential behavior. The primary focus of this process model is on network navigation in integrated destination sites (Hoffman, Novak, and Chatterjee 1995), rather than on mechanisms for search and choice in such environments. Nevertheless, goal-directed processes of prepurchase search and choice in a CME take place against a background of network navigation and involve flow within and across Web sites; we address those issues, as well.

The Process Model

In Figure 2-6, we present a preliminary process model of network navigation in a hypermedia CME. For expository purposes, we diagram only the most important links. The model in Figure 2-6 shows neither the complex set of feedback loops and pathways nor the fully dynamic nature of the process. A consumer enters the hypermedia CME and engages in network navigation. There are several points of exit from the environment, as well as opportunities to continue navigation, with flow in essence serving as the glue holding the consumer in the hypermedia CME.

In the following section, we introduce a series of 15 research issues related to the components of the process model shown in Figure 2-6. We have mapped the research issues on the boxes, and pathways of the Figure to provide an overview of how they relate to the process model. Of the first five research issues, the first three deal with flow measurement, whereas the next two deal with consumer heterogeneity and flow in CMEs. In the second five research issues, we discuss experiential and goal-directed behavior in a CME. In the final five research issues, we deal with the consequences of flow.

RESEARCH ISSUES

Flow Measurement

1. Measurement Approaches

Reliable and valid measurement of flow is necessary for further development of the preliminary process model in Figure 2-6. We view flow in a CME as measurable along a continuum and note that flow can be inferred from its antecedents and consequences. Likert scales provide one approach to measuring flow. Ghani, Supnick, and Rooney (1991) and Ghani and Deshpande (1994) operationalized flow as a self-report scale containing items measuring enjoyment and concentration. Perceptions of control, skill, and challenge were significantly related to this flow measure. Trevino and Webster (1992) used four items to measure flow. The four items dealt with components of control, attention, focus, curiosity, and interest. Webster, Trevino, and Ryan (1993) used a 12-item scale expanded from Trevino and Webster's study

to measure flow, again measuring the same four components of flow. Although these components correspond more to antecedents of flow than to the flow experience, the scales used were significantly correlated with a variety of consequences of flow, such as enjoyment, positive attitudes, and future usage intentions.

Privette (1983) and Privette and Bundrick (1987) take an alternative approach to measuring flow by asking respondents to describe construct events they have personally experienced involving flow, peak experience, peak performance, average events, misery, and failure. Brief descriptions of these construct events are provided, and respondents provide personal examples of and rate each construct event using Privette's (1984) experience questionnaire. Lutz and Guiry (1994) used a modified version of Privette's experience questionnaire in a study on consumption experiences.

The most widely used approach to measuring flow is the Experience Sampling Method (Csikszentmihalyi and Csikszentmihalyi 1988; Csikszentmihalyi and LeFevre 1989; Ellis, Voelkl, and Morris 1994; Mannell, Zuzanek, and Larson 1988). With the Experience Sampling Method, respondents are electronically paged at random intervals throughout the day, at which point they immediately complete a self-report experiential sampling form with open-ended items and rating scales. On a typical experiential sampling form, respondents rate the experience in which they are currently engaged on the challenge of the experience, their own skills in the experience, a series of items measuring affect and arousal, and items measuring motivation, concentration, and creativity.

A comprehensive flow measurement procedure for a CME must include measures of the antecedent conditions (see Research Issues 2 and 3), consequences (see Research Issues 11 through 15), and variables related to the psychological experience of flow (e.g., lose track of time, self-awareness, concentration, mood, control). We anticipate that qualitative research (such as verbal protocol statements obtained from consumers as they interact with a CME), process tracing

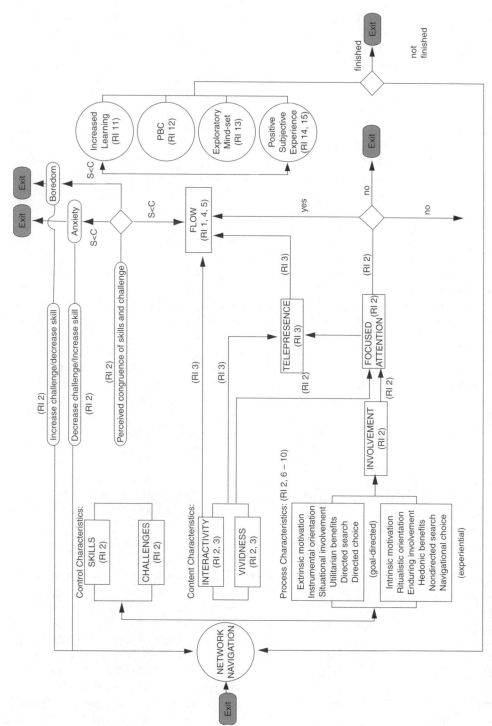

Figure 2-6   A Model of Network Navigation in a Hypermedia CME

measures of actual behavior during the interaction, and survey research (both traditional and electronic) will all be necessary to develop reliable and valid measures of flow in a CME.

2. Primary Antecedents of Flow

Two primary antecedent conditions are necessary for the flow state to be experienced: (1) skills and challenges must be perceived as congruent and above a critical threshold and (2) focused attention must be present. *Skills* are defined as the consumer's capacities for action, and *challenges* as the opportunities for action available to the consumer in a CME. Only when consumers perceive that the hypermedia CME contains challenges congruent with their own skills can flow potentially occur. If network navigation in a CME does not provide for congruence of skills and challenges, then consumers either become bored (i.e., their skills exceed the challenges) or anxious (i.e., the challenges exceed their skills) and either exit the CME or select a more (or less) challenging activity within it (see Figure 2-6).

Csikszentmihalyi's (1997) original model specified that flow occurred when an equal match between skill and challenge was perceived, regardless of whether skill and challenge were equally high or equally low. More recent reformulations (Csikszentmihalyi and Csikszentmihalyi 1988; Csikszentmihalyi and LeFevre 1989) specify that "flow results from experience contexts characterized by a match between challenge and skills only when both challenges and skills exceed the level that is typical for the day to day experiences of the individual" (Ellis, Voelkl, and Morris 1994, p. 338). Congruent skills and challenges that lie below the person's typical level are said to result in an apathy state (Csikszentmihalyi and Csikszentmihalyi 1988). Congruent, above-threshold skills and challenges as a prerequisite for flow are also consistent with the theory of an optimal stimulation level (e.g., Holbrook and Gardner 1993; Raju 1980; Steenkamp and Baumgartner 1992).

Considerable disagreement exists over how many channels, or categories, should be used to represent the various patterns of congruence or incongruence of high and low skills and challenges and how these channels should be labeled. Ellis, Voelkl, and Morris (1994) note that 3-channel (Csikszentmihalyi 1977), 4-channel (Csikszentmihalyi 1988), 8-channel (Csikszentmihalyi and Nakamura 1989; Massimini and Carli 1988), and 16-channel (Massimini and Carli 1988) models have been developed; recently, Clarke and Haworth (1994) proposed a 9-channel model. The labeling of these channels also can be inconsistent. For example, Csikszentmihalyi and Csikszentmihalyi (1988) define low skill and low challenges as *apathy,* whereas Clarke and Haworth (1994) call this combination *relaxation.*

There is also debate about the best way to determine whether skills or challenges exceed the critical threshold or typical level. Most often, within-subject standardization is used (e.g., Csikszentmihalyi and Csikszentmihalyi 1988; Csikszentmihalyi and LeFevre 1989). However, Ellis, Voelkl, and Morris (1994) note that within-subject standardization precludes studying individual differences, which have been found to be an important predictor of flow (see Research Issue 4). Consequently, some researchers (e.g., Clarke and Haworth 1994) do not employ within-subject standardization.

The presence of focused attention is also necessary to experience flow. *Focused attention* is characterized as "a centering of attention on a limited stimulus field" (Csikszentmihalyi 1977, p. 40). Webster, Trevino, and Ryan (1993) note that the computer screen functions as the limited stimulus field and that subjects report being "mesmerized" during their computer interactions. In Figure 2-6, we indicate the role of the content characteristics of vividness and interactivity in attracting attention. The performance characteristics of ease of use, mapping (naturalness of how human actions are connected to actions in the hypermedia CME; Steuer 1992), speed, and range all combine to increase interactivity. *Vividness* is defined as "the representational richness of a mediated environment as defined by its formal features" (Steuer 1992, p. 81), such as its breadth and depth. *Breadth* refers to the number of sensory dimensions presented and is closely related to media concurrency (Valacich et al. 1993) and media richness (Daft and Lengel 1986; Daft, Lengel, and Trevino 1987). *Depth* is the resolution or the quality of the presentation (Steuer 1992) and is highly correlated with media bandwidth. In the hypermedia CME both breadth and depth, in general, are high.

Extrinsic and intrinsic motivation (Csikszentmihalyi 1977, Chapter 1; Davis, Bagozzi, and Warshaw 1992; Graef, Csikszentmihalyi, and Gianinno 1983) are important process characteristics that affect focused attention through involvement (Zaichkowsky 1986). Davis, Bagozzi, and Warshaw (1992, p. 1112), in summarizing the motivational literature, note that extrinsic motivation applies to activities performed because they are instrumental to achieving a valued outcome, whereas intrinsic motivation applies to activities performed "for no apparent reinforcement other than the process of performing the activity." Extrinsic motivation creates situational self-relevance (Bloch and Richins 1983; Celsi and Olson 1988), whereas intrinsic motivation, or *autotelic activities* (Csikszentmihalyi 1977, Chapter 2), create intrinsic self-relevance. We define *involvement* as felt involvement (Celsi and Olson 1988), which is formed by the presence of situational and/or intrinsic self-relevance. Felt involvement affects attention and comprehension effort (Celsi and Olson 1988). In the context of human-computer interaction, Webster, Trevino, and Ryan (1993) find significant positive correlations between factors for intrinsic interest and/or curiosity and focused attention.

3. Secondary Antecedents of Flow

Because of the presence of focused attention and perceived congruence of skills and challenges, two additional antecedents—interactivity and telepresence—enhance flow. These additional antecedents increase the subjective intensity of the consumer's flow state, though they are not sufficient alone to produce a flow state. A strong sense of telepres-

ence (i.e., the mediated perception of an environment) is induced by vividness and interactivity (Sheridan 1992), as well as focused attention. Although the user of a hypermedia CME always experiences some level of telepresence and interactivity, higher levels can boost flow. Feedback loops, however, also must be considered. When telepresence is too high—for example, when the medium is too "hot" (McLuhan, 1964, p. 36)—challenges may become greater than skills and flow cannot be achieved (Steuer 1992).

For marketers, the primary and secondary antecedents of flow suggest that flow is not a constant state. Consumers move in and out of flow—as a function of control, content, and process characteristics. To some extent, all these characteristics may be influenced by marketing activities. The congruence of skills and challenges is something that can be facilitated by interface design. For example, a user-specified difficulty level can be designed to avoid anxiety in novice users and boredom in experienced users. Because lack of congruence may lead the consumer to exit the CME, it is important to provide opportunities for consumers to actively select activities that create congruence. Content characteristics such as interactivity and vividness lead to telepresence and can be affected directly through product design considerations. Process characteristics, specifically the distinction between extrinsically and intrinsically motivated consumers, are an important segmentation basis.

Consumer Heterogeneity and Flow in CMEs

4. The Autotelic Personality

Consumers are heterogeneous in their ability to experience flow in a CME. Csikszentmihalyi (1977, pp. 21–22) distinguishes between autotelic experiences, activities, and personalities. Flow is the autotelic experience; autotelic activities are those activities relatively more likely to lead to flow; and the autotelic personality trait characterizes a person "who is able to enjoy what he is doing regardless of whether he will get external rewards from it"

(Csikszentmihalyi 1977, p. 22) and who thus is more likely to experience flow for a given activity. Csikszentmihalyi (1988) later suggests that the ability to experience flow may be learned in the family, developed through practice, or even have a neurological component. Whatever the underlying explanation for the individual differences, Ellis, Voelkl, and Morris (1994) find that considerable variation in subjective experience was explained by variables that indicated the autotelic nature of the person, over and above the variance explained by the perceived congruence of skills and challenges. For marketers, the crucial implication is that the relative likelihood a person will experience flow is an important segmentation basis in a CME.

5. Optimal Stimulation Level and Flow

People with a higher optimal stimulation level (OSL) are more likely to possess the autotelic personality trait. The fundamental idea of OSL theories (e.g., Zuckerman 1979) is that an intermediate level of stimulation obtained from the environment corresponds to the most favorable affective reaction. Furthermore, there are individual differences in the OSL—with people having a higher OSL exhibiting increased curiosity-motivated, variety-seeking, risk-taking (Steenkamp and Baumgartner 1992), and exploratory behavior (Raju 1980). Holbrook and Gardner (1993) found the duration time of consumption of an experiential good to be related to an optimal arousal level, which has clear implications for experiential consumer behavior in a CME.

As we previously discussed, flow in a CME requires the congruence of above-threshold skills and challenges. Yet, people with low optimal stimulation levels are more likely to experience anxiety in their initial interactions with a CME, as they will be overwhelmed by the wide variety of options available to them and will perceive their skills to be well below the uncomfortably high stimulation level of the CME (i.e., the challenges of the task). Furthermore, people with low OSLs who have mastered the basics of network navigation also are more likely to later become bored with a CME, as they will be relatively less likely to

seek out sufficiently high challenges to maintain congruence with their increasing skills. Thus, we anticipate that people with higher OSLs are more likely to possess the autotelic personality trait and experience flow in a CME.

Experiential and Goal-Directed Behavior in a CME

6. Definition of Experiential and Goal-Directed Behavior

Two broad categories of behavior in which consumers engage during time spent in a CME are goal-directed and experiential behavior. Goal-directed and experiential behavior are characterized respectively by (1) extrinsic versus intrinsic motivation, (2) instrumental versus ritualized orientation, (3) situational versus enduring involvement, (4) utilitarian versus hedonic benefits, (5) directed versus nondirected search, and (6) goal-directed versus navigational choice.

For example, the corporate buyer using the Web to close a deal for computer components experiences an extrinsically motivated, instrumental, goal-directed flow state. On the other hand, net surfers exploring the Web in their daily quest for the latest interesting sites experience an intrinsically motivated, ritualized, experiential flow state. It is important to recognize that consumers engage in both goal-directed and experiential behaviors, flow may occur with both types of behaviors, and the optimal design of a CME site differs according to whether the behavior is goal-directed or experiential.

In the communications literature, a distinction is drawn between instrumental and ritualized orientations to media (Rubin 1984; Rubin and Perse 1987). Ritualized orientations focus "more on the medium, rather than on particular content," are "associated with diffuse motives (e.g., pass time, habit, relaxation)," and are a "less intentional and nonselective orientation, a time-filling activity" (Rubin and Perse 1987, p. 59). In contrast, instrumental orientations are "more intentional and selective," which reflects "purposive exposure to specific content" (p. 59). The distinction between instrumental and ritualized orientations bears considerable resemblance to the classification of expected benefits in the marketing literature into utilitarian and hedonic or experiential benefits (e.g., Havlena and Holbrook 1986; Srinivasan 1987), which as we previously noted are, respectively, extrinsically and intrinsically motivated.

We also can differentiate flow states resulting from goal directed and experiential behaviors on the basis of involvement and search behavior. Most commercial Web sites currently provide information rather than offer an opportunity to purchase a product. Thus, much of today's consumer search activities are more likely to involve what has been termed *ongoing search* than *prepurchase search* (Bloch, Sherrell, and Ridgway 1986, p. 121). Similarly, Biehal and Chakravarti (1982, 1983) distinguish between directed and non-directed learning. Bloch, Sherrell, and Ridgway (1986) note that on-going search is a function of enduring involvement with the product (or with the CME), whereas prepurchase search is a function of situational involvement with the purchase.

For choice, in experiential behavior, "activities are not guided by goals or outcomes, but by the process itself" (Bloch, Sherrell, and Ridgway 1986, p. 121). Similarly, Deci and Ryan (1985, p. 155) note that for intrinsically motivated people engaged in flow, choice is "intuitive and spontaneous" and does not involve conscious, deliberate decisions. Consumer choice in goal-directed behavior is based on a clearly definable goal hierarchy, and movement through this goal hierarchy involves choices among products and services, information sources, and navigational alternatives. Consumer choice in experiential behavior is dominated by choices among navigational alternatives and corresponds to a relatively unstructured and continually changing goal hierarchy.

7. Search Motives and Involvement for Experiential and Goal-Directed Behavior

Goal-directed versus experiential behaviors depend on distinct search motives combined with the object of involvement:

Search Motive	Involvement	Behavior
Task completion	Situational involvement with **goal** →	Goal-directed
Prepurchase deliberation	Situational involvement with **product** →	Goal-directed
Build information bank	Enduring involvement with **product** →	Experiential
Opinion leadership	Enduring involvement with **product** →	Experiential
Recreation	Enduring involvement with **process** →	Experiential

Goal-directed behaviors are characterized by situational involvement and directed search. In general, a CME user is involved with a specific task-completion goal. Marketers are particularly concerned with understanding the prepurchase deliberations for product purchase goals. Search motives in experiential behaviors, however, are more varied. When the consumer exhibits enduring involvement with a product or product category, Bloch, Sherrell, and Ridgway (1986), Biehal and Chakravarti (1982, 1983), and Bettman (1979) indicate that consumers may search to build an information bank or knowledge base in their memories for potential future use. In addition, Richins and Root-Shaffer (1988) find that enduring involvement (occurring in experiential flow) led to opinion leadership, whereas situational involvement did not. Thus, an opinion leader may be motivated to search and engage in experiential behaviors to disseminate product news, advice, and personal experience by word of mouth. Moreover, consider that consumers may be involved with the CME itself. Bloch (1995) suggests that there likely are two segments of consumers who navigate a CME: (1) those who exhibit enduring involvement with an interest area and (2) those who are navigating because they exhibit enduring involvement with computers. We propose that the latter segment is engaged in nondirected search for recreational purposes (Bloch, Sheffell, and Ridgway 1986; Csikszentmihalyi 1983).

Thus, experiential behavior is relevant for (1) word-of-mouth strategies based on influencing opinion leaders, (2) providing entertainment and recreation, and (3) enhancing consumers' product knowledge, whereas goal-directed behavior is relevant for task-specific use of a CME, such as prepurchase deliberation. This distinction is critical and suggests that marketers should take care to focus not only on goal-directed behaviors in a CME (e.g., product purchase), but also on nondirected experiential behaviors (e.g., net surfing), which are strategically important as well.

8. External Memory

A CME can provide devices for external memory. User-generated "bookmark files" containing custom lists of consumers' favorite Web sites are cases in point, as is comparative information about brands (e.g., product reviews), which is directly retrievable through an on-line storefront. Although information gained from goal-directed search activity is more accessible in memory than that from experiential search activity, CMEs provide devices for external memory that negate this advantage. Biehal and Chakravarti (1983) find that information retrieved from directed search (goal-directed) had greater memory accessibility than information retrieved from nondirected search (experiential). Furthermore, the likelihood of choosing a brand for which information was acquired during directed search was not significantly different than the likelihood of choosing a brand for which information was externally available; in both situations, the choice likelihood was greater than when brand information was acquired through nondirected search. However, the external memory devices present in CMEs imply that information retrieved from nondirected search should have a greater impact on subsequent consumer choice behavior than that in traditional environments, because the external memory devices are used by the consumer.

9. Choice Behavior and Decision Making in a CME

We also distinguish goal-directed and experiential behavior on the basis of consumer decision and choice processes. Most research on consumer choice and decision making in marketing deals with activities directly involving or motivated by product purchase (e.g., Payne, Bettman, and Johnson 1993). Although theories of problem-solving behavior have been developed for extensive, limited, and routine problem-solving scenarios, all three scenarios are typically motivated by a purchase outcome. In a CME, however, the process of network navigation continually confronts the consumer with an ongoing series of decisions that are potentially but not necessarily related to a purchase outcome or other task completion. Although existing models of adaptive decision making can explain much of goal-directed choice in a CME, they hold relatively lesser applicability to navigational choice in flow occurring from experiential behavior. In addition, CMEs provide devices that augment the individual decision processes with input from communal or machine agents.

Choice in experiential behavior primarily involves an ongoing series of navigational decisions of what to do next. This is a highly unstructured activity and, as was noted previously, corresponds to an intrinsically motivated, ritualized, hedonic use of the CME. Nonetheless, a key assumption of the nature of adaptive decision behavior expected in goal-directed situations—"that people are motivated to use as little effort as necessary to solve a problem" (Payne, Bettman and Johnson 1993, p. 13)—would realistically hold in nondirected experiential situations as well. Thus, in deciding among navigational alternatives, heuristics and noncompensatory decision rules most likely would be applied in experiential activities. Relatively little research, however, deals with choice behavior during experiential activities, so we must be cautious and not overly dependent on goal-directed decision strategies to provide explanations of consumer choice. We liken flow from experiential behaviors to navigating through an amusement park where the visitor is presented with a wide array of ride choices in a nonlinear fashion.

For flow occurring with experiential behaviors, outcome variables other than choice should

be investigated. For example, Holbrook and Gardner (1993) argue that duration time is a critical outcome measure of consumption experiences, and
Olney, Holbrook, and Batra (1991) use viewing
time as a dependent variable in a model of advertising effects. Indeed, duration times are a useful
behavioral indicator of experiential versus goal-
directed orientations. For example, 43% of all
calls to the French Minitel system are for the electronic telephone directory (a goal-directed activity) but account for only 21% of the total connect
time. On the other hand, only 6% of all calls to
Minitel are for the chat services (an experiential
activity), but they account for 15% of the total connect time (Cats-Bafil and Jelassi 1994).

In structured decision environments, such as
an on-line storefront offering a variety of goods,
the strategies typically applied by consumers in
traditional environments (e.g., Payne, Bettman,
and Johnson 1993, Chapter 2) are likely to be
used. These strategies, however, will be augmented by powerful decision aids (e.g., Payne,
Bettman, and Johnson 1993, Chapter 7) that are
feasible only in a CME. At the most basic level,
these decision aids involve information displays
that increase the consumer's processing capacity,
whereas more sophisticated approaches use decision support systems to assist the decision maker.
Both of these categories of decision aids are local,
rather than network-based, because they involve
only information presented at a given location in
a CME.

Intelligent interface agents (e.g., Maes 1994)
provide a network-based decision aid, which is
particularly useful for vastly enhancing the consumers' ability to perform search activities by reducing information overload. An example of an
agent present on the World Wide Web is Digital
Research Laboratory's Alta Vista search engine
(www.altavista.digital.com), a robot program that
automatically traverses the World Wide Web in
search of hypermedia documents and stores and
categorizes them in an extensive and rapidly growing database that can be accessed by an intelligent
search interface. As of March 1996, the Alta Vista

database can access 11 billion words found in over
22 million Web pages.

Although agents have been portrayed in the
popular media as engaging in semiautonomous,
high-level, humanlike interactions, "the most successful interface agents are those that do not
prohibit the user from taking actions and fulfilling
tasks personally" (Maes 1994, p. 31). Thus, agent's
can serve as effective decision aids in an information intensive environment. One promising approach in a networked environment such as a CME
are collaborative interface agents (Lashkari,
Metral, and Maes 1994), which combine decision
aids across a segment of similar consumers, rather
than rely on a single consumer's input.

10. Development Patterns of Flow States

We expect that experiential behavior dominates
a user's early flow experiences. Early interactions
in the hypermedia CME that lead to flow are characterized by a nondirected, time-passing, ritualized quality. Over time, ritualized use evolves into
instrumental use as consumers accumulate experience navigating within the medium. A greater degree of technical skill is required to successfully
perform goal-directed behaviors than experiential
behaviors. Experiential behaviors, in which the
consumer experiments and becomes familiar with
the CME, are accompanied by an increase in skills
that the consumer develops to meet the challenges
presented by the environment. In other words,
learning occurs and consumers begin to seek
greater challenges. Thus, an "instrumental" orientation is likely to dominate a consumer's later
interactions in the environment, though both
orientations may be present at different points in
time, depending on consumer characteristics.

This discussion has important implications for
the adoption of CMEs, particularly for those people
seeking the "killer application." Developmental
patterns of flow states suggest that goal-directed
behaviors such as home shopping and home banking do not necessarily lead to flow for new users of
a CME. On the other hand, experiential behaviors,
such as browsing on-line magazines, participating

in interactive chat rooms, and exploring a Web corporate home page for a topic with which the consumer exhibits enduring involvement, would be more likely to lead to flow and thus stimulate adoption in new users.

The Consequences of Flow

In the final set of research issues, we address consequences of flow. Based on the existing literature, consumers who experience flow in a hypermedia CME achieve increased learning, increased perceived behavioral control (PBC), increased exploratory and participatory behavior, and positive subjective experiences. In addition, we briefly consider potentially negative consequences of flow. Research Issues 11 through 15, seen in the context of the network navigation model in Figure 2-6, contrast consumers who experience the flow state versus those who do not. These research issues apply to both heterogeneity *across* consumers according to their ability to experience flow (Research Issue 4) and heterogeneity *within* consumers according to whether flow is experienced (Research Issues 2 and 3). Thus, flow is viewed as both a trait and a state, much as Webster and Martocchio (1992) view playfulness as both a trait and a state. Note that other researchers have viewed positive mood as both a trait and a state (e.g., George 1991).

11. Consumer Learning

Consumers who experience the flow state are more likely to retain more of what they perceive than consumers who do not. Playfulness (Webster and Martocchio 1992) and flow (Webster, Trevino, and Ryan 1993) have been found to relate to learning. Early ritualized use of a CME (i.e., scanning, exploring, and wandering; see Canter, Rivers, and Storrs 1985) facilitates the learning needed to progress to instrumental usage involving browsing and searching (i.e., purposive search behavior to identify on-line vendors selling products or services desired by the consumer). Webster, Trevino, and Ryan (1993) suggest that because consumers develop and apply

their abilities through exploratory behaviors that characterize flow interactions, learning is a reasonable outcome of the flow state.

The distinction between directed and nondirected learning (Bettman 1979; Bichal Chakravarti 1982, 1983) further differentiates flow occurring in goal-directed and experiential behaviors. In experiential behavior, ongoing, nondirected search produces latent learning (Hilgard and Bower 1966, pp. 199–200), in which the consumer learns about the environment even if the specific knowledge gained has no direct relevance to current purchases" (Bettman 1979, p. 88). In goal-directed behavior, a product choice decision or specific task completion is the primary goal for learning. Consumer learning suggests that flow resulting from goal-directed behaviors leads to more informed decisions, whereas flow resulting from experiential behaviors leads to greater recall and word-of-mouth activity.

12. Perceived Behavioral Control

Consumers who experience the flow state in a hypermedia CME are expected to have greater PBC than those who do not. *Perceived behavioral control* is defined as "the perceived ease or difficulty of performing the behavior and . . . is assumed to reflect past experience as well as anticipated impediments and obstacles" (Azjen 1988, p. 132). Perceived behavioral control is a component of Azjen's (1988, 1991) theory of planned behavior, extends the well-known theory of reasoned action (Azjen and Fishbein 1980), and is useful for predicting behaviors that are not under complete volitional control. Similar to the original expectancy-value model, the theory of planned behavior posits that conceptually independent determinants of attitudes toward the behavior, subjective norms with respect to the behavior, and a new component—*perceived control over the behavior*—affect behavioral intentions. In addition, PBC directly affects behavior. Thus, usage of a hypermedia CME (for those people with the prerequisite technology) depends jointly on motivation (intentions) and ability (behavioral control).

Perceived behavioral control (cf. Bandura's [1977, 1982] earlier notion of *perceived self-efficacy*) also can be interpreted as a confidence construct and is an important determinant of CME usage, because behavior in a CME is strongly influenced by consumers' confidence in their ability to engage in network navigation. A consumer's perception of behavioral control over CME use and its impact on intentions and actions is more important than real control (Azjen 1988).

Flow significantly correlates with perceived control (Ghani, Supnick, and Rooney 1991). Webster, Trevino, and Ryan (1993) define control as one of four dimensions of flow and find that it significantly correlated with two of the other three dimensions (curiosity and intrinsic interest, but not attention focus). Webster and Martocchio (1992) find a significant correlation between microcomputer playfulness and self-rated computer competence. Because the hypermedia CME is, first and foremost, an interactive environment, it affords the foundation for consumer control that is impossible in traditional, passive media. Control comes from both consumers' perception of their ability to adjust the CME and their perception of how the CME responds to their input, with consumer adjustment taking the form of network navigation.

We here imply that flow resulting from experiential behavior results in increased PBC over network navigation, whereas flow resulting from goal-directed behavior results in increased PBC over task completion. Because the former is a prerequisite for the latter, experiential behavior flow facilitates the learning necessary to goal-directed activities.

13. Exploratory Behavior

We expect that consumers who experience the flow state in a hypermedia CME exhibit more exploratory behaviors than those who do not. Webster, Trevino, and Ryan (1993) found that flow correlated positively with experimentation and perceptions of software flexibility and modifiability. Other researchers have found that higher levels of playfulness or flow in human-computer interactions correlate with

higher experimentation (Ghani and Deshpande 1994; Ghani, Supnick, and Rooney 1991; Katz 1987). This argues for a flexible hypermedia environment that encourages exploratory behavior on the part of consumers. Implications of increased exploratory behaviors are increased risk taking in goal-directed behaviors (Raju 1980; Steenkamp and Baumgartner 1992) and broader exposure to content in experiential behaviors. Furthermore, increased exploratory use has been found to lead to greater extent of use (Ghani and Deshpande 1994).

14. Positive Subjective Experiences

We expect that consumers who experience the flow state in a hypermedia CME exhibit more positive subjective experiences than those who do not. Webster, Trevino, and Ryan (1993, p. 412) note that "higher playfulness results in immediate subjective experiences such as positive mood and satisfaction" (Csikszentmihalyi 1977; Levy 1983; McGrath and Kelly 1986). Previous research on human-computer interactions (Sandelands and Buckner 1989; Starbuck and Webster 1991; Webster and Martocchio 1992) has shown that higher degrees of pleasure and involvement during computer interactions lead to concurrent subjective perceptions of positive affect and mood. A study conducted by Gardner, Dukes, and Discenza (1993) shows that the more people use computers, the more their self-confidence with respect to computers increases. This in turn causes more favorable attitudes toward computers. Csikszentmihalyi (1977 p. 36) notes that "people seek flow primarily for itself;" thus, flow itself serves as a positive reinforcer, which increases the probability of further use of a hypermedia CME.

Together, positive subjective experiences and the increased PBC resulting from flow feed back into the planned behavior model discussed previously and increase the probability that the CME will be used in the future. Webster, Trevino, and Ryan (1993) find flow to be positively correlated with expectations of future voluntary computer interactions. Thus, we anticipate that the positive affect generated by flow translates into longer duration time spent visiting a CME and increased repeat visits.

15. Distortion in Time Perception

The positive subjective experience of flow also has been linked to a distortion in time perception (Csikszentmihalyi 1977), whereby the consumer is unaware of the passage of time. Hauser, Urban, and Weinberg (1993) provide a model of how, in the presence of time pressure, the allocation of search time to negative information sources increases, whereas in the absence of time pressure, the allocation of search time to positive information sources increases. Thus, to the extent that the flow state reduces time pressure and increases time spent at the site, it contributes to a relatively greater amount of time being allocated to searching for positive information sources. Because of the tendency of computer-mediated environments to encourage negative word-of-mouth communications, actions that marketers can take to facilitate positive search behavior become particularly important.

Negative Consequences of Flow

There are some potentially negative consequences of flow that must be considered. Because flow can be its own reward, consumers may explore a CME for its own sake, rather than purposely search for specific information. Thus, too much flow may distract the consumer from purchase-related activities. As Webster, Trevino, and Ryan (1993, p. 422) note, playfulness may produce longer time to task completion; at an extreme, "playful computer systems may be so enjoyable that employees neglect other tasks." However, if one marketing objective of a hypermedia CME is to encourage the consumer to spend time at the site examining product-related information, for example, then this is not necessarily a problem. Flow has also been linked to overinvolvement (Csikszentmihalyi 1977), which leads to mental and physical fatigue. A related source of cognitive fatigue stems from the overwhelming complexity inherent in global hypermedia content (Gygi 1990).

DISCUSSION AND CONCLUSION

The hypermedia CME represents a fundamentally different environment for marketing activities than do traditional media and so-called interactive multimedia. The many-to-many communication model turns traditional principles of mass media advertising (based on the one-to-many model of Figure 2-1) inside out, rendering impossible the blind application of marketing and advertising approaches that assume a passive, captive consumer. Thus, marketers must carefully consider the ways in which advertising and communication models can be adapted and reconstructed (e.g., see Hoffman and Novak 1996) for the interactive, many-to-many medium depicted in Figure 2-3. In that new communication model, consumers can actively choose whether to approach firms through their Web sites and exercise unprecedented control over the management of the content with which they interact.

The opportunity for customer interaction in the hypermedia CME also is unprecedented. This can be utilized in numerous ways, including (1) the design of new products, (2) the development of product and marketing strategy, and (3) the innovation of content. The evolution of content in a hypermedia CME depends on not only the evolution of existing metaphors and communication codes from traditional media, but also new techniques and conventions inherent in the possibilities of the medium itself (Biocca 1992). One implication of this is that the content that makes hypermedia CMEs commercially successful likely has not been invented yet and may require more than a simple continuous innovation of existing content (Grossman 1994).

Because consumers vary in their ability to achieve flow, new bases for market segmentation are needed for marketing in hypermedia CMEs. Scholars must determine the variables that relate to a consumer's propensity to enter the flow state. Such information can be used to develop marketing efforts designed to maximize the chances of the consumer entering the flow state. Because we believe that repeat consumption behavior, that is, repeat visits to a hypermedia CME, are increased if the environment facilitates the flow state, the marketing objective at trial must provide for these flow opportunities.

In summary, the new medium-as-market represented by hypermedia CME—of which the World Wide Web on the Internet currently stands as the preeminent prototype—offers a working example of a many-to-many communication model in which the consumer is an active participant in an interactive exercise of multiple feedback loops and highly immediate communication. As such, it offers dynamic potential for growth and development, as well as a virtual revolution in both the way marketing academics and practitioners alike approach the problem of effective, consumer-oriented marketing in emerging media environments.

Donna L. Hoffman and Thomas P. Novak are Associate Professors, Owen Graduate School of Management, Vanderbilt University. This research is based on work supported by the National Science Foundation under Grant No. SBR-9422780, Interval Research Corporation, Sun Microsystems, and the Dean's Fund of the Owen Graduate School of Management. The authors acknowledge the many helpful comments of seminar participants at the Owen School and at Interval Research Corporation, as well as those of three anonymous *JM* reviewers and the editor. The authors contributed equally to this article.

REFERENCES

Ajzen, Icek. *Attitudes Personality, and Behavior.* Chicago: Dorsey Press, 1988.

———. "The Theory of Planned Behavior," *Organizational Behavior and Human Decision Processes,* Special Issue: Theories of Cognitive Self-Regulation. 50 (2), 1991, 179–211.

——— and Fishbein, M. *Understanding Attitudes and Predicting Social Behavior.* Englewood-Cliffs, NJ: Prentice-Hall, 1980.

Bandura, A. "Self-Efficacy: Toward a Unifying Theory of Behavioral Change," *Psychological Review,* 84, 1977, 191–215.

———. "Self-Efficacy Mechanism in Human Agency," *American Psychologist,* 37, 1982, 122–47.

Berners-Lee, T., R. Cailliau, N. Pellow, and A. Secret. "The World-Wide Web Initiative," in *Proceedings 1993 International Networking Conference,* http://info.isoc.org/ftp/isoc/inet/inet93/papers/DBC. Berners-Lee, 1993.

Bettman, James. *An Information Processing Theory of Consumer Choice.* Reading, MA: Addison-Wesley Publishing Company, 1979.

Biehal, Gabriel and Dipankar Chakravarti. "Information Presentation Format and Learning Goals as Determinants of Consumers' Memory-Retrieval and Choice Processes," *Journal of Consumer Research,* 8 (March 1982), 431–41.

——— and———. "Information Accessibility as a Moderator of Consumer Choice," *Journal of Consumer Research,* 10 (June 1983), 1–14.

Biocca, Frank. "Communication Within Virtual Reality: Creating a Space for Research," *Journal of Communication,* 42 (2), 1992, 5–22.

Blattberg, Robert C., Rashi Glazer, and John D. C. Little, eds. *The Marketing Information Revolution.* Boston: Harvard Business School Press, 1994.

Bloch, Peter H. Personal e-mail communication, University of Missouri, (April 12, 1995).

——— and Marsha L. Richins. "A Theoretical Model of the Study of Product Importance Perceptions," *Journal of Marketing,* 47 (Summer 1983), 69–81.

———, Daniel L. Sherrell, and Nancy M. Ridgway. "Consumer Search: An Extended Framework," *Journal of Consumer Research,* 13 (June 1986), 119–26.

Bornman, H., and S. H. von Solms. "Hypermedia, Multimedia and Hypertext—Definitions and Overview," *Electronic Library,* 11 (4/5), 1993, 259–68.

Bush, V. "As We May Think," *Atlantic Monthly,* 176 (1), 1945, 101–108.

Canter, David, Rod Rivers, and Graham Storrs. "Characterizing User Navigation Through Complex

Data Structures," *Behaviour and Information Technology,* 4 (2), 1985, 93–102.

Carroll, Jon. "Guerrillas in the Myst," *Wired,* 2 (August 1994), 69–73.

Cats-Baril, William L. and Tawfik Jelass. "The French Videotex System Minitel: A Successful Implementation of a National Information Technology Structure," *MIS Quarterly,* 18 (March 1994), 1–20.

Celsi, Richard L. and Jerry C. Olson. "The Role of Involvement in Attention and Comprehension Processes," *Journal of Consumer Research,* 15 (September 1988), 210–24.

Clark, Tim. "Net Savings," *Inter@ctive Week,"* (October 23, 1995), 66.

Clarke, Sharon G. and John T. Haworth. "'Flow' Experience in the Daily Lives of Sixth-Form College Students," *British Journal of Psychology,* 85 (4), 1994, 511–23.

Csikszentmihalyi, Mihaly. *Beyond Boredom and Anxiety.* San Francisco: Jossey-Bass, 1977.

———. "Measuring Intrinsic Motivation in Everyday Life," *Leisure Studies,* 2 (May 1983), 155–168.

———. "The Future of Flow," in *Optimal Experience: Psychological Studies of Flow in Consciousness.,* Mihaly Csikszentmihalyi and Isabella Selega Csikszentmihalyi, eds. Cambridge: Cambridge University Press, 1988, 364–83.

———. *Flow: The Psychology of Optimal Experience.* New York: Harper and Row, 1990.

——— and Isabella Selega Csikszentmihalyi. *Optimal Experience: Psychological Studies of Flow in Consciousness.* Cambridge: Cambridge University Press, 1988.

——— and Judith LeFevre. "Optimal Experience in Work and Leisure," *Journal of Personality and Social Psychology,* 56 (5), 1989, 815–22.

——— and J. Nakamura. "The Dynamics of Intrinsic Motivation: A Study of Adolescents," in *Handbook of Motivation Theory and Research,* Vol. 3, R. Ames and C. Ames, eds. New York: Academic Press, 1989, 45–71.

Daft, Richard L. and R. H. Lengel. "Organizational Information Requirements, Media Richness and Structural Design," *Mangement Science,* 32 (5), 1986, 554–71.

———, ———, and L. K. Trevino. "Message Equivocality, Media Selection and Manager Performance: Implications for Information Systems," *MIS Quarterly,* 11, 1987, 355–66.

Davis, Fred D., Richard P. Bagozzi, and Paul R. Warshaw. "Extrinsic and Intrinsic Motivation to Use Computers in the Workplace," *Journal of Applied Social Psychology,* 22 (14), 1992, 1111–32.

December, John and Neil Randall. *The World Wide Web Unleashed,* 2d ed. Indianapolis, IN: Sams.net Publishing, 1995.

Deci, Edward L. and Richard M. Ryan. *Intrinsic Motivation and Self-Determination in Human Behavior.* New York: Plenum Press, 1985.

Dennis, Everett E. and Joseph S. Valacich. "Rethinking Media Richness: Towards a Theory of Media Synchronicity," working paper, Terry College of Management, University of Georgia (May 3, 1994).

Ellis, Gary D., Judith E. Voelkl, and Catherine Morris. "Measurement and Analysis Issues With Explanation of Variance in Daily Experience Using the Flow Model," *Journal of Leisure Research,* 26 (4), 1994, 337–56.

Gardner, Donald G., Richard L. Dukes, and Richard Discenza. "Computer Use, Self-Confidence, and Attitudes: A Causal Analysis," *Computers in Human Behavior,* 9 (4), 1993, 427–40.

George, J. M. "State or Trait: Effects of Positive Mood on Prosocial Behaviors at Work," *Journal of Applied Psychology,* 76 (April 1991), 299–307.

Ghani, Jawaid A. and Satish P. Deshpande. "Task Characteristics and the Experience of Optimal Flow in Human-Computer Interaction," *Journal of Psychology,* 128 (4), 1994, 381–91.

———, Roberta Supnick, and Pamela Rooney. "The Experience of Flow in Computer-Mediated and in Face-to-Face Groups," in *Proceedings of the Twelfth International Conference on Information Systems,* Janice I. DeGross, Izak Benbasat, Gerardine DeSanctis, and Cynthia Mathis Beath, eds. New York: The Society for Information Management, 1991, 229–37.

Gifi, Alert. *Nonlinear Multivariate Analysis.* Chichester, England: John Wiley & Sons, 1990.

Glazer, Rashi. "Marketing in an Information-Intensive Environment: Strategic Implications of Knowledge as an Asset," *Journal of Marketing,* 55 (October 1991) 1–19.

Godwin, Mike. "Electronic Frontier Justice and the 'Green Card' Ads," *Internet World,* 5 (6), 1994, 93–95.

Graef, Ronald, Mihalyi Csikszentmihalyi, and Susan McManama Gianinno. "Measuring Intrinsic Motivation in Everyday Life," *Leisure Studies,* 2, 1983, 155–68.

Grossman, Lawrence K. "Reflections on Life Along the Electronic Superhighway," *Media Studies Journal,* 8 (1), 1994, 27–39.

Gygi, Kathleen. "Recognizing the Symptoms of Hypertext . . . and What to Do About It," in *The Art of Human-Computer Interface Design,* Brenda Laurel, ed. Reading, MA: Addison-Wesley, 1990, 279–87.

Hafner Katie and Mattthew Lyon. *When Wizards Stay Up Late: The Origins of the Internet.* New York: Simon and Schuster, 1996.

Hambrecht & Quist [http://www.hambrecht.com/], 1996.

Havlena, William J. and Morris B. Holbrook. "The Varieties of Consumption Experience: Comparing Two Typologies of Emotion in Consumer Behavior," *Journal of Consumer Research,* 13 (December 1986), 394–404.

Hauser, John R., Glen L. Urban, and Bruce D. Weinberg, "How Consumers Allocate Their Time When Searching for Information," *Journal of Marketing Research,* 30 (November 1993) 452–66.

Hilgard, Ernest R. and Gordon H. Bauer. *Theories of Learning,* 3d ed. New York: Appleton-Century-Crofts, 1966.

Hoffman, Donna L. and Jan DeLeeuw. "Interpreting Multiple Correspondence Analysis as a Multidimensional Scaling Method," *Marketing Letters,* 3 (3), 1992, 259–72.

———, William D. Kalsbeek, and Thomas P. Novak. "Internet Use in the United States: 1995 Baseline Estimates and Preliminary Market Segments," working paper, Owen Graduate School of Management, Vanderbilt University (April 1996) [http://www2000.ogsm.vanderbilt.edu/baseline/1995.Internet.estimates.html].

———, Thomas P. Novak, and Patrali Chatterjee. "Commercial Scenarios for the Web:

Opportunities and Challenges," *Journal of Computer-Mediated Communication,* Special Issue on Electronic Commerce, 1 (December 1995). [http://shum.huji.ac.il/jcmc/vol 1/issue3/vol1no3.html]

——— and ———. "A New Marketing Paradigm for Electronic Commerce," working paper, Owen Graduate School of Management, Vanderbilt University (January 1996).

Holbrook, Morris B., Robert W. Chestnut, Terence A. Oliva, and Eric A. Greenleaf. "Play as a Consumption Experience: The Roles of Emotions, Performance, and Personality in the Enjoyment of Games," *Journal of Consumer Research,* 11 (September 1984), 728–39.

——— and Meryl P. Gardner. "An Approach to Investigating the Emotional Determinants of Consumption Durations: Why Do People Consume What They Consume for as Long as They Consume It?" *Journal of Consumer Psychology,* 2 (2), 1993, 123–42.

IBM Corporation. "Electronic Purchasing," IBM Electronic Commerce Services (February 8, 1995). [http://wwwl.ibmlink.ibm.com]

Katz, E. and P. F. Lazarsfeld. *Personal Influence.* Glencoe, IL: The Free Press, 1995.

Katz, J. A. "Playing at Innovation in the Computer Revolution," in *Psychological Issues of Human Computer Interaction in the Work Place,* M. Frese, E. Ulich, and W. Dzida, eds. Amsterdam: North-Holland, 1987, 97–112.

Kaul, Aditya. Personal email communication, University of Tasmania (April 27, 1995).

Kotler, P. *Marketing Management: Analysis, Planning, Implementation and Control,* 8th ed. Englewood Cliffs, NJ: Prentice-Hall, 1994.

Lashkari, Yezdi, Max Metral, and Pattie Maes. "Collaborative Interface Agents," working paper, MIT Media Lab, 1994. [http://agents.www.media.mit.edu/groups/agents/abstracts.html]

Lasswell, H. D. "The Structure and Function of Communication in Society," in *The Communication of Ideas,* Lyman Bryson, ed. New York: Harper and Brothers, 1948.

Levy, J. *Play Behavior.* Malabar, FL: Robert E. Krieger, 1983.

Lutz, Richard J. and Michael Guiry. "Intense Consumption Experiences: Peaks, Performances, and Flows," presented at the AMA's Winter Marketing Educators' Conference, St. Petersburg, FL (February 1984).

Maes, Pattie. "Agents That Reduce Work and Information Overload," *Communications of the ACM,* 37 (July 1994), 31–40.

Malone, Thomas W. "Inventing the Organizations of the 21st Century: Control, Empowerment, and Information Technology," presentation for the Harvard Business School Colloquium, Multimedia and the Boundaryless World (November 16–17, 1995).

Mannell, Roger C., Jiri Zuzanek, and Reed Larson. "Leisure States and 'Flow' Experiences: Testing Perceived Freedom and Intrinsic Motivation Hypotheses," *Journal Leisure Research,* 20 (4), 1988, 289–304.

Massimini, Fausto and Massimo Carli. "The Systematic Assessment of Flow in Daily Experience," in *Optimal Experience: Psychological Studies of Flow in Consciousness,* M. Csikszentmihalyi and I. Csikszentmihalyi, eds. New York: Cambridge University Press, 1988, 288–306.

McGrath, J. E. and J. R. Kelly. *Time and Human Interaction.* New York: Guilford, 1986.

McLuhan, M. *Understanding Media: The Extensions of Man.* New York: Penguin Press, 1964.

Modahl, Mary. "Forecasts of the Core Economy," in *Forrester Research Report.* Cambridge, MA: Forrester Research (September 11, 1995). [http://www.forrester.com/]

Neece, Jerry. Personal communication, Senior Product Manager, Sun Microsystems, 1995.

Nelson, T. "Getting it Out of Our System," in *Information Retrieval: A Critical Review,* G. Schechter, ed. Washington, DC: Thompson Books, 1967.

Network Wizards. *Internet Domain Survey.* Menlo Park, CA: Network Wizards, 1996. [http://www.nw.corn/zone/WWW/top.html]

Oliver, Richard W. Personal communication (November 9, 1995).

Olney, Thomas J., Morris B. Holbrook, and Rajeev Batra. "Consumer Response to Advertising: The Effects of Ad Content, Emotions, and Attitude toward the Ad on Viewing Time," *Journal of Consumer Research,* 17 (March 1991), 440–53.

Open Market. *Commercial Sites Index.* Menlo Park, CA: Open Market, 1996, [http://www.directory.net/]

Payne, John W., James R. Bettman, and Eric J. Johnson. *The Adaptive Decision Maker.* Cambridge: Cambridge University Press, 1993.

Perse, Elizabeth and John A. Courtright. "Normative Images of Communication Media: Mass and Interpersonal Channels in the New Media Environment," *Human Communication Research,* 19 (4), 1993, 485–503.

Potter, Edward. "Commercialization of the World Wide Web" Internet conference on The WELL, (November 16, 1994).

Privette, Gayle. "Peak Experience, Peak Performance, and Flow: A Comparative Analysis of Positive Human Experience," *Journal of Personality and Social Psychology,* 45 (6), 1983, 1361–68.

———. *Experience Questionnaire.* Pensacola, FL: The University of West Florida, 1984.

——— and Charles M. Bundrick. "Measurement of Experience: Construct and Content Validity of the Experience Questionnaire," *Perceptual and Motor Skills,* 65, 1987, 315–32.

Rafaeli, S. "Interactivity: From New Media To Communication," in *Advancing Communication Science: Merging Mass and Interpersonal Process,* R. P. Hawkins, J. M. Wieman, and S. Pingree, eds. Newbury Park, CA: Sage Publications, 1988, 110–34.

Raju, P. S. "Optimum Stimulation Level: Its Relationship to Personality, Demographics, and Exploratory Behavior," *Journal of Consumer Research,* 7 (December 1980), 272–82.

Rangaswamy, Arvind and Yoram Wind, "Don't Walk In, Just Log In! Electronic Markets and What They Mean for Marketing," working paper, Pennsylvania State University (December 1994).

Reardon, Kathleen K. and Everitt M. Rogers. "Interpersonal Versus Mass Communication: A False Dichotomy," *Human Communication Research,* 15 (2), 1988, 284–303.

Rheingold, Howard L. "A Slice of Life in My Virtual Community," 1992, [gopher://nkosi.well.sf.ca.us/ 00/Community/virtual_communities92]]

Rice, Ronald E. "Task Analyzability, Use of New Media, and Effectiveness: A Multi-Site Exploration of Media Richness," *Organizational Science,* 3 (4), 1992, 475–500.

———. "Media Appropriateness: Using Social Presence Theory to Compare Traditional and New Organizational Media," *Human Communication Research,* 19 (4), 1993, 451–85.

Richins, Marsha L. and Terri Root-Schaffer. "The Role of Involvement and Opinion Leadership in Consumer Word-of-Mouth: An Implicit Model Made Explicit," in *Advances in Consumer Research,* Vol. 15, Michael J. Houston, ed. Provo, UT: Association for Consumer Research, 1988, 32–36.

Rogers, Everett M. *Communication Technology: The New Media in Society.* New York: The Free Press, 1986.

Rubin, Alan M. "Ritualized and Instrumental Television Viewing," *Journal of Communication,* 34 (3), 1984, 67–77.

——— and Elizabeth M. Perse. "Audience Activity and Television News Gratifications," *Communication Research,* 14 (1), 1987, 58–84.

Sandelands, L. E. and G. C. Buckner. "Of Art and Work: Aesthetic Experience and the Psychology of Work Feelings," in *Research in Organizational Behavior,* L. L. Cummings and B. M. Staw, eds. Greenwich. CT: JAI Press, 1989.

Sheridan, Thomas B. "Musings on Telepresence and Virtual Presence," *Presence: Teleoperators and Virtual Environments,* 1 (1), 1992, 120–26.

Smith, Pauline A. and John R. Wilson. "Navigation in Hypertext Through Virtual Environments," *Applied Ergonomics,* 24 (4), 1993, 271–78.

Srinivasan, T. J. "An Integrative Approach to Consumer Choice," in *Advances in Consumer Research,* Vol. 14, Melanie Wallendorf and Paul Anderson, eds. Provo, UT: Association for Consumer Research, 1987, 96–101.

Starbuck, W. J. and J. Webster. "When Is Play Productive?" *Accounting, Management, and Information Technology,* 1, 1991, 71–90.

Steenkamp, Jan-Benedict and Hans Baumgartner. "The Role of Optimum Stimulation Level in Exploratory Consumer Behavior," *Journal of Consumer Research,* 19 (December 1992), 434–48.

Steuer, Jonathan. "Defining Virtual Reality: Dimensions Determining Telepresence," *Journal of Communication,* 42 (4), 1992, 73–93.

Stewart, David W. and Scott Ward. "Media Effects on Advertising," in *Media Effects, Advances in Theory and Research,* Jennings Bryand and Dolf Zillman, eds. Hillsdale, NJ: Lawrence Erlbaum Associates, 1994.

Trevino, Linda Klebe and Jane Webster. "Flow in Computer-Mediated Communication," *Communication Research,* 19 (5), 1992, 539–73.

Valacich, Joseph S., David Paranka, Joey F George, and J. F. Nunamaker. "Communication Concurrency and the New Media: A New Dimension for Media Richness," *Communication Research,* 20 (2), 1993, 249–76.

van Dijk, Jan A. G. M. "The Mental Challenge of the New Media," *Medienpsychologie: Zeitschrift fur Individual & Massenkommunikation,* 5 (1), 1993, 20–45.

Verity, John W. and Robert D. Hof. "The Internet: How It Will Change the Way You Do Business," *Business Week,* (November 14, 1994), 80–86, 88.

Webster, Jane and Joseph J. Martocchio. "Microcomputer Playfulness: Development of a Measure With Workplace Implications," *MIS Quarterly,* 16 (June 1992), 201–26.

Webster, J., L. K. Trevino, and L. Ryan. "The Dimensionality and Correlates of Flow in Human Computer Interactions," *Computers in Human Behavior,* 9 (4), Winter 1993, 411–26.

Williams, Frederick, Sharon Strover, and August E. Grant. "Social Aspects of New Media Technologies," in *Media Effects, Advances in Theory and Research,* Jennings Bryand and Dolf Zillman, eds. Hillsdale, NJ: Lawrence Erlbaum Associates, 1994.

Yahoo. 1996, [http://www.yahoo.com/]

Zaichkowsky, Judith L. "Conceptualizing Involvement," *Journal of Advertising,* 15 (2), 1986, 4–14.

Zuckerman, Marvin. *Sensation Seeking: Beyond the Optimal Level of Arousal.* Hillsdale, NJ: Lawrence Erlbaum Associates, 1979.

Bruce H. Clark

"Agencies See Gold on the Web," "Small Business Hits It Big on the Web," "Industry Taps Into Web Power," "No Explosion Yet," "E-Commerce Fears Persist," "Internet, Schminternet: When's the Thing Going to Start Paying Off?" The media are filled with headlines about the World Wide Web. Proponents proclaim it the most important phenomenon since the personal computer, and insist that it will transform business. Skeptics see a heady mix of hype and hope that so far has generated profits mostly for consultants. Otherwise-sophisticated marketing professionals find themselves intimidated by a Web culture that sometimes seems to exclude anyone over age 25 who did not go through college working in a computer room filled with Mountain Dew, cold pizza, and video games (see "What's a World Wide Web?" . . .).

Marketing on the World Wide Web is currently a grand experiment. No dominant business model has emerged, and the majority of commercial Web sites do not report profits. Nonetheless, the Web's potential has drawn tens of thousands of companies on-line. In this rapidly evolving arena, all parties are grappling with critical issues familiar to marketers: How do we communicate effectively with customers? How do we provide value to customers in a way that differentiates us from competitors? And how do we make a profit doing this?

The Web presents a couple of major opportunities for marketers. First, a large and growing number of individuals and businesses access the Web. Research firm Find/SVP estimates that as of September 1996 some 20 million Americans accessed the Web weekly. And the growth rate of consumer access appears high: CommerceNet/Nielsen notes a 50% increase in Web usage between September 1995 and April 1996, while investment-banking firm Morgan Stanley predicts that 152 million people worldwide will use it by the year 2000. Aside from their numbers, Web users represent an attractive target market (see "Who's Out There?" on page 13). Furthermore, these individuals are beginning to buy products. Forrester Research estimates a total of $518 million in commercial transactions over the Web in 1996, and Nielsen claims some 2.5 million people have purchased at least one item on-line.

The business-to-business market opportunity appears to be even greater than the consumer one. A late-1995 survey by O'Reilly and Associates revealed that 51% of large businesses, 25% of medium-sized businesses, and 8% of small businesses had access to the Internet, with many more planning to go on-line by the end of 1996. The crush of commercial Web sites developed in the last year suggests a substantial increase in the number of companies with Internet access. A Netcraft Web Server Survey received responses from 373,000 commercial sites in December 1996, compared with 171,000 the previous June.

The second opportunity on the Web lies in the economics of Web sites. Most costs involved in hosting a Web site—site development, site personnel, site maintenance, and so forth—are fixed. In particular, the information on a given Web page is not consumed when it is accessed—it remains available to the next customer. Therefore, the direct cost of providing this information to the first customer, the second customer, or the 100th customer is close to zero. Once the fixed costs of site development and maintenance have been covered, the revenue from additional customers is virtually all profit. Note, however, that these fixed costs can be quite large, and that customers requiring a personal response do create variable costs.

Reprinted with permission from *Marketing Management,* published by the American Marketing Association, Bruce H. Clark, Winter 1997, pp. 11–22.

VISIONARIES OR LEMMINGS?

The hype about the Web suggests the opportunity of the future, but the reality is considerably more prosaic, with companies learning by trial and error how to use the Web effectively in marketing. In June 1996, a survey of more than 1,100 commercial Web sites by the research firm ActivMedia revealed a dramatic difference in success across sites. Some 31% of sites reported that they were "profitable now from sales," with total revenues in June of $102 million and Web maintenance costs of $22 million. Meanwhile, the 69% of sites that were unprofitable reported June revenues of $39 million and Web maintenance costs of $50 million. Business-to-business sites were somewhat more

What's a World Wide Web?

"Honey, Is Judith Home from School Yet? I Need Her to Show Me How to Use the Internet."

The Internet and its well-known offspring, the World Wide Web, inspire apprehension as much as fascination in many adults. While 12 year old children gleefully swim in cyberspace, some of the rest of us need a native guide. Herewith, some definitions:

- *Internet.* The Internet is a decentralized network of computers that communicate over a variety of phone and data lines provided by the government, phone companies, and private organizations. Its backbone was created by the U.S. Department of Defense as a backup method for the military to communicate in the event of a crisis. Other networks of computers, both in the United States and abroad, have connected to the original network, increasing its usefulness. The Internet is thus an "international network of networks." Because of this decentralization, no one organization owns or controls it.

- *World Wide Web.* The World Wide Web is a multimedia (text, sound, and graphics) subset of the Internet as a whole. After the Internet was first established, it spread to universities, where scientists used it to exchange data and messages. Data exchange was quite cumbersome, however, partly due to conflicting standards for programs and storage formats. In 1989, a scientist at the European Particle Physics Laboratory (CERN) in Geneva, Switzerland, put forth a proposal to establish a single standard across all computer platforms that would allow users to easily view and exchange data. Sites that adopted this standard became part of the World Wide Web.

- *Web site.* A Web site is a set of multimedia material that computer users can access electronically.

- *Web page.* A Web page is a single document at a Web site.

- *Link.* A link is a selection of highlighted text or an image on a page that, when the visitor clicks on it with a mouse, gives the visitor access to another page. Virtually all Web pages contain links that connect visitors to different pages on the site and to interesting pages on other Web sites.

- *Browser.* Browsers are programs that automatically read and display information from a Web site. They also allow a visitor to move from one Web page to another by pointing and clicking on a link to access the new page. The easy access to information on the Web provided by browsers has been an important factor in the Web's soaring popularity.

- *Search engine.* A search engine is a computer program that searches for information on the Web. Although the term "browser" evokes images of a leisurely stroll through a familiar library, in reality the Web is much too large and disorganized to make browsing an attractive way to find information. To solve this problem, several sites have sprung up that feature search engines (e.g., Yahoo!). An individual visits one of these engines and types in a keyword or phrase. The engine then displays titles and brief descriptions of all Web sites that contain this word or phrase in its text.

Who's Out There?

Measuring the size of the World Wide Web market has proven both difficult and controversial. I present a "snapshot" of consumer Web usage in the first six months of 1996 compiled from a number of studies, but all these statistics are part of a "moving picture" of the Web that must be updated over time.

Sources such as the CyberAtlas Internet Research Guide, the CommerceNet/Nielsen Internet Survey, and the Find/SVP American Internet User Survey show that, in general, the Web is moving from a medium dominated by high-income technologically-inclined males to a broader market of college-educated, upper- and upper-middle class men and women, as follows:

- Gender: 65% male, 35% female. Earlier studies reported about a 67%–33% split, but new users of the Web in the second half of 1996 appear to include more females, along the lines of 60%–40% male–female.

- Age: about 32. Nearly 10% of Internet users are children under 18. New users are older, which should drive this number up over time.

- Race: 80%–90% white.

- Geography: about 70%–75% of users live in the United States, but international usage is growing almost twice as rapidly as American usage.

- Education: 64% had college degrees late in 1995; new users are somewhat less educated.

- Median income: about $60,000, but new users appear to have somewhat lower incomes.

- Usage time: about 2.5 hours per week (roughly equivalent to time spent on videocassette rentals), although this number varies widely by study. New users appear to use the Web less, though this may be a learning phenomenon.

- Usage substitutes: watching television and making long-distance phone calls.

- Usage activities: e-mail and finding information.

successful than consumer sites, but both markets had success stories. ActivMedia notes that many of the successful sites are smaller companies, as opposed to the more frequently reported stories of commercial failures by large organizations.

While no answers are certain in an industry chronicled in "Internet years" (every two months equals a year on the Internet), there are two general approaches to marketing on the World Wide Web. The first is for companies to use the Web as a supplement to traditional marketing, delivering additional benefits to customers and building relationships with customers. This is often used as part of general branding and communication strategies. The second is for companies to use the Web to construct "virtual" businesses—profitable, stand-alone ventures that exist only on the Internet.

The Supplemental Approach

Looking at Web marketing as another tool in the company's marketing arsenal, alongside traditional advertising, personal selling and sales promotion, is the most common use of the Web for marketing today. International Data Corp. reports that, as of June 1996, 57% of Fortune 500 companies have publicly accessible sites, but fewer than 5% of those sites support transactions. More generally, another survey of 290 commercial Web sites revealed that only 18% were on-line storefronts.

The Web has a number of advantages as a promotional tool. First, it allows a company to provide large quantities of information to customers quickly and with negligible variable cost per customer. Second, it gives the company an instant global presence, 24 hours a day, 365 days year. Third, there is little "wasted coverage"—people exposed to your ad who aren't in your target market—in Web advertising. Because people have to choose to go to your Web site, their arrival is proof that they are interested in what they believe the site offers (always assuming good search engine descriptions and good advertising by the site, of course). Finally, the Web opens a new communication channel with customers, allowing a company to develop or cement relationships with them.

In the beginning, the most common reaction to the Web was "Hey, let's put our catalog on line." This can represent a tremendous convenience to customers: rather than call a company to request a catalog, a customer can immediately look at the entire catalog via his or her computer. Furthermore, an on-line catalog can mean substantial cost savings to the company: while it might cost $3 to produce and mail a catalog, once it's available on the Web, the cost of each additional customer using it is virtually nothing. Updating the catalog is much easier as well. One simply changes a Web page rather than resetting and reprinting thousands of catalogs. And, the Web's growing world-wide accessibility means that companies can easily and cheaply reach markets to which they do not ordinarily mail. General Electric's Plastics division has been a business-to-business pioneer in this area, putting up a Web site providing catalogs and extensive technical background data on polymers and resins purchased by a wide variety of industrial customers. Consumer direct marketers such as L.L. Bean and Lands' End also have gone online with their catalogs.

Another promotional tack has been to use the Web to build brand awareness and image. Reebok's Web site lets visitors read about sports and fitness, hear from Reebok-sponsored athletes, and learn about Reebok's human-rights activities, among other things. A particularly clever example of building a brand from scratch on the Web is Clnet, which has promoted both its global name and particular services by acquiring strong generic brand

names on the Web (e.g., news.com, a news service, and shareware.com, a library of free software).

Supplemental promotion on the Web can produce significant sales in other areas of business. Some 1,400 car dealers spend $250–$1,500 a month to promote themselves through Auto-By-Tel, a car-buying service. Consumers buy as many as 15,000 cars per month based on information they obtained from the service. Aside from direct sales, companies have found they also can generate numerous marketing and sales leads. Insight Direct, a discount computer cataloger selling mostly to businesses, generates only 1% of its sales from its on-line catalog, but more than 50% of its new customers come from the site.

In addition to promotion, companies have begun to use the Web as a cost-effective way to augment their core products with related information and services. At Microsoft Corp.'s site, for example, visitors can access voluminous support material, listen to live audio broadcasts of Microsoft conferences, interact with other Microsoft customers electronically, and copy (download) free supplemental programs for Microsoft software. Marshall Industries, an electronics distributor, reports "thousands" of leads from its extensive site. which includes a searchable database, parts availability and pricing, UPS tracking and a special NetSeminar series on the Internet. At Fidelity Investments' Web site, visitors can obtain extensive information on the company's products, from fund prospectuses to profiles of fund managers. The site also offers guides to retirement planning, on-line quizzes, and other interactive pages.

Cost savings from automating routine customer service functions can be substantial. In a 1996 *Journal of Marketing* article, Donna Hoffman and Thomas Novak report that Sun Microsystems has saved a minimum of $4 million in answering standard customer inquiries since reorganizing its customer service around the Web. Federal Express receives over 200,000 shipment tracking requests on its Web site per day, and its internal research indicates that more than half those people would have used an 800 number had the Web site been unavailable.

A final supplemental approach to the Web is to use it to build a customer database. Many sites ask visitors to register or subscribe to the site at no cost. As part of the registration process, the company collects demographic and other information from the visitor. Often, the company will ask for an e-mail address so the visitor can be informed of new products or services. While unsolicited e-mail is still frowned upon on the Internet, these more targeted lists of consenting inquirers can be highly responsive; one software company reports a 12% response rate to its e-mail customer list *within 24 hours* of sending a message. Companies can also offer periodic surveys that visitors fill out, further increasing the information collected. Companies can use this information to tailor what appears on the Web site the individual visitor, for example, calling up specific ads or highlighting particular areas that the visitor has indicated would be of interest.

A particularly intriguing example of database building on the Web is the Firefly site, run by Agents Inc., a startup spinoff from the Massachusetts Institute of Technology. Firefly has a visitor give his or her musical and movie preferences and then matches this preference profile with other customers in the Firefly database to suggest further titles that the visitor might enjoy. Over 130,000 individuals have registered their preferences with Firefly, and advertisers use the database to target very specific groups of Firefly visitors with ads.

Virtual Businesses

The true visionaries of Internet commerce expect this medium to fundamentally transform business. New businesses will appear, they argue, that are unlike any in the real world. Rather than having physical businesses, with tangible storefronts, inventories, and products, they will create "virtual" businesses, existing only on the Internet. Successful virtual-business opportunities can be realized by creating a Web site with: a larger or more specialized selection of products than competitors can offer; superior information (higher quality, higher quantity), economic benefits, and convenience; and a sense of community for customers.

One way virtual businesses can succeed is by creating a retail presence larger than any physical store could. A commonly cited example is Amazon.com, an on-line bookstore that offers over 1 million titles (compared with a Barnes & Noble superstore, for example, which might hold 150,000 titles). Customers can search the database by subject, author, or title, and read staff recommendations and author interviews. When they select a book, Amazon automatically suggests related titles customers might find interesting. If customers volunteer their e-mail addresses and preferences, Amazon will send recommendations as new books arrive in the store. Even more intriguing, customers can write and post their own book reviews for others to read, creating a community of readers and reviewers.

Operationally, Amazon also is unlike any standard bookstore. It special orders most titles from distributors: this allows it to stock only quick-turning bestsellers and turn over its inventory a staggering 150 times a year. The entire operation is run out of a warehouse in an industrial neighborhood. Unlike many commercial Web sites, Amazon is generating substantial sales after barely a year in existence; *Business Week* reports insider estimates of annual revenues approaching $17 million, with operating profits since January 1996. Amazon founder Jeffrey Bezos reports that revenues are growing 34% a month, with 44% of business coming from the repeat customers that selection and sense of community encourage.

A second approach is to create a virtual business that provides extra information in a form competitors can't imitate. Virtual Vineyards is an on-line wine retailer, selling California varietals ranging in price from $6–$100 a bottle. What sets Virtual Vineyards apart from conventional wine merchants is that it provides a level of information and expertise beyond the reach of other retailers. At the heart of this strategy is cofounder Peter

Ganoff, one of only 25 master sommeliers in the United States, who selects and extensively reviews every wine Virtual Vineyards sells. Furthermore, the site includes sales of specialty foods, a food and wine matching guide, and a popular section called "Ask the Cork Dork," in which customers can pose questions for Granoff about wine. This experience, combined with the company's contacts at wineries both famous and obscure, provides a product offering and service level that conventional wine retailers cannot match. Founded in January 1995, Virtual Vineyards sold over $1 million worth of wine in its first year, and sales growth is estimated at 20% a month.

A third way to start a virtual business is to take a specialty product or collectible and sell it world wide. Because one Web "store" reaches the world, markets that are too small on a local basis can become viable on a global one. A popular example of this type of business, albeit one attached to a successful retail store, is the Hot Hot Hot Web site. The 300 square foot Hot Hot Hot store in Pasadena, Calif., sells some 400 "hot" food items, notably salsas from all over the world. A customer who ran a Web service company suggested to the owners that they could further publicize their business via the Internet. On-line since September 1994, sales are currently running at about one-quarter of the store's total volume, but annual growth is projected at a 100% rate, compared with only a 15% growth in walk-in business.

A fourth virtual-business opportunity lies in creating a business that uses the Web to produce superior economic benefits to customers that competitors cannot imitate. Security First Network Bank (SFNB) is one of the Web's first full-service banks, offering standard banking products such as checking accounts, money market accounts, and certificates of deposit—all FDIC-insured. What sets SFNB apart from real-world banks is an extremely low cost structure. Based in Pineville, Ky., the bank does not have the expense of building and managing branches, which allows it to offer free checking with $100 minimum balances and superior CD rates as much as a full percentage point

above national averages. Customers also have the benefit of complete 24-hour access to their accounts, simple electronic payment, and ready interface between their account and popular financial planning software such as Quicken. In its first six months, SFNB signed up 2,000 customers across all 50 states.

A fifth virtual-business opportunity comes from providing convenience to customers that competitors cannot match. An intriguing hint of the future in Web marketing can be seen at Peapod. Using proprietary software and negotiating relationships with local grocers in four cities, Peapod has developed a surprisingly powerful tool for grocery shopping from the home. For a monthly fee of about $5, users can shop from home across more than 20,000 items and have these items delivered to their door for an additional charge. Users navigate product categories and shelves in the Peapod "store," view packaging and nutritional information and search for and compare items using several different attributes. The Peapod "cart" keeps a running total of what has been purchased and can store frequent requests (e.g., "gallon of milk") for future trips. At the end of the trip, the order is confirmed and then delivered within a 30- or 90-minute window. As of May 1996, the company had 17,000 customers and an annual revenue rate of $16 million.

A final opportunity comes from providing a sense of community that competitors cannot match via "chat rooms" or "bulletin boards." Chat rooms and bulletin boards are electronic forums on which individuals can converse or post messages. By hosting a forum in which customers can connect with each other, companies hope to offer valuable informational and emotional benefits that will make customers more loyal to the core product and more likely to become regular visitors to the company's site. Some experts believe that this is the application that represents the greatest potential for revolutionizing business via the Web.

The *Los Angeles Times* estimates that 30%–50% of America Online's revenue comes from the ferocious popularity of its chat rooms. A particularly popular room is the Motley Fool investment room, an irreverent site where some 230,000 amateur and professional investors interact, trading news and gossip with all the decorum of what site managers have described as "a seventh-grade detention room on substitute teacher day." Stocks that capture the attention of "the Fools" can move noticeably in price, according to the *New York Times*.

America Online has made its money on chat rooms by selling access time. Other sites use community as a way to bring together people with particular interests who can then be exposed to advertising or products. Parents Place, which describes itself as "the parenting resource center on the Web," features general chat rooms plus extensive specialized rooms on topics ranging from parenting teens to adoption to interfaith families. Discreet ads and separate shopping areas dot the Parents Place home page. Amazon's Bezos describes community as "the secret weapon of the electronic merchant," and plans to rely on it as much as his vast selection to face down planned Web sites from book superstores Barnes & Noble and Borders.

MONEY MAKING MODELS

Some companies might be satisfied with using the Web as an advertising tool to build awareness or provide information. As Web sites and technology become more elaborate and expensive, however, many worry about their return on investment. Although there is no dominant business model for making money on the Web, in undertaking an extensive review of commercial Web sites, I found a number of common models that companies are using to make revenues, and sometimes profits, on the Web. Allowing that the future will change the potential of some of these models, marketers may want to consider them in thinking through their own approach to the medium: the Retail Model, the Mail Model, the Broker Model, the Broadcast Model, the Subscriber Model, the Cable TV Model, the Arcade Model, and the Customization Model.

The Retail Model

Set up an electronic storefront on the Web and make money by selling products directly to customers. The retail model covers most of the examples cited in the discussion of virtual businesses. At its simplest, this model entails putting a catalog on a Web site. While this makes for a simple, low-cost site, a static catalog is not the kind of content that will attract a lot of visits. Many catalog sites now provide additional information to give people other reasons to visit; L.L. Bean, for example, provides a variety of information on National Parks and outdoor sports, while Lands' End includes a library of its quirky "Dateline Dodgeville" catalog features, as well as essays and short fiction that have appeared in its catalogs.

Some sites have developed elaborate retail storefronts. One popular site is the CyberShop, an upscale on-line department store run by former Bloomingdale's buyer Jeff Tauber. Established in September 1995, CyberShop offers some 12,000 products from more than 300 manufacturers covering product categories such as fragrance, bed and bath, and home furnishings. CyberShop charges manufacturers an initial setup fee of $2,000–$20,000 depending on the number of products the store carries, and then follows the standard retail model of buying products from manufacturers at wholesale and selling them at retail for a 30%–60% gross profit margin. The 10-person company projects first-year revenues of $6 million. Some 400 visitors purchase products on-line every week.

The Mall Model

Develop a "location" on the Web and make money by charging Web retailers fees. A Web retailer can either run its own Web server (computer) or rent space on someone else's server. The latter choice is equivalent to renting space in a mall. With hundreds of thousands of Web sites, Web mall businesses believe there is a virtue in consolidation. For customers, the benefit of a Web mall is that it allows them to visit just one site for all their shopping needs. For stores, attractive, well-promoted locations attract many more visitors than any individual store could. Netmart, for example, which sells memberships to small Web stores for a monthly fee as low as $25–$50 per month, attracts over 1 million visits a week. Some Web retailers choose to have the mall physically host their Web site on the mall's servers, while others simply purchase a link in the mall that sends customers to the retailer's site.

The mall model is not limited to consumer marketing. Industry.net, for example, billed over $25 million in 1995 by providing a mall for manufacturers and resellers of business equipment and services. Currently hosting some 4,500 businesses ranging from small machine shops to well known suppliers such as Allen-Bradley, Honeywell, and Westinghouse, Industry.net has some 275,000 free "subscribers" representing 36,000 corporations. Subscribers are typically purchasers or specifiers who can access news, product information, professional organizations and interactive discussions at the site.

Mall sites must develop an attractive mix of stores and effectively promote the mall; customers won't want to visit unless the site houses a lot of attractive stores, but stores won't want to locate in a given mall unless it has a lot of visitors. Mall sites thus incur substantial promotional investment to attract both customers and stores to the site. Furthermore, malls are most valuable to visitors who do not have a specific product in mind, for example, when browsing for a gift. If a visitor knows what he or she wants to buy, the increasing sophistication of search engines means a visitor does not need to visit a mall to find a particular type of store.

The Broker Model

Bring together buyers and sellers on the Web, and charge a portion of the transaction for the service. Various businesses have now cropped up on-line to create electronic markets and exchanges. The most prominent example of this is the growth in on-line stock trading. Going discount brokers one better, these companies conduct trades at extremely low cost because of the low variable overhead and costs inherent in a Web site. One such company, E-trade, charges as little for $15 for a single stock transaction, compared with hundreds of dollars at full-service brokers.

Business-to-business marketers also are setting up exchanges. TRADE'ex, for example, is a company operating an electronic market in computer equipment. Vendors offer products over the exchange and customers purchase them. TRADE'ex manages the transaction, including taking on the credit risk, while charging a registration fee to vendors of $300 plus $49 for each transaction. Currently it serves customers from more than 50 countries.

The Broadcast Model

Provide attractive free content to consumers and charge advertisers to appear with that content. Like television networks and print media, some Web businesses are earning revenues by selling ads on their sites. Typically, images in the form of banners appear next to content, and visitors may click on the image to be transported to that advertiser's site. Among prominent sites using advertising are search-engine sites such as Yahoo! and on-line magazines such as *HotWired.*

While this model is very appealing in theory, in practice it is unclear if there is enough advertising money to go around. Jupiter Communications reports that $66 million was spent on Web advertising in the third quarter of 1996, almost equaling the $72 million total for the first six months of the year. Even Jupiter's projection for the year 2000, $5.3 billion, is still a small portion of an estimated $88 billion total advertising market for that year. And ad dollars appear to be concentrated on a few successful sites, many of them search engine sites. Of over 900 sites accepting ads, Jupiter reports that the top 10 sites alone accounted for 64% of advertising revenues in the third quarter. Many major advertising-supported sites are losing money. For example, despite ad revenues of some $2 million in 1995, Time-Warner's Pathfinder site is estimated to have lost $8 million in that year, prompting a frustrated Time CEO Don Logan to complain that it gave "new definition to the term black hole." Similarly, the *Wall Street Journal* estimates that *Wired* magazine's HotWired site is losing $3 million a quarter.

The Broadcast Model is currently the scene of much experimentation. One of the most followed Web broadcasters is Pointcast, which has developed a very clever technology allowing customers to create customized news feeds that Pointcast automatically assembles and downloads to the customer's computer. The service is free to customers, but features animated 30-second commercials in one corner of the news screen. Pointcast expects fourth quarter 1996 advertising revenues to exceed $3 million.

The Subscriber Model

Charge customers to view content. The perils of the Broadcast model have led many businesses to begin supplementing their meager advertising revenue by charging for "subscriptions" to content. The most prominent experiment of this type is the interactive edition of the *Wall Street Journal,* which, after months of free content, began charging $29 to $49 a year for access on September 21, 1996. Approximately 30,000 of the 650,000 customers who had registered for the free trial agreed to pay for the service.

The drawback is that once content providers begin requiring subscription fees, visits can drop off dramatically. Subscriptions may turn out to be well below projections. Furthermore, advertising revenue drops, as most advertisers are unwilling to pay for poorly visited sites. Rich Masterson, an interactive marketing consultant, has written that, "the Internet audience will reject retail subscriptions because they will be presented with too many [free] options from which to choose." Indeed, while quality is varied, there is a vast amount of free content on the Web, from both traditional publishers and "hobby" publishers who place their creative or journalistic work on personal Web pages; organizations following the Subscriber Model need to find a way to create unique "must have" content. So far, financial and investing information seem to have the strongest draw; Quote.com is an example of a site profitably selling investment information. More generally, businesses, already accustomed to subscribing to research services, may be a better target than consumers for this model.

The Cable TV Model

Provide a selection of advertiser-supported free content while charging customers for premium content. A hybrid of the two previous approaches, the Cable TV Model attempts to offer the best of both worlds. A prominent example of this type is ESPN's SportsZone, where 230,000 visitors a day browse thousands of pages of free, frequently updated sports information, while 40,000 subscribers pay $4.95 per month to access detailed background information, columns, ESPN sports reporters, and more. By providing substantial free content, the Cable Model site retains the large number of visitors attractive to advertisers, while earning money from the hard-core visitors who become subscribers. A further advantage of this model is that the free content acts as a sampling device for the premium content. Occasional free trials of the premium content may convert visitors into subscribers.

The Arcade Model

Charge customers small amounts of money per use of materials. This is a relatively new model of commerce even for the Web, but has the potential to generate substantial revenues assuming current obstacles can be overcome. Information and entertainment properties are considered likely users of this model. Virtual Vegas, for example, provides a variety of betting aids for under $1 per week. Mind's Eye Fiction is selling downloadable short fiction over the Web for about 50¢ per story. While currently the focus of small companies, both the Discovery Channel On-Line and the *Los Angeles Times* plan to use the arcade model for per-use access to information.

Given the large size of the video game and pay-per-view movie market, this seems a likely revenue generator. However, transactions this small (sometimes called "microtransactions") are not worth the processing fees for credit card companies, so the ultimate potential of this business model relies on the popularity of what is called "digital cash."

The Customization Model

Charge customers for content that is customized to meet their preferences. This model, also relatively new, takes advantage of database software and the Web's low marginal cost of information transmission. Subscribers to a personal information service provide a description of what kind of articles and information they would like to see. The company then culls articles matching each reader's preferences from its overall information database. A pioneer in this model is the *San Jose Mercury News'* Newshound, which charges $4.95 a month for a custom information service. Time-Warner expects to launch a similar "Personal Edition" on its Pathfinder site in the near future. While this model represents a clever use of Web technology, it is unclear how large a paying market exists for this kind of information, considering that companies such as Pointcast provide an advertiser-supported version of this service at no charge. As with the Subscription Model, business customers, already used to paying for research reports and clipping services, seem more likely than

consumers to purchase these kind of custom Web services.

Hidden Obstacles

That the Web will grow as a commercial medium is inevitable; whether it will be profitable anytime soon is more problematic because a number of obstacles currently stand in the way. While most of these obstacles will diminish as the market grows and technology improves, companies should be aware of them before investing in the Web.

Cost of Site Development

While a simple Web site can cost very little to produce, and the cost to transmit messages to a customer can be less than a penny, building Web sites with large amounts of searchable content and transaction capabilities can be very costly. Cyber-Shop, for example, spent $850,000 to build its online department store.

Development costs vary greatly. In a survey of large corporate Web sites late in 1995, Forrester Research reported that sites used simply to promote a brand were the least expensive to build, averaging $98,000. Content sites featuring news, weather, information, or games cost $419,000 to launch on average. Transactional sites were the most expensive to build, averaging $593,000. ActivMedia's broader site sample estimates development spending of between $10,000 and $100,000 for companies with more than 500 employees. Joel Snyder of Internet consultants Opus One suggests small companies can hire developers for as little as $100 per simple page on a site.

Advertising Age's NetMarketing group sent out requests for bids on three typical Web sites to 21 Web developers. The medium bid to build a small site (20 pages) was $26,100. The corresponding figure for a medium site (100 pages) was $102,025, and for a large site (custom programming, secure transactions, data-base handling) was $596,073. Most interestingly, the range on bids was very large. For large sites, the low bid was $15,000 and the high bid was $2.8 million. In general, expect development costs to go up as firms use sophisticated site design to compete for visitor attention in an increasingly crowded commercial Web market.

Cost of Operations and Maintenance

Once built, the cost of operating and maintaining a popular Web site often proves surprisingly large. The *New York Times* estimates that Starwave, the operator of ESPN SportsZone, is earning revenues of approximately $7 million annually, but that costs are running $20 million. Forrester Research quoted average one-year operating costs of $206,000 for large promotional sites, $893,000 for content sites, and $2.8 million for transactional sites.

Where does this money go? Part goes to promoting the site. CyberShop, for example, has a $2.6 million promotional budget for 1996. The top 10 advertisers in Jupiter Communication's WebTrack study spent between $200,000 and $600,000 each in advertising on other Web sites in the fourth quarter of 1995. As with site development costs, promotion will continue to be a growing expense for many sites. As Web sites proliferate, attracting visitors to a particular site will only become more difficult.

Another expense of operating a Web site is updating the content. Depending on the nature of the site, content may have to be updated frequently. Starwave, for example, updates the ESPN SportsZone front page more than 20 times a day. Some of this can be fairly automatic, but companies should plan on staff time devoted to ongoing design and content improvements.

The last and often most difficult part of operating a Web site is managing the interaction with visitors. If interaction is the thing that the Web does better than many other marketing tools, then companies must do a good job of fulfilling this function. Perhaps because the Web is a very responsive medium (you click on something and it

appears), visitors expect a rapid response when they contact a company through its Web site. This is particularly true of visitor communication via e-mail; if visitors send a company e-mail, they expect a timely and useful answer. The consensus of participants at a recent Internet marketing workshop was that 24-hour response was a good goal to aim for. Most companies appear to be nowhere near this goal. An October 1996 *Wall Street Journal* report indicated that the vast majority of companies had trouble simply responding to e-mail questions, much less responding within 24 hours.

This is a lost opportunity for the offending company and a corresponding competitive advantage for those who do act responsively. Being responsive to customers is especially important on the Web, as word-of-mouth is magnified by the ease of sending e-mail to multiple recipients and the widespread availability of and participation in computer discussion groups (newsgroups). As Bezos noted in the *Wall Street Journal,* "If someone thinks they are being mistreated by us, they won't tell five people—they'll tell 5,000."

Moving beyond simple communication, a full-fledged transactional Web site presents additional operational challenges. If a company does not already have a direct marketing operation, it will need one to provide shipping and customer service. International customers will require extra logistical support and thoughtful pricing policies.

Large companies typically will have to dedicate staff to managing and servicing customers through a Web site. They will also have to prepare other parts of the organization for on-line transactions and service. New staff may have to be hired, as the blend of marketing skills and Internet knowledge required to support a Web site can be difficult to find.

Small-company owners may find themselves absorbed in the day-to-day business of Web site operations. Hot Hot Hot changes its site content at least once a month so that people keep visiting. Co-owner Monica Lopez spends two hours a day answering customer e-mail. International business proved initially daunting for the store; for example, shipping rates calculated for the domestic market became irrelevant when orders started coming in from overseas. "When we started the business," Lopez notes, "we had planned to open a second shop in the second year. The Web was our second shop."

Transaction Security

Transaction security has been a concern for consumers and businesses shopping on the Web. The fear is that credit card numbers or other purchase authorizations may be stolen by third parties. Indeed, some experts have pointed to the perception of insecurity on the Web as a prime reason that Web commerce has been slow to develop.

In response, a variety of security solutions have been proposed. The one that appears most likely to dominate in the near future is the Secure Electronic Transactions (SET) standard, put forth by Visa and MasterCard and endorsed by influential companies such as Netscape Communications and Microsoft. Expected to be in use by early 1997, SET uses sophisticated encryption technology to mask data as they are transmitted across the Internet. Forrester Research predicts SET will take off in 1997. For business-to-business marketing, the familiar Electronic Data Interchange format is gradually making its way onto the Web.

A different solution to transaction security is the concept of digital cash. With digital cash, a customer sets up an account by depositing money with one of several providers. Merchants accepting that provider's digital cash automatically debit the customer's account for each use. Any size of transaction is easily supported and only the cash amount is transmitted over the Web—no credit card numbers are endangered. Unfortunately, there is no current standard in digital cash, so a variety of providers are competing both to acquire customers and to sign up merchants.

Some merchants seem unconcerned about security. While nearly half of respondents to a survey by Arthur D. Little rated security and privacy as the most significant barriers to commerce on the Web, an informal survey by *Web Week* magazine revealed only 16% of on-line merchants were using some kind of security technology; over half of respondents relied on unencrypted transmission of credit card numbers. Forrester Research found few merchants had experienced on-line fraud, leading to little demand for special systems such as digital cash. Forrester predicts that secure credit card transactions will eventually dominate consumer transactions while digital cash may find its niche in providing business-to-business solutions.

Technically, it appears that security problems are well on the way to being solved. The more important issue is customer perception. Creating customer trust in the security of the Web, and trust in Web sites generally, remains a challenge. Some consumers are willing to use their credit cards on-line: Amazon.com reports that 80% of its customers submit their credit card numbers over the Web, and the Atlanta Olympics sold over 50,000 tickets to the Olympic Games via on-line credit card transactions. However, others remain wary.

WHO CAN BENEFIT?

For all those obstacles, the overall evidence supports that many kinds of businesses can benefit from being on the Web. There is every indication that the Web will only become more attractive to commerce over time through market growth and improved technology. Following are some specific suggestions about which companies are most likely to benefit, from marketing on the World Wide Web:

• If a product or service can be transmitted electronically, the Web is likely to prove an effective distribution and marketing channel, because it allows instantaneous direct marketing with virtually no distribution costs. Coming technological improvement will dramatically increase the speed and volume of electronic products that may be transmitted via the Web. Thus, digital products in industries such as computer software, publishing, music, movies, games, financial services, and travel services are most likely to be transformed by the Web.

- If a product is highly technical or would benefit from a quantity of information to sell or service, it's a good candidate for the Web because that information can be presented effectively at little cost.

- If a company already sells products directly via catalogs or telemarketing, the Web is likely to be a viable additional marketing method. If customers feel comfortable ordering from a catalog or advertisement, they are likely to feel comfortable ordering over the Internet.

- If a product appeals to a broad geographic market, the Web can provide a cost-effective marketing medium. Many commercial Web sites report customers from dozens of countries, a trend that will increase as more of the world catches up with the United States in Internet access.

- If the product is a planned purchase for which customers gather information before purchase, it's a good candidate for Web marketing. The Web provides an effective way to help with customer research; indeed, a company can build research aids into its sites.

The single most important factor, however, is whether a company's customers are on the Web. For consumer markets, the Web is not yet a mass medium—and may never be one. Young, highly educated upper- and upper-middle class consumers will likely continue to be the primary Web purchasers for the foreseeable future. The Web has achieved broader penetration of business-to-business markets, but large companies and technology-intensive companies are the ones that currently have the greatest Internet access.

Making Web Marketing Work

Many companies seem to fall prey to the "if we build it, they will come" mentality regarding Web sites. One of the most important factors in Web marketing success is an organizational commitment to ongoing support and development of a site, but several other factors play significant roles.

Have a strategy. Companies must know their goals for being on the Web and plan how to achieve those goals. It is important to consider how the Web site will relate to the rest of the organization's marketing, and how the company will measure the site's success.

Collect customer feedback. Ideally, one should research building a Web site, but at a minimum, customers should be able to send the company e-mail directly from its site. Track how customers visit the site—e.g., which pages are popular, which pages should be linked to other pages. Consider on-line surveys as a way of building a database of information. Include phone numbers and addresses on your site.

Respond to customers. When you receive customer feedback or questions, respond in a timely, effective manner. Offer e-mail updates or newsletters to customers who volunteer their e-mail addresses. Update and redesign your site based on customer feedback.

Integrate Web marketing into all marketing. Coordinate Web marketing approaches with other marketing in the company. Use the Web site to support advertising messages and promotional activities. Provide sales leads to other parts of the company. Include e-mail and Web addresses in all advertising and promotional materials. Most important, prepare the rest of the company to provide on-line sales and service.

Make a unique offer. On-line purchasing is a new behavior for most customers. Companies must give customers a reason to change their purchase habits. Why should a customer purchase a company's product on the Web? Why should a customer purchase from the company's Web site rather than a competitor's?

Web Sites Mentioned in This Article.
- Amazon.com, http://www.amazon.com
- Auto-by-tel, http://www.autobytel.com
- CyberShop, http://www.cybershop.com
- The Discovery Channel, http://www.discovery.com
- ESPN SportsZone, http://espnnet.sportszone.com
- E-trade, http://www.etrade.com
- Federal Express, http://www.fedex.com
- Fidelity Investments, http://www.fidinv.com
- Firefly, http://www.firefly.com
- General Electric Plastics Division, http://www.ge.com/plastics/
- Hot Hot Hot, http://www.hothothot.com
- HotWired, http://www.hotwired.com
- Industry.net, http://www.industry.net
- Insight Direct, http://www.insight.com
- Lands' End, http://www.landsend.com
- L. L. Bean, http://www.llbean.com
- *Los Angeles Times,* http://www.latimes.com
- Marshall Industries, http://www.marshall.com
- Microsoft, http://www.microsoft.com
- Mind's Eye Fiction, http://www.ghgcorp.com/mindseye/

- Motley Fool, http://fool.web.aol.com
- Netmart, http://www.netmart.com
- News.com, http://www.news.com
- Parents' Place, http://www.parentsplace.com
- Pathfinder, http://pathfinder.com
- Peapod, http://www.peapod.com
- Pointcast, http://www.pointcast.com
- Quote.com, http://www.quote.com
- Reebok, http://www.reebok.com
- *The San Jose Mercury News,* http://www.sjmercury.com
- Security First Network Bank, http://www.sfnb.com
- Shareware.com, http://www.shareware.com
- Sun Microsystems, http://www.sun.com
- Trade'EX, http://www.tradeex.com
- Virtual Vegas, http://www.virtualvegas.com/cybercoin/beta.html
- Virtual Vineyards, http://www.virtualvin.com
- *The Wall Street Journal,* http://www.wsj.com
- *Yahoo!,* http://www.yahoo.com

A Multivariate Analysis of Web Usage

Pradeep K. Korgaonkar
Lori D. Wolin

Applying the uses and gratification theory to improve the understanding of Web usage, the authors explore Web users' motivations and concerns. These motivations and concerns, as well as demographic factors, were studied in three usage contexts: (1) the number of hours per day spent on the Web, (2) the percentage of time spent for business versus personal purposes, and (3) the purchases made from a Web business and, if purchases were made, the approximate number of times purchasers placed orders on the Web. Multivariate factor analysis suggests the presence of seven motivations and concerns regarding Web use. Additionally, the results suggest that these seven factors, along with age, income, gender, and education levels, are significantly correlated with the three usage contexts.

As a business tool, the World Wide Web, or the multimedia interactive component of the Internet, is fast becoming as common as the telephone. An estimated 55 million people surf the Web (Green, Himelstein, and Judge, 1998), and on-line traffic has been doubling every 100 days (Ingersoll, 1998). Much like telephone technology changed the way people did business in the past, the Web is dramatically changing the way people do business today. No other Internet feature offers as much versatility as the Web. The Web's technology allows businesses to use it for several purposes: as an information retrieval source, as a sales tool, as a distribution channel, and as a customer support tool (Sandberg, 1998; Peterson, Balasubramanian, and Bronnenberg, 1997). Not surpris-

ingly, many studies indicate that the number of consumers clicking on the Web is on the increase (e.g., Hagel and Armstrong, 1997). Paradoxically, the studies suggesting disappointing corporate experiences with the Web also continue to increase (e.g., Wolff, 1998). For many companies, the commercial experience with the Web has been disappointing. Even companies known for their media innovation are perplexed by this new medium; Procter and Gamble recently conducted a pivotal seminar with key Internet executives to discuss the underperforming Web. Topics included measurement standards, Web banner formats, consumer acceptance of on-line advertising, and making on-line advertising easier to purchase (Elliott, 1998). According to e-land, an Internet research company, in all of 1997, Web users spent only $1.5 billion buying products and services, and 1998 on-line spending projections are at $3.7 billion (e-land, 1998). In perspective, these amounts are a fraction of the $2.5 trillion spent shopping in 1997. Not surprisingly, many marketing executives are skeptical about the claims that the Web is the global marketplace of the future. We believe, in this stage of promises and doubts, the key to realizing the underutilized potential of the Web rests with understanding the needs of the Web user.

Sellers once had an advantage because only they held the knowledge that gave them power with reference to a product or service they sold; in the past, consumers had to work hard to become well-informed about products and services. However, today's Web search software is yielding information that puts consumers on the same level with the professional (Martin, 1996). As a result, it is clear to many Internet experts that to succeed in this environment, we need a better understanding of the Web user. For example, Hagel and Armstrong (1997) state, "To become profitable, the organizers of the virtual community must understand and address this newly empowered customer's needs." A study by the Gartner Group (1995) found that 90 percent of Web sites were developed without asking existing customers what they wanted. In their rush to have an Internet presence, many firms that ordinarily employ sound research practices abandon their logic and develop ineffective Web sites (Nadilo, 1998).

Curiously, little is actually known about how and why consumers are using this technology to interact with businesses and other consumers. For example, are they using the Web only to acquire information? Are they also using it to socialize? What are their concerns or fears? Finally, does all of this information have any relationship or bearing on how they use the Web? It seems that researchers have studied the issues of Web advertising in more detail (e.g., Maddox, Mehta, and Daubek, 1997; McDonald, 1997) than the fundamental issues related to the use of the Web as a medium.

Although some research exists indicating the demographic profile of the Web user, little is known about the consumers' reasons, as well as concerns, as they relate to Web usage. We studied these issues in the context of different levels or types of Web usage:

Level 1. The number of hours per day spent on the Web.
Level 2. The percentage of time spent for business purposes versus personal purposes.
Level 3. The purchases made from a Web business and, if purchases were made, the approximate number of times purchase orders were placed on the Web in the past 12 months.

In order to understand the motivations and the concerns of Web users, we reviewed the past published literature on Web usage as well as the usage of other mass media such as television, radio, cable television, and newspaper. Additionally we conducted six focus groups with users of the Web to get a deeper understanding of the topic. Proceeding with the focus group studies, we developed a survey of the Web to validate the focus group findings and to test specific research hypotheses. In the next section we review the past literature which, in conjunction with the focus groups, guides us in developing the study's hypotheses.

LITERATURE REVIEW

Although it is clear that using the Web is an important activity for many people, there is less consensus regarding their reasons for using it. As the Web has grown, the reasons for its use, as well as concerns related to its use, have also proliferated.

The Web was founded for government and educational use, so it's no surprise that its early adopters were students, professors, and scientists. Given the educational emphasis in its early years, commercial activity was originally frowned upon (Strangelove, 1993). Today, a great variety of people have found that they could use the Web for reasons beyond educational information retrieval. It reflects the fact that the Web users of today are very diverse and not limited to the professors, students, and scientists of the early days. Interestingly, the most recent Georgia Tech Graphic, Visualization, and Usability Center World Wide Web Survey from April 1998 states that the general demographics of the Web's user population moved closer to the characteristics of the general population for the first time (GVU, 1998).

In order to get a better understanding of possible reasons and concerns of the Web users, we examined the past published literature on why people use the mass media and the gratifications derived from media use. Uses and gratifications have been elaborated extensively by several researchers (e.g., Katz, Blumer, and Gurevitch, 1974; Rosengren, Wenner, and Palmgreen, 1985; McGuire, 1974). For example, Mendelson's (1964) study of radio listeners suggested several types of gratifications including forming companionship, counteracting boredom, and acquiring information. Berelson's (1959) study of newspapers suggested many motives such as the need for information, social prestige, social contact, and respite. Rubin's (1983) study of television gratifications led to several typologies including relaxation, habit, entertainment, information, and escape.

Contemporary researchers have applied the gratifications concept to the study of new technologies. Shaver (1983) conducted focus group interviews and found two gratifications related to cable television. They were "variety" and "control over viewing." The studies (Phillips, 1982; Waterman, 1984; Levy and Fink, 1984) on video cassettes suggested gratifications of choice, time, and mobility. Rafaeli (1986) found that users of electronic bulletin boards felt "recreation, diversion, and entertainment" as the principal motivations for use followed by "communications" and "learning what others think." In recent years, it has also been used to examine the audience experience associated with Web sites (Eighmey and McCord, 1998; Mukherji, Mukherji, and Nicovich, 1998). Thus, the user gratification research has been quite fruitful in understanding consumers' motivations and concerns for using various media. Uses and gratifications theory rests on several basic assumptions, which emphasize the underlying belief that the audience is actively involved in media usage. The interactive element of the Web requires a significant consumer involvement. For example, a study conducted by Saatchi & Saatchi (1996) reveals that the typical Web user is alert, absorbed, and enjoying the surfing experience. As a result, the application of uses and gratification theory to improve our understanding of Web usage seems appropriate. Thus, based on the past research, we hypothesize that motivations and concerns of Web users will be varied and correlate significantly with the usage of the Web.

We expect the usage of the Web to also vary based on the demographics, i.e., the characteristics of the audience. Each of the major media has unique capabilities and unique audience characteristics. For example, middle income, high-school-educated viewers and their families are the heaviest viewers of television (Bov'ee and Arens, 1996). Additionally, older women view television the most and teenage females the least. In the context of the Web, measuring precisely who is using it is still difficult to establish. The national research companies define a Web user differently, and the Web continues to grow in its popularity. Thus,

Table 2.3	**Research Company Web User Estimates**			
Company Survey Results Source	**Cyber Dialogue**	**Media Metrix at Home Survey**	**Nielsen**	**Relevant Knowledge**
Number of U.S. users	41.5 million	38 million	52 million	55.4 million
Gender	58% male 42% female	58% male 42% female	57% male 43% female	57% male 43% female
Percentage with college degrees	43%	49.9%	40.4%	51%
Percentage with household income above $60,000	N/A	48.1%	35.8%	N/A
Largest age group	30–49 (54%)	35–50 (37.3%)	N/A	18–34 (34%)
Size of sample	500	10,000	8,000	2,000
Sample error	+/−4.4%	+/−.75%	+/−.6%	+/−1.5%

Source: Wang Nelson, "Measuring Who's On Web Is Still Difficult Business," *Internet World,* February 9, 1998.

companies such as Nielsen Media Research, Cyber Dialogue, Relevant Knowledge, and Media Metrix provide different estimates.

Despite these differences, Table 2.3 suggests that a typical Web user is more likely to be: male, well-educated, middle income and middle-aged or younger. Hence, we hypothesize that Web usage will correlate significantly with the demographic factors of gender, education, income, and age. The following section describes the methodology used to test the two research hypotheses.

METHODOLOGY

The research effort began with a series of six focus groups with undergraduate and graduate students of a comprehensive urban university in the southeastern United States. For the purpose of the focus groups, the student population was considered appropriate as the urban and commuter setting of the university allowed us to select the students who were either moderate or active users of the Web and also reflected diversity in terms of gender, age, ethnicity, education, and income levels. The series of focus groups were designed and anchored to elicit responses in terms of the Web in general, rather than a specific Web site. The participants were probed to indicate their reasons for using the Web, as well as any concerns they might have about its usage. The participants' information on the various gratifications obtained from the usage of the Web, along with their concerns and how they use the Web, was used to construct the survey instrument used in the second stage of the study.

Questionnaire Development

The survey instrument included several statements designed to measure the motivations related to the usage of the Web. The survey also gathered additional information on the respondents' views on advertising on the Web, the types of Web sites the respondents visit, and the regularity of the respon-dents' usage of various Web sites, e-mail, bulletin boards, and chat rooms. Additionally, we asked the respondents to compare Web advertising with others types of media advertising. Finally, we collected demographic information including gender, age, income level, occupation, education, and ethnicity.

In constructing the survey items specific to this study, we reviewed the items in prior studies in media uses and gratifications research (e.g., Rubin, 1983; Greenberg, 1973) as well as the results of six focus groups. The participants in the focus groups were asked to provide detailed information on ways in which they use the Web and to provide reasons for their use along with any concerns they might have regarding the Web. The information was collected individually, grouped, and then reviewed. A large majority of the items included in the survey instrument came directly from the focus groups. Ultimately, we designed the survey with 41 items intended to capture eight underlying constructs: companionship, entertainment, interactivity, learning about things, privacy concerns, security concerns, shopping, and to pass time. Each survey item was measured on a five-point scale of (1) strongly disagree to (5) strongly agree. The detailed discussion of the operationalization of these constructs is provided in the measurement section.

Sample and Data Collection

The study sample consisted of 420 consumers from a large southeastern metropolitan area. They were contacted on different days of the week and times of the day for their study participation. Given the nature of the study topic, only those who indicated they had used the Web were selected to participate in the study. The participants were interviewed in their homes. Of the surveys collected, 401 were usable for the analyses in this research. The sample consisted of an almost equal number of males (53 percent) and females (47 percent), primarily in professional jobs (30 percent), with some college-level education (40 percent), mostly under 40 years of age (79 percent), with incomes between \$20,000 and \$40,000 (29 percent). Compared to the demographic composition of the area, the sample was overrepresented in terms of younger and professional composition. This overrepresentation was not surprising given that we surveyed only those consumers who had a previous experience with the Web. The following measurement section gives a full description of how the motivations and concerns of using the Web, demographics, and usage of the Web were operationalized and measured.

MEASUREMENT

Operationalization of Gratifications and Concerns

The first step in the analysis was aimed at validating the underlying measurement of eight factors designed to capture the gratifications and concerns. To accomplish this objective, we factor analyzed the 41 items with principal component extraction with iterations and varimax rotation. With eigenvalues of 1.00 or higher as the criterion, we found a presence of nine factors as opposed to the hypothesized eight factors in our data. The nine factors explained 63.71 percent of the variance. But a closer examination of the factors, including the results of the scree test, led us to narrow the number to seven factors. The seven factors accounted for 58.88 percent of the variance. By using a criterion of factor loadings of .40 or higher, we selected the items pertaining to each factor. The results of the factor analysis are shown in Table 2.4. The statements themselves and the prior focus group discussions provided insights into the interpretation of the factors.

Factor 1: Social Escapism Motivation

The first factor consists of statements that characterize the Web as a pleasurable, fun, and enjoyable activity that allows one to escape from reality. This factor is very similar to the notion of entertainment, as the statements indicate that the Web is

gratifying in its ability to provide diversion, to arouse emotions and feelings, and to provide aesthetic enjoyment. Thus, we see the Web being used as a relaxant to relieve day-to-day boredom and stress. It also includes the concept of overcoming loneliness (companionship), which we originally envisioned as a separate and distinct factor. The loading of these statements designed to measure loneliness, with the entertainment-oriented statements, led us to label this factor Social Escapism. The eigenvalue of this factor was 9.759.

Factor 2: Transaction-Based Security and Privacy Concerns

This factor captures one of the two concerns expressed by the respondents. After years of media reports that have focused on security lapses on the Web, consumers have become cautious. In a recent *USA Today* poll, 95 percent of Americans said they would not give out their credit-card number on-line (Schavey, 1998). This factor captures the misgivings respondents have giving credit-card information on the Web, the security fears of buying products and services on the Web, the reluctance of computer banking, and privacy issues that are transaction-based. It captures the concerns related to sharing personal financial information as well as the perception that the Web usage will improve if there were privacy safeguards (Beck, 1998). These real or imagined concerns of transaction-based privacy and security were also separate from the control-based security and privacy (Factor 6) discussed later. The eigenvalue of this factor was 5.270.

Factor 3: Information Motivation

The statements that load on this factor describe how consumers use the Web for their self-education and information needs. As noted by many academics, as well as practitioners, this information-seeking orientation led to the earlier popularity of the Web and still continues to draw new users to the medium. As stated by Schwartz (1997), if the Web

TABLE 2.4	Factor Analysis Result[1]		
Factor1—Social Escapism Motivation	Loadings Eigenvalue	Reliability	
		.91	*9.759*
So I can escape from reality	.824		
Because it stirs me up.	.756		
Because it arouses my emotions and feelings.	.755		
Because it make me feel less lonely.	.740		
So I can get away from what I am doing	.738		
So I can forget about work.	.734		
Because it shows me how to get along with others	.732		
Because it helps me unwind.	.728		
So I won't be alone.	.716		
I do not like to use the web alone.	.562		
Because it takes me into another world.	.557		
Factor 2—Transaction-Based Security and Privacy Concerns			
		.80	*5.270*
I am worried about the security of financial transactions on the Web.	.791		
I am concerned that my personal financial information may be shared with businesses without my consent.	.759		
I am uncomfortable giving my credit card number on the Web.	.662		
I am concerned over the security of personal information on the Web.	.658		
When I send a message over the Web, I feel concerned that it may be read by some other person or company without my knowledge.	.634		
I am uncomfortable conducting personal banking transactions via the Web.	.526		
To me, the use of the Web will be more appealing if proper safeguards were in place.	.517		
Factor 3—Informatlon Motivation			
		.77	*3.604*
Because it gives quick and easy access to large volumes of information.	.750		
Overall, I learn a lot from using the Web.	.748		
So I can learn about things happening in the world.	.677		
Overall, information obtained from the Web is useful.	.661		
Because it make acquiring information inexpensive.	.521		

TABLE 2.4 Factor Analysis Result[1] *(continued)*			
Factor 4—Interactive Control Motivation	**Loadings Eigenvalue**	**Reliability**	
		.83	1.531
Because I decide if I want to continue scrolling through the sites or not.	.736		
Because it gives me the control over what and when I want to use it.	.719		
Because it is interactive.	.607		
Because I enjoy it.	.574		
Because it is thrilling.	.573		
Because I find it exciting.	.504		
Factor 5—Socialization Motivation			
		.80	1.434
When I visit my friends we often use the Web.	.714		
With my friends.	.697		
Often, I talk to my friends about sites on the Web.	.601		
I enjoy telling people about the Web sites I like.	.456		
Because it is a part of my usual routine.	.426		
Factor 6—Nontransactional Privacy Concerns			
		.76	1.345
I detest the fact that the Web is becoming a haven for electronic junk mail.	.768		
I wish I had more control over unwanted messages sent by businesses on the Web.	.754		
I dislike the fact that marketers are able to find out personal information of on-line shoppers.	.768		
Factor 7—Economic Motivation			
		.65	1.199
I enjoy the convenience of shopping on the Web.	.660		
When I want to buy a big-ticket item, I use the Web to search for bargain prices.	.597		
To research a company, industry, or stock.	.549		
Because it saves money.	.523		

[1] 58.881% of the variance is explained in this factor analysis.

is good at anything, it's good at presenting tons of information and involving people in the process of sorting through it. Thus, the respondents agree strongly with the statements describing their usage of the Web for acquiring useful information quickly, easily, and in an inexpensive manner. The eigenvalue of this factor was 3.604.

Factor 4: Interactive Control Motivation

The interactive element of the Web puts the users in charge of the medium. Now, the user can choose which Web sites to view, when to view them, who to interact with in chat rooms, and what to say to others. The interactive feature of the Web allows consumers to personalize and customize their experience by choosing among its huge selection. By doing so, the Web has become the first successful interactive medium. According to Ghose and Dou (1998), Web users gravitate to sites with many interactive features. Clearly, this factor captures perhaps the most gratifying feature of the Web as seen by consumers. Because of the interactivity, the Web has the potential to also become a niche medium, as opposed to a mass medium such as television or radio. The eigenvalue of this factor was 1.531.

Factor 5: Socialization Motivation

The socialization factor represents the role of the Web as a facilitator of interpersonal communication and activities. Past studies of television viewing have frequently mentioned the usefulness of the medium in terms of its conversational value (e.g., Tooley, 1989). A similar sharing of experience and knowledge with friends about different Web sites provides a strong reason for using the Web. This information suggests that consumers are looking for more than information when they go on the Web. Consumers look at the Web as a place in which they can interact and socialize with others with similar interests. The widespread use of e-mail, bulletin boards, and chat room features testify the importance of the socialization motive for many Web users. Hagel and Armstrong (1997) suggest that a

key to profitability on the Web for many companies will be their abilities to build virtual communities on the Web for their customers, catering to the socialization motivation captured by this factor. The eigenvalue of this factor was 1.434.

Factor 6: Nontransactional Privacy Concerns

This factor differs from the transaction-based security and privacy concerns (Factor 2) in that it is concerned about privacy in general rather than the security and privacy issues related to Web transactions. As stated by Malcolm Fitch (1998), on-line swindlers include everyone from whiz-kid hackers to the old boiler-room operators who sell bogus products and services to unsuspecting consumers. However, seemingly less benign activity such as sending an unsolicited e-mail could provide fodder for consumers' concerns with privacy. Further, as database marketing to Web users becomes more sophisticated, users will receive increasingly more unsolicited advertisements (Weber, 1997). If not properly addressed, this barrage could lead to a backlash against the companies as well as the Web (Markoff, 1998). A few recent articles suggest that over two-thirds of consumers consider the privacy concern to be very important (e.g., Wang, Lee, and Wang, 1998). The recent establishment of the Online Privacy Alliance—an industry group designed to offset these concerns—attests to the volatility of this concern (Quick, 1998). The eigenvalue of this factor was 1.345.

Factor 7: Economic Motivation

The factor shows that the users collect information for learning and educational purposes (informational purposes), as well as for shopping and buying motivations, such as buying a stock or bond or making investment decisions. One sees less impulse purchasing here than in a typical store. However, when shopping for big-ticket items where price comparisons in an information-rich environment is fairly easy, and the potential for savings significant, the economic motivation to shop on the Web could be strong (Anders, 1998). Another part of the economic motivation is consumers' ability to get free products. Netscape is a glaring example of a successful company catering to the economic motivation. By allowing users to download its Navigator software for a charge, Netscape became a household name. The eigenvalue of this factor was 1.199. The statements loading on each of the seven factors were summated to form a measurement scale corresponding to the particular construct and used in the subsequent analysis.

Operationalization of Demographic Information

The demographic information collected in the study included gender (1) male, (2) female; occupation measured on a scale of (1) unskilled through (6) professional; education measured on a five-point scale of (1) high school through (5) post graduate/professional training; age measured on a six-point scale of (1) under 20 years through (6) over 60 years of age; annual household income measured on a six-point scale of (1) under $20,000 through (6) over $100,000; and ethnicity measured on a five-point scale of (1) African-American, (2) Anglo-American, (3) Asian-American, (4) Hispanic-American, and (5) other.

Operationalization of Web Usage

Finally, the dependent variable Web usage was conceptualized as a three-types-of-activity variable and measured to capture the various types of usage as indicated by the respondents. The first usage variable captured the average amount of time spent per day on the Web on a five-point scale of (1) zero hours through (5) more than four hours. The second usage variable captured the percentage (from zero to one hundred) of estimated time spent on the Web for business and personal purposes. This variable was measured by asking the respondents to indicate the estimated percentage for each separately as an

open-ended response. Third, a set of usage variables were designed to capture purchasing activities from the Web. Two questions related to purchasing on the Web were included: (1) if the respondents had purchased merchandise or a service from a Web business in the previous 12 months, measured as either a yes or a no and, if yes, then (2) approximately how frequently they ordered the merchandise from the Web, in the past 12 months, on a six-point scale of (1) 1 to 2 times through (6) 11 or more times. Thus, our analysis of usage is capturing three different activities of (1) overall usage, (2) business and personal usage, and (3) shopping-oriented usage. The data were analyzed separately for each of the usage variables. Using the resulting seven motivational and four demographic variables as independent variables and each usage factor as a dependent variable, discriminant and regression analyses were carried out.

RESULTS

Hours Spent per Day on the Web

The respondents to this question were classified into two groups of (1) those who spend less than an hour per day on the Web, and (2) those who spend more than an hour per day on the Web. A multivariate discriminant analysis between these two groups was carried out, again using the seven motivational and concern factors and the four selected demographics. Missing values of the discriminating variables were replaced with the mean values. The discriminal function was developed by randomly splitting the sample in half and using the other half for cross validation purposes. The results are shown in Table 2.5. The discriminal function for this usage variable was significant ($p < .001$). The classification results indicated that 74 percent of the cases were correctly classified. This result was a 45 percent improvement over chance for the total sample. The z-test for proportional chance criterion rejected the null hypothesis ($p < .05$) that classification accuracy is no better than chance. Seven out of eleven discriminating variables were found to be significant at a level of .05 or better. The significant variables were social escapism motivation ($p <$ .001), information motivation ($p < .05$), interactive control motivation ($p < .001$), socialization motivation ($p < .001$), economic motivation ($p < .05$), education ($p < .05$), and income ($p < .05$).

The comparison of means between the groups for the significant variables indicates that compared to those who spend an hour or less per day on the Web, the heavier user of the Web is more likely to (a) find gratification in using the Web as

an escape from real acquiring useful info pensive way, (c) enjo the Web, (d) enjoy talk ent sites and use the We activity, and (e) find grat to shop for "good" prices for big-ticket items. Not su quent users of the Web had income levels than their coun ...10 used the Web less frequently. The results are shown in Table 2.5.

TABLE 2.5 Discrimination Analysis: Hours Spent per Day on the Web

Summary of Fit Independent Variable	Significance
Social escapism motivation	.000
Transaction-based security and privacy concerns	.306
Information motivation	.020
Interactive control motivation	.001
Socialization motivation	.000
Nontransactional privacy concerns	.179
Economic motivation	.037
Gender	.131
Education	.046
Age	.287
Income	.088

Test of Functions	Wilks' Lambda	Chi-square	df	Sig.
1	777	96.331	11	.000

Cross-Validated Classification Results[1]	Predicted Group Membership of Less Than One Hour per Day	Predicted Group Membership of More Than One Hour per Day	Total
Less than one hour per day	66.9%	33.1%	100.0%
More than one hour per day	25.2	74.8	100.0

[1]74.0% of the original cases were correctly classified and 71.7% of cross-validated ground cases were correctly classified.

Purpose Web Usage

respondents were asked to indicate what percentage of the time spent on the Web was for business purposes. Those who spent 25 percent or less were grouped as light users of the Web for business purposes, and those who spent more than 25 percent were grouped together as heavy users. Again, a discriminant analysis between the two groups was undertaken with the 11 independent variables. Missing values of the discriminating variables were replaced with the mean values. The sample was split in half and the resulting discriminant function was cross-validated us-

ing the hold-out sample. The results are shown in Table 2.6.

The resulting discriminant function was significant at $p < .001$ level. The z-test for proportional chance was significant at ($p < .05$) with 20.66 percent improvement in predictions over chance alone. Thus, the null hypothesis that the classification accuracy is no better than chance was rejected. Four out of eleven factors were found to be significant in discrimination between these groups. The significant variables were nontransactional privacy concerns ($p < .10$), economic motivation ($p < .001$), age ($p < .05$), and income ($p < .05$). Overall, the respondents who

---

TABLE 2.6   **Discriminant Analysis: Percentage of Business Web Use**

Summary of Fit

Independent Variable	Significance
Social escapism motivation	.445
Transaction-based security and privacy concerns	.261
Information motivation	.160
Interactive control motivation	.406
Socialization motivation	.119
Nontransactional privacy concerns	**.052**
Economic motivation	**.001**
Gender	.706
Education	.110
Age	**.009**
Income	**.003**

Test of Functions	Wilks' Lambda	Chi-square	df	Sig.
1	.921	30.974	11	.001

Cross-Validated Classification Results[1]	Predicted Group Membership of 0–25% Business Use	Predicted Group Membership of 26–100% Business Use	Total
0–25%	58.2%	41.8%	100.0%
26–100%	43.7	56.3	100.0

[1]60.4% of the original cases were correctly classified and 57.3% of the cross-validated grouped cases were correctly classified.

were heavier business users of the Web were less worried about the nontransactional privacy issues and more interested in shopping for economic and convenience reasons. Demographically, they were older and came from higher income strata.

Personal Purpose Web Usage

The respondents were asked to indicate what percentage of time spent on the Web was for personal reasons. Once again, the responses could vary from zero to one hundred percent. As expected, the frequency distribution of the responses indicated that the respondents favored the personal use of the Web more so than the business use. Therefore, we split the data into two groups of heavy versus light use by splitting the sample at 50 percent use. That is, the respondents who indicated that they spent 50 percent or less time on the Web for personal use were grouped as light users, and those who spent more than 50 percent of their time were grouped together as the heavier users. A discriminant analysis of the two groups with the 11 independent variables was carried out. Again, the sample was randomly split in half and the hold-out half was used for classification validation. Missing values of the discriminating variables were replaced with the mean values. The results are shown in Table 2.7.

The resulting discriminant function was significant at $p < .001$. The cross-classification results

TABLE 2.7	Discriminant Analysis: Percentage of Personal Web Use

Summary of Fit

Independent Variable	Significance
Social escapism motivation	.513
Transaction-based security and privacy concerns	.140
Information motivation	.908
Interactive control motivation	**.046**
Socialization motivation	.213
Nontransactional privacy concerns	.125
Economic motivation	**.026**
Gender	.410
Education	**.018**
Age	**.001**
Income	**.003**

Test of Functions	Wilks' Lambda	Chi-square	df	Sig.
1	.919	31.980	11	.001

Cross-Validated Classification Results[1]	Predicted Group Membership of 0–50% Personal Use	Predicted Group Membership of 51–100% Personal Use	Total
0–50%	56.3%	43.7%	100.0%
51–100	43.8	56.2	100.0

[1]59.9% of the original cases were correctly classified, and 56.3% or the cross-validated grouped cases were correctly classified.

indicate that the improvement in classification was 24 percent higher than expected by chance. The results of the z-test rejected the null hypothesis ($p < .05$) that the classification accuracy is no better than chance. Five out of eleven variables were significant at the .05 level or better. Thus, information motivation ($p < .05$), economic motivation ($p < .05$), age ($p < .001$), and income ($p < .05$) were able to discriminate successfully the two groups of Web users. Compared to the light users, the heavier users of the Web for personal purposes were younger, less educated, and lower in income. These results are starkly in contrast to those who frequented the Web more for business purposes. The heavier user of the Web for personal reasons sought higher enjoyment from the Web for seeking information as well as for economic reasons. These younger, middle-income consumers enjoy performing a whole slew of tasks on the Web without paying a cent. No wonder many Web businesses are not able to persuade consumers to pay for the privilege of using their Web services (Sandberg, 1998).

Purchased Merchandise/Service

The respondents were asked to indicate if they had purchased merchandise or services from a Web

TABLE 2.8	Discriminant Analysis: Web Purchases over the Past Year

Summary of Fit Independent Variable	Significance
Social escapism motivation	.665
Transaction-based security and privacy concerns	**.006**
Information motivation	**.075**
Interactive control motivation	**.008**
Social motivation	**.000**
Nontransactional privacy concerns	.896
Economic motivation	**.000**
Gender	**.006**
Education	.962
Age	**.001**
Income	.224

Test of Functions	Wilks' Lambda	Chi-square	df	Sig.
1	.793	89.024	11	.000

Cross-Validated Classification Results[1]	Predicted Group Membership of Subjects Who Purchased	Predicted Group Membership of Subjects Who Did Not Purchase	Total
Purchase	69.9%	30.1%	100.0%
Did not purchase	30.5	69.5	100.0

[1]73.0% of the original cases were correctly classified, and 69.6% of cross-validated grouped cases correctly classified.

business in the previous year. The differences between those who had purchased a product or service and those who had not were analyzed via multivariate discriminant analysis. The seven motivational and concern factors and the four selected demographics were used as the discriminating set. The sample was split in half and the resulting discriminant function was cross validated using the hold-out sample. Missing values of the discriminating variables were replaced with the mean values. The resulting discriminant function was significant at $p <$ .001. The cross-classification results indicated that the classification accuracy is significantly ($p < .05$) better than by chance alone. The percentage improvement in classifications over the chance factor was 43. The z-test for proportional chance criterion rejects the null hypothesis ($p < .05$) that classification accuracy is not better than chance. Seven out of eleven factors were found to be significant. The significant discriminating variables were transaction-based security and privacy concerns ($p < .05$), information motivation ($p < .10$), interactive control ($p < .05$), conversation motivation ($p < .01$), economic motivation ($p < .01$), gender ($p < .01$), and age ($p < .01$). Those who purchased from a Web business were more likely to accept the privacy and security pitfalls associated with purchasing on the Web, enjoy the information-rich environment of the Web, and relish the interactive features and the socialization value of the Web. As expected, the Web users who have purchased a product or service from a Web business also enjoy the convenience of shopping for big-ticket items on the Web. Demographically, they are more likely to be older men. The results are shown in Table 2.8.

How Often Items Were Ordered

We asked those who indicated they purchased an item from a Web business in the past year ($n =$ 176), to indicate on a six-point scale of (1) 1–2 times, (2) 3–4 times, (3) 5–6 times, (4) 7–8 times, (5) 9–10 times, and (6) 11 or more times, the frequency of their order in the past 12 months. The results were analyzed via multiple regression

analysis. The 11 variables were the descriptors and the frequency of purchase was the dependent variable. Missing values of the independent variables were replaced with the mean values. The results are shown in Table 2.9.

The multiple regression was significant at $p <$ .001. Five out of eleven variables were significant. The significant variables were: social escapism motivation ($p < .001$), interactive control motivation ($p < .10$), economic motivation ($p < .05$), age ($p < .05$), and income ($p < .10$). Those consumers who are frequent patrons of Web businesses are more likely to enjoy using the Web for social escapism, economic shopping incentives, and interactive control features. Demographically, they

TABLE 2.9   Regression: How Often Subjects Ordered Products and Services on the Web in the Last Year

Parameter Estimates Independent Variable	Significance
Intercept	**.010**
Social escapism motivation	**.000**
Transaction-based security privacy concerns	.260
Economic motivation	.932
Interactive control motivation	**.096**
Social motivation	.126
Nontransactional privacy concerns	.323
Economic motivation	**.004**
Gender	.971
Education	.408
Age	**.038**
Income	**.099**
Summary of Fit	
R-square	.169
R-square adjusted	.113
F-value	3.046
F-value significance	.001
Mean square error	3.167
Observations	176

are likely to be older and of higher income levels than those who are less frequent shoppers on the Web.

DISCUSSION

Gratification Factors

Social Escapism Motivation

This motivation factor correlates positively and significantly with the number of hours respondents spent on the Web daily and how often those who ordered products on the Web did so in the last year, indicating that users who use the Web to escape from reality may be viable targets for marketers. Furthermore, users who are motivated by social escapism assert they use the Web to avoid loneliness. Paradoxically, researchers at Carnegie Mellon University have found that people who spend even a few hours a week on-line experience higher levels of depression and loneliness than they would if they used the computer less frequently (Harmon, 1998). This study suggests that the interactivity of the Web may be no more socially healthy than older mass media. Participants in the two-year study used social features such as e-mail and chat rooms more than they used passive information, yet they reported a decline in interaction with family and a reduction in time spent with friends that directly corresponded to the amount of time they spent on-line. While the results depended upon the user's life patterns and type of use, the researchers hypothesize that *non* face-to-face interaction does not provide the kind of support that typically contributes to a sense of security and happiness like human contact does. Hence, this portion of the social escapism motivation factor may relieve boredom and stress but may not overcome loneliness as we originally expected.

Transaction-Based Security and Privacy Concerns

This concern factor correlated significantly and positively with the percentage of business Web-use respondents reported and, if respondents made Web purchases over the past year, asserting that users concerned with the Web's lack of financial and personal safeguards are likely to make Web purchases if these concerns are abated. Understanding consumers' transaction-based security and privacy concerns is paramount to recognizing the Web's potential. Less than 1 percent (0.07 percent) of 1997's total shopping dollars were spent by the Web's users, with 1998 projections at only 0.2 percent (e-land, 1998). Much of this reluctance is due to consumer security and privacy concerns (Quick, 1998; Kiely, 1997). The resolution of some of these problems is already developing. In an attempt to jump-start electronic commerce, an international consortium including the three largest U.S. banks is creating a joint venture to certify corporate and employee identities of the Internet (Bulkeley, 1998). By mid 1999, the certification should be completed, allowing consumers to identify bona-fide merchants and become more comfortable purchasing from them on-line.

Information Motivation

The information motivation factor correlated significantly and positively with the respondents' number of hours spent on the Web per day and if they made Web purchases in the past year. Those users seeking information on the Web may be more likely to eventually make purchases on the Web. From a consumer perspective, the Internet's information role is its main legitimizing function, with free information exploding on the Internet. In order to cater to this gratification factor, the information provided must have quick and easy access. The information provided must also be relevant. The businesses that offer this or are a rich source of information attract an important segment of the Web users. For example, Eshare Technologies, a major provider of Internet chat technology, provides companies like AT&T, Merrill Lynch, and leading universities the capabilities to have real-time communications with consumers (Marriott, 1998).

Interactive Control Motivation

The interactive control motivation factor corresponded significantly and positively with the respondents' number of hours spent on the Web per day, the percentage of personal Web use, if Web purchases were made over the past year, and how often those who ordered products on the Web did so in the last year. Web users have control over the presentation order of the information they view, the amount of information they view, and the style in which they view information (i.e., video, audio, pictorial, and text formats). This interactivity feature unique to the Web iterates between the firm and the user, requiring information from both parties to align the needs of the user. These iterations allow firms to build databases that enhance both the consumers' experiences and the firms' marketing efficiencies (Bezjian-Avery, Calder, and Iacobucci, 1998). Thus, Web users who enjoy the interactivity of the Web are likely to be important targets for marketers.

Socialization Motivation

This motivation factor correlated significantly and positively with the number of hours respondents spent on the Web per day and if they made Web purchases over the past year. The results indicate that those who use the Web with friends and as a part of their social routine are likely to make purchases over the Web. Frankel (1998) suggests that while users may initially use a site for its interactive features, it is the sense of community that keeps them there, which has implications for the marketer. If marketers want to reach users in particular Web sites, the length of time and repetitive use of the site become important factors. Thus, Web-site designers may consider building a sense of community to promote firm offerings.

Nontransactional Privacy Concerns

This concern factor correlated significantly and positively with respondents' percentage of Web business use, suggesting that those who dislike the lack of control over junk e-mail and unwanted messages are more likely to be using the Web for business purposes. The privacy concerns are not limited to the well-known cases of spamming and improper Web cookie distribution, but are expanded to include activities such as selling consumer databases to other companies for direct marketing solicitations. To address these concerns, the Interactive Services Association, which represents online information services, and the Direct Marketing Association have proposed guidelines that would limit unsolicited electronic junk mail as well as marketing to children over the Internet. However, it may still take considerable time and effort to alleviate consumers' irritation over the privacy issue. The companies that take steps to protect privacy will win consumers' trust and confidence.

Economic Motivation

The economic motivation factor correlated significantly and positively with the hours per day respondents spent on the Web, the percentage of Web business use, the percentage of Web personal use, if respondents made Web purchases over the past year, and how often those who ordered products on the Web did so in the last year. Users who enjoy the convenience and money-saving attributes of Web shopping are likely to purchase from the Web. Selling products on the Internet can save companies as much as 15 percent compared to selling through the regular channels. However, many companies are still reluctant to sell products at a lower rate on the Internet in order to avoid alienating their sales force and distributors (Andres, 1998). Nevertheless, the success of companies such as Amazon.com and Dell Computers suggests that opportunities exist for companies to cater to the economic incentives sought by consumers.

Demographic Factors

We considered the demographic factors of gender, education level, age, and income level. Gender correlated significantly and positively only with Web purchases made over the past year. This finding suggests that males are slightly more inclined to make Web purchases; however, with respect to the other dependent variables, gender had no significance, implying no gender distinction over the amount of time spent on the Web, the percentage of business or personal use, and how often Web purchasers ordered products and services. These findings are consistent with the GVU survey stating that the general demographics of the Web's 1998 user population moved closer to the characteristics of the general population for the first time (GVU, 1998).

Education correlated significantly and positively with the hours spent per day on the Web and the percentage of personal Web use, suggesting that subjects with higher education levels tend to spend less time on the Web, perhaps due to heavier time constraints. In terms of personal Web use, subjects with higher education levels are more likely to be light personal users, using the Web less than half the time for personal purposes, which asserts that occupations held by those with higher education levels are more likely to require Internet usage.

Age is correlated significantly and positively with the percentage of business Web use, the percentage of personal Web use, if respondents made Web purchases over the past year, and how often those who ordered products on the Web did so in the last year. The results indicate that older Web users are more likely to be light users, spending less than half of their Web time for personal use. Conversely, older Web users were more likely to be heavy users for business purposes. Older users are also more likely to make Web purchases than younger users, and the older Web users are more likely to make more frequent purchases.

Income level is correlated significantly and positively with the hours spent per day on the Web, the percentage of business Web use, if respondents made Web purchases over the past year, and how often those who ordered products on the Web did so in the last year. Subjects with higher household income are more likely to spend less than an hour a day on the Web and are more likely to use this time for business purposes. The higher income household Web users are more likely to make Web purchases in which the frequency of purchasing increases with household income.

Future Implications

The evolution of the Web has profound implications for the way businesses perform marketing tasks. As stated by Hanson (1998), the Web's commercial growth parallels that of the growth of radio. In 1922, radio advertising transitioned from a point-to-point communication medium to a broadcast medium; the industry participants knew there was incredible demand but could not determine how to collect revenue. By the end of 1922, there were 576 broadcast stations in the United States, and the attention poured on the broadcasters parallels that of the explosion of Web servers in the mid 1990s. Additionally, the rapid expansion of Web connections and browser use is reminiscent of radio in 1922 and 1923. Much like the way we look back at radio today, Web users may be looking back at the Web in several years with amusement at our antiquated technologies and fledgling marketing tasks. However, like radio, it may take years to determine the economic and social impact of the medium. If we are to learn lessons from radio, we must consider the motivations and concerns of Web users to develop advertising and segmentation effectively.

Interactive technology has the capability to change technology in a variety of ways. First, technology developments include greater contingency, frequency, simultaneity, and sensory involvement (Haeckel, 1998). Next, the Web's future includes high fragmentation similar to what we have seen in television. Much like CNN delivers information, ESPN delivers sports, and The Home Shopping Network delivers shopping goods, the Web is beginning to fragment. *Women's Wire* and *iVillage* are two sites catering to women, a growing segment, that provide information on health, parenting, financial services, technology, and shopping (Green 1998; Stem, 1998). Further, America On Line has launched *Electra,* an on-line resource for women focusing on career, money, mind and body, relationship, style, and leisure issues (Sacharow, 1997). Female-oriented sites are rushing to develop a presence on the Web to capture this growing market as women are using the Web as a time-saving device. The future of the Web indicates further fragmentation. The Internet may be used as a tool for entrepreneurs to provide new services and opportunities to narrow user groups. Alas, the Web is a happening, evolving medium whose murky future is likely to be constructed, in part, by examining users' reasons for using the Web. Understanding the motivations and concerns of its users will open the doors to its future.

CONCLUSION

The findings of this study add significantly to our understanding of why and how consumers use the Web. Hoffman and Novak (1996) addressed the implications of the Web as an important and different environment faced by consumers and marketers. Many entrepreneurs and established businesses who have plugged into this new and different environment without understanding it have been disappointed with their results (see, for example, Wolf, 1998). Thus, for practitioners and researchers alike, understanding why and how consumers use the Web may be the key to unlocking the Web's capacity. The Web has turned into a resource as well as a new form of electronic commerce, for everything from buying stocks, books, and computers to grocery shopping. However, to succeed, one has to realize that the Web is, for all intents and purposes, a society unto itself, with its own culture, its own people, and even its own language (Testerman, Kuegler, and Dowling, 1996). It has drastically changed the buyer-seller relationship, tipping the balance of power in favor of consumers, as the interactive feature of the technology puts the consumer in control. As stated by Sheth and Sisodia (1997), industrial-age marketing of the past is trying to cope with the information-age consumer behavior of today and of the future, thus creating a misalignment. How consumers view the new medium and use it have a significant impact on the future of marketing.

This study suggests that consumers use the Web for many more reasons than the often overemphasized reason: to retrieve information. Consequently, in an information age, simply providing information may not be enough (Egan and Pollack, 1995). This study documents Web users' motivations and concerns in relation to different types of usage. It suggests that Web users' motivations and concerns correlate significantly with the number of hours per day spent on the Web, the percentage of time spent on the Web for both personal and business purposes, and the users' purchasing behavior. Although the study asserts that Web users' behavior varies based on gender, education, income, and age, motivations and concerns play a greater role than demographics alone in determining subjects' actions with respect to Web usage. Furthermore, as the Web becomes more mainstream, demographics will continue to play less of a role in determining Web usage characteristics. Males and females of all ages, income levels, and education levels will use the Web in a similar fashion.

In sum, it is clear that practitioners and researchers need to pay more careful attention to the needs of Web users. Examining these needs may provide the means to understanding the underutilized potential of the Web. The growth of advertising on the Web indicates that further studies should analyze users' perceptions of the medium as well as the advertising on the medium (Hirschman and Thompson, 1997; Ducoffe, 1996). Investigation of Web users' needs and perceptions will benefit researchers and practitioners eager to unravel this new and different medium's potential.

Pradeep K. Korgaonkar a professor of marketing at Florida Atlantic University. He received his Ph.D, in business administration at Georgia State University. His teaching interests are in marketing management, marketing strategy, direct marketing, and services marketing. His research has been published in numerous journals and periodicals including the *Journal of Advertising,* the *Journal of Advertising Research,* the *Journal of Business Research,* and the *Journal of Marketing Research,* among others. He has won several teaching and research awards.

Lori D. Wolin is a marketing Ph.D. student at Florida Atlantic University. She received her B.A. at the University of Illinois and her M.B.A. at Florida Atlantic University. Her teaching interests are in sales and sales management, marketing management, promotions, and hospitality marketing. Her extensive industry background in the hospitality industry included senior vice president level positions with major hotel management groups.

REFERENCES

Anders, George. "Some Big Companies Long to Embrace Web but Settle for Flirtation." *Wall Street Journal,* November 4, 1998.

———. "Amazon.com's Shares Illustrate How Wild Internet Stocks Can Be." *Wall Street Journal,* July 23, 1998.

Backchannel. "The Interactive Consumer; A Saatchi and Saatchi Study." *Backchannel,* February 1996.

Beck, Russell. "World Wide Web May Mean World Wide Lawsuits." *Direct Marketing* 61, 3 (1998): 60–65.

Berelson, B. "The State of Communication Research." *Public Opinion Quarterly* 23, 1 (1959): 1–6.

Bezjian-Avery, Alexa, Bobby Calder, and Dawn Iacobucci. "New Media Interactive Advertising vs. Traditional Advertising." *Journal of Advertising Research* 38, 4 (1998): 23–32.

Bov'ee, and Arens. "Contemporary Advertising." Homewood, IL: Richard D. Irwin, Inc., 1986.

Bulkeley, William M. "New Method for Web Ads Stirs Attention." *Wall Street Journal,* October 22, 1998.

Ducoffe, Robert H. "Advertising Value and Advertising on the Web." *Journal of Advertising Research* 36, 5 (1996): 21–35.

Egan, Jack and Kenan Pollack. "Cashing in on the Internet." *U.S. News and World Report,* November 13, 1995.

Eighmey, John and Lola McCord. "Adding Value in the Information Age: Uses and Gratifications of Sites on the World Wide Web." *Journal of Business Research* 41, 3 (1998): 187–94.

Elliott, Stuart. "Procter and Gamble Calls Internet Marketing Executives to Cincinnati For a Summit Meeting." *New York Times,* August 19, 1998.

e-land. "e-stats." Available: WWW URL *http://www.e-land.com/e-stat.*

Fitch, Malcolm. "The New Faces of Cybercrime." *Money,* Summer 1998.

Frankel, Alex. "Customer Knowledge: Ahead of the Game." *Web Business Magazine,* May 1, 1998.

Gartner Group Research. "Web Sites: What Customers Want and Do Not Want." Gartner Group Research, November 9, 1995.

Ghose, Sanjoy and Wenyu Dou. "Interactive Functions and Their Impacts of the Appeal of Internet Presence Sites." *Journal of Advertising Research* 38, 2 (1998): 29–43.

Green, Heather, Linda Himelstein, and Paul Judge. "Portal Combat Comes to the Net." *Business Week,* March 2, 1998.

———. "A Site of One's Own." *Business Week,* July 20, 1998.

Greenberg, B. S. "Viewing and Listening Parameters among British Youngsters." *Journal of Broadcasting* 17, 2 (1973): 173–88.

GVU. "GVU's 9th WWW Survey Results." Available: WWW URL http://www.gvu.gat-ech.edu.

Haechel, Stephan H. "About the Nature and Future of Interactive Marketing." *Journal of Interactive Marketing* 12, 1 (1998): 63–71.

Harmon, Amy. "Researchers Find Sad, Lonely World in Cyberspace." *New York Times,* August 30, 1998.

Hagel, John III and Arthur G. Armstrong. *Net Gain: Expanding Markets through Virtual Communities.* Boston: Harvard Business School Press, 1997.

Hanson, Ward. "The Original WWW: Web Lessons from the Early Days of Radio." *Journal of Interactive Marketing* 12, 3 (1998): 46–56.

Harvey, Bill "The Expanded ARF Model: Bridge to the Accountable Advertising Future." *Journal of Advertising Research* 37, 2 (1997): 11–20.

Hawkins, Robert P., Nancy Reynolds, and Suzanne Pungree. "In Search of Television Viewing Styles." *Journal of Broadcasting and Electronic Media* 35, 3 (1991): 375–83.

Hirschman, Elizabeth C. and Craig J. Thompson. "Why Media Matter: Toward a Richer Understanding of Consumers' Relationships with Advertising and Mass Media." *Journal of Advertising* 26, 1 (1997): 43–60.

Hoffman, Donna L. and Thomas P. Novak. "Marketing in Hypermedia Computer-Mediated Environments: Conceptual Foundations." *Journal of Marketing* 60, 3 (1996): 50–68.

———, Thomas P. Novak, and Patrali Chatteriee. "Commercial Scenarios for the Web: Opportunities and Challenges." *Journal of Computer Mediated Communication* 1, 3 (1995): online.

Ingersoll, Bruce. "Internet Spurs U.S. Growth, Cuts Inflation." *Wall Street Journal,* April 16, 1998.

Katz, Elihu, Jay G. Blumler, and Michael Gurevitch. "Uses and Gratifications Research." In *The Uses of Mass Communications,* J. G. Blumler and E. Katz, eds. Beverly Hills, CA: Sage Publications, 1974.

Kiely, Thomas. "The Internet: Fear and Shopping in Cyberspace." *Harvard Business Review* 75, 4 (1997): 13–14.

Levy, M. R. and E. Fink. "Home Video Recorders and the Transience of Television Broadcasts." *Journal of Communication* 34, 2 (1984): 56–71.

Maddox, Lynda M., Darshan P. Mehta, and Hugh G. Danbek. "The Role and Effect of Web Addresses in Advertising." *Journal of Advertising Research* 37, 2 (1997): 47–58.

Markoff, John. "Security Flaw Discovered in E-Mail Programs." *New York Times,* July 29, 1998.

Marriott, Michael. "The Blossoming of Internet Chat." *New York Times,* July 2, 1998.

Martin, Michael H. "Why the Web Is Still a No-Shop Zone." *Fortune,* February 5, 1996.

McDonald, Scott. "The Once and Future Web: Scenarios for Advertisers." *Journal of Advertising Research* 37, 2 (1997): 21–28.

McGuire, William J. "Psychological Motives and Communication Gratifications." In *The Uses of Mass Communications,* J. G. Blumler and E. Katz, eds. Beverly Hills, CA: Sage Publications, 1974.

McQuail, Denis. "With the Benefit of Hindsight: Reflections on Uses and Gratifications Research." *Critical Studies in Mass Communication* 1 (1984): 177–93.

Mendelson, H. "Listening to Ratio." In *People, Society, and Mass Communications,* L. A. Dexter and D. M. White, eds. Glencoe: Free Press, 1964.

Mukherji, Jyotsna, Ananda Mukherji, and Stef Nicovich. "Understanding Dependency and Use of the Internet: A Uses and Gratifications Perspective." Paper presented to the American Marketing Association, Boston, MA, August 1998.

Nadilo, Rudy. "On-Line Research Taps Consumers Who Spend." *Marketing Research,* June 8, 1998.

Peterson, Robert A., Sridhar Balasubramanian, and Bart J. Bronnenberg. "Exploring the Implications of the Internet for Consumer Marketing." *Journal of the Academy of Marketing Science* 25, 4 (1997): 329–46.

Phillips, A. F. "Attitude Correlates of Select Medial Technologies: A Pilot Study." Annenberg School of Communication, University of Southern California, unpublished, 1982.

Quick, Rebecca. Computer-Industry Group Presents Plan to Regulate Consumer Privacy On-Line." *Wall Street Journal,* July 22, 1998.

Rafaeli, S. "The Electronic Bulletin Board: A Computer-Driven Mass Medium." *Computers and the Social Sciences* 2, 3 (1986): 123–36.

Rosengren, Karl Erik, Lawrence A. Wenner, and Philip Palmgreen (eds.). *Media Gratifications Research: Current Perspectives.* CA: Sage Publications, 1985.

Rubin, Alan M. "An Examination of Television Viewing Motives." *Journal of Communication Research* 8, 3 (1984): 141–65.

Sacharow, Anya. "AOL Studios Spawns Electra, A Women's Site." *Adweek,* December 8, 1997.

Sandberg, Jason. "It Isn't Entertainment That Makes the Web Shine; It's Dull Data." *Wall Street Journal,* July 20,1998.

Schavey, Aaron. "Retailing On-line: Today's American Promise and Tomorrow's Opportunity." *Business America,* January 1998.

Schwartz, Evan I. *Webnomics.* New York: Broadway Books, a Division of Bantam Doubleday Dell Publishing Group, Inc., 1997.

Shaver, J. L. "The Uses of Cable TV." Master's thesis, University of Kentucky, 1983.

Sheth, Jagdish N., and Raiendra S. Sisodia. "Consumer Behavior in the Future." In *Electronic Marketing and the Consumer,* Robert A. Peterson, ed. CA: Sage Publications, Inc., 1997.

Stern, Gary M. "Women's Wire." *Link-Up* 15, 2 (1998): 20.

Strangelove, Michael. "Advertising on the Internet: Myths, Facts, and Tips." The *Internet Business Journal,* 1, 6 (1993): 4–5.

Testerman, Joshua 0., Thomas J. Kuegler, Jr., and Paul J. Dowling, Jr. *Web Advertising and Marketing.* Rocklin, CA: Prima Publishing, 1996.

Tooley, J. A. "'Talk, Talk, Talk." *U.S. News & World Report,* May 15,1989.

Wang, Huaiqing, Matthew K. O. Lee, and Chen Wang. "Consumer Privacy Concerns about Internet Marketing." *Communications of the ACM* 41, 3 (1998): 63–70.

Wang, Nelson. "Measuring Who's on Web Is Still Difficult Business." *Internet World,* February 9, 1998.

Waterman, D. "The Prerecorded Home Video and the Distribution of Theatrical Feature Films." Presented to the Arden Teachers' Conference on Rivalry among Video Media. Hariman, NY, 1984.

Weber, Thomas E. "Software Helps Target Internet Advertising." *Ft. Lauderdale Sun Sentinnel,* April 22, 1997.

Wenner, Lawrence A. "Model Specification and Theoretical Development in Gratifications Sought and Obtained Research: A Comparison of Discrepancy and Transactional Approaches." *Communications Monographs* 53 (1986): 160–79.

Wolff, Michael. *Burn Rate: How I Survived the Gold Rush Years on the Internet.* New York: Simon and Schuster, 1998.

BUSINESS-TO-CONSUMER INTERNET MARKETING

The economics of business-to-consumer web marketing are compelling. In the traditional brick-and-mortar world, retailers face the constant constraint of store size and location. Traditionally, retailers have dealt with these constraints by altering the breadth and depth of the product mix in a unique way to achieve competitive advantage. Holding store size constant, retailers could either offer a greater number of product lines with fewer alternatives within each product-line class or offer fewer product lines but present a greater number of alternatives within each product-line class.

These constraints are, at least in theory, absent on the web. New product lines and product-line options can be added to web sites simply by creating new pages or bullets. Breadth and depth of product line can be expanded without limit. Store location, store size, and time become irrelevant. Some believed that freedom from these constraints would portend a new era in retailing.

To some extent, heady predictions of e-tailing have been realized. In 1999, we witnessed the first "e-Christmas" with billions of dollars in sales. Revenue growth shows no sign of slowing. Consumers' interest in online shopping continues to increase. All forecasts point to a bright future.

Yet not all have been successful. Witness the failure of Levi Strauss online. In 1999 shortly before the Christmas season, this giant of the apparel industry announced that it was closing its online e-commerce operations. Levi Strauss, despite the strength of its world-class brand names and resources, simply could not find a way to make its online operations succeed.

The failure of Levi Strauss online represents an important lesson for business-to-consumer web marketers. To succeed online, electronic retailers must offer a shopping experience superior to both online and offline competitors. Online retailers cannot simply expand the breadth and depth of product mix without also considering the specific shopping needs of consumers.

In the first reading of this chapter, Joseph Alba and his co-authors present a framework for analyzing what benefits various shopping environments provide to consumers. These researchers suggest that the web may present a greater threat to some retail formats than to others. Least threatened by the web is the catalog marketer, according to the authors, since catalog marketers already have the direct marketing skills and backend fulfillment systems in place. Most threatened by the web are retailers that compete on price alone since the web exacerbates price competition.

In the second reading of this chapter, researchers note that despite growth, Internet shopping is still not a mainstream activity. The Internet shopper continues to show distinctiveness on a variety of demographic and behavioral measures.

Please visit the textbook's web site for additional resources and exercises related to the business-to-consumer web environment.

Interactive Home Shopping: Consumer, Retailer, and Manufacturer Incentives to Participate in Electronic Marketplaces

Joseph Alba, John Lynch, Barton Weitz,
Chris Janiszewski, Richard Lutz,
Alan Sawyer, Stacy Wood

The authors examine the implications of electronic shopping for consumers, retailers, and manufacturers. They assume that near-term technological developments will offer consumers unparalleled opportunities to locate and compare product offerings. They examine these advantages as a function of typical consumer goals and the types of products and services being sought and offer conclusions regarding consumer incentives and disincentives to purchase through interactive home shopping vis-à-vis traditional retail formats. The authors discuss implications for industry structure as they pertain to competition among retailers, competition among manufacturers, and retailer-manufacturer relationships.

A confluence of technological, economic, and cultural forces has made possible a new and revolutionary distribution channel known generically as interactive home shopping (IHS). Although only in its infancy, IHS has the potential to change fundamentally the manner in which people shop as well as the structure of the consumer goods and retail industries. Projections about the diffusion of IHS are sometimes breathtaking: Forecasts of IHS sales range from 55 billion to $300 billion by the year 2000 (Reda 1995; Wilensky 1995). In contrast to such projections, current sales are barely perceptible. Internet sales in 1996 were estimated at $500 million—less than 1% of all nonstore shopping (Schiesel 1997). Combining Internet,

Reprinted with permission from the *Journal of Marketing,* published by the American Marketing Association, Joseph Alba, John Lynch, Barton Weitz, Chris Janiszewski, Richard Lutz, Alan Sawyer, and Stacy Wood, July 1997, Vol. 61, pp. 38–53.

other online services, television home shopping, CD-ROM catalogs, and conventional catalogs, all nonstore retailing combined accounts for only 5% to 10% of all retail sales, with little growth in recent years. Therefore, IHS will need to offer benefits superior to current nonstore channels in order to realize the more ambitious sales forecasts that have been set for it.

Our goal is to examine the effects of consumer, retailer, and manufacturer behavior on the diffusion of IHS and the impact this new retail format could have on the retail industry. In the first half we analyze the demand-side issues, examining what IHS offers consumers that could motivate them to alter their present shopping behavior. In the second half we examine the impact of this new channel on industry structure and the competitive positioning of individual firms.

INTERACTIVE HOME SHOPPING DEFINED

In defining IHS, we conceptualize *interactivity* as a continuous construct capturing the quality of two-way communication between two parties. (For an elaborated treatment of interactivity in the context of electronic media, see Hoffman and Novak 1996.) In the case of IHS, the parties are the buyer and seller. The two dimensions of interactivity are response time and response contingency. Because IHS involves electronic communication, the response can be immediate—similar to the response time in face-to-face communications. Response contingency is the degree to which the response by one party is a function of the response made by the other party. We use the term *home* merely to indicate that the customer can engage in this interaction in a location other than a store. Figure 3-1 illustrates a somewhat futuristic form of IHS.

The scenario portrayed in Figure 3-1 is highly interactive. Judy, the consumer, using an electronic

Judy Jamison sits in front of her home electronic center reviewing her engagement calendar displayed on her television screen. She sees that she has accepted an invitation to a formal cocktail party on Friday night and she decides to buy a new dress for the occasion. She switches to her personal electronic shopper, BOB, and initiates the following exchange:

BOB: Do you wish to browse, go to a specific store, or buy a specific item?

JUDY: Specific item

BOB: Type of item?

JUDY: Black dress

BOB: Occasion? (menu appears on screen)

JUDY: Formal cocktail party

BOB: Price range? (menu appears)

JUDY: $300–$500

BOB: 497 items have been identified. How many do you want to review?

JUDY: Just 5

[Five pictures of Judy in each dress appear on the screen with the price, brand name, and the IHS retailer selling it listed beneath each one. Judy clicks on one of the dresses and it is enlarged on the screen. Another click and Judy views the dress from different angles. Another click and specifications such as fabric and laundering instructions appear. Judy repeats this routine with each dress, She selects the one she finds most appealing. BOB knows her measurements and picks the size that fits her best.]

BOB: How would you like to pay for this? (menu appears)

JUDY: American Express

BOB: Nieman Marcus [the firm selling the dress Judy selected] suggests a Xie scarf and Koslow belt to complement this dress.

[Judy clicks on the items and they appear on the screen. Judy inspects these items as she inspected the dresses. She decides to purchase both accessories. BOB then asks Judy about delivery. Judy selects two-day delivery at a cost of $5.00.]

BOB: Just a reminder. You have not purchased hosiery in 30 days. Do you wish to reorder at this time?

JUDY: Yes

BOB: Same shades?

JUDY: Yes

Figure 3-1   Illustration of IHS

shopper, BOB, can specify the type of merchandise sought and then screen the located alternatives to develop a smaller set of options that she can view in detail. The interaction requires the parties to query each other's databases. In contrast, this level of interactivity and selection is not available from current Internet retail sites, which function as an unwieldy collection of electronic catalogs (Rigdon 1996). Consumers cannot search quickly and easily for specific items of merchandise, nor can they screen and compare merchandise on the basis of their idiosyncratic desires. Individual retailers provide road maps to facilitate search within their sites but avoid formats that would satisfy consumers' comprehensive needs. However, capabilities such as those described in Figure 3-1—along with the design and production of customized clothing—soon could become available to consumers (Cortese 1996; Hill 1995; Maes 1995; Negroponte 1995).

The scenario illustrates the following critical attributes affecting the adoption of IHS:

- faithful reproduction of descriptive and experiential product information,
- a greatly expanded universe of offerings relative to what can be accessed now through local or catalog shopping,
- an efficient means of screening the offerings to find the most appealing options for more detailed consideration,
- unimpeded search across stores and brands, and
- memory for past selections, which simplifies information search and purchase decisions.

Our scenario implies that the consumer owns the intelligent search agent BOB, which might be a software package bought by Judy and parameterized to fit her needs on the basis of data she provides. However, other search engines also might be owned and controlled by the retailer (e.g., http://www.landsend.com) or an independent third party, as in Continuum Software's "Fido the Shopping Doggie" (http://www.shopfido.com) or Anderson Consulting's Bargain-Finder (http://bf.cstar. ac.com/bf). The consumer might enter a site to be interrogated by the retailer's search engine. Finally, the search engine might be operated by a third-party expert in a product category, as in *Business Week*'s Maven agent for finding personal computers (http://www.maven.businessweek.com). The consumer might pay a service charge to use the site, or retailers might pay to have their information available at the site.

We assume that all of these types of search agents will exist but will have different mixes of information desired by the other parties. However, consumers must have access to vendors' databases if the scenario portrayed in Figure 3-1 is to become reality. In the current transitional period, product search often is dictated by the vendor. Moreover, global search across vendors can be thwarted by actions taken by individual vendors. In the end, technological and market forces will determine the extent to which consumers can gain access to the

information they desire. In the latter half of this article we consider vendors' incentives to inhibit information exchange and their likelihood of success. First, however, we consider the critical attributes affecting consumers' incentives to adopt IHS.

THE DEMAND SIDE: CONSUMERS AND IHS

Consumer Trade-offs

Similar to any innovation, IHS will need to match or exceed the utility provided by traditional formats to succeed. In Table 3.1 we compare six retail formats in terms of benefits and costs to the consumer. The three in-store formats are a prototypical convenience-goods store (supermarket), a specialty-goods store (department store), and a shopping-goods store (category specialist) (cf. Copeland 1923); the nonstore formats are the traditional catalog, the present Internet offering and the IHS format described in Figure 3-1. Although the scenario in Figure 3-1 is intriguing, department and specialty stores afford buyers the opportunity to touch and feel merchandise and obtain information from sales associates. "Category killers" such as Best Buy and Office Depot offer comparisons across a wide array of alternatives in a specific merchandise category. Also, all in-store formats allow immediate delivery.

It is important to clarify our orientation and assumptions before discussing the relative merits of these retail formats in detail. First, our analysis assumes that technology has developed to the point in which a highly evolved IHS system is readily available to a significant number of households. Therefore, as characterized in Table 3.1, IHS enables consumers to access merchandise unavailable in their local markets, gather veridical information about merchandise at a low cost, efficiently screen the offerings of a broad cross-section of suppliers by avoiding unwanted alternatives and unimportant features, and easily locate the lowest prices at which a specific item is offered. As we discuss in

					Current	
Dimension	**Supermarket**	**Department Store**	**Category Specialist**	**Catalog**	**Internet Retailer**	**IHS Format**
Providing Alternatives for Consideration						
Number of categories	Medium	Medium	Low	Low	Low	Low or High
Alternatives per category	Medium	Low	Medium	Medium	Low	High
Screening Alternatives to Form Consideration Set						
Selecting consideration set	Medium	High	Medium	Low	Low	High
Providing Information for Selecting from Consideration Set						
Quantity	Medium	Medium	Medium	Medium	Medium	High
Quality	High	High	High	Medium	Low	Low or High
Comparing alternatives	Medium	Medium	High	Low	Low	Depends on Supplier
Ordering and Fulfillment: Transaction Costs						
Delivery time	Immediate	Immediate	Immediate	Days	Days	Days
Supplier delivery cost	Low	Low	Low	High	High	High
Customer transaction cost	High	High	High	Low	High	Low
Supplier facility costs	High	High	High	Low	Low	Low
Locations for placing orders	Few	Few	Few	Everywhere	Many	Many
Other Benefits						
Entertainment	Low	High	Medium	Low	Low	Medium
Social interaction	Medium	High	Medium	Low	Low	Low
Personal security	Low	Low	Low	High	High	High

TABLE 3.1   Dimensions Affecting Relative Attractiveness to Consumers of Alternative Retail Formats

the following sections, IHS retailers currently enjoy considerable latitude in designing their offerings to exploit or subvert such activities.

Second, the values used to describe a format are illustrative. It is not our intention to argue the specifics, which can vary across retailers within a given format (e.g., across those selling products that can rather than cannot be digitized, those emphasizing depth rather than breadth of selection). Our assessment of performance of the six retail formats is based on the well-developed retail industry structure in the urban and suburban United States. In less developed retail environments, non-

store formats could be much more attractive (Quelch and Klein 1996).

Table 3.1 illustrates three main points:

- For a given product category a comparison of traditional retail formats (e.g., department stores, category specialists, catalogs selling clothing or consumer electronics) makes apparent the basis for competition. The benefits provided by different formats influence the types of merchandise that can be sold successfully; product, situation, and consumer characteristics affect the relative weights of these benefits when consumers select a format (Day, Shocker, and Srivastava 1979; Dickson 1982). For example, most apparel is sold in department and specialty stores because these outlets offer the service and accessories sought by customers buying clothing. In contrast, apparel sales make up a smaller percentage of total sales at discounters. Catalog apparel sales skew toward unfitted clothing items. Catalogs are especially attractive for occasions where the purchaser cannot achieve a superior fit by visiting a store (as when buying a gift for a relative in a distant city).

- Catalogs dominate current Internet retailers. It is therefore unsurprising that there are so few examples to date of businesses making significant revenues by selling merchandise on the Internet.
- The IHS format differs from current Internet retailers primarily by providing more alternatives for consideration, the ability to screen alternatives to form consideration sets, and information to facilitate selection from the consideration set.

We expect changes in the benefits relating to consumer information acquisition to drive any change from the current, nearly nonexistent penetration of Internet retailing to the more optimistic sales projections for IHS. Consequently, we focus our analysis on the dimensions in the first three sections of Table 3.1, which bear on the cost of information search, rather than on those in the bottom half of the table.

Retailers and retail formats compete in the types of information they convey effectively to customers. Just as in Erlich and Fisher's (1982) analysis of "derived demand for advertising," we analyze "derived demand for retailer information about products." Erlich and Fisher note that information reduces the wedge between the market price received by the seller and the "full price" paid by the buyer. The wedge between market price and full price includes the costs of obtaining information about products and of dissatisfaction

from disappointing purchases. Consumers demand information that reduces this wedge. Such information alternatively can be derived from their own prior knowledge, advertising, or "other selling efforts"—notably information from retailers.

Although we focus on retail competition through information, we recognize that retail formats differ on many factors, such as entertainment and personal safety, that contribute to the utility consumers obtain from the "total shopping experience" (cf. Tauber 1972) and that transaction costs related to ordering and fulfillment are an important basis for competitive advantage. For example, Verity and Hof (1994) suggest that it could be 25% less costly to engage in direct marketing with electronic channels. Although consultants and the popular press widely draw similar conclusions, we regard this as an open question. On the one hand, the IHS retailer is not burdened with the cost of locally convenient stores. On the other hand, the IHS retailer faces the cost of delivering merchandise in small quantities to individual consumers. It is premature to assess the relative efficiencies. Using catalogs and electronic grocery shopping (e.g., Peapod [Donegan 1996]) as guides, however, it is not clear that consumers will enjoy large monetary cost savings by using IHS.

However, here, we focus on the informational effects of electronic commerce as they pertain to retailer-consumer interaction. Excellent discussions of enhanced consumer-to-consumer interaction and the implications for marketing are available elsewhere (Armstrong and Hagel 1996; Hoffman and Novak 1996).

Providing Alternatives for Consideration

A significant benefit of IHS compared with other retail formats is the vast number of alternatives that become available to consumers. Through IHS, a person living in Florida can shop at Harrod's in London in less time than it takes to visit the local Burdines department store.

Economic search theory implies that if there are N alternative brands or sellers available in a market, and the consumer considers only a subset $n < N$, the utility of the chosen (best) alternative from the subset increases with n (Hauser and Wernerfelt 1990; Ratchford 1980; Stigler 1961). However, in terms of the benefits of search, there are strong diminishing returns. As additional alternatives are examined, the potential increase in benefits offered by the next alternative is small. Inasmuch as the cost of searching for and evaluating new alternatives continues to increase, a point is reached at which the expected cost of considering additional alternatives is greater than the potential increase in benefits. At this point, the consumer terminates search for additional alternatives. Research also indicates that consumers reach this point quickly: Consumers rarely visit more than one or two outlets when they are buying expensive consumer durables (e.g., Newman and Staelin 1972; Wilkie and Dickson 1985).

Because IHS search costs are low and decline with experience using the interface, simply providing consumers an opportunity to consider a thousand alternatives versus ten alternatives could be enough to switch some of them from in-store shopping to IHS. However, other consumers could find it too tedious and stressful to look through information on hundreds of products identified for consideration, unless there is reason to expect that the added alternatives are systematically different from the first ones considered, with a different distribution of utilities. Consequently, the mere capability of IHS to increase the universe of potential options is not a major reason for its adoption.

Screening Alternatives to Form Consideration Sets

The attractiveness of the opportunity to inspect an expanded number of alternatives is dependent in part on the consumer's ability to sort efficiently through a potentially daunting amount of information. A particular advantage of IHS over alternative formats is that consumers can screen information so that they can focus on alternatives that match their preferences.

In most product categories, consumers have prior beliefs and preferences about alternatives (Hauser and Wernerfelt 1990; Ratchford 1982; Roberts and Lattin 1991; Simonson, Huber, and Payne 1988). Consumers use this information to make purchase decisions more efficiently by forming a small consideration set and then evaluating alternatives within this subset in more detail. The savings in search costs involved in using this two-step process often overwhelms the potential opportunity cost of overlooking the "best" alternative that would have been uncovered by carefully inspecting the entire universe of alternatives.

Interactive home shopping enables the formation of consideration sets that include only those few alternatives best suited to a consumer's personal tastes. This screening can be done almost instantaneously using electronic agents that use information about an individual consumer's specific preferences and the alternatives available (Maes 1994). In Figure 3-1, for example, BOB located 497 "suitable" black dresses from a potentially much larger universe and rank-ordered these dresses on the basis of criteria (black/formal/ $300–$500) supplied by Judy. An additional screening phase that is based on criteria derived from prior interactions and stored in the agent's memory (such as the style she prefers and her trade-offs between price and quality) might reduce the set dramatically. The remaining alternatives then could be searched in more detail to choose the "best" of this reduced set. If the screening criteria are highly correlated with Judy's full utility function, Judy can be reasonably confident that the alternative chosen after screening has utility close to that associated with the choice she would have made if she had inspected all 497 alternatives exhaustively (Feinberg and Huber 1996).

Others have noted that consumers often rely on memory for the generation of alternatives for consideration (Alba and Chattopadhyay 1985; Hutchinson, Raman, and Mantrala 1994; Kardes et al. 1993; Nedungadi 1990). In such cases, memory plays a screening function that is often only imperfectly correlated with the consumer's utilities. An efficient and dispassionate search agent should produce appropriate brands that otherwise would not have been considered, implicitly replacing memory with explicit product criteria for screening the universe of available options to a manageable consideration set.

Note that both BOB and retail store buyers have access to the same universe of merchandise and screen that universe to offer a subset intended to appeal to end consumers. However, the assortments offered by store-based retailers are developed for market segments with significant within-segment heterogeneity. Store customers are required to expend resources to form smaller consideration sets tailored to their needs. Consumers could find that the set provided by the retailer is insufficient and opt to visit another store.

Interactive home shopping has the potential to tailor consideration sets from a much broader set of alternatives for specific individual consumers. The usefulness of these customized approaches will depend on the consumer effort necessary to calibrate the screening mechanism and the accuracy with which the mechanism correlates with the consumer's full utility function for meaningful alternatives. The lower bound on effort to calibrate screening criteria comes from the use of past purchase history—as in the Peapod grocery shopping service, which keeps lists of regularly purchased items for automatic rebuy. At the other extreme, the screening criteria in many current Internet retailing sites are cumbersome in requiring the consumer to enter many responses to calibrate the function (e.g., *Money Magazine*'s Best Places to Live site on Pathfinder.com, Firefly a http://www.agents-inc.com for music and films).

Some search agents require less data input from the consumer but at a cost of including only a few criteria that collectively explain a relatively small percentage of variance in a consumer's overall preferences. A good example is the use of a standard Internet search engine like Alta Vista to shop for Advanced Photo System cameras. Others strike a better balance in asking for a compact set of preferences highly related to a person's tastes

but only allow search of a limited set of alternatives (e.g., Dell's computer site http://dell.com for computers, RackesDirect women's clothing site at http://www.rackes.com/rackes.html, Fido the Shopping Doggie service for shopping in a broad cross-section of categories). Therefore, screening criteria can be established in different ways. In the BOB example, Judy explicitly stated her criteria when initiating the search. In the Internet sites mentioned previously, screening criteria are limited to a small set specified by the retailer.

Providing Information to Evaluate Alternatives in the Consideration Set

One of the primary benefits offered by traditional retailers is information that enables consumers to predict how satisfied they would be if they purchased various offerings. The degree to which this information is useful to consumers depends on the nature of the information provided and its reliability. Consumers should seek out formats that enable them to make selections that maximize consumption utility net of price and search costs (Ehrlich and Fisher 1982), even if competing retail formats offer identical merchandise (Hauser, Urban, and Weinberg 1993).

Quantity of Information

Retail formats differ in the sheer amount of information provided about the merchandise they offer. For example, Lands' End not only provides faithful visual information but often gives great detail about the construction process, stitching, and materials. Other catalogs provide only a few specifications per item, such as price, weight, and brand or model. More information could increase ability to predict consumption utility but add to processing costs.

Store-based retailers also differ in the information they make available to consumers. Specialty and department stores often provide trained and knowledgeable sales associates, whereas discounters do not. Consequently, the effective "database" of attributes available to consumers is much greater at specialty and department stores than it is at discounters and catalogers. Store-based retailers have an additional characteristic that radically increases the usefulness of the information available to consumers, that is, interactivity. Interaction between a customer and sales associate enables store-based retailers to provide information about the attributes that matter to the customer. Such selectivity gives consumers all the advantages of a large database without the large information processing costs. Perhaps for this reason, post-purchase reports from buyers of major durables indicate that the salesperson was the most useful information source consulted, outstripping *Consumer Reports,* advertising, and friends (Wilkie and Dickson 1985).

Conversely, catalogers, discounters, and present Internet retailers are forced to make decisions about which attributes to promote on the basis of what is most desired by the market as a whole or by relatively crude segments of the market. However, consumers differ in their needs and therefore if the information that will be of interest to them. Consequently, the information provided by catalogers and discounters will be less valuable because it is not tailored to idiosyncratic desires.

Interactive home shopping should prove superior even to specialty and department store retailers in terms of the sheer quantity of attribute information it can provide about each stock-keeping unit. As a result of the interactivity of IHS, retailers need not fear that the provision of information about an attribute that matters only to a few will impose search costs on the majority. In this respect, IHS resembles department and specialty stores. However, because attribute information is available consistently from a central database, IHS effectively becomes a "supersales associate" (i.e., one that never gets sick, is not moody, learns quickly, and never forgets). In contrast, store-based retailers have a difficult time retaining knowledgeable sales associates, and in many cases it is not cost-effective for

them to do so. It should cost far less to add information to an IHS database than to attempt to disseminate the same information to sales associates through conventional training.

Quality of Attribute Information

Information economists often distinguish among search, experience, and credence goods (Darby and Karni 1973), typically in terms of consumers' ability to know quality before and after buying. In economic parlance, search goods are those whose quality and value to the consumer can be assessed easily prior to purchase. The quality of experience goods is difficult to assess prior to purchase and usage; however, because quality can be assessed accurately after one use, the consumer knows quality when an opportunity arises to repurchase the same brand. For credence goods, quality cannot be known even after repeated purchase and use.

A tempting conclusion that is based on this trichotomy is that merchandise now selected in store environments primarily on the basis of search and credence attributes is most amenable to electronic retailing (because direct experience is not required), whereas merchandise purchased on the basis of experience attributes will be purchased in stores. By similar reasoning, IHS and catalogs should be more successful with merchandise dominated by visual attributes and should fare less well when touch, taste, and smell are important for evaluating quality. The latter senses require direct experience consuming or sampling the product (Anderson 1995).

However, these conclusions fail to consider the key issue regarding the quality of information. The quality or usefulness of information is determined by the degree to which consumers (or their agents) can use the information obtained prior to purchase to predict their satisfaction from subsequent consumption, which in turn depends intimately on consumers' inference rules (Alba and Hutchinson 1987; Broniarczyk and Alba 1994) and consumers' confidence in the reliability of these rules (Wright and Lynch 1995). In the analysis that follows, we adopt Wright and Lynch's (1995) reinterpretation of the search/experience/credence distinction in terms of consumer inferences. Specifically, for experience and credence (but not search) goods, there is at first a low subjective correlation between product attributes observable prior to purchase and benefits at the time of consumption. For experience goods, brand names enable highly reliable inferences about consumption benefits after one purchase and use. This is not true for credence goods, presumably because feedback from the first use takes a long time to materialize and is not predictive of consumption utility if the same brand were to be repurchased.

In addition, though information economists initially spoke of search, experience, and credence "goods," it is now clear that all goods have some combination of search, experience, and credence attributes. A search good is simply one for which the consumption benefits most important to consumers are predicted reliably by attribute information available to them before buying. This reasoning implies that the same product can be a search, experience, or credence good, depending on the benefits that are important to consumers and the inferences consumers make about how well those benefits are predicted by information available prior to purchase.

These observations have important implications in the present context because retail formats differ greatly in their capability to provide information about attributes linked to consumption benefits. Consequently, attributes that are search attributes in one format might be experience attributes in another—and this dictates patterns of competition among retailers over time. For example, if the key attributes of ice cream relate to experienced flavor, Ben & Jerry's Cherry Garcia might be a search good at a Ben & Jerry's store, which allows a consumer to taste the ice cream prior to purchase. It would be an experience good at first if a person were buying at a supermarket that sells ice cream only in cartons and does not

allow tasting prior to purchase. Consequently, the Ben & Jerry's store initially would have an informational advantage over the supermarket. However, when the consumer learns that Cherry Garcia on the carton label reliably predicts experienced flavor, the supermarket no longer would be at a disadvantage. Similar dynamics explain why mail order computer giants Dell and Gateway have a customer mix dominated by experienced users (Templin 1996).

Similar principles govern the relative advantage or disadvantage of store-based retailers relative to nonstore retailers that sell through catalogs or IHS. For example, critical information in the purchase of apparel might include search attributes such as color and style—which ostensibly can be assessed accurately in a department store or catalog—as well as experiential attributes such as fit, which can be searched readily before purchase only in the department store. However, when buying the item through nonstore outlets, the ability to assess color depends on consumers' inferences about the faithfulness of photographic reproduction and piece-to-piece variation in dyeing. Also, fit might seem unpredictable unless the nonstore retailer has consistent sizing and the consumer has learned over time to infer what fit is implied by a particular brand and size.

These examples illustrate three important points. First, consumers make inferences about product attractiveness on the basis of information provided by retailers, and retail formats compete on the information they provide as cues for these inferences; second, different consumers possess different rules, and this affects the extent to which the information provided by any particular format leads to competitive advantage; and, third, the cues that are deemed to provide a reliable basis for inference are likely to change with experience with the brand. The following issues further emphasize the need to consider predictability of satisfaction rather than a simple classification of suitability of "goods" to IHS that is based on the traditional search/experience/credence distinction:

1. *The (in)adequacy of searchable experiential information.* In certain purchase situations, information for some products with important experiential attributes cannot be gathered prior to consumption. In such cases, in-store shopping offers little advantage over IHS. For example, flowers and wine are consummate sensory products. However, consumers who send flower arrangements via FTD must base their decisions on pictures in the florist's shop, and purchasers of wine frequently must rely on labels or advice from a retail sales associate. Therefore, some products possessing important experience attributes could be no less amenable to IHS than to traditional shopping. In yet other cases, experiential attribute information could be conveyed *more* effectively electronically than in-store. For example electronic bookseller Amazon (http://www.amazon.com) has space for customers to post their own reviews of books, with positive word of mouth clearly influencing sales.

2. *Consistency and predictability.* The ability to predict satisfaction from observable attributes is not inherent in the specific consumption benefits driving satisfaction, nor is it inherent in the retail format. Actions by retailers and manufacturers can increase consumers' ability to predict post-purchase satisfaction from attributes observable before purchase. Consider the case of running shoes purchased by a consumer who cares about comfort and protection from injury. We might expect that these features could be assessed better when buying from a store, such as Athletic Attic, than from a cataloger. Road Runner Sports, however, provides information for each shoe in its catalog, making it easy to assess suitability for underpronators and overpronators, and customers can submit their old shoes for a custom analysis and suggestions for suitable replacements. Manufacturers' actions also influence the customer's ability to predict consumption

satisfaction from pre-purchase information. If manufacturers become more consistent in the characteristics they build into differing models in their product lines, consumers' ability to predict satisfaction will rise accordingly. Comfort and sizing are important attributes of running shoes that require direct experience with the product. However, when a particular brand is consistent in the height of its arch support and the roominess of its toe box, the predictability of comfort and size is enhanced. In essence, brand name converts experience attributes to search attributes that can be effectively communicated verbally or visually (see Agins 1994).

3. *Other determinants of satisfaction.* Satisfaction is determined by more than the consumption experience with the product: it also is affected by the belief that one has exhaustively searched the set of acceptable alternatives such that there is no regret regarding a missed opportunity (Gilovich and Medvec 1995). Interactive home shopping provides the potential for a more extensive search than that which consumers could accomplish in a store.

These considerations imply that consumer adoption depends on more than the (retail format-independent) importance of search, experience, and credence attributes to the consumer.

Comparison of Alternatives

Retail formats differ in the extent to which they facilitate the comparison of alternatives in the consideration set. For example, most in-store retailers stock alternative colors, styles, and brands in each product category. An appealing characteristic of category specialists such as Circuit City and Office Depot is the breadth of selection and customers' ability to make side-by-side comparisons of brands. Similarly, consumers shopping for apparel can compare the fit of different alternatives. Current Internet retailers do not offer this opportunity. In addition current IHS retailers are selective in the information presented, whereas in-store retailers allow the consumer to control the basis for comparison of alternatives.

Research shows that consumers acquire and process information in ways made easiest by the constraints of the information format (Bettman and Kakkar 1977). However, consumers prefer formats that promote maximum flexibility to engage in either attribute- or alternative-based processing (Bettman and Zins 1979). This preference for flexibility to engage in attribute-based processing should be stronger for novices in a product class than for experts (Bettman and Park 1980); experts know what levels of an attribute are attractive without having to rely on relative information to make that assessment (Mitchell and Dacin 1996).

It is argued that effort looms large when decision makers consider the effort-accuracy trade-off required in any given decision task—so much so that decision makers could focus more on effort reduction than on accuracy maximization (for a discussion, see Todd and Benbasat 1994). In this context, the advantages of IHS are apparent. The initial (and effortful) decision phase involving attribute-based, side-by-side comparisons will be compressed if an efficient screening mechanism is available. This should inspire consumers to learn and use more information in the course of decision making (cf. Kardes and Kalyanaraman 1992; Russo 1977). In addition, the transformation of the decision from a memory-based to a stimulus-based choice should enhance the precision of the decision process and therefore the optimality of the ultimate decision (see Alba, Marmorstein, and Chattapadhyay 1992; Biehal and Chakravarti 1983; Lynch, Marmorstein, and Weigold 1988).

The combination of IHS search, screen, and comparison features also should prompt consumers to make their decisions more rapidly (cf. Greenleaf and Lehmann 1995). Research shows that the addition of attractive alternatives to a choice set could prompt consumers to delay their choice (Tversky and Shafir 1992), perhaps because of the perceived possibility that even more attractive options have yet to be inspected (Karni and Schwarz 1977). Insofar as search and comparison minimize the possibility of regret over choosing a suboptimal product, both decision speed and satisfaction with the decision process should increase.

A caveat is appropriate at this point. Most aspects of an efficient search engine point to improved decision quality. However, it has been noted recently that though some decision aids could improve decision making, abuse is possible (Todd and Benbasat 1994). In particular, Widing and Talarzvk (1993) show that the decision aid most likely to be a part of an electronic search agent (i.e., a cutoff rule that enables formation of a consideration set containing only those alternatives that pass consumer-specified attribute cutoffs) can lead to suboptimal decisions in efficient choice sets. In addition, a separate stream of research shows that a second likely characteristic of IHS—visually rich presentation—can distort the decision process by diverting attention to peripheral cues and away from information that is most important for the task at hand (Jarvenpaa 1989, 1990; cf. Edell and Staelin 1983).

Summary of Key Consumer Factors Affecting Use of the IHS Format

Many factors will influence a consumer's decision to shop electronically versus in-store. We focus on the benefits pertaining to the consumer's information acquisition and processing that enable consumers to locate and select merchandise that satisfies their needs, because the fundamental benefit of IHS is to lower the cost of information search (Bakos 1991). In summary, then, the growth of IHS is dependent on the following factors:

- *Vast selection:* If the format does not allow for quick and comprehensive inspection of an expanded set of options, electronic commerce will mimic the shopping experience now available through catalogs and achieve a relatively low level of penetration.

- *Screening:* If consumers cannot screen the large number of options made available, the advantages of vast selection will be outweighed by the costs of search.
- *Reliability:* If consumption benefits are predicted more reliably from experiential information searchable in stores than from surrogate information searchable through IHS and consumers are unwilling to bear the risk, in-store shopping will continue to prosper.
- *Product comparisons:* To be successful, IHS must allow the consumers to tailor the basis for comparison of alternatives in order to make the system compatible with the process by which consumers prefer to make decisions. Interactive home shopping has the potential to provide superior information presentation formats for making these comparisons.

Without these benefits, IHS will not develop beyond the relatively unattractive collection of electronic catalogs representing the present Internet offering. In the next section we review the incentives and disincentives for retailers and manufacturers to stimulate the development of the IHS channel and provide the appropriate information to attract consumers.

THE SUPPLY SIDE: RETAILERS, MANUFACTURERS, AND IHS

For many retailers the most significant threat posed by IHS is that profits will be eroded drastically by intensified price competition that will ensue as consumers' search costs are lowered. Consequently many retailers are making limited, experimental investments in electronic commerce that, ironically have none of the characteristics we describe previously as necessary for IHS to be preferred to existing formats. Many firms participate through stand-alone sites (such as World Wide Web home pages) that increase the costs of conducting cross-store companions. When third-party electronic search agents such as Bargain Finder (http://bf.cstar.ac.com/bf/) are created to compare prices charged by different vendors for the same compact disc, some retailers deny access. When participating in interactive malls, some firms require exclusivity agreements that protect them from the kinds of cross-store comparisons that would make IHS truly useful to the consumer.

It is reasonable to assume that firms that have made substantial commitments to an existing business format or technology will adopt defensive responses to radical change (Leonard-Barton 1995). In the case of IHS and other radical changes, we argue that these defensive approaches are likely to fail in the long run, because the ultimate nature of the IHS channel and its appeal to consumers is beyond the control of individual firms. Firms might attempt to build walls around their offerings that make comparison across retailers and manufacturers difficult. However, consumers will prefer retailers that freely provide such information and make cross shopping easy; therefore, isolationist vendors could be bypassed in the search process. Eventually, intelligent agents will allow consumers to search across vendors to find offerings that possess the set of attributes desired. Attempts to limit information will be met with new formats that disseminate information (Bakos 1991). Therefore, an electronic version of *Consumer Reports* could emerge that makes recommendations and informs consumers of where to find the best deal.

In the remaining portion of this article, we discuss that nature of competition in an IHS environment, approaches that firms can take to build competitive advantage in this environment, and some important issues confronting IHS retailers and manufacturers.

The Role of Price and Quality

To complete a sale, a vendor must be considered by a consumer and the consumer must fail to consider a superior alternative (Nedungadi 1990). Retailers believe that an IHS presence can increase the probability of being considered, but conditional on the achievement of that goal, IHS can have only a negative effect on profits by intensifying price competition with other IHS alternatives. Inasmuch as established retailers have less to gain in terms of increasing consideration probability, it is perhaps unsurprising that few of the most aggressive entrants into IHS have a large store-based presence. But the conclusion that IHS must lower profits through higher price competition does not necessarily follow. Generally speaking, information that is easy to obtain or that can discriminate unambiguously among options tends to receive higher weight in the consumer's decision process. Price information possesses both properties, which suggests that the concerns of retail firms are well founded. However, just as in the debate on economic effects of advertising (Mitra and Lynch 1996; Rosen 1978), IHS also can reduce the cost and increase the discriminating power of information regarding merchandise quality.

A strong parallel can be drawn between the introduction of IHS into the present retail environment and the development of discount stores 40 years ago (Sheffet and Scammon 1985). Discount stores offered consumers an opportunity to forgo personalized service in return for lower prices. The result was an increase in price competition followed by attempts to avoid such competition through fair trade laws. Proponents of fair trade laws argued that, without some protection for department and specialty stores, discounters would drive them out of business; this, it was argued, would leave a shopping environment in which price could be discerned easily but nuances of quality could not. Consequently consumers would become more price sensitive, sellers would adjust over time to compete more on price and less on quality, and consumers would suffer through the lack of interest in providing superior merchandise and service quality. Although the advent of discount stores did increase price competition in some merchandise categories, many consumers shop at retailers, such as Nordstrom, that provide

superior information and services even though they charge a higher price. Such inherent consumer heterogeneity suggests that no one retail format can dominate all segments.

The potential impact of IHS on the nature of competition in the retail industry should be considered in this context. Although consumers shopping through an IHS channel will be able to collect price information with little effort, they also will be able to review at a low cost quality-related information about most search attributes and some experience attributes. For example, an electronic merchant of custom oriental rugs can convey clearly real differences in patterns and materials used for construction. An electronic grocery service such as Peapod can enable customers to sort cereals by nutritional content, thus making it easier to use that attribute in decision making. Insofar as (1) quality-related information is important to consumers and (2) brands within a category are differentiated, IHS can lead to less price sensitivity at the brand level and more sensitivity to search attributes associated with quality than does traditional shopping (cf. Mitra and Lynch 1995).

This is a critical point for manufacturers that offer differentiated merchandise with superior performance attributes. Similarly, retailers that carry unique merchandise and/or provide superior information about merchandise could face less rather than more price competition. Perhaps this is why vendors cooperating with multiple-category search agents such as Fido the Shopping Doggie (http://www.shopfido.com/Vendors.html) are predominantly manufacturers and retailers selling highly unique merchandise such as arts and crafts, alternative music, hot sauces and spices, and gourmet foods and wines. Conversely, manufacturers of "me-too" brands competing on cost can expect more intense price competition with the diffusion of IHS, and retailers carrying nationally branded merchandise with limited service also will face increased price competition.

Therefore, the introduction of the IHS channel will intensify the competitive environment, but this need not shift the emphasis from quality to price. By providing more information to consumers with minimal search cost, manufacturers and retailers with differentiated offerings will have a greater opportunity to educate consumers about the unique benefits they offer, and consumers will find it easier to access and compare the offerings of firms competing on price.

Developing Competitive Advantage in IHS

"Location, location, location" is the classic response to the question about the three most important factors in retailing. The development of IHS certainly reduces the importance of location. The IHS retailer will need to adopt strategy that seeks competitive advantage in one or more of the following areas: (1) distribution efficiency, (2) assortments of complementary merchandise, (3) collection and utilization of customer information, (4) presentation of information through electronic formats, and (5) unique merchandise.

Distribution Efficiency

Consumers perform a major portion of the distribution function when purchasing from stores. They transport merchandise from stores to their homes and bring unsatisfactory merchandise back to the store. In an IHS system, these substantial costs of home delivery and returns will be fully borne by the seller and must be factored into the price. Because these costs are substantial, IHS players that can select and package multiple items for delivery to individual households will have a competitive advantage over IHS competitors that lack such skills. The importance of this advantage naturally is greater when the preparation for shipping constitutes a large fraction of the overall price of the product.

Assortments of Complementary Merchandise

The opportunity to make multiple-item sales is important for two reasons. First, by making multiple-

item purchases from an IHS supplier, customers reduce the shipping costs, which thereby reduces the net price. Second, the IHS retailer is in an ideal position to tailor a secondary offering to a customer on the basis of the customer's primary purchase objective. We might suggest that electronic agents will put together complementary bundles of products from multiple suppliers. However, to accomplish this task, the agents would need to possess an extremely broad knowledge base, such as information on what ties and shirts go together and what ingredients are needed to make a good Brunswick stew. Even without the presence of electronic agents, IHS offers retailers an opportunity to merchandise their wares in ways not previously possible. Traditional merchandising is limited by physical constraints. Floor space and shelf space limit the number of complements that can be placed in close proximity to any given product. However, even the Internet allows nearly unlimited cross-referencing through hypertext. Interactive home shopping faces no such problems, and the efficient IHS merchandiser should realize superior gains in customer retention and cross-selling—goals that are increasingly important regardless of distribution channel (e.g., Reicheld 1993). The opportunity to cross-sell extends well beyond shirts and ties. Diversified vendors that own subunits that are only modestly related to each other in terms of the consumer goal they serve could realize synergies not possible with conventional channels (cf. Benjamin and Wigand, 1995 on "virtual value chains").

Collection and Utilization of Customer Information

Database marketing is an important capability for IHS retailing (cf. Blattberg and Deighton 1991; Peppers and Rodgers 1993. Interactive home shopping will increase the importance and accelerate the development of database marketing because more comprehensive customer-specific data can be captured. All consumers who shop electronically can be identified at the individual level. Moreover unlike other formats, consumer browsing can be tracked. That is, records can be constructed not only of what consumers bought but also what they inspected and for how long.

Interactive home shopping retailers can use these data to provide information-based value to the customer by (1) using technology to identify and display consideration sets most suited to individual consumer tastes and (2) providing information about those options that enables consumers to predict their satisfaction after purchase. Consumers, in turn, are likely to become loyal to an IHS retailer offering this service. This loyalty advantage could be sustainable for two reasons: First, consumers who experience high satisfaction may not defect to competing IHS retailers; and second, as consumers patronize a particular IHS retailer more frequently, more information can be collected. Thus, a cycle is created wherein consumer satisfaction provides the opportunity to learn how to provide greater satisfaction. Consumers would incur switching costs and an initial decrease in customer service if they took their business to a competing IHS retailer. Insofar as information about the consumer is proprietary, sustainability ensues.

Presentation of Information

Traditionally, some stores have sought differentiation on the basis of atmospherics and service. Both still could play a role in IHS, and each will require a new technical skill set, as evidenced by the recent acquisition of software company Davidson and Associates and interactive entertainment company Sierra On-Line by CUC International, a leading direct marketing and interactive retailer.

Unique Merchandise

From the retailer's perspective, the most straightforward method for increasing differentiation and reducing price competition is to sell merchandise that cannot be offered elsewhere. Uniqueness traditionally has been achieved in several ways:

- *Private labels:* IHS retailers can develop their own private label merchandise that they offer exclusively.
- *Branded variants:* Alternatively, retailers can work with manufacturers to provide "branded variants" sold exclusively through that retailer (Bergen, Duna, and Shugan 1996). The intent is to provide incentives for retailers to provide better service when inter-store (but not inter-brand) competition is reduced. (As noted subsequently, however, this method of achieving uniqueness could lose some effectiveness in the context of IHS.)
- *Offering assortments of complements tailored to customer needs:* One way for retailers to make their merchandise "unique" is by creating bundles of complements that are available only separately elsewhere. For example, with each bottle of wine offered by Virtual Vineyards (http://www.virtualvin.com), customers can get complementary recipes from noted Bay-area chefs. Although some of the wines are available elsewhere, Virtual Vineyards allows its customers to anticipate satisfaction when serving the wine with a particular meal. In essence, the wine-recipe bundle rather than the bottle of wine becomes the unit of analysis. Interactive home shopping retailers can use customer information skills noted previously to suggest bundles that lead to multiple sales and increased customer satisfaction—with the side benefit of reducing shipping costs.

IMPLICATIONS FOR FIRMS IN THE RETAIL INDUSTRY

The success of consumer product manufacturers and retailers in the IHS environment will be determined by the degree to which their strengths and weaknesses match the capabilities required to

TABLE 3.2	IHS Success Capabilities Possessed by Firms			
Skills for Developing Advantage	**Catalog Retailers**	**Traditional Stores**	**Category Specialists**	**Merchandise Manufacturers**
Distribution efficiency to homes	High	Medium to High	Medium	Low
Provision of complementary assortments	High	High	Low	Medium
Collection and use of customer information	High	Medium to High	Low	Low
Presentation of merchandise information	High	Medium to High	Low	Medium
Ability to offer unique merchandise	Medium	Medium	Low	High

build competitive advantage (Aaker 1989). In Table 3.2 we provide such a comparison. In this table, we assess each type of firm in terms of the skills previously identified as bases for competitive advantage in the IHS channel. We consider the likely impact of IHS on their businesses and how their businesses are likely to adapt. Afterward, we examine the impact of IHS on manufacturers.

Entry Into IHS by Retailers

Table 3.2 leads to some interesting insights when contrasted with Table 3.1. Table 3.1 suggests that catalog retailers are more vulnerable to IHS than are other retail formats. Interactive home shopping retailers and catalogers share the same limitations in terms of delivery timing and providing information about experience attributes; interactive home shopping dominates catalogs in terms of the information provided. However, Table 3.2 indicates that catalog retailers are best prepared to exploit IHS, inasmuch as they possess order fulfillment systems and database management skills that match the requirements of IHS. As an example, Lands' End (http://www.landsend.com) has a "Specialty Shopper Service" that coordinates outfits for a whole wardrobe, helps the customer find his or her correct size, and keeps a file on sizes, tastes, past purchases, and address and credit card numbers. Also, the skills necessary for effective visual presentation of information in IHS follow closely the visual merchandising skills necessary

for catalogs. Catalogers can reap efficiencies by listing their products electronically rather than in a more expensive print format when penetration of IHS justifies the production of electronic assets by savings of significant paper and postage costs.

However, the ability of currently successful catalogers to adapt to IHS can be expected to vary sharply, depending on the strategy the catalog retailer has used to establish competitive advantage. For example, Spiegel sells primarily branded merchandise, which is susceptible to price comparisons. Catalog retailers that emphasize branded merchandise will be particularly vulnerable compared with a retailer such as Lands' End, which has developed high-quality, private brand merchandise.

Interactive home shopping is ideal for retailers, such as Nieman-Marcus, Harrod's, Gumps, and Saks, that enjoy strong national reputations for high-quality, unique merchandise, but that have only spotty or regional penetration. Such retailers are well positioned to take advantage of the market-expanding feature of IHS by attaining an international presence without making significant investments in store locations, visual merchandising, and leases (Rennie 1993). Most of these stores currently possess an effective mail-order catalog operation. Interactive home shopping also is ideal for niche retailers that appeal to a far-flung customer base (cf. Quelch and Klein 1996; Wernerfelt 1994). For example, Hot Hot Hot (http://www.hothothot.com) is a specialty store that carries more than 450 brands of hot sauce. The Internet gives this firm international exposure without significant advertising and only 300 square feet of store space (Carlton 1996).

Conversely, national chains such as Sears have far less incentive to participate. These chains possess high levels of penetration through their ubiquitous stores. Even among national department store chains, there are clear differences in incentives to enter IHS. Both Sears and JCPenney have saturated the domestic market with stores, but JCPenney is also the largest catalog retailer in the United States. This catalog operation provides the infrastructure for fulfillment and visual merchandising that is well suited to IHS. Sears exited the "Big Book" catalog business largely because its catalog fulfillment operations and technology were antiquated and because the cost of rebuilding these systems was prohibitive. This absence of efficient fulfillment systems for individual orders creates a further disincentive for Sears to engage in IHS.

Adaptatation of In-Store Retailers to IHS

The DEFENDER model (Hauser and Shugan 1983) suggests that in-store retailers should react to emerging IHS retailers by emphasizing attributes of their offering for which they have a comparative advantage. Therefore, store-based retailers should (1) focus on merchandise that has important experiential attributes that are search attributes in a store but experience attributes in IHS, (2) capitalize on their relative advantage in providing information tailored to the needs of specific customers, (3) emphasize the noninformational benefits of shopping, (4) complement IHS with their in-store business, and (5) place more emphasis on unique merchandise.

Because it is more difficult to provide some experience information through IHS, in-store retailers must focus on merchandise that possesses characteristics consumers can assess veridically only through contact with the merchandise. For example, bedding and linens come in standard sizes and are amenable to IHS; consequently, de-

partment stores might need to decrease space allocated to this merchandise and increase floor space devoted to tailored clothing. They also might need to increase resources devoted to personalized service associated with those items (e.g., alterations). Similarly, department stores should shift their merchandise mix to emphasize items for which immediate, low-cost access to the merchandise is important.

To offset the ability of IHS retailers to provide personalized information at home, in-store retailers should improve the personalized information they offer using their sales associates or in-store kiosks. For example, Best Buy uses kiosks extensively to alleviate physical store constraints and provide detailed product information. Media Play uses in-store listening stations to enable acoustic sampling of compact discs prior to purchase. Used-car superstore CarMax provides kiosks that allow flexible screening criteria, side-by-side viewing of screened options, and the printing of car lot location maps for candidate cars—all of which greatly reduce search costs inherent in navigating a huge and heterogeneous on-site inventory.

Because IHS retailers can provide greater informational benefits, in-store retailers must emphasize ancillary benefits such as entertainment and opportunities to socialize. For many consumers, shopping is an experience that transcends product purchase. One method of differentiating a retail outlet is to provide benefits that enhance the experience. Traditionally, this has involved improvements in ambiance. Increasingly, the entertainment value of shopping is being emphasized. Incredible Universe, Niketown, and the Mall of America are possible harbingers of the future. (For a discussion of how IHS retailers might respond to these efforts by in-store retailers and improve the social experience benefits for IHS customers, see Armstrong and Hagel 1996.)

In-store retailers with an IHS presence can use IHS as a source of advertising to presell merchandise and to check its availability in local stores. This would enable the customer to pick it up or have it delivered from the local store.

In-store retailers and IHS retailers will need to reduce their reliance on nationally branded merchandise to lure people into their sites and will need to redouble their efforts to develop private label brands. Therefore, the trend seen in store-based retailers such as JCPenney—which increasingly promotes private-label brands such as Arizona jeans—could accelerate.

Impact on Category Specialists and Discounters

In light of the consumer analysis in Table 3.1, category specialists appear particularly vulnerable to IHS retailing. Aside from the immediacy of delivery, this shopping format offers few informational and noninformational benefits. In addition, these formats emphasize branded merchandise for which price competition will increase with the advent of IHS. However, the nature of these outlets varies greatly in terms of their operation, merchandise, and relationships with suppliers.

Toys 'R' Us enjoys national (and increasingly international) penetration. If Toys 'R' Us were to sell electronically, it might experience significant cannibalization of its in-store sales, making IHS less attractive to it than to an entrepreneur entering the toy business through IHS or even to an F.A.O. Schwartz, which is smaller and more specialized.

Circuit City appears to be as vulnerable as Toys 'R' Us is to competition from IHS retailers. However, the structure of the consumer electronics industry is considerably different from the toy industry. The consumer electronics industry is dominated by a few suppliers that make most of their profits from sophisticated, high-technology products. The benefits of these products can be credibly demonstrated only in a store environment. To motivate electronics retailers to provide this information to consumers, manufacturers employ several mechanisms designed to protect specialty retailers from price competition from mass merchandisers that sell only the low-end and mid-range models that dominate the market. (For example, co-op ad-

vertising offers to mass merchandisers can be made contingent on pricing cooperation.) Moreover, distribution of high-end products to IHS retailers would encourage free riding and reduce in-store retailers' incentive to provide product-differentiating information.

Home Depot is similar to Toys 'R' Us in terms of distribution intensity but is less vulnerable because many of its goods demand immediacy, highly tailored advice from expert associates, or direct (non-video) inspection of size, specifications, or colors. Home Depot also offers a level of hand-holding from expert sales associates that cannot be duplicated electronically. Moreover, bulky do-it-yourself merchandise can be expensive to ship directly to homes.

Implications for Manufacturers and Retailers

Disintermediation

The most important structural change that could be brought about by IHS is disintermediation, wherein manufacturers bypass the retailer and sell directly to consumers. Although the IHS channel does offer manufacturers an opportunity to deal directly with consumers (cf. Benjamin and Wigand 1995; Pine, Peppers, and Rovers 1995), Table 3.2 illustrates the limited capabilities of most manufacturers to succeed as IHS retailers—which suggests that the degree of disintermediation will not be significant.

Manufacturers cannot easily and efficiently duplicate a variety of services that retailers perform for both manufacturers and consumers (see Sarkar, Butler, and Steinfield 1996). The classic functions undertaken by retailers and other firms in a distribution channel include breaking bulk (converting caseload shipments into individual items); providing assortments that permit one-stop shopping; holding inventory to make merchandise available when customers want it; and providing a variety of transaction features and services that include credit, alteration and assembly of merchandise, attractive display, dressing rooms, personal assistance in selecting merchandise, repair services, return services, and warranties (Levy and Weitz 1995). Although these functions *can* be provided by manufacturers selling directly through IHS, present retailers might be more efficient at performing these functions. Manufacturers are not highly skilled at selling directly to customers. They lack the efficient systems to fulfill orders at a household level and have limited capability to offer the complementary products that increase customer satisfaction and reduce shipping costs. Similarly, manufacturers may not be able to deal with high return rates encountered in nonstore retailing formats.

We noted previously that JCPenney's catalog operation is the largest in the United States. It is undergirded by an extremely efficient and capital-intensive system for accepting orders, packaging them together, and shipping them to customers to be picked up at local stores and catalog distribution centers. The difficulty and expense of duplicating such a system drove Sears from the catalog business; the scale economies are high. It seems unlikely that many manufacturers would find it worthwhile to build such a fulfillment operation from scratch or to replace retailers in the supply chain with outsourcers to handle the functions now performed for them by retailers.

These fulfillment-based disincentives to disintermediate will be lower among products for which fulfillment costs contribute only a small fraction of the sales price to consumers. Products such as computer software, branded jewelry, and high-end perfumes fit this description.

Finally, although manufacturers might be tempted to generate incremental sales by adding a direct IHS channel to their store-based channels, entry into IHS could alienate the stores that now carry their lines. Unless the manufacturer believes it would be more profitable to sell directly than through stores, it will hesitate to disintermediate for fear of alienating those stores that currently carry its lines.

These considerations implicitly identify those manufacturers that might have an incentive to disintermediate. Manufacturers possessing extremely strong brand names and the ability to produce complementary merchandise might consider disintermediation. Consider Levi Strauss. Its brand names are among the strongest in the apparel industry. Network externalities are weak for the markets it faces, either because it produces complements demanded by consumers (e.g., Dockers slacks and shirts) or because, for core products such as Levi's 501 Blue Jeans, consumers can be assured of a match without buying the complementary items from the same seller. In contrast, a maker of dress slacks such as Savane would have less incentive to consider disintermediation because its brand name has less pull and because demand for Savane slacks benefits from significant network externalities when sold in department and specialty stores carrying other manufacturers' lines.

The foregoing discussion applies to manufacturers of nationally branded merchandise that distribute through store-based retailers. Small manufacturers and entrepreneurs, conversely, are more prone to disintermediate because their alternatives to IHS are less attractive. Small or new firms—even those with superior new products—find it difficult to obtain shelf space or awareness. For these producers, IHS could reduce barriers to entry by making it possible for consumers to locate them. In this sense, IHS functions just like advertising in helping heterogeneous consumer segments find products that match their tastes (Rosen 1978).

Brands and Branding

A brand is a search attribute that assures consumers of a consistent level of product quality. It might be the only attribute available to assess some credence goods. Because a brand offered by different outlets can be easily compared by IHS shoppers, manufacturers of branded merchandise are particularly vulnerable to price competition at the retail level; consequently, IHS retailers will find it unattractive to sell their merchandise. It is ironic that strong brands increase the attractiveness of IHS to consumers by providing sufficient information to predict satisfaction without experiencing the merchandise, but that this same mechanism makes these brands less attractive for retailers to carry in the face of IHS.

In the present retail environment, branded-goods manufacturers employ restricted distribution in a territory, relying on location to reduce price competition among retailers and ensure retailer cooperation. This mechanism is not feasible in the low search cost environment of IHS retailing. Therefore, manufacturers of branded merchandise must focus on other methods for insulating IHS retailers from price competition. One method is the production of private-label brands for each retailer. Alternatively, the manufacturer can produce "branded variants" of nationally branded products. These branded variants might be retailer-specific manufacturer model numbers (e.g., Sony Model MA 3150, which is sold only by Service Merchandise).

Neither of these alternatives will be relished by manufacturers that have developed strong national and international brands. It is obvious why such manufacturers would be loathe to find themselves mainly as suppliers of private label merchandise. The prospect of employing an expanded branded-variant strategy also is perilous, albeit in more subtle ways. Increasing the number of branded variants could have the effect of lowering the average attractiveness of the manufacturer's offerings. The easy search-and-compare aspects of IHS could render transparent the existence of trivial differences between models, forcing manufacturers to create larger differences in their variants to satisfy retailer demands of noncomparability across retailers. However, if a significant amount of purchasing still occurs in store, the manufacturer risks losing sales because the variant carried by the store is not the variant desired by the consumer. It seems that manufacturers will be driven to produce variants that are exclusive to each retailer with which they do business (e.g., "Liz Claiborne for Macy's").

The preferred solution for manufacturers is to create a level of brand power that ensures cooperation from retailers in terms of resale price mainte-nance and other tactical mandates. Manufacturers that hold such power could threaten defectors subtly (Barrett 1991). Few brands hold such sway, however, and it is likely that even fewer will be able to maintain such power with distribution through IHS. Nonetheless, "brand building" is another option for manufacturers that fear the leveling effects of IHS. On the surface this could seem counter-intuitive: The threat of IHS to vendors is that its information features will speed commoditization and expose parity where it exists; parity should decrease the value of the brand.

Nonetheless, in product classes in which technology cannot provide advantage and for firms that cannot win technological battles, image building becomes an option. For example, in the case of fashion goods, brands can attain cachet through a carefully crafted marketing strategy. Plainly, brands will have least influence in nonimage, parity product classes. However, parity is not a limiting factor when credence attributes are important—and nearly all products possess credence attributes (Levitt 1981). For example, when quality is difficult to assess, brand name serves as a surrogate (see our previous discussion). And, as marketers long have known, brands can signal quality or other dimensions of differentiation falsely through long-term positioning tactics or explicit attempts to frame consumer decisions (cf. Gardner 1983; Hoch and Deighton 1989). Therefore, another irony of IHS could be that the technology that enables consumers to make more intelligent comparisons in some cases can induce manufacturers to take actions intended to produce an opposite outcome in other cases. As with other determinants of IHS success, the importance of the brand and the viability of a brand-building strategy will vary as a function of the product class and firms' individual competencies.

RESEARCH OPPORTUNITIES

The advent of IHS raises significant questions pertaining to consumer behavior and industry structure. Previous research focuses on heuristics used by consumers to make choices when search and comparison are relatively difficult and costly. Such a focus has been appropriate because the environment, often aided by the retailer, tends to discourage consumer search (see Hoch and Deighton 1989). In contrast, the potential IHS search environment is highly interactive, information intensive, and low in cost. In this alternative environment, research questions in need of attention include the following:

- What fundamental changes occur in information processing as a function of the availability of electronic search agents? With few exceptions (e.g., Widing and Talarzyk 1993), consumer research fails to examine the heuristics and resulting decision quality that are enabled by the search and screening operations that constitute the most attractive features of IHS. A related question involves the influence of search agents on consumer learning. Traditional shopping affords consumers the opportunity to learn the distribution of attribute values across alternatives; search agents merely produce a set of alternatives that satisfy particular criteria. Thus, on some dimensions of product knowledge, search agents can produce undesirable outcomes.
- How does the balance of memory-based versus stimulus-based processing shift as the search environment changes? Some researchers criticize research on consumer choice for focusing on stimulus-based paradigms and ignoring important memory-based aspects present in nearly all consumer decisions (Alba, Hutchinson, and Lynch 1991). Our assumptions regarding an effective IHS system, conversely, argue in favor of greater attention to stimulus-based processing inasmuch as electronic search agents will reduce memory constraints significantly. An especially large effect should be observed when the optimal choice set includes items from different product categories (Ratneshwar and Shocker 1991). Although human memory might be bounded by temporarily salient options, electronic agents

can retrieve all alternatives tagged with the consumer's goal or desired benefit (e.g., "gift").

- Important questions also exist regarding short-term memory and perceptual issues. Just as the cognitive implications of hypertext are virtually unexplored (Rouet et al. 1996), consumer researchers must understand how memory constraints affect decision making as consumers move from brand listings to brand attributes to third-party evaluations to complementary product information, and so on. From a vendor's perspective, there is an information vacuum regarding optimal display format. Insofar as search agents efficiently retrieve requested alternatives, impulse purchasing will occur less frequently (cf. Park, Iyer, and Smith 1989). Vendors must understand the cognitive and perceptual rules that can prompt consumers to make electronic detours in their search for goods and services.
- How do the content and presentation of product information affect consumers' willingness to make choices without directly experiencing the product? Are there ways to create "consumption vocabularies" (West, Brown, and Hoch 1996) that increase consumers' willingness to infer experiential benefits from descriptive, electronically provided information?
- How are consumer confidence and satisfaction affected by search processes that enable efficient screening? The ability to screen products by attribute creates a much more manageable information environment but simultaneously allows some attractive options to go unnoticed. Do consumers experience a greater but illusory sense of confidence in choices made from effortfully but incompletely constructed consideration sets?
- How will consumers react to the collection of detailed information about their needs and purchase behavior by IHS retailers? The utilization of this information to tailor merchandise presentations provides a benefit to consumers, but will consumers be willing to

make this personal data available? What can IHS retailers do to assure consumers that personal information will not be misused?

- What are the true dynamics of price sensitivity in this environment? Although greater amounts of information should increase sensitivity among comparable goods and reduce sensitivity for differentiated goods, empirical research is required to understand how this general conclusion is moderated by type of good, branding, and the manner in which vendors present information.

- How will the nature of the relationships among manufacturers, retailers, and consumers evolve as a function of technology-based reductions in search costs (cf. Zettelmeyer 1996)?

- To what extent will vendors be able to control the search environment? In part, technological developments can determine the ability of vendors to inhibit search and comparison. At present, Internet vendors can prevent entry by search agents. However, irrespective of technology, to what extent will market forces determine not only control of entry but also search procedures allowed by vendors?

- We argue that disintermediation will not blossom in the present environment because of the critical functions now performed by retailers. Looking to the future, how will IHS interact with developments in distribution and flexible manufacturing to enable manufacturers to mass customize their offerings and deliver them efficiently to customers?

- Many traditional retailers will find themselves in multiple channels—maintaining their bricks-and-mortar operations while also creating an electronic presence. What are the economics of such dual systems and how sustainable are existing stores if electronic sales grow to significant levels? In other words, if total sales do not increase, at what point does cannibalization reduce the viability of stores?

These questions are a mere sample of a much larger set both within and beyond the scope of our analysis. Clearly predictions about the ultimate fate and form of IHS are risky. However, it is equally clear that this emerging channel provides marketing researchers and practitioners with much opportunity to test their theories and apply their tools.

Joseph Alba is Holloway Professor of Entrepreneurship, University of Florida. John Lynch is Hanes Corporation Foundation Professor of Business Administration, Duke University, Barton Weitz is JCPenney Eminent Scholar of Marketing. Chris Janiszewski is Associate Professor of Marketing, Richard Lutz and Alan Sawyer are Professors of Marketing, and Stacy Wood is a doctoral candidate in Marketing, University of Florida. The authors gratefully acknowledge the support of the IBM Retail Group, especially Dan Hopping and Dan Sweeney. The views expressed in the article represent those of the authors.

REFERENCES

Aaker, David. "Managing Assets and Skills: The Key to a Sustainable Advantage," *California Management Review,* 31 (Winter 1989): 91–106.

Agins, Terry. "Go Figure: Same Shopper Wears Size 6, 8, 10, 12, *The Wall Street Journal.* (November 11, 1994): B1.

Alba, Joseph W. and Amitava Chattopadhyay. "Effects of Context and Part-Category Cues on Recall of Competing Brands." *Journal of Marketing Research,* 22 (August 1985): 340–49.

——— and J. Wesley Hutchinson. "Dimensions of Consumer Expertise." *Journal of Consumer Research,* 13 (March 1987): 411–54.

———, ———, and John G. Lynch. "Memory and Decision Making," in *Handbook of Consumer Theory and Research,* Harold H. Kassarjian and Thomas S. Robertson, eds. Englewood Cliffs. NJ: Prentice Hall, 1991, 1–49.

———, Howard Marmorstein, and Amitava Chattopadhyay. "Transitions In Preference Over

Time: The Effects of Memory on Message Persuasiveness." *Journal of Marketing Research,* 29 (November 1992): 406–16.

Armstrong, Arthur and John Hazel III. "The Real Value of On-Line Communities." *Harvard Business Review,* 74 (May/June 1996): 134–41.

Anderson, Christopher. "The Accidental Superhighway: A Survey of the Internet," *The Economist,* (July 1, 1995): 50–68.

Bakos, J. Yannis. "A Strategic Analysis of Electronic Marketplaces," *MIS Quarterly,* 15 (September 1991): 295–310.

Barrett, Paul M. "Anti-Discount Policies of Manufacturers Are Penalizing Certain Cut-Price Stores," *The Wall Street Journal.* (February 27, 1991): B1–B5.

Benjamin, Robert and Rold Wigand. "Electronic Markets and Virtual Value Chains on the Information Superhighway," *Sloan Management Review,* 37 (Winter 1995): 62–72.

Bergen, Mark, Shantanu Dutta, and Steven M. Shugan. "Branded Variants: A Retail Perspective," *Journal of Marketing Research,* 33 (February 1996): 9–19.

Bettman, James R. and Pradeep Kakkar. "Effects of Information Presentation Format on Consumer Information Acquisition Strategies," *Journal of Consumer Research,* 3 (March 1977): 233–40.

——— and C. Whan Park. "Effects of Prior Knowledge, Exposure, and Phase of the Choice Process on Consumer Decision Processes: A Protocol Analysis," *Journal of Consumer Research,* 7 (December 1980): 234–48.

——— and Michel A. Zins. "Information Format and Choice Task Effects in Decision Making," *Journal of Consumer Research,* 6 (September 1979): 141–53.

Biehal, Gabriel and Dipankar Chakravarti. "Information Accessibility as a Moderator of Consumer Choice," *Journal of Consumer Research,* 10 (June 1983): 1–14.

Blattberg, Robert C. and John Deighton. "Interactive Marketing: Exploiting the Age of Addressability," *Sloan Management Review,* 33 (Fall 1991): 5–15.

Broniarczyk, Susan and Joseph W. Alba. "The Role of Consumers' Intuitions in Inference Making,"

Journal of Consumer Research, 21 (December 1994): 393–407.

Carlton, Jim. "Think Big," *The Wall Street Journal,* (June 17, 1996): R27.

Copeland, Melvin T. "Relation of Consumer's Buying Habits to Marketing Methods," *Harvard Business Review,* I (April 1923): 282–89.

Cortese, Amy. "Software's Holy Grail," *Business Week,* (June 24, 1996): 83–92.

Darby, Michael R. and Edi Karni. "Free Competition and the Optimal Amount of Fraud," *Journal of Law and Economics,* 16 (April 1973): 66–86.

Day, George S., Allan D. Shocker, and Rajendra K. Srivastava. "Customer-Oriented Approaches to Identifying Product Markets," *Journal of Marketing,* 43 (Fall 1979): 8–19.

Dickson, Peter R. "Person-Situation: Segmentation's Missing Link," *Journal of Marketing,* 46 (Fall 1982): 56–64.

Donegan, Priscilla. "High Tech in a High Touch Way," *Progressive Grocer,* (December 1996): 133.

Edell, Julie A. and Richard Staelin. "The Information Processings of Pictures in Print Advertisements," *Journal of Consumer Research,* 10 (June 1983): 45–61.

Ehrlich, Isaac and Lawrence Fisher. "The Derived Demand for Advertising: A Theoretical and Empirical Investigation," *American Economic Review,* 72 (June 1982): 366–88.

Feinberg, Fred M. and Joel Huber. "A Theory of Cutoff Formation Under Imperfect Information," *Management Science,* 42 (January 1996): 65–84.

Gardner, Meryl Paula. "Advertising Effects on Attributes Recalled and Criteria Used for Brand Evaluations," *Journal of Consumer Research,* 10 (December 1983): 310–19.

Greenleaf, Eric A. and Donald R. Lehmann. "Reasons for Substantial Delay in Consumer Decision Making," *Journal of Consumer Research,* 22 (September 1995): 186–99.

Gilovich, Thomas and Victoria Husted Medvec. "The Experience of Regret: What, When, and Why," *Psychological Review,* 102 (April 1995): 379–95.

Hauser, John R. and Steven Shugan. "Defensive
Marketing Strategies," *Management Science,* 3 (Fall
1983): 327–51.

———, Glen L. Urban, and Bruce D. Weinberg. "How
Consumers Allocate Their Time when Searching for
Information," *Journal of Marketing Research,* 30
(November 1993): 452–66.

——— and Birger Wernerfelt. "An Evaluation Cost
Model of Consideration Sets," *Journal of Consumer
Research,* 16 (March 1990): 393–408.

Hill. G. Christian. "Cyberslaves," *The Wall Street
Journal,* (June 17, 1996): R20.

Hoch, Stephen J. and John Deighton. "Managing What
Consumers Learn from Experience," *Journal of
Marketing,* 53 (April 1989): 1–20.

Hoffman, Donna L. and Thomas P. Novak. "Marketing
in Hypermedia Computer-Mediated Environments:
Conceptual Foundations," *Journal of Marketing,* 60
(Winter 1996): 50–68.

Hutchinson, J. Wesley, Kalyan Raman, and Murali K.
Mantrala. "Finding Choice Alternatives in Memory:
Probability Models of Brand Name Recall," *Journal
of Marketing Research,* 31 (November 1994):
441–61.

Jarvenpaa, Sirkka L. "The Effect of Task Demands and
Graphical Format on Information Processing
Strategies," *Managment Science,* 35 (March 1989):
285–303.

——— "Graphical Displays in Decision Making—The
Visual Salience Effect," *Journal of Behavioral
Decision Making,* 3 (3), (1990): 247–62.

Kardes, Frank R. and Gurumurthy Kalyanaraman.
"Order-of-Entry Effects on Consumer Memory and
Judgment: An Information Integration Perspective,"
Journal of Marketing Research, 29 (August 1992):
343–57.

———, Gurumurthy Kalyanaraman, Murali
Chandrashekaran, and Ronald J. Dornoff. "Brand
Retrieval, Consideration Set Composition,
Consumer Choice, and the Pioneering Advantage,"
Journal of Consumer Research, 20 (June 1993):
62–75.

Karni, E. and A. Schwarz. "Search Theory: The Case of
Search with Uncertain Recall," *Journal of
Economic Theory,* 16 (October 1977): 38–52.

Leonard-Barton, D. *Wellsprings of Knowledge.*
Cambridge. MA: Harvard Business School Press,
(1995).

Levitt, Theodore. "Marketing Intangible Products and
Product Intangibles," *Harvard Business Review* 59
(May/June 1961): 94–102.

Levy, Michael and Barton Weitz. *Retailing
Management,* 2d ed. Burr Ridge, IL: Richard D.
Irwin, Inc., (1995).

Lynch, John G., Jr., Howard Marmorstein, and Michael
F. Weigold. "Choices from Sets Including
Remembered Brands: Use of Recalled Attributes
and Overall Evaluations," *Journal of Consumer
Research,* 15 (September 1988): 169–84.

Maes, Patricia. "Agents that Reduce Work and
Information Overload," *Communications of the
ACM,* 37 (July 1994): 31–40.

———. "Intelligent Software." *Scientific American,*
(September 1995): 84–86.

Mitchell, Andrew A. and Peter A. Dacin. "The
Assessment of Alternative Measures of Consumer
Expertise," *Journal of Consumer Research,* 23
(December 1996): 219–39.

Mitra, Anusree and John G. Lynch, Jr. "Toward a
Reconciliation of Market Power and Information
Theories of Advertising Effects on Price Elasticity,"
Journal of Consumer Research, 21 (March): 644–59.

——— and ———. "Advertising Effects on Consumer
Welfare: Prices Paid and Liking for Brands
Selected," *Marketing Letters,* 7 (March 1996):
644–59.

Nedungadi, Prakash. "Recall and Consumer
Consideration Sets: Influencing Choice without
Altering Brand Evaluations," *Journal of Consumer
Research,* 17 (December 1990): 263–76.

Negroponte, Nicholas. *Being Digital.* New York: Alfred
A. Knopf, (1995).

Newman, Joseph W. and Richard Staelin. "Prepurchase
Information Seeking for New Cars and Major
Household Appliances," *Journal of Marketing
Research,* 9 (August 1972): 249–57.

Park, C. Whan, Easwar S. Iyer, and Daniel C. Smith.
"The Effects of Situational Factors on In-Store
Grocery Shopping Behavior: The Role of Store
Environment and Time Available for Shopping,"

Journal of Consumer Research, 15 (March 1989): 422–33.

Peppers, Don and Martha Rodgers. *The One to One Future.* New York: Currency Doubleday, (1993).

Pine, B. Joseph II. Don Peppers, and Martha Rogers. "Do You Want to Keep Your Customers Forever?" *Harvard Business Review,* 73 (March/April 1995): 103–114.

Quelch, John and Lisa Klein. "The Internet and International Marketing," *Sloan Management Review,* 38 (Spring 1996): 60–75.

Ratchford, Brian T. "The Value of Information for Selected Appliances," *Journal of Marketing Research,* 17 (February 1980): 14–25.

———. "Cost-Benefit Models for Explaining Consumer Choice and Information Seeking Behavior," *Management Science,* 28 (February 1982): 197–212.

Ratneshwar, S. and Allan D. Shocker. "Substitution in Use and the Role of Usage Context in Product Category Structures," *Journal of Marketing Research,* 28 (August 1991): 281–95.

Reda, Susan. "Interactive Home Shopping: Will Consumers Catch Up with Technology?" *Stores,* (March 1995): 20–24.

Reicheld, Frederick F. "Loyalty-Based Management," *Harvard Business Review,* 71 (March/April 1993): 64–73.

Rennie, W. R. "Global Competitiveness: Born Global," *McKinsey Quarterly,* (September 22, 1993): 45–52.

Rigdon, Joan. "Caught in the Web." *The Wall Street Journal,* (June 17, 1996): R14.

Roberts, John H. and James M. Lattin. "Development and Testing of a Model of Consideration Set Composition," *Journal of Marketing Research,* 28 (November 1991): 429–40.

Rosen, Sherwin. "Advertising, Information, and Product Differentiation," in *Issues in Advertising.* David Tuerck, ed. Washington, DC: American Enterprise Institute, (1978): 161–91.

Rouet, Jean-Francois, Jarmo J. Levonen, Andrew Dillon, and Rand J. Spiro. *Hypertext and Cognition.* Mahwah, NJ: Lawrence Erlbaum Associates (1996).

Russo, J. Edward. "The Value of Unit Price Information," *Journal of Marketing Research,* 14 (May 1977): 193–201.

Sarkar, Mira, Brian Butler, and Charles Steinfield. "Intermediaries and Cyberintermediaries: A Continuing Role for Mediating Players in the Electronic Marketplace," *Journal of Computer-Mediated Communications,* 1 (3) (1996) (http://jcmc.huji.ac.ii/vol1/issue3/).

Schiesel, Seth. "Payoff Still Elusive on Internet: Gold Rush," *The New York Times.* (January 2, 1997): C17.

Sheffet, Mary Jane and Debra L. Scammon. "Resale Price Maintenance: Is it Safe to Suggest Retail Prices?" *Journal of Marketing,* 49 (Fall 1985): 82–91.

Simonson, Itamar, Joel Huber, and John Payne. "The Relationship between Prior Brand Knowledge and Information Acquisition Order," *Journal of Consumer Research,* 14 (March 1988): 566–78.

Stigler, George. "The Economics of Information," *Journal of Political Economy,* 69 (January/February 1961): 213–25.

Tauber, Edward. "Why Do People Shop?" *Journal of Marketing,* 36 (October 1972): 42–49.

Templin, Neal. "Veteran PC Customers Spur Mail-Order Boom," *The Wall Street Journal,* (July 17, 1996): B1.

Todd, Peter and Izak Benbasat. "The Influence of Decision Aids on Choice Strategies: An Experimental Analysis of the Role of Cognitive Effort," *Organizational Behavior and Human Decision Processes,* 60, (1994): 36–74.

Tversky, Amos and Eldar Shafir. "Decision Under Conflict: An Analysis of Choice Aversion," *Psychological Science,* 6 (November 1992): 358–361.

Verity, John and Robert Hof. "The Internet: How Will It Change the Way You Do Business," *BusinessWeek,* (November 14, 1994): 80–86, 88.

Wernerfelt, Birger. "An Efficiency Criterion for Marketing Design," *Journal of Marketing Research,* 31 (November 1994): 462–70.

West, Patricia M., Christina L. Brown, and Stephen J. Hoch. "Consumption Vocabulary and Preference Formation," *Journal of Consumer Research,* 23 (September 1996): 120–35.

Widing, Robert E. II and W. Wayne Talarzyk. "Electronic Information Systems for Consumers:

An Evaluation of Computer-Assisted Formats in Multiple Decision Environments," *Journal of Marketing Research,* 30 (May 1993): 125–41.

Wilensky, Dawn. "The Internet, The Next Retailing Frontier," *Discount Store News,* (December 4, 1995): 6–7.

Wilkie, William L, and Peter R. Dickson. "Consumer Information Search and Shopping Behavior," Management Science Institute paper series, Cambridge, MA (1985).

Wright, Alice and John G. Lynch, Jr. "Communication Effects of Advertising Versus Direct Experience When Both Search and Experience Attributes are Present," *Journal of Consumer Research,* 21 (March 1995): 708–18.

Zettelmeyer, Florian. "The Strategic Use of Consumer Search Cost," working paper, Massachusetts Institute of Technology (1996).

The Internet Shopper

Naveen Donthu
Adriana Garcia

Based on a telephone survey, the authors found that Internet shoppers are older and make more money than Internet non-shoppers. Internet shoppers are more convenience seekers, innovative, impulsive, variety seekers, and less risk averse than Internet non-shoppers are. Internet shoppers are also less brand and price conscious than Internet non-shoppers are. Internet shoppers have a more positive attitude toward advertising and direct marketing than non-shoppers do. Implications of these findings are discussed.

Today the world is facing an "electronic" change that is affecting the way people communicate and which is transforming the entire value chain, from manufacturers and retailers to consumers. The Internet is revolutionizing marketing, which is often defined as the exchanges between individuals and firms. Internet shopping is becoming a well-accepted way to purchase many kinds of products and services including computer products, automobiles, travel products, investment products, clothing, flowers, books, music, and homes. In 1998 businesses expected to exchange goods and services of over $22 billion on the Internet. The number is expected to be as high as $3.2 trillion in the year 2003 (Forrester Research, 1998).

Many factors are helping the development of the Internet market, some related to technological advances, some related to the corporate world has changed its perceptions, and some related to changing lifestyles of consumers. The increasing number of companies that offer Internet access are providing consumers with a convenient and inex-

Reprinted from the *Journal of Advertising Research,* © 1999, by the Advertising Research Foundation.

pensive way to become members of the Internet community. The development of better navigation software and search engines are making Internet visits a more pleasant and exciting experience. The increase in the quantity and quality of the available information on the Internet and the presence of well-known corporations and brands on the Internet are also generating higher interest among consumers. In addition, the development of secure systems that allow secure monetary transactions are accelerating Internet shopping.

Shopping has become the fastest-growing use of the Internet, and almost 40 percent of Internet users report shopping as a primary use of the Web (GVU, 1998). The total number of Internet shoppers has reached more than 20 million, and it is expected to continue growing. Even consumers who have not used the Internet to purchase goods and services claim to have used it for information searching that ultimately led to shopping in the traditional channels (*USA Today,* 1998).

The growth of Internet commerce is evidenced not only by the popularity of the Web sites but also by the increase in revenue and profitability of some of its key players. In a survey conducted using 2,069 Web-based businesses, ActiveMedia found that 46 percent claimed to be profitable, and 29 percent said that they would be profitable in the next 12 to 24 months (*Business Week,* 1998).

To summarize, the electronic commerce industry is growing, with Internet shopping becoming a very popular activity among Internet users. Recently there have been several industry and academic studies investigating and profiling the Internet user. For example, it has been established that the Internet *user* is young, educated, male, etc. What is still not very well known is who the Internet *shopper* is. While it is useful to profile the Internet user, from a marketing or advertising point of view it is more important to understand the Internet shopper. There is no evidence that suggests that the typical Internet user is also the typical

Internet shopper. For example, knowing that the typical Internet shopper is young, does that mean that companies planning to sell on the Internet should target only young adults? It is possible that while the typical Internet user is young, it is the older Internet user, who probably has access to more discretionary money, who is the typical Internet shopper. While market segmentation principles tell us that the shopper is going to be different for different products, just as the Internet user is likely to be different for different Internet applications, it is still useful to understand and profile the typical Internet shopper. This is especially important if the typical Internet shopper is going to be different from the typical Internet user. This research is a step in that direction.

Managers recognize the importance and the potential impact of the Internet on advertising, retailing, direct marketing, and other related fields, but little research has been conducted profiling the Internet shoppers. The bulk of the formal research has been conducted on the evolution of the Internet, the way people surf on the Internet, designing Web sites, profiling Internet users, etc. This exploratory study is intended to gain insights to better understand the characteristics, motives, and attitudes of the Internet shopper. Results of this study will help the development of effective Internet marketing strategies.

UNDERSTANDING INTERNET SHOPPERS

This exploratory study will help us understand how Internet shoppers differ from non-Internet shoppers (people who have not made purchases on the Internet). We profile the characteristics of those who purchase and those who do not purchase from the Internet in three main categories: socioeconomic, motivational, and attitudinal characteristics. Due to the lack of formal research on the profile and behavior of Internet shoppers, we will use in-home shopper studies and recent statistics that describe Internet users to draw the hypothesis of our study.

Socioeconomic Characteristics

Despite the extraordinary increase of new Internet users, their socioeconomic profile has not significantly changed. Internet users continue to be young and well-educated people with above-average income even though the disparity is gradually disappearing. The median age of the Internet user is 35 years, and more than half of them have college degrees. Only 38 percent of Internet users are females (GVU, 1998).

The majority of the in-home shopper studies described in-home shoppers as above-average in socioeconomic status as measured by household income, social class, education, and occupation of the household head (Gillet, 1976; Croft, 1998). Berkowitz, Walton, and Walker (1979) also found that in-home shoppers have higher than average education and occupational levels. The same study evidenced that in-home shoppers are younger than store shoppers. Darian (1987) found that in-home shoppers are from households which are in the highest income group, are above average in education, and tend to be younger than in-store shoppers.

In the case of Internet shoppers, the combination of two profiles, Internet users and in-home shoppers, should be considered jointly. Given that Internet users are mainly young males with above-average education, income, and occupation, very similar to the socioeconomic characteristics found in most of in-home shoppers studies, we hypothesize that:

> Hl: Internet shoppers differ from nonshoppers in age, education, income, and gender.

Motivational Characteristics

Darian (1987), describes five types of convenience that in-home shoppers could perceive: (1) reduction of time spent shopping; (2) flexibility in the timing for shopping: (3) saving the physical effort of visiting stores; (4) saving of aggravation; and

(5) the opportunity of buying on impulse or in response to an advertisement.

Considering Internet shopping as a new alternative for in-home shopping, Internet shoppers could receive any of the benefits described by Darian when shopping on the Internet.

H2: Internet shoppers seek more convenience than nonshoppers.

In-home shoppers are more willing to try new things and are less concerned with the risk involved with their purchases. They are also more likely to engage in different ways of in-home shopping such as catalog shopping, mail order, and other similar sources (Berkowitz, Walton, and Walker, 1979; Donthu and Gilliland, 1996). The aversion of risk among in-home shoppers is below average. In-home shoppers tend to be more adventurous, cosmopolitan, and self-confident in their shopping behavior (Gillet, 1976). Fifty percent of the Internet population belong to the Actualizer segment (active, discriminating, and adventurous), and eighteen percent belong to the Experiencers segment (innovative, stimulation seekers, and fashionable) (SRI International, 1995). Nearly seven out of ten Internet users have the innovator and risk-taker personality type.

H3: Internet shoppers are more innovative than nonshoppers.

H4: Internet shoppers show less adversity to risk than nonshoppers.

Despite considering Internet shoppers as convenience-seekers, Internet shoppers can also be considered recreational shoppers as their perceived cost of shopping, in terms of the time and the hassle of searching, do not exceed their perceived value gain in terms of pleasure and information. On the recreational side, the Internet offers consumers the possibility of get in "flow" (Hoffman and Novak, 1997). When consumers are "in flow" on the Web, they lose track of time and become so involved in what they are doing that they feel more present in the interactive environment than in their immediate physical surrounding

(Hoffman and Novak, 1997). Through this experience Internet users interact with the computer in a recreational manner.

Recreational shoppers tend to be less traditional, more innovative, more actively involved in information seeking, and tend to make more impulsive purchases (Bellenger and Korgaonkar, 1980; Donthu and Gilliland, 1996) even though the latest GVU survey found that most Internet shoppers made "intentional" searches.

H5: Internet shoppers are more impulsive than nonshoppers.

The key players on the Internet are well-known companies and strong brand names. Moreover, Fortune 500 companies were the first to present their companies and products on the Internet, which means that a significant portion of the information available on the Web is about branded products. The type of products presented on the Web, coupled with the difficulty of finding information on the Web, requires that the people that are looking for something on the Web need to be aware of the name or key related words of what they are looking for. Internet shoppers need to be well-informed consumers and need to be aware of brand names to find them on the Web.

H6: Internet shoppers are more brand conscious than nonshoppers.

Hoffman and Novak (1997) refer to the Internet user as a well-informed consumer, as a result of the variety of information available on the Net and the control over the search process consumers have in this medium. They also mention that the control over the search process facilitates price comparison. Moreover, the Web is a very good source of product information that provides relevant, timely, up-to-date, convenient, complete, and accessible information (Ducoffe, 1996). Internet shoppers often look for many alternatives when purchasing because the medium is very appropriate for searching, and the process of shopping on the Internet is totally controlled by the consumer. In-home shopper studies show that product assortment and price are among the most important reasons for purchasing from home (Croft, 1998). Therefore, Internet shoppers are interested in both: the availability of product assortment and the possibility of price comparison.

> H7: Internet shoppers are more price conscious than nonshoppers.
>
> H8: Internet shoppers are more variety seekers than nonshoppers.

Attitudinal Characteristics

In the preceding discussion, the hypothesis developed described Internet shoppers as above-average income young males with above-average occupations, innovative and impulsive, who were categorized as recreational shoppers. As recreational shoppers, they consider shopping a leisure activity and enjoy using their free time shopping (Bellenger and Korgaonkar, 1980). Also, some in-home shoppers studies found that in-home shoppers enjoy shopping as much as any other shopper and sometimes make even more frequent in-store purchases than many other shoppers (Gillet, 1976; Reynolds, 1974). Based on these observations from in-home shoppers, and the assumption that Internet shoppers are recreational shoppers, we believed that Internet shoppers have a more positive attitude toward shopping than nonshoppers.

> H9: Internet shoppers have a more positive attitude toward shopping than nonshoppers.

In-home shoppers are risk takers, adventurous, and self-assured, which makes them more likely to purchase from many different sources. Specifically, Berkowitz, Walton, and Walker (1979) found that in-home shoppers tend to purchase different types of merchandise from different in-home sources and that they have a more positive attitude toward direct marketing.

> H10: Internet shoppers have a more positive attitude toward direct marketing than nonshoppers.

Many Web sites have corporate listing directories, free sample offers, billboard-type logos, branded messages, on-line catalogs, corporate information, and other forms of advertising (Ducoffe, 1996). Ducoffe found that Internet users rated Web advertising as somewhat valuable; they also rated Web advertising as slightly more informative than it is valuable. In his study that measured attitudes toward Web advertising, Internet users stated that the Internet "is a good source of up-to-date product information," "is useful," and "is entertaining." These results suggest an overall positive attitude toward advertising among Web users.

> H11: Internet shoppers have a more positive attitude toward advertising than nonshoppers.

METHODOLOGY

To collect data with which to test the hypotheses, trained interviewers called 2,000 household telephone numbers selected randomly from a large city telephone directory. Seven hundred and ninety interviews were completed successfully with "one of the adults" (at least 16 years old) in the household who was Internet active (used the Internet at least once in the past month). Others refused to participate, were not available by phone (in spite of at least one callback), did not have Internet access, and/or had their answering machines on. The gross response rate of 39 percent was determined to be acceptable for our exploratory study and is well within the range of reported response rates found in studies published in the *Journal of Advertising Research* in the past three years.

Respondents were first asked some general questions about their Internet use and demographics. Then they responded to questions about their in-home shopping behavior (use of catalogues, direct-marketing and telemarketing solicitations, and television shopping channels to purchase goods and services). Next, they were asked whether they had purchased products from the Internet.

Finally, they were asked a series of short questions to measure their attitudes (toward shopping, direct marketing, and advertising), brand and price consciousness, risk aversion, variety-seeking propensity, innovativeness, importance of convenience, and impulsiveness. The constructs measured by this series of questions and the Cronbach alpha coefficients of reliability are reported in Table 3.3. These questions have been used previously in a study of Infomercial shoppers and published in the *Journal of Advertising Research* (Donthu and Gilliland, 1996) and have very high reliability.

TABLE 3.3	Constructs Measured[a]	
Construct	**Questions**	**Alpha**
Risk aversion	I would rather be safe than sorry. I want to be sure before I purchase anything. I avoid risky things.	0.77
Innovativeness	I like to take chances. I like to experiment with new ways of doing things. New products are usually gimmicks.[b]	0.74
Brand consciousness	I usually purchase brand name products. Store brands are of poor quality.[b] All brands are about the same.[b]	0.80
Price consciousness	I usually purchase the cheapest item. I usually purchase items on sale only. I often find myself checking prices. A person can save a lot by shopping for bargains.	0.81
Importance of convenience	I hate to spend time gathering information on products. I do not like complicated things. It is convenient to shop from home.	0.75
Variety-seeking propensity	I like to try different things. I like a great deal of variety. I like new and different styles.	0.84
Impulsiveness	I often make unplanned purchases. I like to purchase things on a whim. I think twice before committing myself.[b] I always stick to my shopping lists.[b]	0.87
Attitude toward advertising	Advertisements provide useful information. I think that advertisements are often deceptive[b] I usually do not pay any attention to advertisements.[b]	0.78
Attitude toward shopping	Shopping is fun. I get a real high from shopping. Buying things makes me happy.	0.88
Attitude toward direct marketing	Phone solicitations are an invasion of my privacy.[b] I enjoy receiving junk mail. I often use catalogues to shop for products.	0.72

[a]Responses to all questions were on a 5-point scale ranging from "strongly agree" to "strongly disagree." Responses to multiple-item scales were averaged. [b]Reverse scaled.

TABLE 3.4	Internet Shopper versus Nonshopper		
Hypothesis Number: Construct	**Internet Shopper** ($n = 122$)	**Internet Nonshopper** ($n = 668$)	**diff. sig. at the 0.05 level?**
H1: Age[a]	3.3	2.8	Y
H1: Education[b]	2.8	2.6	N
H1: Income[c]	3.4	2.8	Y
H1: Gender[d]	1.5	1.5	N
H2: Importance of convenience	4.0	2.9	Y
H3: Innovativeness	4.0	2.8	Y
H4: Risk aversion	2.5	3.2	Y
H5: Impulsiveness	3.5	2.0	Y
H6: Brand consciousness	3.4	3.2	N
H7: Price consciousness	3.9	3.7	N
H8: Variety-seeking propensity	3.8	2.9	Y
H9: Attitude toward shopping	2.4	2.3	N
H10: Attitude toward direct marketing	2.9	2.2	Y
H11: Attitude toward advertising	3.4	2.9	Y

[a]age: 1 = <20; 2 = 20–35; 3 = 36–50; 4 = 51–65; 5 = >65.

[b]education: 1 = some school; 2 = high school diploma; 3 = some college; 4 = college degree; 5 = postgraduate degree.

[c]income: 1 = <15K; 2 = 15–30K; 3 = 31–45K; 4 = 46–60K; 5 = >60K.

[d]gender: 1 = female; 2 = male.

RESULTS

The study results are reported in Table 3.4. Respondents were divided in two groups, a group of Internet shoppers ($n = 122$), those respondents who have purchased goods from the Internet, and a group of Internet nonshoppers ($n = 668$), those who had never purchased from the Internet. T tests (Chi-square tests in the case of ordinal-scaled variables) were conducted for each of the hypotheses in order to confirm or reject each of them. As mentioned before, we replicated the methodology used by Donthu and Gilliland (1996). They profiled Infomercial shoppers while we profile Internet shoppers.

Results show that Internet shoppers do not differ from nonshoppers on education and gender. However, Internet shoppers are older and make more money than non-Internet shoppers. Based on these results, we partially reject Hypothesis H1.

While Internet users are young in general, it is the older Internet users who have a higher purchasing power and easier access to credit cards as a result of higher incomes that are actually shopping on the Internet. These results indicate that young Internet users are mainly looking for fun and entertainment when surfing the Internet while older users are more likely to purchase products on the Internet.

In terms of motivational characteristics, results confirm H2, H3, and H4, as Internet shoppers are more convenience seekers, more innovative, and less risk averse than Internet nonshoppers are. Also, Internet shoppers are more impulsive and more variety seekers than nonshoppers, which confirms H5 and H8. However, we reject H6 and H7, as Internet shoppers are less brand and price conscious than nonshoppers are. The lack of price consciousness could be a result of Internet shoppers belonging to an above-average socioeconomic class.

Price is less important than other benefits the Internet can provide them. They are not looking for the best deal; they are looking for the product that satisfies their needs. In traditional purchase decisions brand and price could be used as a surrogate for quality of the product. For Internet shoppers, however, brand and price are no longer symbols of quality of the product as detailed product quality information is usually available on the Web sites.

While not hypothesized, we found that Internet shoppers spend longer time surfing the Net per week. The process of finding products and information on the Net makes Internet shoppers take more time using the Internet versus nonshoppers.

Internet shoppers have a more positive attitude toward advertising and direct marketing than nonshoppers do, which confirms H10 and H11. However, Internet shoppers do not have a more positive attitude toward shopping than nonshoppers, therefore we reject Hypothesis H9. Internet shoppers seem to be more economic and convenience shoppers, as opposed to recreational shoppers that we had hypothesized. Internet shoppers are not any more recreational shoppers than Internet nonshoppers, as they do not have any more positive attitude toward shopping than Internet nonshoppers.

Discussion

Researchers have concentrated much of their Internet research efforts on understanding the "mechanics" of the Internet. Researchers have been describing the evolution of the number of hosts, number of users, and general characteristics of key players in their new medium. As Berthon et al. (1996) state, "most of the work done so far has been of a descriptive nature—what the medium is." The lack of understanding of the consumer and consumer behavior on the Internet motivated us to conduct this exploratory study. From a marketing/advertising point of view it is very important to

understand who the Internet shopper is and what his or her attitudes and opinions are. Berthon, Pitt, and Watson (1996) state, "serious advertising and marketing practitioners and academics are by now aware that more systemic research is required to reveal the true nature of commerce on the Web." Our study is a step in this direction.

In order to profile the Internet shoppers, we conducted 790 telephone interviews with Internet users in a metropolitan area. The results revealed that the typical Internet shopper is different from a typical Internet user. The finding that the Internet shopper is older and earns more money than the average Internet user is not an obvious one and has profound managerial implications. The study also revealed that the Internet shopper is a convenience seeker who is innovative and more impulsive and variety seeking than the non-Internet shopper. However, the Internet shopper is no different from a nonshopper when it comes to brand and price consciousness. The Internet shopper also has a positive attitude toward direct marketing and advertising. Such a profile can be very useful for a marketing or advertising manager developing Internet marketing strategies.

These results would be useful to guide the definition of target markets for Web commerce sites as well as for fine-tuning positioning and the benefits offered by those sites to the Internet shoppers. The Internet shoppers' characteristics make promotions and launch of new products ideal marketing practices on the Internet. Promotions may attract Internet shoppers as they are more likely to make impulsive purchase decisions and the launch of a new product may be of particular interest to Internet shoppers as they are always looking for new things. Variety and convenience are key features that a Web site should offer to Internet shoppers. Also, detailed information about the products should be presented to prospective customers. They are not likely to judge the quality of a product based on price and brand name alone.

Further research is needed to better understand the specific needs and expectations of Internet shoppers. These are likely to vary by product category, which was not investigated in this study. More research is needed to understand how to increase electronic commerce by converting non-Internet users into Internet users and converting Internet nonshoppers into Internet shoppers. The study results need to be generalized over larger and national/international populations. Further research is also necessary to understand how the Internet would impact the marketing mix and how to integrate this new technology with conventional marketing activities. Given that the Internet is one of the fastest-changing environments, changes in consumer attitudes are expected. Continuous researching of

Internet shoppers and profiling should be done in the future.

Naveen Donthu is professor of marketing at Georgia State University. He received his M.S. in management science and Ph.D. in marketing from the University of Texas at Austin. He has published in several marketing and advertising journals including *Marketing Science,* the *Journal of Marketing Research,* the *Journal of Consumer Research,* the *Journal of the Academy of Marketing Science,* the *Journal of Advertising,* the *Journal of Advertising Research,* the *Journal of Retailing,* and the *Journal of Business Research.*

Adriana Garcia currently works for United Parcel Service of America (UPS). She is responsible for managing the customer relationship marketing process within the customer strategies group. Her previous work experience was in market research and brand management at Procter & Gamble. She holds a Bachelor of Science in computer engineering from the Universidad Simon Bolivar in Caracas, Venezuela and a Master of Science in marketing from Georgia State University.

REFERENCES

Bellenger, Danny N., and Pradeep K. Korgaonkar. "Profiling the Recreational Shopper," *Journal of Retailing,* 56, 4 (1980): 77–92.

Berkowitz, Eric N., John R. Walton, and Orvile C. Walker, Jr. "In-Home Shopper: The Market for Innovative Distribution Systems." *Journal of Retailing* 55, 3 (1979): 15–33.

Berthon, Pierre, Leyland F. Pitt, and Richard T. Watson. "The World Wide Web as an Advertising Medium: Toward an Understanding of Conversion Efficiency." *Journal of Advertising Research* 36, 1 (1996): 43–54.

Business Week. "Doing Business in the Internet Age." *Business Week,* June 22, 1998.

Croft, Martin. "Shopping At Your Convenience." *Marketing Week,* 21, 18 (1998): 36–37.

Darian, Jean C. "In-Home Shopping: Are There Consumer Segments?" *Journal of Retailing* 63, 3 (1987): 163–86.

Donthu, Naveen, and David Gilliand. "The Infomercial Shopper." *Journal of Advertising Research* 36, 2 (1996): 69–76.

Ducoffe, Robert H. "Advertising Value and Advertising on the Web." *Journal of Advertising Research* 36, 5 (1996): 21–35.

Forrester Research. "Worldwide Internet Commerce Will Reach As High As $3.2 Trillion In 2003." *http://www.forrester.com/,* 1998.

Gillet, Peter L. "In-Home Shoppers—An Overview." *Journal of Marketing* 40, 4 (1976): 81–88.

Griffin, Jill. "The Internet's Expanding Role in Building Customer Loyalty." *Direct Marketing* 59, 7 (1996): 50–53.

GVU. "GVU's WWW User's Survey." *http://www.gvu.gatech.edu/,* 1998.

Hoffman, D. L., and T. P. Novak. "A New Paradigm for Electronic Commerce." *The Information Society* 13, Jan.–Mar. (1997): 43–54.

Plummer, Joseph T. "Life Style Patterns and Commercial Credit Card Usage," *Journal of Marketing,* 35, 2 (1971): 35–41.

SRI International. "Exploring the World Wide Web Population's Other Half." *http://future.sri.com/,* 1995.

USA Today. "America's Online: 70.5 million adults." *http://www.usatoday.com/,* 1998.

SHOPPING AGENTS AND CONSUMER BEHAVIOR

The Internet is having an enormous impact on how buying decisions are made. This is true for both consumer and industrial markets.

On the consumer side, a growing army of web sites are changing the way consumers shop. By visiting Autobytel.com, for example, consumers can easily learn real invoice price data and, in a matter of hours, have dealers bidding for their business. At mobshop.com consumers can aggregate their buying power to get the best prices for an array of products. Or, by visiting Respond.com, consumers can let others broker purchases for them.

The Internet is revolutionizing business-to-business purchase behavior as well. Industrial exchanges, spot markets, auctions, e-procurement sites, and catalog aggregation sites are springing up so fast that it is difficult to keep pace. It is fair to say that businesses can now procure most operating supplies, industrial parts, and direct materials online in price efficient markets that did not even exist three years ago.

Marketers have known for years that purchases involve a distinct series of steps. First, there is the awareness that a need exists. Next, alternatives for need satisfaction are sought. Alternatives are then compared in terms of attributes or other values. On the basis of comparison, a preferred alternative arises. Next, payment, shipping, service, and warranty alternatives are compared before a final decision is made.

For simple consumer purchases, many of these steps may be skipped. Or, in the case of industrial buying, long-term supply contracts may minimize the costs of constantly reevaluating suppliers. The higher the order and search costs of the product relative to price, the greater the likelihood that consumers and businesses will pay fixed prices for commodity-type products of an acceptable quality without extensive search of alternatives.

The Internet is driving the costs of searching for alternatives, evaluating alternatives, and negotiating terms lower and lower. Both consumers and businesses are finding that they no longer have to accept fixed prices even for commodity-type products. The Internet allows buyers to quickly and easily find the lowest priced, highest quality suppliers. In addition, web-based auctions provide a forum through which qualified vendors may be forced to bid for the business.

In the first reading of this chapter, Pattie Maes shows how intelligent agents are creating a new form of agent-mediated internet buying behavior. Maes describes how intelligent brokers may automate virtually every step of the purchasing process.

In the second reading of this chapter, researchers Stef Nicovich and T. Bettina Cornwell describe how the Internet represents a facilitation of meaning transfer between cultures. These researchers suggest that the Internet may have a dramatic effect on communication and consumer behavior as a result.

In the third reading of this chapter, Kim Bartel Sheeba assesses online privacy concerns and resultant behaviors. Results suggest that online consumer behavior is often driven by the desire to protect privacy. Implications are for firms to increase trust and confidence in transactions and data privacy.

Smart Commerce: The Future of Intelligent Agents in Cyberspace

Pattie Maes

How will dramatic developments occurring today, including the sophistication of intelligent agents, affect the future of electronic commerce? Pattie Maes discussed this question and more in her keynote address at the Direct Marketing Association Conference in Miami, April 6, 1998.

THE ELECTRONIC MARKET OPPORTUNITY

Why should we take this new medium, Web-based commerce, seriously? First, let's consider the numbers: There are about 64 million people on-line in the United States and Canada—approximately 22% of the population. The average Internet user is 33 years old. Sixty percent of those users are male, and their average annual household income is $59,000. Eighty percent access the Internet on a daily basis, and an even higher percentage report that e-mail and the Web have become an indispensable part of their lives. So far, 25% of these users have purchased products on-line. We expect that these numbers will keep growing rapidly for two reasons: First, 42% of U.S. households have computers, but many of them are not yet on-line. Second, we expect that by the year 2000, just two years away, 60% of U.S. households will have computers. The predicted growth stems from rapidly declining computer prices. Next year, a basic personal computer will cost around $499. The merging of consumer electronics items, such as the television and telephone, with the computer, will also increase the number of computerized households.

On the other hand, today's on-line retail sales numbers might not seem as encouraging at first glance. In 1996, on-line retail sales totaled about $600 million. In 1997, that figure is estimated at over $2 billion. But almost half of those sales, or $800 million, occurred between Thanksgiving and Christmas—during a period of a little over a month. By the year 2001, Forrester Research expects about $17 billion of retail sales revenues. Most of these numbers are on the low side because they include only sales where the entire transaction, including payment, occurs on-line. People may shop on the Web and even place orders online, but the payment and fulfillment systems—the back office systems—are not yet automated for many retailers. For example, about 16% of the people who bought new cars last year used the Web as part of the car-shopping process, but only 2% of them actually ordered and paid via the Web. By 1999, J. D. Power expects that about 50% of all new car sales will involve customers' looking up information about cars on the Web.

In terms of business-to-business sales, the numbers are a bit higher. In 1997 there were approximately $8 billion in business-to-business sales. Forrester Research predicts that number to jump to about $327 billion by 2002. A recent survey by Hambrecht and Quist showed that while most of the Fortune 500 companies interviewed still see the phone and fax as the primary channels for today's business-to-business sales, most of these companies expect that the Internet will be the most important channel for selling in the year 2000. The companies surveyed envision that, within two years, about 42% of their sales and revenues will be generated from the Internet, while just 32% will come from the phone or fax.

The numbers above illustrate the enormous opportunity for companies that are willing to experiment with Web-based commerce: The channel is very efficient, the cost is low, and the potential global market is huge. But of course, the challenges are daunting. For example, let's look at customer attention. How do you attract customers to your site? How do you keep them there? How do you keep customers loyal when they can go to your competitor's site and compare offerings with the click of a mouse?

For the customer, or the buyer, there are tremendous opportunities as well. The Web offers customers choice and convenience—they can shop easily from their desks or at home. But consumers also face major challenges. Finding the products that they want is still incredibly difficult for consumers. Trust and privacy are also often mentioned as prime challenges that consumers face in e-commerce.

Agents are a key technology in overcoming both business and consumer challenges in Web commerce. What are agents? They are pieces of software that profile a user or buyer. Agents keep a detailed profile of demographic information such as the ZIP code, age, and gender of the user or consumer. Agents also track interests and preferences of consumers. These are derived from a number of possible sources: purchase history, expressed user preferences, and inferred user preferences— preferences that a company gathers by watching a user's behavior on its site. Agents thus keep a detailed profile of every one of a business's customers and use that profile to offer personalized services to those consumers. Such personalized service and attention typically mean higher-quality service. An agent compares a particular user's profile with the business's catalog of products and then personalizes the whole user experience at the site. The agent dynamically generates Web pages for the user, pages that are completely tailored to the particular user—to his or her interests, preferences, age, gender, and location.

In this way, agents link business goals and consumer interests. Agents can fulfill business goals of Web commerce such as consumer loyalty. If a company offers personalized services to its customers, and if that company knows its customers better than anyone else, those customers will be very loyal to the company—assuming that

they can't get that same high-quality, personalized service elsewhere. Agents also help to grow sales. A company's customers are more likely to find the products they want because the shopping experience is personalized to their needs and preferences. In addition, this technology helps businesses to understand their markets by keeping detailed profiles of each and every customer. Companies can mine the aggregate data and look for patterns. For example, a company may discover that some of its products appeal more to one type of user than to another.

Agents serve the consumer's interests as well. Agents allow consumers to receive personalized service. Each consumer is treated like an individual. He receives the information and product offerings that are most likely to interest him. This makes it much easier for customers to find information relevant to them. A customer often receives recommendations for products based on a company's understanding of the user's profile and what that reveals about which products that customer may want to buy. Another benefit for customers is that they are kept informed about new products that meet their particular profiles.

THE BUYING PROCESS

If we look at buying behavior, both in consumer-to-business and business-to-business sales, we can identify six stages. The first stage is often called *need identification*. This stage occurs when a customer recognizes a need for a particular product. The second stage is called *product brokering,* wherein a customer compares different products in order to determine which product to buy. The third stage, which sometimes occurs before the second stage, is *merchant brokering*— deciding from whom to buy the product. The fourth stage is *negotiation*—negotiating the price, delivery, or other conditions of the sale. The fifth stage is the *purchase and delivery* of the product. Finally, the sixth stage is *product evaluation and service.* Agent technology has proven critical in automating or assisting the first four stages in the buying process.

How Agents Automate Need Identification

First, agents help people identify their needs. How? By keeping track of each user's interests and notifying a user when a new product matches her profile. For example, my book agents at Barnes & Noble or at Amazon.com might know that I'm interested in new books by John Grisham or new science fiction paperbacks. Or my agent may know that I want a particular book, but that I think the book is too expensive. Perhaps I've told the agent that I'd be willing to buy the book if it becomes available for less than $25. My agent knows what I'm in the market for, and can compare this information with the business's catalog. Whenever that catalog is updated (new books become available, prices change, and so on), my agent compares my profile with the updated catalog information. If my agent identifies a match, perhaps a new book by John Grisham, a new science fiction paperback, or the book I want to buy at the price I'm willing to pay, then my agent notifies me by e-mail. This means that I don't have to go to the store regularly to find out whether it has added new products that I may want to buy. Instead, the store runs an agent for me, and the agent encourages me to come to the store to make that purchase.

Notification agents are very easy to implement, and there are many examples of them on the Web. Any personalized Web server technology that allows you to keep a database of information about your users makes it possible to implement this functionality. Examples of sites that use notification agents, in addition to the Barnes & Noble and Amazon.com examples described above, include FastParts.com and Classifieds2000. At FastParts.com, an auction site, an agent notifies a user via e-mail when a new bid may affect his bids. The user can then return to the site and place a new bid. Classifieds2000, a classified ads site, allows a user

to create a notification agent that will tell her when a particular product becomes available at a particular price.

How Agents Automate Product Brokering

During product brokering, the second stage of the buying process, consumers determine which products to buy to meet a particular need. Recommendation agents help users figure out which of the many products available best suit their needs and interests. Like notification agents, these agents are offered at retail or business Web sites and keep profiles of user interests. They also match user profiles with a business's catalog. But recommendation agents have an additional function: They make predictions about which products will interest a user based on the user's profile, past behavior, and preferences. These predictions are often the result of an automated analytical process such as data mining, which looks at large databases of customer buying behavior and makes correlations between classes of customers and specific products.

Recommendation agents use a number of techniques to predict which products will interest a particular customer. For example, an agent may learn that a customer is interested in products with certain features—for example, that the customer likes several movies from the 1940s that star Humphrey Bogart. Once the agent has detected such a pattern, the agent can automatically recommend similar products that may interest the customer. Many agents use collaborative filtering, a technology developed at the MIT Media Lab, to make product recommendations. An agent that uses collaborative filtering makes recommendations based on the opinions of like-minded people. The agent identifies users with profiles similar to the customer's, then makes recommendations based on what those users purchased. . . .

Collaborative filtering has been tested and deployed successfully by large retailers such as Amazon.com, Barnes & Noble, ZDnet, and

MyLaunch. Collaborative filtering products include the Firefly personalization and recommendation product Broadvision, Net Perceptions, and others. Constraint-based filtering is another well-known technique used in making recommendation agents. PersonaLogic is a retail site that uses constraint satisfaction techniques. . . .

This site helps users choose between products in several categories. In the example above, the user is shopping for a mountain bike. The user gives the agent a set of product constraints—both hard and soft constraints, such as how much the user is willing to pay and how light the frame of the mountain bike should be. The user also tells the agent how important these constraints are. Then the system considers all of the user's constraints and orders the set of available products—in this case, the set of mountain bikes available that match the user's preferences. The agent presents an ordered list of products that tells the user how different products score with respect to her constraints and preferences.

HOW AGENTS AUTOMATE MERCHANT BROKERING

The third stage of the buying process, which sometimes precedes product brokering, involves choosing a merchant from which to buy a particular product. Agent technology helps consumers choose between merchants. Because these agents are used to compare a number of different retailers, they are usually offered by a third-party service. These agents know which specific product the user seeks. They contact a number of Web sites and compare prices and other conditions at these sites. For example, BargainFinder is a price-comparison shopping agent built several years ago by Andersen Consulting. A user enters the title and artist of a music CD into BargainFinder. Then the BargainFinder agent shops for that CD at the various on-line stores that sell music. BargainFinder accesses many on-line music stores, and it knows how to extract information such as the CD's availability, price, shipping costs, and so on. Within two minutes, Bargain-

Finder returns with a screen that tells the user where and at what price the CD is available.

Andersen Consulting built BargainFinder as an experiment, and learned much from it. Initially, many businesses reacted to the BargainFinder technology by blocking the agents from their sites. These businesses learned to recognize the IP addresses from which the agents originated and blocked all requests from those addresses. Why? Some of these businesses did not want to be compared with their competitors on price alone. Others blocked the technology because the huge number of requests from these robots overloaded and slowed down their servers. But eventually, most of the businesses involved decided to participate in the BargainFinder comparison-shopping experiment. At this point, only one on-line music retailer, the largest one, still blocks the BargainFinder agent. All of the other on-line music retailers realized that appearing in BargainFinder gave them exposure to more customers. In fact, when a customer accesses a retail site through BargainFinder, that customer buys an average of two CDs from that retailer. Therefore, a retailer that attracts customers by offering a low price for a particular item could actually sell other items to those customers at much higher prices. It's not known whether on-line music stores modify prices on items requested through BargainFinder. However, the payoff of such a strategy is obvious: The low BargainFinder price brings the customer in the door. The customer then buys more items, at higher prices, without returning to BargainFinder between purchases.

BargainFinder is not the only merchant brokering agent. Other examples include Fido and Jango. Fido accepts it user's natural language query and then searches a number of sites for the product indicated. Jango was developed by Netbots Inc., a small startup in Washington that was recently acquired by Excite. The Jango agent allows users of the Excite search engine site to comparison shop for a full range of products. This agent not only tells a user where a particular product is for sale, but also returns any product reviews it can find. Another recent entry in the merchant-brokering business is priceline.com, which allows consumers to shop for inexpensive airline tickets. Users access the priceline.com site and enter a request such as, "I want to fly from Boston to Brussels on April 20, and I'm only willing to pay $500." The agent then searches a number of sites to find a ticket for that destination, day, and price.

Of course, these comparison-shopping agents have limitations: First, they're consumer biased. A retailer may cooperate with these agents, or it may deliberately provide incorrect information when it detects that an agent, rather than an end user, is accessing its catalog. Second, and more important, price is not the only factor in a consumer's decision about where to buy a product. For example, imagine that a user accesses Jango to find out where to buy an Apple Powerbook. Jango provides the user with a list of merchants and their prices. But the consumer has no information about the reputations of these merchants or whether the merchants offer extended warranties, service contracts, gift services, and so on. Furthermore, the consumer has no way of knowing whether the product is in stock, how fast can it be delivered, or whether it can be personalized or configured according to the user's specifications. As a result, today's merchant-brokering agents are limited by their focus on price as the sole factor in purchasing decisions. The second generation of comparison shopping agents . . . overcame these limitations by performing a complete value-based comparison of vendors and their products.

HOW AGENTS AUTOMATE NEGOTIATION

After a customer decides what product to buy and where to buy it, he enters the fourth stage of the buying process: negotiation. In this phase, buyers and sellers negotiate price, delivery conditions, and so on. Negotiation agents can automate much of this negotiation process. Usually this phase involves both a buyer's agent and a seller's agent that negotiate with one another. The buyer's agent understands the buyer's needs and preferences,

while the seller's agent understands the seller's sales and pricing rules. This phase of the buying process has spurred much research, and commercial products are slowly becoming available. BusinessBots, a small start-up in the San Francisco Bay Area, is one example of a company that is developing negotiation agents. . . .

Using this system, consumers can buy and sell from other consumers and from retailers. For example, a user who wants the book *Eva Luna* by Isabel Allende can create an agent to buy the book. The user outlines her conditions and bargaining strategy for the agent: She wants a paperback, brand new, by a particular date and time, and she's offering $8 to start but is willing to pay as much as $15. The agent should employ a tough bargaining strategy, keeping the price as low as possible. If the agent can't obtain the book at the lower price, it should gradually increase the offer. The user also specifies whether she wants to buy the book from a local retailer or from sellers the world over, how often she wants the agent to report to her, and how much autonomy the agent has in representing her. It takes the user about 15 seconds to fill out the form that creates the agent. In doing so, she's created a little program that understands her conditions for buying the book and will represent her in negotiations with other parties, both retailers and other consumers who bought the book and want to resell it.

On the seller's side, retailers can use this system to create agents that determine which price to quote to a particular buyer's agent for a particular product. These agents use a number of criteria in determining price. For example, the agent may quote a lower price if the seller has quantity stock of the item, or it may quote a higher price if market demand outpaces current supply. The agent also considers the customer: Is this a loyal consumer who buys regularly from the seller? The agent may quote that customer a better price than it would a new customer. Is the customer buying other books or many copies of one book? The agent may quote a lower price for quantity sales. Seller's agents also look at the market. For example, what's the average sale price of the book on the electronic market? The seller's agent takes these factors into account when negotiating with buyer's agents.

AuctionBot, created at the University of Michigan, performs a similar function. At the AuctionBot site, users create agents to run auctions for them, both for buying and selling of goods. AuctionBot lets the user choose the type of auction—Dutch, English, Vickrey, and so on. The user then specifies the parameters of the auction: the minimum price and the length of the auction. The robot, or agent, then runs the auction on the user's behalf, automating negotiations with all interested parties. While many Web sites conduct auctions for users, not many of them automate the entire process using agent technology. Agent-run auction sites offer one important advantage over other auctions: the user needn't be present to enter bids or run his auction.

Another negotiation system developed at MIT is the Tête-à-tête system, mentioned earlier, which helps users differentiate among merchants' offerings. This system differs from standard merchant-brokering agents that base recommendations on price comparison. Tête-à-tête considers price, but it also takes into account a number of other parameters defined by the user. This agent undertakes an integrated negotiation that looks at many products and many merchants using many user-defined preferences and conditions.

CHALLENGES IN IMPLEMENTING AGENT TECHNOLOGY

By automating much of the buying process, agents promise to redefine electronic commerce. But in order to ensure success, agent technology must address customer concerns about trust and privacy. Trust is an issue in electronic commerce because it's very difficult for consumers to trust unknown parties. An agent may help consumers find the merchants who meet their conditions for buying particular products—the best price, desirable delivery time frames, and so on—but can consumers trust a merchant they never heard of? New, third-party escrow services are making this trust gap their place of business. For example, MoneySave.com is an

escrow site that holds a consumer's credit card number until the consumer receives the goods ordered from a vendor. MoneySave releases that credit card information to the vendor only after the consumer verifies the product. MoneySave earns revenue from this escrow service by charging buyers a percentage of the sale. Also, the equivalents of Better Business Bureaus are emerging in the electronic world—for example, the reputation systems provided by auction sites such as E-Bay and OnSale.com. These Web bureaus rate the trustworthiness of Web vendors for consumers.

The second important challenge is consumer concerns about privacy. Consumers will provide businesses with information about their interests, preferences, product needs, and demographics only if they feel comfortable that the information is safeguarded and ultimately under their control. In the future, sites that collect consumer information will need to follow several important principles if they want to ensure customer comfort with agent-assisted shopping. First, the consumer should ultimately own the collected data. Second, the vendor should remove profile data at the customer's request. Third, a user should be asked for her consent any time a site collects information about her. Finally, users should receive some value in exchange for personal information collected.

DEVELOPING TRENDS IN AGENT TECHNOLOGY

At this point, we've seen just the beginning of agents' effect on the electronic commerce space. Currently, agents reside on servers at particular retail sites. This means that retailers can develop personalized relationships with their consumers and thus offer higher-quality service. But several future trends will change and deepen the impact of agents on Web commerce.

First, developers are working on agents that will store user profiles on the user's client, in the user's browser. Microsoft, Netscape, and Firefly are together authoring a major initiative under the approval of the W3 Consortium. This Open Profiling

Standards (OPS, also referred to as P3P) initiative states that the browser will store information about particular users: their interests, needs, credit card information, demographics, past book reading and purchasing preferences, videos purchased, travel interests, and so on. All of this information will be stored on the browser's site. When a user accesses a retail site, that retailer's server can automatically request information from the user's profile. For example, if a user visits an on-line bookstore, the bookstore might request information on the user's age, gender, and past book preferences. The user then approves or denies the information request. Another advantage of storing user profiles on the client is that these profiles can be stored on smart cards for use in the physical world. For example, a user who shops regularly at Barnes & Noble may want to carry a card that contains his profile information. When he visits a Barnes & Noble in his neighborhood, he can swipe his card through a reader and obtain personalized recommendations for books based on his profile, notification that the book he's waiting for has arrived, and so on.

A second development underway is the sharing of profile information among networks of sites. This development follows naturally from the way individual sites collect user profiles. For example, four different sites may collect information on a user's preferences in books, music, travel, and software. These sites may become interested in linking that information to verify whether, for example, something can be learned about the user's book preferences from her movie preferences. Or perhaps her travel preferences indicate her possible restaurant preferences. Several sites are beginning, with user consent, to share user profile information—for example, the sites in the Engage network. In this way, information collected about the user at one site is used to generate a personalized experience when that user visits another site for the first time.

A third trend is the integration of on-line and off-line systems. Agent technology is not limited to the Web. If retailers provide in-store kiosks, much of the agents' functionality can be provided in physical stores at the point of sale.

The last development—one which is still being researched but will quickly affect the marketplace—is the integration of agent technology with mobile computers (next-generation mobile phones, two-way pagers, car computers, and so on). The MIT Media Lab is building a system based on two-way pagers that matches a user's profile to his current physical location. This system provides a user's profile to businesses within 200 yards of his current location. Those businesses in turn have agents that understand their catalogs of offerings and look for a match with the user's interests. For example, the user's profile might indicate that he's currently looking for a sushi restaurant. If he happens to be in the vicinity of a Japanese restaurant, the user's pager notifies him that if he turns right at the next intersection and then turns left, he'll find a restaurant that has reserved a table for him. If his agent carries detailed information about the user's sushi preferences, the restaurant may have begun to prepare his favorite sushi. The Media Lab is building this system in devices that people carry with them as well as in cars. A user may want an agent in her car that constantly radiates information about her needs and preferences. Local businesses can then determine whether their products and services match the user's needs and respond to her. For example, an antique store's agent may convince the user to turn right at the next intersection and visit the store because the user's agent indicates that she's interested in antiques.

Interoperability will be one of the challenges in making these agents ubiquitous. Major interoperability initiatives, such as the OPS initiative described earlier, are in various stages of the W3 Consortium approval process. Microsoft, for example, already offers support for OPS in its current browsers. These major standards initiatives will ensure that agents become more common and easier to build. For example, Extended Mark-up Language (XML) is a standard language that tells computers how to interpret information on Web pages. Retailers use XML tags as a standard way to call out product references, prices, and so on. Then the user's computer can read the retailer's

Web pages and automatically catalog what is available at a site. Another important initiative is the joint Electronic Payment Initiative JEPI), a standard for payments on the Web undertaken by the W3 consortium.

HOW AGENTS WILL CHANGE THE GAME

All of these initiatives will have a tremendous effect on our economy. Perhaps middlemen will be cut out, or new types of middlemen like the MoneySave escrow site will emerge. Because marketing is less expensive in this on-line environment, producers of goods, content, and services may grow in number. Agents will make it easier for businesses to find consumers who are interested in their products. This will reduce the capital required to set up a business and start selling products. This technology will make smaller niche markets viable by helping to identify that subset of consumers interested in a unique product. Finally, agents will spark diversity in the products, content, and services provided.

For businesses, this technology means the beginning of a new game. The on-line markets benefit the buyer more than the seller—they are buyer-centric. Increased competition and ease of comparison shopping will make prices fall. On the other hand, new efficiency in marketing and sales will reduce operating costs.

Agent technology will also encourage new developments in advertising and marketing. One example of this trend is reverse advertising— buyers advertising what they want, rather than re-tailers and marketers advertising to buyers. In addition, cartels, or aggregations of consumers, will develop more easily. For example, if a user's agent knows that the user wants to buy a Saab 900SE in the next month, the agent can communicate with the agents of other users who seek the same car in the same time frame. Thus agents will enable users to form consumer cartels, which can negotiate a lower price for a number of purchasers of the same product.

The new market will be tough on retailers, but retailers can't afford not to play by these new market rules. Even traditional businesses with strong market shares and established brands will be forced to play by these rules as more start-ups use agent technology to capture market share.

How can businesses respond to these challenges today? They can implement agent technology on their sites. They can provide several types of agents for their customers—agents that offer notifications, that make recommendations, that help customers choose among products. Businesses can also provide agents that build communities by introducing customers to others with similar tastes and profiles. The business benefits of agent technology are significant. Agents increase customer loyalty by offering personalized service. Agents increase sales. Studies of sites that have adopted this technology show that sales increase as a result. Customers who ask a site's agents to recommend products buy more than customers who don't use the site's agent technology. Agents provide continuous, detailed feedback about a business's products and customers. Agents allow businesses to produce and market products that are aimed at a narrower consumer base. Finally, agents gather information about user age, gender, preferences, and so on, which can be used for targeted advertisements.

Electronic markets will soon become ubiquitous. In these electronic markets, agents will act as brokers, automating much of the buying process. This change will create a market that is largely buyer centric. But sellers must learn to play this new game, because not playing will mean losing.

One of the 100 Most Influential Netizens, Pattie Maes is a research pioneer in the area of software agents, semi-intelligent computer programs that help users with information overload and the complexity of the on-line world. Dr. Maes's expertise spans electronic publishing, electronic commerce, human-computer interaction, artificial intelligence, and artificial life. An Associate Professor at MIT's Media Laboratory, she founded and currently directs the software agent group. She is also a former visiting professor and research scientist at MIT's Artificial Intelligence Laboratory. In addition, as founder of Firefly Network, Inc., Dr. Maes has helped to commercialize agent technology software. Frequently quoted in television and the popular press in this increasingly important area, Dr. Maes is an organizer of leading conferences on this topic.

An Internet Culture?: Implications for Marketing

Stef Nicovich
T. Bettina Cornwell

Abstract

The internet is explored in light of its ability to enhance cross-cultural communications. The internet exhibits many of the characteristics of a culture and as such can be used by marketers for enhancing meaning transfer between national cultures. We present the concept of a bridge culture as exhibited by the internet and discuss the implications of such a phenomenon for marketers in terms of interactive international communication.

> *Transport of the mails, transport of the human voice, transport of flickering pictures— in this century as in others our highest accomplishments still have the single aim of bringing men together.*
>
> Antoine de Saint-Exupéry (1900–1944)

INTRODUCTION

One of the most important issues facing marketers today is how to effectively compete in today's economy, and marketing professionals are realizing that the internet holds much promise as a means of facilitating direct customer, client and partner exchange. The internet, however, has yet to prove itself. The promise of internet commerce, while intriguing, has yet to fully develop. Because we tend to look at new technologies in terms of what *existing* technologies can do, the most common interest in the Internet comes from its adver-

tising and mass communications abilities (Peterson et al., 1997). Consequently, web sites now routinely support advertising banners in an attempt to apply the traditional rules of mass communication to this new medium. Savvier marketers, however, are exploring alternative, interactive technologies such as web phones and video conferencing, as well as more traditional technologies such as email and newsgroup postings, in an effort to foster more intuitive bidirectional, real-time communications. Marketers have been handed an exciting new tool with which to exercise their trade; while most companies seem content to just have a presence on the Web, few are exploring the full extent of the new technology and even fewer are focusing on its potential in cross-cultural communication.

As familiar as the internet appears to us now, it has elements that do not exist with any other type of communications vehicle. For example, it manifests properties that give it an almost lifelike quality, and this quality is what makes the internet so intriguing. There is no doubt that the internet is more than strictly a vehicle for communications; it has developed a social organism that is more than the sum of its parts. As Giese (1996) states, "While it might have been overlooked early on, the internet cannot now be ignored as a cultural phenomenon." (p. 51) What is this manifestation and how can we as marketers define it and understand it?

A first step into the scientific inquiry of a new phenomenon is the attempt to classify it in terms of existing knowledge structures and then to examine the implications of the, as it were, model fit. We have taken this approach here. The premise of this paper is that the internet exhibits a social mechanism, or society, definitive to itself, and that it can be used as a bridge for facilitating exchanges between different nationalities and cultures by relating to their common elements. The goal of this paper is to examine the internet in terms of its exhibited social elements, as well as the process of meaning transfer between societies and the implications of a social common ground, or bridge culture as presented by the internet for international interactive marketing activities.

THE NATURE OF THE INTERNET

One of the more intriguing elements of the internet has been its fantastic growth. The internet has exploded over the globe at a rate unheard of for any other technological advance. The internet's use of existing telecommunications infrastructures has quickly made it a truly global communications system. What was almost exclusively a U.S.-based phenomenon has expanded to the point where there are now more internet host sites outside than inside the United States (Friedman, 1996). The global nature of the internet, combined with the nature of the communications that it can convey, makes it a perfect vehicle for international interactive marketing.

While many attempt to mold the internet into a new form of mass communication, a few are realizing that the internet is a vastly different form of communications device that combines many of the elements of previous forms. The internet combines the real-time audio communications of the telephone and adds video capabilities, as well as text-based communications, to become a new, more interactive and intimate, medium. As with television, we view internet communications via a video delivery device that sits on our desk or tabletop. This device "broadcasts" information directly to our homes or offices; however unlike other broadcast media the internet also has a static component where the information that comes across does not change in real time (Web sites are by nature static and become animate only with extra effort on the part of the site provider). Another distinguishing aspect of the internet is its ability to create different environments in which we can experience new forms of reality. Members of the internet do not just communicate, they interact with a total environment. We can travel to other countries via cyber-

tours (http://homepages.ihug.co.nz/~denisg/nztour. htm), travel through cybermalls, and go shopping (http://vvww.majon.com). We can even leave the planet and view the sunset on Mars (http://users. redrose.net/constitution/default1.html). This type of cyberreality, combined with the one-to-one personal nature of the medium, makes for an extremely powerful device that has capabilities that we have not yet begun to explore. Since culture is a total environmental phenomenon, we feel that the internet's ability to create new "cyberworlds" lends itself well to examination vis-à-vis this perspective.

CULTURE

In order to understand the internet's social manifestations, it is necessary to understand the nature of culture and how it impacts the social context in which we communicate. Culture has been defined as "sets of learned behavior and ideas that human beings acquire as members of society. Human beings use culture to adapt to and to transform the world in which we live." (Schulz and Lavenda, 1995: 5) Culture can therefore be viewed as an artificial phenomenon devised by humans for the purpose of interacting with the environment.

The manifestations of culture are the institutions that are created to manage social relationships. These include family, language and communication, religion, government and politics, education, technology, society, and economic structures and activities (Baligh, 1994; Dunning and Bansal, 1997). These components are devised by society to facilitate generally accepted, learned, values, attitudes and beliefs. Culture, therefore, is a rather vague generic term that is made up of a host of interrelated components that impact our social interactions.

Three common threads run through these views of culture: (1) Cultures are learned; (2) Cultures serve as a barrier between members and something else; and (3) Cultures facilitate the social relationships between their members. To this extent society has been defined as ". . . a population or a group of individuals united by some common principle of principles." (Hoebel and Frost, 1996, p. 29) Hoebel further adds that societies exhibit identifiable boundaries, patterned and ordered relationships that are distinctive, culturally defined and limited, as well as bonded by common linguistic and symbolic representations.

The three common threads of culture discussed above equate very nicely with the three elements of a society as discussed by Hoebel and Frost. In order for cultures to be learned they must be communicated via a common social symbolic language. As a boundary between its members and something else, a culture exhibits barriers to entry that must be overcome, as well as impacting the social relationships within a society. It has been suggested that the proper method of examining a culture is in context of its parts or components (Baligh, 1994). This is the approach that we will use here; we will examine the Internet in terms of the "culturally impacted social elements" of identifiable boundaries, ordered relationships and common linguistic and symbolic representations.

THE SOCIAL NATURE OF THE INTERNET

Identifiable Boundaries

Traditional social boundaries have consisted of elements such as geographic locality, skin color, economic wealth, religious affiliation, and ethnic heritage. These visible distinctions are often used as a proxy for ascertaining these individuals' beliefs, attitudes and behaviors. These boundaries are often necessary in order to give definition, and thereby protection, to the group. The distinction of who is in and who is out is necessary in order to maintain the established community norms and beliefs. As such, community boundaries are often strongly established and defended in an attempt to reaffirm the center's position in the group (McMillan and Chavis, 1986; Schouten and

Alexander, 1995). The members of the intern_ pear to have a very firm understanding of who is _ member and who is not. This understanding, however, does not stem from traditional means of proxy delineation. It is impossible to ascertain skin color, economic status, or geographic locality just from casual interaction. Discourse with internet community members and agitators is the only way of determining community acceptance. This discourse between members is not only necessary but desirable in order to develop a sense of belonging, or community. The community boundaries that are set are reflections of group acceptance of views and discourse as well as the individual's psychological sense of community. A psychological sense of community refers to what extent members of a community actually perceive themselves to be members (McMillan and Chavis, 1986). The recent explosion of chat room participation on the internet appears to be a reflection of the growth in psychological community membership. Marketers have responded to community growth by adding extra rooms devoted to topics of interest. For example, many, sites including those of CNN (http://cnn.com/), ESPN (http://ESPN.SportsZone.com/) and the Wall Street Journal (http://interactive.wsj.com/edition/current/summaries/front.htm) now offer chat rooms that are geared toward specific topics of conversation. The Usenet newsgroups likewise are formed around topics of interest and conversation as well. These forums serve to inform the members of the community norms, attitudes and interests, at least to the extent that the vocal members of the community are representative of the community whole.

Similarity of understanding through learning is one of the culturally driven elements of a community. Members of a community agree, more or less, to certain ideals and are expected to abide by if not accept them. This can be seen with the internet and the recent attempts to make it conform to U.S. norms. Attempts to regulate the nature and form of the communications content that the internet carries have been stymied. For example, in

1996 the United States Supreme Court declared the Communications Decency Act unconstitutional (Quittner, 1996). The implication of this for marketers is that anyone who wishes to engage in any kind of exchange behavior via internet channels must understand and operate by its rules. This may be no easy task; witness the general disregard exhibited by members of internet society for e-mail and newsgroup advertising. The negative response to Sanford Wallace's junk e-mail solicitations for business opportunities and diet supplements was overwhelming (Sanchez-Klein, 1996). Similar outrage was exhibited toward two Phoenix-based immigration lawyers who posted information about their services to thousands of Usenet newsgroups in April 1994 (Wilder, 1996). Responses to these initial attempts at traditional direct marketing methods ranged from polite comments to the Usenet administrator to e-mail letter bombing the return address. Marketers who are not sensitive to the sociocultural boundaries of the Internet risk community backlash.

Ordered Relationship and Communication Flows

Cultures impact the social relationships that occur when any large group of individuals come into contact and institutions are typically created to perform this task. Perhaps the most visible institution for managing the relationships on the internet comes from the different domains in use there. As in traditional societies, institutional relationships are established to define functional needs: the internet has "created" domains in order to facilitate its communications exchanges. The traditional domain designations are .edu (educational facility), .gov (government institution), .net (network), .org (organization), and .com (company), with the .com designation experiencing phenomenal growth. There were over 400,000 .com domain names registered to U.S. businesses as of October 1996, a 37% increase over the previous three months

(Dickinson, 1996). Member sites of each domain have specific purposes for inhabiting the internet. Government sites trace their roots back to the old ARPAnet days when the internet was strictly a military tool for coordinational communication. Similarly, educational facilities used the internet for the development of military communications. This latter, however, grew into a general sharing of research not directly related to military needs. The last two domains were added in response to the increased commercialization of the internet. The two are separate based largely on the economic purpose of their organizations, profit as opposed to not for profit. Each subdomain has its own primary purpose for the communications it pursues on the internet. New domains are still being proposed and accepted, including country designations such as .uk for United Kingdom. As the internet grows and evolves these designations will evolve as well to support the needs of internet communications.

Distinctive delineations have been made in traditional marketing as to the linear nature of information flow. The two models are (1) the dyadic, bidirectional information flow of interpersonal communications used in direct selling and relationship marketing, and (2) the mass communications model of unidirectional information flow used in advertising, promotional, and to a large extent, traditional direct marketing techniques. Interpersonal communications is characterized by immediacy, true feedback to the communications cycle and knowing who the recipient of the communications is. The mass communications model is characterized by a lack of immediacy, proxy measure to determine feedback, and anonymity on the part of the recipient. It has been suggested that the internet is a new force that will merge many of the qualities of both of these models (Deighton, 1997). With the dynamic linking nature of the World Wide Web it is possible to produce mass and interpersonal communications at nearly the same time. One can produce original content for a web page and link it to others for their use as well as one's own. In this arena the distinctions between mass and interpersonal information flow becomes muddied. Indeed, the dynamic linking nature of the internet may broaden our conception of communication to include the idea of mass interpersonal communication. The Usenet newsgroups are a perfect example of how these two modes of communication are being blurred. They exhibit unidirectional mass communication that can be responded to in an interpersonal manner. A posting can be delivered to an individual or individuals. It can be responded to on an interpersonal basis by any who read it, yet it is available for mass consumption. The internet has some of the same fundamental concepts of ordered social relationships, as do traditional cultures; however, it also has special flow characteristics that mix the traditional elements of mass and interpersonal communication.

Common Linguistic and Symbolic Representation

As societies have evolved and become more complex, the language that they use has also become more complex. What was once a fairly simple method of communication for purposes of cooperation in hunting has become a very intricate system complete with its own formal rules and regulations. However, the symbolic nature of language has remained constant. Even from the earliest times language has been used as a representative for something else. Just as the cave drawings of early peoples symbolized life in the primitive community, combinations of pictures words, and sounds symbolize life in our modern communities. In order to understand the social meanings that surround us we must decipher the mode in which those meanings are communicated. Language is the prime channel for such meaning transfer.

Cultural institutions, therefore, can be understood as the manifestations of transferred meaning. Everything that we have developed can be viewed as coming about through the symbolic interpretation of ideas that have been communicated

through a community. This phenomenon has been explored through the ideal of the dialogic community (Arnold and Fischer, 1994). Arnold and Fischer state, "The community is characterized by a sense of collective identity and by voluntary participation in purposive social action. . . . Through dialogue the community collectively creates new understanding." (p. 57) Culture helps define generally accepted views of behavior, which are transferred throughout the community via symbolic communication. The goal of communication is the transference of meaning; a common language and context will facilitate this process, whereas different languages and contexts will inhibit it.

Culture and Meaning Transfer

As we have stated, culture and the social mechanisms that are derived from it are learned and language is the primary means of knowledge transfer. The internet, as a communications medium, is particularly sensitive to the mechanisms of meaning transfer. To this end, a brief examination of meaning transfer is in order; for this we draw upon Peirce's semiotic triangle. Peirce's views of semiotics "stresses the import of people, social institutions, and culture." (Mick, 1986) For Peirce, communication consisted of three elements, the object, its sign and an interpretant (Peirce, 1931–1956). Meaning is transferred through symbolic representations of an entity through the interpretation of the recipient. If the object is a physical entity such as an apple, then the process is relatively simple. The object is a piece of fruit, the sign is the word "apple;" the interpretant, however, will depend as much on the individual who is interpreting the sign as on the object. In this case, the interpretant may include color, flavor, and textural meanings. Thus, the interpretant varies with each individual. If the object of the sign, however, is a complex concept, the process is more complex, with a greater possible discrepancy between the object and the interpretant. As complexity is added into this system either in terms of language

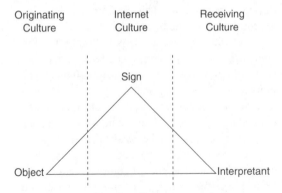

Figure 4-1 Meaning Transfer via the Internet through Peirce's Triadic Semiosos

translations or the sophistication and subtlety of the idea being communicated, the chances of a successful transfer of meaning become smaller. Meaning is transferred through a process of applying known meanings (interpretants) to new symbols (signs) in known contexts (cultures). It is in this manner that the Internet can facilitate the transference of meaning from one culture to another. By using the common society of the internet, a common context is established between two national cultures that is different yet affiliated with each.

It is important to note that the internet is not a culture proper, for it has no natural world with which to contend. This placelessness was termed *cyberspace* by the science fiction writer William Gibson in his 1981 novel *Neuromancer* (Giese, 1996). As a place without a place, the internet simplifies its cultural and social elements. If we accept the internet as a place with a distinct social mechanism, then what kind of a social environment does a place without a place have? We argue that the internet exhibits elements of a culture of occasion without measurement (McCracken, 1981). This statement needs some elaboration. The internet has its own elements of cultural occasion that are familiar to members, yet these elements are viewed in the context of measurement of each individual's home culture. The term measurement refers to the use of a known symbolic scale for

purposes of objective understanding. Each time meaning is transferred, it is related to the home cultural context. It is "measured" in terms of cultural understanding. Physical properties are absolute but the interpretant can become varied in its understanding. More subtle and complex scales of social and psychological constructs are more susceptible to miss communication. It is therefore necessary to examine the cultural and social elements of the internet with the understanding that all meanings will be understood in the context of the host culture of the recipient.

Time

All cultures exhibit perceptions of time. These perceptions will impact how we interact with others, both of the same culture as well as from different cultures. Perceptions of time as exhibited by societies include the linear-separable, procedural-traditional and circular-traditional models (Graham, 1981). The linear-separable model of time perceives time as linear and separated into the discrete compartments of past, present, and future. The circular-traditional model views time as a circular motion of events that repeat according to cyclical patterns. The procedural-traditional model perceives time as largely irrelevant; activities that occur are procedure-driven and not dependent on time factors. It is understandable that members of cultures with different perceptions of time will have difficulty in coordinating activities. What is less obvious is that different perceptions of time will affect the ability to transfer meaning between cultures as well. For example, the concept of interest and discounting money that is common in linear-separable cultures would be meaningless in a circular-traditional culture that views events as repeating.

Similarly, the internet exhibits a distinct perception of time. The internet exhibits a perception of time as "present" with limited reference to past or future. The immediacy of connectivity on the internet means that there is very little waiting involved compared with traditional modes of communication. As a result, there is less reason to "discount time" into the future. Time on the internet, however, is severely impacted by the passing of minutes. Since most internet providers charge by the time users spend money on-line, this time is usually carefully monitored. Since the Internet is user controlled, all events happen only when the user is logged on. All e-mail messages, all newsgroup communications, all web surfing happens during log-on time. Events that transpire during time when the user is not logged on do not really "happen"— that is, they are not experienced— until the user logs on. Similarly, it is the action of reading newsgroup postings, or the routine of receiving and reading e-mail every day that is part of the on line experience. In this manner the Internet exhibits nonlinear perceptions of time. Activities are important in cyclical and procedural ways. This means that the internet exhibits the characteristics of several perceptions of time and as such can aid in the transfer of meaning between cultures with different time perceptions.

IMPLICATIONS FOR MARKETERS

The basic focus of this paper has been the exploration of the internet as a bridge mechanism for the facilitation of meaning transfer between cultures. The question now must be asked, how can marketers benefit from such a communications channel? Marketers, in the spirit of the marketing-oriented company (Kohli and Jaworsky, 1990; Kohli, Jaworsky, and Kumar, 1993; Narver and Slater, 1990) must contend with three categories of communication, or information flow. Incoming communications that the company uses to develop an understanding of current and potential exchange partners, outgoing communications that inform potential and current exchange partners of the offerings that are available, and true bidirectional communications used for the purposes of servicing and generally engaging current and potential exchange partners.

Incoming Communications

The process of information gathering is critical to any business today. In this age of increased competition it is the company that best matches its offerings to its markets that stands the best chance of success. There have been complaints that the internet does not allow for the establishment of who exchange partners are in the "real world" and that measures of site effectiveness need to be developed (Hoffman and Novak, 1996). This seems to be contrary to the strengths of the internet. The internet allows the gathering information about attitudes, personality, and behaviors. This information is often freely given to companies when customers e-mail and request information about products. E-mail, newsgroup, and chat room exchanges can be analyzed for patterns of satisfaction and dissatisfaction among customers. In this manner a company can actually observe and analyze the process of word-of-mouth information flow. Furthermore, companies are now in a position to affect community discourse through the same channel. Traditionally, a company could only examine the relationship between the company and the customer; now the company can examine and impact the dynamics of the market community in relation to the company.

The internet can now deliver the types of information that marketers have only been able to obtain at great expense. We have traditionally relied on focus groups, interviews, and questionnaires for gathering such information as attitudes, motives, and personality; however we have not, to date, really been able to match this information to behavior. By examining the dynamic community around the company or industry this information can be obtained by recording and analyzing the discourse between members. For companies that distribute over the internet a direct relationship between what members discuss and what they exchange can be recorded and analyzed. Since the internet is an addressable form of communication (every participant has a unique IP address), it is possible to equate patterns of behavior to individuals. While many institutional computers have more than one user, it is possible to segregate users via a password either on log-in to the machine or for access to specific sites. In this manner it is possible to equate the opinions and attitudes of a person with purchase behavior, since the location of every transaction is recorded. This type of analysis will obviously benefit companies who distribute products and services over the internet as well as information.

In order for companies to gather the types of information they need to compete on the internet, new techniques and methods will most likely be needed that can gather this type of information. These techniques will be based on digesting large amounts of information in order to find patterns of interest. This type of research is already being applied in database mining and database marketing. The next step is to analyze this information, not for specific references to company name or product mentioned, but for patterns of attitude toward the products mentioned as well as mentions of purchase and use behavior. We will need to go beyond such traditional techniques as content analysis and key word frequencies to methods that will gather the subtler meanings exhibited in these communications. For marketers who communicate between national cultures, this type of understanding of subtle meanings, as expressed by exchange partners, becomes very important when designing goods, services, and communications for export.

Outgoing Communications

If the incoming information that can be gathered on the internet allows marketers to expand their understanding of their exchange partners, it follows that the outgoing information that is disseminated by marketers can be better formulated in order to form and maintain these exchange partner relationships. It is therefore a logical conclusion that the better the information that is gathered by a company, the better that company is able to meet

its customers needs. This logic is manifested in the product design process. Offerings on the internet must be communicated in light of the common context of the internet. Marketers must, therefore, design a product that will reflect the attitudes and views as exhibited by the dynamic community. Marketers can design a product that will reflect the attitudes and views exhibited by the dynamic community. For example, the community surrounding an industry will often have opinion leaders who will help formulate the opinions of the community as a whole. Traditionally, unless marketers could find and question these leaders, vital elements of attitude and behavior about the market would be missed. Due to the addressable nature of the internet, these opinion leaders are much easier to locate and target with the appropriate communications. It has been traditionally assumed that these opinion leaders have a discernible impact on the market; it is possible, however, that opinion leadership on the internet has less impact than has been previously thought (Smilowitz et al., 1988). The market may now become a self selected body of interested people who are actively forming opinions and may not be as susceptible to the impact of opinion leaders. Additionally, opinion leaders have been used by marketers as a proxy for measuring the greater market. The internet allows for a more accurate measurement of the market, so that the need for opinion leaders may again be reduced. A more accurate profile of the interested internet market should allow for better design of offerings. Doing so will provide a better match between company and customer.

One of the social mechanisms of culture is the development of economic institutions. The internet is in the process of developing such institutions for the purpose of commerce. The development of new forms of secure monetary transmission, such as e-cash and cybercash, is taking the risk out of purchasing products and services on the internet. A consistent monetary currency facilitates a business's ability to price its offerings. With the type of information that can be gathered now, a company's offerings can be based on its perceived value to the market, as opposed to the demographic ability of the market to support a certain price. In other words, market-based pricing decisions disappear. This is a two-edged sword for companies marketing on the internet. The ability to price according to perceived value will allow a company to consummate an exchange more effectively. The increased availability of information about substitute goods and competition means that the consumer is in a better position to compare competing offers. Companies that intend to compete on the internet will be forced to develop new methods of determining the value and consequently the price of their offerings.

Promotion

The promotional element of the marketing mix will need to cater to the cultural norms as exhibited by the market. Dynamic community views and attitudes will dictate to a large extent what type of promotional communications will be accepted and what will not. Some areas of the internet are less tolerant of advertising than others. There is still a vocal sentiment against advertising in the Usenet newsgroups and email, yet little outcry has been registered regarding advertising on sites on the Web. Similarly strong language appears to be accepted in the newsgroups as a normal mode of expression, yet posting messages to groups that have little to do with the topic of conversation seems to be dimly regarded (Nicovich, 1996). It is here that the traditional views of direct marketing come into conflict with the society of the internet. Direct marketers have traditionally relied on contacting as many people as possible in a target market in order to receive a small percentage of replies. This mass marketing distribution process appears not to fit with the internet culture. New methods for making contacts will need to be developed. These methods will need to contact users and elicit information without violating the norms exhibited

about commercial speech. The way to accomplish this is for marketers to become members of the communities in which they wish to communicate. In this manner, marketers will learn the social values and attitudes exhibited by the community as well as garner a greater appreciation of the communications they present.

Interactive Communications

The telephone has long been the standard tool for customer service. Dissatisfied exchange partners would use the phone in order to get immediate attention for a problem or to resolve a pressing issue. Technology is advancing to the point where the immediacy of the phone can be achieved by using web phone technology, and video conferencing will soon be able to enhance this ability. The impact, however, of electronic communication on customer service lies in the synergy of using computers for both communications and analysis. Customer information could be directly entered into customer databases from email and newsgroup information, bypassing manual entry. Similarly companies are now posting FAQs (Frequently Asked Questions) to newsgroups that answer the most common problems. This frees tip customer service representatives to handle more difficult problems.

The impact of the internet on customer service is profound, but perhaps of more importance is the impact the internet can have on negotiations. Seventy-two percent of U.S. companies interviewed stated that they used phone or telex with overseas suppliers for the purposes of negotiation (Min and Galle, 1993). It is not possible for the many details of a complex negotiation to be completed in the few days of face to face contact. The internet can provide a better proxy for negotiating the details than can either the phone or the fax. With the immediacy of real-time bidirectional communications and the context setting of a familiar culture, the finer points of a negotiation can be addressed with a greater chance for an equitable decision. Studies have indicated that the negotiation site can have an influence on the outcomes of the negotiation (Min and Galle, 1993). With a negotiation handled via the internet, this concern can be lessened due to the common, familiar context provided to all parties.

Marketers must be aware of the impact of time on the internet as it interfaces with different host cultures. Most notably, the members of the internet community are not always there. Since the members of the internet are only active when they are logged on, communication is not always as immediate as we would like. The internet lends itself well to asynchronous communications, such as e-mail and newsgroup posting. In order to coordinate between exchange partners, it is necessary to understand that time moves in jumps and spurts. Things happen quickly when all involved are logged on at the same time, and more slowly when they are not. Marketers must also realize that there is little difference between reading a chat room post live and a newsgroup post that has been up for some time. Both happen during log-on time and the only difference is in timing of reply. Until technology can advance enough to allow for more intuitive real-time communication, time perceptions as exhibited by the internet will continue to be largely nonlinear in perception and very linear in experience.

The internet will have an effect on all types of communications that a company uses: incoming, outgoing, and interactive. In all cases the increased understanding of the communicated message is a desired goal. The internet provides for a culturally consistent language that enhances the chances of the communicated message being understood. This is done through the use of jargon common to the internet. Terms such as "spam" (unwanted newsgroup or e-mail advertising) and "newbie" (someone who is new and not yet accepted by the community) appear to be commonly understood on the internet regardless of native tongue. Such common linguistic references increase the richness of meaning in the channel, and subtler and more complex messages may be transmitted.

Ethical Issues

When marketers attempt to send communications across cultural boundaries it is important to keep in mind the norms and attitudes of the receiving culture. Attitudes toward such issues as corruption and child labor in various countries have been well documented. Any marketer who attempts to cross cultural boundaries must be aware of these and a host of other issues. Newer to the marketing arena, however, is the issue of electronic privacy. What is permitted for a company to learn about its customers and what isn't will undoubtedly vary from one country to the next. Where does the internet fit into these discussions? The use of "cookies" to track the movement of internet users after they have left a site is already generating controversy. Is it possible to behave ethically on the internet and at the same time behave unethically in the larger culture and vise versa? For many cultures, junk mail is a fact of life that is tolerated if not accepted. In certain parts of the internet this practice is not tolerated and has been all but eliminated. If the internet does indeed have its own culture then we must argue yes. Yet at the same time the individuals who "inhabit" the internet also inhabit the larger culture of their perspective countries. The question of what behavior is acceptable on the Internet will be fought in the courts of this and other countries around the world. We as marketers can either wait and see what these rules will be or we can take a proactive stance and attempt to help mold and form what these rules will be, the choice is ours.

CONCLUSIONS

The internet has been given the status of a *deus ex machina* as the contraption that will save commerce and give businesses a new life in terms of increased profitability through electronic market expansion. In truth, the internet may prove to be just a new form of the telephone surrounded by hype and broken promises. It certainly has proved to be slower than expected in becoming the great cybermall. We, in marketing have traditionally viewed new technologies of communication in terms of previous ones and have lagged behind the technologies in coming to grips with their advantages and short comings (Deighton, 1997). The internet with its exhibited culture does appear to be an excellent channel of communication for cross-cultural meaning transfer. Direct marketers can use the internet to develop and maintain direct exchange relationships with customers and clients all over the world. In this manner, this new form of communication could very well lower the barriers to cultures that have traditionally been so hard to overcome. The use of the internet as a means of satisfying partner exchange needs is just starting to be explored and it will be sometime before we, as marketers, have exhausted all the possibilities.

Stef Nicovich is a doctoral student in the Fogelman College of Business and Economics at the University of Memphis, Memphis, TN.

T. Bettina Cornwell is a professor in the Fogelman College of Business and Economics at the University of Memphis, Memphis, TN.

REFERENCES

Arnold, S. J., and Fischer, E. "Hermeneutics and Consumer Research," *Journal of Consumer Research, 21,* (June 1994): 55–70.

Baligh, H. H. "Components of Culture: Nature, Interconnections, and Relevance to the Decision of the Organization Structure," *Management of Science, 40,* (January 1994): 14–27.

Deighton, J. Commentary on "Exploring the Implications of the Internet for Consumer Marketing," *Journal of the Academy of Marketing Science, 25* (4) (1997): 329–346.

Dickinson, M. "Businesses Continue Rush to Claim Web Sites," *Rochester Business Journal, 12, 27,* (1996): 1.

Dunning, J. H., and Bansal, S. "The Cultural Sensitivity of the Eclectic Paradigm," *Multinational Business Review,* 5, (Spring 1997): 1–16.

Friedman, M. "Net's Globalization Creating Tension," *Computing Canada, 22,* (July 18, 1996): 1, 4.

Giese, J. M. "Place Without Space, Identity Without Body: The Role of Cooperative Narrative in Community and Identity Formation in a Text-Based Electronic Community, dissertation." State College, PA: Pennsylvania State University, 1996.

Graham, R. J. "The Role of Perception of Time in Consumer Research," *Journal of Consumer Research, 7* (1981): 335–342.

Hoebel, E. A., and Frost, E. L. *Cultural and Social Anthropology,* 4th ed. New York: McGraw-Hill, 1976.

Hoffman, D. L., and Novak, T. P. "Marketing in Hypermedia, Computer-Mediated Environments: Conceptual Foundations," *Journal of Marketing, 60, 3* (1996): 50–68.

Kohli, A. K., and Jaworski, B. J. "Market Orientation: The Construct, Research Propositions, and Managerial Implications," *Journal of Marketing, 54,* 2 (1990): 1–18.

Kohli, A. K., Jaworski, B. J., and Kumar, A. "MARKOR: A Measure of Market Orientation," *Journal of Marketing Research, 30,* 4 (1993): 467–477.

McCracken, G. "Culture and Consumption: A Theoretical Account of the Structure and Movement of the Cultural Meaning of Consumer Goods," *Journal of Consumer Research, 13,* (June 1981): 71–84.

McMillan, D. W., and Chavis, D. M. "Sense of Community: A Definition and Theory," *Journal of Community Psychology, 14,* (1986): 6–23.

Mick, D. G. "Consumer Research and Semionics: Exploring the Morphology of Signs, Symbols, and Significance," *Journal of Consumer Research, 13,* (September 1986): 196–213.

Min, H., and Galle, W. "International Negotiation Strategies of U.S. Purchasing Professionals," *International Journal of Purchasing and Materials Management, 29,* 3 (1993): 41–50.

Narver, J. C., and Slater, S. F. "The Effect of a Market Orientation on Business Profitability," *Journal of Marketing, 54,* 4 (1990): 20–35.

Nicovich, S. G. "An Examination of the Internet Usenet Newsgroups as a Subculture of Consumption: Implications for Marketers." In Wilson, E. J., and Hair J. Jr., (Eds.) *Developments in Marketing Science, Proceedings of the Annual Conference of the Academy of Marketing Sciences,* 1996.

Peirce, C. S. "1931–1958" *Collected Papers.* In Hartshorn, C., Weiss, P., and Burks, A. W. (Eds.). Cambridge, MA: Harvard University Press, 1960.

Peterson, R. A., Balasubramanian, D., and Bronnenberg, B. J. "Exploring the Implications of the Internet for Consumer Marketing," *Journal of the Academy of Marketing Science, 25,* (1997): 329–346.

Quittner, J. "Free Speech for the Net," *Time* (June 24, 1996): 56.

Sanchez-Klein, J. "Meet the Most Hated Man on the Internet; Spamming on the Net, Sanford Wallace's Junk Mail Solicitations for Business Opportunities and Diet Supplements Are About as Welcome as a Virus," *Baltimore Sun,* (May 28, 1996): 1 D.

Schouten, J. W., and McAlexander, J. H. "Subcultures of Consumption: An Ethnography of the New Bikers," *Journal of Consumer Research, 22,* (June 1995): 43–61.

Schultz, E. A., and Lavenda, R. H. *Cultural Anthropology: A Perspective on the Human Condition.* Mountain View, CA: Mayfield Publishing, 1995.

Smilowitz, M., Compton, D. C., and Flint, L. "The Effects of Computer Mediated Communication on an Individual's Judgment: A Study Based on the Methods of Asch's Social Influence Experiment," *Computers in Human Behavior, 4,* (1988): 311–321.

Wilder, C. "How It All Began," *Information Week,* (August 6, 1996): 42.

An Investigation of Gender Differences in On-Line Privacy Concerns and Resultant Behaviors

Kim Bartel Sheehan

Abstract

This study examines whether gender differences are apparent in attitudes and behaviors toward advertising and marketing practices involving information gathering and privacy on-line. As part of a larger study, 889 internet users nationwide were surveyed using electronic mail. Results indicated that women and men differed significantly in their attitudes toward several practices, with women generally appearing more concerned about the effect the practice would have on their personal privacy. Additionally, the study found that men were likely to adopt behaviors to protect their privacy when they became concerned; women, however, rarely adopted protective behaviors. Implications for web advertisers are provided.

Recent estimates suggest that the internet is doubling in size every 100 days (U.S. Department of Commerce, 1998), with much of this growth fueled by the huge numbers of women who are engaged in on-line activities (Kehoe, Pitkow, and Morton, 1997). By some estimates, women account for almost half of all internet users (Garrubbo, 1998), and it is anticipated that women will account for 48% of on-line users by the year 2000. The percentage of women subscribing to the popular America Online network grew from 16% in 1994 to a majority of 51% in 1998 (Sukamar, 1998). As internet usage by both men and women continues to grow, it is becoming apparent that men and women

"An Investigation of Gender Differences in On-Line Privacy Concerns and Resultant Behaviors," Kim Bartel Sheehan, *Journal of Interactive Marketing*, © 1999 John Wiley & Sons, Inc. Reprinted by permission of John Wiley & Sons, Inc.

make use of the internet in distinctive ways. Differences have been seen in how men and women use the internet (e.g., Kehoe, et al., 1997; Roper Center, 1998), their on-line communication styles (e.g., Herring, 1993; Witmer and Katzman, 1997), and their purchasing habits (e.g., Kehoe, et al., 1997).

These current studies in gender differences on-line tend to be descriptive studies of proportions of men and women using specific internet applications. Studies of gender differences in on-line communication styles have primarily researched the interpersonal and social communication aspects of the internet and have been conducted in somewhat "social" settings such as chat rooms and newsgroups. Reactions by men and women to on-line marketing practices, including the collection and usage of information, are just beginning to be assessed. This study attempts to observe if gender differences are apparent in attitudes and behaviors toward marketing practices involving information gathering and privacy on-line, and, if so, to assess the strength of these differences.

REVIEW OF THE LITERATURE

Studies of the communication patterns of men and women indicate that gender differences in communication are clearly apparent. Men are seen as dominant, aggressive, competent, and persuasive in communication, while women are seen as passive, reticent, and cooperative (Regan Shade, 1993). Women choose language that is nurturing, expressive, and supportive, while men use language that is opinionated, reactive, and self-oriented (Pearson, 1985). Boys talk more than girls, men talk more than women, and men interrupt others more than women do (Pearson, 1985). These communication patterns are modeled and passed from one generation to another (Kramarae and Taylor, 1993).

The advent of the internet, though, suggests an opportunity for communication that would minimize these gendered behaviors. The internet presents both men and women with the opportunity to express ideas in a way that transcends their biological bodies (We, 1993). The internet has been described as a place where women can be released from the "prison of appearance" (We, 1993). However, recent studies of on-line communication indicate this gender-free potential is not coming to fruition. Numerous differences between the sexes in orientation to computers and their use have been seen in the past decade, differences which in turn appear to influence on-line language and behaviors.

GENDER AND COMPUTER USAGE

To many individuals, the stereotypical image of a "computer nerd" is that of a Dilbert-like man who has a closer relationship with his computer than with other human beings. Studies show that this stereotype holds somewhat true in that men are more interested than women in many computer applications, including the internet, on-line services, interactive information and entertainment, and virtual reality (Roper Center, 1998). Turkle (1988) suggests that the computer has no inherent gender bias, but computer culture is socially constructed as male. For example, men are more interested than women in experimenting and playing with technology (Roper Center, 1998). As previously mentioned, fewer women than men use the internet: in a 1997 survey by Kehoe, et al. about 40% of on-line users were women. Interestingly, from preschool through third grade, girls spend more time on home computers than do boys (Find/SVP, 1998). Girls and boys view computers differently, with girls viewing computers as compact, flexible communications machines, and boys seeing computers as fast, powerful weapons and entertainment machines (Brunner and Bennett, 1997). Girls' interest in computers appears to wane between grades four and seven. By the time they reach high school, girls use computers about two hours a week less than boys.

This fall-off in usage by high school girls may eventually limit the total number of women who go on-line (Find/SVP, 1998). Additionally, it has been argued that equivalent usage of the internet by men and women may be impossible for socioeconomic reasons (Truong, 1993). Since women's average incomes are lower than those of men, women have less disposable income for computers, modems, software, services, and phone charges (Truong, 1993). Additionally, women's responsibilities in society demand that they juggle many different areas of their lives so that they do not have the time necessary for many to learn about new technologies such as the internet (DeBare, 1996).

Once on-line, men and women use the internet differently. Men spend about two hours more per week on-line than women (Roper Center, 1998). Men are slightly more likely than women to use on-line services and e-mail (Kehoe et al., 1997). More men than women have web pages, and men read and post to newsgroups more frequently than women (Kehoe et al., 1997). Men are also more likely than women to use home computers for personal business such as banking (Roper Center, 1998). More men than women are likely to purchase products on-line (Briones, 1998).

Women are more likely than men to form personal relationships on-line (Parks and Floyd, 1996) and women view community as an important reason for going on-line (Femina, 1996). One indication of this is the success of a New York–based internet service iVillage. This service repositioned itself in 1997 its a "woman-oriented" site, and has since seen an 88% increase in membership (Kuchinskas, 1998). Services like iVillage and Hearst Publishing's HomeArts page offer connections to information and issues that interest women, such as health, career management, and relationships. Women's sites tend to integrate various aspects of women's lives, where men's sites tend to be more focused on a single aspect (Teicholz, 1998).

GENDER AND ON-LINE COMMUNICATION

Differences are seen in communication patterns of men and women on-line that are similar to off-line patterns. Traditionally, women's communication consistently is involved with maintenance of social and emotional group process roles, and men consistently perform task-oriented roles (Savicki, Lingenfelter, and Kelly, 1997). Regan Shade (1993) found that women on-line engage in a *rapport* style of communication on-line while men engage in a *report* style of communication. The rapport style encourages community building and places a high value on the wants and needs of others (Ferris, 1996). Herring (1993) described this as a *supportiveness* style: characterized by expressions of appreciation, thanking, and other activities that make other participants feel welcomed into the environment. Women are more focused on positive interaction on-line than men (Ferris, 1996) and women adopt an *attenuation* style that includes hedging, expressing doubt, and apologizing (Herring, 1993). In contrast, men tend to be more adversarial on-line (Herring, 1993). The report style tends to be factual, and assigns greater value to freedom from censorship, forthright and open expression, and agnostic debate (Ferris, 1996). While women may view this adversarial style as rude, men might think otherwise (Herring, 1993).

Regarding the use of language on-line, research has found that men swear more than women on-line and women use more "emotions," such its "smileys"— :-) (Ferris, 1996). Gurak (1995) believes that the rhetorical purpose of these symbols is to deflect from the seriousness of a woman's argument or point. She compares this to the verbal practice adopted by many women of ending statements with question-mark inflections, a practice that takes away from the emphatic nature of a statement. While men and women both report a dislike of sending highly negative messages to others on-line (a practice known as *flaming*), women expressed a stronger dislike of flaming than men (Herring, 1994). Women are also less likely than men to start or continue "flame wars"(Herring, 1994). However, Witmer and Katzman (1997) found that men do not use more challenging language than women, nor do they flame more often than women.

The lack of a physical presence on-line might suggest that women would be less likely to experience some types of communication problems encountered in face-to-face communication; e.g., men not listening to women, men negating women's opinions, or men interrupting women when they are speaking (Herring, 1994). However, this is not always the case. Kramarae and Taylor (1993) found that in almost any open network, men monopolize the talk, and Herring (1994) suggested that men occasionally stifle women's voices on-line. Women's on-line contributions are often ignored, downplayed, or criticized (Herring, 1994). In newsgroups, topic choices are predominantly "male" (Ferris, 1996). In newsgroups, men post more frequent and longer messages than women and tend to ignore postings by women (Herring, 1994). Additionally, women experience on-line sexism: many women have reported harassment in chat rooms (DeBare, 1996) and Femina (1996) reported that 26% of women report being sexually harassed on-line. Sutton (1996) has characterized participation in newsgroups, for women, as equivalent to "walking down a city street in a short skirt" (p. 171).

Others have suggested that computer-mediated communications actually improve communication between men and women (e.g. Selfe and Meyer, 1991; We, 1993). We (1993) found, for example, that women and men communicate more easily on-line than face-to-face. Additionally, we found that men interrupt women less often on-line than in face-to-face conversations, and that both men and women are less aware of gender when communicating on-line. Truong (1993) found that some women purposely choose gender-neutral identities on-line to safeguard their ability to speak freely.

INTERACTIVITY AND PRIVACY

Beyond the scope of interpersonal communication on-line, research suggests that there are some gender differences in terms of advertising and marketing communications. Men are more likely than women to purchase products and services on-line than women (Briones, 1998; Kramarae and Taylor,

1993). More men than women say they don't care whether a site maintains a customer profile about them (Kehoe et al., 1997). Men are also less concerned about women in regards to entities selling information that has been collected on-line (Kehoe et al., 1997). Women tend to be more cautious than men when they make on-line purchases, and women tend to require that on-line entities maintain an off-line presence (like a retail store) before they purchase their products and services (Kehoe et al., 1997).

These findings, then, suggest that women may be more concerned than men about information-gathering and their privacy on-line. There is some evidence that there are similar concerns about these issues in off-line communication. Survey data indicate American women are highly concerned about threats to the privacy of their medical, insurance, and financial information (Westin, 1997). More women than men were "very concerned" about threats to privacy today (58% of women compared to 53% of men). Westin (1997) found that these strong privacy concerns of American women were a driving force behind an unprecedented wave of state privacy laws in 1997, which addressed a wide range of privacy issues such as confidentiality in handling of medical records, limiting telemarketing calling hours, and controlling third-party access to driver's license information. Specific to information gathering and direct marketing, however, Nowak and Phelps (1992) found that concerns about threats to personal privacy did not vary between sexes. They also found that the propensity of individuals to request removal from a mailing list did not correlate with gender, indicating that perhaps no gender differences exist in the actions men and women take to protect their privacy in direct marketing contexts. In the on-line context, Kehoe, et al. (1997) found that women are more concerned about privacy than men, and that more women than men feel that new laws are needed to protect privacy on-line. Women are more likely than men to provide false information to web sites, therefore attempting to protect their privacy on-line (Kehoe et al., 1997).

PURPOSE OF THE STUDY

The literature addresses interpersonal communication on-line (through newsgroups, chat rooms, and the like) and broad-based concerns about consumer privacy issues. However, there are few studies investigating gender differences in perceptions of specific marketing communications and practices on-line as well as what behaviors men and women can adopt in order to protect privacy. The purpose of this study, then, is to move beyond the current investigations of the social contexts of the internet to the commercial context and investigate gender differences using a national sample of on-line users.

Understanding gender differences is important given that on-line commerce is growing very quickly; by the year 2000, it is estimated that every US adult will be spending $350 a year on-line (CyberAtlas, 1998). Since women account for about 70% of consumer spending off-line, it is likely that in order for cyberconsumerism to succeed, women need to feel confident in their on-line activities and protection of privacy there. As on-line advertisers and marketers provide information and request the same from both men and women on-line, understanding the attitudes towards these practices will assist advertisers in determining proper policies for the web sites.

This study asks two key research questions:

1. Are there differences in women's and men's concerns with privacy and marketing activities that involve collection of information?
2. Are there differences in women's and men's responses to marketing activities that involve information gathering?

METHODOLOGY

Overview

To investigate the research questions, an e-mail survey was sent to 3,724 individuals whose e-mail addresses were randomly generated using the Four11 directory service (http://www.four11.com). The 889 completed surveys constitute a 24% response rate and provide a nationally representative sample of on-line users. The survey included questions that assessed privacy concerns with various on-line marketing-related scenarios, as well as computer usage, and demographic information

Sampling Procedure

The sampling frame consisted of individuals with personal e-mail addresses who could be identified via the Four11 Directory Service, a global directory of 15 million names and e-mail addresses (www.four11.com). The Four11 search engine allows a search of an individual's e-mail address based on completing some or all of the following search fields: name, city, state/province, country, or domain name of the ISP. The search field used to generate e-mail addresses for this study was "domain name." Thirty-five domain names were systematically selected from Network USA's Internet Service Provider Catalog, which is a comprehensive on-line list of commercial personal ISPs in the United States organized by state and area code. Every sixth service provider was selected for inclusion on the list resulting in representation of all regions of the country. No duplicate providers were selected.

When only a domain name is supplied, the Four11 search engine provides either a complete list of entries (if less than 200 people subscribe to the ISP) or a randomly selected sample of 200 names and e-mail addresses within that domain (if there were more than 200 entries). A random sample of provided addresses was used for the current study.

Survey Measures

Fifteen statements were presented reflecting scenarios that represented three different levels of predicted privacy concern (low, moderate, high)

for each of five different dimensions that influence privacy concern (awareness of data collection, information use, information sensitivity, familiarity with entity, and compensation for information provided). These were derived either from previous studies of privacy in the off-line context (Nowak and Phelps, 1992) and adapted for the online environment, or from pretests of available measures (see Table 4.1 for scenarios). These 15 statements were presented in random order. The respondents were instructed to consider each statement from the point of view of an individual using the internet for personal (as opposed to business) use. They were then asked to indicate their level of privacy concern for each scenario using a seven-point bipolar scale with 1 (not at all concerned) to 7 (highly concerned) as endpoints. The use of the word "concern" to measure privacy has been used in similar research (Nowak and Phelps, 1992; Sheehan and Hoy, 1997; Sheehan and Hoy, 1998). Respondents were profiled in terms of computer usage and demographics. The demographic section concluded the survey and measured gender, age, education, household income and state of residence.

Survey Administration

One week before the survey was distributed, each prospective sample member received a solicitation e-mail, which described the study and invited the individual to participate. This technique is frequently used in traditional mail surveys to enhance response rates and secure cooperation, but is imperative in the on-line environment due to concerns with "spam" and other mail issues. The e-mail solicitation provided potential respondents with the opportunity to respond via e-mail to indicate that they did not wish to receive the survey. Individuals who did not respond received the e-mail survey along with instructions on how to reply via e-mail and an assurance of confidentiality. If the respondent had not returned the e-mail survey within one week, a reminder e-mail was sent

TABLE 4.1	Practices and Behaviors Assessed

Practices

You receive e-mail from a company you recently e-mailed.

You receive e-mail from a company you currently do business with.

A company requests your e-mail address only to send information of interest.

You register for a web site with e-mail address and receive a discount.

You receive e-mail from a company whose web page you visited in the past.

You register for a web site with e-mail address and are entered in a contest.

You receive e-mail about a new product from known company you don't do business with.

You provide your name to access home page.

You register for a web site with e-mail address and receive a mousepad.

Information about you is used by other divisions of a company you patronize.

You receive e-mail from a company you've never heard of.

You provide names of newsgroups read to access home page.

You receive e-mail and having no idea how the company got your address.

Information about you is sold to other companies.

Behaviors

Register for web site
Provide inaccurate information
Provide incomplete information
Read unsolicited e-mail
Notify ISP about unsolicited e-mail
Request removal from mailing list
Send highly negative response ('flame')

along with another copy of the survey. Because return e-mail can include the sender's e-mail address, it was possible to identify individuals who had not yet responded and to insure that there were no duplicated responses.

Two pretests of the procedure involving a total of 350 selected e-mail addresses revealed a 25% undeliverable e-mail rate, a 14% decline rate and a completed survey response rate of 23%. A target sample size of 864 was set, and therefore (assuming a 23% response rate) 3,756 viable e-mail addresses would need to be solicited. To compensate for estimated undeliverable e-mail solicitations and replacement of individuals who declined to participate, 5,000 e-mail addresses were selected. Actual administration of the solicitation and survey showed an undeliverable rate of 26%, a decline rate of 12% and a completed survey rate of 24%.

Of the 889 respondents, 622 (70.0%) were male, 259 (29.1%) were female, and eight (0.9%) did not provide their gender. Table 4.2 provides demographic and computer usage profiles of both male and female respondents. Demographically, the male and female respondents were similar in their ages (about 40% of both men and women were under the age of 30) and their household incomes (56% of men and 54% of women had incomes under $60,000). Men were somewhat better educated than women, with 62% of men having a bachelor's degree or higher and 56% of women attaining these levels (chi-square = 9.078, $p = .028$).

As seen in other studies (e.g. Kehoe et al, 1997; Roper Center, 1998), men and women differed in their computer usage habits. Men have been using computers longer than women (12.34 mean years for men, 10.90 mean years for women, $t = 3.07$, $p = .0022$). Men go on-line more often than women, with men going on-line during 11.3 days out of the past fourteen and women going on-line during 9.67 days out of the past fourteen ($t = 5.15$, $p = .0001$). Women spent more time on the computer for their personal use at home (77% of their on-line time, compared to 71.5% for men), where men spent more time on the computer for their personal use at work. Both men and women check their e-mail frequently, with 88% of men and 83% of women checking e-mail at least once per day.

TABLE 4.2	Demographics of Respondents			
Descriptor	**Men**	**Women**	**Value**	**Prob.**
Age				
18–24	17%	16%		
25–34	26	23		
35–44	25	32		
45–54	21	19		
55–64	7	8		
65+	4	1	9.17[a]	.102
Education Level Attained				
High School	38%	44%		
Bachelors	40	38		
Masters	15	15		
Doctorate	7	3	9.078[a]	.028
Household Income				
Less than $20K	5	7		
$20K to $39.9K	21	24		
$40K to 59.9K	30	26		
$60K to $79.9K	20	23		
$80K to 99.9K	13	13		
$100K or more	10	9	3.259[a]	.660
Adopt Personae				
Yes	31%	23%		
No	69	77	5.353[a]	.021
Check E-mail				
Several times/day	67%	61%		
Once/day	21	22		
Several times/wk	10	14		
Once/wk	2	2		
Less often	0	1	4.804[a]	.308
Place of use (% of time)				
at home	71.48%	77.03%	−2.21[b]	.0275
at work	23.84	16.35	3.38[b]	.0008
at school	3.48	5.86	−1.78[b]	.0752
at other locations	1.17	0.74	0.91[b]	.3601
Years Using Computers				
(mean)	12.34	10.90	3.07[b]	.0022
Number of Days Online				
(in past 14 days)	11.30	9.67	5.15[b]	.0001

[a]Chi-square value.
[b]T value.

RESULTS

Concerns with Privacy

The first research question asked whether women's and men's concerns with privacy and marketing activities differed. For each of the fifteen situations provided to respondents to assess, mean scores for women and men were calculated (each situation was assessed using a 1 to 7 scale, where 1 = not a concern and 7 = extremely concerned). The mean scores of women's and men's responses were compared for each situation (Table 4.3). Five of the fifteen situations generated significant differences among women and men in terms of their concerns about their own privacy in the given situation. In these five situations, women's concerns with their personal privacy was higher than the men's.

Of the five situations predicted to cause a low level of concern, one situation generated significantly different responses between women and men: the situation where the respondent received

TABLE 4.3 Gender Differences in Situations				
Situation	**Men**[a]	**Women**[a]	**T**	**Prob > |t|**
Situations predicted to cause a low level of concern				
You receive e-mail from a company you recently e-mailed.	1.93	1.84	.8687	.3699
You receive e-mail from a company you currently do business with.	*2.04*	*2.24*	*−1.87*	*.0609*
A company requests your e-mail address only to send information of interest.	2.12	2.22	−0.91	.3655
You register for web site with e-mail address and receive a discount.	3.36	3.56	−1.47	.1410
You provide your name to access home page.	4.02	4.04	−0.14	.8876
Situations predicted to cause a moderate level of concern				
You receive e-mail from a company whose web page you visited in the past.	3.43	3.54	−0.71	.4770
You register for web site with e-mail address and are entered in a contest.	3.64	3.75	−0.72	.4723
You receive e-mail about a new product from known company you don't do business with.	*3.61*	*3.88*	*−1.78*	*.0755*
A notice on a web site informs you that information about you is used by other divisions of a company you patronize.	*3.98*	*4.41*	*−3.09*	*.0020*
You provide names of newsgroups read to access home page.	4.57	4.45	.73	.4623
Situations predicted to cause a high level of concern				
You register for a web page with e-mail address and receive a mousepad.	4.08	4.19	−.73	.4611
You receive e-mail from a company you've never heard of.	*4.10*	*4.42*	*−1.99*	*.0471*
You receive an e-mail and having no idea how the company got your address.	*4.60*	*4.95*	*−2.19*	*.0284*
A notice on a web site informs you that information about you is sold to other companies	5.66	5.63	.27	.7842
You provide your Social Security Number to access home page.	6.82	6.86	−.77	.4364
Total Concern	47.18	48.57	−1.25	.2215

[a] 1 = not a concern, 7 = extreme concern.

an e-mail from a company with which they currently did business. Given this situation, women and men both felt a relatively low level of concern. The mean level of concern for women was 2.24 (on a 1 to 7 scale, where 1 = not at all concerned and 7 = extremely concerned). Men's mean level of concern was 2.04, significantly lower than that of the women ($t = -1.87, p = .0609$).

Of the five situations predicted to cause a moderate level of concern, two generated significantly different levels of concern for women and men. The situation in which individuals received e-mail about a new product from a known company with which the respondent currently does not do business generated a mean level of concern of 3.88 for women and 3.61 for men ($t = 1.78, p = .0755$). Additionally, the situation where information about the respondents being used by other divisions of a company patronized by the respondent generated a mean level of concern of 4.41 for women and 3.98 for men ($t = 3.09, p = .0020$).

Of the five situations predicted to cause a high level of concern, two situations generated significantly different levels of concern for women and men. Receiving an e-mail from a company the respondent had never heard of generated a mean level of concern of 4.42 for women and 4.10 for men ($t = 1.99, p = .0471$). Receiving an e-mail and having no idea of how the company got their address generated a mean level of concern of 4.95 among women and 4.60 among men ($t = -2.19, p = -.0284$).

Given that five of the fifteen situations generated significantly higher levels of concern about privacy for women than men, it seems appropriate to suggest that women are sometimes more concerned about their privacy on-line than men. Some similarities can be seen across the five situations where women appear more concerned than men about their privacy. Women seem more concerned about unsolicited e-mail, regardless of its origin, than men. Women also appear more concerned about secondary usage of information than men. In several situations, these two concerns are related: that is, e-mail was received and the respondent could not clearly tell how the entity sending the

mail found their address. One way that the address could be generated would be through on-line entities selling their address lists with other entities. This secondary usage, then, resulted in the respondents receiving e-mail and not being able to identify how the sender found their name. As Westin (1997) pointed out, women were responsible for a large number of state privacy laws that addressed confidentiality and control of specific types of information (e.g., medical records and driver's license information). Women evidently are also concerned about sharing of types of information beyond merely medical information and drivers license information; it is possible that the sharing of different types of information also causes concern for women.

Kehoe et al (1997) found that women are more cautious when it comes to shopping online, and often require an off-line presence in addition to an on-line presence. In this study, women may be expressing this caution when they indicate a higher level of concern with unsolicited contact by entities. For several situations, the women were unfamiliar with the entity sending the mail. It is not known if they were aware that the entity had an off-line presence. It could be that women as a group are simply more uncomfortable with entities with which they are unfamiliar than men. This, then, suggests that women feel relationships with entities are very important for on-line commerce relationships. This is not surprising, given that women view building communities as an important part of their social on-line behavior (Ferris, 1996). Therefore, women view the commercial and social realms of the internet similarly; that is, they view building relationships as important in both realms.

Gender Differences in Behaviors

The second research question asked if there were differences between women's and men's responses to marketing activities that involve information gathering. To address this question, a new variable was created called *total concern*. This variable sums each of the concern scores for the 15 situations (Cronbach's alpha for this new variable is .92). The total concern scores ranged from 15 to 105. A score of 15 would reflect an individual for whom none of the situations caused concerns about privacy. A score of 105 would reflect an individual for whom *every* situation caused extreme concern with privacy.

The total concern score was then correlated with each of the seven behaviors measured in the survey. The survey asked each individual to indicate the frequency with which they adopted seven behaviors on-line: reading unsolicited e-mail, requesting removal of their name from mailing lists, informing ISPs about unsolicited e-mail, sending a 'flame' message, registering for web sites, providing inaccurate information when registering for web sites, and providing incomplete information when registering for web sites (Table 4.4). When correlated with total concern, the correlation coefficient can assess whether persons with higher concern about privacy are more or less likely to adopt specific behaviors. A comparison of men's and women's responses to questions about frequency of adopting behaviors and this correlation with total concerns is found in Table 4.5.

The mean total concern score was 58.35 for men and 60.00 for women; the difference between these mean scores is not significant ($t = -1.12, p = .2622$). However, propensity to adopt behaviors in

light of this privacy concern indicates significant differences. As women's concern increased, they exhibited a propensity to adopt only two of seven measured behaviors. As men's concern with privacy increased, their propensity to adopt all seven behaviors to protect their privacy also increased. Each of these behaviors will be discussed in turn.

Reading unsolicited E-mail

Women and men both reported that they read unsolicited e-mail slightly less than half of the time they received it, with women's mean frequency (3.89, where $1 =$ never and $7 =$ always) significantly higher than men's (mean frequency for men $= 3.40, t = -3.23, p = .0013$). Women's propensity to read unsolicited e-mail did not change based on changes in their total concern with privacy. As men's total concern with privacy increased their propensity to read unsolicited e-mail decreased (correlation coefficient $= 14\ r = .0018$).

Notifying ISP about Unsolicited E-mail

Women and men both reported that they rarely notified their internet service provider about unsolicited e-mail, with men providing notification more often than women (mean frequency for men $= 1.91$, for women $= 1.41, t = 4.94, p = .0001$). For both men and women, increases in total concern with privacy resulted in increases in the frequency

TABLE 4.4　**Frequency of Adopting On-line Activity**

Activity	Men[a]	Women[a]	T	Prob > |t|
Provide incomplete information when registering for web sites	3.51	3.92	−2.46	.0138
Read unsolicited e-mail	3.40	3.89	−3.23	.0013
Register for web sites	3.08	3.39	−2.32	.0203
Request removal from mailing lists	2.89	2.66	1.40	−.1608
Provide inaccurate information when registering for web sites	2.13	2.12	0.03	.9768
Notify ISP about unsolicited e-mail	1.91	1.41	4.94	.0001
Send a 'flame' message to those sending unsolicited e-mail	1.49	1.65	−1.39	.1644

[a] 1 = never, 7 = always

TABLE 4-5	Correlations between Activities and Total Concern						
	Men			Women			
Activity	Mean Freq[a]	Correlation Coefficient[b]	R	Mean Freq[a]	Correlation Coefficient[b]	R	T
Read unsolicited e-mail	3.40	−.14	**.0018**	3.89	.07	.2950	−3.23[c]
Notify ISP about unsolicited e-mail	1.91	.32	**.0001**	1.41	.21	**.0017**	4.94[c]
Request removal from mailing lists	2.89	.17	**.0002**	2.66	.02	.7582	1.40
Send a 'flame'	1.49	.22	**.0001**	1.65	−.08	.2258	−1.39
Register for Web site	3.08	−.22	**.0001**	3.39	−.22	**.0007**	−2.32[c]
Provide incomplete information	3.51	.21	**.0001**	3.92	−.06	.3968	−2.46[c]
Provide inaccurate information	2.13	.16	**.0011**	2.12	−.07	.2485	0.03

[a] 1 = never, 7 = always
[b] Correleated with total Concern.
[c] Significant at .05.
[d] t test of mean frequencies for men and women

of notifying ISPs about unsolicited e-mail (for women, correlation coefficient = .21, $r = 0017$; for men, correlation coefficient = .32, $r = .0001$).

Requesting Removal from Mailing Lists

Both women and men occasionally requested removal from mailing lists (mean frequency for women = 2.66, for men = 2.89; no significant difference between the two means). As women's total concern with privacy increased, their frequency of requesting removal from lists did not change. As men's total concern with privacy increased, their frequency of requesting removal from lists also increased (correlation coefficient .17, $r = .0002$).

Sending a Flame

Both women and men reported that they rarely sent "flame" messages (mean frequency for women = .65, for men = 1.49; difference in means is not significant). The frequency of women sending

flames did not vary with increases in total concern with privacy. As men's total concern with privacy increased, the frequency that they sent a flame also increased (correlation coefficient = .22, $r = .0001$).

Registering for Web Sites

Both women and men occasionally register for web sites, with women registering somewhat more often than men (mean for women = .339, for men = 3.08; $t = 2.72$, $p = .0203$). For both women and men, the frequency of registering for web sites decreased as their total concern with privacy increases (correlation coefficients for both women and men = .22, $p = .0007$ for women and $p = .0001$ for men).

Providing Incomplete Information

Both men and women reported providing incomplete information about half of the time that they registered of web sites, with women providing incomplete information more often than men (mean frequency for women = 3.92, for men = 3.51, $t = -2.46, p = .0138$). Women's propensity to provide incomplete information did not change as their concern with privacy increased. As men's privacy concerns increased, the frequency that they provided incomplete information increased (correlation coefficient = .21, $r = .0001$).

Providing Inaccurate Information

Both men and women occasionally provided inaccurate information when registering for web sites (mean frequency for women = 2.12, for men = 2.13; differences are not significant). The likelihood of women providing inaccurate information did vary with increases in their total concern with privacy. Men were more likely to provide inaccurate information as their total concern with privacy increased (correlation efficient = .16, $r = .0011$).

This analysis suggests that there are several significant differences between women's and men's behaviors on-line, even without regard to privacy concerns. Women more frequently read unsolicited e-mail and register for web sites than do men. This indicates that women are more likely to comply with certain activities that entities wish them to do. Again, this could be a reflection of women's attempts to create a community with minimal animosity on-line. Of the other behaviors, it was apparent that men notify ISPs about unsolicited e-mail more often than women and women provide incomplete information more often than men. With this, we can see a reflection of the aggressive and passive dichotomy on-line. Men more frequently complain, which is an aggressive, confrontational behavior. Women more frequently provide incomplete information, which is a passive behavior in that they aren't directly confronting another entity with their dissatisfaction. Instead, they are avoiding a confrontation by limiting the amount of information that they give out instead of refusing to give out the information altogether. This dichotomy is further seen in the correlation analysis.

The results of the correlation analysis suggest that men are much more likely to react to privacy concerns with some type of confrontational behavior (like complaining to entities) than women. The correlation analysis also indicated that women take much less aggressive actions when faced with privacy concerns than men. It is again evident that men are much more active when it comes to protecting their privacy: the more concerned they are, the more frequently they adopt an entire range of behaviors in order to address privacy concerns. Women, however, differ considerably in their reactions. Of the behaviors measured, only two behaviors changed when privacy concern increases: women are less likely to register for web sites and more likely to contact their ISP. Both of these actions avoid direct confrontation with the entity that is causing the concern.

The indication that men adopt a wider range of behaviors is similar to findings regarding men's behavior in interpersonal or social communications. In interpersonal communications on-line, men tend to be adversarial and are not as concerned about positive interactions than women (Ferris, 1996). This gender difference also seems to be apparent in their approach toward marketing communications. The passiveness of women may be related to their tendency to be supportive rather than adversarial and more focused on positive interactions (Ferris, 1996). Women do not seem to appear to want to offend entities that they may find offensive.

Off-line, men and women tend to be similar in their complaining behavior (Speer, 1996). Off-line, research has indicated that men and women both take time to complain when they feel connected to the particular entity with which they have a complaint. Instead of searching for a replacement (i.e., another store with which to do their business), both men and women will try to make the entity perform the way they believe it should perform (Speer, 1996). This does not seem to be the case with on-line users. This may be due to a lack of information in the study about the relationship between on-line user and entity. Since the questions in this study did not indicate whether the respondent had a relationship with the entity that sent the e-mail or required registration, it could be that the respondents assumed a relationship did not exist, and were responding to the questions based on this lack of relationship. Perhaps if women had relationships with the e-mail senders or web page owners, they would have responded differently.

Discussion and Implications

In order for the advertisers and marketers to successfully develop commerce, it seems imperative that women be comfortable and confident in their on-line transactions, The findings of this study should raise a red flag to on-line advertisers and marketers. Research has already shown that currently women are less likely than men to shop on-line (Kehoe et al., 1997). Given that there are certain activities that cause women higher levels of concern than men, it could be that this concern will limit the potential for women to participate in on-line marketing and advertising activities. If women are concerned about unsolicited contact and sharing of information, they may be likely not to wish to transact business on-line. This could limit the effectiveness of the internet as an advertising and marketing communication vehicle in the future.

The fact that women are adopting few behaviors that protect or safeguard their privacy on-line should raise concerns among on-line advertisers and marketers. Research (Speer, 1996) has shown that those people who do not complain directly to an offending entity instead tend to complain about the entity to their friends, family and acquaintances. Given the evidence of women's need to develop communities on-line, some of women's communication to develop communities may be alerting others to sites with inappropriate web practices. Additionally, this passivity on the part of women makes it simply more difficult for web content providers to determine what constitutes appropriate behavior when dealing with women on-line. Without even knowing they are acting in-

appropriately, on-line advertisers and marketers may be limiting their own potential.

One solution may be for web content providers who have minimal communication with women to partner with other entities that are endorsed by women. These could be web sites that are clearinghouses for women's issues and interests (such as Women's Wire) or sites that have both an on-line and off-line presence that is acknowledged to be appropriate for women (for example, Hearst Publishing's HomeArts web site). These partnerships not only can lend some credibility to the entity among women, but they will also allow entities to learn about the wants and needs of women who use on-line services and are interested in their types of offerings. Web advertisers must try to find out how both men and women feel about their own privacy and information collection policies before the policies are implemented. Additionally, advertisers need to determine how the rapport/report orientation of the genders affects how they will communicate with their customers on-line. Given that both men and women seldom adopt any behaviors to denote their dissatisfaction with practices that on-line entities undertake, entities must not assume that "no news is good news." It may be in the best interest of advertisers to investigate the communication patterns of their customers in an off-line environment, when men and women are not involved in a particular task and may be more willing to discuss the best way to create on-line relationships.

Conclusion

Despite the opportunity for both men and women to adopt gender neutral personalities on-line, or even to choose to be anonymous on-line, there appear to be gender differences in on-line communication and behavior styles in both the social and the commercial contexts. This study has indicated that women are more concerned than men about their personal privacy in several types of information gathering situations. Even though women appear somewhat more concerned than men, men are more likely than women to change their behavior on-line in the face of privacy concerns. Men appear to adopt a range of behaviors in reaction to privacy concern, both active and passive, while women adopt primarily passive, nonconfrontational behaviors when faced with privacy concerns.

This study has several limitations. First, it used correlation to determine the relationship between privacy concern and behaviors. Since correlation does not imply causation, further study specifically examines whether privacy concern causes the changes in privacy. Additionally, the response rate of 23% may raise issues regarding nonrespondents and whether responses are skewed. Research must be done to determine if there are ways to influence or increase these response rates.

This study indicated a similarity between communication and behavior in the social and commercial realms on-line. Future research can explore whether individuals draw strong distinctions between these realms or whether there is a blurring on-line of different contexts. This research could also explore gender differences in communications with known or unknown entities in different contexts on-line (e.g., social, commercial, research, business, education). Finally, this study suggests that further research into complaining behavior on-line should be attempted. This research can look at the different outlets that on-line entities have for complaining and which outlets they adopt in which situations.

As more and more individuals go on-line, it has been predicted that the on-line universe will mirror the off-line universe (Kehoe et al., 1997). This study has begun to explore whether this prediction is accurate, and an initial assessment indicates that on-line and off-line contexts are different. In the near future, the similarities and the differences between the on-line and off-line universes should become more apparent.

Kim Bartel Sheehan is with the School of Journalism and Communication, University of Oregon.

REFERENCES

Briones, M. "Online Retailers Seek Ways to Close Shopping Gender Gap," *Marketing News,* (September 14, 1998): 2.

Brunner, C. and Bennett, D. "Technology and Gender: Differences in Masculine and Feminine Views," *NAASP Bulletin, 81,* (592) (1997): 46–52.

DeBare, I. "Women Lining Up to Explore On-line." *Sacramento Bee,* http://www.sacbee.com/news/projects/women/wconline.html, 1996.

Femina. @Cybergrrl electronic survey, http://www.femina.com/, 1996.

Find/SVP. On-line web page, http://www.finds-vp.com, 1998.

Garruboo, G. "What Makes Women Click?" *Advertising Age,* 69 (5) (1998): 12a.

Gurak, L. J. "On Bob, Thomas, and Other New Friends: Gender in Cyberspace," *Computer Mediated Communication Magazine,* 2 (1995): 2.

Herring, S. "Gender and Democracy in Computer-Mediated Communication," *Electronic Journal of Communication,* 3 (1993): 2.

Herring, S. "Gender Differences in Computer Mediated Communication: Bringing Familiar Baggage to the New Frontier," keynote talk. "Making the Net *Work*: Is There Gender in Communication?" panel discussion. American Library Association annual convention, Miami, June 27, 1994.

Kehoe, C., Pitkow, J., and Morton, K. Eighth WWW User survey [on-line web page]. http://www.cc.gatech.edu/gvu/user_surveys/survey-1997-04/, 1997.

Kramarae, C. and Taylor, H. J. "Women and Men on Electronic Networks: A Conversation or a Monologue?" In C. Kramarae (Ed.). *Women, Information Technology, and Scholarship.* Urbana, IL: Center for Advanced Study, University of Illinois at Urbana-Champaign, 1993.

Kuchinskas, S. "It's a Woman's Web." *Brandweek,* (September 17, 1998): xx.

Nowak, G. J. and Phelps, J. "Understanding Privacy Concerns: An Assessment of Consumers' Information Related Knowledge and Beliefs." *Journal of Direct Marketing,* 6 (4) (1992): 28–39.

Parks, M. R. and Floyd, K. "Making Friends in Cyberspace." *Journal of Communication,* (1996): 46.

Pearson, J. C. *Gender and Communication.* Dubuque: William C. Brown Publishers, 1985.

Regan Shade, L. "Gender Issues in Computer Networking." Talk presented at Community Networking: The International Free-Net Conference, Carleton University, Ottawa (August 1993): 17–19.

Roper Center for Public Opinion Research. On-line web page. http://www.ropercenter.uconn.edu, 1998.

Savicki, V., Lingenfelter, D., and Kelly, M. "Gender Language Style and Group Composition in Internet Discussion Groups." *Journal of Computer Mediated Communications,* http://www.ascusc.org/jcmc/vol2/issue3/, 1997.

Selfe, C. and Meyer, P. "Testing Claims for Online Conferences." Written Communication, 8 (1991): 162–192.

Sheehan, K., and Hoy, M. "Warning Signs on the Information Highway: An Assessment of Privacy Concerns of Online Consumers." Presented at the Association for Education in Journalism and Mass Communications Annual Conference, Chicago, August 2, 1997.

Sheehan, K., and Hoy, M. "Privacy and Online Consumers: Comparisons with Traditional Consumers and Implications for Advertising Practice." Presented at the 1998 American Academy of Advertising Conference, Lexington, KY, March 28, 1998.

Speer T. L. "They Complain Because They Care," *American Demographics* (May 1996).

Sukamar, R. "Managing the Marketplace: Netting the Better Half," *Business Today,* (October 10, 1998): 156.

Teicholz, N. "Women Want It All, and It's All Online," *New York Times* on the Web, http://archives.nytimes.com/archives/, October 22, 1998.

Truong, H. "Gender Issues in Online Communication," BaWIT, http://bawit-request@cpsr.org., 1993.

Turkle, S. "Computational Reticence: Why Women Fear the Intimate Machine." In C. Kramarae (Ed.). *Technology and Women's Voices.* New York: Routledge Kegan Paul, (1988): 41–61.

U.S. Department of Commerce. "The Emerging Digital Economy" [on-line document]. http://www.ecommerce.gov.emerging.htm, 1998.

We, G. "Cross-Gender Communication in Cyberspace," unpublished manuscript, Simon Fraser University, 1993.

Westin, A. "Privacy and American Business Study" [on-line web page]. http://shell.idt.it/p̄ab/women.html, 1997.

Witmer, D. and Katzman, S. "Online Smiles: Does Gender Make a Difference in the Use of Graphic Accents?" *Journal of Computer Mediated Communication* [on-line journal]. http://www.ascuse.org/jcmc/vol2/issue4/witmer1.html, 1997.

CHAPTER

5

INTERNET MARKETING COMMUNICATIONS

Expenditures on Internet marketing communications continue to skyrocket year after year. According to the Internet Advertising Bureau, online advertising spending has increased from $267 million in 1996 to over $4.5 billion in 1999. Already, advertising on the Internet exceeds that of outdoor advertising.

Yet, advertising is just one form of Internet marketing communications. Internet web sites are often called upon to perform critical customer support and communication functions. Corporate web sites are also emerging as the most important vehicle through which to launch public relations initiatives. Of course, corporate web sites are also used in direct e-mail promotion and multichannel marketing campaigns.

In the past, web sites informed visitors how the firm operates in the offline world. Now, web sites show visitors how the firm operates in both the online and the offline worlds. In this sense, web sites are advertisements for the firm and the firm's products and services.

As individuals visit a web site, attitudes may be formed or changed on the basis of the navigation experience. Only a small percentage of those who visit will likely become serious leads and/or new customers for the firm. However, it is from these "converts" that the firm may generate new profits and loyal customers over time. In this sense, Internet marketing is similar to direct marketing in that the offer and creative must be tailored to maximize the probability that targeted prospects or visitors will buy the firm's products.

In this chapter, important research concerning Internet marketing communications is presented. In the first reading, researchers Qimei Chen and William D. Wells show how consumers' "attitude toward the site" can be measured. In addition, Chen and Wells show how multidimensional factors correlate with this construct. Chen and Wells' research offers important guidelines to Internet marketers wishing to improve web site quality.

In the second reading, Bill Harvey shows how the classic ARF model can be expanded to incorporate the Internet. According to Harvey, advertising on the web can be explained in a hierarchical manner consistent with other media. In addition, Harvey addresses weaknesses associated with the original ARF model.

In the third reading, Rex Briggs and Nigel Hollis report results of an experiment that tested the effect of one banner advertisement on consumer attitudes. According to results, banner ads can have a significant effect on attitudes even for established

mature brands. Their results suggest that banner advertising has economic value even if consumers do not click-through to the sponsoring site.

Finally, in the fourth reading, Xavier Drèze and Fred Zufryden detail the results of several experiments that call into question the reliability of Internet reach and frequency measures. These researchers note that the identification of unique visitors (reach) and exposures (frequency) is problematic given the nature of Internet technology. Their results may explain the growing reliance on sponsorships, affiliate marketing, and other non-exposure-based advertising models.

Please visit the textbook's web site for additional resources.

Qimei Chen
William D. Wells

Attitude toward the Ad (A_{AD}) is widely used in studies of traditional mass media advertising. As e-commerce becomes more important, Attitude toward the Site (A_{ST}) will gain parallel status in evaluating effectiveness. In this study, we develop and present a reliable and valid scale that measures Attitude toward a Website (A_{ST}). We then develop and present additional scales that provide more detailed information. Reasons for high and low evaluations are discussed and illustrated.

The year 1998 saw a breakthrough for electronic commerce—buying by modem. This development not only changed the nature of holiday shopping but the face of retailing itself. *Newsweek* (December 1998) quoted Amazon.com founder Jeff Bezos as calling 1998's Christmas a "Web Christmas" instead of a "White Christmas." According to Jupiter Communication (*Newsweek*, December 1998), almost 17 million people purchased something from a website in 1998, up from 10 million in 1997 and 5 million in 1996. Observers predicted that within a decade, "mouse clickers will eclipse catalog buyers" (*Newsweek*, December 1998). The actual growth of online retail is even faster than expected. According to the Boston Consulting Group, the revenue from online sales is likely to top $36 billion by the end of 1999, more than double 1998's total (*Marketing News*, August 16, 1999).

Of course these developments beget competition. In 1998, approximately a million-and-a-half new web pages appeared each day, and many of them were ineffective (*Ventures,* January 1999). Internet advertisers now need to wonder whether their communications will be noticed and accepted.

Marketing News (November 1998) reported that new media research firms hope to grow rich by inventing an industry standard for measuring responses to web pages. Although many approaches have been proposed, chaos presently exceeds agreement (Krauss, 1998; *Marketing News*, July 1998; November 1998).

The most obvious parallel to evaluating web advertising is evaluating traditional mass media advertising. Although researchers have devoted much attention to this topic, no single system is preeminent. However, one approach—measuring Attitude toward the Ad (A_{AD})—has proved useful in applied and academic settings (Shimp, 1981; MacKenzie, Lutz, and Belch, 1986; Baker and Lutz, 1988; Brown and Stayman, 1992). It therefore seems likely that as the Internet becomes more important, Attitude toward the Site (A_{ST}) will prove useful for similar purposes. Hence, this paper presents a practical, reliable, and valid scale that measures Attitude toward the Site (A_{ST}) and gives examples of its applications.

Academic and applied researchers have also found that a single measure of Attitude toward the Ad does not convey all the information in consumers' ratings of advertisements (Schlinger, 1979; Pashupati, 1994). It therefore seems likely that dimensions that correlate with Attitude toward the Site will yield insights into surfers' reactions. After describing development of an Attitude toward the Site (A_{ST}) scale, we present and discuss three scales that profile more detailed dimensions.

ATTITUDE TOWARD THE SITE (A_{ST})

Although some marketers initially regarded the Internet as quite measurable (Gibson, 1997), many soon realized that "web surfers are getting harder to measure" (Taylor, 1997). They came to understand,

Reprinted from the *Journal of Advertising Research,* © 1999 by the Advertising Research Foundation.

for instance, that the once popular click-throughs approach might well be distorted by online robots that imitate human surfers. In response to these technical limitations (ARF, 1995, 1996; Chen, 1996), some academic researchers focused on counting reach and frequency (Leckenby and Hong, 1998). This development increased the need to find a way to assess individual website effectiveness.

Previous research on Attitude toward the Ad (A_{AD})—a "predisposition to respond in a favorable or unfavorable manner to a particular advertising stimulus during a particular exposure situation" (MacKenzie, Lutz, and Belch, 1986)—has shown that A_{AD} is an indicator of advertising effectiveness. In a well-known study sponsored by the Advertising Research Foundation, Haley and Baldinger (1991) found that how well viewers liked an ad was the best single predictor of sales effects. Aaker and Stayman (1990) found that A_{AD} was the best single effectiveness index. Shimp (1981), Batra and Ray (1986), and MacKenzie, Lutz, and Belch (1986) found that A_{AD} influences brand attitudes and

purchase intentions. Brown and Stayman (1992) provide an integrated review of this evidence.

By analogy, we assume that Attitude toward the Site (A_{ST}) will be an equally useful indicator of site value. In this study, we emphasize web surfers' predispositions to respond favorably or unfavorably to web content in natural exposure situations.

Method

Scale Items

One way to measure Attitude toward the Site (A_{ST}) would be to employ one or more bipolar rating scales patterned after the "evaluative" factor of the semantic differential (Osgood, Suci, and Tannenbaum, 1957). Indeed, many of the studies cited above used good–bad," "like–dislike," and "nice–awful" to measure affective responses to advertisements.

However, a website can be good or bad in specific ways. It can be easy or difficult to use, it

---

The following items assess your general favorability toward the website you just visited. Circle the number that best indicates your agreement or disagreement with each statement.

	Definitely disagree				Definitely agree
This website makes it easy for me to build a relationship with this company.	1	2	3	4	5
I would like to visit this website again in the future.	1	2	3	4	5
I'm satisfied with the service provided by this website.	1	2	3	4	5
I feel comfortable in surfing this website.	1	2	3	4	5
I feel surfing this website is a good way for me to spend my time.	1	2	3	4	5
	One of the Worst				One of the Best
Compared with other websites, I would rate this one as	1	2	3	4	5

Figure 5-1   Six Ways to Measure Attitude toward the Site (A_{ST})

can be active or passive, or it can make a positive or negative impression of the sponsoring company. Accordingly, we asked a sample of experienced web users how they would describe "good" and "bad" websites. Consensus developed around the expressions shown in Figure 5-1: "makes it easy for me to develop a relationship with the company"; "would like to visit this website again in the future"; "satisfied with the service provided"; "feel comfortable in surfing the website"; and "surfing the website is a good way to spend my time." These specifics accompanied and enriched more general evaluations.

In this context, one important question would be: Do these various ways of operationalizing Attitude toward the Site (A_{ST}) all tap into the same latent dimension, or do they measure two or more independent aspects of evaluation? To answer that question, we asked judges to use these six expressions (see Figure 5-1) to rate 120 websites chosen to represent the corporate and institutional (not personal) website population. If the six expressions in Figure 5-1 all tap into the same latent evaluative dimension, sites that score high on one of them should also score high on all the others. On the other hand, if the expressions shown in Figure 5-1 tap into two or more separate evaluative dimensions, correlations among them should fall into unique patterns. Note that our purpose at this point was to assess correlations among the expressions, not to compare individual websites with each other.

Site Pool

The websites came from three sources: (1) *The Internet Source Book—The Executive's Guide to the Internet/Intranet World* (High-Tech Media, 1998); (2) experts' recommendations—in this case the experts were Information Decision Science department faculty members in the Carlson School of Management; and (3) web users' recommendations of sites they most like and most dislike to surf. The objective here was to obtain a pool of corporate and institutional (not personal) websites that would vary greatly in user evaluation.

Judges

Each website was evaluated by three judges using the items shown in Figure 5-1. The judges were experienced website users, both in industry settings and for personal entertainment and information. Seventy-two were MBA and undergraduate students at the Carlson School of Management, University of Minnesota; forty-eight were undergraduate students at the University of Kentucky.[1]

Again, the purpose at this point was not to evaluate the individual websites but to determine whether the items shown in Figure 5-1 all tap the same dimension. If the expressions in Figure 5-1 all tap into the same latent evaluation dimension, they would correlate highly with each other. If they did not correlate highly, two more evaluative dimensions would be indicated. Each judge rated three websites over a period of one week. Three hundred and sixty usable judgments were collected.

The A_{ST} Scale

The three judges' evaluations of each website were averaged to eliminate between-judge variance. Bivariate correlations among the mean ratings are shown in Table 5.1. These correlations are all strong and positive, suggesting the presence of a single latent evaluative dimension.

To further test unidimensionality, we factor analyzed the items. All six items loaded on one factor that accounts for 73 percent of the matrix variance. Coefficient Alpha (Cronbach, 1951) of the six-item scale was .92, and no item deletion significantly increased reliability. These findings, together with the overt semantic meaning of the six items, enhance confidence that the six items in the aggregate tap a single latent evaluative dimension—Attitude toward the Site (A_{ST}).

---

[1]JAR's policy is not to publish research that depends entirely on student samples. In this case, however, the purpose was methodological—instrument development—rather than normative, and the judges were web users in industry and personal settings, as well as students. Future work with new sets of judges will be reported in this journal.

TABLE 5.1 Correlation Matrix	Q1	Q2	Q3	Q4	Q5
Q1. This website makes it easy for me to build a relationship with this company.					
Q2. I would like to visit this website again in the future.	.62				
Q3. I'm satisfied with the service provided by this website.	.71	.61			
Q4. I feel comfortable in surfing this website.	.67	.60	.84		
Q5. I feel surfing this website is a good way for me to spend my time.	.63	.78	.58	.55	
Q6. Compared with other websites, I would rate this one as (one of the worst–one of the best).	.68	.73	.70	.68	.73

Note: The correlations are all statistically significant at the .01 level (2-tailed).

Interpretation of the A_{ST} Scale

One way to understand the meaning of A_{ST} scores is to examine differences among sites that scored high, medium, and low on this measurement. To create A_{ST} scores, we averaged each site's scores on the six items listed in Table 5.1 and divided by .05 to convert the average to scores that could range from 20 to 100. Table 5.2 lists websites that received high A_{ST} scores (80 or higher on a 20 to 100 scale), medium A_{ST} scores (58 to 60), and low A_{ST} scores (40 or lower). The purpose here is to gain some understanding of the meanings of high and low A_{ST} scores, not to assert that a score produced

TABLE 5.2 A_{ST} Scores of Selected Websites					
URL	A_{ST}	URL	A_{ST}	URL	A_{ST}
Highest A_{ST} scores (80)		*Medium A_{ST} scores (60)*		*Lowest A_{ST} scores (40)*	
dell.com	96	uhc.com	60	Low site S	40
toysrus .com	91	cisco.com	60	Low site T	40
chicagocubs.com	90	erahome.com	60	Low site U	39
amazon.com	90	gsnetworks.com	60	Low site V	38
norwest.com	88	qeb.com	58	Low site W	35
abcnews.com	87			Low site X	27
musicblvd.com	87			Low site Y	27
pillsbury.com	86			Low site Z	24
umn.edu	86				
bettycrocker.com	84				
disney.com	80				
ticketmaster.com	80				
channel4000.com	80				

by three judges can be generalized to the entire web user population.

Among the websites that received high A_{ST} scores, dell.com represents a high technology business; toysrus.com and disney.com represent children-oriented marketers; amazon.com and musicblvd.com sell entertainment products (books, CDs, etc.); pillsbury.com and bettycrocker.com offer cooking ideas and recipes; chicagocubs.com is a sports site; norwest.com, ticketmaster.com, and channel4000.com are service sites; abcnews.com is a news broadcasting site; and umn.edu is an institutional site. This diversity of content indicates that a high A_{ST} score can come from many different content areas and that a website can earn a high A_{ST} score even when its content is not completely congruent with judges' interests.

Among websites with low A_{ST} scores, Low site S is in the car business; Low site T provides archived historical information; Low site V conducts online auctions, Low site X aims to introduce Asian films, while Low site Y reports political events. Thus, low-scoring websites also differ greatly in content, and a site can earn a low A_{ST} score even when its content is congruent with judges' interests. Ironically, three of the lowest-scoring sites (U, W, and Z) represent "online publishers," "consultants," or "eAgents" who claim to be able to help their clients generate attractive web presentations.

As a group, the judges regarded the lowest-scoring websites as doing a poor job of building relationships with the audience, being too boring to visit again, being frustrating to deal with, and a waste of time and effort. A more detailed diagnosis of high and low A_{ST} scores will be presented later.

BEYOND OVERALL EVALUATION

While it is important to know a site's A_{ST} score, it is also important to know the underlying perceptual dimensions that contribute to and account for that evaluation. As Siegel (1998) noted, commercial web design is an exciting and noble undertaking yet is fraught with pitfalls. Websites with low

A_{ST} scores suffer from these pitfalls, and it is important to understand the reasons. Hence, in the second part of this study, we developed some explanatory dimensions.

Theoretical Foundation

Previous researchers created scales that provide useful ratings of print advertisements and television commercials (Wells, 1964a, 1964b; Leavitt, 1970; Schlinger, 1979; Aaker and Bruzzone, 1985; Aaker and Stayman, 1990; Pashupati, 1994). Figure 5-2 gives an overview of the dimensions that emerged from these investigations.

The present study provides a similar analysis of a new medium. It attempts to generate a set of rating scales that account for overall evaluation.

Item Pool

The rating form that included the items shown in Figure 5-1 also included 141 adjectives that could be used to describe websites. The following paragraphs detail the ways the adjectives were selected.

We started with adjectives that have been used to describe human personality. To select these adjectives, we began with the widely accepted "Big Five" personality dimensions (Norman, 1963; Tupes and Christal, 1958; McCrae and Costa, 1989). This well-embraced paradigm includes: Negative Emotionality, Extraversion, Openness, Agreeableness, and Conscientiousness. Approximately six adjectives represented each of these dimensions.

To address the possibility that the "Big Five" might not be sufficiently comprehensive, we added adjectives that describe other aspects of human personality: Sexuality (Buss, 1996), Attractiveness (Henss, 1996; Saucier, 1997), Negative Valence (Tellegen and Waller, 1987; Benet and Waller, 1995; Almagor, Tellegne, and Waller, 1995), Narcissism, Thrift, and Humor (Saucier and Goldberg, 1998). Two or three adjectives represented each of these dimensions.

A website is also a brand carrier and an extension of the sponsoring organization's operations

Wells (1964)	Leavitt (1970)	Wells, Leavitt, and McConville (1970)	Schlinger (1979)	Aaker and Bruzzone (1981)	Moldovan (1985)	Aaker and Staymen (1990)	Pashupati (1994)
Attractiveness	Energetic/ Amusing	Humorous	Entertaining	Entertaining	Stimulating	Amusing/clever	Entertainment
Meaningfulness	Personal relevance	Relevant	Relevant	Relevant	Clear	Informative/ Effective	Cognitive/ Utilitarianism
		Irritating	Alienating	Irritating	Tasteless	Irritating/silly	
	Sensual	Sensual	Empathetic	Warm	Empathetic/ self-involving	Warm	
	Familiar		Familiar			Familiar	Executional distinctiveness
					Credible	Believable	
Vitality		Vigorous				Dull	
		Unique				Lively	
		Brand reinforcing	Brand reinforcing				

Figure 5-2   Ad Perception Factors across Studies

(Palmer and Griffith, 1998). From work on brand and corporate personality (Marineau, 1957; Vitz and Johnson, 1965; Dolich, 1969; Ackoff and Emsoff, 1975), we borrowed five dimensions: Sincerity, Excitement, Competence, Sophistication, and Ruggedness, with each represented by two to four adjectives (Aaker, 1997). These additions increased the item pool to 78.

We were still concerned that some important features of websites may not be captured by either human personality or brand personality. Palmer and Griffith's (1998) model (see Figure 5-3) prompted us to address basic marketing functions as well as technical characteristics. We therefore asked 63 web users to list adjectives that specifically describe characteristics of websites they regularly visit. We also asked them to consider one website they liked and one website they disliked and describe the differences between them. After eliminating duplications, 63 adjectives were added to the adjective pool. This procedure produced a pool of 141 adjectives for scale generation.

The Dimensions

The judges who rated the 120 websites on the A_{ST} scale items also rated these sites on the 141 adjectives, using a 5-point Likert scale that ranged from "not at all applies" to "very much applies." A choice of "not applicable to any website" was also provided. Adjectives that more than 10 percent of the judges said were "not applicable to any website" were deleted. This procedure decreased the item pool to 76.

Since our objective was to develop scales that would correlate with A_{ST}, we computed correlations between the A_{ST} score and each of the remaining 76 items. Eleven items did not correlate significantly ($p < .01$) with A_{ST} and were eliminated. This procedure reduced the pool to 65 adjectives that correlated significantly with overall website evaluation.

We then factor analyzed the mean scores that each of the 120 websites received on each of these 65 items, using an eigen value of 1.00 as the stopping criterion. Use of mean scores eliminated the variance due to differences among individual judges and left variance across websites as the determinant of the factor structure (Schlinger, 1979). Principle component analysis with Varimax rotation yielded 11 factors. The first three factors explained 54 percent of the matrix variance (see Table 5.3). The remaining factors accounted for no more than 4 percent each. Because we were most interested in locating a small number of major factors, we dropped the eight minor factors from further consideration.

For clarity of presentation, we reversed the signs of the items that loaded on Factor 3. Hence, Factor 3—Organization—consists of four items: (not) messy, (not) cumbersome, (not) confusing, and (not) irritating.

Discussion of the Explanatory Dimensions

In previous work on consumers' evaluations of television commercials and print advertisements, two factors—entertaining/amusing and informative/

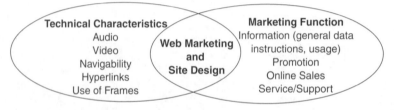

Figure 5-3   Emerging Web Marketing Model
Source: Palmer and Griffith, 1998

TABLE 5.3	**Three Main Factors**				
	Factors				
	1	**2**	**3**	**Alpha**	**Variance Explained**
Factor 1: Entertainment				.92	36%
Fun	.87				
Exciting	.82				
Cool	.81				
Imaginative	.78				
Entertaining	.78				
Flashy	.77				
Factor 2: Informativeness				.94	13%
Informative		.85			
Intelligent		.84			
Knowledgeable		.81			
Resourceful		.78			
Useful		.77			
Helpful		.75			
Factor 3: Organization				.84	5%
Messy			−.78		
Cumbersome			−.78		
Confusing			−.76		
Irritating			−.74		

relevant—always seemed to emerge. Website-flavored versions of two factors reemerged as dominant factors in users' evaluations. This finding supports Krauss's (1998) prediction that the future of Internet advertising will look a lot like today's television advertising since, fundamentally, advertising is about controlled message delivery and persuasion. The dimensions found here reflect consumers' main requests in net surfing.

Factor 1: Entertainment

The "Entertainment" factor was best defined by six adjectives (Alpha = .92): fun, exciting, cool, imaginative, entertaining, and flashy. These terms are similar but not identical to terms that loaded high on an "entertaining" dimension often found in raters' evaluations of TV commercials, e.g., merry, amusing (Wells, Leavitt, and McConville,

1971); "lots of fun to watch," "clever and quite entertaining" (Schlinger, 1979); and fast, held attention, and interesting (Moldovan, 1984).

To create scores on this factor, we averaged sites' ratings on the six adjectives and again divided by .05 to produce scores that could range from 20 to 100. Examination of sites that score high on this factor shows that different sites achieve high Entertainment scores in different ways. The Chicago Cubs site (E score = 89) emphasizes exciting and cool aspects of baseball games. Pillsbury and Disney sites (E score = 84 and 86, respectively) use highly imaginative characters. The Disney site is flashy and fun to watch while the Pillsbury site evokes the feeling of cute and entertaining by using the Pillsbury Doughboy icon.

Previous academic research suggests that a high E score is likely to be a valuable advantage.

Stern (1990) found that consumers who regard an advertisement as "entertaining" are more likely to credit the brand with positive attributes and are more likely to intend to purchase the brand. In these cases, the websites position themselves as fun sites, and their Entertainment scores reflect the extent to which they successfully embody this dimension.

Factor 2: Informativeness

The Informativeness factor is best defined by: informative, intelligent, knowledgeable, resourceful, useful, and helpful (Alpha = .94). This factor resembles the Informative/Relevant scales that have emerged in previous studies of print advertisements and TV commercials. However, while TV-based Informative/Relevant scales focus on terms like "meaningful," "worth remembering" (Wells, Leavitt, and McConville, 1971), "convincing," and "valuable" (Leavitt, 1970), the website Informativeness factor focuses on the site as an interactive provider. Specifically, "intelligent," "resourceful," and "knowledgeable" fit websites very well but seem less appropriate to TV commercials. With almost unlimited virtual space, and the capacity to be interactive, a website is expected to offer more personal and insightful content than a fleeting TV impression.

The relevance of Informativeness is supported by Market Facts' TeleNation survey. Market Facts found that the No. 1 online usage is "gathering news or information" (Maddox, 1998a).

Scale 3: Organization

Organization is operationalized by four adjectives (Alpha = .84): (not) messy, (not) cumbersome, (not) confusing, and (not) irritating. Similar factors were discovered in some (but not all) previous attempts to locate the basic dimensions of mass media advertisements. Schlinger (1979) found a dimension she called "confusion" defined by the terms "distracting," "hard to follow," and "too complex." Aaker and Stayman (1990) found a similar factor that had only one high loading: confusing (.97).

Compared with a print advertisement's limited physical space and a TV commercial's rigid time limit, a website is virtually free from both limitations. Thus, the website's "unlimited shelf space" (Stewart, 1998) gives advertisers more freedom to put whatever they want online. The web breaks through the physical restrictions of time and space and moves advertising to new, virtually unlimited venues (Palmer and Griffith, 1998). But still, the advertiser must plan well or lose the audience.

The Organization factor gauges how well a website presents itself and tour-guides its users. A low score on Organization suggests that the website does a poor job of leading surfers to their destination. Examination of low-scoring websites indicates that a poor Organization score can be caused by too many links, too many layers, too many animations, or too bright colors. However, information intensity does not necessarily mean information overload. Websites such as amazon.com not only convey rich, intensive information to the audience but also stay easy to follow.

Regression

To understand how Entertainment, Informativeness, and Organization relate to the overall A_{ST} Score and to each other, we regressed mean scores representing each of these factors on A_{ST}. All three factors accounted for significant variance in overall attitude. The regression formula for this particular set of websites rated by this particular set of judges was as follows:

$$A_{ST} \text{ Scale} = .348 \text{ (Factor 1: Entertainment)} + .572 \text{ (Factor 2: Informativeness)} + .227 \text{ (Factor 3: Organization)} (R^2 = .63)$$

It should be noted that this formula represents evaluation of this particular set of websites by this particular set of raters. When individual websites or less diverse sets of websites are evaluated by other raters, the R^2, and the relationships among A_{ST}, Entertainment, Informativeness, and Organization might well be different.

TABLE 5.4	Correlations among Descriptive Dimensions and Attitude toward the Site		
	A_{ST}	Entertainment	Informativeness
A_{ST}			
Entertainment	.51**		
Informativeness	.68**	.23*	
Organization	.44**	.14	.34**

*Correlation is significant at the 0.05 level (2-tailed).
**Correlation is significant at the 0.01 level (2-tailed).

We also calculated bivariate correlations among A_{ST} and the descriptive dimensions. As the formula given above would predict, Informativeness correlated the highest (.68), followed by Entertainment (.51) and Organization (.44).

The correlation matrix (Table 5.4) shows that correlations among Entertainment, Informativeness, and Organization are lower than the correlations of each with A_{ST}. Though Organization strongly correlates with Informativeness, it does not correlate significantly with Entertainment.

More discussion of these relationships will be presented later.

USING THE FACTORS TO UNDERSTAND HIGH, MEDIUM, AND LOW A_{ST} SCORES

The A_{ST} score lets us know the overall evaluation raters give to a certain website. Although this evaluation is useful and important by itself, the dimensions that contribute to it provide still further

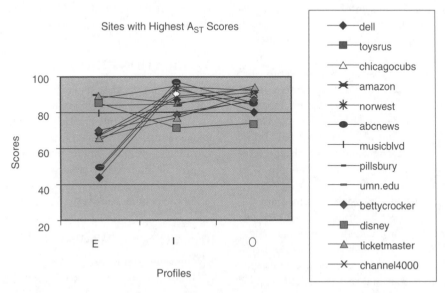

Figure 5-4 **Entertainment, Informativeness, and Organization Profiles of Websites with Highest A_{ST} Scores**

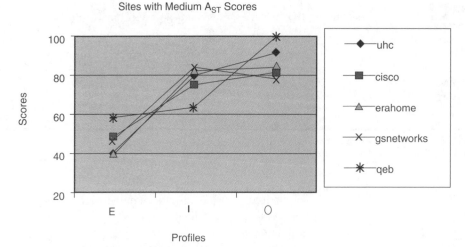

Figure 5-5 **Entertainment, Informativeness, and Organization Profiles of Websites with Medium A_{ST} Scores**

information. Therefore, in this section, we take a closer took at the dimensions that profile high-, medium-, and low-scoring sites in this situation.

Figure 5-4 shows Entertainment, Informativeness, and Organization scores for websites with high A_{ST} scores. Though Informativeness and Organization scores for this group are generally high (>70), Entertainment scores vary substantially.

This variation in Entertainment scores indicates that when websites like dell.com and abcnews.com are intended primarily to convey information, users put more weight on Informativeness and Organization, and less on Entertainment. This finding also explains why Informativeness and Organization correlated relatively highly with each other and less highly with Entertainment.

Figure 5-5 profiles websites with medium A_{ST} scores. These sites all have fairly low Entertainment scores (E < 60), and their Informativeness scores are not especially high (from 63–84). However, they are all rated as exceptionally well organized. It seems this advantage offset relatively poor approaches in dealing with the other dimensions.

Figure 5-6 profiles websites with low scores. This graph shows that the variances within Informativeness and Organization scores are relatively large, while Entertainment value is low (below 42, with one exception). With no offset from Information or Organization, a low Entertainment value produced low overall evaluation.

APPLICATIONS IN PRACTICE

Just as "common sense and experience . . . caution that no one rating dimension can measure advertising success across all brands" (Schlinger, 1979), no one rating scale can measure all the responses a website can generate. In the following paragraphs, we provide more descriptive detail to show how A_{ST}, Entertainment, Informativeness, and Organization can profile website performance.

High AST Score Websites

Ticketmaster.com received a high A_{ST} score (80). What was the key to its success? First of all, it used eye-catching color, violet and dark blue, plus

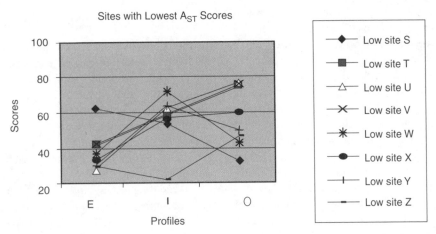

Figure 5-6   **Entertainment, Informativeness, and Organization Profiles of Websites with Lowest A_{ST} Scores**

daily-updated movie or concert clips to enhance its Entertainment value (E score = 66). Second, it also offered information on how to buy tickets for movies and how to arrange travel. These attributes gained it a 76 Informativeness score. Third, the information was presented in an eye-pleasing and orderly way. A high Organization score (90) confirms the easy flow of information.

Pillsbury's website earned a high Entertainment score (84) by adding the image of the Pillsbury Doughboy and other entertaining icons. It also earned a high Informativeness score (84) by offering mealtime ideas and diet advice and earned an even higher Organization score (95) by using sky blue sharply contrasting to a snow-white background. High scores on these dimensions led to an A_{ST} score of 86. Thus, the high A_{ST} scores earned by Ticketmaster and Pillsbury were achieved through somewhat different approaches.

A website does not need an exceptionally high score on every dimension to gain a high A_{ST} score. As noted earlier, Dell's website is not high on Entertainment (44). However, a high Informativeness score (93) indicates that it fulfilled its goal and sent its message (A_{ST} = 96).

Low A_{ST} Score Websites

Just as websites received high A_{ST} scores for somewhat different reasons, websites earned low A_{ST} scores through various configurations. Some, like a film magazine's website and an e-Agent's website, received low scores on all three main dimensions.

Given its topic, the film magazine site (Low site X) might be expected to be quite interesting and inviting. However, it is virtually all black-and-white (Entertainment Score = 33), and the movies it reviews are out of date. Under the "current issue" link, the most recent movie listed is from 1995. The descriptions of the movies do not give enough detail to be informative (Informativeness Score = 57). Under the link that promises to show "Videos," there is virtually nothing. Third, the site is presented as a single page, and surfers have to scroll endlessly to complete the reading. In the end, no anchors offer surfers a chance to return to the top of the page. Consequently, they have to scroll back (Organization Score = 60). One of the links prompts viewers to order. However, the description of videotape availability is so confusing that ordering is far from easy.

The presentation of Low site Z—an e-Agent who describes itself as an "Internet consultant"—is even less inviting. Entering into this website, all the surfer can see is blank white or black space. No specific content or introduction of the business is given (Informative Score = 22). Contrary to its own suggestion that websites should "add some animation to your site to help create a focal point on your web page," it contains no animation, graph, or icon (Entertainment Score = 29). When surfers enter the "About Us" link—trying to obtain more information about this company—they can get lost in a new window and may be unable to find their way back (Organization Score = 47). Ironically, this site says its mission is to help companies offer surfers a "unique," "versatile," and "imaginative" experience.

Low site W claims its mission is to "tie together different information systems so organizations can distribute that information anywhere it needs to go, whenever it needs to arrive." This site featured links to computing, data warehousing, and web computing resources (Informativeness Score = 72). However, it failed to be entertaining (Entertainment Score = 37) and apparently lacked logical arrangement (Organization Score = 43). The homepage contained no animation, and the links there seemed unrelated to each other. The result, despite a relatively high Informativeness Score, was an A_{ST} score of 35.

When we revisited the same URL five months later, we found that this website had been rebuilt. Some animation had been added. The background of the homepage was made more attractive with a picture of tender color. Links were arranged on the right-hand side of the screen instead of scattered.

When the rebuilt website was retested, its Attitude toward the Site score increased from 35 to 71, its Entertainment score increased from 37 to 62, its Informativeness score increased from 72 to 86, and its Organization score increased from 43 to 62. In this case, the A_{ST} and Profile scales identified problems and tracked solutions.

SUMMARY AND CONCLUSION

In this study, we developed an Internet-specific evaluative scale that can be used by any set of raters. While this scale resembles other evaluative scales, it has its own Internet specific flavor. We also derived a set of dimensions that can give more detail on how well a website is doing. Taken together, these scales complement each other and offer some clues on how to improve website design and presentation.

According to *Advertising Age* (October 1998), "it's becoming increasingly clear that just about every business must be looking at whether they should be implementing an electronic commerce strategy" (Maddox, 1998b). The question challenging today's entrepreneur is not whether to have a website but how to become the winner in Internet competition.

"Web commerce is still in its infancy. The companies that have started down this route are still learning lessons and figuring out what makes sense for them" (Maddox, 1998a). The findings reported here indicate that a good website is one that delivers relevant and well-organized information in an engaging manner. While this principle may sound obvious, many websites—even websites created by website consultants—manage to violate it in one way or another. The Attitude toward the Site (A_{ST}) scale and associated Profile scales offer simple and reliable instruments that calibrate success and single out important failures.

Qimei Chen is a Ph.D candidate in the School of Journalism and Mass Communication at the University of Minnesota. Prior to that, she served as project manager in Sino Field Ltd. in Hong Kong and prior to that, she worked for Siemens AG in Erlangen, Germany. Her research interests include advertising effectiveness, e-commerce, IT usage, and cross-culture consumer behavior.

William D. Wells is the Mithun Land Grant Professor of Advertising in the School of Journalism and Mass Communication at the University of Minnesota. Before joining the Minnesota faculty, he was executive vice president and director of marketing service in the Chicago office of DDB Needham Worldwide.

REFERENCES

Aaker, David A., and Donald E. Bruzzone. "Viewer Perceptions of Prime-Time Television Advertising." *Journal of Advertising Research* 21, 5 (1985): 15–23.

———, and Douglas M. Stayman. "Measuring Audience Perceptions of Commercials and Relating Them to Ad Impact." *Journal of Advertising Research* 30, 4 (1990): 7–17.

Aaker, Jennifer L. "Dimensions of Brand Personality." *Journal of Marketing Research* 34, 3 (1997): 347–56.

Ackoff, R. L., and J. R. Emsoff. "Advertising Research at Anheuser-Busch, Inc. (1963–68)." *Sloan Management Review* 16, 2 (1975): 1–15.

Advertising Research Foundation. *Getting Started on Interactive Media Measurement.* New York, NY, 1995.

———. *Transcript Proceedings: Interactive Media Research Summit II.* "Bringing Clarity to New Media." New York, NY, 1996.

Almagor, M., A. Tellegen, and N. G. Waller. "The Big Seven Model: A Cross-Culture Replication and Further Exploration of the Basic Dimensions of Natural Language Trait Descriptors." *Journal of Personality and Social Psychology* 69, 2 (1995): 300–307.

Baker, William E., and Richard J. Lutz. "The Relevance-Accessibility Model of Advertising Effectiveness." *Nonverbal Communication in Advertising,* Sidney Hecker and David W. Stewart, eds., Lexington, MA: Lexington Books, 1988.

Batra, Rajeev, and Michael L. Ray. "Affective Responses Mediating Acceptance of Advertising." *Journal of Consumer Research* 13, 2 (1986): 234–49 .

Benet, V., and N. G. Waller. "The Big Seven Factor Model of Personality Description: Evidence for Its Cross-cultural Generality in a Spanish Sample." *Journal of Personality and Social Psychology* 69, 4 (1995): 701–18.

Brown, Steven P., and Douglas M. Stayman. "Antecedents and Consequences of Attitude toward the Ad: A Meta-analysis." *Journal of Consumer Research* 19, 1 (1992): 34–51.

Buss, D. M. "Social Adaptation and Five Major Factors of Personality." In *Theoretical Perspectives for the Five-Factor Model,* J. S. Wiggins, ed. New York: Guilford Press, 1996.

Chen, Paul. "Measuring Site Effectiveness." *Technology-Powered Marketing Special Report.* Atlanta, GA: Threshold Group, 1996.

Cronbach, L. J. "Coefficient Alpha and the Internal Structure of Tests." *Psychometrika* 16, 3 (1951): 297–334.

Dolich, I. J. "Congruence Relationships between Self-images and Product Brands." *Journal of Marketing Research* 6, 1 (1969): 80–84.

Gibson, Stan. "Spin a Website to attract more customers." *PC Week,* March 31, 1997.

Haley, Russell I., and Allan L. Baldinger. "The ARF Copy Research Validity Project." *Journal of Advertising Research* 31, 2 (1991): 11–32.

Henss, R. "The Big Five and Physical Attractiveness." Paper presented at the *Eighth European Conference on Personality.* Ghent, Belgium, 1996.

High-Tech Media. *The Internet Source Book—The Executive's Guides to the Internet/Intranet World.* High-Tech Media, 1998.

Krauss, Michael. "The Next Step for Internet Advertising." *Marketing News,* November 23, 1998.

Leavitt, Clark. "A Multidimensional Set of Rating Scales for Television Commercials." *Journal of Applied Psychology* 54, 5 (1970) 427–29.

Leckenby, John D., and Jongpil Hong. "Using Reach/Frequency for Web Media Planning." *Journal of Advertising Research* 38, 1 (1998): 7–21.

MacKenzie, Scott B., Richard J. Lutz, and George E. Belch. "The Role of Attitude toward the Ad as a Mediator of Advertising Effectiveness: A Test of Competing Explanations." *Journal of Marketing Research* 23, 2 (1986): 130–43.

Maddox, Kate. "E-commerce Become Reality." *Advertising Age,* October 26, 1998a.

———. "Survey Shows Increase in Online Usage, Shopping." *Advertising Age,* October 26, 1998b.

McCrae, Robert R., and Paul T. Costa, Jr. "The Structure of Interpersonal Traits: Wiggins's Circumplex and Five-Factor Model." *Journal of Personality and Social Psychology* 56, 4 (1989): 586–95.

Marineau, Pierre. *Motivation in Advertising.* New York: McGraw-Hill, 1957.

Moldovan, Stanley E. "Copy Factors Related to Persuasions Scores." *Journal of Advertising Research* 24, 6 (1984): 16–22.

Norman, Warren T. "Toward an Adequate Taxonomy of Personality Attributes: Replicated Factor Structure in Peer Nomination Personality Ratings." *Journal of Abnormal and Social Psychology* 66, 6 (1963): 574–83.

Osgood., C. E., Suci, G. J., and Tannenbaum, P. H. *The Measurement of Meaning.* Urbana: University of Illinois Press, 1957.

Palmer, Jonathan W., and David A. Griffith. "An Emerging Model of Website Design for Marketing." *Communications of the ACM* 41, 3 (1998): 44–51.

Pashupati, Kartik. "The Dimensions of Attitude toward the Ad: A Re-exploration." In *Proceedings of the American Academy of Advertising.* Cincinnati, OH: American Academy of Advertising, 1997.

Saucier, Gerard. "Effects of Variable Selection on the Factor Structure of Person-descriptors." *Journal of Personality and Social Psychology* 73, 6 (1997): 1296–1312.

———, and Lewis R. Goldberg. "What is Beyond the Big Five?" *Journal of Personality* 66, 4 (1998): 495–525.

Schlinger, Mary Jane. "A Profile of Responses to Commercials." *Journal of Advertising Research* 19, 2 (1979): 37–46.

Shimp, Terence A. "Attitude toward the Ad as a Mediator of Consumer Brand Choice." *Journal of Advertising* 10, 2 (1981): 9–15.

Stern, Barbara, and Judith Lynn Zaichowsky. "The Impact of 'Entertaining' Advertising on Consumer Responses." *Australian Marketing Researcher* 14, 1 (1991): 68–80.

Stewart, Martha. "My Big Bet on the Net." *Newsweek,* December 7, 1998.

Taylor, Catharine P. "But there's a cache: Web surfers are getting harder to measure." *MEDIAWEEK.* November 17, 1997.

Tellegen, A., and G. N. Waller. "Re-examining Basic Dimensions of Natural Language Trait Descriptors." Paper presented at the 95th Annual Convention of the American Psychological Association, 1987.

Tupes, Ernest C., and Raymond E. Christal. "Stability of Personality Trait Rating Factors Obtained Under Diverse Conditions." *USAF WADS Technical Report* No. 58-61. Lackland Air Force Base, TX: U.S. Air Force, 1958.

Vitz, P. C., and Johnson, D. "Masculinity of Smokers and the Masculinity of Cigarette Images." *Journal of Applied Psychology* 49, 3 (1965): 155–59.

Wells, William D. "EQ, Son of EQ, and the Reaction Profile." *Journal of Marketing* 28, 4 (1964a): 45–52.

———. "Recognition, Recall and Rating Scales." *Journal of Advertising Research* 4, 3 (1964b): 2–8.

———, Clark Leavitt, and Maureen McCon "A Reaction Profile for TV Commercials." *Journal of Advertising Research* 11, 6 (1971): 11–17.

The Expanded ARF Model: Bridge to the Accountable Advertising Future

Bill Harvey

The Web is the first interactive medium presented to the advertiser. As such, it offers important opportunities for learning how to use interactivity within the advertising process to add to advertising effectiveness. Like any other new medium, the advertiser's predictable initial concern is "how cost effective is this medium compared to those I use already?" This paper proposes how the ARF Model for Evaluating Media can be updated and predicts that the use of our version or a similar underlying agreed industry model will facilitate the growth of more accountable advertising opportunities into the next Millennium.

The year was 1955. The advertising industry was challenged by the ascension of a new medium—television—whose audience numbers needed to be compared with radio and print numbers. Questions were being raised which magnetized to a *lumpen* complexity of confusion: Is a viewer the same as a reader? Is a viewer equal to a listener? How do we compare the cost/value equation when alternate media want our money and cite their apples-and-oranges numbers?

Clearly, the advertising industry had to get down to some overdue concentration on thinking out the basic principles of what advertising is, what media are, and how the whole process works. This was a historic moment. It could not have been possible earlier in the history of advertising, because the basic conceptual tools had just appeared, courtesy of WWII.

Propaganda research during WWII trained some of the people who were later to become leaders in advertising research, including giving the Advertising Research Foundation one of its vice

Reprinted from the *Journal of Advertising Research,* © 1997, by the Advertising Research Foundation.

presidents, Charles Ramond, who was also editor of this *Journal* for about 20 years—and it also gave the industry a scientific underpinning of attitude research, which led to studies by agencies such as Foote Cone, Grey ("The Study of Brand XL"), and others, proving that attitude shift and sales were empirically related.

Between 1955 and 1961, many of the brightest minds in the advertising industry focused on the basic questions of how media might be compared—which always returned the discourse to the one basic question: *How does advertising work?* Because one cannot think about comparing media until one first thinks about what these media are supposed to help accomplish.

In 1961, the ARF published a monograph entitled *Toward Better Media Comparisons,* which offered a six-stage model of the advertising process, and recommended that media be compared *within* each of these six stages whenever the difficult conditions of experimental purity were reached which would allow any such comparisons at all. Simplistically, this means that you should not take a Vehicle Distribution number from Medium A and compare it to a Vehicle Exposure number from Medium B. But the implications of this historic document go far beyond that intuitively obvious imprecation. The ARF Model, as it has come to be called, is a conceptual roadmap, a master model of advertising. Its inherent logic and its clarity are powerful aids to thinking about what constitutes the advertising value equation between any medium and any advertiser. It is a framework that can be operationalized through specific research initiatives, the broad strokes of whose requirements are innately embodied in the Model itself.

The ARF Model has lasted over a third of a century and has promise to last potentially forever. However, it appears upon closer inspection to have certain correctable omissions. This paper is an inspection of those omissions, with recommendations on how to correct them.

Why today? What is the impetus for this dusting-off of a hallowed and yet largely forgotten old scroll? It is because we live in another time right now just like the time that was then—the start of an important, and world-changing, new medium. Then it was television. Now it is the Internet. New times make us think deeply again about what we are trying to accomplish and how we can measure it, and how we can compare accomplishment costs across old and new media alike.

Today the Net is not growing its adspend as fast as it would like. Because the Net is the intended beneficiary of this work, before proceeding into the general subject of the ARF Model and its updating let us pause for a moment to consider some of the current debates raging within the Internet advertising medium.

CURRENT QUESTIONS

The most prevalent advertising form within the Web today is the *banner.* This is a diminutive advertising unit whose appearance within the visual field is approximately equal to the experience of seeing an outdoor billboard from a low flying plane. The two cost-efficiency measures which have become typical collateral for pricing ad buys are *adviews,* the number of times that the banner is presumably seen; and *clickthroughs,* the number of times that the banner is clicked upon. This results in connecting the user to the *advertiser's website* (or in the mode we prefer, to a mini-site still within the cybermedia vehicle's space; we will defer discussion of this preference for later).

Adviews

The debate about adviews centers on Cost Per Thousand. Outdoor has a CPM of under $1, but cybermedia are selling adviews for CPMs ranging generally between $20 and $80. Why? What is the additional value that is being paid for? In reality, in many cases this CPM is being paid (or in some cases *was* being paid) for extraordinary reasons

which will not support rollout of the medium. These extraordinary reasons include research and the need to drive traffic to the advertiser's website (to justify having built it, but without necessarily positive implications to the continuation of this activity). Today many cybermedia are feeling the pinch of a more difficult sell on these CPMs as the medium matures into a sustaining mode.

Yet there could be a reason to pay a higher CPM for banners. What if being seen in cyberspace by a Netizen results in the brand instantly achieving a friendlier status in the Netizen's mind? This posits a relationship effect conferred by the medium upon a brand seen in the medium. What if the Netizen is so sold on his or her medium that any brand seen in that medium will be seen in a new and more positive light, as a ruboff effect?

Our 1974 study for *Black Enterprise Magazine* found such an effect. A proportion of upscale blacks consciously sought to repay advertisers seen to be supporting a black medium dedicated to promotion of the process of blacks joining the American success system. This drove recall and persuasion rates two to three times higher than the control publication, *Newsweek,* holding the ads constant. The effect of environment, a subset of spokesperson bias is well documented in the advertising research literature and within the broader academic and scientific attitude research surrounding it.

A semihypothetical anecdotal example might be Ragu. The Mama Cucina site was for a long time the best-liked site on the Web. It is easy to imagine that 16- to 49-year-old males, still the mainstay audience of the Web even as it begins to massify, might have had little tendency to prefer Ragu over Prego or vice versa before 1995, and that the website could have created brand preference for Ragu in the exposed segment of males 16 to 49 that might otherwise never had existed.

The Millward Brown study for *Hotwired* is the first to begin to investigate such effects and could turn out to be a landmark study in the development of the Internet as an advertising medium. (See the Briggs and Hollis paper in this issue.)

Clickthroughs

The debate on clickthroughs is classical, in that it raises the question of what is the medium's job: is it merely to deliver eyeballs/ears, or is it to also create an environment conducive to furthering the attention paid by those eyes and ears? If the latter, then the medium's job includes the creative factor, because the ad itself is that which creates attention—but isn't this the agency's job? The exact same debate flowed out of the publication of the ARF Model over 35 years ago, when the media took the position that all ARF Model levels above advertising exposure are the advertiser's and agency's job, not the media's job.

In today's version of the argument, the, advertiser says, "The banner is not the ad, it's the *ad for the ad!* I'll pay you for the number of people that are reached by the actual ad." In other words, the advertiser offers to pay on a per-clickthrough basis. Procter & Gamble continued their fine tradition of setting industry practices by pioneering such a deal with Yahoo in April 1996.

"But wait!" the seller says, "Your banner creative is terribly uncreative. You won't generate many clickthroughs, and then you'll penalize us for that. Our job is just getting you the opportunity for clickthrough, and unless we control the creative in the banner, we can't be held responsible for the clickthrough rate; that's your job." In other words, the medium objects to the fairness of being paid for clickthroughs, because some of the clickthrough rate lies beyond their control in the hands of the agency preparing the banner creative.

The acid test of the relevancy of the ARF Model will be its ability or inability to add constructively to the resolution of these current questions standing in the way of more rapid utilization of the advertising potentials of the Web.

Purpose

The objectives of this paper are to:

1. Advertise the availability of the ARF Model as a constructive element in facing current questions regarding Internet advertising
2. Review the ARF Model and update and/or improve it for today's use. Apply the updated Model to the questions facing us, and draw conclusions for recommended action.

The Original ARF Model

The 1961 ARF Model (see Figure 5-7) still standing today has six levels at which media can be compared:

1. *Vehicle Distribution*—a count of the physical units through which the advertising flows (TV or radio sets tuned to the program, copies of the magazine/newspaper issue, etc.).
2. *Vehicle Exposure*—the number of individuals exposed to the media vehicle (program, magazine, etc.).
3. *Advertising Exposure*—the number of individuals exposed to the advertising itself (commercial, ad, etc.).
4. *Advertising Perception*—the number of individuals noticing the advertising.
5. *Advertising Communication*—the number of individuals receiving some level of substantial communication from the advertising, more than the simple act of noticing.
6. *Sales*—the actual sales created by the advertising.

At each of these six levels, the ARF Model distinguishes between Prospects and Non-Prospects, with some Non-Prospects participating in all but the Sales level (by definition, Non-Prospects will not buy despite all the advertising that might be directed to them). And at each level, within each of the two segments, there is not a single number but rather a diminutive barchart symbolizing a reach/frequency distribution. In other words, we might take any level, say Advertising Exposure, and we will find that any media campaign will result in

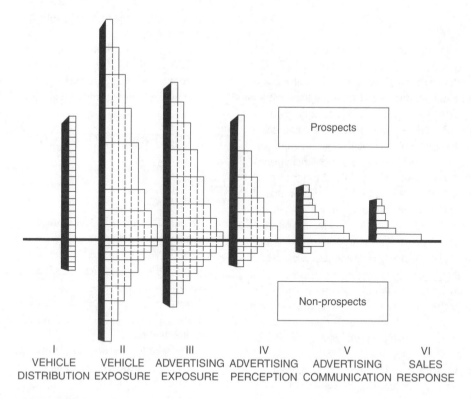

Figure 5-7   ARF Model for Evaluating Media

repeated Advertising Exposure occurring with more frequency among some individuals than among others, and with some receiving only one Advertising Exposure, or none at all. This same kind of frequency distribution occurs at every level within each segment.

Problems with the Model

Even before the development of the Internet, the ARF Model ran into problems which eventually caused it to be essentially put aside out of the mainstream day-to-day media buying and selling process.

One major problem was that of funding the necessary research to actually measure each medium at each of the six levels. Individual advertisers with the exception of General Foods were generally unwilling to spend enough on research to take advantage of the Model, at least until BehaviorScan came along. And then when BehaviorScan and scanner data came along, the advertisers leaped to the Sales level and tended to ignore Advertising Communications as never before; calibrations were not made among the levels which would have led to generalizations about how much of one level led to how much of another level. Scanners caused so much focus on the Sales level that the Model underneath Sales was forgotten, and as agency research department headcounts went down, we entered a Dark Age where questions about cause and effect, where concepts of *diagnostic explana-*

tion and *understanding process* were at their minimum perceived value. This unfortunate historical trend was documented by Cook and Dunn in their 1996 *JAR* Paper analyzing the agency decline in copy testing.

At the same time, those research organizations who kept the conceptual flame alive by incorporating the ARF Model in their services (including brand-share-prediction modeling), such as ASI and Millward Brown among others, thrived while other major research companies experienced flatter growth.

Media were similarly unmotivated to spend enough to prove their advertising effectiveness. Because, for the most part, those able to consider such investment were riding high on the status quo state of knowledge, and why upset the apple cart? Who knew what such research would really show. Only those out of power would be likely to consider such research, and then only if they truly had the confidence that the results would prove their own advertising efficacy. But those out of power would generally not be able to afford such research, which would have always been costly.

Looking back to 1983, Paul Chook, then Chairman of ARF, wrote: "Today, twenty-odd years after the Model's formulation, it is undeniably true that the main focus of industry media research is still on Stage Two—Vehicle Exposure ... it might appear that we have made no progress at all."

Another problem that the Model had was that its creators recommended that Advertising Perception become the level to be most fully funded by industry research coffers. This thorny stumbling block had two sharp edges: the media considered that the Advertising Perception level exceeded their fair job—shades of clickthroughs—and the research community admitted that it could never measure Perception at all. As Erwin Ephron reminds us, it was Alfred Politz who first explained to the creators of the Model that the only way to measure Perception would be through Memory; therefore we will wind up with Recall (then

considered part of Advertising Communication) whenever we try to measure Perception. (Today we might actually be able to operationalize Perception—or "noticing"—by measurement of Cortical Evoked Potential P300 waves, something that was not yet in the ken of the creators of the Model. This would take Memorability out of the Perception equation at last.)

This is perhaps why Paul Chook in 1983 recommended that the industry refocus one level down, on Advertising Exposure, which would still be an improvement over the industry's traditional focus, still one floor lower at Vehicle Exposure (the realm of Nielsen, Arbitron, MRI, and Simmons).

One might criticize the ARF Model by saying "Why have a level that can never be operationalized as itself, a level that turns into a different level when we try to measure it (as Perception turns into Recall when we try to measure it)? Why not leave such a level out entirely?" A thorough inspection of the Model would leave the rational observer to conclude that the Model is incomplete. For one thing, sales are the highest level. But the advertiser seeking *profitable sales sustained for as long as possible,* not just Sales. This means that the Model is useless or counterproductive for comparing advertising and promotion, two competing uses of the marketing budget. For example, coupons are likely to drive up Sales, but all too frequently drive down profits, and also undermine brand loyalty which is related to the *"sustained for as long as possible"* part. Use of the Model as is would bias the outcome toward shifting all advertising into promotion, which would be lethal. Therefore the Model in this respect is simply "wrong in that, if used as originally intended, would lead the industry in the opposite direction from the in-reality success direction, simply as a result of being incomplete and therefore Reductionist.

Finally, the Model omits all reference to Leads, a critically important stage in all direct marketing, database marketing, and relationship marketing— three modern tools which were in pre-embryonic condition in 1961. Without a separate level for Leads they would presumably be tossed into Sales level, making practical implementation of the Model clumsy at best for practitioners of the direct arts. This is a particularly troublesome issue with regard to the Web, already proven as a direct marketing medium.

And when one removes the fetters of the past and stares straight at the one-to-one personal communications potentials of the Internet, they transcend direct marketing and look more than anything else like direct selling. The difference is the veracity of the communication: only in direct selling—and on the Internet—is there the potential for realtime branching to a new stimulus based on the nature of the last response. These direct selling considerations correspond to the direct marketer concept of ever-more-qualified, information-seeking *Leads*.

Therefore to fully realize the promise of the Web as an advertising medium, the needs of direct marketers cannot be overlooked, and the Leads dimension summarizes the gap between Persuasion and Sales where the Prospect is taking communication action. The Model cries out for updating—for the inclusion of Leads if for no other reason—if we as an industry are to be equipped with the necessary conceptual tools with which to appreciate and apply the Internet as a means of marketing communication.

PROPOSED NEW ARF MODEL

In order to make the Model more fully usable in helping to solve today's problems, we propose the following changes to the Model: the addition of four missing levels—*Leads, Profits, Loyal Customers,* and *Return On Investment* (ROI). These are described by Craig Gugel in his fine article in the 4As magazine *Agency.* I cannot improve upon the language and so with kind permission here is how Craig describes the four new levels:

> More recently, Bill Harvey of Next Century Media endeavored to extend the historical ARF model by adding four stages that coincided with the unique one-to-one communica-

tion properties of the Internet and other response-based media.

Situated between the advertising communication and ad sales response levels, the first of the four additional stages has been logically labeled *Advertising Leads,* a measure of those who have received some form of communication from the advertising and have actively sought more information on the product or service being advertised (e.g., requested a brochure via an 800 number, activated information request hotlinks within an advertiser's website, etc.).

Positioned following the ad response level, the second extended stage, *Loyal Customers* is essentially a count of leads converted to purchasers who are favorably predisposed to the offering and who have continued purchasing the product or service over time.

The third extended stage, *Profits,* can best be summed up as the positive dollar difference resulting from the interactive sale of the product or service to Loyal Customers, versus the cost of producing the product or service.

The final extended stage, *Return on Investment (ROI),* is defined as the annual percentage rate of return on profits attributable to the interactive capital investment (e.g., costs for building, promoting, hosting and maintaining an Internet website).

The addition of these four missing levels makes the Model complete in terms of mapping to real-world effectiveness requirements (see Figure 5-8). In particular they prepare the Model for life in the Age of Interactivity, where Leads will become even more important as a level of advertising effectiveness, and where clickstream accountability capabilities will make Sales and the three levels above Sales a more constant part of the picture, improving the cost effectiveness of marketing in general, with unknown but presumably salutary effects upon the world economy and the quality of life.

Note that we have slightly changed the order of the new levels in the diagram. At the stage of its evolution at which Craig Gugal saw the new

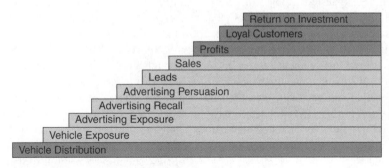

Figure 5-8   ARF Model Expanded for Interactive

Model, Loyal Customers were situated just above Sales. We have since refined our thinking such that we see better placement of Profits just above Sales, since Profits can be calculated based upon a point-in-time Sales figure, and since both Loyal Customers and ROI are more long-term, rather than point-in-time measures.

We also propose a nomenclature change with regard to the next two levels above Advertising Exposure, aimed at solving the operationalizability problems the industry has had with the level called Advertising Perception. As Alfred Politz had predicted, all use of the Perception level involved Recall/Recognition measures. Why then continue to refer to it as the "Perception" level—why not simply call it "Recall," the most-often-used word in the industry to describe the advertising memorability dimension?

This then requires a new word also at the Advertising Communication level, since Recall had been defined as part of the Advertising Communication level. "Advertising Communication Other Than Recall" would be ugly, and since Persuasion is the industry's most-often-used word for the rest of what advertising does, why not call that level simply "Persuasion"?

It is recognized that different advertisers have different ways of measuring Persuasion, often using tools that do not even use the word "Persuasion." Commonly used terms include brand building, brand equity building, increase in competitive share of choice, purchase intention increase, brand rating increase, etc. We consider all of these to be differently operationalized variations of Persuasion level. Even measures of corporate image changes, reflecting consumer awareness of the company's good works in the community, are defined as falling within Persuasion.

On the other hand, consumer learning of sales and copy points are defined as falling within Recall. For example, Belief and Liking clearly fall within Persuasion, but Comprehension is a more borderline dimension. Our recommendation is to include it in Persuasion, so that the Recall level is left to be purely a function of Memorability, and *anything beyond Memorability falls into Persuasion.*

The New Model Implies Sublevels

Just as there are sublevels of more-qualified and less-qualified Leads in the direct marketing field, there are obviously sublevels of the other nine levels of the new Model. The most significant sublevel phenomena are believed to exist at the Persuasion level. Here the realization that there are gradual stages in the Persuasion process is classical.

An early industry model was AIDA, which stands for Attention, Interest, Decision, Action.

This model assumed that all consumer processes are rational and involve decisionmaking. Later industry research suggested that, in low-involvement product categories, much of the purchasing does not involve rational decisionmaking but is impulsively driven by price and awareness dimensions ("Low Involvement Theory").

In Internet advertising, the first sublevel within Persuasion that can be easily measured is the clickthrough, and further clicks related to paying more attention to that advertiser's content can be equated to further upward movement among sublevels of Persuasion.

Let us remember that the first goal of the ARF Model was to provide transportability of measures across media. One might be concerned that measures originating in Internet practice, such as clickthroughs, might not be transportable across media. However, by establishing clickthrough as an initial sublevel of Persuasion (i.e., the consumer would not have clicked if there was not already some Persuasion toward taking action), we ensure transportability of the clickthrough measure across media—albeit only the media allowing a measurable consumer action to get more information, such as ITV, kiosks, and other Interactive media.

Erwin Ephron proposes that five important stages in Internet advertising success are Attraction, Reaction, Interaction, Transaction, and Sales. He defines Attraction as a "count of persons landing on the source site page carrying the banner . . . this corresponds to the mass media's 'ad exposure'." (The term "Attraction" usually implies that some perception or attention has taken place, which is certainly the case here; however, it is to the URL and subsequently to the initial content of the site's home page, not necessarily to the banner. Attraction to the content of the site would correspond to Vehicle Exposure in the ARF Model, where the banner has come along as a side effect, in fact, the visitor may fail to see the banner if it is below what appears on the screen before scrolldown. Therefore use of the term "Attraction" could mislead some to think of Vehicle Exposure

or Advertising Exposure or even Perception, when Ephron's apparent intent is to link it to "ad exposure," i.e., Advertising Exposure. Therefore although the term "Attraction" is itself attractive, it might add to confusion in practice.)

Reaction is defined by Ephron as the clickthrough. Interaction is defined as further interaction, specifically, downloading more pages from the advertiser after the first clickthrough. We would propose making the term more generally apply to further interaction with the advertiser short of becoming a Lead (i.e., to include measures of time spent even without further clicking, interacting with complex pages even without downloading other pages, etc.).

Transaction is the same as Leads. (At the recent ARF/CASIE Symposium in Monterey, California in February, the extension of the ARF Model was much discussed, and several people were concerned that the term "Transactions" would imply "Sales" to most of the industry.) Sales are Sales.

What Ephron's analysis proves to us is that the new ARF Model, as proposed here, stands up to the ongoing need to incorporate other valuable new ideas. The Ephron Model maps onto the proposed ARF Model as shown in Figure 5-9.

Following Ephron's lead a bit further, we might be tempted to expand the new ARF Model still further, to 12 levels as shown in Figure 5-10. In this 12-stage Model, Persuasion becomes a zone in which there are 3 levels; Clickthrough, Interaction, and Attitude Shift. This has the advantage of pointing directly to an operational definition of terms, since each of these three things can be measured today, the first two quite inexpensively.

The drawback with the 12-stage Model is that it reduces Persuasion to just Clickthrough, Interaction, and Attitude Shift. It leaves out Comprehension, Mood, and other dimensions which fit within the process of Persuasion but do not fit within the more narrow term "Attitude Shift." The latter is more specific than Persuasion, i.e., Attitude Shift may be the core of Persuasion but it is not necessarily all of Persuasion. Rather than conclude that one of these two new Models is better than the

Figure 5-9   **ARF Model Expanded for Interactive Including the Ephron Model**

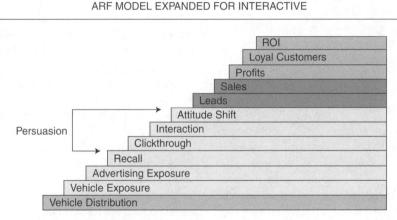

Figure 5-10   **ARF Model Expanded for Interactive (to 12 levels)**

other, we will propose both as variations on a theme and leave room for further debate and evolution of industry thought on the subject.

The New Model in the Old Visual Metaphor

Because we see the Model as a progression of states through which advertising induces prospects, we automatically picture the Model as a staircase ascending to the heavenly heights of brand success. However, the creators of the Model had their own picture to which we must pay respect. Therefore, here is the proposed new 10-stage Model in the visual clothing of the original Model, showing

the Prospects/Non-Prospects dimension and the reach/frequency dimensions.

Applying the New Model to the New Questions: Implications

If this the New Model, then how does it solve our advertising measurement and advertising pricing problems on the Internet today? The job of any model is to help us think, and the test of whether this new Model helps us think is whether or not the Model leads us to any new solutions for our problems.

Our first problem was the value and price of an adview. The new Model tells us that this is at the Advertising Exposure level (better than the Vehicle Exposure level at which most other media are sold), but it can also have Persuasion effects as postulated above for Ragu, and as shown for several advertisers in the Briggs and Hollis (1997) study. The Model implies that an adview is worth much more when it can be proven to have effects at the Persuasion level as well as at the Advertising Exposure level. This leads to at least two important action implications:

1. Enlargement of the banner so that Persuasion may be better accomplished by the inclusion of sales points, imagery, etc.
2. Measurement as in the Briggs and Hollis study should be pursued by more major cybermedia individually or together, or perhaps an all-industry study ought to be organized by the ARF, to determine the Persuasion effects of (Internet Persuasion Type A, Media Effect) merely being seen in cyberspace and (Internet Persuasion Type B, Creative + Media Effect) larger banners containing more persuasive elements than allowed by current size banners.

We hypothesize that the "Type A" effect stems from *Associative Bias,* or "The friend of my friend is my friend, etc." In other words, a consumer who is positive toward the Internet may (as in the *Black Enterprise* experience recounted earlier) become positively disposed toward advertisers who support that person's preferred medium. Such an effect, we hypothesize, will more frequently obtain for brands not expected to be seen in cyberspace, such as packaged goods, and will not as frequently or not at all for computer-related products, cars, and other categories that users are used to seeing in cyberspace, because the linkage is expected. And that therefore this Type A halo effect will tend to diminish over time, as the medium becomes home to all the usual advertisers seen in other media.

Pursuit of larger banners and landmark Persuasion measurement will tend to have positive effects on the growth of Internet advertising revenues. And the measurable value derived by advertisers will lead to more accountability in advertising. These are good effects of a better new Model but are really derived from the goodness of the original ARF Model in the first place.

Our second problem was the value and price of a clickthrough and whether clickthroughs should even be used as a basis for pricing. The new Model casts clickthrough a part of Persuasion, which makes it very important and valuable. TV commercial pretesting shows that the percentage of the advertising-exposed audience which shifts attitude favorably toward a brand is on the order of magnitude of 0 percent to 8 percent. Interestingly, this is remarkably close to today's average-to-better clickthrough rates. An advertiser may test five new TV commercials to find one that does better than 6 percent positive shift, thought to be the cutting point at which to run a new commercial. At this point far fewer than one in five banners has such a high clickthrough rate. The classification of clickthroughs as an initial sublevel of Internet Advertising Persuasion perhaps gains face validity given that the average order of magnitude of the clickthrough phenomenon is on an approximate par with the average order of magnitude of Persuasion measures in TV commercial pretesting.

What this implies is that *there should be a price per clickthrough, additive to a price per adview.* Each has some value, the adview having value at least at the Advertising Exposure level and sometimes at the Persuasion level (Types A and B as elaborated above), and the clickthrough having value at the Persuasion level. Persuasion research using experimental design (controlling all variables except one) is recommended in order to establish the value and, therefore, the fair price for adviews and clickthroughs. This suggests further use of the Briggs and Hollis type study, where experimental design is used to establish a matched control group without which Persuasion measures are likely to be nondefinitive. We predict that more cybermedia will be using that and other research company suppliers for more sure experimental-design Internet Advertising Persuasion studies in the near future.

Another important implication of the new Model (and, less visibly, of the old Model) is that advertising "work" takes place over a staircase of dimensions, and that to the extent that a media vehicle can prove that it did part of that work, the media vehicle ought to be compensated accordingly by the advertiser. This in turn implies that a cybermedia vehicle ought to want to do more advertising work for each advertiser, which in turn implies that the user ought to be taken through a series of Persuasion sublevels within the cybermedia vehicle's own space, where the cybermedia vehicle can take credit for the work accomplished.

For example, a cybermedia vehicle could charge for the value of (a) the adview of an enlarged banner containing more persuasive elements than present sized banners; (b) the value of the first clickthrough to a mini-site containing subset of the advertiser's website; (c) a lead captured at the mini-site, and finally for (d) passing the warmed-up prospect off to the advertiser's own website. The advertiser could verify the value of this warming-up process by comparing the accomplishments (e.g., Sales), at the advertiser's website among "warmed-up" versus "direct-from-small-banner" prospects arriving at the advertiser's website. Such a multistage process could create a win/win situation for the advertiser and cybermedium by providing for "pay for performance," and by giving the cybermedium opportunity to do valuable and measurable advertising work as outlined by the new Model.

CONCLUSIONS, SUMMARY, NEXT STEPS, AND A PREDICTION

We conclude that the new Model, mostly by building upon and elucidating the benefits in the old Model, serves a useful purpose and leads to potentially valuable action implications testable in the real world.

We have added four new levels to the ARF Model and renamed two of the old levels. This appears to add to the current applicability of the Model in a world which offers the opportunity of fusing the advantages of image advertising plus direct marketing via the New Media.

The next steps we recommended are banner enlargement for more Persuasion, the increased use of mini-sites, the capturing of Leads at mini-sites, cybermedia pricing for each piece of provable advertising work done at prices agreed based on measured value, and therefore the increased use of Persuasion (and Recall) measures of Internet advertising.

We predict that the clearer thinking engendered by a better Model will lead to fuller and sooner exploitation of Internet advertising opportunities beyond mere mass media techniques, where the linkages between Interaction, Interest, and Persuasion will become better understood and utilized. This will be part of a general trend to utilize the clickstream plus traditional survey research tools to make advertising as practiced a more accountable part of the total corporate budget. In this process, the long-awaited integration of copy research and media research, held up by so many years by their conceptual separation into specialized, suboptimizing "silos" within advertiser/agency organizations, may finally be achieved as the perspectives of all parties find a single, explanatory codex. This assimilation of media and advertising research will strengthen planning, execution, and analysis. That will promote more impactful advertising, whatever the medium.

Bill Harvey is Cofounder, Chief Executive Officer, and president of Next Century Media, Inc. He has more than 30 years experience in advertising and media research. He and his companies have been involved with most of the interactive media ventures launched since the medium's inception.

Recognized as one of the most influential media research innovators of the past three decades, as well as an interactive media expert with singular accuracy in predicting the evolution of the medium, Harvey has many accomplishments in the media research field. Some include: Inventing the Area of Dominant Influence (ADI) concept for Arbitron; designing a touch screen, executive friendly system that presaged *Metaphor* in its look and feel; coining the word "audiotex" in his 1983 report, "Audiotex vs. Videotex," triggering the rollout of 900 numbers from a base of 4 cities to 43 cities in one year; conceptualizing and cofounding International Rating Services, Inc.; coining and popularizing the term, "New Electronic Media"; in part via a special study conducted with Arbitron in 1978, subscribed to by the major TV networks, film studios, cable companies and top ad agencies; and editing and publishing *The Marketing Pulse* since 1972, a newsletter which focuses on the ongoing "new electronic media" revolution.

Considered one of the leading experts on new electronic media, Harvey is a frequent speaker before many advertising/media industry groups. He is one of the few consultants to have worked with all three TV networks and all seven Hollywood studios.

Prior to founding Next Century Media's predecessor company, New Electronic Media Science, Inc. in 1972, Harvey held various media research management positions at Grey Advertising, Kenyon & Eckhardt, Interpublic, Arbitron, and Brand Rating Index.

REFERENCES

Advertising Research Foundation. *Toward Better Media Comparisons.* New York, NY: Advertising Research Foundation, 1961.

Bhatia, Manish. "The Nature of Advertising on the Web." In *Transcript Proceedings of the Advertising Research Foundation's Interactive Media Research Summit II.* New York, NY: Advertising Research Foundation, 1996.

Blair, Margaret Henderson. *End of Battle, Beginning of Knowledge.* Presented by Advertising Research System Division of Research Systems Corporation Inc. at the 18th Annual Advertising Research Foundation Conference, November 14, 1972.

Briggs, Rex, and Nigel Hollis. "Advertising on the Web: Is There Response before Click-Through?" *Journal of Advertising Research* 37, 2 (1997): 33–45.

Chook, Paul. *Advertising Research Foundation Model for Evaluating Media: Making the Promise a Reality.* New York, NY: Advertising Research Foundation, 1983.

Coalition for Advertising Supported Information & Entertainment. *CASIE Guiding Principles of Interactive Media Audience Measurement: Second Edition.* New York, NY: CASIE Committee, December 1996.

Cook, William A., and Theodore F. Dunn. "The Changing Face of Advertising Research in the Information Age: An Advertising Research Foundation Copy Research Council Survey." *Journal of Advertising Research* 36, 1 (1996): 55–71.

Earl G. Graves Publishing Co., Inc. *A Study of Advertising Responsiveness among Upscale Blacks and Upscale Whites.* New York, NY: Earl G. Graves Publishing Co., Inc., 1973.

Ephron, Erwin. "Or Is It an Elephant? Stretching Our Minds for a New Web Pricing Model." *Journal of Advertising Research* 37, 2 (1997): 96–98.

Foote Cone. *Brand XL Study.* Chicago, IL: Foote Cone, 1957.

Gugel, Craig. "Tracking The Web: Measuring Results From Ad Exposure To ROI." *Agency Magazine* 6, 4 (1997): 42–44.

Harvey, Bill. "Prodigy Proves Itself as Advertising Medium." *The Marketing Pulse* 12, 2 (1991): 5–6.

———. "Internet Beats Direct Mail." *The Marketing Pulse,* 15, 11 (1995): 8.

———. "Nissan Sells Cars to 3.8% of Banner Clickers Via Hachette Online." *The Marketing Pulse* 16, 11 (1996): 5.

———. "The Nature of Advertising on the Web." In *Transervice Proceedings of the Advertising Research Foundation's Interactive Media Research Summit II.* New York, NY: Advertising Research Foundation, 1996.

Information Resources, Inc. *How Advertising Works.* Chicago, IL: Information Resources, Inc., 1991.

National Broadcasting Company. *Why Sales Come in Curves.* New York, NY: National Broadcasting Company, 1953.

Next Century Media, Inc. *Interactive Media: What Have We Learned To Date: Dial-A-Mattress Electronic Marketing Test.* New Paltz, NY: New Century Media, Inc., 1995.

Pakula, Andrew. "The Nature of Advertising on the Web." In *Transcript Proceedings of the Advertising Research Foundation's Interactive Media Research Summit II.* New York, NY: Advertising Research Foundation, 1996.

Spaeth, Jim. "Can Website Marketing Pay?" *Transcript Proceedings of the Advertising Research Foundation's Interactive Media Research Summit II.* New York, NY: Advertising Research Foundation, 1996.

Starch, Dr. Daniel. *Scope, Method and Technique of the Starch Continuing Study of Outde Advertising.* New York, NY: Daniel Starch, 1955.

———. *Analysis of 12 Million Inquiries.* New York, NY: Daniel Starch, 1955.

———. *How Do Size and Color Affect Ad Readership?* New York, NY: Daniel Starch, 1956.

———. *Measuring Product Sales Made by Advertising.* New York, NY: Daniel Starch, 1966.

——— and staff. *Virtual Impression Studios (1956–1968),* New York, NY: Daniel Starch and Staff, 1968.

———. *Measuring Advertising Readership and Results.* New York, NY: McGraw Hill, Inc., 1968.

Advertising on the Web: Is There Response before Click-Through?

Rex Briggs
Nigel Hollis

A study of Web banner advertising that measured attitudes and behavior found important attitudinal shifts even without click-through. By using Millward Brown's BrandDynamics™ system, along with other copytesting measures, the authors have documented increases in advertising awareness and in brand perceptions to Web banner ads for apparel as well as technology goods.

Since advertising on the world wide web began in 1994, marketers have asked the same question they ask of all advertising in any media: Does it work? More specifically, do banner ads (those small, hyperlinked pixel displays popping up on public Web sites) actually provide a vehicle for effective commercial communication? As marketers are projected to spend billions of dollars on Web advertising in the next few years, this question becomes increasingly important.

Until now, the only available answer has been partial at best. The accepted wisdom suggests that, yes, ad banners *do* work as direct marketing vehicles—but only when viewers click on them for transport to the advertiser's own Web site, where a wide range of customized marketing processes begins.

The problem is that only a fraction of all viewers click on the banners they see. As a consequence, a few marketers have elected to pay only for proven click-throughs, while the rest of the marketing community, which pays for ad placements according to CPM (cost per 1,000 impressions), is left to wonder whether the millions of impressions its banner ads generate without click-through are simply wasted.

Are advertisers throwing away money on byte-sized electronic billboards which go unnoticed and un-noted in an environment unfriendly to advertising? Or do Web banners, even without the benefit of click-through, stimulate brand awareness, brand affinity, and purchase interest as effectively as more traditional advertising does?

To answer these questions, two research teams collaborated in an on-line experiment. The researchers came from the research department of HotWired, Inc., the Internet publisher that innovated the ad banner, and Millward Brown International, a recognized leader in advertising effectiveness research. The experiment was the first significant research study on Web advertising effectiveness, a study which dealt successfully with the unique research challenges posed by the Internet environment. This article describes the methodology of this important study and details its findings.

WHAT TO MEASURE

Many people have argued that the best measure of advertising response on the Web is the click-through rate. The advantages of this metric are that it is a behavioral response and easy to observe, and that it indicates an immediate interest in the advertised brand. But many other factors are also likely to influence the click-through response, and these factors may have more to do with the original predisposition of the audience than with the advertising itself. Thus the practice of evaluating Web advertising on the basis of click-through is like evaluating television ads for automobiles on the basis of how many people visit a showroom the next day. A showroom visit is an ideal response, but hardly the most likely one, since relatively few people will be in the market for a new car on a particular day.

Because most advertising does not evoke an immediate behavioral response, we designed our

Reprinted from the *Journal of Advertising Research,* © 1997, by the Advertising Research Foundation.

study to observe and measure both the attitudinal and the behavioral responses to a Web banner. In particular, our objective was to measure whether or not banners themselves have the potential to build brands, by creating awareness and image. We divided the population of our experiment into two cells: an exposed cell, which saw a banner for a tested brand on HotWired's homepage, and a control cell, which did not. Using these two groups, we sought to assess the impact on an advertised brand of one single incremental banner exposure.

HOW WE MEASURED THE RESPONSE

The question we then faced was how to define and measure the "impact" of one Web banner exposure. Traditionally, researchers have relied upon measures of awareness, recall, and reported response to indicate whether or not advertising has had an impact. These measures allow us to assess the degree to which an ad has been noticed (a necessary precursor to any more fundamental effect) and the degree to which the advertisement is likely to lead to a purchase. We adapted Millward Brown's proprietary measurement systems to the Web environment to assess the awareness of, and reaction to, the ad banners themselves. However, we sought to go beyond measures of awareness, recall, and reported purchase probability. We sought to determine the contribution the ad banner makes to building the brand. To do this we adapted Millward Brown's Brand-Dynamics™ System to work in the context of an online interview (Dyson, Farr, and Hollis, 1996).

The BrandDynamics™ System

The BrandDynamics™ System is composed of two modules: the Consumer Value Model and the BrandDynamics™ Pyramid.

The Consumer Value Model

The Consumer Value Model allows us to identify the probability that an individual will choose a particular brand for their next purchase. We call this measure *Consumer Loyalty*. The prediction of Consumer Loyalty is based on:

- consumers' claimed brand consideration
- a measure of brand size
- the price of the brand relative to others in the category

The Consumer Value Model has been validated against behavioral data and market share in many different categories in both North America and Europe. A higher average Consumer Loyalty in the exposed cell than the control would suggest that the banner exposure had positively affected the likelihood that people would buy the advertised brand.

The BrandDynamics™ Pyramid

Based on a consistent set of survey measures that can be applied across different brands, categories, and countries, the BrandDynamics™ Pyramid allows us to explain the variation we observe in respondents' Consumer Loyalty scores. Each level of the Pyramid is a composite of awareness and imagery measures. We use these levels as building blocks to define an individual's relationship with a brand, as shown in Figure 5-11.

As we move up the levels of the Pyramid we describe a deepening attitudinal involvement with

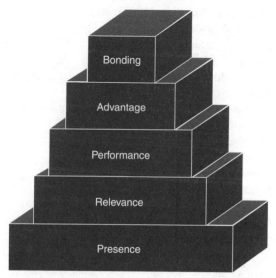

Figure 5-11   BrandDynamics™ Pyramid

the brand. The brand relationship moves from consciousness of the brand (*Presence*), through acquaintance and examination (*Relevance and Performance*), and to experience (*Advantage*), and then, finally, to the point where the consumer finds it difficult to consider alternative choices (*Bonded*). By comparing the percentage of people in the control and exposed cells who attain each level of the BrandDynamics™ Pyramid, we explain any observed changes in Consumer Loyalty.

Immediate vs. Delayed Effects

An important point to note is that the findings reported in this document relate to consumers' reactions a day or so after exposure. Tracking advertising response in traditional media suggests that the observed increases would erode over time without the reinforcement of further exposure. A positive response to advertising, while obviously desirable, is of little benefit to a brand unless it positively influences the consumer's choice on the next purchase occasion. Therefore, a key function of advertising is not only to establish but to *maintain* key brand associations in long-term memory so that they come to mind the next time the person encounters the brand. Unfortunately, it is beyond the scope of this project to evaluate the advertising in this respect. The objective of our study was to identify the immediate effect of one additional banner exposure. However, since exposure is rarely limited to one occasion, we assume there would be additional effect with repeated exposure (and the results of this study suggest as much).

THE STUDY DESIGN

We designed our research to address the particular concerns of both the advertiser and the researcher. Advertisers need to accurately measure the impact of advertising. Therefore, we measured the communication value of the advertising banner (i.e., its impact on consumer's attitudes), as well as its ability to elicit an immediate behavioral response (the click-through). We controlled exposure carefully

to ensure that observed differences were due to the advertising and not extraneous variables. And we tested ads which had varying levels of preexisting advertising "weight" in order to gauge diminishing returns.

The research objective was to execute a rigorous and carefully controlled study which avoided the bias sometimes encountered in on-line research. We represented the "real world" as precisely as possible, by ensuring that the true nature of the research was not immediately apparent to participants. Our recruitment methodology guaranteed us a true cross-section of users, and our ability to record the Web site behavior of both Responders and Nonresponders enabled us to look for significant differences between Responders/ Nonresponders and Control/Test Cells. No significant differences were observed.

First Day

From the universe of users who accessed Hot-Wired between September 9 and September 16, 1996, a random sample was solicited for participation in a short research study, "To Help HotWired Better Understand Their Audience." Thirty-eight percent of those solicited participated. Respondents completed a seven-minute survey covering demographics and webographics. The survey avoided any indication of the true purpose of the research. Upon submission of the survey, respondents were returned to HotWired's homepage. Respondents were randomly assigned to Control or Exposed (test) cells. One of three test ads, or a control ad, was randomly placed in the designated advertising space on HotWired's homepage.

Second Day

Respondents were sent an email thanking them for their participation and inviting them to participate in a second survey (with the added incentive of a chance to win $100). Respondents were provided a URL (Web address) in the email and directed to link to the Web page in order to participate in the survey. Sixty-one percent of the original respondents participated in the second survey.

TABLE 5.5

	Total	Exposed	Control
Total sample	1,232	910	293
Men's apparel brand	397	301	82
Telecommunication			
company ISP	422	312	95
Web browser	413	297	116

Respondents from the test cells were served one of three category-specific surveys based on their exposure to the advertisement on the first day. Respondents from the control cell were randomly directed to one of the three exposure surveys. The resulting final base sizes for each cell are shown in Table 5.5.

There was no special selection process for the creative used in the experiment. We believe it is possible for advertisers to create banners that compare favorably to the ones tested in this study. What was significant about the ad banners used was that each one represented a brand at a different stage of developing a "presence" on the Web.

Men's Apparel Brand

For reasons of client confidentiality we have used debranded data in this paper. At the time of this study, the men's apparel brand was preparing to launch their Web site. In fact, the very first Web advertising impressions that were seen for this brand occurred as part of this study. Thus we expected the banner exposure to increase *Presence* (consciousness of the brand) and *Relevance* (perception that the brand might suit their clothing needs). We expected the advertising to sway individuals who identified with the Web toward purchasing the brand that had recently become "wired." Seeing the advertising might also cause people in this target audience who had previously rejected the brand to reevaluate their opinion, perhaps even to perceive an *Advantage* and then *Bond* with it. This could result in an increase in their

likelihood to purchase the brand, as measured by the difference in Consumer Loyalty scores between the exposed and control cells.

A Telecommunication Company's Internet Service Provider Brand

While the telecommunication company helped pioneer Web advertising, the ISP brand had not been advertised on the Web prior to our study. Given the telecommunication company's strong overarching brand name, we expected that the ad banner might reinforce the parent company's generic presence rather than generate significant awareness for the ISP brand specifically. And because the telecommunication company's objective was to create an immediate behavioral response (a click-through), we wondered whether we would observe an attitudinal response at all.

Web Browser

The latest version of this Web browser was released with a significant Web advertising campaign. The browser was a new product but with pervasive presence and a well-known parent company; therefore, we were prepared to see little response at all to just one more banner exposure. If, however, users did show a measurable response to one additional exposure to the ad banner, then we would conclude that Web advertising has the potential to impact consumers even at higher levels of frequency.

DID THE ADVERTISING AFFECT ATTITUDES?

To answer this question, we will start by considering the overall impact of an additional ad banner exposure on the various brands tested using the Consumer Loyalty score. We will then explore the factors that may have caused the observed differences on a brand-by-brand basis.

Consumer Loyalty

The Consumer Loyalty score, which measures the likelihood that the consumer will purchase the product on the next purchase occasion, has been shown to be highly predictive of consumer purchase behavior. In each of our three test cells, the Consumer Loyalty score is higher than that for the control cell, suggesting that the extra exposure did have an effect. (When considering the implications of these scores, it is important to bear in mind how they are derived. The basic component of the Consumer Loyalty score is a consideration scale. Another key component is the relative price of the different brands within their category. For the men's apparel and ISP brands we calculated a *perceived* relative price from the brand image data. The men's apparel brand indexes 10 percent higher than the average khaki pants, and the ISP 30 percent higher than the average Internet service provider. To the extent that this perception-based measure differs from the actual relative prices in the market, the absolute Consumer Loyalty will be biased up or down. However, any bias will be consistent between the two cells. In the case of the Web browser, the price index is set to nearly zero, given that it could be downloaded for free.) The difference is most significant in the case of the men's apparel brand, reflecting the fact that the exposure was the first time the brand had ever advertised on the Web. The impact of a single Web banner exposure on the Consumer Loyalty score ranged from a 5 percent increase for the Web browser to an increase of over 50 percent for the men's apparel brand as shown in Figure 5-12.

Why does the Consumer Loyalty score increase so strongly for the men's apparel brand? Do those who are exposed to the advertising banner suddenly say that this brand is the only brand they will buy? Though the impact of the advertising is not this dramatic, Figure 5-13 shows how the advertising makes some people a bit more likely to consider this brand compared to other brands. The differences noted are statistically significant. (Statis-

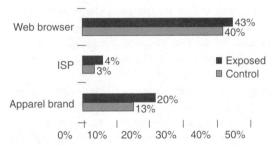

Figure 5-12   Effect on Consumer Loyalty

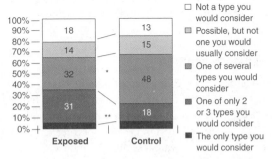

Figure 5-13   Consideration of Apparel Brand

tically significant differences have been marked as follows: 95 percent confidence level denoted with **, 90 percent confidence level denoted with *.)

The first appearance of a banner for the men's apparel brand seemed to cause some people to move the brand higher up in their consideration hierarchy. A complementary question, designed to determine if the brand might fulfill a specific role in relation to other brands people might consider, demonstrates that exposure to the men's apparel brand ad banner increased the likelihood that the brand will be bought for a purpose that other competing brands don't fulfill (exposed: 14 percent versus control: 5 percent).

The ISP and Web browser brands show a different pattern of response, perhaps indicating a degree of diminishing returns associated with increased advertising weight on this particular measurement. Neither brand shows statistically significant increases in the consideration hierarchy. However, those exposed to the ISP banner clearly demonstrate an increased propensity to "'buy" the service for a purpose that other competing brands don't fulfill (exposed: 26 percent versus control: 14 percent).

It is important to note that the differences reported refer to future purchase consideration. There is no difference between the exposed and control cells in terms of prior brand experience or ownership for any of the three brands, confirming that exposure to a single additional advertising banner has the potential to increase purchases.

Name Recognition

Given that a basic function of all advertising is to increase the presence of the advertised brand in the marketplace, and that the men's apparel brand had never advertised in this medium before, it is not surprising that awareness of the men's apparel brand is higher in the exposed cell than the control, as shown in Figure 5-14. This result is also observed with the Web browser, despite the fact that the level of awareness of that brand is already extremely high.

It appears that, in addition to increasing the Consumer Loyalty scores, the advertising increases passive name recognition as well. So, how does the advertising appear to affect the levels of the BrandDynamics™ Pyramid for each brand?

THE BRANDDYNAMICS™ PYRAMID: MEN'S APPAREL BRAND

All levels of the pyramid increased from the Control to the Exposed cell, with the largest effect observed at the *Presence* level (see Figure 5-15). The score at each of the Pyramid levels is a composite of awareness and image measures. By looking at the individual measures which comprise each level, we can further diagnose the effects of the advertising. This increase in *Presence* is driven entirely by an increase in just one of the measures used to define *Presence*—endorsement of the statement, "Comes readily to mind when you think about (clothes)." (Fifty percent of the exposed agree with this statement, compared to thirty-two percent of those in the control cell.) The increase of the *Presence* dimension then fuels the majority of the increase at higher levels of the Pyramid, suggesting that many people held latent good opinions of the men's apparel brand which emerge upon exposure to the advertising banner. There are also some modest increases observed for attributes that affect the higher levels of the Pyramid. These are shown in Figure 5-16.

As can be seen from the chart, the largest difference is in the attribute "just the same as other brands." While not expressly used to build the Pyramid, this attribute contrasts "offers something

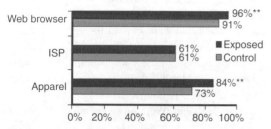

Figure 5-14   Aided Brand Awareness

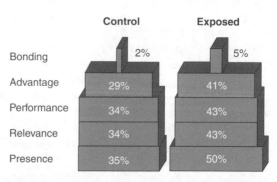

Figure 5-15   BrandDynamics™ Pyramid— Men's Apparel

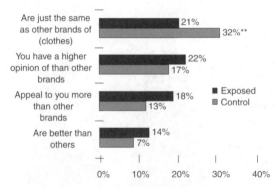

Figure 5-16   Apparel Brand Attributes

different," which is used, in part, to derive *Advantage* and *Bonding.* This finding suggests that the advertising has a positive effect on perceptions as well as *Presence,* by creating a distinctiveness for this brand among the Web audience.

The hypothesis that Web advertising can positively impact perceptions is confirmed by the fact that other diagnostic measures also exhibit a difference between the exposed and control cells. Out of 18 adjectives which might describe the men's apparel brand with which people can agree or disagree, 5 are higher in the exposed cell compared to the control (see Figure 5-17).

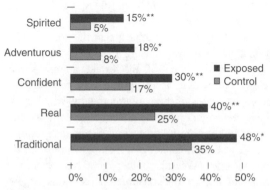

Figure 5-17   Apparel Brand Personality

For this brand, the findings appear conclusive. The effect of its first exposure on the Web has a strong immediate effect on the brand. Consumer Loyalty and brand *Presence* increase, perceptions of the brand's personality are positively impacted, and the advertising helped to differentiate the brand from its competition. We attribute these effects both to the context in which exposure takes place and the power of the banner on the target audience. The Web and the HotWired site have strong positive images for these people; HotWired delivers content they find relevant through a medium—the Web—which they find exciting. Advertising on the Web transferred some of this excitement and relevance on to the men's apparel brand itself.

THE BRANDDYNAMICS™ PYRAMID: ISP

As might be expected from the Consumer Loyalty results, we do not see quite the same degree of impact resulting from the first exposure to the ISP banner (see Figure 5-18).

The results for this brand may suggest that increasing brand awareness for new products and services (especially when branded under a strong parent name) may take more than a single banner impression to have a dramatic impact on consumers' perceptions and purchase intentions. While there is little change in the overall Pyramid, there are two individual attributes that exhibited a significant difference.

One measure, "is growing more popular," helps define perceptions of *Advantage* and *Bonding* (38 percent of the exposed cell agreed with this statement compared to 26 percent of the control). The other attribute, "is a good Internet service provider," helps to define the *Performance* level of the pyramid but only among those who have first achieved the level of *Relevance.* Overall, 43 percent of the exposed cell agrees that this ISP would be a good Internet service provider versus 31 percent among the control. The increase observed in

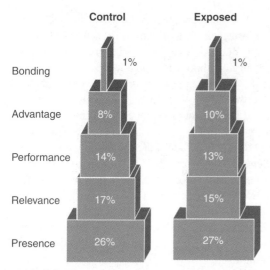

Figure 5-18   BrandDynamics™ Pyramid— ISP Brand

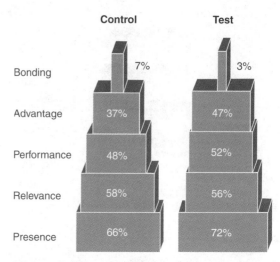

Figure 5-19   BrandDynamics™ Pyramid— Web Browser

these two measures occurred among people who had failed to qualify for either the *Presence* or *Relevance* levels of the Pyramid.

THE BRANDDYNAMICS™ PYRAMID: THE WEB BROWSER

The overall Pyramid and its underlying attributes provide intriguing insight into consumer perception of the parent brand, as well as the advertising for this particular product (see Figure 5-19).

Even with ubiquitous advertising levels, there is a modest positive increase in *Presence* as a result of one more exposure to the Web browser's ad banner on HotWired's homepage. We also see some marginal increase at the levels of *Performance* and *Advantage*. The *Bonding* score, however, declined. This decline may have been caused by the negative press surrounding the brand during the time of the advertising effectiveness test.

To a similar point, the *Presence* level comprises not just an active awareness of the brand, but an active awareness of the brand promise (defined by an acceptance or rejection of the notion

that the brand is relevant to the individual's needs). In the case of the Web browser brand, the awareness component for the exposed cell is higher than the control cell (47 percent versus 41 percent). However, active rejection is also 5 percentage points higher (12 percent in the exposed cell versus 7 percent in the control cell). Similarly, when we turn to the higher levels of the Pyramid, "have a higher opinion of than other Web browsers" is lower among the exposed cell (6 percent versus 12 percent among the control). This increase in active rejection, in part, accounts for the reduced score at the *Bonding* level.

Overall, it would appear that the single additional advertising exposure increased the awareness and *Presence* of the brand among some viewers; however, it also reminded a few of their negative views of the parent company, which may have been generated by the intense scrutiny focused on the security provisions within the product.

These findings suggest that exposure to an ad banner on HotWired's homepage can have an immediate impact on consumer perceptions of the advertised brand. We now turn to the advertising-specific data to better understand these reactions.

REMEMBERED EXPOSURE: BRAND-LINKED AD AWARENESS

We know that all those in the exposed cell had one more opportunity to see the ad banner than those in the control cell. This additional exposure should result in those exposed having both a higher level of brand awareness, in general, and a higher level of ad banner awareness specifically.

We will now assess the results for specific brand-linked ad awareness, a measure that has been found to have a strong predictive relationship with sales in traditional media (Hollis, 1994). Figure 5-20 confirms that the proportion of people who claimed to remember seeing the tested brand advertised on the World Wide Web in the past seven days was higher in all cases. The chart shows that the increase in ad awareness varies by brand. This variance is a function of the overall power of the banners, diminishing returns related to the individual brands' Web advertising weights, and the original level, the "base," from which ad awareness had been increased.

To properly understand the last factor, we need to consider the fact that it must be incrementally more difficult to raise awareness from a base level of 73 percent than from 7 percent. Millward Brown's FORCE score (the *First Opportunity to see Response Created by the Execution*) (Dyson and Farr, 1995) accounts for the effects of diminishing returns and consequently allows a like-for-

like comparison of the three banners ability to create brand linked ad awareness.

Millward Brown utilizes the FORCE score in traditional media such as television and print. As the FORCE score models out the effects of time, exposure weight, diminishing returns, and base level, FORCE scores can be directly compared across media types. While time-series modeling is normally employed to calculate the FORCE measure, in this case it was not necessary. The aspects of time, exposure weight, and base level were all controlled for by the test design and a simple calculation can be used to allow for the diminishing returns effect.

As the median FORCE score for television advertisements is only 10 percent the scores reported in Figure 5-21 (an average score of 20) suggest that the Web banners we tested compare very favorably to most TV ads in terms of creating brand-linked ad awareness.

Though this finding may seem surprising at first glance, previous work done by Millward Brown in the United Kingdom suggests that print also compares very favorably to TV in its ability to create brand-linked awareness of advertising (Farr, 1994). The median FORCE score for print ads is 18 percent, as can be seen in Figure 5-22.

While TV has the advantage of being more intrusive (moving visuals, sound, etc.), it is nonetheless a passive medium. The content is displayed to the viewer irrespective of whether they are actually

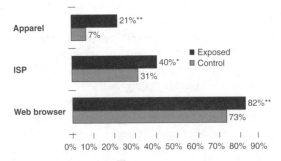

Figure 5-20   Ad Awareness

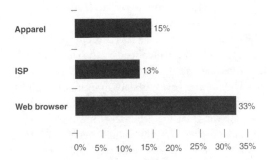

Figure 5-21   FORCE Score

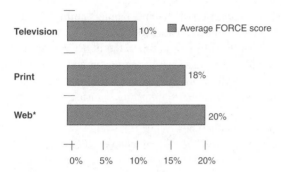

Figure 5-22   Comparison of FORCE Score by Media Type

attending to it. Conversely, Web- and print-based media both have the advantage of active reader involvement. The consumer actively engages with the content as they peruse it and search for items of interest. This engaged state, that the nature of the Web encourages, seems to result in higher initial recall of advertising than might otherwise be expected.

We have now observed that, overall, Web advertising can create strong increases in brand-linked ad awareness, the necessary precursor to the changes in brand-related measures. But how do the individual banners compare?

As the men's apparel brand banner had not run anywhere else on the Web prior to the study, we are able to see a true picture of the effect of one exposure. Seven percent of the respondents in the control cell claim to have seen an ad for the brand in the past seven days. While we know this to be contrary to fact, this level of base awareness is not unusual; in fact, it is to be expected from an established and relatively well-known brand like the one tested. The increase of 200 percent for the exposed cell is considerable, even by the standards of television and print advertising. The resulting FORCE score, however, is only marginally higher than the observed increase in ad awareness. This is due to the fact that the effects of diminishing returns and exposure weight (which negatively impact the absolute increase observed for the other brands) are minimal in the case of the men's ap-

parel brand, since it started with a low level of awareness.

The telecommunication company's banner generated a 29 percent increase in general awareness of advertising for the brand on the Web. The higher base level and the increased impact of diminishing returns account for the difference in the size of this increase relative to the one observed for the men's apparel brand.

The results for the Web browser's FORCE score stand out from the others. Though the base awareness level in the control cell is extremely high in comparison to any point-in-time measure for traditional media, it is clear that an extra exposure on HotWired's homepage is capable of improving even on *that* high level of awareness. The FORCE score indicates that the browser's banner created a high level of brand-linked memorability—a level far higher, in fact, than the averages for television and print. The publicity and other marketing activity surrounding the browser's introduction may well have played a part in the increased attention that people paid to this ad, but the score is dramatic nonetheless.

THE EFFECT OF DIMINISHING RETURNS

What is the incremental value of the additional ad banner exposure? Analysis of Web server-log files by one Web media company suggests that diminishing returns on the behavioral click-through begin immediately and that, at a frequency of three exposures, little to no additional click-through benefit is garnered. If this suggestion is correct, does the brand communication value generated from the exposure of the banner exhibit a similar pattern?

To fully analyze the diminishing returns function requires a tightly controlled experiment which measures the effect at multiple levels of exposure for each banner ad. While this type of measurement is beyond the scope of this study, the following analysis does provide some insight into the incremental benefit one might expect to find at different levels of frequency. The analysis is based on a comparison of the single exposure for the three different ads tested. On average, these brands have different levels of weight ranging from the men's apparel brand (no previous exposure) to the Web browser (significant exposure on average).

For instance, specific banner awareness (elicited by showing people the actual ad banner) displays a classic diminishing returns function consistent with findings from traditional media. Initial banner awareness is highest for the Web Browser (see Figure 5-23), since many of these people are likely to have been exposed to this banner, or one like it, elsewhere, but the incremental benefit of one additional exposure is the lowest of the three (see Figure 5-24). The converse can be seen for the apparel brand. Initial awareness is lowest, but one additional exposure results in the strongest increase. The suggestion that there may be diminishing returns does not preclude the fact that there is likely to be (as in the cases tested) measurable incremental effects at higher levels of frequency. Whether the incremental benefit warrants the cost of exposure is a question that can only be answered on a brand-by-brand basis.

A key finding is that the benefits are likely to be derived even after multiple exposures. In addition, findings for the men's apparel brand seemed to indi-

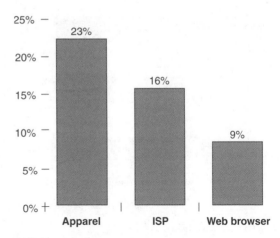

Figure 5-24   Incremental Effect on Specific Brand-Linked Awareness

cate that the communication power was partially a function of the surrounding program context.

AD REACTION

The questions employed to understand consumer reaction to the advertising banners themselves were adapted from Millward Brown's Link copy test. The results reinforce the notion that the Web is a unique medium. It resembles traditional print media in some respects but exhibits some similarities with outdoor advertising in the way people describe their reaction to the content.

The main finding in this area is the lack of variation in response to the ad banners. It tends to confirm that part of the ad awareness increase observed for the Web browser's banner could be due to synergy with other marketing activity and exposure. While the lack of variation in this diagnostic data might be a function of the banners tested, it does suggest that the high-involvement, prominent placement aspects of advertising on the Web dominate the differences in creative impact.

An example of this uniformity of response can be seen in how the banners exhibit little difference

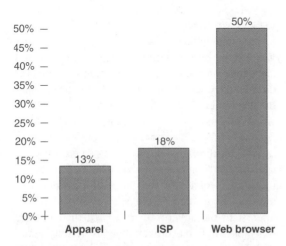

Figure 5-23   Baseline Specific Brand-Linked Awareness

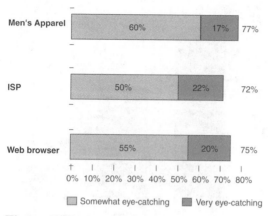

Figure 5-25   Standout Power

in the degree to which people thought they were "eyecatching," as shown in Figure 5-25. The similar results are especially noteworthy given that the men's apparel brand and ISP were animated banner ads, while the Web browser was not. The power of an advertisement to hold a consumer's attention and be remembered at a later date varies widely in other forms of media, even given a constant level of exposure. The main causes of the variation differ by medium. In print, category interest is key, since people are actively searching for items of interest; the creative power of an ad plays a supporting role. For TV advertising, creative power dominates and viewer involvement is key. (Viewer involvement is a function of enjoyability and the degree to which attention involves active processing rather than passive) (Hollis, 1995). Our results from this study suggest that the Web is far more similar to print than TV in this respect.

DETERMINING FACTORS OF CLICK-THROUGH

A focus of the Web advertising debate has centered on the value of click-through. Click-through on ad banners transports readers from content focused Web sites to advertiser sites where direct marketing

can occur. From this point of view, ad banners are similar to direct mail envelopes, enticing the recipient to open it up, browse further, and take action. Using this logic, many people have argued in favor of the click-through rate as the best measure of advertising response on the Web. However, we believe that the click-through response is determined by five basic factors, three of which relate to the predisposition of the audience, not the advertising itself.

Audience-related factors are:

- innate tendency to click on advertisements
- immediate relevance of the product to the audience
- preexisting appeal of the brand or company

Advertising-related factors are:

- immediate relevance of the message to the audience
- involvement or intrigue created by the ad

The results of this experiment indicate that those who click through had, as might be expected, actual recall of the ad banner (which they may have seen in locations other than HotWired). More importantly the brand had immediate personal relevance to the user. People who remembered the ad and who said the product category was of interest to them were three times more likely than the average to claim to have clicked-through. The fact that we observe little difference between the reported click-through rates for any of the banners tested indicates that click-through in itself may not predict the level of brand building likely to be realized.

While more extensive studies need to be conducted to fully understand other factors that might drive click-through, these findings suggest that ad agencies and content providers who agree to be remunerated solely on the basis of click-through rates are tying their revenues to current levels of interest in the advertised brands of their clients. Since our study has proven that advertising on the Web has sizable effects on brand loyalty and attitudes which are not reflected in click-through, the use of click-through rates alone are likely to undervalue the Web as an advertising medium.

If this finding proves to be a general one, then tactics designed to generate click-through may also underutilize the power of Web advertising. The practice of running "unbranded" banners, which has been reported to yield high click-through rates, surely runs counter to the concept of brand building through ad banner exposure. In short, click-through certainly has value (especially if the goal is to create an immediate behavioral response such as downloading software), but the clickthrough rate itself is unlikely to be indicative of the overall value of a banner exposure.

Conclusions

So what do our findings tell us about Web banner advertising? Our results tell us, simply and unequivocally, that it works. Moreover, it works with or without the added benefit of click-through. One single banner exposure generated increases in Consumer Loyalty scores ranging from 5 percent for the Web Browser to 50 percent for the men's apparel brand. Advertising awareness increased from a low of 12 percent (for the brand with the highest base of ad awareness) to a high of 200 percent for the previously unadvertised men's apparel brand. The FORCE scores we calculated for the three banner ads suggest that Web banners may rival or surpass TV and print advertising in producing brand-linked ad awareness. We observed, as expected, a diminishing returns factor associated with levels of advertising weight. This factor dampened but did not extinguish the advertising effects.

In addition, our findings to date suggest that the high-involvement nature of the Web and the prominence of the advertising seemed to play a larger role in defining ad effectiveness than did consumer reaction to any particular execution we tested. In this respect advertising on the Web appears to work similarly to print rather than TV. A combination of factors appear to generate click-through, the primary one being the nature of the audience and the inherent interest the product category holds for them. The appeal of the creative plays a secondary role at best.

The Web offers unique and undeniable advantages over other media in terms of targeting and direct marketing. One such advantage is the ability of advertising banners to serve as gateways to an advertiser's own Web site. But our results suggest that the ad banner is a legitimate advertising vehicle in its own right. This experiment shows that banner ads on the HotWired Network have a significant impact on their viewers, an impact that demonstrably builds the advertised brand. Banner ads remind people of a brand's existence, stimulate latent or dormant brand associations, and can cause people to change their attitudes toward the brand, thus increasing their likelihood to purchase. The unique marketing power of the on-line environment and the established communication benefits of traditional advertising combine to make the Web a powerful new advertising medium with real potential for brand building.

Rex Briggs is vice president of MBinteractive, a division of Millward Brown International. Formerly, Mr. Briggs was director of research for HotWired. Mr. Briggs began analyzing the impact of the Internet on marketing in 1993. San Francisco-based MBinteractive is a full service research practice dedicated to helping clients measure and understand interactive marketing.

Nigel S. Hollis is the Group Research and Development Director at Millward Brown International. In his current role he has global responsibility for all projects related to improving Millward Brown's current services or developing new ones. Over the last two years he has worked on projects related to brand equity, and interactive and on-line research.

Mr. Hollis started work in market research at Cadbury Schweppes in the United Kingdom. After gaining a broad experience of different research methodologies at Cadbury, he joined Millward Brown in 1983. There he had a key role in the development of Millward Brown's successful TV Link pre-test. In 1988 he transferred to the United States and, until moving to his current role, worked on a variety of client businesses, mostly related to the analysis of tracking research.

He has had papers published in the *Journal of Advertising Research*, *Admap*, *plunung und analyse*, and the *Journal of the Market Research Society*.

REFERENCES

Dyson, P., A. Farr, and N. Hollis. "Understanding, Measuring, and Using Brand Equity." *Journal of Advertising Research* 36, 6 (1996): 9–21.

———, and A. Farr. "Effective Frequency, New Evidence on an Old Debate." In the Proceedings of the 1995 Market Research Society Conference.

Farr, A. "Ad Track 94." A study of magazine advertising effectiveness, available from IPC Magazines or Millward Brown International.

Hollis, N. "The Link Between TV Ad Awareness and Sales." *Journal of the Market Research Society,* January 1994.

———. "Like It or Not, Liking Is Not Enough." *Journal of Advertising Research* 35, 5 (1995): 7–16.

Is Internet Advertising Ready for Prime Time?

Xavier Drèze
Fred Zufryden

Advertising on the World Wide Web is growing at a fast pace. However, it is difficult to compare advertising effectiveness on the Internet relative to standard media, such as broadcast and print, because current measures of advertising effectiveness on the Web are not standardized and incorporate significant measurement errors. In this study, we investigate issues relating to the accurate measurement of advertising GRPs, Reach, and Frequency on the Internet. Moreover, we suggest critical measurement issues that need to be resolved before Internet advertising can be considered as an integral part of a company's media mix.

Online advertising revenues reached $906.5 million in 1997 (Internet Advertising Bureau, 1998). Although advertising expenditures on the Internet remain relatively small in contrast to standard media, this figure is approaching that of outdoor advertising and represents nearly a threefold increase over the last two years. In 1995, only $312 million were reported on Web advertising in contrast to $38.1 billion for the television medium (Jupiter Communications, 1996).

The spectacular growth trend in online advertising revenues, that has been experienced so far, is expected to continue. Thus, it has been projected that Internet advertising revenue will reach $1.9 billion in 1998, grow to $3 billion in 1999, and reach a level of $4.3 billion in the year 2000 (Jupiter Communications, 1998). Indeed, the latter growth statistics suggest that the Internet is quickly becoming a very significant advertising medium. Moreover, a substantial increase in rev-

Reprinted from the *Journal of Advertising Research,* © 1998, by the Advertising Research Foundation.

enues, from $1.5 billion in 1996 to a level of $3.7 billion in 1998, has been noted for expertise, access, software, content, and commerce on the Internet (*Advertising Age,* 1998). Thus, the concurrent growth of electronic commerce is expected to further fuel the growth of advertising activities and revenues on the Internet in the future.

Along with the growth of electronic commerce and advertising on the Web, the number of Web users has also been growing rapidly (*Electronic Advertising and Marketplace Report,* 1997). The number of Web users has been estimated at 36 million in 1996 and is expected to grow to 170 million users by the year 2000 (I/PRO, CyberAtlas, 1996). All of these factors suggest that Web-based advertising will ultimately become a very important component of a company's media mix. Already, numerous companies are committing large budgets to advertising on the Web. For instance, "Amazon.com," an online book retailer, has recently signed a contract for $19 million with America Online to rent space on the latter's home page to feature its banner ads for the next three years (see Online Money News, 1997).

Internet advertising has now reached the point at which many companies are considering it as being a viable alternative to traditional media. However, to render the Internet fully viable as an advertising medium, companies need standardized measures (such as Reach and Frequency) that will allow them to compare advertising effectiveness on the Internet to that of other media. Unfortunately, this is where a number of major measurement shortcomings currently exist on the Web. This is because Web servers typically provide statistics that can tell advertisers how many pages were requested, how much time was spent on each Web page, and what types of computers made the page requests. However, it is generally very difficult to translate the page requests into specific audience-viewing-behavior estimates. In particular, due to the present problems associated with identifying unique visitors to a site, it is difficult to accurately measure the impressions, Reach, and Frequency of banner advertising exposures for a target audience. Thus, the fundamental questions of "How many people visit a Web site?" and "What types of people visit a Web site?" are generally unanswered by current Web-based measures. Hence, it is difficult to compare advertising effectiveness on the Internet relative to that in media such as broadcast and print. Although standardized measurements exist for the latter media, standards have not yet been formalized for assessing advertising effectiveness on the Web. Until these standards emerge for the Internet, we argue that Internet advertising will not be truly "ready for prime time" in the sense that its effectiveness will not be comparable to the advertising effectiveness of other media. Hence, advertisers will not be able to justify shifting significant advertising budgets away from traditional media and allocate them to online advertising. This means that it is important to provide accurate measures of *impressions* as well as *Reach* and *Frequency* of banner advertising exposures relative to target audiences on the Web.

The purpose of the study is to determine the nature and magnitude of the errors that exist in current Web-based advertising effectiveness measures. We evaluate the accuracy of current methods in measuring Reach, Frequency, and Gross Rating Points (GRP) for banner ads on the Web. We also provide guidelines that will allow for a better interpretation of results from current measures and enable more meaningful comparisons to be made between advertising effectiveness on the Web relative to standard media.

MEASURING ADVERTISING EFFECTIVENESS ON THE WEB

Measurement Problems

At the present-time, despite ongoing efforts toward this end, there does not appear to be any widely accepted measurement standards for adver-

tising on the Web. Third-party companies, such as Netcount and I/PRO, have proposed Webspecific measures such as click-through rates (i.e., clicks on banner ads on a publisher's Web page that result in the transfer of a surfer to the advertiser's Web site) and advertising transfers (pages containing an advertiser's advertising message downloaded to a surfer's PC), developed from server log file records, to assess the effectiveness of banner ads within the Web-based multimedia environment. Interestingly, recent empirical evidence has suggested that the use of click-through rates is likely to undervalue the Web as an advertising medium (Briggs and Hollis, 1997). In contrast, to the aforementioned third-party census-based measurement procedures, companies such as Media-Metrix or Millward Brown Interactive have developed market-measurement methods based on a *sample* of home-based PCs in the United States (see Coffey and Stipp, 1997). Despite the advantages of the latter data source for evaluating individual visitor behavior on the Web, a potential limitation of online panel data is the sampling bias due to the omission of work- and school-based PCs from their sample. Another problem is that of representativeness. The number of panelists required to accurately reflect the behavior of Internet surfers is far larger than the number of households required to track 50 TV channels or 100 cereal brands. Some researchers (e.g., Drèze, Kalyanam, and Briggs, 1998) are working on methods that improve the representativeness of these online panels. However, these methods are still at the prototype stage.

Some Web-based companies have taken steps to provide Reach and Frequency measures on the Web in an effort to provide comparability with standard media (I/PRO-DoubleClick, 1997). However, the accuracy of these measures is limited by the current measurement problems that exist on the Web. In particular, there are two essential measurement problems that may bias such measures in connection with the measurement of the effectiveness of banner ads on the Web:

1. The Problem of Identifying Unique Site Visitors on the Web

In traditional media, advertising effectiveness measurements are usually collected through some kind of survey or panel. In these surveys or panels, potential viewers or listeners are uniquely identified (by a phone number or household address) and can, if needed, be tracked over time. Using this procedure, each record made can be linked to its originator without ambiguity. On the Internet, measurement companies have done away with costly surveys and can track users' actions from the log files of the sites they visit. Measurements of visitor traffic and flow patterns to, from, and within a given site are generally established on the basis of the visitors' IP (Internet Protocol) addresses. Unfortunately, these addresses may not be uniquely assigned to visitors by their Internet Service Provider. For example, several Internet users can be assigned the same IP address in multi-user systems such as America Online. In addition, from one session to another, Internet users who use Internet Service Providers that use dynamic IP allocation may have different IP addresses assigned to them. To complicate matters further, users can be assigned multiple IP addresses even within a single Internet session by Internet Service Providers that use multiple "proxy servers[1]." All of these problems make it difficult to accurately link the actions recorded on a Web site's log file to *unique* visitors of that site. Consequently, these problems may seriously affect the accurate measurement of advertising effectiveness measures such as advertising Reach on the Internet.

The following provides four alternative scenarios that illustrate the potential problems encountered when IP addresses are used to measure visitor behavior:

[1]A proxy server is a centralized computer that consolidates requests from multiple client computers. For example, if 20 different AOL users request the same MSNBC page, the AOL proxy server will make only one request to MSNBC and forward the answer to the 20 originating computers.

1. Visitor 1 accesses the Internet from two different PCs:

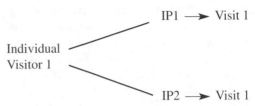

2. Visitor 2 makes one visit but uses an ISP with proxy servers. His requests are handled by two different proxy servers (with two different IP addresses) during the same visit:

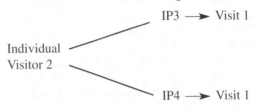

3. Visitor 3 makes two visits and is assigned a different IP by his ISP at each visit:

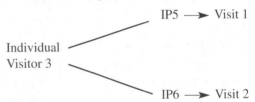

4. Visitor 4 makes two visits and uses the same ISP as user 3. For his second visit, he is assigned the same IP address as used by visitor 3 on his first visit:

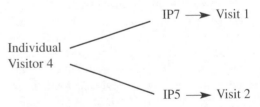

Looking at the log file of the site visited by our four individuals, we would erroneously conclude that seven different individuals visited the site. We would also believe that visit 1 of visitor 3 and visit 2 of visitor 4 were made by the same individual.

2. The Problem of Caching

An important determinant of the measurement of banner advertising effectiveness is the number of pages requested by a surfer on the Internet. A Web page is a document that may contain text as well as graphics, sound, and video files. A Web page thus provides a basic building block for a Web site, which will typically be comprised of one or more interlinked Web pages. Consider an individual surfer (Jane) who requests a page (A) from a Web site. This page contains a series of links to other pages as well as a banner advertisement for a car manufacturer (Ad 1). After reading the page, Jane follows one of the links to another page (B). Upon reading this second page, she clicks on the "Back Button" to go back to the first page (A). This results in a second exposure to the advertisement. Unfortunately, in an attempt to speed up the information flow, Jane's browser will not make a second request for page one (and the car advertisement) but will rather retrieve the information (both page A and Ad 1) from a local cache (typically on the surfer's PC hard drive)[2] where it stores pages after receiving them. This means that the Web site's server will not record Jane's second or any of her subsequent exposures to the banner advertising. Consequently, caching seriously biases advertising effectiveness measures, such as impressions and exposure Frequency, for banner ads. In fact, our study revealed that an average of 30 percent of page requests are not recorded by servers, either because the Web pages were cached on the surfer's PC or by "proxy servers" somewhere between the server and the surfer. Although the specific problem of caching is not encountered in traditional media, similar problems have plagued the measurement in standard media as well. For example, the time-shifted viewing of television programs by means of video recorders also leads to understatements of viewing behavior for the TV medium.

A third problem affecting the reliability of reported measures lies in the fact that there is a difference between requesting a page and actually reading it, or even receiving it. A lot of things can happen between a user request and the actual processing of the information contained in that page by the user. He or she can decide that the request takes too long to complete and cancel it. He or she can be attracted by a message displayed at the top of the requested page and request another page without reading all the information contained on the first one. The page might even be too long to fit on the screen, and the user does not have the time to scroll it to view its entirety. This type of problem plagues any medium. Newspaper subscribers do not necessarily read a newspaper in its entirety. When watching TV, a viewer could be distracted by the telephone or go to the kitchen and miss a particular commercial advertisement. Obviously this problem will tend to bias reported measures upward. Although we recognize this problem, we do not specifically consider it in our study in view of the associated measurement difficulties.

Defining and Measuring Ad Effectiveness on the Web

Consider the measurement of advertising effectiveness for a banner advertisement on the Web. The currently favored Web measures are Page Views and Click-through rates. However, to ensure comparability with standard media, the following standard measures need to be defined and measured for banner ads on the Web:

1. *Reach:* The net unduplicated number, or percentage, of a target audience that have had opportunity to see a banner ad one or more times.
2. *Frequency:* The average number of times an individual has had the opportunity to see a banner ad (conditional on the fact that he or she has been exposed to the banner ad at least once).

---

[2]Caches are temporary storage areas in which a computer system stores information that may be too lengthy to retrieve from their original location and that it may need in the near future.

3. *Cross Rating Points:* This measure, also called impressions, is the sum of all potential exposures to a banner ad without accounting for audience duplication. GRP may also be defined as the product of Reach and Frequency (i.e., GRP = Reach * Frequency).

As noted earlier, the development of advertising effectiveness measures, such as Reach, requires that the exposure patterns of individuals be known. This means that we must be able to identify and differentiate *unique* individual Web-site visitors. Currently IP addresses of visitors are the most common means of identifying unique Web-site visitors. Consequently, the number of distinct addresses that access a given page are used to compute the Reach of a banner ad on the Web. Unfortunately, because of the nonuniqueness of IP address assignment to Web users that has been described above, the resulting Reach figures are severely biased.

Likewise, the development of effectiveness measures, such as Frequency, requires that the complete exposure patterns to banner ads of unique individuals be known. This measurement is also complicated by the problems of identifying unique visitors and those of caching that have been described above.

Study Methodology

Our study focuses on the evaluation of the nature and magnitude of errors that now exist in measuring Reach, Frequency, and GRP for banner advertising on the Web with current measurement methods. We proceed according to the following four study steps: (1) We first examine five Web sites that track their visitors by the means of unique visitor IDs to estimate the bias created by the use of IP addresses as a means of visitor identification; (2) in the next study, we explore the implications of study 1 for measuring advertising effectiveness measures, including GRP, Reach, and Frequency; (3) next, we evaluate the effectiveness of three methodologies that attempt to re-

cover cached pages; and (4) last, we set up a test site to evaluate the impact, on surfers, of using procedures to uniquely identify them and to prevent caching.

Our approach (in study 2) involves the computation of Reach, Frequency, and GRP by means of current measurement procedures. That is, the Internet users' IP addresses are used to identify unique visitors to a Web site. At this stage, the recording of page requests from Web-site servers are used to measure potential exposures to banner advertising without accounting for potential repeat exposures to pages that may have been cached on individual surfers' PCs.

In order to examine the magnitude of the errors inherent in current measurement methods, we examined various Web sites that use unique visitor IDs. The visitor IDs were generated using a combination of cookies and user password.[3] These visitor IDs allow us to compute actual measures of Reach, Frequency, and GRP that accurately accounted for unique visitors.

We gathered data from five Web sites. These Web sites had widely different target audiences (education, news, entertainment, and information database) as well as sizes (1,000 to 90,000 visits per site). Our methodology involved a comparison of statistics generated using only IP address information (as would generally be the case for current measurement methods) and an IP address analysis supplemented by information from visitor IDs (to obtain contrasting estimates of the actual levels of the advertising effectiveness measures).

The third stage of our research evaluates the effectiveness of three cache recovery strategies. Three techniques are currently used to measure the requests of cached pages: (1) Do Nothing, (2) Full Path Recovery, and (3) Partial Path Recovery. We test the ability of these techniques to produce

[3]One must note that this tracking methodology is likely to impact the behavior of visitors (see study 4 for an analysis of this impact). However, the purpose of this study is not to describe the behavior of the Internet population but rather to evaluate how accurately one can measure this behavior. Hence we do not see this as a significant problem.

accurate statistics of ad exposure Frequency (caching does not affect Reach measures).

The purpose of our last study (study 4) was to evaluate the impact of implementing procedures for better monitoring Web surfers. Specifically, does the use of Cookies[4] as a visitor tracking mechanism or the implementation of a cache-defeating scheme alter surfers' behavior? To study this question, we modified an existing site to implement a 2×2 experimental design. In this setup, half of the site visitors were issued Cookies and the other half were not. The second (and orthogonal) treatment was to issue an immediate expiration date on the pages served to half the visitors. This would force the browsers of these visitors to reload the page from the server each time they want to access it, instead of retrieving them from their cache. Because of implementation issues, we were not able to test whether the use of passwords significantly impacts the behavior of online surfers.

STUDY RESULTS

Study 1—Current Biases in Estimating Number of Visitors and Visits

We first investigate the biases inherent in current measurement methods, which rely on IP address identification, in connection to the estimation of number of visitors and visits. Using Visitor ID information we find an average ratio of 1.16 IP addresses per visitor. This suggests that there is a significant problem in using IP addresses as a measure of number of unique visitors as different IP addresses were assigned to the same visitor in 16 percent of the address assignment instances. We also find an average ratio of 2.1 visitors per IP address. This suggested that a given address is assigned on the average to approximately 2 visitors. Moreover the nonuniqueness of IP addresses is further supported by the fact that the average number

of visits with multiple IP addresses (within a visit) was 3.5 percent. These represented cases where multiple proxy servers were used to satisfy a given visitor's requests within a given Internet session.

To assess the importance of using the proper procedures to identify users, we first compute basic descriptive statistics for each of the five sites—first, by using visitor IDs as the means of differentiating users and, second, by using IP addresses for that purpose. The summary results are shown in Table 5.6 (complete results are shown in Appendix A). As one can see, using IP addresses as a means of identification will lead to an underestimation of the number of visitors (39 percent on average) as well as number of the true number of visits (35 percent on average). Naturally, underestimating the number of visitors and visits leads to an overestimation of the number of pages seen by each visitor (64 percent as well as the time spent during each visit (79 percent). Finally, the reallocation of IP addresses to multiple users leads to an overestimation of the number of repeat visits of about 9 percent.

Study 2—Implications for Measurement of Advertising Effectiveness

Next, we investigate the accuracy of IP-based methods when measuring Reach, Frequency, and GRP. We look at banner ads appearing in two of the five Web sites that we studied (the other sites did not display advertising). Specifically, we stud-

TABLE 5.6	Measurement Error
Measurement	Average Error (%)
Number of visitors	−39*
Number of visits	−35
Number of pages accessed/visit	+64
Time spent/visit	+79
Number of repeat visits	+9

*−39% means that IP-based measures underestimate the true number of visitors by 39%.

[4]Cookies are small strings of text that are sent by a Web site to a visiting surfer's PC, stored on that PC, and retrieved by the Web site on subsequent page requests (i.e., these requests are tagged with the cookie).

ied three advertisements from site 1 and two advertisements from site 2. For the purpose of this test, we ignore the impact of caching on GRP measures. (The issue of caching is studied in detail in the next section.) At this stage, we only consider biases induced by visitor identification. The results of this investigation are summarized in Table 5.7 (detailed results appear in Appendix B).

As noted in Table 5.7, the measurement of advertising Reach is subject to the greatest error magnitude, with an average error of +25 percent and an error ranging from +12 percent to as high as +42 percent. Frequency was least subject to error by current measurement methods with an average of −1.1 percent. Here, the error ranged from a low of −13 percent to a high of +9 percent. Finally, GRPs were shown to result in an error of +22.7 percent with a variation over a narrow range of +22 percent to +23 percent. There is less variance in GRP error than in the two other measures because the error on Reach and Frequency are negatively correlated. Indeed, the numerator of the Reach formula and the denominator of the frequency formula are the same (number of people having seen the ad). Since GRP is equal to the product of Reach and Frequency, the numerator and denominator cancel each other. In fact, the only source of error in the GRP formula comes from the estimation of the total number of visitors (assuming that caching is not an issue). This means that, within a site, the error in GRP is *constant*. It is equal to the inverse of the error in

unique visitor count. For instance, using IP addresses to measure GRP, we overestimate Site 1's measures by 23.09 percent. This is due to the error in visitor identification of −18.76 percent (1/0.8124 = 1.2309). Similarly, the errors for Site 2 are 22.14 percent and −18.12 percent for GRP and visitor identification (1/0.8188 = 1.2214). In short, if one can estimate the error rate in using IP addresses to identify users for a given site, one can correct all GRP measures for that site.

The Frequency distribution of exposures often provides a useful media analysis tool for studying the impact of a given media schedule on a target market. Several different model approaches have been proposed in the literature to measure the Frequency distribution of exposures (e.g., see Metheringham, 1964; Headen et al., 1977; Zufryden, 1987; Pedrick and Zufryden, 1991). The results of Table 5.7 suggest that the Frequency of exposures distributions, that are developed from current measurement methods, may be subject to significant errors.

To illustrate the specific nature of the potential errors in exposure distributions that may be produced by the current methods, we used the commonly applied Beta Binomial Distribution (BBD), first proposed by Metheringham (1964), as a model of the distribution of banner advertising exposures over a target population. Here, this model is used to describe $P(i\backslash N;m,n)$, the probability that a Web surfer is subject to i banner advertising exposures, given a maximum of N exposures, and may be stated mathematically as:

TABLE 5.7	**Errors in Measurement of Advertising Effectiveness Based on IP Address Identification**			
			% Error Range	
Average	**% Error**		**Low**	**High**
Reach	+25*		+12	+42
Frequency	−1.1		−13	+9
GRP	+22.7		+22	+23

*i.e., IP-based measurement overestimate true Reach by 25%.

$$P(i \mid N;m,n) = \frac{N!}{(N-i)!i!} \frac{\Gamma(m+n)}{\Gamma(m)\Gamma(n)}$$

$$\frac{\Gamma(m+i)\Gamma(n+N-i)}{\Gamma(m+n+N)} \quad (1)$$

for $i(= 0, 1, 2, \ldots, N$ banner advertising exposures, with $m, n > 0$ model parameters.

We considered the exposure patterns to a banner ad on a given Web page based on measurements of Reach = 0.75 and GRPs = 1.75 from current methods by using only IP address identification. Then, we obtained estimates of actual

Reach and Frequency for the banner ad by applying the average percent error corrections developed in Table 5.7. Thus, the actual Reach and GRP figures were estimated as 0.56 and 1.35, respectively. We then fitted BBD distributions to the corresponding Reach and GRP figures by a method of means and zeroes (e.g., see Pedrick and Zufryden, 1991). Figure 5-26 illustrates the distributions based on actual and estimated Reach and GRP values that were so developed for a case situation where the maximum number of banner advertising exposures in the target market is $N = 16$. Here, we note that the exposure distribution estimated from

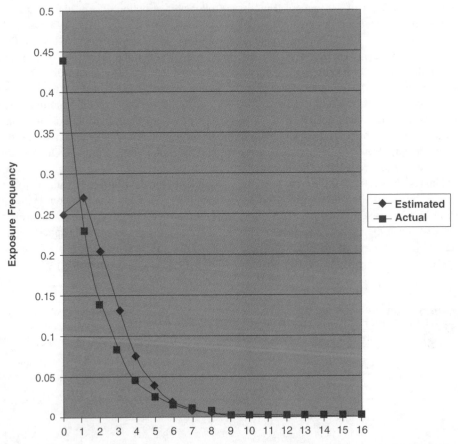

Figure 5-26   Contrast of BBD Exposure Distributions Based on Estimated and Actual Levels of Reach and GRPs

current measurement methods resulted in frequencies that overstated the actual frequencies over intermediate values of exposure levels and then slightly understated actual Frequency values for higher levels of exposures. Thus, Figure 5-26 suggests that errors in Reach and GRP may create significant skews and consequent biases in the resulting patterns of distributions of exposures.

Study 3—Cache Recovery Algorithms

We now turn to the implications of caching. As we mentioned earlier in this paper, the purpose of caching is to increase the apparent speed of data transfer between a user's computer and the site he or she is visiting. This is done by saving some information on the user's PC and accessing that information more speedily instead of the Web site when it is needed. As a result, Web site logs will record only one exposure per visit from any visitor (assuming that the visitor's caching algorithm works perfectly). This is a problem when measuring GRP since repeat exposure to an advertisement during a single visit will not be recorded. Only repeat exposures across multiple visits or sites are.

To measure the impact of caching on GRP measures, we modified an existing Web site so that it would send a special instruction, along with each page, that would disable caching on the user's computer. This yielded a log file with a complete record of all pages accessed. We then simulated the impact of caching by keeping only the first exposure of each of the pages during each visit (i.e., Perfect Cache). Lastly, we applied three different cache recovery strategies to this file and compared various statistics obtained after cache recovery with the statistics obtained on the raw (no cache) file. The three strategies, described below, are: (1) No Path Recovery, (2) Full Path Recovery, and (3) Partial Path Recovery.

To illustrate these strategies, consider a Web site, which consists of a tree-like structure linking its pages, defined as nodes on the network (A to G), as shown in Figure 5-27. Consider now the situation of a surfer who visits the site in the follow-

Sample Site Visit

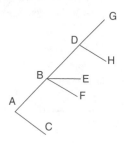

Visit: A B D G D[1] H D[1] B[1] E B F A[2] C

Log with Cache: A B D G H E F C
[1]Use the "Back" button
[2]Use the "Go" menu

Figure 5-27   Illustration of Cache Recovery Algorithms

ing way: He or she starts at A, then goes to B, D, and G. At this point our user presses the "Back Button" on the browser to go back to D, then goes to H. Now, he or she backs up through D and B, visits E, backs down to B, and goes to F. At this point, the user decides that he or she has gone deep enough and uses the browser's Go Menu to jump back directly to the starting point A and then finishes the visit in C. The total visits yielded 13 page exposures. Nevertheless, only 8 page requests would have been made.

Possible algorithms for inferring page requests and thus recovering the sequence of cached pages include the following:

- *Partial Path Recovery* When the server notes a user jumping from page H to page E, it can infer that the last jump was made from B to E, and thus a dummy hit to B is added. This is a safe correction to make since along with a page request, a browser is sending information about the page from which this request originated.
- *Full Path Recovery* A bolder approach is to infer the shortest path from page H to E. In this case: H–D–B–E. And then account for the two unseen pages by adding dummy hits D and B.

TABLE 5.8	Implications of Caching Alternatives on the Measurement of Average Number of Pages Accessed per Visit*			
	No Cache	Perfect Cache (No Recovery)	Full Path Recovery	Last Page Recovery
Average number of pages per visit	2.63	1.63	1.87	1.64
Accuracy	100%	62%	71%	62%

*Based on a sample of 627 visits.

- *No Path Recovery* Make no attempt to recover cached pages.

  Before looking at GRP measures, we can look at a more basic statistic of site visits: the number of pages accessed per visit. Table 5.8 summarizes the results that were obtained in measuring the average number of pages per visit for no cache, perfect cache (i.e., No Path Recovery), full path recovery, and recovery algorithms.

  As may be noted in Table 5.8, we found that 38 percent (100 − 62%) of the pages in our test case were cached. Moreover, the full-path-recovery algorithm recovered 24 percent (9%/38%) of the cached pages while the last-page-recovery algorithm recovered less than 1 percent of the cached pages.

  We can now turn to the impact of cache recovery on GRP measures. We selected two advertisements that were running on the server during the test and computed GRP measures for the *No Cache* situation as well as for each of the cache re-

covery strategies (see Table 5.9). As might be expected from the results of Table 5.8, the *Partial Path Recovery* algorithm did not yield much improvement over the *No Recovery* option. For the first of the two advertisements, the *Full Path Recovery* algorithm recovered 40 percent of the missing, pages (the amount of error decrease by 40 percent from 50 percent to 30 percent). For the second one, it did not recover any.

  Despite the significant improvements obtained for the first Advertisement with the *Full Path Recovery* algorithm, we do not favor the use of this approach. This is because there are problems with its use. For example, if users do not take the shortest path between one page to the next, then the path recovered will be incorrect, and thus this will lead to missing Web pages (i.e., only Partial Page Recovery). In addition, if a surfer uses his or her browser's "Go" menu to jump back to the last page, then the path recovered will contain pages that were not seen a second time and extra

TABLE 5.9	Path Recovery Effectiveness						
		No Recovery		Partial Path Recovery		Full Path Recovery	
	No Cache		% Error		% Error		% Error
A Reach	0.20	0.20	0%	0.20	0%	0.20	0%
D Frequency	2.75	1.38	50%	1.39	49%	1.92	30%
1 GRP	0.54	0.27	50%	0.27	49%	0.38	30%
A Reach	0.19	0.19	0%	0.19	0%	0.19	0%
D Frequency	1.41	1.05	26%	1.05	26%	1.05	26%
2 GRP	0.27	0.20	26%	0.20	26%	0.20	26%

TABLE 5.10	Full Path Recovery Statistics
	Occurrences %
No page recovered	58%
Partial recovery of pages	23%
Perfect recovery	0%
Overcorrection	19%

TABLE 5.11	Reliability of Measures	
	Mean Percent Error	Standard Deviation
No recovery	19%	0.20
Full path recovery	6%	0.33

pages will be recorded (i.e., overcorrection). By looking at each of the 627 visits analyzed in Table 5.8, we can compute the number of times that the Full Path Recovery method (a) does not recover any cached pages, (b) recovers only a fraction of the cached pages, (c) recovers the exact number of cached pages, or (d) overcorrects number of cached pages. Table 5.10 shows the Frequency of occurrences for these possibilities.

In particular, Table 5.10 suggests potential problems with Full Path Recovery. Although Full Path Recovery improves the numbers on average, we note that it often overcompensates (19 percent of the time) and consequently leads to estimates that are actually less reliable than the raw numbers. As shown in Table 5.11, even though the overall imprecision (Mean Percent Error) of the measures is greater when using Full Path Recovery than when using raw data, the reliability of these measures (Standard Deviation) suffers greatly.

Study 4—Implications of Visitor Monitoring

The previous studies showed that the overall accuracy of some specific current methods leaves a lot to be desired. However, they also show that with appropriate monitoring instruments in place one can remedy this lack of precision. In our case, the monitoring that needs to take place relates to two areas: first, an accurate tracking of visitors needs to be performed, and second, one needs to be able to account for cached pages.

The monitoring of visitors can be performed in a variety of ways (e.g., passwords, digital certificates, cookies, etc.). Passwords are widely used by commercial sites that have a membership element. Companies such as E*Trade or *The Wall Street Journal* require their users to be registered and to use a password to access their sites.

Digital certificates provide third-party certification of a user's or Web Server's identity. They are provided by an entity that both the Web Site and the users trust (such as VeriSign). The digital certificates are unique to the individuals to whom they are issued and are encrypted to prevent tampering. They are used by such companies as Kmart or the Virtual Vineyard.

Cookies are much simpler devices than either digital certificates or passwords. As noted before, cookies tag requests from individual users (or more accurately, the requests from the computer used by the surfer). With this simple mechanism, Web-site operators can tag individual users with unique cookies and then track their progress through the Web site or their subsequent site visits. Thus, cookies provide a simple and effective way to track users. However, they do not provide any information about who the users are as do digital certificates or the registration processes associated with requesting a password would. In addition, cookies may have other measurement limitations. For example, cookies cannot distinguish multiple users of one computer (except for multiuser operating systems such as Unix). Furthermore, Web users who may be sensitive to privacy issues could delete the resident file on their hard drive which stores the cookies and thus erase their previous viewing history. Indeed, although benign in nature, Cookies have received a lot of negative press with respect to the issue of invasion of privacy and have been the subject of controversy (e.g., Komando, 1997).

Monitoring cache access is more straightforward than tracking individuals. However, it also interferes more with their actions. The simplest way to deal with caching is to disable the caching of pages. This can be done by sending an immediate expiration date along with every page served by a Web site. This will have the effect that each time a user will try to access a cached page, his or her browser will realize that the cached page is outdated and that it needs to request a newer one from the Web server. In short, the browser will never retrieve pages from its cache.

One would expect that such monitoring may interfere with surfer behavior. That is, the delays caused by disabling caching are likely to frustrate surfers and cause them to leave a site earlier than they would if caching was enabled. Similarly, users who are sent cookies and do not want to register with a site are likely to leave it immediately. As a result, one would expect to see a sharp decrease in the average number of pages requested by surfers in an environment where monitoring is taking place as compared to an environment that is free of monitoring.

To test this hypothesis, we set up a test Web site with the ability to implement a 2×2 factorial design as shown in Figure 5-28. The site would dispense cookies to half of the visitors who are accessing it. It would also prevent caching during half of the visits. That is, when a visitor comes to our test site, he or she would have a 50–50 chance of being assigned to the cookie treatment. In this case the visitor would be issued cookies, which the visitor would keep for any subsequent visit. At the same time, each visit is assigned to a cache or no-cache condition. This second assignment is made at the visit level and not the visitor level. Hence, a surfer who visits the site repeatedly will make some visits in a cached environment and some in a noncached one. He will, however, see only one of the two cookie conditions.

We collected data for 1,074 visits. Of these visits, 52 percent were made in a no-cache environment, while 67 percent were made in a cookie environment. Similarly to Drèze and Zufryden (1997) we used a Poisson regression approach to test whether cookies and/or cache-disabling impact surfer behavior. Our dependent variable is the number of pages requested during a visit. Our independent variables are two treatment variables (Cookies and No-Cache) as well as a series of control variables that are not reported here for the sake of conciseness.

Our analysis shows that contrary to our prior belief, the use of cookies did not have a negative impact on the number of pages requested by visitors (see Table 5.12). Indeed, the regression coefficient for cookies is not significant. In contrast, the coefficient for the no-cache treatment is significant at the $p = 0.01$ level. Moreover, this coefficient is positive. This means that more pages are requested in the no-cache environment. This makes sense given the nature of caching.

However, if one looks at the number of unique pages requested (eliminating duplicate pages requested within a visit), the coefficient for the no-

Treatments	Issue Immediate Expiration Date on Pages Served (i.e., No Cache)	Do Not Issue Expiration Date on Pages Served (i.e., Cache)
Issue cookies	$n_{11} = 388$	$n_{12} = 359$
Do not issue cookies	$n_{21} = 169$	$n_{22} = 158$

*n_{ij} represent the samples sizes tested in each cell

Figure 5-28 2×2 Experimental Design to Study the Impact of Surfer Monitoring Procedures

TABLE 5.12	Poisson Regression of Number of Pages Requested as a Function of Cookie Issuance and Cache Disabling					
	Coef.	Std. Err.	z	$P > \backslash z \backslash$	[95% Conf. Interval]	
Cookies	.08	.07	1.100	0.271	−.06	.22
No-cache	.43	.05	8	0.000	.32	.54

cache situation becomes negative at −0.21 (still significant at the $p = 0.01$ level). This means that although more pages are requested, the breadth of the visits made by surfers in a no-cache environment is smaller than the visits made in a cached environment. This is an indication that visitors may resent the delays caused by the disabling of their caches.

CONCLUSION

This paper suggests that significant problems of advertising effectiveness measurement must be resolved before Internet advertising is "ready for prime time." More specifically, our study has demonstrated that measurements based on current techniques are subject to significant errors and thus will tend to make Web-based advertising effectiveness difficult to compare to standard media. In order to ensure comparability with standard media, we need to identify unique visitors rather than use current methods that rely on IP address identification. This can be done in a variety of ways: through password, a rather obtrusive method; cookies, an unobtrusive but controversial method (e.g., see Komando, 1997); or even better through unique serial numbers assigned to individual copies of the browser programs (a feature said to be upcoming in future versions of Netscape and Internet Explorer).

Another problem we highlighted, with respect to current measurement methods, is that they do not record cached page requests. However, we have shown that it is quite important to account for page requests from cache to accurately account for the number of potential exposures to banner ads inserted on Web pages. Our

investigation of the use of path-recovery algorithms has shown that they are either ineffective, or unreliable (i.e., do more harm than good). Here, some mechanism which forces all page requests to be made from a Web site's server, rather than retrieving pages from cache, would solve the problem of failing to record exposures on a log file because of caching. However, we have shown that this technique may detrimentally affect surfers' behavior. Obviously, this solution increases the download times of Web pages and may contribute to the impatience and irritation of surfers. The irritation that surfers may experience when faced with long download times has been suggested as a potential adverse effect which may decrease a surfer's interest in the contents of a Web site (e.g., Ducoffe, 1996). Perhaps a technique that allows for the partial caching of Web pages may offer a compromise to this potential problem. For example, on the one hand, components of a page that take relatively more time to download, such as graphics, video, and sound files may be cached. On the other hand, the text portions of a page (which can be reloaded quickly) might have an instantaneous expiration date so that the text of the page will always be requested from the Web-site server and hence recorded. This method would provide a record of all potential exposures to Web pages whether or not they were partially cached. Furthermore., it is expected that such a method would not significantly increase the resulting download time, relative to complete page caching, as text may quickly be downloaded from a Web-site server to a user's PC screen. Consequently, there should be minimum irritation and loss of patience on the part of Web surfers.

APPENDIX A Measure Error for Five Web Sites

	Site 1 ID-based	Site 1 IP-based	% Error	Site 2 ID-based	Site 2 IP-based	% Error	Site 3 ID-based	Site 3 IP-based	% Error	Overall % Error
No. of visitors	709	576	−18.76	63832	52263	−18.12	25260	14006	−44.55	−39.31
No. of visits	830	663	−20.12	90039	69290	−23.04	42997	29894	−30.47	−35.28
Page/visit	2.54	3.19	+25.19	8.89	11.67	+29.96	13.36	19.22	+43.82	+63.90
Time spent	60.98	98.46	+61.47	385	531	+37.92	396	536	+35.35	+79.47
Repeat visits	1.17	1.15	−1.68	1.41	1.33	−6.01	1.70	2.13	+25.39	+9.18

	Site 4 ID-based	Site 4 IP-based	% Error	Site 5 ID-based	Site 5 IP-based	% Error
No. of visitors	26099	9790	−62.49	14506	6870	−52.64
No. of visits	36761	15183	−58.70	18437	10310	−44.08
Page/visit	17.38	42	+141.66	25.99	46.5	+78.91
Time spent	335	903	+169.55	274	529	+93.07
Repeat visits	1.41	1.55	+10.11	1.27	1.50	+18.08

APPENDIX B Measurement Error for Three Advertising Alternatives

	Ad 1 ID-based	Ad 1 IP-based	% Error	Ad 2 ID-based	Ad 2 IP-based	% Error	Ad 3 ID-based	Ad 3 IP-based	% Error	Overall · % Error
Site 1										
Reach	0.25	0.34	+40.07	0.18	0.21	+20.16	0.30	0.43	+41.90	+25.37
Frequency	2.31	2.03	−12.12	1.22	1.25	+2.44	2.21	1.92	−13.25	−1.10
GRP	0.57	0.70	+23.09	0.22	0.27	+23.09	0.67	0.83	+23.09	+22.71

	Ad 4 ID-based	Ad 4 IP-based	% Error	Ad 5 ID-based	Ad 5 IP-based	% Error	Overall % Error
Site 2							
Reach	0.0218	0.0245	+12.55	0.0094	0.0105	12.16	
Frequency	1.1541	1.2523	+8.52	1.2167	1.3249	+8.89	
GRP	0.0251	0.0307	+22.14	0.0114	0.0140	+22.14	

Alternatively, current problems could be solved if browser programs had a way to uniquely identify their users and informed sites about the users' identities whenever they retrieved a page from cache. Once the current measurement problems are resolved, Internet advertising should indeed achieve its full potential as a significant component of a company's media mix.

Xavier Drèze is an assistant professor of marketing at the Marshall School of Business at the University of Southern California. He received his Ph.D. in marketing from the University of Chicago. Dr. Drèze has published in the *Journal of Marketing,* the *Journal of Retailing,* and other journals. He has been involved with database marketing for the past five years.

Fred S. Zufryden is the Ernest W. Hahn Professor of Marketing at the Marshall School of Business at the University of Southern California. He received a Ph.D. in business administration from the University of California at Los Angeles. Dr. Zufryden's numerous publications have appeared in the *Journal of Advertising Research Management Science,* the *Journal of the Operational Research Society,* the *Journal of the Royal Statistical Society,* the *Journal of Marketing,* the *Journal of Marketing Research, Marketing Science,* and other journals. He has served as consultant to various market research and consumer products firms.

REFERENCES

Advertising Age Interactive. Advertising Data Place, 1998. http://adage.com.interactive/articles/19980406/article6.html

Briggs, Rex, and Nigel Hollis. "Advertising on the Web: Is There Response before Click-Through?" *Journal of Advertising Research* 37, 2 (1997): 33–45.

Coffey, Steve, and Horst Stipp. "The Interactions between Computer and Television Usage." *Journal of Advertising Research* 37, 2 (1997): 61–67.

Drèze, Xavier, Kirthy Kalyanam, and Rex Briggs. "The Ecological Inference Problem in Internet Measurement: Leveraging Web Site Log Files to Uncover Population Demographics and Psychographics." Working paper, 1998.

———, and Fred Zufryden. "Testing Web Site Design and Promotional Content." *Journal of Advertising Research* 37, 2 (1997): 77–91.

Decoffe, Robert H. "Advertising Value and Advertising on the Web." *Journal of Advertising Research* 36, 5 (1996): 21–35.

Electronic Marketplace and Advertising Report. January 1997.

Headen, Robert S., Jay E. Klompmaker, and Jesse E. Teel, Jr. "Predicting Audience Exposure to Spot TV Advertising Schedules." *Journal of Marketing Research* 14, 1 (1977): 1–9.

Internet Advertising Bureau. "Report on On-line Advertising Revenue." April 1998.

I/PRO CyberAtlas, 1996.

I/Pro-Doubleclick. "Web in Perspective: Ad Response, What Makes People Click?" Presented at the Advertising Research Foundation Interactive Media Symposium, Monterey, CA, February 3–5, 1997.

Jupiter Communications. "Ad Revenues Jump 83% in Second Quarter, According to Jupiter AdSpent Data." Press release, September 3, 1996.

———. "Web Ad Revenues." Press release, April 6, 1998.

Komando, Kim. "No Milk Needed With These Cookies." *Los Angeles Times,* June 9, 1997.

Metheringham, Richard A. "'Measuring the Net Cumulative Coverage of a Print Campaign." *Journal of Advertising Research* 4, 4 (1964): 23–28.

Online Money News. "Amazon.com and America OnLine Announce Multi-Million Dollar Advertising and Promotional Agreement." Press release, July 8, 1997.

Pedrick, James H., and Fred S. Zufryden. "Evaluating the Impact of Advertising Media Plans: A Model of Consumer Purchase Dynamics Using Single-Source Data." *Marketing Science* 10, 2 (1991): 111–30.

Zufryden, Fred S. "A Model for Relating Advertising Media Exposures to Purchase Incidence Behavior Patterns." *Management Science* 33, 10 (1987): 1253–66.

6

INTERACTIVITY AND COMMUNITY

In Chapter 2, researchers Hoffman and Novak presented a model of network navigation. In their model, interactivity plays an essential role in determining the quality of the surfing experience. These researchers noted that the web allows for individuals to interact with web site content and with others through the web medium.

Interactivity is closely related to personalization. Personalization tailors the nature and form of interactivity according to unique individual needs. The goal of personalization is the creation of a customized surfing experience for each visitor.

Online communities are formed when individuals interact with one another on the web. One of the most surprising discoveries concerning Internet marketing is that virtually anything can be, and is being, sold on the web. Furniture, designer clothing, jewelry, perfume, cars, homes, and even coffins are all successfully marketed online.

One reason that even sensory-intensive products sell well on the web is because of the influence of online communities. Communities act as unbiased, helpful purchase agents in purchase decisions. Communities perform the role of salesperson and product expert simultaneously. Communities act as a kind of Department of Consumer Affairs online.

Smart marketers not only allow but encourage the creation of communities on web sites for several reasons. First, communities allow marketers to better understand the needs of their customers. This information is ordinarily quite expensive to obtain via market research. Second, communities act as important centers of product knowledge and information. Those new to the web site will learn that the sponsor can be trusted and that the purchases can be made online without risk. Finally, communities show that that firm is customer focused and willing to live by the judgments of its customers even at the risk of bearing criticism in an open forum.

In the first article of this chapter, Professors Ghose and Dou test the degree to which specific interactive features in various categories impact web site quality. These researchers find that some classes of interactivity matter more than others in determining web site quality.

In the second article, John Hagel, author of the widely acclaimed book *Net Gain: Expanding Mar-* *kets Through Virtual Communities,* suggests that virtual communities present a new market model called reverse markets. Mr. Hagel details the dramatic implications of this emerging market model on customer relationship management.

Please remember to visit the textbook's web site for related resources.

Interactive Functions and Their Impacts on the Appeal of Internet Presence Sites

Sanjoy Ghose
Wenyu Dou

Internet Presence Sites (IPS) are becoming important mechanisms for marketing communication. Therefore it is vital to understand what affects the attractiveness of a firm's IPS. In this research, we focus on the multidimensional factor of interactivity. We use statistical models such as Logit to evaluate the effects of interactivity on IPS appeal. We find that the greater the degree of interactivity, the more likely it is for the IPS to be considered as a top site. Additionally we find that the "customer support" component of interactivity has a significant positive impact on the likelihood of an IPS being included in a list of high-quality Web sites. The findings are discussed in terms of their implications for design of corporate Web sites.

The importance of the World Wide Web as an advertising medium has been rapidly gaining ground in recent years. According to a recent On-line Advertising Report released by Jupiter Communications (1997), total annual ad spending on the Internet reached $301 million in 1996, was expected to total $940 million in 1997, and reach $4,352 million in 2000. An interesting trend is that marketers are focusing more (by spending more) on advertising their products/firm at their own corporate sites than on advertising in somebody else's site (Williamson, 1997). The range of Web site objectives could, of course, be anything from pure advertising of the firm's name to implementing customer support or online sales. It is, therefore, becoming increasingly important for companies to be able to successfully attract potential customers to their own Web sites.

How does a firm hope to attract target customers or compete for them especially among sites of the same nature (e.g., personal-computer sites)? With the explosion in the number of Web sites (the site of companiesonline.com contains more than 100,000 sites for public and private companies as of October 1997), this has become a challenging question. To help consumers navigate the "wild jungle," Ducoffe (1996) suggested that a regularly published series of rankings of Web sites would increase the public's expertise as Web consumers. When search engines (such as Yahoo) are used with keywords (such as "personal computers"), they still tend to generate a very long list of URLs. Couple this with the fact that downloading times are often long (Dreze and Zufryden, 1997), and we can see why a reputed ranking list would increase the search efficiency of Web users. Just as manufacturers of consumer products would like to see their products ranked high by *Consumer Reports,* it also appears reasonable that firms would like their sites to be included among the attractive ones in such a list.

In this research, we use the well-known Lycos Top 5% list to assess the quality of corporate Web sites. Analogous to the profile of *Consumer Reports,* sites cannot pay to be listed in the Top 5% directory, thus ensuring impartiality. This Web site review service has been rated very highly by the reputed publication *Internet World* magazine (Vendittp, 1997). This list is published by Lycos which has been given an A grade as a search engine by the noted publication *PC World* (Scoville, 1996).

Overall then, the Lycos Top 5% list appears to have substantial credibility. The task of increasing potential customer visits to a firm's Web site should clearly be facilitated, once the Web site is included in the Lycos Top 5% list.

What factors might be influential in improving the quality of company Web sites? One factor that appears to be a good candidate is that of *interactivity*. In contrast to the traditional one-to-many marketing communications media, the Web exemplifies an *interactive* many-to-many communication scenario (Hoffman et al., 1995). Berthon et al. (1996) have even suggested that the *level* of interactivity in a Web site might be critical in getting surfers involved in the marketing communication process. It would thus seem logical for firms to explore whether interactivity plays any significant role in affecting the overall quality of their Web sites.

Consequently, in this paper we are interested in examining the impact of interactivity on the attractiveness of corporate Web sites. We perform statistical analysis with data and information obtained from the Internet to perform this evaluation.

STUDY OBJECTIVES

The overall goal of this study is to examine the role of interactivity in increasing the attractiveness of Web sites of firms. To do this we consider information related to 101 sites. About half of these sites were included in the Lycos Top 5% list, while the remaining were not. Given that *interactivity* activity is a multidimensional concept and can thus manifest itself in various forms, we visited each of these 101 sites to gather the interactivity information of each of these sites. By using descriptive statistics, we are able to generate a profile of the nature and usage frequency of different forms of interactivity functions in corporate Web sites.

In this research, we *hypothesize* that the degree and nature of interactivity have a significant effect on the quality of corporate Web sites, as indicated by their inclusion/noninclusion in the Lycos Top 5% list. In other words, we expect that the attractiveness of sites would increase with the increase in the number of interactive functions. In addition, we also expect that certain types of interactive functions could have relatively stronger effects on the standing of sites. Recognizing the difference in sites' goals, we explore the existence and differential benefits of alternative types of in-

teractions and also examine whether the impact of interactivity differs by site goals.

We use Chi Square Analysis and the Logit model to test our hypothesis. Our results provide specific directions on how Web site designers can modify their site attributes to increase the quality recognition of their sites.

In our next section, we primarily focus on discussing the multidimensional aspects of interactivity; we also discuss characteristics of the Lycos Top 5% list. This is a precursor to the next section, where we describe our research design linking interactivity features to site attractiveness. Following that, we provide the results of our analysis. Finally, our last section contains discussions and managerial implications of our study and also indicates directions for future research.

INTERACTIVITY AND SITE ATTRACTIVENESS

In this section, we first briefly review the current thinking in the literature about interactivity and Web sites. Second, we discuss in details the various forms of interactivity that we observed in our considered sample of Web sites. We follow this with a discussion on the subject of site attractiveness.

Building Interactive Internet Presence Sites

The nomenclature of "Internet Presence Site" (IPS) is nowadays being commonly used to denote a corporate Web site (Hoffman et al., 1995) that provides a virtual "presence" for a firm and its offerings. Firms may have different objectives in setting up their IPSs. Some desire full-scale content or image-rich sites for visitors to explore and enjoy, while some may aim to be more like cyberbrochures with flat ads containing general company and product information. Since image-rich or content-rich IPSs have a greater ability than flat ad sites to motivate consumers with messages embedded with interactive presentations, Hoffman and Novak (1995) have posited that they represent the future of advertising and marketing communications on the Web.

Interactivity, in the context of the Web, is a multidimensional concept. Blattberg and Deighton (1991) defined interactivity as the facility for individuals and organizations to communicate directly with one another regardless of distance or time. In Steuer's (1992) model of computer-mediated communication, interactivity is ". . . the extent to which users can participate in modifying the form and content of a mediated environment in real time." Deighton (1996) interpreted interactivity as two features of communication: the ability to address an individual and the ability to gather and remember the response of that individual. Those two features also make possible a third: the ability to address that individual once more in a way that takes into account his or her unique response.

A number of researchers have identified the roles of interactivity in firms' efforts to build a good relationship with their customers. Hoffman and Novak (1995) pointed out that the Web frees customers from their traditionally passive role as receivers of marketing communications, gives them much greater control over the information search and acquisition process, and allows them to become active participants in the marketing process. Upshaw (1995) also argued that the interactive nature of the Web offers marketers new opportunities to create stronger brand identities that have the potential to translate into brand loyalty. Cuneo (1995) stated that the potential for customer interaction, which is largely asynchronous under current implementations, facilitates relationship marketing and customer support to a greater degree than ever before possible with traditional media (TV, broadcasting, etc.). Berthon et al. (1996) have suggested that the level of interactivity of the site would be critical in converting site visitors from interested contacts into interactive customers. Therefore, it seems reasonable to infer that surfers who visit interactive sites may be more likely to positively evaluate the sites and their surfing experience than surfers who run into less interactive sites with static information and humdrum presentations.

It is important to recognize, however, that corporations may have varying motivations when they decide to set up their IPSs. The importance of interactivity seems obvious for "content/image" rich sites as firms that spend efforts in building such sophisticated IPSs should expect customers to get actively involved in surfing their sites. Yet, interactivity may still play an important role for "flat ad" sites. As suggested by Davis (1997), pure information sites such as cyber-brochures can make their site visitors' probes more fruitful and enjoyable by providing positive interaction mechanisms, examples of which would be key-word search, inquiry, and so on. Thus, the impact of interactive mechanisms on site attractiveness may be present regardless of site goals. It would also be beneficial to empirically assess how firms might be drawing on the differing benefits offered by alternative types of interactions, in order to be compatible with their overall site objectives. The following subsection describes different forms of interactive functions.

Forms of Interactive Functions in IPSs

At the current level of Web technology development, there already exists a variety of technical tools that enable visitors to interact with Web sites. Marrelli (1996) gave an excellent point-by-point analysis of how a firm utilizes various forms of interactive functions in its Web site (the Zima site). His step-by-step analysis illustrated how such functions as "e-mail feedback loop," "multimedia presentation," "Web questionnaire," "affinity (user) groups," and "software downloading" had helped Zima to build a massive advertising presence in cyberspace. Emerick (1995) has also identified "end user news group," "end user information gathering," "product/service utilization service," "product/service explanation and problem solving," and "ordering" as forms of interactive functions that can be utilized by IPSs.

It should not be a surprise that as Web technology evolves, new forms of interactivity are going to emerge. To summarize the latest developments in this area, our study here presents a broad spectrum, if not an exhaustive, list of various forms of interactivity tools that are employed by IPSs in their marketing communications. We do this by actually observing 101 Web sites and relating our findings to past discussions in the literature. A complete list of the 23 functions and their brief definitions are given in Table 6.1; more explanations, including a discussion of associated benefits, are given below.

TABLE 6.1	**Forms of Interactive Functions**

Customer Support
- *Software downloading:* surfers download software from a site, usually for free.
- *Online problem diagnostics:* customers report their problem spots and this function helps them to locate the problem exactly. Whenever possible, "trouble shooting" suggestions are given.
- *Electronic-form (e-form) inquiry:* e-forms on which customers can type in online inquiries regarding the products or the firm.
- *Order status tracking:* customers can track the status or whereabouts of their orders online in real time.
- *Comment:* customers can fill out e-forms to express their opinions about the company, products and the site.
- *Feedback:* customers can type in their feedback in e-forms with regard to specific questions raised by the site.

Marketing Research
- *Site survey:* e-form survey for visitors that solicits their comments on the content and design of the site.
- *Product survey:* e-form survey designed for measuring customer satisfaction about firm's offerings and service.
- *New-product proposal:* e-forms for customers to write about their expectations of new products and their suggestions for new products.

Personal-Choice Helper
- *Key word search:* a function that allows a visitor to pinpoint the particular information he or she is interested in.
- *Personal-choice helper:* a function that can make relatively sophisticated recommendations on consumers' choices based on their input of preferences and decision criteria.
- *Virtual reality display:* a function that permits consumers to virtually "feel or experience" the product.
- *Dealer locator:* a function that allows users to pinpoint a dealer closest to his or her residence.

Advertising/Promotion/Publicity
- *Electronic coupon:* distributed online and can be used in retail stores.
- *Usergroups:* cyber community for product users.
- *Online order:* an option to order products online.
- *Sweepstakes/prize:* events held to attract surfers and to encourage surfer participation by special incentives.
- *Multimedia shows:* quicktime movie, streamline video, and other forms of multimedia presentations.
- *Push media:* similar to TV channels. Users select to participate and receive information directly to their screens on a regular basis.
- *Interactive job placement:* online resume building, personal career goal check, etc.

Entertainment
- *Electronic post card:* written by senders online and to be retrieved by recipients.
- *Surfer postings:* a section for surfers to write their stories, opinions, or others.
- *Games:* online games.

1.–3. **Online forms for customer feedbacks, inquiries, or comments**   Our visit to The BASF site showed that it had an online feedback form for visitors to fill out on their screens. On this form, visitors can comment on anything related to the company—either product-related or company-related. Berthon et al. (1996) had discussed the merits of such functions.

4. **Downloading of software**   In the Epson site, or instance, visitors can download operating software for Epson printers to upgrade their existing ones. This approach is much faster and convenient compared to traditional methods. If a firm can upgrade its product or service continuously then it is likely that the company may "lock in" the customers by building a long-term relationship.

   Another variation of "software downloading" is found in a section where a customer can download images from an IPS and save them as his or her screen saver. For example, Guinness allows surfers to download its latest TV commercial and use it as a screen saver. Conceivably, this approach builds affinity with the corporate brand by encouraging fun and involvement, and the screen saver provides a constant reminder of the advertising message (Berthon et al., 1996).

5. **Online problem diagnostics**   The Whirlpool site has a built-in function that allows Whirlpool to diagnose product problems pointed out by site visitors. The function works just as if the customer is engaging in a conversation with the Whirlpool service representative who asks the customer a series of questions. Based on the customer's input, the function can usually nail down the problem spot and provide trouble-shooting suggestions. Advantages of this function are manifold. First, the need to maintain a complete service center is reduced. Second, such routinized service assistance will be available around-the-clock.

Third, service instructions to the customers could be aided by multimedia thus making it much easier for customers to follow, e.g., by showing a three-dimensional figure of the machine being examined. Finally, service quality will always be guaranteed as long as the server and the software are functioning well, since the function can boast of a better memory than the most diligent service person, and has none of the service person's distaste for repetitive work (Deighton, 1996).

6. **Order status checking**   The Dell site enables customers to track their orders online in real time. This capacity challenges the firm to stick to its delivery time claims, and this, in turn, may give customers added confidence in purchasing Dell products. If this function performs satisfactorily, then customers may achieve positive post-purchase reinforcement of their product decisions.

7. **Site survey**   The BMW USA site had online survey forms for visitors to fill out, with a view to understanding their perceptions and evaluations of the site. This function provides one way of establishing a dialogue (Berthon et al., 1996) between site visitors and the firm's site design team which can then use such feedback to improve the site.

8. **Product survey**   The BMW USA site also has an electronic form of survey about the company's products. Again, as in a site survey, a dialogue between the customers and the firm itself can be established through this channel.

9. **New product proposal**   The Kenwood USA site allocated a special section in which visitors can express their opinions on their ideal new products. By doing this, surfers are likely to feel that the firm values their opinions and their self-perceptions might therefore be positively enhanced.

10. **Key word search**   A surfer interested in Kodak's foreign operations can simply type a

key phrase "foreign operations" in the "search" section of the site. Then all the relevant information contained in the Kodak site will be shown on the screen. Since the organization of Web site content is nonlinear in nature (Hoffman and Novak, 1996), it is crucial that a Web site is equipped with such a function to help surfers easily locate the exact information they are looking for. This function enables an IPS to provide an individual visitor with personalized information while it can still contain a full spectrum of information to meet the potentially diversified information needs of site visitors.

11. **Personal choice helper**   The Internet gives firms the unique opportunity of moving consumers from being potential buyers to purchasers by actively helping them make their final purchasing choices. This is illustrated in the Ford site: once a surfer indicates that he or she is interested in a certain model, (say, Escort), then the site can instantly calculate the required monthly payment for the model if they specify the amount of down payment and APR rate. A comparison of lease versus buy option is also immediately available. Getting the financial information in a handy fashion significantly reduces consumers' time spent and lessens their efforts in the prepurchase information search phase.

As posited by Winer et al. (1997), the applications of new information technology (such as Peapod) may significantly affect the traditional ways consumers make choices. They argued that the ability of Peapod to sort brands easily on any of the product attributes may affect consumers' decision rules and ultimately their brand choice.

12. **Virtual-reality presentation**   A visitor to the BMW USA site who is interested in getting a real "feel" for the M3 model can virtually examine the interior and exterior of the car and experience the fast ride. While

physically the visitor is not moving, the virtual-reality function enables him or her to "test drive" the vehicle—an experience that is unimaginable in a traditional marketing setting. This interactive function ensures that potential consumers of the BMW model are no longer passive recipients of its Web marketing communication. They can actually participate and be a part of it. Again, this is yet another interactive technique that firms can employ to help their potential consumers make their purchasing choices.

13. **Dealer locator**   A fundamental issue consumers must address during decision making is where they should buy a product (Engel et al., 1993). A firm can provide such information in its presence site by employing a dealer/retailer locator function. For instance, the "where to buy" function in the Acer site can direct a visitor quickly to the closest retail store that carries Acer products.

14. **Electronic coupon**   The Burpee site offers electronic coupons for its gardening products. Surfers can print the coupons and use them in retail stores. Compared to traditional coupon distribution, the company can monitor and even control the number of e-coupons in circulation. For instance, the company can withdraw the e-coupon section once there are too many downloads. In addition, the cost of setting up the e-coupon section is nominal for the firm. Further, since the e-coupon is there for the consumers to *actively* seek out, it is quite likely that consumers who download e-coupons will use them in real purchasing. Thus, the firm sending out e-coupons will have a better estimate of how many of them might be redeemed whereas in traditional situations the company has no idea how many consumers have actually clipped the coupons from the print media.

15. **Online ordering of goods**   A visitor to the Gateway2000 site can order his or her computer online. After specifying the

designed model, the visitor can choose from a number of modes of payment, e.g., secured server credit, telephone, or check by mail. While online shopping at this time is relatively infrequent (Gupta, 1997), this option provides innovative visitors with an alternative way of making a purchase. With the continual growth of Web commerce, it is not surprising that the online ordering function is continuing to find applications on more and more IPSs.

16. **Online contests/prize** The Acer site has a monthly sweepstakes campaign that invites visitors to participate by filling out an electronic entry form in which they are also asked to provide some personal information. While visitors are likely to view such message types as advertising (Ducoffe, 1996), they might benefit (e.g., by winning prizes) from such events and the participation requires very little effort. Further, if such an event is held constantly, it is quite likely that visitors may come back regularly. An online contest with prizes may serve the same purpose.

17. **Push media** The GM site can "broadcast" its content to interested users. Once a visitor registers to participate, the GM site will deliver multimedia-rich information content about GM products and events to the user's screen. Users of the GM channel can even specify which type of information they would like to receive (e.g., new vehicle information). This technique allows visitors of the GM site the convenience of receiving information tailored to their personal interests. While it still retains the interactive nature of the new media, it also provides users with the same ease associated with TV viewing.

18. **Interactive job placement** The presence site of Texas Instrument (TI) is one of the best examples of how companies can utilize their Web sites to improve their recruiting

procedure. The "employment" section in the site contains a list of openings, a job-search planning guide, a fit-check questionnaire which "measures" the degree of the applicant's fit with TI's culture and organizational goals, and an online resume builder which allows the visitor to type in relevant information for constructing a resume. The highly interactive nature of this section provides the means to treat each online applicant in an individual manner. Even for those who are not applying for TI jobs, this section may project a favorable image of a company that is considerate to its potential employees.

19. **Electronic post card** Kellogg's site allows visitors to send electronic post cards to their friends right from the site. Senders can simply type in their messages and then choose the graphics, settings, etc., to build their cards. The recipients, on the other side, will come to the Kellogg's site to check the cards out. Borrowing the concept of aesthetic enjoyment (McQuail, 1983), we anticipate that this function serves not only to furnish real benefits to surfers but also to entertain visitors by fulfilling their needs for aesthetic enjoyment.

20. **Surfer postings** The BMW site asks customers to write down their driving experience with BMW cars on an online form. It will publish those details on the site. In a sense, consumers are also content providers to the site. In encouraging consumers to write out their consumption experience, BMW is also encouraging them to relate their personal experience to the site content. The possible self-referencing effect is desirable to the firm in that the likelihood of information retrieval may be enhanced (Engel et al., 1993).

21. **Usergroup** The Agfa site has a special section for its user groups on different topics, e.g., scanners, or photo imaging. Users of

Agfa products can share their experience with others and also ask questions which may be answered by others. According to Berthon et al. (1996), user groups may build a community atmosphere in the site, which in turn may make this site a satisfying and adaptive marketplace option.

22. **Games**   Young people are known for their fondness of computer games since they provide escapism and emotional release (McQuail, 1983). This is also illustrated in the fact that the 1996 sales in the United States for software games totals $1.1 billion (cnn.com, 6/22/97). Given that an average surfer in the United States is in the lower 30s (Gupta, 1997), it is not surprising that firms are increasingly using games as incentives to attract surfers to visit their IPSs. For instance, the Electrolux site offers several cleverly designed games that can be related to the firm's product, such as a game featuring an Electrolux vacuum cleaner sucking bugs in a room. The interactive games aim not only to entertain consumers in the cyberspace but also to reinforce their impressions about the company's products. Though a majority of visitors may recognize that games are part of the firm's advertising (Ducoffe, 1996), they may still love to play because games provide escapism, diversion, and possibly emotional release (McQuail, 1983).

23. **Multimedia presentations**   The Coca-Cola site neatly slides in multimedia presentations that have several interesting themes, e.g., mini-movies about its animated spokesperson the "Sun." New inventions in Web technology today such as Quick Time movies and xlivescreen now allow multimedia techniques to make much more sophisticated and integrated presentations in the form of video, sound, music, graphics, and text. This enhanced capability not only makes surfers' experiences more fun and stimulating (Spalter, 1996) but also gives surfers the

flexibility to activate only a needed part of the presentation, e.g., movie frames four to eight.

Assessing Site Attractiveness

In their exploratory work concerning new metrics for Web-measurement standards, Novak and Hoffman (1996) argued that the degree to which the visitor interacts with the target ad should be measured in addition to examining purely exposure measures such as "click through rates." They suggested that such an interactivity metric could be based upon duration of time spent viewing the ad, the depth or number of pages of the target ad assessed, or the number of repeat visits to the target ad. Such measures inevitably require in-depth monitoring from Web masters, and it is quite unlikely that such information will be disclosed to a firm's competitors.

The typology of measuring Web-site efficiency proposed by Berthon et al. (1996), in which awareness, locatability/attractability, contact, conversion, and retention efficiency measures are constructed, seems to be applicable for an individual site that is aiming to *improve* its site efficiency. All the information the firm can collect will be site specific, and it can only compare its current site attractiveness to its past records. If the firm wants to compare its site attractiveness to its competitors' by using such absolute measures, then it has to gather such information from its competitor's sites. Obviously, the difficulty in obtaining such competitive information is easy to realize. A new Web-based methodology of measuring the effectiveness of promotional content (Dreze and Zufryden, 1997) by tracking time spent and page visited also seems to fall into this category. In general, the above measures might be difficult to implement for a site (e.g., Nike site) that is concerned about its Web-site attractiveness for target surfers (e.g., young sports fans) relative to its competitors (e.g., Reebok site). In this scenario, an aggregate level indicator of relative Web-site efficiency (such as Web-site rankings or a list of "top sites") may be a more practically available benchmark for firms to refer to.

Lycos Top 5% Sites List

Previous research (Holbrook, 1992) has used product-rating reports such as *Consumer Reports* to study important issues such as "brand equity." In a similar vein, we also need Web-site rankings to carry out our research. Fortunately, at the aggregate level, a few indicators now exist for signaling the excellence of Web sites. They differ in the objects they survey and in the ways they conduct survey's to construct such indicators. For example, the "Hot 100 Web Sites List" is primarily based on a ranking of the real number of hits (which itself is under criticism for its incomparability across sites, see Novak and Hoffman, 1996). Another approach is to rely on expert reviews; an example of this approach is the Lycos Top 5% sites list. As a pioneering Web-site rating agency, the Lycos Top 5% sites list has been reviewing Web sites and recommending "top 5% sites" in lists since 1994. Being an integrated operation of the popular Lycos search engine, the Lycos Top 5% sites list is regarded as one of the most authoritative Web-site rating agencies in the WWW (Vendittp, 1997). Another nice feature of the lists is that it maintains a separate list for different categories, e.g., business, education, etc. Since there is a special list for top 5% corporate homepages, this makes the Lycos Top 5% sites list especially relevant to our study which probes for factors that lie behind successful IPSs of companies.

The Lycos Top 5% sites list also has publicly announced reviewing guidelines that make it more credible. According to the guidelines, Web sites are evaluated by independent reviewers (experts) on three aspects—content, presentation, and experience. Content refers to the broadness, thoroughness, accuracy, and updatedness of the information. Presentation refers to the beauty and originality of de-

sign. Finally, experience refers to the intangible asset of Web-site fun or personality.

Firms following conventional marketing practices seek to enhance consumer trials of their products through various means, e.g., samples, coupons, advertising, or publicity (such as being recommended by *Consumer Reports*). Similarly in Web marketing, firms seek to bolster their Web presence by attracting more visitors to their IPSs. To accomplish this goal, firms can spend more on advertising their Web site—clearly an important way. The second mechanism can take advantage of positive reviews of their IPSs from independent experts—something comparable to *Consumer Reports'* ratings. In our opinion, being included in the Lycos Top 5% sites list represents such a mechanism. In this research, we use the Lycos list and focus on investigating how firms can get their IPSs into this list.

RESEARCH DESIGN

Sample

Our sample consists of 101 Internet presence sites (IPSs). Forty-nine of them were in the Lycos Top 5% list for corporate homepages, whereas the remaining fifty-two were not in that list. We also classified the IPSs into "flat ad" sites and "content/image" sites following the guidelines of Hoffman and Novak (1996). The time frame of the sampling was restricted to mid January and mid March in 1997, during which period there was no change in the Lycos list with respect to our sample sites.

All of the corresponding companies are manufacturers of consumer goods—both durables (e.g., automobiles) and nondurables (e.g., soft drinks). We picked general consumer-goods companies (e.g. foods, electronics, medicines, etc.,) because they appear to be more relevant to "average" consumers than are companies that produce industrial goods or specialty goods (e.g., hearing-aids).

Our sample encompasses a wide spectrum of product categories, and it includes well-known companies from North America, Europe, and Asia. Since we are also interested in cross-comparison among sites in the same industry, we also deliberately selected some from the same product category (e.g., personal care) of companies that are usually categorized as market leaders (e.g., P&G), market challengers (e.g., Unilever), and market followers (e.g., the Bodyshop). In terms of its variety and depth, we can assume that our sample is "representative" of major manufacturers of consumer goods. Yet we caution that it is still a judgmental sample.

Table 6.2 gives a list of product categories and the number of firms selected within each category. Sites classified as "top 5% sites" or "flat ad sites" are also indicated in this table.

Data Processing

We chose to apply content-analysis-type techniques to our investigation of the 101 Web sites. While the application of this technique has been reported in the advertising and marketing literature (e.g., Resnick and Stern, 1977), its application in Web advertising is relatively new. A recent work by Philport and Arbittier (1997) expanded the guidelines by Resnick and Stern (1977) and applied the traditional content-analysis technique to examine the information content of Web advertising. Their results were then used in comparing different brand communication styles in established media and the Internet.

TABLE 6.2	IPSs Used in the Study
Category	**Sites Selected**
Athletic foot wear	Adidas, Asics^, Reebok
Automobile	BMW USA*, Chrysler*, Ferrari, Ford*, GM, Honda*, Hyundai, Toyota*
Battery	Duracell*
Beer	Budweiser, Guinness, Heineken*, Molson
Clothes	Guess, Levi
Film	Agfa*, Kodak*, Konica, Fuji Film*^
Food	Beechnut*, Birdseye*, Butterball*^, Hersheys, Kellogg's*, Nestle
Gardening supply	Burpee*
Gasoline	Chevron*^, Mobil*^, Texaco*^, Shell*
Home appliances	Electrolux*, Frigidaire*, Kirby^, Maytag*, Westinghouse*^, Whirlpool
Home electronics	Aiwa^, AVFlsher*, Casio USA, GE*, Hitachi*^, JVC^, Kenwood USA, Magnavox*, NEC^, Panasonic*, Pioneer^, Polaroid*, RCA Electronics^, Samsung, Sanyo^, Sharp^, Sony*, Toshiba USA*, Uniden^, Yamaha^, Zenith^
Office supply	Canon, Epson, Motorola*^, 3M*, Siemens, Xerox*
Personal care	Avon, Bodyshop*^, Clinique*, Colgate^, Mentadent^, Kimberly-Clark^, Procter & Gamble, Unilever^
Personal computer	Acer, Apple*, AST, Compaq, Dell*, Gateway2000, Hewlett Packard*, IBM*, Packard Bell, Texas Instruments*
Pharmaceutical	BASF*^, Bayer*^, Bristol-Myers^, Johnson & Johnson*^, Hoechst^, Merck & Co*, Novartis^, Pfizer^, Warner-Lambert*
Soft drinks	Coca-Cola*, Dr. Pepper, Pepsi-Cola
Tires	Bridgestone^, Goodyear*, Dunloptire^
Toys	Lego, Playmobil^

*denotes Lycos Top 5% site, ^denotes "flat ad" site.

Following guidelines similar to those adopted by Philport and Arbittier (1997), we constructed an "Interactivity Index" for each site to denote the maximum number of interactive functions within that site. This interactivity index (II) then can be used to quantify the highest possible level of interactivity a visitor may experience in this site.

Since our analysis also endeavors to explore what type of interactivity functions may be more effective, we also constructed five groups of interactive marketing functions, each consisting of interactive functions that are associated with a marketing function (see Table 6.1). Our mutually exclusive grouping here was largely based on two previous studies: one study (Berthon et al., 1996) outlined possible utilities of Internet presence sites and the other one (Emerick, 1995) specified dialogue, research, service, support, lead acquisition, and ordering as major forms of interactivity. As discussed earlier, Web sites could have varying goals. Following Hoffman et al. (1995), we divided the IPSs we visited into two groups: "content/image rich" type and "flat ad/cyber-brochure" type sites.

lowing structure. It first gives a summary of our findings followed by the analytical details.)

Usage Frequency of Different Interactive Functions

We examined our Web-site sample to get an idea of how often various forms of interactive functions were being used. We found, for example, that the following forms occurred relatively more frequently in the sites we studied: "key word search," "dealer locator," "software downloading," "comment," "online ordering," "sweepstakes," and "surfer postings." Their exact percentage of occurrences are shown in Figure 6-1.

The overwhelming presence of the "key word search" function (64 out of 101) clearly illustrates a primary perceived advantage of Web-based communications, i.e., firms can set up complicated IPSs to cater to a wide audience yet still easily retain the sensitivity to be able to respond to individual-level information needs. "Dealer locator" also has a high 36 percent occurrence rate as we expect that firms

RESULTS

Overview of Our Findings

Supporting our basic hypothesis, we found that the degree and nature of interactivity have a statistically significant effect on the quality of corporate Web sites. We found that the greater the degree of interactivity in a site, the greater was its likelihood of being included in the Lycos Top 5% Sites list. Examining different groups of interactive functions, we found that the interactive function group of "customer support" had a significant positive effect on the quality rating of Web sites. We also found that forms of interactions used varied logically with the differing objectives of the Web sites. Finally, we observed a pattern where the impact of interactivity mechanisms was a little stronger for content/image type of sites than for flat ad/cyber-brochure type sites. (Each of the following subsections has the fol-

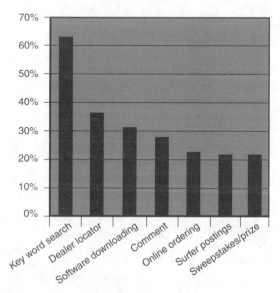

Figure 6-1   Usage Frequency of Seven "Popular" Interactive Functions

provide purchasing location knowledge in order to convert interested potential buyers to actual purchasers. "Software downloading" also appears to be popular with its 31 percent rate, probably because it provides unique benefits which are otherwise unavailable in traditional media environments. "Comment" enjoys a 28 percent percentage rate, indicating perhaps that surfers prefer two way communications to simply being passive recipients of firms' communications. The relative popularity of "online ordering," "sweepstake /prize," and "surfer postings" also seemed to suggest that Internet surfers value not only the tangible benefits (convenience in ordering or a prize) but also less tangible benefits such as good feelings (postings) in an IPS.

The percentage occurrence rates of most of the remaining interactive functions are in the neighborhood of 10 to 20 percent: personal-choice helper (18 percent), site survey (17 percent), product survey (17 percent), multimedia show (16 percent), games (15 percent), user group (12 percent), interactive job placement (12 percent), and feedback (11 percent).

The percentage occurrence rates for the remaining few interactive functions are lower. These functions may be industry specific as in "problem diagnostics" (6 percent) which are commonly used by computer companies, or they might be site idiosyncratic as in "electronic post card" (9 percent), "new-product proposal" (4 percent), and "electronic coupon" (2 percent). The very low rates (1 percent) for the remaining three interactive functions may be due to the innovative nature of the marketing communication used (e.g., push media) or due to high expense (e.g., for virtual reality or order-status tracking)—making them less appealing for a majority of the IPSs.

Site Goals versus Forms of Interactive Functions

Considering that firms may have different goals in setting up their IPSs, we would expect that the type of interactive functions employed might also vary with site types. Our analysis did uncover some interesting patterns. For example, we found that the presence of

"dealer locator" was not related to site goals whereas that of "online order" was significantly related to site goals. It was evident from the data that "online ordering" was more frequently associated with content/image sites than with flat-ad-type sites. In contrast, the "dealer locator" function was fairly evenly associated with both categories of Web sites. This kind of finding indicates that differences in site objectives are related to the differential benefits of alternative types of interactions. Consider two sites, one which is not more than a cyber-brochure, and another which has enhancing product sales as a goal. The former might include the "dealer-locator" function simply to provide a broader range of information about the company's setup to readers of its corporate brochure. The latter type of site may want to include the "dealer-locator" function with an intent to increase the probability of sales in the near future.

Our calculations here applied the Chi-square-analysis method to situations not involving small-cell counts. We tested null hypotheses of the form: "There is no significant relationship between Web site goals and the existence of a certain type of interactive function." For each of the 12 forms of interactive functions, we performed a Chi-square analysis with the existence /nonexistence of the individual function as a categorical variable and the classification of site goals (content/image versus cyber-brochure) as the other categorical variable. The test results indicated that "dealer locator," "games," postings," and "comment" were not associated with goals. In other words, our data suggested that there was no relation between each of these four specific functions and different types of site goals. Thus, these functions might be suitable for use by "content/image" type of sites as well as by "flat ad/cyber-brochure" type of sites. On the other hand, we did find that the following functions were associated with different types of site goals: "online ordering," "downloading," "site survey," "product survey," "contest/prize," "personal choice helper," "multimedia show," and "site search" ($p < .05$ in each case.). Since these functions were used more frequently among "content/image" type of sites, we could conclude that these functions might be more closely aligned to the goals of the more complicated "content/image" sites and less so with those of "flat ad/cyber-brochure" sites.

Impact of Interactive Functions on the Lycos Top 5% Site List

Here we present different aspects of the issue of how interactivity impacts Web-site attractiveness—as indicated by the probability of a site's inclusion in the Lycos Top 5% Sites List. First, we found that increase in the degree of interactivity had a significant positive effect on Web-site attractiveness/quality. Second, we detected that certain types of interactive marketing functions, e.g., the "customer support" function, have relatively stronger effects on site attractiveness. Third, we also observed that the impact of interactive marketing functions might differ in their magnitudes by site goals—though such a difference was not statistically significant. We did observe the general pattern that as sites goals change from those of a "cyber-brochure" to those of a "content/image," the impact of "customer support" functions on an IPS' likelihood of getting into the Lycos Top 5% list becomes slightly stronger.

In our logit model 1, we used the inclusion/ noninclusion of the Lycos Top 5% Sites List as a dependent variable; the independent variable was the "interactivity index" (II)—the total number of interactive functions found in a given IPS. Our results here indicated that as II gets larger, the probability that the IPS will get into the Lycos list also gets larger. For example, if an IPS has no more than four interactive functions, then the odds of it being "in the top list" versus "not in the top list" will favor the latter. However, when II is more than four, the odds start to favor "in the top list." In fact, the odds of "top list" versus "not in top list" are two to one for an IPS that has eight interactive functions.

The analytic form of our logit model 1 is given as follows.

$$\text{Prob (in Lycos list)} = \frac{e^{\alpha+\beta*II}}{1 + e^{\alpha+\beta*II}}$$

where II is the interactivity index or the predictor, α is the intercept, and β is the slope coefficient in the model.

The model fitting was performed by the logistic procedure in SAS (1990), and major output results are listed in Table 6.3. The log-likelihood ratio test (Agresti, 1990) used in this procedure

TABLE 6.3	Results from Logit Model Runs	
	Logit Model 1	**Logit Model 2**
Model fit: p-value of the log-likelihood ratio test	$p < 0.07$	$p < 0.05$
Variable	Interactivity Index 0.178 ($p < 0.08$)	CUS: customer support MKR: marketing research PSC: personal-choice helper ADP: advertising and promotion ENT: entertainment
Coefficient estimates	0.178 ($p < .08$)	CUS: 0.885 ($p < 0.01$) MKR: -0.343 PSC: 0.140 ADP: 0.087 ENT: 0.093
Percentage of correct predictions for Logit model 2 using the leave-one-out method		61

indicated that our model fit was significant at $\alpha = 0.1$ level ($p < 0.07$). The parameter estimate of the Interactivity Index (II) was also significant ($p < 0.08$). Further, the positive parameter estimate (0.178) clearly suggested that the probability of an IPS being classified into the Lycos Top 5% list increases with the increase in II.

In our logit model 2, we again used the inclusion/noninclusion of the Lycos Top 5% Sites list as a dependent variable; the independent variables were the five interactive marketing functions as defined previously in our "Data processing" section. Our results here indicated that as the value of "customer support" (i.e., total number of individual interactive functions belonging to the "customer support" domain) gets larger, the probability that the IPS will get into the Lycos list also gets larger.

Major output results of our logit model 2 are listed in Table 6.3. The log-likelihood ratio test (Agresti, 1990) used in this procedure indicated that our model fit was significant at $\alpha = 0.05$ level ($p < 0.05$). Among the five predictors, only the parameter estimate of "customer support" was significant ($p < 0.01$). Further, the positive parameter estimate (0.885) clearly suggested that the probability of an IPS being classified into the Lycos Top 5% list increases with the increase in the value of "customer support."

For example, if the value of "customer support" is just 1 in an IPS (e.g., it has a "software downloading" section on site), then the odds of it being in the Lycos "top list" versus "not in top list" is about 1:1. However, if this IPS adds another interactive form of "customer support" (e.g., it now adds a "comment" section), then the odds can be elevated to about 2.5:1 (holding other forms constant). That is, this IPS is now more than twice as likely to be classified into the Lycos list.

One interesting question that might naturally arise from the above discussions is: How well does this logit model predict the classification of Lycos Top 5% Sites List for a "future" observation? One way of answering this question was to split our original sample into a model calibration sample and a holdout sample for prediction. In view of our sample

size (101), such an approach might be appropriate. A better way to provide an answer to the above question is to use the "leave-one-out" method (closely related to jackknifing)—which we used here.

Lachenbruch and Mickey (1968) originally proposed the "leave-one-out" technique. Not only does this method yield almost unbiased estimates of misclassification probabilities but also it is not sensitive to normality assumptions (Dillon, 1979). The method involves removing one observation i from a sample size of n, estimating model parameters with the n-1 size sample, and predicting the binary response (in our case) probability for the removed observation i, using parameters obtained from the calibration sample size of n-1. The procedure is then repeated n-1 times resulting in a total of n holdout predictions.

Using this method on our logit model 2, we obtained a correct prediction rate of 61 percent. This is higher than a prediction rate that one would get by random chance—clearly indicating that our model has satisfactory predictive ability.

This study also probed into other aspects of the effect of interactivity mechanisms on site attractiveness. For example, we examined whether this effect differs across sites with different site goals. To answer this research question, we used a standard procedure in logistic regression to look for the existence of possible interaction effects between site goals and the most important interactive marketing function—"customer support." We observed a general pattern in the data which showed that increase in an interactivity mechanism (i.e., customer support) was more likely to propel a "content/image" type site (than a "cyber-brochure" type site) into the Lycos Top 5% List; the difference in the magnitude of this effect across site types was, however, not significant.

We used a standard variable selection procedure in logit models (Hosmer and Lemeshow, 1989) to search for any interaction effect. First, a logit model with "customer support" as the only independent variable and the classification of Lycos Top 5% sites as the dependent variable was built and the model fit was established ($p < 0.05$). The coefficient estimate for "customer support" was 0.89. Then, a categorical "site goal" variable (1 for content/image type of sites and 0 for cyber-brochure type of sites) was added into the model. A Log-likelihood ratio test indicated that the addition of the "site goal" variable significantly increased the logit model fit. Thus, this variable should be kept in our logit model. Coefficient estimates for "customer support" and "site goals" were 0.76 and 0.51, respectively.

Following that, an interaction term of "customer support" and "site goals" was included in the logit model as the third predictor. For this model, coefficient estimates for "customer support," "site goals," "customer support × site goals" interaction term were 0.62, 0.38, and 0.18, correspondingly. The positive coefficient estimate for the interaction term thus implied that the impact of "customer support" on Lycos Top 5% Sites List was larger for "content/image" types of sites than for "cyber-brochure" types of sites. According to those coefficient estimates, for a content/image site, the predicted probability of getting into the Lycos list is 14 percent higher than that for a cyber-brochure site—when the value of customer support is 1. In addition, such a difference in predicted probabilities increases to 17 percent when "customer support" is increased to 2. However, a closer examination through a Log-likelihood ratio test revealed that the inclusion of the interaction term did not significantly improve the logit model fit ($p > 0.10$). In other words, this interaction term was not significant.

Based on the above three different logit model runs, we could conclude that the impact of "customer support" on site attractiveness seemed to be greater for content/image type of sites than for cyberbrochure type of sites; such a difference in the magnitude of impact was, however, not statistically significant.

DISCUSSIONS AND MANAGERIAL IMPLICATIONS

This study identifies the interactivity mechanism as a significant factor affecting the attractiveness of Internet Presence Sites (IPSs). It also highlights the importance of certain dimensions of "interactivity," namely those interactive functions that serve primarily as customer-support functions. Hence, this research contributes to a better understanding of the success factors of quality IPSs. In accordance with our conclusions, we suggest that firms should critically examine the degree and forms of interactivity in their corporate Web sites and improve the designs accordingly. This will provide two benefits. First, it will help them get their Web sites included in a Lycos type list. Quality recognition of this type will encourage Web users to visit the firms' IPSs. Second, the Web sites themselves will be more appealing to those people who actually visit the sites. If that happens, then as Berthon et al. (1996) pointed out, visitors to those highly interactive sites will be more likely to get actively involved in those firms' Web communications—which is a very important reason for many firms to set up their IPSs in the first place.

This research also summarizes a variety of interactive functions that are currently employed by major consumer goods companies. Some of them are becoming "near standard" (e.g., key word search) while some of them are just emerging (e.g., push media). While a firm does not need to incorporate every single interactive function into its IPS, it is definitely desirable for a firm to increase the level of interactivity in its IPS at least to the same level that is being employed by its best Web competitor (which might be in the Lycos Top 5% list). This rationale follows from one of our main conclusions that the increase in site interactivity will be helpful in elevating site recognition (i. e., being included in the Lycos Top 5% Sites List). Hence, given other things constant, an IPS with a better "Web" reputation (e.g., Frigidaire in the Lycos Top 5% Sites List) is more likely to attract and get them involved than its competitor site (e.g., Whirlpool—not in the list), even though otherwise they may be providing similar kind of information (e.g., product and usage information about home appliances).

Another finding from this study calls for firms to choose different combinations of interactive functions that fit well into their Web communication strategy and site goals. For instance, such interactive functions as "dealer locator," "games," "postings," and "comment" are used by "content/image" types of sites as well as by "cyber-brochure" types of sites. So both types of sites can experiment with these four functions. On the other hand, interactive functions such as "online ordering," "downloading," "site survey," "product survey," "contest/prize," "personal-choice helper," "multimedia show," and "site search" are used more frequently among "content/image" types of sites. If we can make the realistic assumption that such market practices are compatible with firms' overall communication strategies and objectives, then we can suggest that IPSs that are more oriented toward image-building or selling should consider planting these functions into their sites.

Our study also highlighted the particular importance of those interactive functions that are primarily geared toward "customer support." This includes activities such as "software downloading," "online problem diagnostics," "inquiry," "order tracking," "comment," and "feedback." Clearly, this interactive marketing function group can efficiently handle a portion of conventional customer support tasks that are commonly performed by firms' customer-support representatives. Not only is such service less costly, it is also less subject to quality variations caused by human errors. In essence, we would argue that this interactive marketing function exemplifies the new model of customer support in the interactive age—taking customers' inputs and serving each of them as a unique individual.

On the other hand, we also have to be reminded that the pace of change in Web communications is very fast. Thus, a firm should not be content with its present high Web site ratings but should closely monitor how other interactive marketing functions may be gaining momentum. For instance, "personal-choice helper" is one remarkable interactive marketing function that may in the future significantly affect how people make product choices in the hyper-media mediated environment (Winer et al., 1997). The "push media"

technology in the "advertising/promotion/publicity" interactive marketing function domain is also gaining ground very rapidly as can be seen by its integration into the latest release (October 1997) of the Netscape Navigator and Microsoft Internet Explorer (version 4.0). In fact, with the rapid increase in the usage of corporate Web sites as firms' communication vehicles (Williamson, 1997), the competition in building interactive IPSs to attract more surfers is likely to get more intense.

After all, just as firms in the same industry compete in the traditional marketplace, their IPSs are also competing for a common target population on the Web. If a company can provide a better-designed IPS then it is more likely to be noticed by Web-site rating agencies. As a result, it may be subsequently put into the lists of popular Web sites such as the "Lycos Top 5% Site" or some other list of a similar nature. Once the IPS is recommended in such a list, then it is more likely to attract more surfers. In addition, visitors are more likely to stay longer in browsing the more interactive IPSs (Novak and Hoffman, 1996).

Future studies can extend our research in several directions. For example, a more comprehensive study may look at a probabilistic sample of Web sites. However, the difficulty in obtaining a unified unbiased sampling frame would be a deterrent to appropriately using a probabilistic sampling approach. In future research, a more comprehensive study may apply the content-analysis technique to a probabilistic sample of IPSs, *provided* that the sampling frame problem can be tackled. Another approach researchers may take is to directly survey surfers on the interactive aspects of IPSs. Under this scenario, to help a firm to evaluate its IPS relative to those of its competitors, researchers may have to get surveys from a number of sites.

Secondly, since our study used the Lycos Top 5% Sites ranking as a reference for Web-site excellence, we did not consider advertising spending level in our study. Thus the potential effect of advertising spending on site effectiveness was not examined in this study. Even though Lycos reviewing guidelines did not seem to suggest that there could be any disadvantage to smaller firms with less advertising spending, it still might be interesting to investigate whether firms' widely different advertising spendings (e.g., P&G spent $2,622 million in 1996 whereas Packard Bell spent $114 million) had an impact on the contents of such a list. We also consider this an area for future research.

Another interesting subject of future research might be to investigate if different levels of ad spending directly affect the number of visits to a site. The data required for such research would be, however, difficult for researchers to get access to. At the minimum, it will require actual site-visit information from many firms plus information about advertising spending specifically designed to increase site visits. As exemplified by the increasing availability of the state-of-the-art scanner data in conventional marketing research, we expect that growth in Web-based studies will spawn creation of innovative data sets (e.g., click-stream data) that will facilitate implementation of some of the suggested areas of future research.

In the present research, we have focused on the variable of interactivity mechanisms in the World Wide Web. Specifically, our empirical analysis using econometric models has demonstrated that usage of interactive functions is likely to increase the attractiveness of corporate Web sites. Our findings also provide diagnostic information, which should help firms to redesign their Web sites for achieving greater marketing communication effectiveness.

Sanjoy Ghose is an associate professor of marketing at the University of Wisconsin-Milwaukee. He holds a bachelor's degree in electrical engineering from the Indian Institute of Technology, Kharagpur, India; an M.B.A. from Washington State University; and an M.S. and a Ph.D. in marketing from Carnegie Mellon University. His research interests include various methodological and substantive issues in modeling consumer perceptions and consumer choice and the marketing/manufacturing interface. His articles have appeared several times in the *Journal of Marketing Research* and in *Marketing Letters, Omega, Production and Operations Management, Communications in Statistics: Theory and Methods,* the *International Journal of Forecasting, Computers and Operations Research,* and the *European Journal of Operational Research.*

Wenyu Dou is a doctoral candidate in marketing in the School of Business Administration at the University of Wisconsin-Milwaukee. He received both his B.S. and M.S. in meteorology from Beijing University. He also holds a masters' degree in atmospheric science from the University of Wyoming. His research interests include various issues related to electronic commerce such as consumer-choice behavior, advertising and distribution. He also has research interests in marketing and in quantitative modeling.

REFERENCES

Agresti, A. *Categorical Data Analysis.* New York: John Wiley & Sons, Inc., 1990.

Blattberg, R. C., and J. Deighton. "Interactive Marketing: Exploring the Age of Addressability." *Sloan Management Review* 33, 1 (1991): 5–14.

Cuneo, A. Z. "Internet World Show Spurs Online Commerce Debate," *Advertising Age,* April 17, 1995.

Davis, C. "Most b-to-b sites don't meet customers needs." *Net Marketing (http://www.netb2b.com)* September 21, 1997.

Deighton, J. "The Future of Interactive Marketing." *Harvard Business Review* 74, 6 (1996): 151–61.

Dillon, W. R. "The Performance of the Linear Discriminant Function in Nonoptimal Situations and the Estimation of Classification Error Rates: A Review of Recent Findings." *Journal of Marketing Research* 16, 3 (1979): 370–81.

Dreze, X., and F. Zufryden. "Testing Web Site Design and Promotional Content." *Journal of Advertising Research* 37, 2 (1997): 77–91.

Ducoffe, H. R. "Advertising Value and Advertising on the Web." *Journal of Advertising Research* 36 5 (1996): 21–35.

Emerick, T. "Media and Marketing Strategies for the Internet: A Step-by-Step Guide." In *Interactive Marketing,* E. Forrest and R. Mizerski, eds. Lincolnwood, IL: NTC Business Books, 1995.

Engel, J. F., R. D. Blackwell, and P. W. Miniards. *Consumer Behavior,* 7th ed. Texas: The Dryden Press, 1993.

Erthon, P., L. F. Pitt, and R. T. Watson. "The World Wide Web as an Advertising Medium: Toward an Understanding of Conversion Efficiency." *Journal of Advertising Research,* 36, 1 (1996): 43–54.

Gupta, S. "Hermes Project: Consumer Survey of WWW Users." *http//www.umich.edu/~sgupta.,* 1997.

Hoffman, D. L., T. P. Novak, and P. Chatterjee. "Commercial Scenarios for the Web: Opportunities and Challenge." *Journal of Computer-Mediated Communication,* Special Issue on Electronic Commerce 1, 3 (1995).

———, and ———. "A New Marketing Paradigm, for Electronic Commerce." *The Information Society,* Special Issue on Electronic Commerce 13, 1 (1996): 43–54.

Holbrook, M. "Product Quality, Attributes, and Brand Name as Determinants of Price: The Case of Consumer Electronics." *Marketing Letters* 3, 1 (1992): 71–83.

Hosmer, D. W., and S. Lemeshow. *Applied Logistic Regression.* New York: John Wiley & Sons, 1989.

Jupiter Communications. "1998 Online Advertising Report: Revenue Models, Market Strategies, Projects." *http://www./jup.com/,* 1997.

Lachenbruch, P. A., and M. R. Mickey. "Estimation of Error Rates in Discriminant Analysis." *Technometrics* 10, 1 (1968): 1–11.

Marrelli, C. "Anatomy of Web Advertisement." In *Interactive Marketing,* E. Forrest and R. Mizerski, eds. Lincolnwood, IL: NTC Business Books, 1996.

McQuail, D. *Mass Communication Theory: An Introduction.* London: Sage, 1983.

Novak, T. P., and D. L. Hoffman. "New Metrics for New Media: Toward the Development of Web Measurement Standards." *World Wide Web Journal* 2, 1 (1997): 213–46.

Philport, J. C., and J. Arbittier. "Advertising: Brand Communications Styles in Established Media and the Internet." *Journal of Advertising Research* 37, 2 (1997): 69–76.

Resnick, A., and B. L. Stern. "An Analysis of the Information Content of Television Advertising." *Journal of Marketing* 41, 1 (1977): 50–53.

SAS Institute Inc. *SAS/STAT User's Guide,* version 6, 4th ed. North Carolina: SAS Institute Inc., 1990.

Scoville, R. "Special Report: Find It on the Net." *PC World,* January 1996.

Spalter, M. "Maintaining a Customer Focus in an Interactive Age: The Seven I's To Success." In *Interactive Marketing,* E. Forrest and R. Mizerski, eds. Lincolnwood, IL: NTC Business Books, 1996.

Steure, J. "Defining Virtual Reality: Dimensions Determining Telepresence." *Journal of Communication* 42, 4 (1992): 73–93.

Upshaw, L. "The Keys to Building Cyber-brands." *Advertising Age,* May 29, 1995.

Vendittp, G. "Critic's Choice." *Internet World,* January 1997.

Winer, R., J. Deighton, S. Gupta, E. J. Johnson, B. Mellers, V. G. Morwitz, T. O'Guinn, A. Rangaswamy, and A. G. Sawyer. "Choice in Computer-Mediated Environments." *Marketing Letters,* 8, 3 (1997): 287–96.

Williamson, D. A. "Marketers Spend on Sites, but Not on Ads." *Advertising Age,* April 14, 1997.

Net Gain: Expanding Markets through Virtual Communities

John Hagel

Abstract

*What are virtual communities? How do they oper-
ate? How can they help expand markets, increase
visibility, and improve profitability? What effects
have they had on business models and marketing
strategies? John Hagel discussed these issues in
his keynote speech at the Direct Marketing Association's 1998 net.marketing Conference held April
1998.*

Introduction

Electronic Networks as Communities

The real opportunity on the Internet is not just doing what you have always done cheaper and faster,
but instead the real opportunity is to rethink at a
fundamental level the business models that you
employ on this new platform, both in terms of what
kind of value you can deliver to your customers and
also the kinds of relationships that you can build
with customers. I would like to illustrate this message by describing a new kind of business model
and the marketing environment associated with it
on electronic networks. I will use that as a context
to discuss some new approaches to marketing, enabled by (and I would argue even required by)
these new business environments and networks.

My focus in particular is on *virtual communities.* Virtual communities actually started as
spontaneous social events on electronic networks,
whether it was CompuServe or America Online,
the early Internet, or the thousands of independent
bulletin board services that sprouted up around the
US. People gathered around common areas of interest, engaging in shared discussions that persisted
and accumulated over time that led to a complex
network of personal relationships and an increasing
identification with the group as a community. We
believe these spontaneous social events provide the
foundation for a very attractive business model.

New Business Models

While I am going to focus on virtual communities as
a business model, I want to be clear that it is not the
only model emerging on the networks. Virtual communities illustrate the fact that these networks enable
different approaches to business. We have worked
with clients around the world in designing and building this kind of business model. I would like to highlight some of the key themes that have emerged from
this work and also from my book *Net Gain.* We circulated the manuscript to a number of people after
we wrote it to ask for some endorsements. One of the
people who responded is Esther Dyson, who as you
well know is extremely influential in the computer
industry. Her response was to call the book "a subversive book." This caused a fair amount of conster-
nation among my partners at McKinsey. Many of
them were concerned with whether this was really
an endorsement or not. I think good sense prevailed
and we featured it as an endorsement, because Esther, with characteristic sharpness, had zeroed in on
one of the key messages that underlay our work with
virtual communities. This first message explains
why the book is "subversive." If you think about
what will draw people into these virtual communities online, it is the notion that they provide a powerful environment to enable customers to extract ever
more value from the vendors that they deal with.
This will really be what draws people in and keeps
them in these virtual communities.

The second message is that the organizers of
the virtual community who recognize this opportunity and help customers to organize these kinds of

environments online will have an attractive business model of their own as a result of helping the customer.

The third message concerns the economics of this business model. One of the key implications of what drives the economics is that there is substantial advantage to being an early mover, particularly in building a critical mass of customers and vendors within these virtual communities.

The fourth message addresses what it takes to be successful other than moving quickly. While many people have emphasized the technological aspects of virtual communities, we actually downplay them. Technology is a key enabler, but there are other important factors at work. There are many different kinds of skills required to be successful. At the core is the mind-set that one brings to the business model. What are your assumptions about the key elements that are important for success? The mindset we believe is fundamentally different than the mindsets that most executives have brought to traditional businesses. We think this is going to be one of the biggest challenges, particularly for large, established companies as they seek to address this opportunity.

Finally, we believe this virtual community business model is going to become prevalent on the network. Increasingly the choice among management will be not *whether* to participate in virtual communities, but *how*. What role do we want to take? Do we want to help organize one of these virtual communities? Or do we instead choose to participate as vendors, selling products and services within these environments? These will be the choices; participating will be a necessity.

VALUE PROPOSITION

I would like to briefly expand on a few of these key messages, starting with the concept of the virtual community value proposition (the ability to help customers to extract value from vendors) and use that to present a definition of what we mean by the business model of a virtual community. What would

you need if you wanted to deliver on that value proposition of extracting value on behalf of customers? You really need three ingredients. First of all, you would need many customers with a similar set of buying needs to exert strength of buying power relative to the vendors that they deal with. Secondly, you would have to arm those customers with as much information as possible about the vendors, products and services that they are interested in. Finally, you would want to bring a large range of relevant vendors together to enable the customers to easily compare offerings, choose among the vendors, and to switch from one vendor to another if they are not satisfied with the service of the first. This serves to create a situation where vendors are bidding for that customer's business, as opposed to trying to target customers. So we use these three elements to frame our definition of what we mean by the business model of a virtual community.

The first element is having a distinctive focus. Virtual communities are defined by bringing people together with a common set of needs or interests. Those needs or interests could span a variety of dimensions. Virtual communities could be organized around an area of interest (like sports or stock investments), a demographic segment (certain age groups within the population), or a geographic region (metropolitan areas). We believe this also has relevance for business-to-business markets. In those situations, virtual communities might be defined around an industry, certain types of job categories (for example, purchasing managers of large companies), or perhaps types of businesses (small home office based businesses or franchisees). In any event, the point is to create a shared focus to aggregate customers together who have similar concerns and requirements.

Types of Virtual Communities
Personal Interests
Let me just quickly describe a few of the virtual communities that are emerging to underscore some of these different dimensions of interests. One of

the earliest ones is a group called the Motley Fool (*www.fool.com*). Originally founded on America Online, it is now available on the Internet. Despite a frivolous name, it has a serious purpose. The intent is to bring together people who are interested in stock investments. Now it has well over 800,000 active members, and has gotten to the point where the impact of discussions in their bulletin board actually have a material effect on stock prices. In some cases, you can track favorable comments in these discussion forums, leading to stock prices going up, unfavorable comments to stock prices going down. So there is a relatively large degree of influence emerging even at an early stage of development. Mediconsult (*www.mediconsult.com*) is another example of a virtual community organized around an area of interest—in this case health care targeted to consumers. It helps consumers to find information about various kinds of medical treatments for diseases, compare those treatments and choose the best one for themselves.

Demographic and Geographic

Parent Soup (*www.parentsoup.com*) targets a demographic group: parents with small children. It has created an environment where parents can talk about the challenges of raising small children, and in the process represents a quite attractive marketplace for a large range of consumer products vendors. Tripod (*www.tripod.com*) targets a different demographic group. These are people leaving college, facing their first job, the challenge of renting their first apartment or house, and all the lifestyle changes that goes on in that transition. An example of a geographically-oriented virtual community would be Boston.com (*www.boston.com*), targeting people who live in the Boston area or who are interested in events there, creating a diverse set of resources for them.

Business-to-Business

In the business-to-business environment you can look at virtual communities like Physicians' Online (*www.po.com*). You have to be a registered physi-cian to participate, and roughly 25% of all physicians in the US are now members. It provides an environment where physicians can talk not only about the medical challenges of treating certain diseases, but also the business aspects of their practice, such as what to pay a receptionist and how to collect from an insurance company faster. It covers a variety of important issues for physicians.

Another example in the business-to-business realm is @griculture Online (*www.agriculture. com*). This met with a fair amount of skepticism when it was formed because it targets farmers. The stereotype is that farmers do not know anything about computers, so why would they ever participate in a virtual community? In fact, most farmers are intensely computer literate, using them every day for managing their farms. The value of coming together in a geographically isolated job and being able to connect anytime, anywhere with other farmers is a powerful proposition. It is also an attractive marketplace for a broad range of product and service vendors who are trying to reach those farmers.

COMMUNICATION IS KEY

So that is the first element of the definition of the value proposition of virtual communities: a distinctive focus that brings together people with a common set of needs. The second element involves integrating published content with discussion forums in this environment. This could be through chat areas, bulletin boards, e-mail facilities—a wide range in communication capability. The third element is that over time, an increasing amount of the value in participating in these virtual communities will be concentrated in those discussion areas. That is based on the assumption that even if you were able to aggregate all the published content relevant to a certain area of interest, it would merely represent a small fraction of the insight that is available in our heads. If you could bring together a group of people who have experience and expertise in an area, and provide an environment where they can be accessed on demand with targeted questions, that is an infinitely deeper information environment than simply bringing together published content. Another element in the definition entails aggregating competing vendors and publishers over time to maximize the selection available to the members of the virtual community to ensure that they can get the best value as they engage in transactions relevant to their area of interest. Finally, the fifth element of the definition is the need for a commercial motivation for the community organizer. As I mentioned, many of the early virtual communities were spontaneous social events. Somebody bought a server and put it in their spare bedroom or their garage, and operated it after hours because they had passion around a topic. Our view is in order to really deliver on the value proposition of enabling customers to extract more value from vendors, it will be important to have a commercial motivation. This is a resource-intensive exercise, and unless you have the prospect of earning a return on those resources, you are unlikely to be able to aggregate enough customers, equip them with enough information, and provide them access with enough vendors to make this all work in terms of extracting value.

CASE IN POINT: LEISURE TRAVEL

Let me illustrate the value proposition with an example. If you thought about leisure travel as an area of common interest, you could imagine a broad range of published content that could be brought together—everything from special interest magazines to travel directories to flight schedules, all easily indexed and organized for people who have this interest. Combine that with a wide range of bulletin board services to enable people to communicate around their interest in leisure travel, and to share their own experiences. Include a set of chat areas, where people could talk in real time to others about areas of the world that they are planning trips to. Then add transaction capability. You could not only plan your next travel vaca-

tion, you could book the airline reservation or the hotel reservation as part of this virtual community experience. So there is a pretty interesting set of services targeted to people who have a strong interest in leisure travel.

This is not a theoretical example; this is in fact one of the most heavily targeted areas in the virtual community world. One of the early entrants was a group called Travelocity (*www.travelocity.com*). Travelocity was founded by a small startup in the San Francisco Bay Area. It is now owned by a much larger company with an intense interest in leisure travel—American Airlines. They decided that there is a strong value in being able to connect with leisure travelers in general and not just their own frequent flyers in a way that simply was not possible in other kinds of media or markets.

Essentially, that is the concept of a business model based in virtual communities. It is taking distinct customer segments defined by a special interest or need, combining abundant sets of published content and transaction capability, with a particular focus on communication. This involves not just bilateral communication in the sense of vendors connecting directly with customers, but a network that increasingly involves the members themselves exchanging information with each other around their areas of interest.

Economic Potential

To illustrate some of the economic potential of virtual communities, let us continue with the example of leisure travel. This is a hypothetical economic model, driven off a computer-based model that we use with our clients. First, we considered how much growth the leisure travel virtual community could experience over time. Obviously, the answer is based on a whole set of assumptions embedded in the model. Our belief is that a leisure travel virtual community in a five year period could generate as much as $90 million in revenue to the organizer, and as much as $600 million in revenue by the tenth year. So it is a reasonably sizable economic venture, and a substantial portion of it is advertising-oriented. We chose travel as an economic model because we thought it would be transaction-intensive. However, even though the transactions are quite sizable in dollar volume, once you include a commission of about 5% (roughly what a travel agent gets today), they generate a relatively small portion of the total revenue potential for the virtual community organizer. The bulk of the revenue potential is in interactive advertising. There are substantial opportunities to make this an attractive advertising medium because of the kinds of profiles you can develop of the members in leisure travel. Note that we make no assumption about subscription revenues. The assumption here is that this is a *free* virtual community from a member viewpoint, where the consumer does not pay anything to participate. That is conservative, because there are certainly opportunities to at least charge for value-added services around leisure travel. We are also assuming no sale of profiles to third parties. That is another revenue source, but because of privacy concerns, we counsel our clients not to sell that information to third parties.

If you look at the cash flow of this model for a leisure travel virtual community, it shows that a total cash investment of about $20 million would be required to achieve the kind of revenue growth predicted above over that period of time. You would turn cash flow positive in roughly the third or fourth year, and by the tenth year generate substantial positive cash flow. Most of the cash investment up front is not in technology or content, but in marketing expense. We are modeling a very aggressive preemptive entry strategy into this area, and so we are assuming heavy spending to aggregate that critical mass of members and vendors into the virtual community.

Following Traditional Models

For those of you who are inclined to be skeptical, this model has a certain profile to it that is well-known in senior management boardrooms around the country and around the world. It is called the *hockey stick:* a long, slow period of investment with no returns. Trust me, at some point this is going to turn cash flow positive, and at some point reasonably far in the future, it will be quite an attractive business.

For those who are more open to the opportunities created by these networks, this profile actually matches that of many other kinds of successful businesses, which are in a general class called *increasing return businesses.* The essence of an increasing returns business is that the product or service becomes more valuable as more customers purchase it. A classic example is the fax machine. If there is only one fax machine in the world, it has negative value. You have to pay something for the device, and then you cannot do anything with it. If there are two fax machines in the world, at least then I can receive a fax and send a fax to one other person. If there are hundreds, it becomes interesting; with thousands or millions, it becomes extremely valuable. That is the essence of an increasing returns business, and that is what explains the long slow ramp up, followed by an inflection point, and then a rapid acceleration in revenue and profitability. That is true in all of these businesses, and it explains the profile in a virtual community, because the value of a virtual community is in the number of people who participate in it. If you walk into a discussion forum online, and there is nobody else in that discussion forum, it is not that valuable to you. If there are hundreds of people who have a deep expertise in a certain area, it becomes quite attractive and valuable to you. That is why there is this long slow ramp up. There are a variety of increasing returns dynamics in the economic model that drive the performance and determine when you will hit that inflection point, and the pace and acceleration of growth. If you look at the cash flow profile that I showed you, that translates into roughly a $4 billion shareholder value business by the tenth year. In this case of leisure travel, a $20 million cash flow investment upfront generating a $4 billion shareholder value business is a reasonably attractive profile, despite the hockey stick aspect of it.

CONTENT AND DEPTH

There are also important reasons to be quick if you want to target this opportunity. There are added challenges if there is an early entrant who has built a rich set of resources in this leisure travel community, exploiting what we call *fractal depth,* which is the opportunity to increasingly segment the virtual community's offerings around narrower topics of interest. This leads to the point where in leisure travel I could present to a prospective member a wealth of resources around a particular place that includes members who have been there, and can talk about what they did there, what they liked and did not like.

Now imagine yourself as a new entrant trying to challenge a virtual community that has developed this level of fractal depth. How are you going to compete with that virtual community? Are you going to try to replicate the depth level that this early entrant has achieved? Even if you had the money—and by the way, we are no longer talking about $20 million in cash flow investment, we are talking about an order of magnitude greater—could you replicate it? Much of the content and value in these virtual communities is member-generated. How do you replicate that without members? This poses an interesting challenge. Or do you come into this virtual community with a thin, superficial layer of resources around leisure travel? How compelling is that relative to somebody who can deliver such fractal depth? That is why we counsel our clients to move quickly if they are interested in organizing virtual communities in order to get to the critical mass of members and vendors.

MINDSET—CHANGE HOW YOU THINK

There are a broad range of skills required to build these virtual communities. We believe the real issue however, is not skills, but mindset. I want to highlight three different levels of mind set challenges that senior management typically encounter

as they get interested in this idea. The first one is the question of the source of value in this virtual community. Most large companies approach this, initially at least, as just another distribution channel. It is merely another way to sell more products and services to more customers than the company has been able to do in other distribution channels or media. Our view is that is the wrong way to think about this. This is a different business. What it provides is an opportunity for a company to, in effect, "cross the table." Instead of being a vendor sitting on one side trying to push ever more product and service out to a target customer, cross that table and sit next to that customer and say, "I'm here to help you get the best value out of the products and services that are important to you." It is a very different mindset. It starts with relatively trivial issues like how excited you are about having your customers talk to each other about your products and services. Most senior managers, when they hear about this, at first are kind of excited or intrigued. They think, "That's great! If I have a good product, my customers will hype it to other customers, and I will sell more of this product or service." But then they go through the second order of thought, which is, "Wait a minute. No product is perfect. Every product has some limitations. Am I going to have my customers talking to each other about the imperfections in my product? Do I really want that? Maybe that is not such a good idea. Maybe we ought to just back off." So there are some profound issues involved in this mindset change.

The second mindset issue has to do with how to enter into this business. The typical reaction of large companies is, "This is a high-risk proposition. We have to be experimental and cautious here. We will put a little bit of money in it and see how it goes. And since it is so high-risk, we cannot afford to depend on anyone else for any part of its success. We have to control it all ourselves." This is a very different mindset from the one that we believe will drive success in this business. If you believe it is an increasing returns business, you have to be aggressive. In fact, you have to be more aggressive than anybody else in that business to win. You need to leverage as much as possible the resources of other companies and businesses, and focus only on the components you absolutely have to deliver to manage your own financial exposure in this.

Finally, there is the issue of creating a management model over time. One of the red flags for us is when we go into senior management and they say, "This is a great idea. First let's put together a task force whose challenge will be to develop a detailed statement of the services and offerings of this virtual community in the tenth year, and associate that with a detailed income statement and balance sheet." This may be an interesting exercise in creativity, but it is unlikely to have any relevance or bearing on what actually evolves in this virtual community, because many of the services and offerings are driven by the interactions among the members themselves. The challenge for management is to understand what drives the economic value creation as a business model, so that you can have what we call *guided organic growth,* where you are encouraging those initiatives that create value for the members, and also deliver value to the organizer of the virtual community— creating a win-win for both sides.

MARKETING: TRADITIONAL MODELS

This business model serves as the context for examining different ways of thinking about marketing in virtual community environments. This stands in contrast to what I characterize as the mass marketing model, which is basically "communicate more and sell more." The idea is if I can blast enough messages out to people, I will eventually sell more of my product or service. It is an image-intensive exercise, because the challenge is how to capture people's attention. These are monologue messages; there is little thought about dialogue here. This is all about getting messages out to people.

Then there is the familiar direct marketing approach. At the risk of oversimplification, I would characterize this as "know more, therefore sell more." Utilizing lists of names and addresses, over time I will learn about these people as I watch their response to various things I send to them, and I will eventually sell more because of profiles that I am developing. However, these are typically narrow transaction-focused profiles. You get to know people as transactors, what they bought and what they did not buy, but you know relatively little about anything else in their lives.

Building Relationships

I would like to propose a third model that is enabled by these networks, which is quite different in its focus and has some real value. It is what I would call *collaboration marketing.* By starting with the focus on helping increase your customers' effectiveness in purchasing products and services, you will end up knowing more about those customers in a different way than you typically know about them in the narrow direct marketing, or transaction-focused, exercise. You will know how they use products and a variety of other aspects about their lives, and in turn that will help you to sell more. The focus here is on building a broad relationship with customers, not just a transaction-focused interaction. You are, in effect, trying to become the customer advisor. It is a somewhat parallel notion to the virtual community model of crossing the table and helping customers to become more effective in purchasing. Part of it is an educational role, helping them to understand the criteria that they might use in evaluating products and services, sort through options to decide which one is best for them, and connect them with vendors. A key issue here is that it is not just a two party vendor-customer dialogue. We are talking about a rich set of relationships or conversations that might be carried out in the process of helping customers. One way that this could be done is with professional advisors in financial product categories. You might think about presenting them with professional financial advisors to help understand their own needs better as a prelude to buying. It could be referring them to complementary service providers or vendors to maximize the value that they can get out of a product once they have bought it. It could even involve connecting them with other customers, so that they can talk to people who have bought the products before, and leverage the experience that those customers have had before they make their own purchases. In essence it is not just one-to-one marketing between a vendor and a customer. While those are the two major parties at work here, the notion is that by helping, you in fact, create an environment where you are connecting customers with a broad variety of people to help them be more effective in their purchases.

Knowledge and Value

By helping customers more, you will in turn get to know about your customers. Not just what they buy and how often they buy, but how they use the product or service, what kinds of things they like about the products and services, and what they do not like. Many vendors spend a lot of money on focus groups. In effect, what you can create in these environments are focus groups that last 24 hours a day, 7 days a week. There is an enormous learning potential in terms of the kinds of product attributes that are most powerful in driving purchases. You can learn about the complementary products and services that customers tend to buy. This allows you to add value, not just to the customer by providing targeted helping functionality, but also to yourself by refocusing your product development and your own business system to deliver greater value to the customer. Ultimately, that enables you to sell more. I think one of the interesting aspects of this, if it is done right online, is that not only are you selling to the online customers, but the learning that you achieve in this "know more" stage ripples out into traditional markets. If you can redesign your products and services to be more helpful to customers, that has an impact on other markets be-

side the online market. So there are a broad range of potential benefits from this approach, and that allows you ultimately to reap the rewards.

Capturing Customers' Attention

We believe that this approach to collaboration marketing helps to achieve two key goals for marketers online, and increasingly for all markets, physical or online. These are reinforcing effects. As you sell and know more, you can be more helpful to the customers. There are some interesting dynamic loops for increasing returns in this collaboration marketing approach as well. The key objective here is two-fold. One is, how do you capture and maintain the attention of your customers? In the years ahead, options will explode for our customers, not just in terms of the products and services that are available to them, but also in the demands on their attention, the proliferation of all kinds of advertising media, and ways of reaching customers. The key challenge all of us will be facing will be how to rise above the noise to capture and retain the attention. Helping as the first stage of involvement with the customer is a much more powerful way of engaging attention than a provocative image or a list with a name on it can be. It is a way to quickly establish a trust with a customer that entitles you to retain their attention. So by knowing more, you can better capture and retain attention effectively over time.

The second objective or challenge is how to maximize return on attention. I would argue that marketers are going to have to spend increasing amounts of money to capture and retain attention. So the demand on earning a return on that expenditure is going to be ever higher. By knowing more about customers than anybody else does, you are in a better position to sell more to them over time, and so this approach to collaboration marketing, we believe, helps to accomplish that objective as well.

There are some key metrics you can use to determine whether or not you are meeting those objectives. In the early stages of helping, it has to do with how much time your customers are willing to allocate to you (frequency of visits, time spent per visit) and how often they come back over time (return rate). Then, as far as earning a return on attention, you get to more traditional metrics like conversion to purchase rates, repurchase rates, and off-line revenue growth as ways of determining whether you are successful on that dimension.

Making It Work

There are two different approaches to how you can implement collaboration marketing. One approach is what I would characterize as the *funnel model*. This involves putting banner ads out in a variety of context sites that are emerging on the network. A context site addresses a broader experience which is relevant to a vendor's product or service. For example, a virtual community for gardeners might be a relevant context site for vendors of gardening tools, or a virtual community for parents with small children might be a context site for financial services providers offering savings plans for college. Essentially, you are using those banner ads as a device to intercept and divert customers to your own site as a vendor in order to engage them there in terms of this "help more, know more, sell more" model. An alternative approach which is just beginning to be developed, is what I call the *sponsorship model*. Rather than intercepting and diverting customers, it involves using some of these context sites that are developing online as the primary environment where you can help more, know more, and sell more. As a result, your own site, the vendor's site, ultimately becomes an invisible back-office fulfillment operation as opposed to the primary marketing environment.

There is no one right way to implement collaboration marketing. It really depends on a whole variety of factors, and difficult choices need to be made. My own bias from having worked with many clients in this area is I think that too much of the effort today is done on the vendor's site, and

not enough has been done to explore the opportunity of sponsorships as a way of executing this kind of collaboration marketing approach.

Reverse Market

There are some broader implications for marketing that emerge from this discussion. We have a strong belief that the network is enabling a different kind of market that we characterize as a *reverse market*. In this reverse market you have to change the way you think about the components of marketing. One of them is the traditional marketing model of vendors seeking out customers. The extensive use of military terminology in describing marketing—everything from blitzes to targeting, all the classic words—are about vendors finding customers and selling more to them. In these reverse marketing situations, we believe it is about customers finding the right vendors at the appropriate time. You often hear talk about vendors owning customers; the measure of success is the extent to which you own your customers. We would argue in these reverse market situations that the real objective is as much as possible to give your customers at least the impression, if not the reality, that they own you as the vendor. That is a different way of thinking about the marketing challenge and how markets function. It also applies to things like information capture. We all think about information capture with respect to customers, as vendors learning more about customers so they can sell more to them. What about customers capturing information about themselves, and then bargaining with vendors for access to that information? That is a different kind of reverse market which has significant implications for a whole range of vendors.

CONCLUSION

Ultimately, where is the source of value in marketing? Traditionally we have all been driven by scarce shelf space as a key constraint. That shelf space can even be in the form of cost of postage and getting catalogs out to customers. Increasingly we believe that because of electronic networks, the scarce resource will be customer attention, and that the challenge will be how to maximize that resource. That in turn has implications for how you think about brands. Most brands today are product-based. They are statements about the vendor, or the product or service that the vendor offers. Increasingly we believe brands will be statements about the customers, about your knowledge of certain customers, and their trust in your ability to deliver the products and services that are relevant to them, based on all understanding of who they are as individual customers.

Finally, the traditional measure of marketing success has been return on assets. We would argue that the real metric over time is going to be return on attention. You are going to have to spend a lot of money to capture and retain attention. How you maximize return on that attention will drive economic success. I hope that has given you some taste of the key message that the networks are enabling some different business models; there is ample opportunity to do things cheaper and faster, but the real opportunity out there is to do things differently, uniquely leveraging the capabilities of these electronic networks.

QUESTION AND ANSWER PERIOD

Can you provide some examples of how to recruit or retain members of virtual communities? Are there membership fees associated with some of the communities out there?

Recruiting and maintaining are obviously the key early challenges. Our view is that companies will often go out and try to pour their money into customer or member acquisition. The real winners out there are those who are focusing in on what we call *leveraged customer acquisition:* looking at the cost per member acquired as a life cycle cost relative to what the member generates over time. I mentioned the example earlier of Motley Fool as one of the early pioneers in this area. The two

Gardner brothers, the founders of Motley Fool, have taken traditional media and used it is a funnel into their virtual community. So they have now written a number of best-selling books, leveraging much of the content and focus of their virtual community, but taking it into a traditional medium and creating a much higher awareness of their virtual community online.

I think focusing in on relationships with other virtual communities is a good approach. What we are seeing emerge now are what I call *nested* virtual communities, so that one virtual community will establish a sub-interest area in another one. ThirdAge (*www.thirdage.com*) has an interesting relationship with a group called New Jersey Online (*www.njo.com*). ThirdAge found that many of their older members live in New Jersey. New Jersey Online is a virtual community targeting people who live in that state. They are using ThirdAge as a way to find out about older people who live in New Jersey and hopefully pull them in to their broader virtual community. So there are some interesting approaches that leverage the unique capabilities of this network to acquire members.

There are some virtual communities charging membership fees. By and large those tend to be business-to-business oriented virtual communities. We at least are strongly advising our clients that if you can possibly avoid charging subscription fees, you ought to do that. This is particularly important in consumer spaces because of the need to build a critical mass of members quickly. Subscription fees tend to put another barrier in front of people, slowing down the process of getting to a critical mass.

What are your thoughts on bulletin board moderators removing negative postings, or postings which are opposed to the organization's view?

There is a broad issue about the role of the moderator in guiding and focusing discussion. It is all very context-specific. Certain forums are no holds barred, anybody can say anything, and that is part of the fun and excitement of participating in them. You get fantasy bulletin boards where this is certainly true. On the other hand, there are other bulletin boards where information really does matter in terms of what is communicated, and being able to at least throw certain people out over time who are being particularly disruptive is an important role that the moderator plays. I think that one has to be extremely cautious about that though. There is a strong desire on the part of companies to censor comments about their products and services, particularly negative comments. One of the exercises I go through with senior management as they get concerned about the notion of their customers saying negative things about them is I will take them online. I would wager that for any large company, at least today, I can find a discussion forum that is already operating about that company. So things are being said, positive and negative, about your company, whether you want it to happen or not. So your choice is, what role do you play with regard to those discussion forums? Our own view is that there is substantial value in creating discussion forums where there are wide-open comments, negative and positive, and that you rely on the other people in the discussion forums to challenge, or where necessary for company spokesmen, appropriately identified, to challenge, but that it is a free market of input for the products and the value of those products.

In your experience, how long does it take to build a virtual community? What is the typical time frame and process involved?

The challenge with this business model is that it is a relatively long-term business model to build. Of all the business models that are out there, it is probably the one that has the most pronounced increasing returns characteristics to it, and so that implies that there is a longer ramp up period than for many other business models. Now that in turn ought to lead to higher returns over time, because the increasing returns create important lock-in and acceleration effects over time. In the near term, you have this long period before you turn cash flow positive. In the model for a relatively large virtual community with roughly two million members of over a ten year period, it took three to four years to go cash flow positive, and that was for a very aggressive entry strategy. Many virtual communities might take longer than that. Part of it has to do with how much skill the organizer applies to things like the use of the profiles that are accumulated in the virtual communities. What drives the revenue and ultimately the profitability of these virtual communities is advertising and transaction activity. We believe that is heavily influenced by the ability to use the profiles to more effectively present things to the right members of the community.

John Hagel is a Principal at McKinsey and Company at their Silicon Valley office. In addition, he heads McKinsey's Global Electronic Commerce Practice. He has worked primarily for clients in the electronics, telecommunications, and in the media industry. His particular focus is on strategic management and performance improvement. Recently his client work has dealt with electronic commerce initiatives and implementing web-based strategies. Hagel has recently published articles in the *Harvard Business Review* and *The Wall Street Journal*. In addition, his third book, *Net Gain: Expanding Markets Through Virtual Communities* (published by the Harvard Business School Press, 1997) has been on the business book bestseller list in the US, and is currently being translated into ten languages. His new book, *Net Worth: Shaping Markets when Customers Make the Rules,* will be published by Harvard Business School Press in March, 1999.

7

BUSINESS-TO-BUSINESS INTERNET MARKETING

Outline

- *Let's Get Vertical*
  Mohanbir Sawhney and
  Steven Kaplan

A recent issue of Business 2.0 trumpeted "The Web's Trillion-Dollar Secret" in reference to the rise of business-to-business marketing on the Internet. Indeed, most estimates point to dramatic growth in this sector. Forrester Research, for example, predicts that the business-to-business Internet market will grow to $1.3 trillion by 2003, making it 10 times larger than the business-to-consumer market.

What is the reason for the stunning success of business-to-business marketing on the web? The reason is simple: Business-to-business marketing on the web focuses on cost savings rather than direct revenue for success. Businesses use the web to improve the efficiency and effectiveness of internal and external operations and processes. These costs savings alone justify investments in web-related technologies. The business-to-consumer marketing model requires direct revenue for success. Amazon.com, for example, will live or die by the number of orders it processes on its web site. FedEx, on the other hand, shows how the web can deliver huge returns on investments through cost savings alone.

Businesses also have the advantage that business relationships throughout the supply chain are already developed. Offline relationships can easily be moved to the online world. As a result, communities of business interest can be formed rapidly leading to a powerful network of relationships. In the business-to-consumer world, communities must often be formed and built from the ground up over a longer period of time.

The Internet is affecting virtually every business process internally and externally. Internally, intranets provide "just-in-time" access to corporate data, directories, training and reference material, and sales tools. Some corporations are saving millions of dollars in printing and distribution costs alone. Increasingly, internal processes such as expense reports,

time sheets, and benefit functions are becoming automated on the web, resulting in even more substantial
savings.

Externally, firms are using the web in a variety
of ways. Some corporations are using the web to
electronically procure indirect materials, repair, and
operating supplies automatically. Other firms are
leveraging the web to find suppliers and purchase
direct materials and capital goods quickly and easily.
Many companies are discovering new web-based
auction markets for surplus parts and inventory. Fi-

nally, corporations are participating in online exchanges that are creating new markets and liquidity
for previously thinly traded commodities.

In this chapter, Mohanbir Sawhney and Steven
Kaplan review business-to-business marketing on the
web. These researchers detail unique characteristics
of the business-to-business environment and the various marketing models currently employed.

When you are finished reading their article,
please visit the textbook's web site for additional resources.

Let's Get Vertical

Mohanbir Sawhney
Steven Kaplan

The great untold story of online commerce is that business-to-business sales have already eclipsed the higher-profile business-to-consumer market by a long shot. Annual B-to-B ecommerce is projected to soar from $43 billion in 1998 to $1 trillion by 2003, according to Forrester Research, while the consumer market swells from $7.8 billion to $108 billion in the same period. In this issue, we deconstruct the new business models—vertical, horizontal, and otherwise—that promise to turbocharge the online B-to-B engine; a handful of ambitious companies piloting those models in different industries; and the latest market data that points in new directions.

It was a busy spring for ecommerce analysts: A whole crop of numbers sprang up to put some definitive, quantitative stamp on the digital economic boom. . . . The U.S. Department of Commerce weighed in with an industry summit in May on the topic of tracking ebusiness, and in June it released its second annual report on ecommerce, "Emerging Digital Economy II." Also in June, a study released by the University of Texas—and funded by Cisco Systems—found that the Internet economy generated $301 billion in U.S. revenue in 1998, buoyed by a work force of 1.2 million people, which puts it in the same macroeconomic neighborhood as cars ($350 billion) and telecommunications ($270 billion).

While the research firms continue to run numbers, the consumer market for ebusiness continues to grab most of the headlines. Last November's declaration from Jupiter Communications that the

Internet would trigger a $2.3 billion holiday shopping bonanza itself triggered an avalanche of media attention on the advent of online shopping that has hardly let up in the months since.

All that has fairly masked a quiet revolution currently under way in the digital economic realm: business-to-business (B-to-B) ecommerce. Up to this point, most of the attention in B-to-B ecommerce has focused on prominent, well-established firms such as Cisco and Dell Computer that eliminate old-economy middlemen and sell directly to business customers. But the real B-to-B ecommerce revolution is taking place outside the boundaries of individual firms.

A new breed of intermediaries is emerging to facilitate B-to-B ecommerce. These new intermediaries go by different names—"vortexes," "butterfly markets," or "net market makers." All in some way serve as electronic hubs, each spinning in a new market. These hubs focus on specific industry verticals or specific business processes (from spare airplane parts to secondary mortgages), host electronic marketplaces, and use various market-making mechanisms to mediate any-to-any transactions among businesses. They create value by aggregating buyers and sellers, creating marketplace liquidity (a critical mass of buyers and sellers), and reducing transaction costs.

What makes any of this revolutionary? First, these intermediaries do for ecommerce transactions what a network hub does for bits: concentrating, routing, and switching transactional traffic in B-to-B ecommerce. Second, they occupy a central position between buyers and sellers, much as airline hubs do between city pairs.

In short, hubs promise to reshape the landscape of B-to-B ecommerce—and here are a few of the lesser-known "numbers" that back it up. First and foremost is the Forrester Research projection that B-to-B ecommerce will surge past $1 *trillion* by 2003. San Francisco-based investment bank Volpe Brown Whelan estimates that overall hub revenue (both transactions and advertising) nationwide will grow from $290 million in 1998 to $20 *billion* by 2002. The Precursor Group's estimates are even higher, putting B-to-B exchange revenue between $50 billion and $130 billion by 2002. Even with the more conservative estimates, hubs could generate transaction fees of more than $10 billion within three years, with gross margins of 85 percent. If these numbers sound too optimistic, consider eBay, a hub in the consumer-to-consumer market. eBay boasts gross margins in excess of 80 percent and, more strikingly for an Internet company, reported a profit within a year of its inception.

Despite their enormous significance for B-to-B ecommerce, hubs remain poorly understood. Like the bulk of an iceberg that lurks below the waterline, they remain largely invisible to the media, investors, and analysts. While the landscape is still blurry, and few hubs have achieved any degree of prominence, it is possible to describe what hubs are, what they do, how they create value, and what the future is likely to hold.

B2B: A DIFFERENT ANIMAL

Returns to Scale

This is the most important and perhaps the least understood difference between consumer commerce ventures and B-to-B hubs. Consumer hubs, even as expansive as Buy.com's, are one-way networks that deal directly with buyers and create benefits mostly for sellers. B-to-B commerce hubs tend to be two-way networks that mediate between buyers and sellers, and create benefits for both sides. *Lots* of benefits: The value created by consumer hubs tends to increase linearly in the number of buyers; the value created by B-to-B hubs increases as the *square* of the number of participants.

Here's the math: At Buy.com, the benefits to an individual buyer are roughly the same whether there are 100 customers or 100 million customers, because the benefits to buyers are primarily the time saved from going to a physical store and

looking for an item. Buy.com does, however, benefit on the supply side, by tallying savings in marketing and procurement. These benefits tend to be linear, so the total value created by Buy.com increases only linearly in the number of customers.

Now, consider a B-to-B hub: It creates value by reducing search costs, reducing information transfer costs, standardizing systems, and improving matching for both buyers and sellers. Buyers benefit because they have more choices and sellers benefit because they have access to more buyers. All of these value drivers increase with the square of the number of participants in the hub.

Take the case of five potential sellers and buyers in a B-to-B market. In the absence of the hub, each seller would have to determine the identity of each buyer, through advertising or a direct sales force. Each seller would have to contact each buyer each time it wanted to do a transaction. Without a hub, the participants would have to undertake 25 searches—each seller looking for five buyers—and then make 25 contacts (either faxes or phone calls) each time the sellers wanted to sell.

Now look at this electronically: the hub finds the buyers and sellers, reducing the number of searches to 10. Similarly, each time the sellers want to sell, there are only 10 contacts—five postings on the hub, and five views by the buyers.

The methodology is similar for matching buyers and sellers, standardizing systems, and transferring information such as credit checks, product descriptions, and evaluations. Further, the complexity of the benefits a hub offers makes it difficult for competitors to offer customers similar benefits. This is particularly true for matching between buyers and sellers in auctions and exchanges. A buyer is far less likely to find a match in an illiquid hub than in a liquid one. Small wonder, then, that eBay is profitable and commands a rich valuation.

Importance of Domain Expertise

Setting up shop as an online retailer does not require deep knowledge of specific categories. The founders of many popular online shops had no previous category experience, and Amazon has quite easily migrated across retail categories. In contrast, domain expertise is a must for creating a hub. Consider a hub like SciQuest.com that mediates between buyers and sellers in the laboratory and scientific equipment marketplace, or PlasticsNet. com . . . that has spawned a new market between plastics manufacturers and plastics processors, or e-Steel, that makes a market between buyers and sellers of steel. The founders of these companies had extensive industry experience and relationships with key buyers and suppliers. Domain expertise and relationships are key barriers to entry for hubs.

Customer Acquisition and Retention

Online retailers typically use advertising and affiliate programs for customer acquisition. But B-to-B buyers and sellers don't simply see a banner advertisement and sign up with SciQuest.com or PlasticsNet.com. Customer acquisition requires sales calls, and the process for signing up buyers and sellers is time-consuming and expensive—supplier catalogs have to be loaded online . . . business processes need to be understood, business rules need to be defined, and the hub's systems need to be integrated with those of its buyers and sellers. Customer switching costs and customer retention rates are also correspondingly higher for hubs, once they embed themselves into the business processes of buyers and sellers, and for them, competition is a lot further away than a mouse click.

All that presents a worthwhile industry-wide tradeoff. The higher entry barriers due to increasing returns to scale, domain expertise, and higher customer switching costs add up to stronger profit potential and more defensible business designs than B-to-C retailers.

B2B HUBS: WHAT'S WHAT

In contrast to pure financial marketplaces, hubs are contextual marketplaces; hubs focus on a specific dimension of it. Attempting to be everything to everybody is a recipe for failure. Nets Inc. was designed as a B-to-B shopping mall across different verticals and different functions. One of the primary reasons it failed is that it had no focus or context. It was neither vertical nor functional, and never able to attract enough buyers and sellers to generate liquidity.

A hub, though, can specialize vertically along a specific industry or market, or it can specialize horizontally along a specific function or business process. Based on these dimensions, the universe of hubs boils down to two primary types: vertical and functional. Together, they form the quilt of B-to-B ecommerce.

Vertical Hubs

Vertical hubs serve a vertical market or industry focus. They provide deep domain-specific content and relationships. Examples: Altra Energy (energy), Band-X (telecommunications), Cattle Offerings Worldwide (beef and dairy), SciQuest.com (life sciences), e-Steel (steel), Floraplex (florists), IMX Exchange (mortgages), PaperExchange (paper), PlasticsNet.com (plastics), and Ultraprise (secondary mortgage exchange). Vertical hubs typically start out by automating and hosting the procurement process for a vertical, and then supplement their offerings with industry-specific content.

The likely success of a vertical hub increases with:

- Greater fragmentation among buyers and sellers.
- Greater inefficiency in the existing supply chain.
- Creating critical mass of key suppliers and buyers.
- Domain knowledge and industry relationships.
- Creating master catalogs and sophisticated searching.
- Adjacent verticals, for leveraging existing supplier or buyer base.

The primary challenge for vertical hubs is the difficulty of diversifying and extending their business into other vertical markets, because their expertise and relationships are fairly domain-specific.

Functional Hubs

Functional hubs focus on providing the same functions or automating the same business process across different industries. Their expertise usually lies in a business process that is fairly horizontal, which means that it is scalable across vertical markets. iMark.com, for example, focuses on buying and selling used capital equipment. Its target participants are investment-recovery managers responsible for the equipment. Other examples of functional hubs include Processors Unlimited (reverse logistics), MRO.com (maintenance, repair, and operating procurement), Employease (employee benefits administration), Celarix (global logistics monitoring and tracking), BidCom (project management), Adauction (media buying), and YOUtilities (energy management).

The likely success of a functional hub increases with:

- Degree of process standardization.
- Process knowledge and work-flow automation expertise.
- Complementing process automation with deep content.
- Ability to customize the business process to respond to industry-specific differences.

The primary challenge for functional hubs is to deliver industry-specific content. They target functional managers who affiliate and organize their work primarily around their functional area, and not their industry. But many functional managers also affiliate with their industry. The risk: They will gravitate toward a vertical hub for their industry and relegate the functional hub to become a back-end service provider for the vertical hub.

SEPARATING THE WINNERS AND LOSERS

Architects of B-to-B hubs must address a number of key design and execution issues. These include:

Choosing a Marketmaker

Hubs can employ a variety of market-making mechanisms to mediate transactions between participants in the hub. These mechanisms can be fixed-price mechanisms that are typical of catalog purchasing, or dynamic pricing mechanisms that include auctions, exchanges, or barter.

A listing or **catalog model** creates value by aggregating suppliers and buyers. It works best in industries characterized by fragmented buyers and sellers who transact frequently for relatively small-ticket items. Given the small transaction size, it is too costly, even on the Net, to negotiate each transaction. The catalog model also works well when most purchasing takes place with pre-qualified suppliers and with predefined business rules, and the occasional purchase requires searching across a number of smaller suppliers. Finally, it works best for situations where demand is predictable, and prices do not fluctuate too frequently. Chemdex, SciQuest.com, and MRO.com are examples of catalog-centric hubs.

Auction models create value by spatial matching of buyers and sellers. They work best in industries or settings where one-of-a-kind, non-standard, or perishable products or services need to be bought or sold among businesses that have very different perceptions of value for the product. Capital equipment, used products, unsaleable returned products, and hard-to-find products fit this description. iMark.com uses an auction model to sell used capital equipment. Adauction.com auctions off perishable online and print advertising inventory.

Exchange models create value by temporal matching of supply and demand. . . . They require a real-time, bid-ask matching process, marketwide price determination, as well as a settlement and clearing mechanism. The exchange model works best for near-commodity items that can have several attributes, but are easy to specify. Exchanges create significant value in markets where demand and prices are volatile by allowing businesses to manage excess supply and peak-load demand. PaperExchange in paper, e-Steel in steel, and Altra in energy are all good examples of hubs that employ exchange models.

Barter models create value by matching two parties that possess reciprocal assets within an asset class or across asset classes. While barter has traditionally been used in inflationary economies with shortages of hard currency as a tool to minimize currency risk, there are other innovative applications, such as bartering manufacturing capacity, bartering services for other services, and bartering high-transportation cost assets (such as paper or steel).

In many cases, a hub will find it valuable to offer more than one market-making mechanism. Customers of hubs will favor hubs that allow buyers and sellers to choose the appropriate market-making mechanism. This means that hub architects need to take care in choosing a technology platform, because technology providers have tended to focus on catalog (Ariba, Commerce One, IBM), auction (Moai Technologies, Dynamic Trade, OpenSite Technologies), or exchange (Tradex Technologies) models, and lack integrated multimechanism platforms.

Solving the Chicken-and-Egg Dilemma

The value created by a hub increases non-linearly in the number of participants. The key goal of any hub, therefore, is to attain liquidity as quickly as possible. The problem, of course, is that it is difficult to attract buyers without sellers and difficult to attract sellers without buyers.

While hubs need to market to both sellers and buyers, they will generally be better off marketing more heavily to the party in the transaction that re-

ceives the most benefit. Once the hub has gained the participation of that side, it can market more easily or even compel the other side to join up. Despite conventional wisdom that hubs tend to be buyer-centric and hence need to attract buyers first, there is no reason why hubs will consistently favor buyers over sellers or vice versa. Chemdex and SciQuest.com, focused on buyers first in order to attract sellers. PaperExchange, in contrast, has focused on sellers first in order to attract buyers.

In its early stages, hubs might also consider injecting liquidity into the market. Consider the strategy that priceline.com adopted in growing its market for airline tickets. It focused on getting buyers, who arguably receive the greater relative benefit, injecting liquidity by buying cut-rate airline tickets in order to attract buyers. Once it achieved critical mass, the incentives for airlines to cooperate increased.

Timing Market Entry

How quickly should a hub open for business? Let's overstate the obvious: Those that start early reach buyers and sellers more quickly, preempt competitors, and begin to learn earlier about the market. But these benefits must be weighed against the risk that premature opening will discourage market participants from returning because of lack of functionality or liquidity and alert potential competitors. Early entry, then, makes good sense. Another strategy can be to open an informational or content-focused hub, and to add transactional functionality as liquidity improves. . . .

Managing Channel Conflict

Some existing intermediaries are initially likely to be hostile to hubs, because of concerns around disintermediation and price erosion. Hub architects should stress that it can complement an intermediary rather than act as a substitute. Hubs can provide more volume and better matches to existing intermediaries. This is particularly useful in industries with uncertain or volatile supply and demand. To counter price erosion, sophisticated hubs should provide value proposition transparency, not merely price transparency. How? By offering metrics related to quality, reputation, reliability, speed, or service, in addition to providing prices. Finally, hubs can create "virtual private marketplaces" that preserve prenegotiated terms and relationships between specific buyers and suppliers.

Expanding the Scope of the Offering

While liquidity is the key determinant of a hub's success, those firms should also try to increase the depth and breadth of its relationships with participants. This can be done by providing complementary services to participants that make it more costly for buyers and sellers to transact elsewhere. Such services might include IT services like system integration and hosting; financial services such as payment processing, receivables management, and credit analysis; logistics services like shipping, warehousing, and inspection; and risk mitigation services like escrow and warranties. Partners such as Skyway (supply-chain management), PaylinX (enterprise payment servers), i-Escrow (escrow), eCredit.com (credit analysis), and USinternetworking (application service provider) help to round out the offering. In addition, each of these complementors are potential sources of referral revenue from the existing participant base.

Managing Growth and Diversification

Over time, the hub will need to diversify beyond its initial choices of strategic position. These growth vectors can be along four key dimensions— horizontal scope, vertical scope, offering scope, and mechanism scope. Consider e-Steel, a vertical hub specializing in the steel industry, the procurement process, using an exchange mechanism, and by largely outsourcing logistics services. Horizontally,

e-Steel could add logistics tracking or investment recovery services. Vertically, it could branch into the packaging vertical. To expand scope, it could offer credit analysis or fulfillment services. Choices should be based on the strength of connection to the new supplier and buyer base, the new business process, the knowledge and relationships needed, and the alternative market-making mechanisms within the current participant base. In some cases, partnerships and acquisitions will drive growth.

Forecasting the Evolution of B-to-B Hubs

A few predictions of what the next year or two holds for hubs:

- Hubs will have winner-take-all characteristics: The strong increasing returns characteristics will create even more scale advantages for the first hub to achieve scale and liquidity than in the consumer portal or retail business. Even being the second-biggest player may not be enough.
- Vertical hubs will find it hard to diversify beyond their verticals: They compete on domain-specific relationships and expertise. Unless they can find closely related domains where they can leverage these assets, they will find it difficult to diversify into other vertical markets.
- Vertical hubs will form a patchwork of alliances with functional hubs: Verticals possess domain expertise but lack functional expertise, while functional hubs possess functional expertise, but lack domain expertise. Alliances will form across the "quilt" between verticals and functionals. In these alliances, vertical hubs will usually emerge as the ones that control the customer relationship.
- Software vendors will climb out of their silos: Currently, software vendors sit in three silos that correspond to their market-making mechanism of choice—transaction software vendors (such as Ariba and Commerce One),

auction software vendors (such as Moai and OpenSite), and exchange platform vendors (such as Tradex . . .). The walls of these silos will break down, and a flurry of mergers and alliances between software vendors will ensue.

- Exchange models will evolve to include derivatives: The exchange mechanisms in hubs currently are limited to spot markets. As participants become more sophisticated and hub software platforms improve in functionality, hubs will begin to offer derivative products like forward contracts and options on commodities and manufacturing capacity.
- All except the biggest firms will give up on hosting hubs: Early generations of B-to-B ecommerce software focused on catalogs, auctions, and exchanges hosted by individual firms. This firm-centric model limits liquidity, and will give way to catalogs hosted by hubs.
- New "metahubs" may emerge with shared infrastructure and services: Although vertical hubs will not consolidate across vertical domains, there is no reason for them to have dedicated infrastructure and supporting services. We may see the emergence of new market hubs with shared back-ends and common functional hubs servicing the different "tenant" vertical hubs.

- The power of conventional commodity exchanges will erode. Conventional commodity exchanges are devoid of context, they will find it difficult to compete with the powerful integration of context and exchange functionalities that hubs will provide. They also lack business process integration capabilities. As a result, hubs will gradually drain liquidity from conventional commodity exchanges.

Market analysis at this stage—like any analysis about the future of ecommerce—boils down to advanced guesswork. But if the recent successful IPOs of online B-to-B companies such as Vertical-Net and Ariba are any indication, and if the market projections are anywhere close, the best is clearly yet to come.

Mohanbir Sawhney (*mohans@nwu.edu*) is the Tribune Professor of Electronic Commerce and Technology at the Kellogg Graduate School of Management, Northwestern University, and heads the ecommerce and technology group.

Steven Kaplan (*steven.kaplan@gsbpop.uchicago.edu*) is the Neubauer Family Professor of Entrepreneurship and Finance at the University of Chicago Graduate School of Business, and the faculty director of the entrepreneurship program.

8

INTERNET MARKETING RESEARCH

Outline

■ *The Impact of the Internet on Data Collection*
Rick Weible and John Wallace

Internet technologies are changing the way marketing research activities are conducted at virtually every level. In the past, secondary research was an expensive and time-consuming task that involved multiple trips to the local library. Now secondary research can be conducted with ease using a variety of web-based databases and resources, many of which are available at no charge. Primary field research was also very expensive prior to the development of the web. Now surveys and experiments can be done online, with results tabulated in a matter of days or even hours.

The web is perhaps the perfect environment for measuring marketing effectiveness. A variety of web-enabled tools and technologies allows marketers to test and measure the relationship between marketing expenditures and results. Marketers can then act on this knowledge and improve marketing effectiveness. This ability is called *closed-loop marketing*.

One example of closed-loop marketing can be found in the realm of banner advertising. With broadcast advertising such as television, it is very difficult to gauge the effectiveness of commercials in generating sales. However, with banner advertising, marketers can measure, sometimes in real time, the percentage of surfers who click on the advertisement, visit the web site, interact with the web site, and make a purchase. Marketers can now experiment not only with different banner advertisements but with different web site content to maximize response.

Live experiments and response measurements are also common in direct e-mail marketing. Using in-house or opt-in e-mail lists, marketers can experiment with different offers, creative prices, and response pages to see what works best. In addition, the low costs associated with such electronic campaigns makes return on investment a much greater possibility.

The Internet also allows smaller firms to implement, in some cases for the first time, comprehensive customer satisfaction and product quality surveys. These surveys can be done affordably in-house or outsourced to web-based survey companies that automatically collect, analyze, and present data findings.

In this chapter, Rick Weible and John Wallace compare the performance of Internet versus non-Internet data collection techniques. These researchers find that Internet-based collection and analysis procedures hold several advantages relative to other more traditional techniques. These results suggest that web-based marketing research has a bright future.

Please do not forget to visit the textbook's web site for additional resources.

Rick Weible
John Wallace

How is the Internet changing the world of market research? This study compares four methods of collecting survey data and reveals that newer methods have significant but not overwhelming advantages over older methods, such as mail. While conventional mail and fax continue to garner slightly higher response rates than e-mail and Web forms, they are of course slower and more expensive. Unlike most earlier studies on this issue, the authors look at fixed and variable costs of the methods and argue that for an increasing proportion of the North American population, the cost and convenience advantages of the newer methods can often make up for lower response rates and inaccurate e-mail addresses.

It is just past midnight and a fax machine receives a call, a computer receives an e-mail message, and a postal worker begins processing the mail picked up earlier that evening. A survey from a researcher is on the way. The researcher might be a university faculty member, an employee of a market research firm, or a staff member of a firm seeking opinions from fellow employees. The fax was sent by a software package that automatically inserts the addressee's information from the database into a fax form of the survey. One e-mail program is sending the survey to recipients selected from a database. Another e-mail program is sending an e-mail invitation asking other recipients selected from a database to visit an electronic form of the survey at a Web site on the Internet. Earlier, the survey was printed, envelopes were stuffed, mailing labels and postage applied, and the survey was placed in the mailbox. Data collection is under way, and the question is: Which method is best?

Research on the competitive advantages of new data collection methods is timely due to the rapid acceptance of the Internet, especially in industrialized countries. It is estimated that more than 31 million North American adults were using the Internet and e-mail at least weekly in 1997, up from 20 million in 1996, and that the number of users should approach 70 million in 1998. The speed that such changes are occurring makes it difficult for researchers to choose the most appropriate method. In addition, new methods, such as faxing over the Internet are becoming available, and some Internet Service Providers (ISPs) already offer Internet faxing.

A RAPIDLY MATURING TECHNOLOGY

Market research on the Internet is growing rapidly. This is exemplified by the members of the Council of American Survey Research Organizations (CASRO). About one-third of the 165 member firms listed in the CASRO Web site membership directory have their own Web sites and 86% of these firms offer Internet-based data collection. At least three such firms offer online panels ranging in size from 1,000 to 170,000 members, and at least five firms offer Web site analysis for organizations wanting to know who is visiting their Web sites, whether the visitors are part of that organization's target market, and how satisfied the visitors are with the site and why.

These progressive research firms promote the same advantages of Internet-based market research that are reported in the literature: faster responses, lower cost, flexibility, and high response rates (of around 70%). Fast response is exemplified by one market research firm that was able to complete

Marketing Research, Fall 1998.

1,000 customer satisfaction surveys in only two hours. The firm presented a banner type ad for the survey to every 85th visitor to the client's Web site. The firm found that about 50% of those presented with the banner clicked on the survey, and about 50% of those (25% in all) completed the survey. The low relative cost of Internet-based consumer research is illustrated by another research firm that charges only fifteen cents per e-mail survey sent to members of its online consumer panel, a price that is less than one-tenth of typical mailed surveys.

Other advantages of Internet-based surveying that are promoted, but not yet established in the published literature, include higher quality responses, lower respondent error, broader stimuli potential (color, graphics, 3D), more complex questionnaire design, unique research tools (versing, skips, rotations, piping, and advanced data driven intelligence), projected results, and online panel focus groups.

In addition, new software products are making it easier to use the Internet as a research tool. Some firms offer complete outsourcing of the process, priced as low as fifteen cents per e-mail addressee. Products are available to convert surveys to a variety of formats including Web-based (HTML) and Java. Thus it appears that market researchers can reap the benefits of conducting research on the Internet without mastering its intricacies.

Studies

There is a long tradition of research on the relative advantages of different survey methods. Many studies have compared older methods such as mail, telephone, and face-to-face interviews. However, it is increasingly difficult to keep up with rapid technological progress. The literature remains sparse concerning the advantages of newer data collection methods, such as e-mail, fax, and Web form. Earlier studies are poor guides for researchers faced not only with limited budgets, but also with rapid technological change. Moreover, some technological changes make it easier for researchers in small organizations to carry out sophisticated surveys that once were the sole prerogatives of researchers in large organizations. Thus the audience for this research includes millions of small firms that increasingly need to poll their customers and suppliers.

Since market researchers continually seek data collection methods that are cheap, fast, and unbiased, any analysis of alternative methods must cover several dimensions. Early researchers suggested three dimensions: *validity, reliability,* and *practicality. Practicality,* which is more commonly called *"efficiency,"* concerns the complexity of the data collection process, and includes cost, ease of administration, and the ease of analyzing and interpreting the data. In other words, the efficiency of a method is a function of how quickly and how cheaply the researcher can complete the data collection cycle.

Few recent studies on data collection media have attempted to compare more than two survey methods. Moreover, few researchers have attempted to completely analyze both the effectiveness and the efficiency of competing methods. Below are eight studies that compare various relationships between data collection and surveying methods. Four studies compare e-mail and mailed surveys; two compare e-mail surveys; one compares phone with online; and the final study compares mail with fax.

Lee Sproull, one of the first people to analyze e-mail as a data collection medium, was attracted by its low cost, especially in a large corporate environment. He was concerned about his audience's access to e-mail, their willingness to respond via e-mail, and whether the data collected would be as reliable as that collected by other methods. He asked employees of the R&D and product development divisions of a Fortune 500 company to save the messages they received for three days and then answer some questions about those messages. Thirty respondents were asked about e-mail messages and 30 were asked about hard copy messages. He found that e-mail responses came back in half the time of that of hard-copy responses, but that the hard copy responses were slightly more complete. He found no bias in the answers from either group of respondents, and no differences in their attitudes towards the two media.

Lorraine Parker, another corporate researcher, reported on a questionnaire distributed company-wide as part of a total quality management project at AT&T. Parker's team surveyed 140 AT&T employees located around the world by sending 100 surveys by e-mail and 40 by the company's internal mail system. Her response rate for e-mail was almost twice that for company mail (68% vs. 38%). She attributed her satisfactory e-mail response rates to the limited volume of junk e-mail at the time as well as to the mystique of the then new medium. Interestingly, 28% of her e-mail recipients returned their responses by mail, thus raising the issue of preferred response modes if the audience is given the option of responding in several ways. Parker did not report on response times or bias.

Barbara Schuldt and Jeff Totten compared the response rates and speeds of a mailed survey and an e-mailed survey sent to a sample of 325 MIS and 218 marketing professors at U.S. colleges and universities. They sent mail surveys to 100 marketing professors and 100 MIS professors, and e-mail surveys to 118 marketing and 225 MIS professors. They received 113 usable mail responses (a 56.5% response rate) and 42 e-mail responses (a 19.3% response rate). The fact that their response rate for mail was nearly three times higher than e-mail was in part that of the 343 e-mail addresses, 125 came back as incomplete or inaccurate. Most of these were from the marketing professors. E-mail responses were faster at first, with nine e-mail responses arriving for every mailed response, but this rate of return shifted in favor of mail within a week. They suggested that as e-mail becomes more standardized, as addressees become more familiar with e-mail, and it becomes "as easy to use as phone or fax," the response rates will improve. Consequently the speed and cheapness of e-mail could make it the preferred data collection medium.

Gary Vazzana and Duane Bachman compared fax and mail in a survey of CAD (computer-aided design) users in small and medium firms. Their response rates and data quality were similar, while their fax responses were faster (4.4 days for fax, versus 7.5 days for mail).

Alan Tse and his colleagues at the University of Hong Kong compared mail with e-mail. The 400 addressees were administrators and teachers at their university and were assigned randomly, 200 by mail and 200 by e-mail. Tse chose business ethics as the subject of the questionnaire because of the high interest in corrupt public and private practices in China, which was slated to take over Hong Kong in 1997. The response rate for the mail survey was 27% while only 6% for e-mail, and the difference was significant at $p = 0.000$. The mean response speeds were 9.79 days for mail and 8.09 days for e-mail. These were not significantly different at the 5% level. Tse's measure of quality—the mean number of questions unanswered—was not significantly different at the 0.05 level. He speculated that his low e-mail response was due not only to the newness of the technology and inconvenience, since respondents needed to be at a computer, but also due to their desire for confidentiality, since e-mail responses could be traced more easily than mail responses.

Martin Opperman reviewed the e-mail literature and found response rates varied between 19% and 73%. In his e-mail survey of 500 members of the Association of American Geographers, he achieved a 31.8% response on the first mailing and a 17% response on the second mailing for a total of 48.8%.

Joan Palmquist and Andrea Stueve, two market researchers in Minneapolis, compared online data collection with phone surveys. They confirmed the fact that, for consumer-oriented research, those who respond to online surveys tend to be younger, more affluent consumers. They found online respondents more willing to respond to their questions than the typical telephone respondent, and they speculated that this willingness may be an effect of novelty that may wear off as more researchers target them. They found that online data collection was cheaper and quicker than telephone surveys, but they felt that telephone surveys would remain in the researcher's arsenal. They concluded that the key to success in market research is to be able to choose and deploy the right method for the right job.

Duane Bachmann, John Elfrink, and Gary Vazzana compared conventional mail with e-mail. They concluded that e-mail was becoming more promising but it still had significant disadvantages and that e-mail surveys continue to be practical only for specific groups, particularly professionals who have access to the Internet and whose e-mail addresses are readily available. They also noted that because it is cheaper and faster than mail, e-mail lends itself to the pre-testing of survey instruments. Pretest subjects can easily offer suggestions and corrections, thereby enhancing the dialog during survey construction. They recommended that researchers follow the progress of these technologies by repeating their type of research periodically.

In summary, the use of the Internet for data collection deserves more study. Response rates for e-mail have been found to vary from 6% to 73%, while those for mail vary from 27% to 56%, with different studies producing contradictory results. Response speeds have not been so well reported, with the mean varying between 7.5 days and 10 days for mail, 8 days for e-mail, and 4.4 days for fax. Measures of response bias have not only been oversimplified in some cases, but also many studies report mostly anecdotal impressions. Cost, an important measure of efficiency, is seldom discussed in the literature. Clearly, more research is needed before we will understand how to best use the new methods for data collection.

A NEW COMPARATIVE STUDY

Our purpose is to build on previous research by comparing four methods of data collection for printed-type surveys: mail, fax, e-mail, and Web form. *Efficiency* was studied in terms of the time and cost needed to complete the data collection cycle: developing the survey instrument, preparing it for delivery, delivery and return of the survey, and

coding the responses. While we recorded and analyzed the time and cost of preparing, distributing and coding the survey, we did not analyze this data statistically because only one experiment was involved. We expected, however, that the newer methods would be less costly and less labor-intensive than mailed surveys. Since one aspect of efficiency, response time, was controlled by the media and the respondents, we subjected it to statistical analysis.

H1: Delivery and return time of the survey instrument will be the shorter for new methods. This hypothesis was tested by measuring response cycle time.

Methodology

A technologically sophisticated population was chosen in order to better explore the effectiveness issues. The survey was distributed to 800 MIS professors chosen randomly from North American professors listed in the *MISRC Directory of Management Information Systems Faculty,* a comprehensive listing of MIS faculty from around the world with more than 4,600 entries, of which 2,276 are located in North America. The sample of 800 addressees was randomly selected from the 1,737 entries that remained after removing 543 incomplete entries. Two hundred addressees were randomly assigned to one of four distribution method groups: mail, fax, e-mail, and Web form.

In order to encourage the addressees to respond, the survey covered a topic that they would be interested in: Internet use. A cover letter was personally addressed to each addressee introducing the survey. Each addressee received the same introduction with specific instructions on how to respond using any of the four methods.

To analyze efficiency, detailed records were kept of each procedural step. The time involved in developing each type of survey was recorded, as were the dates the messages were sent, the postmarked return dates, the date that responses were received back, the method each respondent used to respond, and the time required to code the responses.

Many of the manual steps for the mailed group were automated for the other groups. The common cover letter for the survey was modified for each group by changing the response-option addresses. For the mailed version, personalized cover letters were printed on university letterhead using a mail-merge program, stuffed into envelopes with a copy of the survey and a stamped return envelope. The faxed version included an individualized cover letter with a university letterhead and a printed survey and was automated using mail merge and WinFax Pro. The name, address, and fax numbers were automatically inserted into the letter and faxed by the computer.

The e-mail and Web form versions were both sent as e-mail messages using an e-mail merge program called Campaign. The e-mail version contained a personalized cover letter with the survey as part of the message. The Web form version was a personalized e-mail message that included the address of the Web form, and an invitation to complete the survey there.

The surveys were mailed and e-mailed on Sept 3, 1997 and the faxes were sent the following day. Of the original 800 surveys distributed, only 670 were delivered in the first distribution. Four mailed surveys (3%) were returned. 39 e-mail surveys and 49 e-mail Web-form invitations (67%) were returned as undeliverable and 38 fax numbers (29%) did not connect. (See Exhibit 8-1).

A second notification was e-mailed two weeks later to those who had not yet responded. The postmarks on all mailed and faxed responses were recorded. E-mail and Web form messages were assumed to have been received the day they were sent. This follow-up immediately affected response rates. An additional 78 surveys were undeliverable, thus reducing the usable sample from 800 to 592. One hundred and thirty-eight usable responses were received after the first distribution of the survey, and an additional 82 were generated by the follow-up for a total of 220 usable responses. From this e-mailed follow-up, 34 from the mail group and 44 from the fax group were returned as undeliverable. The 220 usable responses received from the two distributions gave a 32.84% response rate disallowing the bad addresses that were known about, or 27.50% of the original sample of 800 addressees.

Findings

H1: Delivery and return time of the survey instrument will be the shorter for new methods. This was tested by measuring response times and it was found that the new methods are much faster. On average, it took about 10 days to get a response, with mail taking 12 to 13 days, fax taking nine to 12 days, Web-forms taking about half the time at six to seven days, and e-mail taking about six days. E-mail generated responses immediately, with 17 responses the first day and 30 responses by the fifth day. (See Exhibit 8-2). The Web form was the second fastest with thirteen responses on the first day, and twenty responses by the sixth day. Fax was third fastest and mail was fourth. The first mail response was received on the fifth day. In addition, we knew within about ten minutes of sending the e-mail and faxes which addresses and fax numbers were incorrect. Such information is useful to quickly adjust a survey for poor response rates. The fact that information about bad postal addresses comes in so slowly is a problem for researchers seeking to adjust their surveys to account for low-response rates.

Efficiency: Our assumptions were designed to aid researchers in deciding which methods to invest their time and money in learning. We assumed that the cost of designing a survey was the same for each method. In other words, design costs are considered "sunk" and do not affect the choice of distribution method. We assumed that labor costs $20 an hour for survey preparation, distribution, and coding, and the cost of learning the software is sunk. That is, staff are available who can use the required software for faxing, e-mailing, creating Web forms, and word processing.

It took eight hours to carry out the 12 steps involved in preparing and sending the mailed survey

EXHIBIT 8-1	Responses from the Four Methods				
	Mail	**Fax**	**E-mail**	**Web form**	**All methods**
Bad addresses	4	38	39	49	130
Responses	38	38	39	23	138
2nd e-mailing (two weeks later):					
Bad e-mail addresses	34	44	0	0	78
Total responses	70	50	48	52	220
Raw response rate	35.0%	25.0%	24.0%	26.0%	27.5%
Adjusted rate	35.7%	30.9%	29.8%	34.4%	32.7%

EXHIBIT 8-2	Response Period (Days)				
	Mail	**Fax**	**E-mail**	**Web form**	**All methods**
Mean	12.9	8.8	6.1	7.4	9.6
Mode	12	12	0	1	13
Median	12	12	2	5.5	12

for a total cost of $371. It took two hours to do the four steps to prepare and send the fax survey for a total of $169. It took just over two hours to do the four steps in preparing and sending the e-mail survey for a total of $59, and it took just over two hours to do the four steps for the Web form survey, that also cost $59. Based on our assumptions, the disadvantages of mailed surveys are quite dramatic. As indicated in Exhibit 8-3, costs are allocated as either fixed or variable. Fixed costs, those not affected by the number of addresses, include preparing the survey instrument and cover letter, setting up the data base, and performing a mail merge, etc. Variable costs, those that change with the number of people surveyed, include printing, paper, collating, stuffing, and so on. If we were setting up a survey budget, the cost for a mailed survey (per hundred subjects) would be about $215, about $113 for a faxed survey, and about $77 for either an e-mail survey or Web form survey. In

other words, the mailed survey was twice as costly as fax, and three times as costly as e-mail or Web form. The differences in variable cost are even more striking, with each mailed piece costing 156 times that of an e-mail or Web form message. The biggest cost disadvantage for mail was labor, followed by postage, which accounted for about 35% of its cost. Labor, at the assumed rate of $20 an hour for collating, stuffing, carrying, etc., accounted for 42% of the cost. Paper, at $0.05 per sheet, accounted for 23% of its cost. These cost differences underscore the labor intensity of mail, where 77% of its cost comes from the preparation and delivery of physical, rather than electronic messages.

Fast and Cheap

Although the newer methods for collecting survey data have been catching on rapidly, research on their relative efficiency has been scanty and somewhat contradictory. This study attempted to fill in some of the blanks by comparing conventional printed mail surveys with fax, e-mail, and Web forms. The results indicate newer forms have significant, but not overwhelming advantages, especially for technologically sophisticated populations. While mail and fax percentages achieved a significantly higher response rate than e-mail and Web forms, they were slower and more expensive.

EXHIBIT 8-3 Summary of Costs					
Method	Fixed Cost	Unit Cost	Qty	Variable Cost	Total Cost
Mail	$59.00	$1.56	200	$312.00	$371.00
Fax	$57.00	$0.56	200	$112.00	$169.00
E-mail	$57.00	$0.01	200	$2.00	$59.00
Web form	$57.00	$0.01	200	$2.00	$59.00

For example, compared to Web forms, mail was about three times slower in generating responses, more expensive to prepare, and three times more costly to code and analyze. However, some slight response biases that appeared merit further study. Thus, within limits, survey researchers can feel comfortable favoring e-mail and Web form surveys over mail and fax.

Three limitations to consider in choosing among these data collection methods include the cost of making up for bad addresses, the use of incentives to boost responses rates, and the difficulty of reaching technologically unsophisticated populations. It appears to be much less expensive to increase the size of an e-mail/Web form survey to make up for bad e-mail addresses than to do a mail survey of a particular size. A researcher who needs a certain number of responses to generate an acceptable standard error for a given budget might be tempted to use mail because of the accuracy of its addresses compared to e-mail. Only 2% of the mail addresses in our survey were found to be bad while 24.5% of the e-mail/Web form addresses were bad, a 12 to 1 difference. However, it is much less expensive to increase the sample size of an e-mail or Web form survey than it is to do so with mail. In our case, the variable cost of e-mail was $0.01 while the variable cost of mail was $1.56. Thus, we could send e-mail to more than 150 e-mail addressees for the cost of adding one mail addressee to our sample. Of course, we can expect the accuracy of e-mail addresses will improve over time, thus reducing the need for such adjustments. In addition, the researcher will quickly know how many bad e-mail addresses are in his or her sample, while such information about postal addresses trickles in much slower. In addition, the count of bad e-mail addresses is often more accurate than that of bad postal addresses. In mail surveys of large bureaucracies such as universities (as in our survey), it is often a department secretary, not the post office, who controls whether a particular piece of mail will be forwarded, returned to the sender, or discarded.

A second consideration is the use of incentives to increase response rates. Many ways to enhance mail response rates do not translate directly to fax, e-mail or Web forms. Market researchers who are interested in responses from an entire population and not just the easy-to-get ones regularly enclose incentives to boost response rates. Certainly such incentives might have significantly boosted the mail response in our survey from the small 5% to 10% difference that favored mail. Of course, e-mail and Web form surveys can include incentives as well. Marketers increasingly include "electronic coupons" on their Web form sites, while others provide discounts on products and services or contests and giveaways.

Finally, to what extent can the results from a survey of a technologically sophisticated population be generalized to problems of reaching other populations such as homemakers, food service workers or sports fishermen? While this may still be a significant limitation, it seems to be fast disappearing, at least in North America where e-mail is becoming the "killer application" of the Internet with an estimated 70 million people in the United States being connected and an annual growth rate projected to be between 30% to 50%. New methods have a bright future and with continued research we can begin to better understand how to use the new data collection methods.

Rick Weible is assistant professor of MIS at Marshall University, Huntington, WV.

John Wallace is professor of management and director of Small Business Institute at Marshall University, Huntington, WV.

ADDITIONAL READING

Bachmann, Duane, John Elfrink, and Gary Vazzana. "Tracking the Progress of E-Mail vs. Snail Mail," *Marketing Research,* Summer 1996, Vol. 8, No. 2, (1996): 30–6.

Emerging Technologies Research Group. *The 1997 American Internet User Survey: Realities Beyond the Hype,* May 6, 1997, http://etrg.findsvp.com/internet/methodology.html.

Kramer, Matt. "Internet-Based Fax Solutions Will Soon Gain a Standard," *PC Week,* February 24, 1997.

Oppermann, Martin. "E-mail Surveys—Potentials and Pitfalls," *Marketing Research,* Summer 1995, Vol. 7, No. 3, (1995): 29–33.

Parker, Lorraine. "Collecting Data the E-Mail Way," *Training & Development,* July 1992: 52–4.

Palmquist, Joan, and Andrea Stueve. "Stay Plugged In to New Opportunities," *Market Research,* Vol. 8, No. 1, Spring 1996: 13–5.

Riggs, Brian. "ISPs Learning all About the Fax of Life," *Lantimes,* August 18, 1997. http://www.lantimes.com/97/97aug/708b054a.html

Schuldt, Barbara A, and Jeff W. Totten "Electronic Mail vs. Mail Survey Response Rates," *Marketing Research,* Vol. 6, No. 1, (1994): 36–9.

Sproull Lee S. "Using Electronic Mail for Data Collection in Organizational Research," *Academy of Management Journal,* Vol. 29, No. 1, (1986): 159–69.

Thorndike, Robert and Elizabeth Hagen. *Measurement and Evaluation in Psychology and Education,* 3rd Edition, New York: John Wiley and Sons (1969).

Tse, Alan C. B., et, al. "Comparing Two Methods of Sending Out Questionnaires: E-Mail Versus Mail," *Journal of the Market Research Society,* Vol. 37, No. 4, (1995): 441–46.

Vazzana, Gary S, and Duane Bachmann. "Fax Attracts: New Technological Advances Make Fax a Promising Alternative to Mail Surveys." *Marketing Research,* Vol. 6, No. 2, (1994): 19–25.

THE INTERNET AND INTERNATIONAL MARKETING

Outline

- **The Internet and International Marketing: Is There a Fit?**
  Saeed Samiee

The Internet poses tremendous opportunities and challenges for international marketing. By launching a web site, information regarding the firm's products and services may be available to interested buyers in virtually any nation of the world. This increased global reach can result in new leads and revenues. Stories abound on the web of relatively small, domestic firms receiving substantial orders from customers all over the world via the company's web site. These orders are evidence, some argue, that the web creates an even playing field for small and large firms to expand globally.

The web also allows for more efficient supplier search and supplier integration into the firm. Many web-based trading portals aggregate suppliers, product, and pricing formation; post offers and bids; and facilitate international transactions in a variety of ways. Finding high-quality, low-cost suppliers has never been easier for many firms. In this sense, the web operates as a global trade show 24 hours a day, 7 days a week.

The web is also a platform that allows for closer collaboration among disparate divisions of the multinational firm. Corporate intranets, or internal company portals, centralize information, news, expertise, and knowledge of all members of the global enterprise. It is entirely feasible, if not practical, for country divisions to provide more effective assistance in product design and marketing plans for local markets. The web is a communications platform without boundaries.

Yet boundaries have played an important role in the marketing strategies of many firms. Consumers' sensitivity to price varies across national borders. Firms often take advantage of this fact by charging different prices for the same product in different national markets. Government policies concerning taxes and tariffs and local supply conditions also affect price levels in national markets. Prior to the Internet, national borders often hid these price differences.

The Internet creates greater "price transparency" in global markets. Buyers may more easily discover high- and low-cost markets and perhaps take advantage of these differences. It is likely that the Internet will create a greater number of "grey marketing" activities in which identical products are purchased in low-priced nations and resold outside of formal distribution channels in high-priced nations. In some industries, the result may be the convergence of prices to more uniform levels.

In this chapter, Saeed Samiee introduces a model of Internet applications in international marketing.

Samiee notes that most international trade continues to be dominated by the rich nations of the world and that the Internet will not change this. Samiee argues that there are a number of structural issues that will impede the growth of the Internet in international business-to-consumer marketing. These include PC ownership, computer literacy, and Internet access. However, Samiee notes that the Internet is well-suited for international business-to-business marketing since corporations are generally more "wired" than households in this digital age.

Please visit the textbook's web site for additional resources.

The Internet and International Marketing: Is There a Fit?

Saeed Samiee

Abstract

This article critically examines the internet's limitations and roles in international marketing. Within the context of international marketing, applications of the internet can be conceptualized as either process- or product/service-based. Accordingly, the article examines two types of impediments to the internet's adoption and growth in international marketing: structural and functional. Structural issues deal with nations' information technology infrastructures, as well as their languages, cultures, and legal frameworks. Functional impediments, on the other hand, involve marketing program and process issues, including data management and customer discontent. It is apparent from this analysis that the Internet will play a much greater role in business-to-business marketing across national boundaries than it does in international consumer marketing; however, both structural and functional issues are unlikely to be resolved in the foreseeable future. As with other innovations that have impacted international marketing over time, the internet will gradually carve a niche for itself in the conduct of international transactions.

INTRODUCTION

The internet has been touted as one of the most significant, and perhaps the greatest, marketing tools for the global marketplace.[1] Discussion on the in-

"The Internet and International Marketing: Is There a Fit?," Saeed Samiee, *Journal of Interactive Marketing,* © 1998 John Wiley & Sons, Inc. Reprinted by permission of John Wiley & Sons, Inc.
[1]Although the term *internet* principally refers to the computer network infrastructure that enables the delivery of digital data, it is frequently used to represent the interactive graphical communications medium known as the World Wide Web, which was invented in 1989 by Tim Berners-Lee, a physicist at the European Centre for Nuclear Research (Cern). An agreement between Cern, the U.S. Department of Defense, and the European Commission led to the establishment in 1994 of W3C, World Wide Web Consortium, which is managed at MIT. W3C currently has 160 members, including hardware manufacturers,

ternet's use in marketing has accelerated and an increasing number of articles appearing in scholarly journals attempt to conceptualize the internet's role or explain the conduct of marketing in the advent of the internet (e.g., Bessen, 1993; Peterson, Balasubramanian, and Bronnenberg, 1997; Quelch and Klein, 1996). Some scholars have gone as far as suggesting that this new medium may lead to (or require) a new paradigm and that existing marketing knowledge is insufficient to analyze the internet's role in marketing (Deighton, 1997).

Although the discussions, application development, controversies, and problems associated with the use of the internet in marketing are ongoing, no specific effort has been made to address the issues pertaining to its use in the international arena. Given that the internet is essentially a global medium, the absence of specific coverage of the topic is in part understandable. However, its applicability and its appropriateness for use in international marketing are often presumed without a critical examination of the foundations upon which international marketing rests. This article examines the issues and the impediments to the use of the internet in international marketing and the realistic role that the internet might play in assisting firms to reach their international marketing objectives. Since consumer and business-to-business marketing differ in many ways, a distinction between the two is necessary; however, most of the issues highlighted in this study are valid for both markets.

In the discussions that follow, a series of considerations regarding the use of the internet in international marketing are highlighted. In general, these discussions provide evidence that special treatment for using this medium in international marketing is necessary. However, given the near identical technology platforms and international protocol standards around which the internet has evolved, the

software producers, telecommunications firms, internet service providers, government agencies, and academic institutions.

nature of some important considerations is the same everywhere. For example, two basic requirements for using the internet, PC ownership, and computer literacy, influence the appropriateness of this medium for commercial applications.[2]

Much of what has been written to date on the use of the internet in marketing assumes the conduct of business in the United States and other highly developed nations where a reasonably well-developed information technology and internet infrastructure is available. However, the discussion of the internet's role in international marketing in this article takes a broader view, to include all markets of potential interest to a firm.

There are several important reasons for taking a more universal view in considering the internet's role in international marketing. First, even with a liberal definition of *developed,* fewer than 30 nations (of a total 190 countries) currently qualify as developed. An initial focus on these markets may make good business sense, because they constitute the largest markets on a per capita basis and have better-developed information technology (IT) infrastructures. However, IT and the internet are currently available in many other nations and, from an international marketing perspective, the internet's appropriateness should be examined and integrated into the firm's overall international marketing plan. Second, multinational firms typically market their products and services in many countries. IBM and Coca-Cola, for example, operate in over 100 nations, including emerging and developing countries. Third, in contrast to other developed countries, the U.S. exports proportionately more of its products and services to developing markets. One third of all U.S. exports versus about one fourth of those from the European Union are destined for the developing world. In this sense, closer attention to these mar-

kets is appropriate. Finally, significant economic growth is expected to occur in Asia and, to some degree, in Latin America, where most nations do not meet the definition of *developed.*

THE INTERNET'S ROLE IN INTERNATIONAL MARKETING

The internet's first and foremost role is the same in domestic and international marketing: the delivery and the collection of timely information (including transactions) about products and services. Revenue generation from the internet, however, is currently limited to only about 18% of corporate web sites on the WWW (Economist, 1997). This relatively low figure is consistent with other statistics, indicating that the primary reason for developing a corporate web site is cost savings (35%), followed closely by customer service (32%). As innovative methods of using the internet are developed and as an internet purchasing/shopping behavior and culture evolve, more sites will be devoted to generating revenue.

A conceptual view of the role of the internet in international marketing is shown in Figure 9-1. The internet may be used for either business-to-business or consumer marketing. In general, structural issues are likely to have greater impact on consumer internet marketing than on business-to-business transactions. Firms' greater access to resources can alleviate such impediments as PC ownership and training. Therefore, a more rapid move to new technological platforms on the part of business firms should be expected. Contrasted with the domestic experiences of firms, the adoption and the use of such technologies as intranets, virtual private networks, and value-added networks (VANs) through electronic data interchange (EDI) were expensive, complicated, slow, and generally impractical for use in consumer marketing. Likewise, functional issues are likely to have a greater influence on consumer marketing because businesses are easier to identify, segment, reach, and accommodate.

Business-to-business marketing may involve two types of uses. The first type of internet use involves the development and implementation of

---

[2]The distinction between domestic and international uses of the internet is similar to the long standing dialog among some marketing scholars as to whether there is or ought to be a distinction between domestic and international marketing. Clearly, for some issues these distinctions are a matter of degree rather than kind. On the other hand, some considerations are unique to the use of the internet in the international arena. Therefore, some internet-related issues examined in this study have implications for both domestic as well as international marketing.

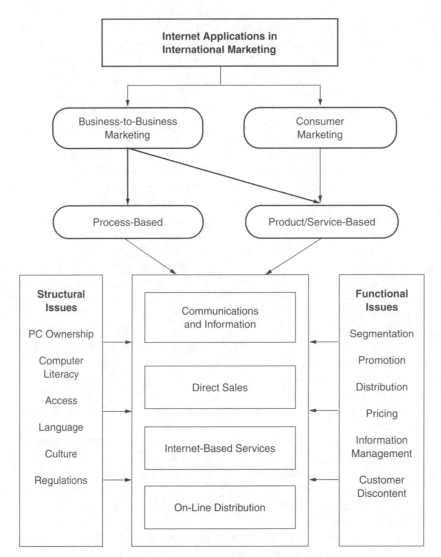

Figure 9-1   Internet-Related Issues in International Marketing

processes which incorporate the internet to more efficiently perform various international marketing functions which may or may not involve business clients and suppliers. Process use of the internet (a.k.a. *Extranets* which is a substitute for VANs) is more complex and must be customized to meet the firm's communications and operating needs.[3] Inasmuch as the manner in which firms operate varies widely, business processes for dealing with internal and/or external constituents need to be developed such that they address very specific firm-level circumstances. The Extranet purchasing processes being implemented by such firms as Carrefour and General Electric are prime examples of process-applications of the internet in international marketing.

The second potential use of the internet in business-to-business exchange involves direct and indirect sales. This category of the internet's application in international marketing constitutes the standard practice in marketing in which the World Wide Web (WWW) represents an outlet for information, promotion, and order processing.[3]

Consumer marketing, on the other hand, involves products and services typically distributed and sold through other means. For example, information about a product may assist a consumer in finalizing a purchase decision, while the product itself is acquired at a local store or purchased on-line and delivered using the firm's normal distribu-

tion network. In this sense, the internet serves as just another method of reaching the consumer.

Since the manner in which the internet works is essentially the same regardless of the application, the marketing areas that are affected remain the same for both business-to-business and consumer marketing. Therefore, the internet may be used for (1) communications (including contract negotiations), information access (including product specification and technical data), and advertising; (2) direct sales of existing products and services; (3) sales of internet-based products and/or services in which the internet is integrated in the offerings itself; and (4) on-line distribution of digital information/data (e.g., software, music, process-related information, and market[ing] research). These four categories represent current uses of the internet.

Clearly, with the passage of time additional possibilities may emerge. Firms are actively seeking innovative new products and services that incorporate the Internet for business-to-business and consumer markets. The internet-based photography service provided by PictureVision Inc., and Kodak is an example of the type of service that fully integrates the internet (the product/service and the internet are practically inseparable). Using this service, customers may store their pictures on an internet account for a monthly fee and, for an additional fee per roll of film, photo finishers scan pictures and post them to the customer's password-coded account. PictureVision in conjunction with Konica initially developed the service which now records over three million pictures per month. Typically, photos are made available on line for 30 days, during which customers can (1) share photos with family and friends by sending the film identification or simply e-mailing the images to them for free, (2) download any or all images to their computers, (3) use their images in web pages, print low-resolution photos, or alter them using image editing software (editors can be downloaded free of charge), (4) order reprints and enlargements of photos, (5) have enlargements mailed to anyone or send them to a preferred store for pick-up (all billing information is collected through a secure

[3]The implementation of business processes for greater competitive advantage and efficiency is certainly not new to businesses. For over two decades, manufacturers, wholesalers, and retailers have invested heavily in EDI systems to accommodate their business processes. EDI systems generally operate over VANs and are the predecessor to Extranets, which are internet-dependent. These systems were developed independently of the internet which, among other things, afforded firms considerable privacy and security vis-à-vis the internet. Furthermore, the investment to these systems was so large that only larger firms were able to participate in implementing such processes. In some firms, such as Procter & Gamble and Wal-Mart, EDI-based processes are so well-developed and the initial investments were so large that it more or less deterred them from shifting to an internet-based system. The advantage of developing firm-based Extranets over the internet is that many smaller firms can now emulate and benefit from business processes that were virtually the monopoly of larger firms. However, such participation is far from "leveling" the competitive arena because larger firms have the critical mass to develop far superior VANs and/or Extranets.

transaction with a Netscape server), and (6) order gift items such as mugs, teeshirts, and mouse pads, personalized with preferred photos ("Kodak Is Launching," 1997; PictureVision, 1998). Although the PictureVision concept is universal in character, its extension to international markets requires (1) the development of an appropriate distribution channel and (2) is limited to areas where computer literacy rate and PC ownership are relatively high.

On-line distribution of digitized information also lends itself to the internet medium. InfoSearch, a prepaid library service, is a prime example. This service permits the user to access and search numerous periodicals in a variety of ways. Security and copyright infringement issues notwithstanding, other possibilities that will gradually take shape include the distribution of music and video, various types of raw and processed data, etc. Given the lack of control of any one firm or nation over the event and the activities on the web, security and piracy issues are unlikely to be resolved in the intermediate term. Such issues have generally played a critical role in the major studios' decision to stay away from digital distribution of their recordings (Brull, 1998).

Structural Issues

PC Ownership

The most basic prerequisite to using the internet in international marketing is the availability of and access to personal computers. International access to consumers through the internet is severely constrained by computer ownership. The United States and the United Kingdom have experienced the greatest penetration of home computers. As of third quarter 1997, for example, the best estimate of computer ownership in U.S. homes was 40% (Carlton and Ramstad, 1997). The low estimates place computer ownership in the U.S. at about 30%, a number expected to grow to just over 50% by 2001 as less-expensive models are introduced by various manufacturers. In the U.K., home computer ownership stands at about 32% (Computer

Retailing, 1996). Ownership figures are lower in other developed countries and much lower in the less-developed nations. Although computer ownership will no doubt grow everywhere, its penetration among households in various countries will probably lag behind the experience observed in the adoption of telephone and fax.

As new technologies are introduced, the cost of computer ownership will continue to decline. However, as computer capabilities expand with each new generation, there tends to be corresponding software development that makes it expensive and difficult for households owning older computer models and software to use the latest benefits that the internet has to offer. Even in the richer developing countries, the cost of acquiring a personal computer often exceeds the monthly salary of a professional employee. Therefore, the Internet as a useful international marketing tool will not grow in importance until ownership significantly increases in target markets

Computer Literacy

As with the adoption and use of any product or service, users (businesses and their customers) must be familiar not only with the use of computers and pertinent software products, but also with the benefits and the potential uses of the internet and World Wide Web. In other words, computer literacy will play an important role in the internet's adoption speed and pattern. Although after 20 years of exposure, domestic businesses and consumers are relatively familiar with the PC and increasingly with the internet, conditions vary considerably in much of the world. The appropriateness and the use of both the PC and the internet in a new market is determined by the antecedents of any adoption situation (i.e., relative advantage, compatibility, complexity, trialibility, and communicability). France Telecom, for example, envisioned the Minitel in the 1970s and flooded households and businesses with countless computer terminals. As a result, on average, the French are very familiar with the notion of accessing data and information, paying bills, making reservations, etc., through computer systems. It is then not surprising that the adoption of the internet in France has been quite rapid.

Although internet-facilitating intermediaries will eventually evolve to manage web site development and maintenance for firms that cannot afford in-house expertise, businesses and consumers must be positioned to sign on to reap the benefits. In other words, inadequate computer and internet literacy, which remain prevalent in many parts of the world, will impede the rate of adoption.

Access

In much of the writing on the applications of the internet in marketing, access to the network by the masses is assumed (e.g., Peterson et al., 1997). However, without convenient and affordable access to the internet, neither businesses nor consumers are likely to become avid users. Access in the developed nations is widely available at reasonable rates and subscribers from these regions constitute about 90% of the 23.4 million households with access to the internet. The U.S. has the lion's share, with 66% of all connections worldwide, a figure which will gradually decrease as the popularity of and access to the internet increases elsewhere. The number of households worldwide with access to the internet is expected to increase to 66 million by the year 2000, with the biggest growth coming from Europe (Economist, 1997).

In many developing and emerging nations, on the other hand, access prices are out of reach for most of the population. This pricing method is partly due to the skimming pricing scheme of government-owned telecommunications agencies. The telecommunications industry in the developing world receives billions of dollars of windfall income by allowing international network access to their local networks. Although an eventual broad-based access to the internet and the WWW will inherently increase demand for telecommunications services, there is the concern that in the short term it may actually decrease international telephone revenues in developing natio. transmission of the more bandwidth- and efficient digitized data replaces the lengthier anal. calls. Limited access to the internet in developing nations is also politically motivated because it makes it possible to access non–government-sanctioned news and views.

China, for example, has only four authorized organizations that offer internet services and international connections are only available through one of these four, i.e., MPT (Triolo, Lovelock, Harwit, and Su, 1996). In addition, connection costs are prohibitively high in many countries. Leased lines for internet providers in China, where personal income is less than $100 per month, cost four times as much as they do in the U.S. Likewise, in Russia, where average professional salaries are about $100–200 per month, a representative rate for internet connection is about $5 per month plus $5 per hour.

Language

At present, single-language sites are by far the most common. These sites are frequently in English but also in other languages depending on the location and the intent. The minority group of web sites consists of those that permit the viewer to choose from among several languages. The majority of multilingual sites offer English as an option and generally assume a reading knowledge of English by the audience. However, the number of languages covered by any site is quite limited and the practical utility of sites that offer translation is quite limited.[4] A casual examination of some of the most prominent and international consumer cata-

[4]For one thing, translation is possible to and from just a handful of languages (see, for example, http://babelfish.altavista.digital.com/cgi-bin/translate? or http://www.japan/english/translate). For another, correct translation of the contextual meanings of statements being translated requires sophisticated artificial intelligence which currently is unavailable (Terazono, 1996). When such artificial intelligence is developed, site owners with an international clientele can license and link it to their sites (i.e., it will not be free). Finally, there remain additional technical problems associated with the type of site which significantly impede timely translation.

.og operations (e.g., Quelle, Neckermann, Lands' End) reveals that their sites are strictly in the home-market language.

Although in the late 20th Century English has evolved into the de facto international language, most of the potential customers neither speak it nor have a reading knowledge of it. Concurrently, the development and maintenance costs associated with multilingual sites make them inappropriate for most businesses. Only the biggest and the richest firms possess the capability to develop sites in a multitude of languages and maintain them on a regular basis.

Even in situations where a client possesses knowledge of the firm's web language, the site's effectiveness is eroded when the information cannot be shared with all responsible parties within the organization. Industrial purchase decision processes frequently involve input from multiple individuals who may not be fluent in the target language. When the information has to be translated for consideration, the usefulness of the site significantly depreciates. Indeed, it is reasonable to expect that industrial users will make the effort to translate relevant information only when the purchase decision is critical to their operations and competitive position.

Culture

Cultural imperatives are likely to have a profound impact on the adoption and the use of the internet in international marketing on a global basis. Local cultures will continue to dictate, as they always have, the necessary level of personal interaction in a purchase situation (Francis-Laribee, 1994). Two considerations influence the role of the internet. First, members of some cultures are unlikely to deal with firms and entities they know nothing about and whose representatives they have never met. Personal knowledge of the vendor and/or its representative is a precursor to the transaction. Second, in situations where business transactions tend to be impersonal, methodical, and/or policy-

driven (e.g., the purchase of standardized industrial products), the local culture is likely to have less influence on the purchase process and, therefore, the internet is likely to thrive and play a key role. On the other hand, the internet's role in purchasing situations of differentiated or customized products and services which rely on personal selling is likely to be less significant.

Personal involvement in purchasing, even for business-to-business transactions, is prevalent among much of the world's population. In particular, in culturally higher-context groups, as well as in Confucian-based cultures, the role and the importance of personal interaction with merchants and business clients is not likely to go away in the advent of the internet. Furthermore, cultures that score high on uncertainty avoidance are less likely to be early adopters of internet marketing schemes, even if other cultural imperatives are met. The development of a personal relationship in higher-context cultures is said to precede the development of a commercial one. Although the implication of this behavioral mode for industrial marketing is clear, high-context consumers are also more likely to favor dealing with individuals about whom they have personal knowledge or who are members of their network. Japanese and Middle-Eastern customers perhaps offer extreme examples of this behavioral pattern, but others elsewhere would also demonstrate such behavior to varying degrees. Even though some observers view internet-based transactions as essentially culture-free and personal due to the perception that it brings the parties closer (e.g., Peterson, Balasubramanian, and Bronnenberg, 1997), these views are rather narrow in that they lack the imperative personal interaction between trading parties in international marketing. In any event, the promise of internet-based marketing is the automation of the process, and to the extent that firms are able to automate the marketing functions, internet-based contacts, in and of themselves, cannot and should not be viewed as personal.

Everything else being equal, is it likely that individuals in higher-context and uncertainty-avoidance cultures will use the internet to deal with businesses that they know and have previously dealt with through the internet? The short-term answer to this question is "not very likely." However, as the personal computer and the internet become more common place, at least some aspects of existing commercial relationships and possibly transactions in these cultures might take place over the internet. Nonetheless, it is unlikely that behavioral patterns grounded in cultural imperatives will be "converted" to automated, technology-based ones in a manner conducive to placing orders for unfamiliar brands through unknown vendors in the foreseeable future.

Regulations

Government regulations will control many of the structural impediments already discussed. In much of the developing world, access to the internet is more a function of government regulations than of the interest of the population at large. In some countries, such as China and Singapore, access to certain sites is controlled for moral, social, and/or political reasons. In China, the Public Security Bureau requires all internet users (Chinese and non-Chinese) to be registered with public security authorities. Only employees of foreign companies with internet access through private networks are exempted from this regulation. Furthermore, access by Chinese users of the internet to such sites as CNN, The Washington Post, The New York Times, Chinese-language publications from Taiwan and Hong Kong, and other politically sensitive sites developed by dissidents living abroad has been blocked (Triolo et al., 1996).

Elsewhere, transnational data flows are hindered by a plethora of regulations aimed at protecting domestic technology and related human resource markets (Goff, 1992; Gupta, 1992). These regulations vary from country to country and may involve tariff structures, data protection and security regulations, and laws that simply prohibit cross-national data transmission (Francis-Laribee, 1994).

French laws, for example, prohibit the transfer employee files across national borders and presumably such rules apply to other sensitive data regarding customer purchases and related information. Other laws, even at the state and provincial levels, control what can and cannot be said, done, or transferred in a wide array of nations including Brazil, Germany, India, and Sweden.

Whereas certain aspects of data and internet regulations are likely to be liberalized over time, the emergence of an open cyberspace marketplace is quite uncertain. The World Trade Organization, operating under the 1993 agreement, will increasingly integrate services into its general trading framework, so it is reasonable to expect that internet regulations pertaining to service offerings will be liberalized. However, there is every indication that the internet will be defined and regulated in each nation according to the cultural, social, political, and quite possibly economic milieu. As digitized television broadcasts become commonplace and the internet becomes a truly multimedia outlet, the differences between the television and the internet are increasingly disappearing. It is therefore reasonable to expect that national and regional regulations pertaining to television will be extended to cover social and commercial applications over the internet. In addition to the national regulations on television broadcasting in Europe, the European Union's directives on distance marketing currently limit local channels to one hour of infomercials and home shopping advertisements per day (Heenan, 1995). Even in Canada, infomercials and home shopping can air only from midnight to 6:00 A.M. Given that firms wish to automate and simplify the conduct of business over the internet, competition over the internet will force companies to use various means of appealing to and attracting individuals to buy. It then appears that the internet's use as an international marketing tool will face a tighter regulatory environment. Thus far in the evolution of the internet, the social and legal forces related to it have been slow to react. Commercial regulations encompass all aspects

...keting program and it is unlikely ...net will escape all regulations every... ...some countries, for example, there are ...language requirements for contests and pro-...tions. In France, the rules of a consumer contest open to residents must be in French (Feldman and Rose, 1996). Likewise, Virgin Atlantic Airways was fined by the U.S. for failing to disclose the fullest of a promotional fare to London on its web site. Commercial regulation of the internet in much of the world, at the very least for the protection of the consumer, is only a matter of time.

Functional Issues

In general, the use of the internet in marketing might take two forms, passive and active. Using the passive mode, a firm recognizes the strategic importance of having a presence on the web, and offers product, service, contact, and other useful information. The majority of corporate web sites at the present time are of this type. The active use of the internet, on the other hand, is much more complex and demands the identification of its appropriate role in the firm's global strategic marketing plan. Since observers generally agree that the internet is little more than an interactive communications medium, this task is not an easy one and demands both innovative and strategic thinking on the part of the firm. Much the same way other media have been deployed scientifically and creatively to achieve firms' marketing objectives, the active mode marketing applications of the internet also need to be defined and integrated into individual marketing plans. In this sense, it is appropriate to examine the internet from the perspective of the key elements of marketing plans.

The Internet as an Information Medium

The internet is a sophisticated information medium that can be of great assistance to both firms and their customers. It offers many efficiencies and cost-cutting opportunities for both parties. Consider, for example, the buyer of new word processing soft-

ware or a printer who can access the firm through its web site and download the relevant and latest printer-driver file in a matter of minutes. Even tracing a shipment via Federal Express and other carriers has been made easier, cheaper, and faster through the magic of the internet. However, the ease with which in formation, can be accessed should not be confused with access to *new information.* Firms had had to satisfy stakeholders' information needs through other means for decades. The internet has merely made the dissemination process automated.

Marketers have developed sophisticated sites that inform their clients as to their policies and increasingly their product and service offerings. Retail firms also offer selling prices and delivery options. However, the prices of business purchases are generally negotiated and are not public domain. The competition will be quick to access a firm's price lists and develop equally (or more) attractive ones for its site(s). Since the outcome of contract negotiations and terms can vary substantially from firm to firm and from client to client, it would be reasonable to expect the internet to serve largely as an information medium for consumers and firms alike. Given the existing structural impediments in the international marketplace, the importance of the role of the internet as an information medium is heightened.

Mass Marketing Versus Market Segmentation

The notion of mass marketing through the internet is constrained, at least for the time being, by the public's limited access to this medium. The early adopters of the internet are likely to be better educated, have higher incomes, and hold white-collar jobs. As computer ownership and internet access increase, the medium's reach will approach that of the radio and the television. These media are commonly referred to as mass media because the broadcaster has no control over who tunes in at any point. Segmentation of audiences for electronic media (i.e., the radio and television) is possible at the most macro level and by time and program type as its key segmentation criteria. For example, Forrester Research expects the number of online computer game players to increase to over 18 million from the current base of about 7 million (Takahashi, 1998). Such game-sites tend to attract younger audiences similar to children's television programs which, barring other limitations of the internet in international marketing, may prove valuable to global brands aimed at youngsters. It is noteworthy, however, that much of the sponsorship of these computer game activities comes from such unlikely candidates as AMD, Cyrix, Logitech International, GTE, and 3Com.

As a mass medium, the internet is hindered by additional limitations. There is no programming, per se to attract the individual "surfer." In fact, most of the advertising on the internet is currently on internet information sites such as PointCast and Yahoo. Thus, the firm must use other means of communications (alternative media) to attract potential clients to its site. Nonetheless, it is a medium that is well-suited for relatively homogeneous products that enjoy a broad appeal. For example, computers and peripherals are generally viewed as homogeneous products that are sold based on performance and price. Dell Corporation has taken advantage of this unique situation and began accepting orders on-line through their English web site in July 1996. The firm is currently recording about $6 million of internet assisted orders daily (approximately 10 percent of sales) (Schonfeld, 1998). Indeed, Dell's web sites are so well thought out that they include customized secured pages for preferred customers and for federal and state agencies. Recently, the firm added a Chinese language web site, with other languages to be added (Flannery, 1997). Through its web sites, customers provide their required specifications, which are linked to assembly lines in Austin, Texas, Malaysia, or Ireland (depending on the location of the customers). Some 50,000 internet calls are received daily and internet-based orders are eventually expected to account for 50% of Dell's sales (Flannery, 1997). Apparently, when correctly applied, the internet is quickly adopted by the target audience and grows rapidly. No doubt the internet's influence

will continue to grow as new uses are conceived and corresponding applications are developed.

Segmentation, however, remains at the heart of contemporary marketing thought and practice, and its displacement would require a change in the macroeconomic theory of monopolistic competition and the microeconomic theory of price discrimination. Most differentiated products and services are aimed at particular segments of the population that are defined based on relevant criteria at the time of product/service conception. Identifying relevant populations of internet users on a global scale, as defined in the firm's marketing plan, is not and may never be a reality. Of course, as with direct mail marketing methods, internet marketers will gain in sophistication and certain software tools might be developed to enable them to closely target the relevant subsets. However, accessing individuals with "well-meaning" commercial messages is likely to be governed by the same laws as for direct mail marketers. Thus, some potential clients, are never reached. Others are hidden under layers of corporate bureaucracy and their mail is screened for relevance and appropriateness by others.

Promotion
Advertising has been the most natural and perhaps best developed use of the internet to date. Aside from corporate sites and targeted e-mail messages, an increasing number of sites (e.g., DoubleClick, PointCast, Yahoo, Prodigy) sell advertising on the internet. Thus far, U.S. and Japan have emerged as the top two internet advertising markets.

Viewed as a multimedium, the internet should be treated with the same principles as other advertising media. The nature of the internet promotes a globally standardized approach to advertising which has been criticized in the international marketing literature as suboptimal for most products and services and is generally inconsistent with the global advertising strategies of many firms (e.g., Aylmer, 1970; Boddewyn, Soehl, and Picard, 1986; Colvin, Heeler, Thorpe, 1980; Peebles, Ryans, and Vernon, 1978). Furthermore, the possibility of offending some populations is always present. Nuns in advertisements are seen as fair game in the U.K., but God is not. However, both are acceptable in Spain. Germany and France possess liberal views toward sex in advertising, but this sentiment is not shared in Greece.

Pricing

As noted earlier, pricing on the internet at the manufacturer level, even for consumer products, makes it easier for the competition to accumulate relevant price data and modify its current marketing program or develop a new strategy to compete for a bigger share of the market. Furthermore, sorting through a plethora of pricing and consumer protection rules for different nations can absorb valuable management time. For example, Virgin Atlantic Airways advertised an APEX fare between Newark and London for $499 on its web site. The firm was fined $14,000 by the U.S. Department of Transportation for not clearly disclosing an applicable tax of $38.91, even though the firm had advised its customers to check with their travel agents for availability, applicable taxes, and various restrictions (Feldman and Rose, 1996). The fact that the price announcement might have been in compliance with the rules in the U.K. did not shelter the firm from legal action in another country. Likewise, the location of the firm's internet server is immaterial to how these cases will be viewed.

Strategic and managerial aspects of pricing on the internet are also significant. Small firms with sites on the internet can develop an international customer base virtually overnight.[5] Technology per-

mits vendors to price in accordance to host market conditions (based on regions, countries, or even by user). However, having competitors' prices on the internet, in addition to legal restrictions over such practices, is likely to soften price discrimination between different markets and buyers. In addition, customers have or can acquire the capability to use the power of technology to find (the vendor's) better values (or prices) through a variety of schemes. Therefore, web-based pricing, if appropriate, should be in accordance with the firm's international marketing strategy and remain consistent across customers being permitted to access a site.

Distribution

The use of the internet as a means of distributing products and services must remain consistent with the firm's overall marketing strategy.

The internet is an ideal distribution channel for any product that can be digitized and sold over the computer network. For example, whereas an average record retailer has a limited collection of music labels, recording studios have the potential of offering everything on the market. Bypassing the firm's traditional international channel may cause conflict and noncompliance by the channel which can have far reaching strategic, legal, and financial implications for the firm.

Firms invest significant sums over a long period to develop their distribution channels which they can risk by attempting to compete with them by distributing their products over the internet. Capitol Records' failed attempt to distribute a new single over the internet reflects the distribution problems that firms face when they compete directly with their distribution channel (Brull, 1998). Thus, the six major recording studios use the web primarily for promotional purposes, including sampling of their music in non-recordable streaming formats. Given the limited global access to the internet at present, the majority of firms will have to remain dependent on their conventional channels for the foreseeable future. If one were to apply the

---

[5]A distinction between becoming "international" and developing an international client base by virtue of a presence on the internet must be made. Some authors suggest that by virtue of a presence on the internet, small firms instantly become multinational (e.g., Quelch and Klein, 1996, p. 62). Since small firms generally lack international experience, international business know-how, and corresponding infrastructure, it is unlikely that they can manage "international" operations overnight. Truly international firms, by contrast, have the ability to proactively design and customize product and service needs, manage international financial functions, efficiently work through a myriad of host market rules and regulations, and so on.

product adoption pattern in various nations, dependence on traditional channels in the international marketplace is not only a must, but is also unlikely to change as a result of the internet. As noted earlier, however, firms apparently have not embraced the internet as a key means of selling or distributing products and services. This posture is consistent with the realities of the international marketplace.

To better understand the role of the internet in distribution, it is useful to recall that the intermediaries must constantly economically justify their presence in the channel, otherwise other channel members will eventually bypass the structure or develop their own more efficient channels and processes. Channel intermediaries have developed capabilities in a long list of functions. They negotiate, buy (or make arrangements for others to buy) in bulk, sort and assort, finance and sell, take title, store, and deliver, and have developed specific technologies and competencies in a variety of services that are not generally the domain of the manufacturer or the retailer. In order for the firm to justify bypassing a channel or portions of it through the internet, it must show that it would be strategically and financially better off to internalize the functions currently performed by the channel. A manufacturer wishing to sell directly to consumers must be willing to deal with the idiosyncrasies of consumer markets, including access to a large inventory (and its financing) for quick delivery, after sales service, offer unconditional returns and credit, and so on. Although some have argued that the Internet will basically eliminate wholesalers and distributors (e.g., Benjamin and Wigland, 1995), most observers question the validity of such predictions because they tend to view exchange in its most basic and simple form (e.g., Peterson et al. 1997). The fact that channel intermediaries have weathered technological innovations that greatly impacted our economic system (e.g., radio, telephone, television, computers, and facsimile machines) demonstrates that through time they have managed to develop their own propri-

etary processes and technologies which have insured their growth. The birth of pharmaceutical distributors in the late 1950s and the subsequent success of such firms as Bergen-Brunswig and McKesson are evidence of distributors' agility and dynamic nature. So far, it appears that the internet has given birth to distributors rather than replacing existing ones Peterson et al., 1997; Sheth and Sisodia, 1997).

Information Management

As new purchasing management software is developed, tested, and implemented, a broader distribution of requests for proposals among approved vendors has become a reality. As the number of responses to requests for proposals from potential suppliers increases, the firm must develop the capability to manage the geometric growth of new data and carefully screen the appropriate vendors for its intended purchases. Vendor proposals will be different in accordance with their marketing strategies, and client firms cannot always impose their version of conditions and negotiations. Thus, each response needs to be carefully considered for fit and negotiated for contract terms. It is likely that at least for some classes of purchases, the cost associated with managing increased vendor participation will more than erode the cost savings associated with the application of the internet.

The interactive nature of the internet also permits businesses to collect a great deal of data about their customers' preferences, information searches, and purchase cycles and behaviors, as well as ordinary market research data. To benefit from this near-windfall access to customer data, internet marketers must develop an infrastructure capable of using these data. Larger firms with market research departments can probably adapt their existing research capabilities to cover data gathered through the internet. Smaller firms without any infrastructure, however, will need to acquire such expertise or such services. Although the management and use of customer data in future marketing plans and strategies is initially an impediment, with sufficient attention and investment the firm can turn it into an opportunity.

Customer Discontent

Several aspects of internet-based marketing have the potential to create buyer discontent. A sound web-site policy and a well-managed and monitored program can avoid such problems. For one thing, some sites (e.g., Sony) reveal suggested retail prices in certain markets. (As noted earlier, the site owner can actually limit access to price information by the addressee's country of origin. However, web surfers tend to be technologically sophisticated and it will be a matter of time before they directly or indirectly access such information.) Even though these prices tend to be at the high end of the price range (i.e., manufacturer suggested retail prices), global access to this information from markets with relatively higher prices can create discontent for consumers and distributors alike. There are clear economic and strategic reasons for price discrimination across markets; however, the availability of price information can reduce firm and brand loyalty among at least some customers.

Most manufacturers' web sites provide distributor and/or retailer access information. It is critical that this information treat all distributors and retailers reasonably equally and be updated on a regular basis so that no one is excluded. For one thing, such exclusion may produce or further heighten channel conflict. For another, such exclusion or significant emphasis on a few, presumably valuable, distributors may be perceived as anti-competitive and subject to antitrust laws. Some web sites link the address directly with a particular web distributor/retailer that typically sells the firm's products as well as many competitive brands. Regardless of whether or not the web retailer is manufacturer-owned unless such connections are distributed across all interested distributors on a proportionally equal basis, they can create managerial, strategic, and legal problems for the firm. In particular, legal problems may be quite serious in regional markets, such as the European Union, which maintain strong community-wide competition and consumer protection regulations.

Finally, manufacturers offering detailed product data through their web sites run the risk of consumer confusion and potential discontent. Firms like Seiko offer dozens of models in hundreds of styles. Distribution strategies in these firms typically limit the range of watches sold through certain classes of retailers. Furthermore, most retailers are unlikely to handle the entire range or even be willing to keep many in inventory. During a conventional purchase decision process, the volume of product information gathered by the typical consumer is quite limited. Consumers using web sites to gather product information are likely to be overwhelmed (and potentially confused) by the sheer amount of data on such sites. In addition, an increasing number of customers who have selected a particular model from the web will be disappointed to learn that their retailer does not carry them and they must place a special order. Mass retailers' strategies generally do not allow special orders, further heightening the possibility of customer discontent.

A POSITION FOR INTERNATIONAL INTERNET-BASED MARKETING

Perhaps the appropriate way to view the internet is as a medium that can deliver and access digitized information. In this sense, the internet is an invaluable marketing tool for providers of services that do not require a provider presence (or at least not always), such as banking, insurance, investments, marketing research and consulting services, software development and distribution, music and video products, among others. Internationally, however, some key service categories such as banking, insurance, and investment services require regulatory approval from host market institutions and/or governments and, therefore, do not lend themselves to internet marketing.

To think of the internet as uprooting the traditional ways of international (or even domestic) marketing is thus naive. Experts agree that the internet's most pronounced impact will be on business-to-business trade rather than consumer marketing (Nairn, 1997). In either case, however, the single most important factor that influences international marketing on the internet is culture. The influence of the internet in international marketing increases with the faster adoption of a generally impersonal internet buying culture (as opposed to patronizing shopping centers or favorite stores). The prime consumer shoppers for the internet are likely to be catalog customers followed by teleshoppers. It is worthwhile to consider that just as catalog shopping did not replace store patronage, the internet will eventually find a similar niche among some consumers in some, but not all, markets. It is also important to emphasize the fact that consumer spending (from which business-to-business purchases are derived) will not increase as a result of the internet.

Estimates of the internet-based market size vary significantly, but invariably they agree that the internet is more relevant for business-to-business marketing than for consumer marketing. Accordingly, estimates for consumer markets by the year 2000 range from $4 billion to $10 billion whereas industrial markets range between $70 billion and $160 billion ("In Search," 1997). It is also noteworthy that this growth does not represent new business. Rather, much of the anticipated internet business will come from other avenues currently in use, e.g., sales calls, telephone, fax, intranets, VANs, and EDI-based Extranets.[6] Thus, for the most part, the internet serves as an accommodating tool and a catalyst to service existing customers and accounts. New business is inherently related to such economic measures as wages, employment, and consumer spending. The only exception to this rule is the innovative ways in which marketers can

[6]Inasmuch as the volume of trade at the wholesale level is typically much larger than consumer trade, the much larger volume of business-to-business marketing on the internet should be expected and is consistent with the patterns of trade in general.

integrate the internet itself into the product or service such as the photographic services being offered by PictureVision and Kodak.

Some observers suggest that the internet and the WWW make it possible for all firms, regardless of size, to compete on equal footing. This position overlooks several important points. First, smaller firms will always be at a disadvantage vis-à-vis larger firms because the latter, by virtue of their greater resources and network of operations, will continue to be better known and potential customers are more likely to know or quickly find their internet addresses. Smaller firms' sites, in contrast, will be accessed far less frequently, simply because their presence, and thus their WWW addresses, are less widely known. In fact, one can argue that smaller firms have virtually no added advantage internationally if their other means of communication do not promote their names and WWW addresses. Indeed, several new "internet" brands such as *Word* and *Charged* recently went out of business and others such as *Amazon* and *Wired Digital* are yet to make a profit (*The Economist,* 1998).

Second, search engines such as Lycos and Yahoo! charge $750–$1,000 per month to direct their internet traffic to firms by "leasing" key words that reflect their businesses, e.g., flower in the case of FTD. In this regard too, smaller firms are clearly disadvantaged vis-à-vis the larger ones that have access to greater resources. Third, although the cost of setting up a simple site is low and affordable by most firms, the cost of setting up comprehensive, high-profile sites is prohibitive for smaller firms. Forrester Research has reported set tip costs in excess of $300,000 for promotional sites, $1.3 million for publication sites, and $3.4 million for catalog shopping (Gould, 1997). Furthermore, the average maintenance cost for such high-profile sites is $3.1 million per year (*The Economist,* 1998).

Fourth, larger firms, by virtue of their greater scope of operations, maintain numerous linked domain names in several countries and in many languages. Some firms have over 100 domain names and possess sites located in dozens of countries. Procter and Gamble and Kraft, for example, have applied for 100 and 134 domain names, respectively (Quelch and Klein, 1996). Since key competitors in virtually all industries maintain one or more internet sites, from a competitive strategy viewpoint it is critical that firms maintain such sites. Finally, since smaller firms can pay to be listed in various internet directories they can be identified and accessed through various search engines.[7] Structural impediments discussed earlier notwithstanding, visibility through the internet places the smaller firm in a better position than was previously the case. Thus, although it can be said that the firm is better off, the playing field is by no means level.

Nonetheless, the importance of a business being found somewhere around the globe through the internet cannot be overstated. There is no question that the internet can, at the very least, widen the playing field even if it cannot level it. Indeed, the internet is serving to further increase the speed of international marketing by providing product and service information on demand. Businesses must still deal with transportation, potential manufacturing and delivery delays, duties and taxes, and customs clearance hurdles, but the savings may be sufficiently large to cover these cost. Manufacturer channel strategies notwithstanding, standardized industrial products that meet international standards and popular brands of known products are the most likely candidates for global internet trade. It is noteworthy, however, that firms invest substantial sums in developing and maintaining their distribution network and will be unlikely to undermine this investment by competing with this channel or promoting an internet channel that creates a conflict with an existing channel. Such moves lead

to the loss of channel coordination and control as well as placing channel member loyalty at risk. For this reason, a large number of manufacturer web sites (e.g., Swiss watches and Sony consumer electronics) offer only product information.

Such linkages afford vendors increased efficiency and faster negotiations of contracts. In the case of Dell, for example, verified web-based orders can be fed directly into the manufacturing process. (Since firms like Dell and Gateway 2000 produce computers to order [i.e., no inventory of manufactured products is kept], orders must necessarily be verified before they are sent to the production line.) This manufacturing automation advantage is available to other firms that, like Dell, do not make the products until an order is received. Selling products and services directly through the WWW, however, is in its infancy and may never mature in the way expected by some internet enthusiasts. Recent surveys indicate that only 3% of business-to-business (in contrast to 9% for consumer marketing) sites are for direct sales.

The internet, however, fully lends itself to business process development and reengineering. For example, the advantage of the system used by Dell is not so much in taking the order through a digital medium, but in enabling Dell to use such orders in its manufacturing processes. Thus, it would be naive to think that firms can close their representative offices and retrench from their current worldwide sales organizations and deal strictly through the internet. Successful European and American consumer catalog operations such as Lands' End and Quelle will retain their buying and local sales organizations throughout the world.

Therefore, firms are expected to continue to depend on their conventional buying and sales offices internationally even as they find innovative ways to utilize the internet for greater efficiency and competitiveness in their business processes. There are many examples of successful uses of the internet in business-to-business trade. General Electric, through its Trading Process Network web site, purchases over $1 billion of supplies annually from about 1,400 vendors. The firm estimates that

[7]It is also noteworthy that search engines are not particularly efficient. The best search engine, HotBot, covers about 34% of approximately 320 million web pages available. Alta Vista, Excite, and Infoseek cover 28%, 14% and 10%, respectively, and Lycos covers only 3% of available pages (Weber, 1998). Although the efficiency of these "software robots" will no doubt improve over time, as the WWW is rapidly becoming bigger and more complex it is doubtful that search engines can keep up with such large volumes of data.

it has lowered its cost of goods between 5% and 20% simply because its has made it easier for its buyers, to contact more suppliers ("In Search," 1997).[8] Carrefour, the French multinational retailer, is testing new software in order to develop a link with its suppliers. The pilot program in Italy links 30 suppliers to their Milan buying office (Carrefour has 6 stores in Italy and 308 stores in 17 countries). Proprietary software developed by QCS is used to negotiate contracts over the internet (Nairn, 1997). Firewalls and data encryption developed by IBM are used to secure negotiating parties' privacy. Carrefour's challenge will be to convince smaller suppliers to invest in the appropriate software and hardware and to convince them to get away from the traditional patterns of doing business (often by fax). Carrefour buys a great deal from smaller firms because they offer competitive deals. As such they cannot simply ignore their views. Their exclusion merely raises Carrefour's cost of merchandise.

It is noteworthy that firms have been using private networks, intranets, and conventional computer linkages to coordinate their contract negotiations, purchasing, and supply delivery for some time. This capability has enabled firms ranging from the Limited, Inc., to Wal-Mart to purchase, manage inventories, and deliver a customized mix of merchandise to designated locations. The internet simply widens the application of this capability on a broader scale.

The trade literature is filled with anecdotal accounts of savings by firms resulting from their use of the internet in purchasing. However, the stated savings are likely to reflect price differences rather than full costing differences that incorporate added time invested in the buying function, delivery delays, tariffs, product quality supply continuity, etc. Although such problems should be minimal through approved vendors, a global invitation to everyone to compete for contracts may result in unanticipated expenses.

It is also noteworthy that in the midst of all the hype and excitement about the internet, few have taken the time to examine the losses being accumulated by key internet firms. Such famous firms as Prodigy (the oldest on-line service provider), CompuServe, America Online, Yahoo, and even Microsoft's internet-based services are frequently surfing the red tides. Only firms that can identify and implement appropriate internet roles and related marketing strategies, combined with a sustainable competitive advantage that can serve a specific client base, will become profitable. However, as the cost of technology is constantly falling, having a presence on the internet or offering services through the internet, in and by itself, is insufficient to secure a firm's future.

Nonetheless, given that from a competitive standpoint a presence on the internet is a must in today's business, firms should be prepared to underwrite its associated costs. That is, a mere internet presence offers competitive survival rather than a competitive advantage in the global marketplace! As noted in this study, these costs can be very high and involve initial investment in equipment and software, maintenance, scheduled upgrading of web pages, training, and the collection and application of customer data. In short, international marketing may become more convenient and faster through the internet, but not necessarily cheaper when the total cost of all phases of business is considered.

---

[8] When product characteristics are reasonably similar across manufacturers and national boundaries, the choice process is made considerably easier than in situations when an assessment of product and vendor attributes precedes purchase decisions. The tremendous success of Dell Computers in internet sales demonstrates this situation well. Although branded, Dell products essentially represent a standardized class of products. The purchase of popular brands of known differentiated products tends to emulate the purchase decision processes of specialty-type products (for example, Sony television sets), i.e., the product is essentially pre-sold. In such cases, the internet is also likely to serve as an effective medium. However, to qualify as a specialty-type product, considerable conventional marketing effort over long periods is required to establish the brand.

Saeed Samiee is Collins Professor of Marketing and International Business in the College of Business Administration, The University of Tulsa, Tulsa, OK.

REFERENCES

Aylmer, R. J. "Who Makes Marketing Decisions in Multinational Firms?" *Journal of Marketing,* 34 (October 1970): 25–30.

Benjamin, R., and Wigland, R. "Electronic Markets and Virtual Value Chains on the Information Superhighway." *Sloan Management Review,* 36, 72.

Bessen, J. "Riding the Marketing Information Wave." *Harvard Business Review* (September–October 1993): pp. 150–160.

Boddewyn, J. J., Soehl, R., and Picard, J. "Standardization in International Marketing: Is Levitt in Fact Right?" *Business Horizons,* 29 (November 1986): 69–75.

Brands Bite Back. *The Economist,* (March 21, 1998): 78–82.

Brull, Steven B. "Net Nightmare for the Music Biz." *Business Week,* (March 2, 1998): 89–90.

Carlton, J., and Ramstad, E. "New Cheap PCs Are Shaking Up the Industry." *Wall Street Journal,* (September 10, 1997): p. B-1.

Colvin, M., Heeler, R., and Thorpe, J. "Developing International Advertising Strategy." *Journal of Marketing,* 44 (1980): 73–79.

Computer Retailing: U.K. Market for In-Home Computers. *Retail Intelligence,* (May 1996): p. 1.

Deighton, J. "Commentary on Exploring the Implications of the Internet for Consumer Marketing." *Journal of the Academy of Marketing Science,* 25 (1997): 347–351.

Feldman, J., and Rose, L. "Advertising and the Law in Cyberspace." *Folio, 25,* 14 (October 1, 1996): 47–49.

Flannery, R. "Dell Using Asian Language Internet "Stores" to Increase Sales." Dow Jones News Service, October 7, 1997.

Francis-Laribee, J. "American Companies Exploring Networks in Europe: Alternatives, Challenges, and Recent Advantages." *Journal of Systems Management,* 45 (April 1994): 6–12.

Goff, L. "Patchwork of Laws Slows EC Data Flow." *Computerworld,* 26 (1992): 15, 80.

Gould, Carole. "Sticker Shock on the Internet." (Report from Forrester Research Finds Huge Set-up and Service Costs for Financial Firms' Internet Sites That Provide Transactions Services). *The New York Times.* June 15, 1997.

Gupta, U. "Global Networks: Promises and Challenges." *Information Systems Management,* 9, 4 (1992): 28–32.

Heenan, D. A. "The Rise of a Worldwide Cybermarket." *Journal of Business Strategy, 16* (May–June 1995): 20–22.

In Search of the Perfect Market, Survey of Electronic Commerce. *The Economist,* May 10, 1997.

Kodak Is Launching Service on the Internet. *Wall Street Journal* (August 26, 1997): p. B-2.

Nairn, G. "Trading Places: From Purchasing to Invoicing, Businesses Are Linking Up." *Financial Times* (August 27, 1997): p. 15.

Peebles, D. M. Jr., Ryans, J. K., and Vernon, I. R. "Coordinating International Advertising." *Journal of Marketing, 42* (1978): 23–34.

Peterson, R. A., Balasubramanian, S., and Bronnenberg, B. J. "Exploring the Implications of the Internet for Consumer Marketing." *Journal of the Academy of Marketing Science, 25* (1997): 329–346.

PictureVision. *http://www.PictureVision.com.* 1998.

Quelch, J. A., and Klein, L. R. "The Internet and International Marketing." *Sloan Management Review* (Spring 1996): pp. 60–75.

Schonfeld, Erick. "The Squeeze is on for the PC Makers." *Fortune* (April 13, 1998): 182–186.

Sheth, J., and Sisodia, R. "Consumer Behavior in the Future." In Peterson, R. A. (Ed.) *Electronic Marketing and Consumer.* Thousand Oaks, CA: Sage Publications (1997): pp. 17–38.

Takahashi, Dean. "Get Serious! Computer Gamers Turn Pro." *The Wall Street Journal,* (March 6, 1998): p. B-1.

Terazono, Emiko. "Fujitso Puts First Japanese Translation Package Online." *Financial Times,* April 29, 1996.

Triolo, P. S., Lovelock, E. H., and Su, J. "Up, Up, and Away—With Strings Attached." *China Business Review,* 23 (November–December 1996): 18–29.

Weber, Thomas E. "Web's Vastness Foils Even Best Search Engines." *The Wall Street Journal,* (April 3, 1998): p. B-1.

10

THE INTERNET AND PUBLIC POLICY

Outline

The internet is a battleground for public policy issues. On the one side are those who believe that the Internet must be tightly regulated to protect society. On the other side are those who argue that web site content represents freedom of expression and is legally protected under the U.S. Constitution.

The first attempt to legislate the Internet in the United States was the Communications Decency Act of 1996. This act sought to make it illegal to publish objectionable material on the World Wide Web. In essence, the act sought to extend the same standards to the web that apply in broadcast media such as television. However, this act was struck down as unconstitutional.

A second area of contention is how to best protect children online. The Child Online Protection Act (2000), currently making its way through Congress, seeks to impose fines on web publishers who do not effectively block minors from access to objectionable material. In related legislation, some lawmakers are trying to pass legislation that would force schools to implement web-filtering technologies in order to be eligible for federal funding. These efforts are opposed by a variety of civil liberty organizations as unconstitutional.

Consumer privacy issues are yet a third area of public policy legislation. The Privacy Commission Act of 2000 is seeking to address a variety of consumer privacy concerns. Already, the Online Privacy Protection Act stipulates that firms must, at a minimum, publish disclosure statements on their web sites indicating how any personal data collected are used. This legislation occurs at a time when the leading Internet advertiser, DoubleClick, is accused of combining online and offline behavioral data without consumers' consent.

A fourth area of public policy is unsolicited commercial e-mail, or spam. The Unsolicited Commercial E-mail Act of 1999 mandates the Federal Communications Commission to collect the e-mail address of anyone who wishes to be removed from unsolicited commercial e-mail lists. Spammers are given 30 days to comply. Earlier legislation also stipulated that spammers must clearly identify themselves with correct contact information, provide correct routing (return e-mail) information, and provide a way to "opt-out" from the e-mail list.

Still other public policy issues relate to Internet gambling, competition in the telecommunications market for Internet access, and export of encryption technology—to name just a few.

In the first reading of this chapter, Ross Petty provides a framework to understand the context in which legislation may take place given the characteristics of the Internet. Petty proposes that legislation will focus on practices that cause unavoidable consumer harm without returning any benefits.

In the second reading, George Milne and Maria-Eugenia Boza present research that shows the critical importance of increasing trust among consumers that personal data will not be misused. Although this research does not apply specifically to the Internet, the implications of this research for Internet marketing are obvious given recent legislation and media attention to privacy issues.

Please visit the textbook's web site for additional information.

Ross D. Petty

ABSTRACT

In the 20th century, the marketing law concept of deception evolved from the earlier legal concept of fraud. Stronger remedies also evolved to address the possibility of deception on a mass scale. In the 21st century, with the rise of interactive marketing, deception will continue as a primary concern, but additional emphasis will be placed on fairness to consumers. Practices that cause substantial unavoidable consumer injury without countervailing benefits will receive greater scrutiny in four areas: consumer control over advertising and the sales transaction, the targeting of vulnerable audiences and discrimination related to such targeting, the provision of information to consumers, and lastly, psychological pressure to buy, particularly as applied to targeted, vulnerable audiences.

"It would be a mistake to underestimate the possibility of additional unfairness enforcement actions by the commission."

FTC Commissioner Starek (1997)

INTRODUCTION

Next to the Federal Trade Commission building in Washington, D.C. is the National Archives Building, which is engraved with the motto: The Past Is Prologue. This maxim appears particularly appropriate as the FTC and other sources of marketing law examine how to appropriately regulate new forms of marketing such as interactive marketing

communications. This paper examines how the law has evolved to regulate changing marketing technologies and practices and, based on the past evolution as well as recent developments, speculates on how the law is likely to react in the future to the rise of interactive marketing.

Marketing law initially developed in the interactive village marketplace of the Middle Ages. Because consumers could examine the wares and at least attempt to judge the honesty of the merchant, the law of deceit or fraud favored the merchant by requiring the consumer to prove the merchant intended to mislead the consumer through a statement known to the merchant to be false and that the consumer reasonably and actually relied upon the statement. This was the time of caveat emptor.

With the development of mass marketing and distance selling, the ability of merchants to deceive large numbers of consumers increased dramatically. The law evolved to provide greater consumer protection. The intent of the merchant and knowledge of falsity was no longer required to prove an advertisement deceptive, only a likelihood that consumers would be misled. Indeed, government regulation and industry regulation both evolved to no longer require the proof of falsity. The advertiser could be liable if its claims were unsubstantiated by a "reasonable basis." (Federal Trade Commission, 1984a) Remedies also were enhanced to include a quick preliminary injunction, corrective advertising, and consumer redress. Indeed, in its twelfth and largest-ever action against internet fraud, the FTC recently obtained both an injunction, asset freeze, and consumer refunds totaling over $5 million against an internet pyramid promoter (Fortuna Alliance, 1997).

Now marketing is evolving away from one-way communication to the masses toward focused interactive communication, often targeted to specific audiences, but still on a broad scale. In other words, with targeted, interactive marketing, marketers can enjoy the persuasive benefits of interpersonal selling combined with the reach of mass marketing. The question arises: will the law evolve to further protect consumers from being induced to purchase products and services that they otherwise would not have purchased? This paper attempts to answer this important question.

One concern that this paper will not address directly is whether the law will develop greater protection of individual privacy, given the fact that marketers are now technologically able to collect detailed purchase data about individual consumers. That issue has been treated extensively elsewhere (Bloom et al., 1994; Foxman and Kilcoyne, 1993; Goodwin, 1991; Jones, 1991; Thomas and Mauer, 1997). Indeed, the FTC released a staff report based on June 1996 hearings on privacy (Federal Trade Commission, 1996b) and has announced that it will conduct a study on data collection from computer files and hold a second workshop on privacy in June 1997 (Federal Trade Commission, 1997).

A second concern not directly addressed here is the question of whether marketing communications, can somehow manipulate consumers to make purchases, either subconsciously or against their will. This concern occurs for each new communication media and is at least as old as Vance Packard's classic book, The Hidden Persuaders (1957). Yet when asked whether advertising was "mind-bending," noted adman George Lois quipped 20 years ago: "No one is that good." The same is true for emerging interactive advertising technologies (Rotfeld, 1997).

Rather than address this amorphous issue, which is still in the realm of science fiction, this paper examines five related areas where the law is likely to evolve as marketing becomes more targeted and interactive: consumer control of the transaction, inappropriate targeting and discrimination, deception, disclosures, and pressure to buy. The law of deception is well established, but the four other areas involve unfairness, to some degree. Before examining each area individually, it is worthwhile to present background information on unfairness.

CONSUMER UNFAIRNESS

In the United States, the tortured history of consumer unfairness under the FTC Act recently has been chronicled by Preston (1995) and Simonson (1995). The current statutory definition, which dates back to a 1980 Policy Statement (Federal Trade Commission, 1980), is both simple and vague. It defines an act or practice as unfair if it "causes or is likely to cause substantial consumer injury which is not reasonably avoidable by consumers themselves and not outweighed by countervailing benefits to consumers or competition" (15 U.S.C. sec. 45).

This language evolved from earlier Commission attempts to define unfairness, the most important of which was first enunciated in the Statement of Basis Purpose of the proposed Cigarette Labeling Rule and later mentioned by the Supreme Court with neither approval nor disapproval in a footnote in FTC v. Sperry & Hutchinson Co. (1972) (Averitt, 1981; Rice, 1983–84). This early attempt defined an act or practice as unfair if it (1) offends public policy; (2) is immoral, unethical, oppressive or unscrupulous; avid (3) causes substantial consumer injury. This standard is still followed by many states under their so called "little FTC Acts."

In Europe, in contrast to this general approach, unfair marketing practices are specified. For example, the August 1979 revision to the proposed Directive concerning unfair and misleading advertising defined unfair advertising as that which:

a. casts discredit on another person by reference to his nationality, origin, private life or good name; or
b. injures or is likely to injure the commercial reputation of another person by false' statements or defamatory comments concerning his firm, goods, or services; or
c. abuses or manifestly arouses sentiments of fear; or
d. promotes discrimination on grounds of sex, race or religion; or

e. abuses the trust, credulity or lack of experience of a consumer, or influences or is likely to influence a consumer or the public in general in any other improper manner; this part of the Directive has not yet been, and may never be, adopted.

Similarly, the Directive Concerning Television Broadcasting (89/552, 3 Oct. 1989, *Official Journal* L 298/23) addresses fairness concerns that television advertising not be discriminatory or encourage behavior prejudicial to health and safety or the environment. Such specific European rules provide useful examples of legally unfair conduct only some of which have been applied in the U.S. Yet many of the European prohibitions arguably satisfy the vague definition of unfairness in the FTC Act. Indeed some of these specific rules can be readily applied to targeted interactive advertising.

DECEPTION

The FTC defines deceptive advertising as that which contains "a representation, practice or omission which is material to consumer choice and likely to mislead consumers acting reasonably (Federal Trade Commission, 1984b). This area of advertising law is well established in the case law and likely to be readily applied to interactive marketing. Indeed, most of the FTC actions to date against internet advertisers are simple fraud cases brought under deception. The use of highly targeted interactive messages in fragmented media make it more difficult to monitor and detect deceptive advertising. Not only must the FTC and other advertising watchdogs find troubling ads, but they may have to interact with the advertisement to find that it is misleading. Not surprisingly, early cases involve blatantly false claims that require no interaction to uncover.

In addition, the FTC and other federal, state and local law enforcement agencies recently "surfed" the web and sent warnings to over 500 websites that might have been operating illegal pyramid scams (Federal Trade Commission, 1996a). It is important to note that these agencies did not interact sufficiently to determine whether each cite had a pyramid, they merely looked for surface evidence and then sent a warning. The websites will be revisited later to determine if they comply with the law. Such informal warnings or education may become more commonplace as the use of targeted interactive marketing increases.

One common deception that occurs whenever new forms of advertising evolve is trying to hide the fact that the new form is advertising rather than some form of objective, and presumably more credible, information. Early infomercial cases challenged the disguising of these 30 minute advertisements to appear like independent investigative television shows (JS&A Group, Inc. 1988; Money, Money, Money, Inc. et al., 1990). A recent direct mail piece challenged the inclusion of what appeared to be a personal note stating: "This really works, J." (Georgetown Publishing House, Ltd., 1996). A related deception which may be challenged in the future is making a "virtual" shadow company appear substantial. Since advertising over the web is extremely low cost, a small, underfinanced firm can appear as substantial as a member of the Fortune 500.

Perhaps the most interesting legal questions concerning interactive marketing have yet to be explored. Does the targeting of highly interested consumers result in an audience that is more easily misled? This question is similar to that associated with the vulnerable audience that the FTC has occasionally applied but is broader in suggesting the possibility that any audience can be vulnerable if targeted effectively both in contacts and the interaction. This issue is examined in the section below on psychological pressure to buy.

DISCLOSURES

Disclosures are often mandated in advertising to prevent a half truth from misleading consumers. For example, in Campbell Soup Co. (1992), the

FTC charged that advertising claiming certain soups were good for the heart because they were low in fat and cholesterol was deceptive because the ads did not disclose that the soups were high in sodium, which can cause other heart problems. However, if Campbell did not claim soups were good for the heart, it did not have to make the disclosure. The disclosure was required only when the otherwise misleading claim was presented.

Unfairness also serves as a basis for requiring that information be disclosed. Failure to disclose the information in question would cause substantial consumer injury that is not readily avoidable and is not outweighed by other benefits. The Commission's Care Labeling (16 C.F.R. sec. 423), Octane Rating (16 C.F.R. sec. 306), and Home Insulation (16 C.F.R. sec. 460). Rules are a few examples where the FTC has mandated important information be disclosed in labeling based on unfairness. In International Harvester Inc. (1984), the Commission also mandated the disclosure of information when the non-disclosure would cause injury. International Harvester's tractor advertising did not mention safety and the tractors in question were found to be reasonably safe. Nevertheless, the Commission found that failing to disclose information on a very rare, but very dangerous, safety problem was unfair because consumers could not avoid the problem without additional information.

The FTC recently obtained a temporary restraining order, which froze the assets of an interactive marketing firm that requested internet customers download a "viewer" program that re-routed the customer's modem to expensive international phone lines. This rerouting continued until the customer's computer was turned off even after the customer was done with the company's website. This rerouting was not discovered until the phone bill was received (FTC v. Audiotex Connection, Inc., 1997). Since nothing was said about connection charges, this is arguably an unfair omission.

The normal remedy for either a deceptive or unfair omission is a "clear and conspicuous" disclosure of information. For deceptive omissions, the disclosure is only required or "triggered" when

the claim is made as in the Campbell Soup case above. Unfair omissions, on the other hand, may require disclosure of the information in labeling or all advertising. Corrective advertising is a disclosure that is ordered, typically for a limited time or specified amount of advertising, to correct "lingering beliefs" from past false advertising. Two questions arise concerning such disclosures when made in targeted interactive electronic media. Is a "click here for important safety information" sufficient? Probably not for safety information, but perhaps so for warranty information. This would be a good area for the FTC, in conjunction with industry and consumer groups, to develop guidelines.

The second important question is whether it is appropriate for more information to be disclosed. Two recent FTC consent agreements have included corrective advertising despite dissents that have argued there was no evidence of lingering beliefs that needed to be corrected (Eggland's Best, Inc., 1994; California SunCare, Inc., 1996). This may suggest a trend that the Commission is more interested in providing information to consumers than the costs of that provision to the advertisers, a traditional Commission concern (Beales, 1981).

Interactive marketing, at least on the internet, is relatively low cost, so that information, including perhaps substantiation materials could be provided for those interested in such information. Furthermore, links to other websites could easily be included to allow consumers to link to those providing objective information. Thus, when the cost is low, interactive marketing could be held to a substantially higher standard of information disclosure, perhaps akin to that for product packaging and labeling, than mass media advertising.

On the other hand, other forms of interactive advertising, such as television home shopping shows, may argue that it is costly for them to disclose information in place of their regular programming. Disclaimers at the bottom of the screen may be difficult for consumers to perceive either because of the small print size or the excitement of the program. Perhaps the operators receiving orders could provide additional information prior to purchase. However, this would be difficult to consistently monitor and might be inconsistent with operators who are paid by commission or are given sales quotas.

CONTROL OF THE TRANSACTION

Electronic interactive marketing suffers from the same legal problems as other forms of distance marketing. Consumers order and pay for products prior to being able to examine them. To address the possibility of unscrupulous marketers keeping the money and not shipping the product, the FTC's Mail Order Rule (16 C.F.R. 435) was updated in 1994 to include sales made by telephone, computer, or fax in addition to the sales made by mail. This rule requires that goods be shipped when promised or in a reasonable period of time or that refunds be offered. Some European countries have, and the European Union has adopted a directive mandating member state rules that would require a seven-day refund period for all "distance" sales, so that consumers could examine the product and then decide whether to keep it or not (Gabbott, 1994; 97/7/EC;O.J. No. 144 June 4, 1997, pp. 19–22). If enough marketers fail to offer and honor money back guarantees in the U.S., the FTC could consider amending its Door to Door Sales Cooling Off Rule (16 C.F.R. 429) to follow the European model and provide a three day (or longer) cooling off period for all distance sales as well.

A second problem that has surfaced for interactive marketing by computer, is the consumer's lack of control over "spamming" or junk e-mail. Some marketers seem not to understand that many consumers feel their telephone or computer belongs to them and is not fair game to unwanted sales pitches. In contrast, the U.S. Postal Service has convinced consumers that their mail boxes actually are controlled by the government so that nonmailed notices or newspapers could not be placed in mail boxes. Perhaps this explains why consumers seem more willing to accept junk mail.

Early battles over advertiser access are being fought between those who wish to advertise through e-mail and those who provide e-mail service (Richards, 1997). To date, the e-mail providers appear to be winning. Two federal district courts have held that there is no First Amendment right of advertisers to have access to the facilities of private e-mail services (Cyber Promotions, Inc. v. America Online, Inc., 1996a; CompuServe Inc. v. Cyber Promotions, Inc., 1997). The latter court issued a preliminary injunction against Cyber Promotions' issuance of any unsolicited advertisements to any CompuServe subscriber. The America Online court also later denied a temporary restraining order against blocking mass unsolicited e-mail based on the theory that e-mail providers were essential facility monopolists under the antitrust laws that had to allow access services (Cyber Promotions Inc. v. America Online, Inc., 1996b). This theory will be litigated if the case goes to trial. While these cases have yet to go to trial and could be appealed after trial, these preliminary decisions are well-reasoned and persuasive in upholding the service provider's right and through it the consumer's right not to receive unsolicited advertisements through the internet.

If the demand for restrictions continues, the FTC or Congress may take action. The Telemarketing Sales Rule (16 C.F.R. 310) bans commercial calls to cellular phones because the consumer gets charged for incoming calls. On the other hand, calls to residential phones are allowed, despite the fact that consumers pay to have such service. To date, e-mail appears more analogous to residential than cellular phone service—there is no charge for incoming messages. However, if e-mail providers charge by mail received (and sent), then consumers would have a stronger argument for restricting unwanted "spam."

INAPPROPRIATE TARGETING AND DISCRIMINATION

These early "spam" decisions begin to establish one of the consumer advantages of electronic interactive marketing technology—the control over information. Consumers seek out interactive information about products and services they are considering for purchase. They both receive targeted solicitations likely to be of interest and request information they want. They are not bothered as much by information they find immaterial. For marketers this also is an advantage since it gets an interested audience, not the mostly disinterested, passive audience of mass media which may freely ignore the marketing message. However, this consumer benefit also may cause two problems that the law might address.

First, despite the death of the FTC's proposed Children's Advertising Rule in the late 1970s, targeting children with inappropriate advertising as an unfair practice has been receiving attention lately. The Food and Drug Administration's proposed rule restricting the sale and distribution of cigarettes and smokeless tobacco products to protect children (21 C.F.R. 897) prohibits a number of marketing tactics thought to target children. The Federal Trade Commission issued a complaint against R. J. Reynolds Tobacco for its use of the Joe Camel cartoon figure as a means of allegedly appealing to minors, too young to buy cigarettes legally (Starek 1997; Petty, 1993).

A California court in Mangini v. R. J. Reynolds Tobacco Co. (1993), found that the targeting of minors with cigarette advertising would be unfair. The court relied on an old FTC case, FTC v. Keppel & Bro. (1934). This case concerned the use of a lottery to market candy to children. The Supreme Court affirmed the Commission's holding that this practice encouraged gambling among children, which induced children to buy a lower quality product. It held that such a practice violated established public policy against gambling, was unethical, and therefore was unfair under the FTC Act. The California court relied on this decision as well as the three part test for unfairness under the FTC Act adopted by the U.S. Supreme Court in FTC v. Sperry & Hutchinson Co. (1972). The California court held that targeting minors with cigarette advertisements: (1) offends public

policy; (2) is immoral, unethical, oppressive or unscrupulous; and (3) causes substantial consumer injury.

The FTC also has taken action against the unfair targeting of children. The Commission's new "900-number" Industry Rule bans 900 number telephone service directed at children under the age of 12 (16 C.F.R. 308). The rule adopts a two-test approach for making this determination. First, it examines the media in which the advertising is placed. If half of the media's audience is under the age of 12, then advertising for a 900-number service can not appear in that programming or publication. The second test is a typical Commission-expertise test: the Commission will examine a variety of factors such as the placement of the advertisement, subject matter, visual content, language, the age of any models and any characters used in the ad.

One final FTC action against involving the unfair advertising to children is Hudson Pharmaceutical Corp (1977) consent agreement. This case involved the use of a comic book character, Spiderman, to sell vitamins. The complaint first alleged that children were not capable of deciding whether they should use a vitamin supplement, so that targeting of children in advertising for such a product was challenged as an unfair practice. The complaint also alleged that the use of the cartoon hero would be particularly appealing to children and might cause them to believe the product had attributes it did not have (e.g., the ability to grant superpowers) and it might cause children to take excessive amounts of the vitamin, thereby injuring their health.

The European Union also is interested in protecting children from being targeted with inappropriate ads. Article 16 of the European Television Directive addresses fairness concerns with television advertising directed towards children. It requires that such advertising not cause moral or physical detriment to minors. Specifically, it states that television advertising not:

a. directly exhort minors to buy a product or a service by exploiting their inexperience or credulity;

b. directly encourage minors to persuade their parents or others to purchase the goods or services being advertised;

c. exploit the special trust minors place in parents, teachers or other persons;

d. unreasonably show minors in dangerous situations

All of these actions suggest that targeting minors with inappropriate interactive advertising is likely to engender legal problems. One commentator found the Real Beer page which allowed the downloading of several drinking games that appeared to encourage drinking to excess and appeal to minors. Other Web pages for alcoholic beverages also included items that would appeal to minors (Pridgen, 1997).

In the context of traditional marketing, it has proven difficult to distinguish between messages and promotions that appeal to adults but have an acceptable level of spillover to minors from appeals which unacceptably target minors. Currently two different tests have been suggested. In adopting the 900 Number Industry Rule, the FTC prohibits advertising in a vehicle where half of the audience or more is under the age of twelve. In contrast, the FDA's cigarette proposal bans event sponsorship promotional items such as clothing in cigarette brand names/logos. It also limits advertisements to text-only, black and white format, if in a publication where more than 15% or 2 million of the readers are below the age of 18. Perhaps the more stringent 15% test for cigarettes is justified by the health consequences of smoking. Advertising has been found to be deceptive when as little as 15% of the audience perceives a misleading message, when the message involves health or safety.

A related question of interest is whether adults can be unfairly targeted. There has been some concern with targeting the elderly, for instance scams that they may find particularly enticing. Targeting heavy drinkers or alcohol abusers is another area of potential challenge. Lastly, U.S. laws prohibit discriminatory advertising based on race and other prohibited bases for certain products: credit (12 C.F.R. 202.5), employment (42 U.S.C. sec. 2000e-3(b)) and housing (42 U.S.C. sec. 3604c). These laws, like those in other countries which are not product specific (Petty, 1994, p. 346), have been interpreted to ban explicitly discriminatory messages, e.g., "men wanted." The same result could be achieved by targeting through media placements an ad with neutral wording in a discriminatory manner.

Such targeting is only beginning to be addressed under the Community Reinvestment Act (12 U.S.C. sec. 2901 et seq.). The Act goes beyond prohibiting the practice of "redlining"—not offering credit to those, typically minorities, who live in certain neighborhoods or postal zones, to evaluating how well banks serve the credit needs of minority communities. In essence, this statute requires community banks to market and provide credit to minority communities, rather than target their efforts elsewhere to the exclusion of these disadvantaged communities. While the statute itself does not address other products or services, it suggests Congress' willingness to address targeted marketing if the disadvantaged are excluded from marketing messages for desirable products. Furthermore, the enactment of the statute suggests an unavoidable consumer injury, not outweighed by other benefits that would allow the FTC to analogize to other products and services and declare targeting that omits minorities to be unfair.

The Fair Housing Act condemns targeting using an implicitly discriminatory message. 1980 Guidelines under the Act require that human models reasonably represent minorities and both sexes and that stereotypes not be used to suggest inferior social status, e.g., African Americans portrayed only as servants (24 C.F.R. 109.30). This area too could be expanding beyond housing, if the FTC found minorities are being injured by such implicit discrimination.

Interactive marketing communications may be targeted both by audience and message. Since targeting is an important factor in the success of interactive marketing, marketers must be sensitive to these social issues and monitor legal developments to see if these narrow prohibitions are broadened to cover marketing generally. Advertisers who merely maintain a home page but do not actively target messages to come view the home page will be less likely to be accused of unfair targeting than those who actively target interactive messages by audience. Yet even home page only advertisers may be challenged if items such as drinking games or logo clothing are shown to appeal disproportionately to minors. Similarly, television shopping shows that design their programs to appeal to, and take advantage of, elderly shut-ins may be liable for message targeting. Standards for targeting are likely to evolve on a case-by-case basis.

PRESSURE TO BUY

One of consumer advantages of mass advertising is that there is relatively little pressure to buy. Magazine and broadcast advertising are easily ignored. Indeed, the recording of television programs on VCRs for later viewing facilitates the "zapping" or fast forwarding through advertisements. Interactive advertising is less easy to ignore. The success of telemarketing as a sales medium attests to this fact.

In Europe, despite the alleged ease of ignoring mass media sales messages, there is substantial concern about psychological pressure to buy. Several European countries ban solicitations that are considered too aggressive or surprising or invasive of consumers' privacy (Maxeiner and Schotthofer, 1992). Belgium, Denmark, France, the Netherlands and the UK all require a seven-day cancellation period for products sold at a distance rather than in person at a store or other place of business. As noted above, a comparable directive for the entire community has been proposed (Gabbott, 1994), but has not been adopted because of controversy whether consumers would select to be on or select to be off mailing lists. Austria, Germany, the Netherlands, and Greece prohibit using psychological pressure to buy such as gratitude for a free gift or the exploitation of emotions such as compassion, fear or superstition (Maxeiner and Schot-

thofer, 1992). For these reasons, Europe may be better able to regulate interactive advertising, at least when it is felt to be too persuasive.

At one time, the FTC also was concerned with high pressure interactive sales tactics. For this it enacted the 3 day cooling off in Door to Door Sales Rule (16 C.F.R. 429). No matter how insistent, persuasive, or simply effective a sales person was, the consumer has the right to cancel the order within three days, after the salesperson has departed and the consumer has cooled off. However, the recently enacted Telemarketing rule (16 C.F.R. 310) ignores both this precedent and the European trend. It does not impose a right of cancellation, but rather only restricts deceptive and abusive practices akin to the sort prohibited in the Fair Debt Collection Practices Act (15 U.S.C. sec. 1592).

Despite the reduction in protection from Door-to-Door Sales to Telemarketing, there is precedent for FTC action to prevent undue pressure to buy. The classic case is Arthur Murray Studio of Washington (1971) where dance salespeople pressured elderly widows to purchase exorbitant numbers of lessons through flattery, playing on their loneliness, and coercion. Television home shopping shows have similarly been accused of preying on the vulnerability of elderly shut-ins by providing both excitement and television-based "friendship." Yet when the FTC recently investigated a shopping network, it obtained a consent order that only addressed advertising substantiation concerns (Home Shopping Network, Inc., 1996). A recent state law case similarly condemned the use of scare tactics to sell a termite protection plan (*Bandura v. Orkin Exterminating Co.,* 1987), but such cases are rare.

The fairness of the persuasiveness of interactive media has yet to be determined. Despite increasing concern about telemarketing fraud, the FTC's rule suggests that fraud is the primary concern causing people to purchase, rather than an unfair pressure to buy. As these media and technology develop, consumer behavior research is needed to attempt to delineate what is fair persuasion that reasonable consumers can resist if they desire as opposed to unfair persuasion that at least some types of consumers have difficulty resisting. Otherwise, the FTC and courts can take action in egregious cases, leaving unclear the location of the dividing line between fair and unfair selling practices other than false and deceptive statements.

CONCLUSIONS

It is important to put the above analysis in context. Deception and fraud likely will continue to be the primary law enforcement concern for interactive marketing. Proving that fraud occurred in blatant cases is relatively easy and allows the FTC to show how it is accomplishing its consumer protection mission (Petty, 1992).

This article suggests that unfairness concerns will increase as advertising becomes more interactive and targeted. Most reasonable people do not believe that new communications technologies can manipulate consumers to buy a product or service they did not want. Nevertheless, several concerns with interactive marketing likely will face increased legal scrutiny in the next century. Consumers demand and the law provides some fundamental consumer control over the transaction. Goods must be received in a reasonable period of time and must be of the promised quality or readily returnable. Consumers want to limit the intrusiveness of advertising, even while enjoying the benefits of advertising targeted toward their particular interests. Targeting may cause unfair consumer injury by excluding some people from access to information about certain products or services. Alternatively, it may unfairly exploit vulnerabilities of the target audience, particularly when the advertising is unduly intrusive or psychologically attractive. Most consumers can defend against such tactics, but U.S. law has probably reached the peak of assuming consumers are economically rational. After all, if consumers are not susceptible to marketing persuasion, marketers would not engage in such practices. It is difficult to say whether the US will approach the level of concern in Europe for pressure to buy, but it is likely to at least move in that direction.

The extent to which the law protects consumers is closely related to the perceived need for such protection. If most marketers behave ethically and legally, consumers will enjoy the benefit of interactive marketing. Unfortunately, the low cost of some forms of such marketing mean that the unscrupulous can easily participate in the marketplace and through targeting reduce the chances of being monitored and caught. For this reason, industry self-regulation and formal consumer protection law will likely increase the sue of unfairness theories to provide enhanced consumer protection.

Ross D. Petty is Professor of Marketing Law at Babson College. He is the Legal Developments Editor of the Journal of Public Policy & Marketing and Chair of the Editorial Advisory Board for the Advertising Law Anthology.

REFERENCES

Arthur Murray Studio of Washington. 78 F.T.C. 401, affirmed, 458 F.2d 622 (5th Cir. 1972) (1971).

Averitt, Neil W. The Meaning of "Unfair Acts or Practices" in Section 5 of the Federal Trade Commission Act. *Georgetown Law Journal* 70(l) (1981): 225—296.

Bandura v. Orkin Exterminating Co. 664 F. Supp. 1219 (N.D.Ill.) (1987).

Beales, Howard J. What State Regulators Should Learn from FTC Experience in Regulating Advertising. *Journal of Public Policy & Marketing* 10(1) (1991): 101–117.

Bloom, Paul N., Milne, George R., and Adler, Robert. "Avoiding Misuse of New Information Technologies: Legal and Societal Considerations." *Journal of Marketing,* 58 (1), (1994): 98–110.

Cain, Rita Marie. "Recent Developments in Telemarketing Regulation." *Journal of Public Policy & Marketing* 15(1) (1996): 135–141.

California SunCare, Inc. FTC No. 942-3218, Nov. 19, 1996.

Campbell Soup Co. 115 F.T.C. 788 (1992).

CompuServe Inc. v. Cyber Promotions, Inc. 1197 U.S. Dist. LEXIS 1997 (S.D. Ohio, Feb. 3, 1997).

Cyber Promotions, Inc. v. America Online, Inc. 948 F. Supp. 436 (E.D. Pa.) (1996a).

Cyber Promotions, Inc. v. America Online, Inc. 948 F. Supp. 456 (E.D. Pa.) (1996b).

Eggland's Best, Inc. FTC No. C-3520, August 15, 1994.

Federal Trade Commission. Commission Statement of Policy on the Scope of Consumer Unfairness Jurisdiction, 104 F.T.C. 1072 (1980).

Federal Trade Commission Advertising Substantiation Policy Statement, 104 F.T.C. 839 (1984a).

Federal Trade Commission Deception Policy Statement, 103 F.T.C. 174 (1984b).

Federal Trade Commission. Federal-State Surfing Catches A Wave of Potential Internet Scams. FTC Press Release Dec. 12, 1996a.

Federal Trade Commission. Staff Report on the Public Workshop on Consumer Privacy on the Global Information Infrastructure, December 1996b.

Federal Trade Commission. FTC Announces Two Significant Efforts in Its Comprehensive Examination of Consumer Privacy. FTC Press Release, March 4, 1997.

Fortuna Alliance L.L.C. FTC File No. X96-0059; Civil Action No. C96-779M. (W.D. Wash. May 29, 1997).

Foxman, Ellen R. and Kilcoyne, Paula. Information Technology, Marketing Practice, and Consumer Privacy: Ethical Issues. *Journal of Public Policy & Marketing* 12 (Spring 1993), 106–119.

FTC v. Audiotex Connection, Inc. FTC No. 972-3079, Feb. 19, 1997.

FTC v. Keppel & Bro. 291 U.S. 304 (1934).

FTC v. Sperry & Hutchinson Co. 405 U.S. 233.

Gabbott, Mark (1994). The European Community Framework for Distance Selling: A Review. *Journal of Public Policy & Marketing,* 13(2) (1972): 307–312.

General Foods Corp. 86 F.T.C. 831 (1975).

Georgetown Publishing House, Ltd. FTC No. C-3692, Nov. 19, 1996.

Goodwin, Cathy. Privacy: Recognition of a Consumer Right. *Journal of Public Policy & Marketing,* 10 (Spring 1991), 149–166.

Home Shopping Network, Inc. FTC No. D-09272, July 11, 1996.

Hudson Pharmaceutical Corp. 89 F.T.C. 82 (1977).

International Harvester, Inc. 104 F.T.C. 949 (1984).

Jones, Mary Gardiner. "Privacy: A Significant Marketing Issue for the 1990s." *Journal of Public Policy & Marketing* 10 (Spring 1991), 133–48.

JS&A Group, Inc. FTC No. C-3248, Nov. 1, 1988.

Manigini v. R.J. Reynolds Tobacco Co. 22 Cal. App. 4th 628, aff'd, 7 Cal. 4th 1057 (1993, 1994).

Maxeiner, James R. and Schotthofer, Peter (Eds.) Advertising Law in Europe and North America, Deventer, Netherlands: Kluwer Law and Taxation Publishers (1992).

Mego Int'l Inc. 92 F.T.C. 186 (1978).

Money, Money, Money, Inc. et al. FTC No. 892-3111. July 3, 1990.

Orkin Exterminating Co. v. FTC. No. 87-8285, (11th Cir., April 19, 1988).

Packard, Vance. The Hidden Persuaders. New York: David McKay Company, Inc. (1957).

Petty, Ross D. FTC Advertising Regulation: Survivor or Casualty of the Reagan Revolution? *American Business Law Journal,* 30(1), (1992): 1–34.

Petty, Ross D. Joe Camel and the Commission: The Real Legal Issues, *Journal of Public Policy & Marketing,* 12(2), (1993): 276–279.

Petty, Ross D. "Advertising Law and Social Issues: The Global Perspective." *Suffolk Transnational Law Review 17* (2) (1994): 309–349.

Petty, Ross D. "Advertising Law in the United States and European Union." *Journal of Public Policy & Marketing* 16(1), (1997): 1–13.

Petty, Ross D. and Kopp, Robert J. "Advertising Challenges: A Strategic Framework and Current Review." *Journal of Advertising Research* 35(2), (1995): 41–55.

Preston, Ivan L. "Unfairness Developments in FTC Advertising Cases," *Journal of Public Policy & Marketing,* 14(2) (1995): 318–321.

Pridgen, Dee. "How Will Consumers Be Protected on the Information Superhighway?" *Land and Water Law Review,* 32(1) (1997): 237–55.

Rice, David A. "Consumer Unfairness at the FTC: Misadventures in Law and Economics." *George Washington Law Review,* 52(1) (1983–84): 1–66.

Richards, Jef I. "Legal Potholes on the Information Superhighway," *Journal of Public Policy & Marketing,* 16(2) (1997): 319–326.

Rotfeld, Herbert. "The FTC and Marketing Abuse." *Marketing News,* 31(6) (1997): 4.

Simonson, Alexander. " 'Unfair' Advertising and the FTC: Structural Evolution of the Law and Implications for Marketing and Public Policy," *Journal of Public Policy & Marketing,* 14(2) (1995): 321–327.

Starek. Roscoe B. III. "Regulatory Enforcement of Your Website: Who Will Be Watching?" remarks before the Online Advertising Workshop, Oct. 1, 1997, available at www.ftc.gov/speeches/starek/onlineweb.htm.

Thomas, Robert E. and Virginia G. Mauer. "Database Marketing Practice: Protecting Consumer Privacy." *Journal of Public Policy & Marketing* 16(1) (1997): 147–155.

Uncle Ben's Inc. 89 F.T.C. 131 (1977).

Trust and Concern in Consumers' Perceptions of Marketing Information Management Practices

George R. Milne
María Eugenia Boza

Abstract

This research examines two constructs, consumers' trust and concern, in information management practices. The authors present empirical evidence from a national consumer survey that suggests improving trust and reducing concerns are two distinct approaches to managing consumer information. Contrary to existing self-regulation efforts, the authors argue that when managing consumer information, the improvement of trust is more effective than efforts to reduce concern.

INTRODUCTION

Database marketing techniques are becoming standard marketing practices across a wide range of organizations ("Database Marketing," 1994). With this increase of database marketing activity comes the heightened concern of consumers over their personal information. On a yearly basis from 1990 to 1995, Equifax conducted studies that found 78% to 84% of respondents, were either very or somewhat concerned about threats to their personal privacy (Harris and Associates, 1990; Harris and Associates, 1991; Harris and Associates, 1992; Harris and Associates, 1993; Harris and Associates, 1994; Harris and Associates, 1995). Much of their concern is due to consumers' feeling they are losing control. Recently, 80% of the public agreed they have completely lost all control of how their personal information is circulated and used by

companies (Harris, 1995). Indeed, data collected for one purpose may be combined with other data and used for an entirely new purpose.

Database marketing has given marketers the ability to compile profiles of each of their customer's purchasing patterns. This information is used to mail offers for goods and services that will likely interest their customers. In addition to using purchase information, marketers are also augmenting their databases with public information and matching their databases with other organizations' databases to further their knowledge about current customers and to prospect for new customers. In some instances, databases are built for the primary purpose of renting out to other marketers.

Concurrent with the rise of database marketing, researchers have emphasized the importance of organizations' complying with fair information practices (Cespedes and Smith, 1993, Culnan, 1993). To implement these practices, many marketing organizations inform consumers of information practices through disclosure statements in communications and offer consumers the option to opt out of lists. In a further effort to reduce concern, the direct marketing industry offers telephone and mail preference services, where consumers can remove their name from all lists. The industry also publishes numerous pamphlets to inform consumers about their rights.

Despite the self-regulation efforts, consumers are still concerned about their personal information. Part of the concern is attributable to the fact that not every business is in compliance with the strictest privacy practices (Milne and Boza, 1998). More importantly, it appears that industry communications are not getting through to consumers. The current study shows that only 41.9% of consumers are aware of opt-out mechanisms. Further, the direct marketing industry reports that less than 2% of consumers use mail or telephone preference service to opt-out from direct mail or telephone lists (Direct Marketing Association, 1994). However, even for those consumers who are aware of opt-out, concern over personal information continues to be high.

Recently, consultants (Peppers and Rogers, 1993; Shaver, 1996) and scholars (Campbell, 1997; Gengler and Leszczyc Popkowski, 1997) in the direct marketing field have offered relationship marketing as an alternative perspective to manage consumer privacy issues. The relationship marketing perspective suggests that being forthcoming in their information practices helps marketers to strengthen consumer relationships. Consumers in turn willingly provide information that enable the marketer to grow the level of trust and advance further consumer relationships through improved offers and targeted communication. While this perspective seems to provide a good complement to opt-out, little empirical research has investigated the effectiveness of gaining trust in database marketing and managing consumer information.

The purpose of this paper is to present empirical evidence to support the claim that improving trust and reducing concern are two distinct approaches to managing consumer information. We demonstrate that consumers' perceptions of trust and concern levels vary by industry and argue that in many circumstances, improving trust may be a more effective strategy than reducing concern, as currently used. Specifically, we suggest that trust can be built through improving the image and reputation of the business and proper customer contact management.

Our argument is based on empirical results of a national sample of 1,508 direct marketing consumers. In the paper, we present three separate studies based on the survey data. In study 1, we examine the relationship between trust and concern. As part of this study, we map consumers' levels of trust and concern toward 17 industries and their information handling practices. In study 2, we examine the antecedents and consequences of trust and concern for both direct marketing and nontraditional direct marketing industries. In study 3, we present qualitative data that suggests what consumers feel leads them to trust an organization with their personal information. In addition, we highlight consumers' concern of organizations

sharing their personal information with third parties. The paper begins by reviewing previous' notions of trust that have appeared in the marketing literature. Next we present a conceptual framework that delineates the concepts of concern and trust in the database marketing context. In the following section we describe the survey methodology. Then we present the three studies, discuss the results, and conclude by offering recommendations for improving trust in database marketing.

TRUST CONCEPTS

Over the years, trust has emerged as a central construct in the study of relationship marketing (Dwyer, Schurr, and Oh, 1987; Morgan and Hunt, 1994) across multiple empirical research contexts. For example, trust has been examined in the context of bargaining (Schurr and Ozanne, 1985), buyer-seller relationships (Doney and Cannon, 1497; Ganesan, 1994), distribution channels (Anderson and Weitz, 1989; Dwyer and Oh, 1987), and use of market research (Moorman; Desphande, and Zaltman, 1993; Moorman, Zaltman, and Desphande, 1992).

Trust is an important concept in relational exchange since it allows exchange partners to look beyond short-run inequities or risks and concentrate on long run gains. In other words, the role of trust in relationships and exchange is to stimulate cooperation (Geyskens and Skeekamps, 1995; Moorman et al., 1992; Morgan and Hunt, 1992) and to create a "reservoir of goodwill" that helps preserve the relationship (Kumar, 1996). In particular, trust supports cooperation through its impact on two main threats to cooperation, namely, fear and greed (Hwang and Burgers, 1997; Kumar, 1997).

Even though Etzioni (1988) argues that some level of trust is a fundamental aspect in all market transactions, the general consensus is that trust is critical in exchanges involving interdependence, uncertainty, and risk. This is in contrast to those transactions that occur under conditions of perfect information and easy monitoring of exchange partners behavior.

Though there is agreement on the importance of trust, there is widespread disagreement about its exact definition, characteristics and dimensions. Trust has been conceptualized in the organizational behavior literature as an expectation (Gabarro, 1978), a behavior (Zand, 1972), a belief (Cook and Wall, 1980) and an attitude (Mayer, Davis, and Schoorman, 1995). In the social exchange literature, trust has been characterized as willingness to place one self in a position of risk (Rempel, Holmes, and Zanna, 1985).

In the marketing literature, two major components that appear in the definition of trust include the psychological and sociological (Moorman et al., 1993). The former includes confidence in an exchange partner, the later a willingness to rely on such partner. The emerging view is that the psychological elements of the definition include trust in the partner's honesty and trust in the partner's benevolence (Ganesan, 1994). The sociological component is less developed in the marketing literature.

The numerous definitions of trust in the literature provide insight to our current study. Moorman and co-authors (1992) defined trust as *the willingness to rely on an exchange partner in whom one has confidence.* Doney and Cannon (1997) defined trust as *the perceived credibility and benevolence of a target of trust.* The former definition focuses on the beliefs and behavior of the party who trusts. The belief component relies on past experience and the behavior component refers to willingness to rely on the partner even in conditions of uncertainty. The latter definition focuses on the perception on the part of the party who trusts the target's credibility (ability to keep a promise) and benevolence (interest to seek joint gain). Taken together, the definitions implicitly assume that the party that trusts is facing uncertainty and concern about possible outcomes from engaging in exchange with the partner and that there are positive outcomes to be achieved from trusting.

In database marketing, consumers face uncertainty and risk when they provide information to marketers. At the same time, database marketing has offered consumers numerous benefits, many of which are realized by customers as a relationship evolves. It follows then that trust may be an important aspect of this exchange process. In our context, we define trust as the expectancy of a customer to rely upon database marketers to treat the consumer's personal information fairly. In the next section we discuss trust more fully in the context of database marketing.

THE ROLE OF TRUST AND CONCERN IN DATABASE MARKETING

Database marketing deals with individual-level data, which raises the possibility that individual privacy may be compromised. Marketers not only use demographic and transactional data for marketing purposes, but many are also starting to capture Internet behavior. Therefore, with the advancement of communication and information technologies such as the internet, consumers' level of concern about privacy is likely to increase. To conduct business in this volatile environment, managers can either focus on lessening concern or increasing trust as alternative strategies in managing consumers' responses toward information practices. This section delineates the differences between the constructs concern and trust and shows that the separate managerial actions to lessen concern and increase trust have different implications.

As shown in Figure 10-1, both trust and concern affect the probability of consumer purchase at various stages of the database marketing relationship. For both prospects and customers, trust and

	Concern	Trust
Prospect	• Lowers probability of purchase	• Increases probability of purchase
Customer	• Lowers probability of repurchase	• Increases probability of strengthened relationship

Figure 10-1   Conceptual Framework

concern have opposite effects on purchase behavior. While concern is likely to reduce purchase probabilities, trust is likely to increase them. Prior reputation of the company and experience in successive contacts with the organization are possibly factors related to consumers' trust. For both prospects and customers, trust may serve as a mechanism that facilitates exchange and strengthens consumer relationships. Stronger consumer relationships imply higher (re)purchase probability but also better cross-marketing opportunities, word-of-mouth support, information exchange and partnering arrangements.

Organizations often pursue either a concern-reduction or a trust-building strategy in managing consumer responses toward information practices. Organizations trying to reduce concern may, for example, avoid mentioning information privacy practices to new prospects until ordering, purchasing or even billing a transaction. In this sense, organizations with strategies to reduce concern may disclose information practices with euphemisms (Milne, 1997). In contrast, organizations attempting to build trust actively disclose their policies. For example, Stop and Shop—a supermarket chain—posted in-store signs disclosing their privacy policy with the introduction of their frequent shopper card program. Similarly, L. L. Bean at their store headquarters places disclosure statements prominently on cash registers outlining their information handling practices. In communicating with customers, organizations seeking to reduce consumers' concern will surreptitiously notify consumers of the option to opt out of mailing lists. In many cases notices will be in fine print, utilize negative check-off boxes, or require the consumer to take some action by phone or mail to remove his or her name from the marketing list. In contrast, in a trust-building relationship, customers are already aware of information practices and fully collaborate with organizations. Customer-organization collaboration may include filling out surveys, participating in pilot programs, and other activities, sometimes in exchange for coupons or other benefits.

Concern-reduction and trust-building strategies are very different. In a concern-reduction

strategy, communication is secretive, in an attempt to avoid consumers' aversive responses. In this strategy, the optimal outcome is to avoid losing sales due to privacy concerns. In contrast, in a trust-building strategy, communication is informative and benefit driven, aimed at developing customer relationships. In this approach, the disclosure of information practices renders benefits, because in fact information practices are tied into a marketing program. Either complete privacy or selective information exchange with other organizations may accrue relationship benefits. In this context, information management practices are a marketing investment and the optimal outcome is to increase business returns.

CONSUMER PRIVACY SURVEY METHODOLOGY

During the first quarter of 1997, we conducted a survey of consumers' attitudes about direct marketing practices in partial fulfillment of supported research by the Direct Marketing Educational Foundation, the Direct Marketing Association, and the Marketing Science Institute. This section describes the survey process.

Survey Development

An eight-page survey instrument was developed for the consumer privacy study project. We adapted questions and items from previous studies, as well as writing items specifically for this study. The survey was revised over a four month period and benefited from the advice and review of a panel of marketing academics and industry practitioners.

The survey was pretested in two waves. The first included expert review as recommended by Hunt, Sparkman, and Wilcox (1992). Colleagues with expertise in survey design filled out the survey and made wording and format suggestions. After these comments were incorporated, the second wave consisted of a small-scale regional mailout of 200 surveys to a random sample of households in three New England cities, of which 173 were delivered. This mailing resulted in 64 completed surveys, for an effective response rate of 37% (64/173). The survey instrument format and items were revised based on reviewing response patterns.

Survey Procedure

The final survey population consisted of 5,003 individuals from a mailing list provided by Metromail. This list represented a random sample from Metromail's known direct mail households. The sample was selected to reflect U.S. adult age distributions.

The survey procedure approximated the guidelines suggested by Dillman (1978). Two mailings were conducted. First, we mailed a 3 × 5 prenotification postcard to each member of the list. On the card we explained the purpose of the study, asked for cooperation, and mentioned a survey would be arriving in a week. The primary author signed the card. Second, after removing 152 names of individuals who had insufficient addresses, we mailed the final instrument to 4,851 remaining individuals. Included with the survey booklet was a signed letter on university letterhead explaining the study purpose, a crisp one-dollar bill, and a business reply envelope.

Response Rate and Sample Characteristics

Responses were collected for a month following the mailout. At the end of this period, we received 1,508 useable surveys and 112 returned surveys which the Post Office was unable to deliver, for an effective response rate of 31.8% (1,508/4,739). This response rate is well within acceptable ranges of academic research, and could be viewed as a high response rate given the length of the survey and the sensitive nature of the topic.

The sample was 62.5% male, older (51.2% older than 50 years of age), and primarily white (92%), with 21% of the sample having household incomes greater than or equal to $50,000. Forty-

seven percent were college graduates and considered their political philosophy to be either conservative (40.9%) or moderate (47.3%). Forty-seven percent used computers.

To check for response bias we compared respondents and nonrespondents on selected demographic variables from the original mailing file. Each mailing piece had an identification number lined to a file with selected demographic information (except the name and address). No significant statistical differences were found for age, gender, or income selects. The only statistical difference was for survey respondents who belonged to households that had higher levels of estimated direct mail response activity (Prob $F < .01$).

Measure Development

Many of the scales used were created primarily for this study. In developing the items, we relied upon the insights and experience from practitioners and other privacy researchers. The questionnaire items and the measurement development details are reported in the Appendix.

STUDY 1: RELATIVE TRUST AND CONCERN BY INDUSTRIES

Both concern and trust are important factors affecting consumers' perceptions of organizations' information management practices. In this study, we compare average consumer ratings of these constructs at a macro level across seventeen different industries. We compare consumers' responses to two questions:

1. How concerned are you with different organizations using personal information they acquire from you in their marketing efforts?
2. How much do you trust the following organizations to use your personal information fairly?

Because we are comparing levels of consumer trust and concern for 17 industries, we were constrained to use a single item measures. While single-item measures are less reliable, we are comforted by the fact that the concepts we were measuring are quite concrete. Further, in prior multiple-item scales that measured trust, there were items that explicitly mentioned trust in a similar way that we asked our question. For example, the two-item scale (α =.84) used by Anderson and Weitz (1989) included the question, "How much do you trust the principal to be fair?" The five-item scale (α =.84) in the study by Moorman et al. (1992) included, "I trust my researcher to do things I can't do for myself"; "I trust my researcher to do things my department can't do itself"; and "I generally do not trust my researcher." Doney and Cannon's (1997) eight-item salesperson scale (α =.90) included the item, "The people

at my firm do not trust this salesperson." Given the high reliability of previous scales (and the high inter-item correlations), we are assured that our item captures the trust construct domain.

Each individual's evaluation of a specific organization was standardized by subtracting the sample's average concern across all industries and dividing by the standard deviation. The same procedure was followed for the trust measure. This scaling adjustment helps facilitate a relative comparison among industries and between the constructs themselves. Concern, was measured on a four-point scale, anchored by *not very concerned* = 1 and *very concerned* = 4. The average level of concern for the 17 industries was 3.15, with a standard deviation of .75. Trust was measured on a 10-point scale anchored by *trust not at*

TABLE 10.1	Consumer Relative Concern and Trust Ratings[a] for 17 Industries				
			Correlations		
Industry	**Concern**	**Trust**	**Industry Concern— Trust Concern**[b]	**Industry Trust— Total Trust**[c]	**Industry Concern— Industry Trust**[d]
Banks	.57	.70	.64	.72	−.11
Credit card issuers	.46	−.14	.71	.71	−.16
Insurance companies	.38	.18	.71	.69	−.19
Telephone companies	.36	.20	.74	.73	−.18
Employers	.30	1.02	.67	.67	−.15
Internet access providers	.21	−.55	.73	.65	−.23
Political organizations	.13	−.62	.76	.66	−.27
Direct mail clubs	.09	−.83	.80	.61	−.26
Charities	−.05	−.06	.79	.70	−.30
Magazine companies	−.12	−.58	.85	.71	−.28
Catalog companies	−.20	−.55	.86	.72	−.28
Drugstores	−.24	.43	.83	.79	−.23
Airlines	−.26	.11	.86	.83	−.30
Alumni associations	−.33	.40	.80	.76	−.26
Video stores	−.36	−.15	.87	.79	−.30
Book stores	−.40	−.09	.87	.81	−.31
Grocery stores	−.46	.26	.85	.80	−.25

[a]Reported Trust and Concern values are standardized scores to facilitate comparison.

[b]Total concern is sum across 17 industries. Correlation based on original scale values.

[c]Total trust is sum across 17 industries. Correlation based on original scale values.

[d]Within industry trust-concern correlations based on original scale values.

all = 1 and *trust completely* = 10. The average level of trust for the 17 industries was 3.98, with a standard deviation of 1.87. Table 10.1 shows the relative values of concern and trust for the 17 industries. In addition, Table 10.1 reports specific industry-total industry correlations for both the trust and concern variables and a within industry correlation between trust and concern.

The data in Table 10.1 are sorted by level of concern. The data indicate that the dimensions of concern and trust are not redundant. Correlation data indicates discriminant validity between the constructs. There are higher levels of within-construct correlation across industries than there is in the within-industry correlation between concern and trust. For example, the correlation of concern for banks and concern for all industries was .64; the correlation of trust for banks and trust of all industries was .72; the correlation of concern for

banks and trust for banks was −.11. While there is a consistent negative correlation between concern and trust with respect to any specific industry (ranging from −.11 to −.31), it does not necessarily follow that industries with high concern ratings have low trust ratings. In fact, the two dimensions of concern and trust are quite robust in terms of describing differences among industries.

To further understand these differences, we mapped the industries by these two dimensions. In addition, we subjected industries' concern and trust ratings to a hierarchical cluster analysis using the average linkage algorithm. In Figure 10-2, we depict the cluster groupings by placing closed loops around industries with similar ratings on the trust and concern dimensions. The analysis revealed that there were four major groupings.

The figure shows that there is one cluster occupied by banks and employers that rate high on

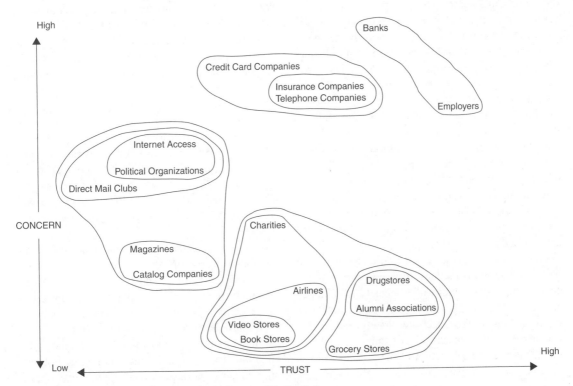

Figure 10-2   Relative Trust and Concern of Industries

both concern and trust. The level of concern for these organizations is probably due to the sensitivity of the information that they store about people. The 1983 Equifax Study (Harris, 1983) reported that these were two areas where concern about privacy was very high. Interestingly, the level of trust for these organizations is also high. Interactions with both banks and employers are heavily-regulated longer-term relationships intensive in personal information. To some degree, the high level of trust is a prerequisite for these interactions.

Insurance, telephone, and credit card companies form a second cluster with the same level of concern but less trust. The reason that trust levels are lower here may be that consumers perceive these organizations as more likely to engage in marketing activity that would involve the exchange of private information.

The third cluster houses industries that engage in information gathering of primarily transactional data. Consumers in this study do not seem as concerned with privacy of transactional data (purchase tracking), but consumers may not be fully aware of the extent to which this happens. Within this cluster there is a group of organizations, namely drugstores, alumni associations, and grocery stores, that have a higher level of trust than other organizations in cluster 3. The other subgroup includes bookstores, video stores, airlines, and charities, which have lower levels of trust. The difference between the subgroups might be in the perceived likelihood of the organization to use customer information for external marketing and data exchanges.

The fourth cluster contains the more active direct marketing industries. This cluster comprises catalog companies, magazines, direct mail clubs, internet access providers, and political organizations. This group is the least trusted of the organizations due to these entities' propensity to capture and share information. However, while the level of concern is higher for this cluster than for cluster 3, it is less than the concern level for first two clusters. This may be a function of the type of information housed on their respective databases.

STUDY 2: MODELING ANTECEDENTS AND CONSEQUENCES OF TRUST AND CONCERN

This study explored the antecedents and consequences of trust and concern of database marketing companies. We examined two models, as depicted in Figure 10-3. The first conceptual model shows the global effect of antecedents on both trust and concern of all database marketing companies. The second conceptual model pertains to specific direct marketers, represented by catalogs, magazines, and direct mail clubs. This model shows the effect of antecedents on trust and concern, and the resulting effect of these variables on direct marketing usage.

The measures of trust and concern are the same as reported in study 1. We summed the ratings of 17 industries to derive aggregate measures. We summed the ratings for the three direct marketing subindustries to derive trust and concern ratings specific to the direct marketing industry. In many respects, our aggregate trust scores follow the same logic as Rotter's (1967) interpersonal trust scale. Rotter asked subjects to express trust of parents, teachers, physicians, politicians, classmates, friends, and so forth. His additive scale expressed trust for a great variety of social objects. In our additive scale of trust for industries, we are measuring trust for a variety of different industries.

Direct mail usage was a single item measure where respondents indicated the number of times they purchased goods or services by mail, phone or internet.

The antecedents we examined are based on previous research on privacy concerns and usage in direct marketing. The antecedents used to explain trust and concern of all industries' information practices included perceived control, knowledge, attitude toward relationship marketing. For the direct marketing industry, we also included the variable attitude toward direct marketing. Following Culnan (1993), perceived control was operationalized in terms of whether respondents were

Model 1: All Industries

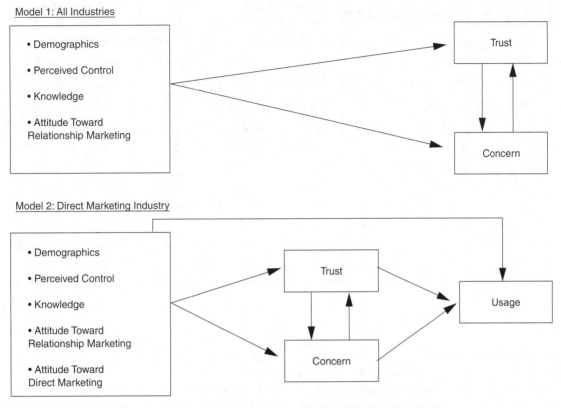

Figure 10-3   Models of Trust and Concern of Database Marketing Companies

aware of opt-out procedures. The question was based on the Equifax studies. Knowledge of information practices, as in Nowak and Phelps (1992), was measured as the number of correct answers in a series of questions about whether organizations could retrieve information from different sources. Attitude toward direct marketing and attitude toward relationship marketing were multi-item measures constructed specifically for this study. Demographics were based on Equifax studies and included measures of sex, age, income, political philosophy, and computer usage. Specific items, factor structures, correlations, and reliabilities of scales are reported in the Appendix.

The general paths of the conceptual model were estimated using OLS regression. Two regres-

sions were estimated for trust and concern across all industries. Three regressions were estimated for trust, concern and usage for the direct marketing industry. The results of this analysis are summarized in Table 10.2.

The regression explaining trust across all industries found that concern and knowledge of information practices negatively impacted trust, and attitude toward relationship marketing positively impacted trust. Also, females were more likely to trust organizations than males. The regression explaining concern found trust to have a negative effect. In addition, older people were more likely to be concerned than younger people.

In the model for the direct marketing industry—as in the overall model—concern has a negative

TABLE 10.2	Regression Model Results[a]				
	All Industries		**Direct Marketing Industry**		
	Trust	**Concern**	**Trust**	**Concern**	**Usage**
Trust		−.35**		−.30**	.11**
Concern	−.35**		−.30**		−.07*
Perceived control	.02	−.05	.05	−.09**	.08**
Knowledge about information practices	−.18**	−.04	−.01	.03	.02
Attitude toward relationship marketing	.11**	−.01	.04	−.04	.08**
Attitude toward direct marketing			.16**	−.02	.04
Sex (female)	.06*	.05	.07*	.05	.03
Age	−.02	.18**	−.04	.21**	−.01
Income	−.01	−.03	−.05	−.06*	.20**
Political philosophy	−.01	−.02	.01	−.02	.04
Computer usage	−.01	−.01	−.05	−.01	.07*
F	29.1**	26.8**	21.3**	22.8**	12.1**
Adjusted R-squared	.18	.16	.15	.16	.10

[a]Standardized betas reported in table.

** $p < .01$. *$p < .05$.

effect on trust and females were more likely to trust organizations than males. However, the effects of knowledge and attitude toward relationship marketing were not significant, apparently because an industry specific variable, attitude toward direct marketing, had a strong positive relationship with trust. The direct marketing model explaining concern had similar results to the overall model; trust was negatively related to concern, and older people were more likely to be concerned than younger people. In addition, perceived control was negatively related to concern and respondents with higher income were less concerned. The regression model explaining direct marketing usage found trust, *attitude toward relationship marketing,* higher incomes, and computer usage to be positively related and concern to be negatively related.

The regression models confirmed the results from the first study that trust and concern are negatively related. The models also found, however, that different antecedents affected these two constructs, the relationships differed for all industries and the direct marketing industry, and that both

trust and concern significantly impacted usage levels.

In addition to the negative impact of concern, the regressions showed that as consumers become more knowledgeable about information practices, they were less likely to trust organizations. Interestingly, this did not hold true for the direct marketing industry. Improving attitudes about relationship marketing and specific attitudes toward direct marketing seem to offer avenues for building trust.

The importance of building trust is seen in the regressions explaining concern. Increasing trust has a very strong impact on reducing concern. Interestingly, in the regression specific to the direct marketing industries, increasing trust had a standardized coefficient that was three times as strong as perceived control. This suggests that trust may be a more effective mechanism of reducing concern in the direct marketing industry than controls through opt out.

Trust and concern have opposite effects on direct marketing usage levels. In general, positive controllable aspects are strong predictors of usage.

Not only is trust positively related, but so is control and attitude toward relationship marketing. Finally, and not surprisingly, targeting affluent people appears to be a viable approach to increase usage.

STUDY 3: QUALITATIVE INSIGHTS INTO TRUST AND CONCERN

In study 2 we found that some preselected antecedents were significantly related to trust and concern. In study 3 we present qualitative data that lends further insight into the nature of these two constructs.

Consumers' Trust of Personal Information

We begin by presenting the results of an open-ended question in which we asked respondents, "What makes you trust an organization with your personal information?" The two authors and a research assistant coded the responses to this question. The coding procedure involved (1) reviewing responses, (2) developing categories, (3) independently coding, (4) meeting as a group to reach consensus on how to classify each response, and (5) reviewing all responses within a category to look for inconsistencies. In coding, we allowed a response to be classified in multiple codes. Of the 1,508 respondents, 1,073 (71%) filled out the open-ended question. These respondents provided 1,325 responses. Table 10.3 presents a frequency distribution of respondents grouped in 17 categories. In addition, to help interpret the results, we organize related response under category headings.

Experience

The number one reason that consumers gave for trusting organizations with personal information was past experience with the company. In the words of one respondent, trust was built "by getting to know them and their integrity. Also by asking others who do business with the organization." Many referred to knowing by experience that

TABLE 10.3	Open Ended Responses to: What Makes You Trust an Organization with Your Personal Information?	
	N	**% Total**
Experience		
Past experience with organization	175	13%
Organization does not share information	76	6%
Good relationship management	69	5%
Personal contacts	31	2%
Reputation		
Reputation	122	9%
Type of business	73	6%
Credibility and fairness	50	4%
Service quality	29	2%
Knowledge of organization	21	2%
Customer initiated contact	9	1 %
Contractucal		
Statement of confidentiality	68	5%
Business asks permission	34	3%
Use of opt out notices	12	1%
Benefits equal the risk	11	1%
Regulation		
Legal statutes	49	4%
Regulatory scrutiny	9	1%
Negative		
No trust	250	19%
No choice	90	7%
Self-centered–no trust	49	1%
Other Responses		
Unclassified	44	1%
Self centered-positive	35	2%
Don't know	19	1%

organizations did not share personal information. Essentially, respondents looked for "no evidence of it being passed around." Many were adamant about not sharing consumer information, as evidenced by the following sentiments: "Never provide information to another company" and "their willingness not to provide others with that information even if it provides them with a profit." Another aspect of experience dealt with relationship management, and expectations about the proper amount of contact between organization and customer. Respondents trusted organizations "if they didn't try to sell me the same product over and over again, if they didn't call me all of the time. . . ." A more positive spin on the same theme was stated as, "They have a vested interest in providing me with the goods and services I would be interested in." Finally, personal contacts with employees were also important in building trust. Typical of these responses is, "I have to know someone within the organization."

Reputation

Reputation was the second broad reason for respondents' trusting organizations with their personal information. Respondents' ideas about an organization's reputation included, "its name and background," and personal experience as indicated by the comment, "repeat business that helps build trust and a reputation for loyalty." Reputation is important because it affects behavior, as noted by the following, "I'll give my credit card number and address to any company that I know to be a reputable firm." Type of business was reported to affect trust. Respondents trusted "those organizations with very little to sell," organizations "not having a profit motive," and organizations "if it is religiously oriented" or "locally owned." Banks, insurance companies, and other financial institutions were also trusted. Other than knowledge of the organization, respondents looked for credibility and fairness and evidence of good service quality. One respondent addressing the issue of credibility wrote, "I trust on a limited basis until they give me reason not to."

Another respondent felt trust for an organization was built by "their professionalism and the way they conducted business."

Contractual

A smaller group of responses dealt specifically with contractual reasons for trusting organizations. By contractual we refer to conditions where the organizations disclose their intentions on how they will use the consumers' information. The top contractual reason provided was in terms of statements of confidentiality. Some respondents wanted "a sworn affidavit saying personal information will not be released without consent." Others wanted a pledge not to sell personal information" or "a policy statement indicating information will be kept confidential." Trust was also built when the organizations asked permission of customers to use information. Respondents felt trust was built if "the organization gives a choice of using our data," or "they give the assurances that they will not give it out unless I give them permission." Other contractual arrangements mentioned by less than 2% of responses include opt-out notices and feeling that the benefits out weighed the risks.

Regulation

Relatively few respondents mentioned regulation as a reason for trusting organizations. Those who mentioned this option were not very trusting in general. One respondent stated, "I don't really trust. Some are obligated by law to keep their information private, so I guess I trust them." Another respondent, similar to others who were not sure of what regulations were in place wrote, "I have little trust but just believe that there are some laws that prevent any/all information going to anyone who asks about my personal information." Finally, there were those individuals who wanted more regulation. One such individual wrote, "giving personal information is part of the process of buying goods and services. The information age is here to stay, but the government must control the use of information to protect peoples' rights to privacy and fair business."

No Trust

Interestingly, the largest group of responses was comments about not trusting any organization. The range of feelings were from very strong, "trust is a strong word to use, I don't trust any of them" to a slightly qualified, "I'm afraid I do not trust any organization with my personal information. The LEAST likely to abuse this privilege would be a religious organization." One respondent, who did not trust because of sharing of information, noted "Nothing. I believe most sell any information they have to mail list companies. A Social Security number is all you need to get a person's total history—financial, health . . ." Another respondent did not trust a company that could improve its profitability using customer information. This respondent wrote, "I don't think you can trust any group or organization with your personal information when there is even a remote chance to help the bottom line." Some respondents felt they had no choice. For them, the issue was not about trust but about not having other choices other than submitting personal information: "Personal information must be given or you will be denied the bank loan, credit, whatever." One respondent stated, "It's really difficult to trust and check any organization to see what they will do but you submit to join or apply and take your chances."

Consumers' Concern About Profiling and Data Transfer

A key concern of consumers, centers on what organizations do with consumers' personal information. The previous qualitative data on what leads consumers to trust an organization indicated that not sharing information with third parties was important. Also, there was a sentiment that the organization needed to exhibit a proper level of contact management and restrained use of data when providing consumers with new opportunities.

In many respects, consumers' concerns about marketers' use of data (profiling and transferring data to third parties) are at the core of the privacy debate. Two questions, in particular, shed light on the intensity of these concerns.

1. Some businesses compile profiles of each customer's purchasing patterns and use this information to mail offers for goods and services that will likely interest their customers. Is this practice *very, somewhat, not very,* or *not at all* acceptable to you?
2. How acceptable is it for organizations to make profits by providing your personal information to other organizations?

For the first question, 68% found profiling to be very or somewhat acceptable. In contrast, for the second question, less than 9% found it very or somewhat acceptable for organizations to make profits providing personal information to third parties. More importantly, 71% found this practice of making profit from data transfer to third parties to be not at all acceptable.

These results suggest that customers do not mind organizations' using data to serve them better. This is not seen as an invasion of privacy. The primary concern is the sharing of data.

CONCLUSIONS

This research presented three empirical studies that were intended to support the notion that trust and concern were different constructs, and help explain their relationships and antecedents. This research suggests that as a marketing strategy in managing consumer information, building trust may be more effective than trying to reduce concern.

The first study described consumers' concern and trust for specific industries. Our results suggest that first, there is enough discriminant validity between trust and concern, and second, that both trust and concern are key to understanding how consumers feel about the information practices of a firm. Based on the pattern of industry clusters and their common information practices, we inferred that concern may be driven by the sensitivity of information and trust driven by whether the organization is likely to share information with third parties.

The second study examined the antecedents of concern and trust. We ran separate models for an aggregate of all industries and the direct marketing industry. In addition, we examined the effect trust and concern had on purchase levels within the direct marketing industry. The results showed that concern and trust are intertwined in a strong negative relationship. Further, we found that antecedents affecting each differ and that trust has a positive effect and concern a negative effect on self-reported purchase levels. Thus, both constructs can affect future outcomes.

The first two studies established that trust and concern are different constructs that both explain consumer attitudes about organization information practices and purchase behavior. The studies showed that customers perceived organizations as differing on these dimensions. Also, consumers' attitudinal and demographic background affects their perceptions. The third study had the objective of gaining insight into what respondents considered antecedents for trust. Interestingly, the unaided themes that emerged from this study confirm the previous conceptualization and measurement of the trust construct in other contexts in marketing. Specifically, the discussion of experience and reputation (Doney and Cannon, 1997; Moorman et al., 1993) in the marketing literature is being reflected by respondents in this study. In the database marketing context, these qualitative results may suggest levers for a building trust strategy. Themes that emerged from these responses indicated different reasons for trusting organizations. Also, a large group of respondents claimed not to trust marketing information practices. Respondents who trusted their organizations referred to experience, reputation, contractual obligations, and regulation. Consumers felt that positive experiences and reputation of the organization were the

overriding factors leading them to trust an organization. Less important were contractual or legal avenues of recourse. One specific behavior that consumers pay close attention to is whether the organization shares information with third parties. In addition, respondents felt good relationship management was important as well as personal contacts.

In many respects, the factors that lead to trust are tantamount to relationship marketing. The findings from the second study corroborate this finding that consumers' attitude toward relationship marketing positively affects levels of trust. It is interesting to note some researchers have stated that trust is the primary facet of good relationship. Morgan and Hunt (1994) put forth a theory of relationship marketing where trust is one of the key factors leading to relationships.

If sharing of information (and the type of information) is a fundamental aspect of information management, the manner in which consumers are informed of policies is a key managerial issue. The direct marketing industry has traditionally approached this from a concern reduction perspective. This resulted in opt out notices and limited communication. The data from this study suggest that consumers want to control their information. Trust can be enhanced by building a reputation for fairness, communicating policies upfront where the relational benefits are stressed, and constantly keeping the consumer informed of the organizational activities to serve them better.

The data from this study represent a comprehensive view of direct marketing consumers' attitudes about database marketing. While the survey covered many topics, the generality led to limitations in the specificity of measures. In addition, because the sample was of known direct mail users (who skewed older and male), the generalizability of the results is narrowed. In addition, we presented studies that crossed multiple levels of analysis that can lead to biases in measures. For example, in the first study we compared organizations based on individuals' perceptions. Despite these measurement limitations, the three studies provide insight into consumers' attitudes toward information management by organizations. The results show that trust is a key positive factor that can reduce consumer concerns and improve organizational outcomes by helping foster strong relationships between consumers and organizations.

APPENDIX MEASURES

We formed traditional reflective scales for the constructs "Attitude toward Direct Marketing." We report their factor structure on the right.

Confirmatory Factory Analysis was run on subsample to evaluate unidimensionality for both the attitude toward direct marketing and attitude toward relationship marketing scales. The model for direct marketing resulted in X^2, 14 d.f. = 130, GOF = .85, CFI = .87, IFI = .87. While exploratory factor analysis found three dimensions which were

Attitude toward Direct Marketing Factor Analysis of Attitude toward Direct Marketing Items	
Items	**Factor 1**
Direct Marketing . . .	
. . . offers result in lower prices for the consumer	.70
. . . is convenient for the consumer	.79
. . . stimulates the development of new products and services	.70
. . . helps save the consumer time	.82
. . . allows for comparative shopping	.77
. . . is a fun way to shop	.81
. . . is hassle-free	.77
. . . provides wider selection	.79
Eigenvalue	4.77

Attitude toward Relationship Marketing Factor Analysis of Attitude toward Relationship Marketing Items			
Items	**Factor 1**	**Factor 2**	**Factor 3**
I like organizations I do business with to keep me informed of new products and services	.78	.09	−.00
Frequent customer programs are a good way to reward me for my loyalty	.72	.14	.05
I appreciate getting phone calls about things the organizations that I do business with feel would be of interest to me	.71	−.01	−.20
I very much enjoy receiving individual attention from the organizations I do business with	.61	.38	.22
It is safe to buy from organizations that I have done business with in the past	.10	.73	−.10
It is easy to buy from organizations that I have done business with in the past	.09	.72	−.06
I really like to maintain long term relationships with organizations	.47	.58	.30
Customers gain from developing long term relationships with organizations	.38	.63	.22
It is unrealistic to expect organizations to have their customer's best interest at heart	.15	−.01	.70
It is boring always to buy from the same organizations	−.24	−.03	.64
I am much more reluctant to buy from organizations that I have *not* done business with in the past	.11	−.40	.29
Eigenvalues	2.53	2.16	1.25

used in creating the measure, a CFA for the eight items resulted in X^2, 14 d.f. = 84, GOF = .90, CFI = .86, IFI = .86.

For the constructs, "Knowledge of Direct Marketing," "Concern About Organizations Using Personal Information," and "Trust of Organizations with Personal Information," we created formative scales (Bollen and Lennox 1991). These scales comprised of a linear combination across a set of items that were not necessarily supposed to be correlated, a priori. Formative scales were used to cover a large range of experience individuals have with numerous marketing practices and organizations. The sum of the items is a causal representation of the construct.

The formative scale for knowledge of direct marketing practices was adapted from items used by Nowak and Phelps (1992). The stem of the question asked respondents the following: "Do you believe organizations can obtain your *name and address,* types of *products purchased,* and *purchase details* from the following sources?" The question asked respondents to check all boxes that were appropriate. These results are reported in the following table. The only source from which organizations, can not obtain any information is tax forms. The formative scale is the product of calculating the number of correct responses to the question about whether organizations could obtain name and address from different sources. The

	Knowledge of Direct Marketing Practices			
	Percent Affirmative Response to Each Question			
Source	**Can't Obtain Any Information**	**Can Obtain Names and Address**	**Can Obtain Products Purchased**	**Can Obtain Purchase Details Like Price and Date of Purchase**
Federal income tax forms	56%	37%	9%	8%
State income tax forms	54%	38%	8%	8%
Medical records	52%	41%	10%	10%
Bank/financial transactions	45%	46%	16%	16%
Checkout scanners	39%	41%	35%	34%
U.S. census questionnaires	37%	57%	12%	11%
Insurance applications	29%	64%	17%	15%
Coupon redemptions	26%	58%	47%	36%
Calls to tollfree numbers	25%	65%	28%	25%
Auto/vehicle registrations	24%	70%	23%	23%
Credit reports or histories	15%	80%	37%	38%
Credit card purchases	15%	77%	57%	55%
Political contributions	15%	80%	19%	22%
Warrantee cards	12%	79%	52%	48%
Club/membership applications	11%	83%	31%	29%
Credit card applications	11%	84%	31%	30%
Internet Usage	11%	79%	43%	42%
Contest/sweepstakes entries	5%	90%	44%	36%
Lists acquired from other companies	5%	91%	53%	51%
Catalogs	4%	91%	76%	67%
Magazine subscriptions	3%	92%	45%	40%

Percentage of Respondents with High Levels of Trust and Concern		
	Percentage of Respondents who Indicated High Levels of Trust and/ or Concern	
	Trust[a]	Concern[b]
Employers	35%	60%
Banks that process checks	28%	71%
Drugstores	19%	41%
Insurance companies	16%	56%
Telephone companies	15%	59%
Alumni associations	15%	35%
Grocery stores	15%	35%
Credit card issuers	11%	34%
Charities	11%	46%
Airline	8%	38%
Book stores	8%	35%
Video stores	8%	37%
Internet access providers	4%	51%
Catalog companies	4%	40%
Political organizations	4%	51%
Magazine publishers	3%	43%
Direct mail clubs	2%	51%

[a]High levels of Concern were those respondents who indicated they were very concerned.
[b]High levels of Trust were those respondents who provided an answer of 8 or above out of 10.

How Many Times in the Last 6 Months Have You Purchased Products or Services by Mail, Telephone, or Internet? (Table 1.3)		
	Purchased by Mail	Purchased by Phone	Purchased by Internet
Base	1361	1325	1080
None	25%	36%	88%
Once	23%	23%	6%
2 or 3 times	35%	25%	3%
4 or 5 times	7%	6%	1%
6 or more times	7%	8%	1%
Don't know	2%	2%	2%

cerned, somewhat concerned, not very concerned, or not at all concerned options. We measured trust in a separate section of the survey. This question asked respondents, "How much do you trust the following organizations to use your personal information fairly (where 1 = trust not at all and 10 = trust completely). The formative scales were the result of adding up the values across 17 different industries. We report the industries and the percent of respondents who had high levels of trust or concern next.

OTHER MEASURES

We used a single question to measure knowledge of name removal mechanisms (perceived control). This item which was used in previous Equifax studies read, "Are you aware of any ways to remove your name from direct response lists for catalogs, products and services?" In this study, 41.8% were aware, 51.5% were not, and 6.7% did not know. For the purpose of analysis, perceived control was a dummy variable defined as 1 for those respondents who knew about name removal mechanisms, and 0 for those who didn't.

mean score was 16.25 correct answers out of 21, with a standard deviation of 3.47.

Formative scales were also used to measure "levels of concern about organizations using personal information" and "trust of organizations with personal information." The question to measure concern was, "How concerned are you with different organizations using personal information they acquired from you in their marketing efforts?" This 4 point scale consisted of very con-

The question that measured usage was a self report item that asked respondents, "How many times in the last 6 months have you purchased goods or services using the following methods. The intervals from the survey were recorded as none = 0, once = 1, 2–3 times = 3, 4–5 times = 5, 6 or more times = 6. The methods included by mail, phone, and by internet. A measure was formed by adding up the total number of times across the three methods.

The demographic questions were taking directly from previous Equifax studies. The specific questionnaire items are listed below:

- What is your age? (less than 30 years old, 30 – 49 years old, 50 years old or over). For analysis, age was converted to a dummy variable that reported 0 for respondents up to

49 years old and 1 for respondents 50 years old or over.
- How would you describe your political philosophy—conservative, moderate, or liberal? Political philosophy was recorded as a dummy variable, 0 for moderate and liberal, 1 for conservatives.
- Do you use a computer at home, at work or any other place? [check all that apply] (Yes, use compter at home; yes, use computer at work; no, do not use a computer, don't know). Computer usage was 1 for respondents who used computers either at home or work.
- Which of the following income categories best describes your total 1996 household income? (<7.5K; 7.5K–15K; 15K–25K; 25K–35K; 35K–50K; 50K–75K; 75K–100K;

Correlations and Summary Statistics of Study 2 Measures

	(1)	(2)	(3)	(4)	(5)	(6)	(7)	(8)	(9)	(10)	(11)	(12)
(1) Direct Mail Usage	1.00											
(2) Trust	.12	1.00										
(3) Concern	−.12	−.37	1.00									
(4) Relationship Mktg. Attitude	.09	.14	−.05	1.00								
(5) Knowledge of Direct Mktg.	.04	−.19	.01	.02	1.00							
(6) Perceived Control	.12	.01	−.05	.02	.12	1.00						
(7) Direct Mktg. Attitude.	.07	.18	−.11	.31	−.05	−.00	1.00					
(8) Age (older than 50 = 1)	−.08	−.10	.22	.02	.03	.12	−.01	1.00				
(9) Income	.23	−.03	−.06	−.07	.09	.10	−.15	−.13	1.00			
(10) Political Philosophy (cons = 1)	.05	.01	−.02	.01	.02	.01	−.01	−.06	−.03	1.00		
(11) Computer User (yes = 1)	.16	.01	−.07	−.05	.03	.05	−.15	−.27	.39	.04	1.00	
(12) Sex (Female = 1)	.00	.06	.03	.03	−.01	.01	.08	−.06	−.20	.16	−.09	1.00
Mean	3.71	68.7	52.9	8.76	16.2	0.42	14.4	0.49	5.31	0.60	0.50	.35
Standard Deviation	3.13	31.2	12.7	1.45	3.34	0.49	4.09	0.50	1.90	0.49	0.50	0.48
n = 1151												
Coefficient Alpha	f	f	f	.88	f	s	.80	s	s	s	s	s

s = single item measure.

f = formative scale.

100K–125K; 125K–150K; 150K+). We assigned values from 1 to 10 to represent the income categories.

- What is your sex? (Male; Female).

The table on page 332 shows the correlations and summary statistics for all the measures used in estimating the model.

George R. Milne is Associate Professor of Marketing and María Eugenia Boza is a doctoral candidate at the University of Massachusetts Amherst. The authors acknowledge the helpful comments of Mary Culnan, Pat Faley, Robert Kestnbaum, and the University of Massachusetts marketing department in the survey development. The authors also thank the Marketing Science Institute for the research grant, the Direct Marketing Education Foundation, the Direct marketing Association, and metromail for their support.

REFERENCES

Anderson, E. & Weitz, B. "Determinants of Continuity in Conventional Industrial Channel Dyads." *Marketing Science,* 8(4) (1989): 310–323.

Bollen, K. & Lennox, R. "Conventional Wisdom on Measurement: A Structural Equation Perspective." *Psychological Bulletin,* 110 (2) (1991): 304–314.

Campbell, A. "Relationship Marketing in Consumer Markets: A Comparison of Managerial and Consumer Attitudes about Informational Privacy." *Journal of Direct Marketing,* 11 (3) (1997): 44–58.

Cespedes, F.V. & Smith. H.J. "Database Marketing: New Rules for Policy and Practice." *Sloan Management Review,* (Summer 1993): 7–22.

Cook, John & Wall, T. "New Work Attitude Measures of Trust, Organizational Commitment and Personal Nonfulfillment." *Journal of Occupational Psychology,* 53, (1980): 39–52.

Culnan, M.J. "How Did They Get My Name?: An Exploratory Investigation of Consumer Altitudes Toward Secondary Information Use." *MIS Quarterly,* 17(3) (1993): 341–364.

"Database Marketing: A Potent New Tool for Selling." *Business Week* (September 5, 1994): 56–62.

Dillman, D. *Mail and Telephone Surveys: The Total Design Method,* New York: Wiley (1978).

Direct Marketing Association. *Fair Information Practices Manual.* New York: Direct Marketing Association (1994).

Doney, P.M. & Cannon, J.P. "An Examination of the Nature of Trust in Buyer-Seller Relationships." *Journal of Marketing,* 61(2) (1997): 35–61.

Dwyer, R.F. & Oh, S. "Output Sector Munificence Effects on the Internal Political Economy of Marketing Channels." *Journal of Marketing Research,* 24 (November 1987): 347–358.

Dwyer, R.F., Schurr, P.H., & Oh, S. "Developing Buyer Seller Relationships." *Journal of Marketing,* 51 (April 1987): 11–27.

Etzioni, A. *The Moral Dimension: Toward a New Economics.* New York: Free Press (1988).

Ganesan, S. "Determinants of Long-Term Orientation in Buyer Seller Relationships." *Journal of Marketing,* 58, (April 1994): 1–19.

Garbarro, J. "The Development of Trust Influence and Expectations," in A.G. Athos & J.J. Gabarro (Eds.). *Interpersonal Behavior: Communication and Understanding in Relationships.* Englewood Cliffs, NJ: Prentice Hall (1978).

Gengler, C.E. & Popkowski Leszczye, P.T.L. "Using Customer Satisfaction for Relationship Marketing: A Direct Marketing Approach." *Journal of Direct Marketing,* 11 (1) (1997): 23–29.

Geyskens, I., Skeekamps, J-B., Scheer, L.K., & Kumar, N. "The Effects of Trust and Interdependence on Relationship Commitment: A Trans-Atlantic Study." *International Journal of Research in Marketing,* 13 (4) (1996): 303–317.

Harris, Louis & Associates. Atlanta: Equifax (1983).

Harris, Louis & Associates. The *Equifax Report on Consumers in the Information Age,* Atlanta: Equifax (1990).

Harris, Louis & Associates. *Harris-Equifax Consumer Privacy Survey 1991,* Atlanta: Equifax (1991).

Harris, Louis & Associates. *Harris-Equifax Consumer Privacy Survey 1992,* Atlanta: Equifax (1992).

Harris, Louis & Associates. *Health Information Privacy Survey 1993,* Atlanta: Equifax (1993).

Harris, Louis & Associates. *Equifax-Harris Consumer Privacy Survey 1994,* Atlanta: Equifax (1994).

Harris, Louis & Associates. *Equifax-Harrris Mid-Decade Consumer Privacy Survey,* Atlanta: Equifax (1995).

Harris, Louis & Associates. *The 1996 Equifax-Harris Consumer Privacy Survey,* Atlanta: Equifax (1996).

Hunt, S.D., Sparkman, R.D. & Wilcox, J.B. "The Pretest in Survey Research: Issues and Preliminary Findings." *Journal of Marketing Research.* 19 (May 1982): 269–273.

Hwang, P. & Burgers, W. "Properties of Trust: An Analytical View." *Organizational Behavior and Human Decision Processes,* 69(1) (1997): 67–73.

Kumar, N. "The Power of Trust in Manufacturer-Retailer Relationships." *Harvard Business Review,* 74(6), (1996): 92–106.

Mayer, R.C., Davis, J.H., & Schoorman, F.D. "An Integrative Model of Organizational Trust." *Academy of Management Review,* 20(3) (1995): 709–734.

Milne, G.R. "Consumer Participation in Mailing Lists: A Field Experiment." *Journal of Public Policy and Marketing,* 16(2) (1997): 298–309.

Milne, G.R. & Boza, M.-E. "Business Perspective on Database Marketing and Consumer Privacy Practices." Cambridge, M.A. Marketing Science Institute, Report No. (1998): 98–110.

Moorman, C., Deshpande, R. & Zaltman, G. "Factors Affecting Trust in Marketing Research Relationships." *Journal of Marketing,* 57 (January 1993): 81–101.

Moorman, C., Zaltman, G. & Deshpande, Rohit. "Relationships Between Providers and Users of Market Research: The Dynamics of Trust Within and Between Organizations." *Journal of Market Research,* 29 (August 1992): 314–28.

Morgan, R.M. & Hunt. S.D. "The Commitment-Trust Theory of Relationship Marketing," *Journal of Marketing.* 58 (July 1994): 20–38.

Nowak, G.J. & Phelps, J. "Understanding Privacy Concerns: An Assessment of Consumers' Information-Related Knowledge and Beliefs. *Journal of Direct Marketing,* 6 (4) (1992): 28–39.

Peppers, D. & Rogers, M. *The One-to-One Future.* New York: Doubleday/Currency (1993).

Rempel, J.K., Holmes, J.G. & Zanna, M.P. "Trust in Close Relationships." *Journal of Personality and Social Psychology,* 49 (1) (1985): 95–112.

Rotter, J. "A New Scale for the Measurement of Interpersonal Trust." *Journal of Personality,* 35 (December 1967): 651–665.

Schurr, P.H. & Ozanne, J.L. "Influences on Exchange Processes: Buyers' Preconceptions of a Seller's Trustworthiness and Bargaining Toughness." *Journal of Consumer Research,* 11 (March 1985): 939–953.

Shaver, D. *The Next Step in Database Marketing.* New York: Wiley (1996).

Zand, D.E. "Trust and Managerial Problem Solving." *Administrative Science Quarterly,* 18, (1972): 229–39.

THE INTERNET AND INFORMATION ECONOMICS

Information products are goods that can be digitized or that originate in digital form. Such products include books, magazines, software, and music. Many products are also augmented by information. For example, equipment may be sold with instruction manuals and warranty. Hence, products may consist of both digital and non-digital components.

The ability to create information goods and distribute them via the Internet is a huge threat to some industries. For example, music recording studios are faced with the prospect of losing billions of dollars in sales because of the explosion of the MP3 format. It is now possible for a single individual to buy one copy of a CD, record each of the songs in MP3 format using a personal computer, and distribute unlimited numbers of copies of these songs to anyone on the Internet.

The threat of MP3 to the music industry also shows a unique aspect of digitization. Digitization means that information products can be broken down into any number of components. In the case of MP3, individual songs, or parts of songs, can be "unbundled" from their associated CD. In fact, digitization allows the information component of any product to be unbundled from the "core" physical product.

One example of this "unbundling" is what has happened at Encyclopedia Britannica. Encyclopedia Britannica used to sell its volumes for thousands of dollars. For any family, the purchase of an encyclopedia set represented a substantial investment in education. Now, at Britannica.com, one can subscribe to the entire encyclopedia "knowledgebase" for just $5.00 a month. In essence, the information contained in the encyclopedias has been unbundled from the physical encyclopedia volume sets.

In fact, the entire book publishing industry is likely to be completely transformed by the Internet. In the past, book publishers could only accept a certain number of new books based on forecasted demand and costs of production. With existing print-on-demand technology, authors can act as their own publishers and enter into their own distributor arrangements with retailers. Publishers, if they so choose, can operate as online retailers, and online retailers, if they wish, can act as publishers. The success of Stephen King's first electronic novel suggests dramatic changes ahead.

In this chapter, Carl Shapiro and Hal Varian educate us concerning the economics of information.

They argue that when the marginal cost of production and distribution is essentially zero (as is the case for information goods on the internet), versioning is critical for profitability. Through versioning, Shapiro and Varian suggest that different forms of the information good can be offered to different customer segments according to demand. They give several examples of how products can be versioned successfully.

When you have finished reading the article, please visit the textbook's web site for more information and resources.

Versioning: The Smart Way to Sell Information

Carl Shapiro
Hal R. Varian

In 1986, Nynex issued the first electronic phone book, a compact disc containing all the telephone listings for the New York area. Charging $10,000 a copy, the company sold the CDs to the FBI, the IRS, and other large commercial and governmental organizations. Sensing a great business opportunity, the Nynex executive in charge of the project, James Bryant, left to set up his own company, Pro CD. His goal was to produce an electronic directory covering the entire United States.

The phone companies, fearing an attack on their lucrative yellow pages businesses, refused to license digital copies of their listings to Pro CD. But that didn't stop Bryant. He went to Beijing and hired Chinese workers—at $3.50 a day—to type into computers every listing from every U.S. telephone book. The resulting database, containing more than 70 million phone numbers, was used to create a master disc, which in turn was used to create hundreds of thousands of copies. The CDs, which cost well under a dollar each to produce, sold for hundreds of dollars, yielding a tidy profit for Pro CD.

But the CD-phone-book boom was short-lived. Attracted by the seemingly strong profit potential, competitors such as Digital Directory Assistance and American Business Information rushed to launch competing products containing essentially the same information. Because their products were indistinguishable, the companies were forced to compete on price alone. Not surprisingly, prices plunged. Soon, CD phone directories were selling for a few dollars in discount software bins. A high priced, high-margin product just months before, the CD phone book had become a cheap commodity.

The rapid rise, and even more rapid fall, of CD telephone directories stands as a cautionary tale for the purveyors of information products, particularly those sold in digital form. It reveals that the so-called new economy is still subject to the old laws of economics. In a free market, once several companies have sunk the costs necessary to create an undifferentiated product, competitive forces will usually move the product's price toward its marginal cost—the cost of manufacturing an additional copy. And because the marginal cost of reproducing information tends to be very low, the price of an information product, if left to the marketplace, will tend to be low as well. What makes information products economically attractive—their low reproduction cost—also makes them economically dangerous.

Many information producers make the mistake of assuming that their products are exempt from the economic laws that govern more tangible goods. But, as Pro CD found out, that's just not so. Although information goods have unusual production economics, they are nevertheless subject to the same market and competitive forces that govern the fate of any product. And their success, too, hinges on traditional product-management skills: gaining a clear understanding of customer needs, achieving genuine differentiation, and developing and executing an astute positioning and pricing strategy.

INFORMATION'S DANGEROUS ECONOMICS

To forge a winning strategy for an information product, you need to understand the economics of information production. Information goods, which we define as goods capable of being distributed in digital form, have always been characterized by a distinctive cost structure: producing the first copy is often very expensive, but producing subsequent copies is very cheap. A book publisher, for example, may spend hundreds of thousands of dollars to acquire, edit, and design a manuscript, but once the first copy of the book has been printed, the cost of printing another is usually only a few dollars. To get a movie made, a producer may spend a hundred million dollars on cast, crew, script, and sets, but making a print of the final cut will cost only a few hundred dollars. The fixed costs of producing information are large, in other words, but the variable costs of reproducing it are small.

The sharp skew toward fixed costs is not the only thing distinctive about the cost structure of information goods. The fixed costs and the variable costs themselves have unusual characteristics. The fixed costs tend to be dominated by sunk costs—costs that are not recoverable if production is halted. If you invest in a new office building or factory and later decide you don't need it, you can recover part of your fixed costs by selling the facility. But if your film flops, you probably won't be able to sell off the script or the sets, and if your CD is a dud, it ends up in the cut-out racks at $4.95.

The variable costs of producing information also have a unique feature: the unit cost of creating an additional copy of an information product typically does not increase even if a great many copies are made. Information producers, in other words, have few capacity constraints, which is quite a different situation from that faced by most manufacturers. If sales of microchips grow, for example, Intel will at some point need to build an expensive new fabrication facility to meet the added demand. And if sales of airplanes increase, Boeing will have to invest heavily in new plants, machinery, and people. When these and other traditional manufacturers reach the limit of their existing capacity, the cost of producing an additional unit goes way up. That doesn't happen with most information products, which can be reproduced with a high degree of automation at very low cost. If you can make one copy, you can make a million copies, or ten million copies, at roughly the same unit cost.

Because of their cost structure, information products offer vast economies of scale: the more you produce, the lower your average cost of pro-

duction. That's why Microsoft, with its dominance in personal-computer operating systems and business applications, enjoys gross profit margins of 92%. But the cost structure has a big downside as well. Because the fixed costs are both large and sunk, companies that don't enjoy market dominance can be caught in devastating price wars. If competition forces a company to reduce its prices to a level near its marginal production costs—as was the case with publishers of CD phone books—that company will never be able to recoup its big up-front investments. It will, in time, face economic doom. What economists call a perfectly competitive market represents a disaster scenario for information producers.

The dangers inherent in the economics of information production become even more pronounced when the information is produced digitally. Copies of information in digital form—such as CDs or digital video disks—are much cheaper to reproduce than analog or print copies. Think of encyclopedias. Printing an encyclopedia set can cost more than a hundred dollars. Cutting a CD-ROM of that same set costs just pennies. By reducing variable costs, digital reproduction further exaggerates the skew toward fixed costs.

And that's not all. When digital information is delivered over a network, the variable costs can disappear almost completely. Because the product has no physical form—it exists purely as bits of data—there's no cost for manufacturing, no cost for packaging, no cost for shipping. Once the first copy of the information has been produced, transmitting additional copies is essentially free. Consider again the case of electronic phone books. Today, if you want to quickly look up phone numbers for people around the country, you don't even need to buy a CD—no matter how cheap they've become. You can search phone listings for free at dozens of Web sites. It costs next to nothing to let an additional customer search an on-line database, so competing providers give the information away, to all comers, hoping to make their money by selling ads.

Many commentators have marveled at the amount of free information on the Internet, but to

The Logic of the Free Version

A refrigerator manufacturer would quickly go broke if it started handing out free samples of its products. But information producers give away free versions all the time. When you buy a computer, you are likely to find a bundle of free software on the hard drive. When you surf the Web, you discover not only oceans of freely distributed news stories and statistics, and other information, but also loads of software demos and "freeware" that you can download with a few clicks of your mouse.

Free, versions of digital goods are common for two reasons. First, the low marginal cost of creating copies of information means that it doesn't require much, if any, investment to give information away. Second, information is an "experience good"—customers don't know what it's worth until they've actually tried it. Free versions provide customers with an easy and attractive way to test out a digital product.

Of course, if all you did was give information away for free, you wouldn't have much of a business. (Many Web site operators are learning this lesson the hard way.) There has to be sound business logic behind the free offer. We have found that the most savvy information producers offer free versions only when they are likely to achieve one or more of the following goals:

Building Awareness

Many companies use free versions simply to create awareness of their products. They give away a version with limited content or feature in order to entice consumers to pay for the full version. Computer game makers, for example, distribute free demos over the Web or on CD-ROMs bundled with game magazines. The demos allow users to play only the first few levels of a game—enough to get hooked but not enough to get bored. The hope is, of course, that the user will rush out to buy the complete game. Using a free version to build awareness works for games because each game is unique; the customer can't buy a substitute. But if you're only one of many providers of the same information, a free version may simply underscore the commodity nature of your product. The customer, spoiled by the free version, will be motivated to find the cheapest possible source of the information.

Gaining Follow-on Sales Gain

A more sophisticated strategy is to give away a version in order to build a base of customers to which you can sell follow-on products, such as extensions, upgrades, and services. The free version, in this case, is usually a complete version; no content is missing and no features are disabled. The idea is to get customers to become dependent on the product. The more they use it, the more interested they'll be in add-ons. McAfee Associates, for example, offers many of its core virus-protection products for free over the Web. It makes money by selling site licenses to companies, upgrades to individuals, and an array of services to both groups. McAfee's products now account for half the sales of antivirus software.

Creating a Network

Because many digital goods are subject to network effects—they only become valuable once a large number of people are using them—free versions can also be a good way to bring a product's use up to a critical mass. Adobe, for example, gives away a simple version of its Acrobat software that enables users to view and print electronic documents even if they lack the software the documents were created with. Because Adobe was the first to seed the market with such a program, it is now able to sell full versions of Acrobat—at between $200 and $600—to anyone who wants to share electronic documents over the Web or through other media.

Attracting Eyeballs

As the war for attention continues to intensify on the Internet, free information becomes ever more valuable as a lure to attract the eyes of surfers. Some information companies, in fact, are finding that they can earn more money from advertising than from selling their own information. Playboy, for example, posts free images of its

The Logic of the Free Version (continued)

playmates on its Web site, along with banner advertisements that it sells for more than $10,000 a month. Each image incorporates a digital watermark, enabling Playboy to track not only how many people view the image on its own site but also how many people view it after it's been copied onto other sites. In this way, Playboy learns more about its on-line customers and how they use its products, further strengthening its ability to sell ads as well as on-line and print subscriptions.

Gaining Competitive Advantage

Sometimes the strategic value of getting a large number of people to use your information is greater than the economic value of getting a smaller number of people to buy it. Microsoft, for example, gives away its Internet browser in order to prevent Netscape from gaining control over computer desktops. That competitive benefit far outweighs the money it could make by selling the browser. Microsoft sometimes finds itself on the other end of such strategies, too. One of the main reasons Sun Microsystems gives away many of its Java programming tools is to reduce the market power wielded by Microsoft. Because Java can be used with any computer, it makes operating systems like Windows 98 relatively less valuable and hardware, such as Sun's servers, relatively more valuable.

---

economists like us it's no surprise. The generic information flowing through cyberspace—phone numbers, news stories, stock prices, maps, and the like—is simply selling at its marginal cost: zero. (See the insert "The Logic of the Free Version.")

LINKING PRICE TO VALUE

The extremely low marginal costs of information production rule out many traditional pricing strategies. You can't, for example, use cost-based pricing. Nor can you set prices according to the competition—that's a sure road to ruin. The only viable strategy is to set prices according to the value a customer places on the information.

But which customer? The value of a piece of information can vary dramatically from one person to the next. A stock market speculator will place a far greater value on stock quotes than will a long-term investor who buys and holds. A computer "power user" will value the latest operating-system upgrade much more than the average home user will. And a drug company executive will likely place more value on the text of the latest FDA rulings than a pharmacist, who, in turn, will

place greater value on it than a premed student. Information never has the same value for every potential customer.

In a perfect world, an information producer would sell its product to each buyer at a different price, reflecting the value that the different buyers place on it. In reality, though, such personalized pricing is rarely possible. For one thing, even in these days of cheap computing, it is awfully expensive to capture, store, and distribute data on the tastes of individual customers. For another, traditional sales channels, like retail stores, cannot set an array of prices for the same good. (Even if they could, it would be next to impossible to get customers to stay within their intended pricing strata—just look at all the gyrations airline customers go through to locate the cheapest routes.) And finally, information producers run the risk of annoying or even alienating their customers if they charge different prices for the same product.

But there is a practical way to set different prices for basically the same information without incurring high costs or offending customers. You do it by offering the information in different versions designed to appeal to different types of customers. With this strategy, which we call *ver-*

sioning, customers in effect segment themselves. The version they choose reveals the value they place on the information and the price they're willing to pay for it.

Traditional information providers have always used versioning, in one form or another, as a way to structure their product lines. Publishers release a book first in hardback and later in paperback, selling the same text at a high price to readers who must have the book right away and at a lower price to people who don't mind waiting. In a similar way, movie houses charge $7 or more for a ticket to a film that can be rented six months later for $3 a household.

When information is produced digitally, versioning becomes an even more flexible and powerful strategy. For one thing, it's easy to manipulate digital data, so the cost and time required to produce and distribute different versions go way down. For another, the proliferation of CD-ROM players, VCRs, and Internet browsers opens many kinds of information to a much larger and more diverse audience. When legal information was conveyed only in heavy and expensive tomes, lawyers were the only people interested in purchasing it. Now that the information can be searched and bought by the bit, there are many more potential customers for it. Versioning provides a way to sell information to those customers in a form that they will value without cannibalizing the existing high-price, high-margin market.

The trick is to identify the best ways to distinguish the different versions of your product. You need to determine which features will be highly valuable to some customers but of little value to others. Then you need to create the right number of versions and set the right prices for them. The goal is to get each customer to pay the highest possible price for the product, thus maximizing the overall returns. Since the customers themselves are selecting the price they'll pay, based on their own calculation of the information's value, they will be far less likely to take offense at paying different prices than they would if the manufacturer were imposing the prices on them,

THE MANY VERSIONS OF VERSIONING

In the past, versions of information products were usually based on timing or, more precisely, delay. For almost any type of information, some people will always be more eager to get their hands on it than will others. That's the rationale for releasing hardcovers before paperbacks and for showing movies in theaters before putting them on tape. Delay is often a good basis for versions of digital information as well. PAWWS Financial Network, for example, offers two versions of its portfolio accounting system, one at $8.95 a month and the other at $50.00. What's the difference? The inexpensive service uses stock quotes that are delayed by 20 minutes to calculate portfolio values, whereas the premium service uses real-time quotes. Those 20 minutes are very valuable to one set of the company's customers.

But with digital information, delay is only one of many possible dimensions for versioning, just consider the wide variety of ways in which digital products are differentiated today:

Convenience

Restricting the time or place at which a customer can access information, or restricting the length of access, is often a good way to get buyers to reveal the value they place on the information. The more a customer needs the information, the more freedom they'll want in accessing it. America Online, for example, offers different monthly membership plans based on convenience. The standard plan, which provides unlimited access, costs $21.95. An alternative plan costs $4.95 but allows only three hours of connection time—if you use more, you pay a high hourly surcharge. By offering the cheaper version, AOL can attract customers who have only a limited need for its service—they may use it solely for e-mail, for example—while maintaining much higher prices for customers with a greater dependence on it. Similarly, some on-line database companies offer discount subscriptions to users who agree to log on only outside of normal business hours.

Comprehensiveness

Some customers will pay a big premium for information that offers a depth of detailing—in geographical coverage, historical scope, or statistical detail. Public affairs specialists and journalists, for example, will value the ability to search the full text of articles from newspapers around the world. Many scholars and students will value extensive historical information. Marketing managers will value information on individual customers and their long-term purchasing patterns.

Many newspapers and magazines are using comprehensiveness as the basis for creating versions of their on-line products. The *New York Times* and *Business Week,* for example, give away their current editions' content on the Web, but they sell access to their extensive archives. Because there are so many sources of news on the Internet, these publications know that the only way to attract readers— and in turn advertisers—is to give away their freshest content. But they can charge for their past articles because the segment of customers that values those articles—writers, researchers, and the like—have no other practical source for them.

Manipulation

Another important dimension that can form the basis for versioning is the ability of the user to store, duplicate, print, or otherwise manipulate the information. Back in the days of copy-protected software, companies like Borland sold two versions of their programs—one was low priced and could not be copied and the other was high priced and could. Many information providers today use similar constraints on information manipulation to distinguish their products. Lexis-Nexis, for instance, imposes additional charges on users who want to print or download information rather than just view it on screen.

Community

The chat rooms and bulletin boards that crowd the Web demonstrate that many people value the opportunity to discuss information with others who have similar interests. By restricting users' ability to join an on-line community, providers can identify customers who place value on the community in addition to the information.

Silicon Investor, a popular Web site for investors in high-tech industries, offers hundreds of discussion boards on individual companies. It allows anyone to read the messages posted on the boards for free. But if you want to post a message—or send a private e-mail to another member—you have to pay an annual membership fee of $100 or a lifetime fee of $200. By allowing free access to the information on the site, Silicon Investor gets more people to visit the site, enabling it to charge more for advertising. By charging an extra fee for posting messages, it makes money on customers who want to do more than read.

Annoyance

People who pay the Silicon Investor membership fee also get an added benefit: they have the capability to turn off the advertisements posted throughout the site. The ability to avoid the annoyance of on-line ads is valued by some Web surfers, and they're willing to pay extra for it.

Similarly, many shareware programs, which are distributed free for trial use, incorporate a start-up screen that asks users if they're ready to purchase a registered version. The only way to avoid the annoying screen is to send in money.

Speed

A common strategy for software makers is to sell versions of their programs that run at different speeds. The most serious users naturally gravitate to the faster versions even if they have to pay a lot more for them; the greater efficiency outweighs the higher cost. Wolfram Research, for example, used to sell two versions of Mathematica, its program for performing symbolic, graphical, and numerical mathematics. The high-priced professional version used a computer's floating-point processor to speed up the calculations. The cheaper student version disabled the processor, slowing the calculations considerably.

Interestingly, Wolfram had to write more code to get the student version to work without the floating-point processor. The inexpensive version thus cost more to produce than did the premium version. But offering the low-speed version made economic sense because it expanded the overall user network, making the professional product even more valuable to the sophisticated users, such as professors who wanted to share files with their students. (See the insert "Value-Subtracted Versions.")

Data-Processing

Various data-processing capabilities can often be built into an information product, enabling certain users to carry out sophisticated tasks. H&R Block, for example, offers the standard version of its Kiplinger's TaxCut software to people who just want an automated way to fill in their tax forms. But it also offers a pricier premium version, Tax-Cut Deluxe, that includes a number of other tools—for example, it has an audit feature that examines your return and highlights entries likely to catch the attention of IRS agents.

User Interface

Varying the way that customers access information can be a particularly good basis for versioning. Sophisticated users will often be willing to invest time learning a complex interface that offers, for example, powerful searching capabilities. (And their up-front investment of time will make them less likely to shift to a competing product later.) More casual users will want a simpler, more intuitive interface even if its capabilities are rudimentary. Adobe's $600 Photoshop software for manipulating photographic images has a complex interface intended for professional designers. But the company also sells a lower-end product, the $50 PhotoDeluxe, that has a stripped-down interface geared for home users. You can't do as much with PhotoDeluxe, but you don't have to spend a lot of time learning how to use it, either.

Image Resolution

Many digital products include images, and different users will place different values on the quality of the images. The stock-photo house PhotoDisk, for example, offers its photographs over the Web at different resolutions. Professional designers creating glossy brochures purchase high-resolution images at $49.95 each, but newsletter producers settle for lower resolution images at $19.95. The myriad pornography sites on the Web often offer low-quality "thumbnails" of their photographs for free but charge for the ability to view and download high-resolution copies.

Support

Some information providers offer different levels of technical support at different prices. You can, for example, download Netscape's Web browser for free over the Net or, for $40, you can become a subscriber and receive not only the software but also an instruction manual and one free phone call to a support technician. Using technical support as a basis for versioning can be tricky, though. Highlighting the added value of support may raise questions in customers' minds about the reliability of the product. And failing to deliver on promises of support can turn into a public relations nightmare.

In addition to being used in isolation, the different dimensions of versioning can also be combined. Dialog, the large on-line information

Value-Subtracted Versions

A few years back, IBM offered two very similar versions of one of its printers—the high-end LaserPrinter and the less expensive LaserPrinter E. The two versions looked the same and functioned the same, with one exception: the LaserPrinter could print ten pages per minute while the E version could print only five. A testing lab for computer equipment examined the two models and found that a special chip had been inserted into the LaserPrinter E to slow down its operation. IBM had, in other words, deliberately degraded the performance of its high-end model in order to create a cheaper model. And because the subtraction of value required the manufacture and installation of a special chip, the low-priced version actually cost more to produce than the high-priced one.

IBM's tactic was unusual. When most manufacturers want to create versions of their products, they start by building a bare-bones model, then add features to create premium versions. The high-end models cost more to create than the low-end alternatives. Toyota, for example, spends considerably more to produce a top-of-the-line Camry XLE, with leather upholstery, antilock brakes and traction control, than it does to manufacture an entry-level Camry CE that lacks the luxury features.

For digital goods, however, the IBM method is the rule, not the exception. Most versions of digital information are created by subtracting value rather than by adding it. The producer first invests in developing the most technologically advanced version—in order to have a distinctive product that will appeal to the most demanding and least price-sensitive customers—and then removes features or capabilities to tailor the product to less demanding customers. As the low-end users' needs advance, they can follow an established upgrade path within the same product family.

PhotoDisk, for example, scans its stock photos at high resolution to create its premium product, then degrades them to produce low-resolution copies. Offering the low-resolution versions requires extra work—and extra server space for storage—so it actually costs the company more to produce its cheap product than its expensive one.

Charging less for products that cost you more to produce may sound illogical, but for digital goods it makes sense. The extra investment required to create degraded versions is usually modest and can be recouped quickly as sales grow. And the revenue from versions designed to appeal to different market segments helps offset the big fixed costs required to create the product initially.

There's an important caveat to value subtraction: you have to make sure that customers can't transform the degraded version back into the original. With a world full of talented hackers, that's no easy feat. There have been reports, for example, that users of Microsoft's $250 workstation version of its NT software have figured out how to turn it into the original and more powerful $1,000 server version with just a few simple tweaks of the code. When you choose the dimensions of your product to manipulate to create different versions, choose carefully.

---

provider, creates versions of its Web-accessible database by altering both its user interface and its comprehensiveness. A high-end version, Dialog-Web, is designed for corporate researchers and other information professionals. It has a powerful but complex interface, allowing highly sophisticated searches, and offers access to the full range of Dialog's content. Another product, DataStar, is much cheaper and much less powerful, offering a subset of the full Dialog database with a simplified interface. DataStar suits casual users well, but because of its limitations it does not siphon away professional users from DialogWeb.

THE MECHANICS OF VERSIONING

So how many versions should you offer? There's no pat answer to that question. The number should be guided by two considerations: the characteristics of the information that you're selling and the value that different customers place on it. If your information can be used in many ways, it probably makes sense to offer a wide array of versions. But if the value of your information hinges on the number of users who access it in the same format—if, in other words, the information is subject to network effects—you may want to restrict the number of versions you offer.

Kurzweil Applied Intelligence, for example, offers many versions of its voice recognition software. Kurzweil understands that voice recognition has many different applications and that they vary greatly in the value they provide to users. College students will be attracted to a simple product that enables them to create documents by speaking into their computers. But given their limited budgets, they'll only buy such a product if its price is low. Doctors, on the other hand, will be drawn to a highly sophisticated product that is able to understand a specialized vocabulary—and because such a product will save them a lot of time, they'll pay handsomely for it.

To capture the different levels of customer value, Kurzweil offers seven different versions of its software, distinguished mainly by the size and specialization of the vocabularies they recognize. The top-of-the-line, $8,000 version for surgeons, Voice Ortho, is 100 times more expensive than the $79 entry-level product for students, VoicePad Pro. Between those extremes are versions tailored to home users, business users, and lawyers, all at different price points. Because each segment's needs are unique, there's little chance that buyers will be confused by the various options. And there's also little chance that customers targeted for high-priced versions will opt instead for lower-priced versions. A version unable to recognize legal terms, for example, would have little value for an attorney. The way customers define the value of the product locks them into their intended segment. (See the table "One Product, Many Versions.")

For other companies, a more limited array of options makes sense. Intuit, for example, offers only two versions of its popular Quicken software for personal financial management. Unlike Kurzweil's product, Quicken doesn't have a wide variety of applications—a lawyer balances her checkbook in pretty much the same way a doctor does—so having to choose from a broad range of versions would simply confuse customers. By limiting the number of versions, Intuit gets other benefits as well. Customer support stays simple, and users are able to share files with less risk of incompatibility.

But by offering only one high-end product and one low-end version, Intuit, like many information companies, may be missing out on an important opportunity. The two-version strategy, though enticing in its simplicity, ignores the psychological phenomenon known as "extremeness aversion." When buying products, consumers normally try to avoid extreme choices—they fear they'll pay too much if they go for the most expensive version, and they worry they'll get too little if they opt for the cheapest. They are drawn instead to a compromise choice—a version in the middle of the product line. Like Goldilocks, they don't want "too big" or "too small"—they want the product that's "just right."

By offering three versions of a product, companies can shift buyers away from the entry-level product and to the more expensive middle offering. The effect can be quite dramatic. In one

One Product, Many Versions		
Recognizing that its voice recognition software can be used in many ways, Kurzweil Applied Intelligence offers a broad array of versions at very different prices.		
Version	**Price**	**Vocabulary**
VoicePad Pro	$79	20,000-word general
Personal	$295	30,000-word general
Professional	$595	50,000-word general
Office Talk	$795	Business
Law Talk	$1,195	Legal
Voice Med	$6,000	Medical
Voice Ortho	$8,000	Special-purpose medical

experiment, researchers offered customers different sets of microwave ovens. When the choice was between a no-frills oven at $109.99 and a midrange model at $179.99, customers chose the midrange oven 45% of the time. When a high-end oven at $199.99 was added to the choice set, people chose the midrange oven 60% of the time. The existence of this phenomenon is the reason McDonald's offers its drinks in three sizes rather than just two.

Information producers can also capitalize on extremeness aversion. If they are currently offering only two versions, they should consider adding a third, high-end product to their line. If Intuit, for example, offered a third version of its Quicken software—Quicken Gold, say—at a price higher than that for the Deluxe version, many buyers who would have bought the standard product will instead move up to Quicken Deluxe. The important thing to recognize is that the product you really want to sell should be positioned in the middle—the high-end product is there mainly to pull people toward the compromise choice.

The optimum number of versions to offer is, as we've seen, rarely clear-cut. The best way to decide is often through trial and error. Because it's usually inexpensive to create new versions of an information product, a company can do a lot of experimentation. Recently, for example, Information America, a company that provides public records to banks, government agencies, and law offices, was trying to decide whether to offer its services to users operating at home. The company felt that demand would be high enough to justify entry into the new market, but it was concerned that a price low enough to attract home users might cannibalize its sales to professionals. To gain insight into the problem, the company created a subsidiary, KnowX, to offer home users access to a subset of its databases via the Web. It turned out that the restricted offering was very popular—and it didn't attract the high-end professionals. With today's powerful technologies for distributing information, more and more companies are, like Information America, finding it easy to explore market segments that were not reachable before.

Old Ideas, New Applications

Information has always played a central role in our economy—a simple fact that too often gets lost in all the hype about the information age. And the total amount of information in existence hasn't expanded all that much in recent decades. What has changed is that the information has become dramatically more accessible. Many of the great technological advances of the twentieth century—telephones, radio, motion pictures, television, computers—have served to speed the flow and widen the availability of information. The arrival of the Internet is just the latest step—albeit a very big step in a process that continues to unfold.

As access to information has expanded, so too have the opportunities for selling information goods to a broader and more diverse set of customers. Versioning provides a way to serve that larger market by tailoring the same core of information to the needs of different buyers. It not only enables you to gain more revenue from an existing product but also provides a basis for thinking creatively about how to distinguish your product from competing offerings. By monitoring how the market reacts to new versions, you gain ever greater insight into how customers define value, allowing you to continually refine your product line. A creative versioning strategy is often the best defense against the commoditization of information.

Success in selling digital goods does not require a whole new way of thinking about business. Rather, it requires the same kind of smart managing and smart marketing that have always set apart the best companies. The real power of versioning is that it enables you to apply tried-and-true product-management techniques—segmentation, differentiation, positioning—a way that takes into account both the unusual economics of information production and the endless malleability of digital data.

Carl Shapiro is the Transamerica Professor of Business Strategy at the Walter A. Haas School of Business at the University of California at Berkeley. Hal R. Varian is the dean of the School of Information Management and Systems at the University of California at Berkeley. They are the authors of *Information Rules: A Strategic Guide to the Network Economy* (Harvard Business School Press, 1998; see http://www.inforules.com).

READINGS LIST BY AUTHOR

READINGS LIST BY TITLE